MARY ELLEN S. CAPEK is Executive Secretary of the National Council for Research on Women. A founding officer of the Council and former Director of Continuing Education at Princeton University, she coordinates the Council's Thesaurus Task Force and Database Resource Committee.

THE NATIONAL COUNCIL FOR RESEARCH ON WOMEN, formed in 1981, is an association of over fifty member centers and organizations that links scholars and practitioners in this country and abroad and serves the academic community, public policy makers, and the general public.

THE BUSINESS AND PROFESSIONAL WOMEN'S FOUNDATION, a Council member center, is an education and research organization established in 1956 by the National Federation of Business and Professional Women's Clubs (BPW/USA), which promotes full participation, equity, and economic self-sufficiency for business and professional women.

A WOMEN'S THESAURUS

Principal Editorial Advisors

Cheryl A. Sloan
Sarah M. Pritchard
Patricia M. King
Susan E. Searing

A WOMEN'S THESAURUS

AN INDEX OF LANGUAGE USED TO DESCRIBE AND LOCATE INFORMATION BY AND ABOUT WOMEN

Edited by

MARY ELLEN S. CAPEK

A Project of The National Council for Research on Women
and The Business and Professional Women's Foundation

1817

HARPER & ROW, PUBLISHERS, New York
Cambridge, Philadelphia, San Francisco, Washington
London, Mexico City, São Paulo, Singapore, Sydney

Users are encouraged to share additional terms and cross-references and to suggest changes in existing entries. Please address:

The National Council for Research on Women
The Sara Delano Roosevelt Memorial House
47–49 East 65th Street
New York, N.Y. 10021

FIRST EDITION

Copy editor: Katherine G. Ness
Designer: C. Linda Dingler

Library of Congress Cataloging-in-Publication Data

A Women's thesaurus.
  "A project of the National Council for Research on Women and the Business and Professional Women's Foundation."
  1. Subject headings—Women. I. Capek, Mary Ellen S.
II. National Council for Research on Women (U.S.)
III. Business and Professional Women's Foundation.
Z695.1.W65W65   1987   025.4'93054   86-46231
ISBN 0-06-015775-5

87 88 89 90 91   10 9 8 7 6 5 4 3 2 1

CONTENTS

PREFACE   vii

ACKNOWLEDGMENTS   ix

THESAURUS CONSTRUCTION AND USE   xiii
   Thesaurus Applications   xiii
   Building the Thesaurus   xv
   Guidelines for Using the Thesaurus   xviii
     Description and Scope   xviii
     Thesaurus Structure   xix
     Form of Entry   xxv
     Cross-References   xxvii
   Thesaurus Subject Groups   xxviii
   Thesaurus Task Force   xxx
   Original Lists Combined to Form the Thesaurus   xxx
   Thesaurus Test Sites   xxxi
     U.S.   xxxi
     International   xxxii
   Selected Bibliography   xxxiii

DISPLAYS

ALPHABETICAL DISPLAY   1

ROTATED DISPLAY   517

HIERARCHICAL DISPLAY   737

SUBJECT GROUP DISPLAY   963

    Communications   964
    Economics and Employment   965
    Education   973
    History and Social Change   977
    International Women   981
    Language, Literature, Religion, and Philosophy   983
    Law, Government, and Public Policy   987
    Natural Sciences and Health   992
    Science and Technology   999
    Social Sciences and Culture   1000
    Visual and Performing Arts   1012

USE/DO NOT USE DISPLAY   1015

    Use/Do Not Use Terms   1016
    Do Not Use/Use Terms   1030

DELIMITERS DISPLAY   1043

    Age Levels   1044
    Cultural and Political Movements   1044
    Education Levels   1045
    Ethnic, Racial, and Religious Descriptors   1046
    Historical Periods   1046
    Laws and Regulations   1047
    National and Regional Descriptors   1047
    Types and Forms of Materials   1049

PREFACE

It is difficult to know where or how to begin the Preface to a project of this scope and magnitude. The Acknowledgments name those individuals who have given so much of their time and imagination to developing *A Women's Thesaurus* over the past five years. Thanks also must go to the untold numbers of women—librarians, teachers, women in the media, scholars, workers in "nontraditional" occupations, mothers, grandmothers, and daughters—all of whom have helped to bring about in the past decade a major shift in attention to women, our histories, and our changing roles in contemporary society.

We have made a difference. The new scholarship about women has added significantly to our contemporary and historical knowledge of women's lives. Cutting across traditional academic disciplines and paradigms, this research has begun to carve out new interdisciplinary inquiries. These explorations have radically critiqued assumptions made about "mankind," assumptions that all too often claimed objectivity based on observations of young, privileged, white males. Feminist researchers have gone on to document links between race, class, and gender bias; linguists, philosophers, theologians, and literary critics have outlined the conceptual errors and false generics that structure our language. All these and many others have offered re-visions and new perspectives on our objectivity, new lenses through which to view our culture and history in its complexity and diversity.

Scholars have also unearthed and made accessible the words of generations of women: lost novels have been rediscovered; diaries, letters, and memoirs newly published. Contemporary women writers are breaking new ground. Artists and historians—older women essayists, ethnic poets and storytellers, women of color novelists—all are overcoming generations of silence and finding new voices.

The impetus of this research and writing about women and girls has created new fields of teaching. Course materials in elementary school, high school, college, and graduate and professional school curricula have increased significantly in recent years. Research and writing have also addressed social issues of immediate public policy impact: women and children living in poverty, occupational segregation, pay equity, the gender gap in voting patterns, and women's participation in world economic development, to name just a few. Advocacy programs designed to strengthen equal access and to assist women at all levels of society and with many types of needs are burgeoning. Even the most cursory surveys of available public resources turn up material ranging from census data and policy analysis throughout levels of government to popular magazine and television journalism and expanded "women's page" coverage in newspapers across the country.

The language used to describe and synthesize this social phenomenon, however, has not kept up with the material and activities generated. And it is this absence, these silences, the words not present, that has shaped our work on the thesaurus: for in spite of technical advances in information storage and retrieval, we have not been able to find, organize, or use effectively the plethora of information available. The language of standard indexing and classification systems—terms used in most journals, libraries, filing systems, and databases—does not offer vocabulary consistently or sufficiently detailed and up-to-date to retrieve the wealth of resources available. Existing classifications frequently overlook emerging topics of special concern to women. As a result, important information is lumped under "women" or is inaccessible. Prefixes and suffixes attached to terminology ostensibly gender neutral reflect implicit male norms and define women in terms of their relationships to men (labels like "nontraditional employment" or "unwed mothers"). Worse, by juxtaposition, indexing systems condition our response to important topics. Grouping lesbian issues and prostitution in categories of sexuality, for example, skews complex social, political, and personal concerns.

For these reasons a standardized vocabulary, a common language that reflects the complexity and subtlety of women's lives and work, has long been a shared goal. Individual researchers, writers, policy makers, and librarians as well as centers of women's research, information, and advocacy have struggled with various dimensions of the problem. Having come this far, we have discovered we have much farther to go—and we are on uncharted territory. This thesaurus is thus more than an index, more than the nuts and bolts of a librarian's "authority" list or a desktop reference guide—although it is and should be able to serve all these functions. For many of us, the thesaurus represents what one of the librarians on our task force called "reclaiming the power of naming." Adrienne Rich gave powerful poetic voice to this need in her collection of poetry *The Dream of a Common Language: Poems 1974–1977.* This first edition of *A Women's Thesaurus* is offered as prosaic contribution to the ongoing efforts to articulate that dream and shared vision.

ACKNOWLEDGMENTS

A Women's Thesaurus would not have been possible without the vision, commitment, and volunteer labor of the many individuals and organizations who contributed untold amounts of time, energy, and imagination to the project.

Collaboration is never an easy process under the best of circumstances. Collaboration on a language list is ripe for conflict, forcing confrontations with how we know ourselves and how the voices of others shape us. No dictionary or thesaurus, even one most leavened by use and tradition, can objectively reflect the complex realities it attempts to describe, and any published list of language should be understood as a work-in-progress.

Yet in spite of the difficulties of juggling emerging interdisciplinary areas of knowledge—and the different styles, requirements, and applications of scholars, librarians, teachers, students, policy makers, writers, and activists—we have carefully, successfully forged a collaborative process in producing this first edition. I am as proud of that process as I am proud of the product of our work.

The Business and Professional Women's Foundation, a Council member center, nurtured the project from its beginnings: without Jenrose Felmley's early and consistent vision, the thesaurus would have remained a good idea in committee. Margaret Siegel continued the Foundation's commitment—contributing energy, encouragement, sane perspectives, and crucial funding.

Cheryl Sloan, Foundation librarian when the project began, provided technical coordination for the first three years of our work. Her confidence, energy, and editing skills helped get us through those critical early phases when a book in print seemed a wistful dream buried in boxes of term forms. Her continued support, good humor, and thoughtful readings of the final manuscript have been critical to the success of our collaboration.

The Foundation contracted with InterAmerica, a Washington-based research and development firm, to do the initial planning, data entry, and first rounds of lexicographical editing. We are grateful to Jan Scheffman, InterAmerica project coordinator, and to Helen

Daniel, their lexicographer, for perseverance, dedication, and patience as the project continued to expand beyond what any of us had anticipated.

The Foundation's financial support for the thesaurus has come from Aetna Life & Casualty; the Atlantic Richfield Foundation; Chevron, USA; the Levi-Strauss Foundation; Mobil Corporation; the Perkin-Elmer Corporation; the Prudential Foundation; Sears, Roebuck and Company; the Sophia Fund; the Tandy Corporation; the Texaco Philanthropic Foundation; and the Xerox Foundation. Additional financial support has been contributed from the Council's core operating grants from the Ford Foundation, and from Council project grants from the Lilly Endowment and the Prudential Foundation. Advanced Data Management, developers of the DRS database software used to build the thesaurus, donated extensive in-kind programming assistance, computer time, and printing resources to complete the last phase of testing and editing.

Even though we can now draw on a rich vocabulary organized in one volume, no words it contains are adequate to express thanks to the Thesaurus Task Force, Subject Groups, Test Sites, and numerous colleagues whose expertise and encouragement broadened our frames of reference and strengthened our spirits.

Mariam K. Chamberlain, National Council president; other Council member center directors; Board chair Catharine R. Stimpson; and other Board and Executive Committee members all have offered encouragement and perspectives that helped to keep the project on track. Barbara Lewis, Saphira Baker, Joanna Mills, and Debra Schultz have provided the efficient, committed staff support without which we would never have gotten organized.

The women's studies database task force of American Library Association (ALA) members and the ALA Committee on the Status of Women in Librarianship contributed early collaboration, data, and essential expertise and vision.

Barbara Parker coordinated the first efforts to organize other interested groups and individuals, and her energy and leadership resulted in the October 1982 Council-sponsored meeting that formed the Thesaurus Task Force.

Donna Allen, Anne Colby, Wendy Culotta, Earnstein Dukes, Carol Falcione, Renee Feinberg, Janet Kaplan, Esther Katz, Patricia King, Sarah Pritchard, Sara Rix, Susan Searing, Cynthia Secor, Karen White, Helen Zimmerberg, and other task force and subject group members put in countless hours of project coordinating, poring over lists of words and editing. A special thanks to Sarah Pritchard, Sue Searing, and Pat King for always being available to read still another draft of the delimiters, answer technical questions, and offer thoughtful support.

The Association of College and Research Libraries' Women's Studies Section provided collective feedback and encouragement at the first critical phase of our testing.

Numerous other colleagues offered help at various stages of the project: Deborah Alterman, Joan Ariel, Mary Edith Arnold, Lynn Barnett, Susan Bellingham, Connie Buchanan, Charlotte Bunch, Lynn Cannon, Lillian Castillo-Speed, Richard Chabran, Gabriela Charnes, Ruth Dickstein, Bonnie Thornton Dill, Gusta Drenthe, Margaret Eichler, Joyce D. Falk, Wendy Foulger, Christine Georgeff, Lori Goetsch, Jane Gottlieb, D. Green, Jane

Guillaume, Barbara Haber, Hiroko Hashimoto, Lorrie Heuser, Suzanne Hildenbrand, Kathleen Hill, Alice Johnson, Patricia Guy, Azar Kattan, Cheris Kramarae, Bernice Lacks, Norma Lundberg, Judith McCaslin, Cynthia McClelland, Mary Drake McFeeley, Rosalie McKay-Want, Casey Miller, Peter Montague, Betsy Nuse, Harsha Parekh, Elizabeth Parent, Leslie Peirce, Katherine Phenix, Wei Chi Poon, Margaret Radcliffe, Frances Rooney, Patricia Roos, Tom Rumer, Sheryl Ruzek, Michelle Schroll, Sarah Sherman, Mafilde Sibille, Jill Gates Smith, Beth Stafford, Elizabeth Stevenson, Kate Swift, Barrie Thorne, Andrea Timberlake, Carol Tobin, Judy Touchton, Paula Treichler, Harriett Walker, Krystyna Wasserman, Sarah Watstein, Sarah Watts, Sara Whaley, Pat Wilson, Leslie Wolfe, Elizabeth Wood, Mary Wyers, and Irving Zaretsky all contributed invaluable perspectives, cleaned up gaffes, and offered suggestions that have considerably strengthened the current edition. A special thanks to Barrie Thorne and Carol Tobin for rereading several sections, raising thoughtful questions, and answering last-minute inquiries.

Thanks also to Jim Houston and Ted Brandhorst of the Educational Resources Information Center (ERIC) Processing and Reference Facility/ORI, Inc., for their suggestions and encouragement.

Our last phase of testing and online editing could never have been completed without the help of Advanced Data Management, developers of our DRS database software. K. Evan Gray donated countless "man hours" of creative programming, patient software instruction, and funny electronic mail support—a gracious, generous perspective that expanded visions of what was possible. Pete Herrick, Glenn Johnson, Hank McCauley, Sue Scott, Jack Twitchell, and other Advanced Data management and staff provided invaluable technical expertise, advice, and a corporate test site with a sense of humor for some of our preferred terms.

Thanks also to Frederic G. Cassidy, whose 1965 lexicography seminar at the University of Wisconsin–Madison first started me thinking about the process of language change and the politics of documenting and standardizing that process—and the potential (and nerve required) for humanists to realize our visions with computer technology.

I am especially grateful to Laura Adams; Charles, Ed, and Michael Capek; Clifford and Kathleen Hill; Claudia Koonz; Jeff Lucker; Ruth Mandel; Leslie Peirce; Cynthia Secor; Donna Shavlik; Anne and John Stagg; Joanne, Nancy, Peter, and Terry Stagg; John Waterbury; Paul Weber; Carolyn Wilson; Rob Woolfolk; and Irving Zaretsky for their continued support, encouragement, and patience. They have been both family and friends without whom, during these last five years, I would never have been able to sustain the energy needed to finish this project.

Finally, thanks go to Charlotte Sheedy and Vicky Bijur of the Charlotte Sheedy Literary Agency for their generous contribution of services and to our editors and the staff we've worked with at Harper & Row for their consistent professionalism and support: to Janet Goldstein, who found us and wisely steered us through to a finished book; to Kathie Ness, whose attention to detail and sense of humor made editing the final draft almost pleasant; to C. Linda Dingler, whose imagination and skill translated complex concepts into readable, classy design; and to Roz Barrow, whose persistence and savvy led to the necessary production solutions and kept us cheerfully on schedule. They all understood the project, took it up with enthusiasm and humor, and provided the vision that has shaped the final design and production of our book. Perhaps as important, they have continued our publishing arrangement in the same spirit that built the thesaurus, a process of collaboration that we hope will continue to shape and give voice to our language.

It is in that collaborative spirit that we would like to dedicate *A Women's Thesaurus:* to all those who gave so generously of their time, energy, and imagination to weave together this first edition.

THESAURUS CONSTRUCTION AND USE

Thesaurus Applications

The thesaurus is designed to support a variety of applications. It can help users develop manual and computerized filing systems, prepare indexes for books, establish categories in bibliographies, catalog special library collections, and index abstracts of research articles. We anticipate that it will be used in libraries, women's centers, classrooms, offices, government agencies, publishing enterprises, local archives, and any other settings that need a detailed language to store and retrieve and explore information.

Not least among these applications is an introduction to the language itself. We hope that users will browse through the displays. They offer rich, graphic access to the rapidly changing worlds of women's lives and ideas and are designed to lead users into the language. Randomly selected sections of the Alphabetical Display yield a diversity of terms that can spark metaphors and historical imagination: **piecework labor policy, the pill, pilots, pimps, pin money, pink collar workers, pioneers, pirates, pituitary hormones, placenta, planned parenthood.** Ready access to this dynamic vocabulary can have applications as diverse as suggesting paper topics for high school students, discussion themes for women's groups, or career opportunities for women reentering the work force.

Used systematically, the thesaurus displays are intended to encourage common usage of terms for sharing information among different types of users—standardized terms for filing information and for indexing books, reports, government documents, magazines, scholarly journals, newspapers, and newsletters, as well as for the compilation of multisource indexes and reference guides.

In addition to strengthening basic forms of information access like file headings and indexing, a primary objective in developing the thesaurus has been to offer needed refinements—cross-references to broader, narrower, and related terms—that can sharpen existing classification and cataloging systems. The thesaurus is not itself a classification system, nor is it intended to replace existing classification and cataloging systems. We expect, however, that the ready availability of terms contained in the thesaurus will enable catalogers working with manual or online card catalogs to add detailed descriptors that will refine existing systems. Catalogers using the thesaurus will be able to describe their collections more accurately and to provide some imaginative correctives for biases embedded in existing classification systems.

Wherever possible, we have attempted to maintain compatibility with existing classification and cataloging systems. We compared terms included in the thesaurus with terms used in the Library of Congress Subject Headings, for example, and have used preferred Library of Congress terms where they fit our own guidelines.

We have also designed the thesaurus for optimum use with electronic retrieval systems. Except where multiword (precoordinated) terms are needed for defining a unique concept (such as **gender gap** or **sex segregation**), we have postcoordinated terms so that both indexers and users will have maximum efficiency in assigning key words and requesting search terms. Instead of "nurses—salaries" or "housewives as authors" (existing Library of Congress Subject Headings), a user can index or retrieve literature on these subjects by pairing terms listed separately in the thesaurus: **nurses** and **wages** and **comparable worth** or **equal pay**. Or **authors** and **homemakers** or **wage earning wives** or **women working outside the home**.

Especially as the cost of mounting and disseminating electronic databases becomes more affordable, we anticipate that a major use of the thesaurus will be to provide a standardized control language for accessing information on computers. By making a more accurate control language available to existing online indexing systems, we also hope that the thesaurus will render more accessible those materials already indexed through many of the discipline-based and other online resources.

We hope that another use of the thesaurus will be to serve as a reference guide for nonsexist use of the language. Users looking up **stewardesses**, for example, will be referred to **flight attendants**. Cross-references will lead users from **housewives** to **homemakers**, from **working women** to **women working outside the home**. As a reference tool, the thesaurus is thus designed to lead users into the language—to provide alternative routes to locating terms and to broaden awareness of some of the ways in which language structures our thinking. Looking up **sexism**, for example, users will be referred to related terms like **doubly disadvantaged, pornography**, and **sexist language**. They will also be referred to the narrower terms **institutional sexism** and **linguistic sexism**. Looking up **institutional sexism** in turn will lead users to key concepts like **blaming the victim, gatekeeping, glass ceiling**, and **structural discrimination**. While no substitute for more comprehensive analyses of linguistic biases, as a working tool for users of the language at all levels of usage, the thesaurus attempts to provide comprehensive, accessible lists of terms that embody these important concepts. A selected bibliography is provided at the end of this introductory section for users who would like to explore these concepts in more detail.

Building the Thesaurus

The thesaurus is a product of many groups' and individuals' ideas and contributions and represents a long-standing awareness of the need for such a shared vocabulary. In 1975 the Business and Professional Women's Foundation (BPWF) convened one of the first meetings to address these needs systematically. A group of twenty-two organizations—including the Federation of Organizations of Professional Women, the Schlesinger Library, Catalyst, the Women's Action Alliance, and the Sophia Smith Collection at Smith College—formed the Women's Information Services Network. Meeting at the Wellesley College Center for Research on Women, the Network defined as a major objective the creation of a cooperative bibliographic database project.

The following year, a 1976 Women's Educational Equity Act grant created the Women's Educational Equity Communications Network, which began to gather and index citations on materials about women. The basic list of terms they produced stopped short of their goal—to generate a machine-readable "translator" between the existing databases and the language women policy makers, educators, and scholars actually use—but their list is one of the building blocks of this first edition of the thesaurus. Similar concerns among feminists in the American Library Association (ALA) resulted in Joan Marshall's 1977 landmark thesaurus, *On Equal Terms,* designed to surmount sexism in Library of Congress Subject Headings. In 1982 a coalition of ALA members formed an ad hoc women's studies database task force that developed standards for evaluating existing databases and for evaluating the extent to which they accurately indexed and made available resources on women (see Pritchard, 1984).

Also in 1982, the Business and Professional Women's Foundation began its thesaurus project. Its immediate aim was to lay the groundwork for developing a bibliographic database for the Foundation library's collection of 20,000 items that document the history and current status of women's employment and economic issues. That same year, Catalyst began to put its collection online, making the Catalyst Resource Center materials available for the first time through a national database vendor.

These projects coincided with the formation of the National Council for Research on Women, a coalition of feminist research and policy centers around the country. As one of its first collaborative projects, the Council undertook development of a thesaurus to improve access to existing research, programs, and work-in-progress. Working with BPWF, the Council identified other projects, centers, and individuals concerned with these issues and in the fall of 1982 sponsored the Task Force on Thesaurus Development as the first stage of a cooperative database project that is currently in the planning stages.

The Task Force produced a first draft of the thesaurus by combining subject lists, catalog headings, filing system guides, and index terms from thirty-five research centers, libraries, publishers, and associations. Duplicates were deleted and sources of the terms coded. This list was shared with librarians, scholars, policy makers, and activists in each of eleven subject categories, categories selected in an attempt to structure the thesaurus into usable and understandable subgroups: Communications; Economics and Employment; Education; History and Social Change; International Women; Language, Literature, Religion, and Philosophy; Law, Government, and Public Policy; Natural Sciences and Health; Science and Technology; Social Sciences and Culture; and Visual and Performing Arts.

The subject specialists in each area were asked to add missing terms and definitions, delete terms, suggest cross-references, indicate preferred terms, and identify potential areas of ambiguity and conflict. Their charge was to produce a revised list of the language—formal and informal, vernacular and scholarly—currently used to define women's lives and research in each of the eleven subject categories. We were concerned that the thesaurus accurately describe whatever would be indexed, sought, or filed. We were also committed to making the thesaurus accessible to the majority of users—using cross-references to related terms, broader and narrower terms, and preferred terms as well as offering subject groupings designed to lead users into the broadest possible scope of language describing their topics.

These recommendations were then collected and edited to conform to our Thesaurus Structure Committee's guidelines, which generally adopted standards of word form and form of entry set by the American National Standard Institute's *Guidelines for Thesaurus Structure, Construction, and Use* (ANSI Z39.19, 1974). We also used variations of the ERIC forms of entry (*Thesaurus of ERIC Descriptors,* 9th edition, 1982) as models for several of our displays.

After this initial round of editing, the cleaned and revised alphabetic and group listings—including definitions and cross-references—were again submitted to subject group specialists for review and revision. The second round of revisions has been edited and shared for testing at sixty-two research, policy, and advocacy centers in this country and abroad. This first published edition of the thesaurus incorporates test site recommendations and suggested revisions and lays the groundwork for a second edition more international in scope.

Building on this history of collaborative effort, *A Women's Thesaurus* has thus evolved as an attempt to define a common vocabulary, a process that is never complete for any culture or language group and one that we hope will grow with continued input from diverse sources. Nor has it been a process without controversy or conflict, for we have attempted to build consensus in areas that are by definition diverse and continually changing. Language is one of the most intimate and most political of human activities. The power of naming in fact shapes and defines the institutions that structure so much of our lives. Attempts to standardize that naming process are intrinsically controversial, especially when they describe concepts, processes, and behavior that in themselves are attempting to redefine dimensions of the language—or at least to wrench some terms free of the assumed, often biased norms that disenfranchise significant groups and individuals in our culture.

There are inevitably trade-offs between descriptions of the language as we have seen it used and our ambition to work toward a common vocabulary that empowers users without prejudice. What are the assumed norms, for example, implicit in a recently coined term like "feminization of poverty"? Do we acknowledge its currency in the literature and continue to use it as a convenient index term? Our task force suggested **women living in poverty** and **pauperization of women** as alternatives, terms perhaps more cumbersome but also more accurate, not perpetuating the process of attaching negative consequences to "feminization." (Wherever coined expressions have been suggested as preferred terms, we have tried to offer several alternatives.)

Other problems are also predictable, given the scope of the project. Sources of our terms are written, and since a primary use of the displays will be to index and retrieve written material, we have included few terms that reflect more exclusively oral traditions. These choices inevitably result in "privileging" a written ("literate") language over the language of women who lack a written language and are thereby even more silenced and marginal than their more privileged sisters. We have included minimal definitions—doubtless a lack that will be frustrating to some—and suggest that users refer to *A Feminist Dictionary* (Kramarae and Treichler, 1986) and other sources listed in the Selected Bibliography for more complete explications of terms. We will have missed preferred terms in some areas and overlooked cross-references in others. Also, given the range of our subject groups, we will have included too much detail for some users and not enough for others. Some users will disagree with our selection of subject groups and what are some inevitably arbitrary assignments of terms to one or more groups. While acknowledging such sources of potential conflict, it is nonetheless essential that this process of standardization, however imperfect, continue in the spirit of collaboration that has produced this first volume.

We do not claim objectivity. Any list of language has its roots in social, political, and economic perspectives. Our choices of terms to include and exclude, to cite as preferred or "do not use," have been shaped by our value systems and those of our organizations. Although terms selected reflect what we hope to be a broad spectrum of cultural and ethnic experience, given the need to limit our scope for this first edition, our choices have been primarily drawn from American English, less from other languages than we will include in subsequent editions. The choices nonetheless reflect our ambition to work toward a less "normed" vocabulary—or at least a vocabulary whose norms are more explicit—but we have few illusions about objectivity. By definition, our choices offer critiques of both current and past practices.

A final word about standardization: it is essential that this process be understood as a means of access. Standardization does not have to mean quashing diversity. What we have learned from the last several decades of work shows us the possibilities for a new kind of institutionalization: building a process of consensus, suggesting standards that themselves call into question assumed norms, defining structures without those structures in turn becoming oppressive. We intend this process to be an opening up, not a restricting of the language. Besides serving the needs of researchers, librarians, and other specialists, we are also attempting to provide a way into the vocabulary for users who may not be as immersed in the language. The standardization that makes this access possible does *not* silence or neutralize the complex world of women's lives. If anything, it is intended to open channels of communication to other users and other disciplines, to document women as linguistically creative speakers and writers who have been systematically excluded or stereotyped in virtually all previous lexicons and classification systems. Subsequent editions of *A Women's Thesaurus* will reflect modifications and additions as more diverse groups and individuals with different languages and different cultures use the thesaurus. All users are encouraged to share their suggestions as they work with the vocabulary and cross-references of this first edition—it is only this shared process that, finally, will begin to realize our dream of a common language.

Guidelines for Using the Thesaurus

Description and Scope

A Women's Thesaurus contains over 5000 terms that can be used as a controlled vocabulary to index and search for materials and information in each of the eleven subject areas. The lists contain preferred terms as well as broader and narrower terms, related terms, and word form variations. Where needed to clarify special meanings, we have provided scope notes (definitions of terms). Cross-references indicate relationships among terms. Our basic rule for including terms in the thesaurus has been a mid-level of specificity: enough detail to convey accurately the texture and substance of a topic or category without overwhelming our lists with details not needed for most indexing or classification uses.

An important editorial task has been to keep the list pared to a manageable size. Obviously, in some contexts any substantive words in the language can be used to describe women's lives. Our choices, therefore, were guided by our collective sense of contemporary or historical language used by women to define women's lives and research. We have tried to include in the main body of the thesaurus terms that have particular significance to women. The exceptions are terms like **organizations** or **corporations** that have considerable impact on women's lives, or terms referring to occupations, the major academic disciplines, and genres that define the scope of the Subject Group Display and the scope of much of our work.

We have also attempted to be suggestive rather than inclusive within categories. Our listing for **images of women**, for example, includes **Cinderella** and **Eve** and our listing for **linguistic sexism** includes **spinsters**, the latter an example of a negative connotation (compared to **bachelors**), but neither listing encompasses all possible examples from fairy tales or mythology or, in the case of **linguistic sexism**, from everyday speech.

With the exception of a suggested system of historical dates, all terms in the thesaurus are listed in the main Alphabetical Display and the Rotated Display. The Hierarchical Display lists only those terms that are assigned to one or more of the eleven subject groups. We have chosen to group the more generally applicable terms needed to narrow or refine a search strategy or standardize a manual filing system in a separate Delimiters Display.

These include lists like Types and Forms of Materials, Age and Education Levels, and Cultural and Political Movements. Many terms in the Delimiters Display are not cross-referenced to other terms in the thesaurus. The exceptions are terms like **womanism** or **children** or **older adults** that are linked to other main terms in the Alphabetical Display and are also assigned to one or more of the subject groups. Other exceptions that are cross-referenced include laws and regulations and delimiters that describe the broadest delimiter categories. Delimiters are also meant to be suggestive, not inclusive. We expect that users will combine delimiter terms with other terms in the Alphabetical Display to fit their own uses and will add their own delimiters as needed.

It should be noted at the outset that these guidelines for use are themselves general and cannot possibly anticipate all the ways in which users will want to use the thesaurus. Those creating files, catalogs, or indexes of specialized collections, for example, may need to establish specific patterns and more detailed guidelines for combining terms to describe their material.

Thesaurus Structure

The thesaurus contains six displays, or presentations, of the terms:

1. The ALPHABETICAL DISPLAY of terms, the "master" list, contains maximum information for each term: scope notes where used, the subject group(s) or delimiters group the term most logically fits into, USE and USE FOR indicators that mark preferred terms, and cross-references to other terms in the list. The Alphabetical Display alphabetizes word-by-word and not letter-by-letter: **child welfare**, for example, will be listed before **childbearing**.

Cross-references, described in more detail in the concluding section of these guidelines, include references to broader or larger terms (BTs), narrower or more specific terms (NTs), and related terms (RTs). Looking up the term **rape**, for example, users will be referred to the larger concept (BT) **sexual violence**; to the more specific examples (NTs) **acquaintance rape, domestic rape, gang rape, racist rape,** and **slave rape**; as well as to other RTs, or related terms: **crimes against children, crimes against women, incest, lynching, sex crimes,** and **slavery** (see Figure 1). Looking up **sexual violence**, users will in turn be referred to a still broader term, **violence**, as well as to another NT, **sexual assault**. BTs, NTs, and RTs for a main entry are arranged alphabetically. The Alphabetical Display lists BTs and NTs *one* level up and down (no grandparents or grandchildren). To see all existing levels up and down for a term (BTs of BTs and NTs of NTs—in other words, the entire extended family), refer to the Hierarchical Display.

The Alphabetical Display also contains definitions, or scope notes (SNs), where needed to clarify a specialized meaning of a term: **tipping**, for example, has a scope note that explains the term is "used to describe point at which status and salaries fall as larger numbers of women or minorities enter a profession or occupation" (see Figure 2). Where a term's use assumes a standard dictionary definition, scope notes are not provided. Subject group (SG) and delimiters group (DG) indicate the broad subject groupings or delimiter categories into which terms fall. Note that some terms are listed in more than one subject group. Some terms are also listed as delimiters as well as in subject groups. The entry **abortion**, for example, is listed in History and Social Change; Law, Government, and Public Policy; and Natural Sciences and Health. Terms like **feminism** and **diaries** will be listed in both a subject group and a delimiters group.

FIGURE 1

rape

SG Social Sciences and Culture
BT sexual violence
NT acquaintance rape
domestic rape
gang rape
racist rape
slave rape
RT crimes against children
crimes against women
incest
lynching
sex crimes
slavery
violence against women

FIGURE 2

tipping

SN *Used to describe point at which status and salaries fall as larger numbers of women or minorities enter a profession or occupation.*
SG Economics and Employment
UF feminization of occupations
feminization of professions
RT backlash
critical mass
equilibrium
occupational sex segregation
organizational behavior
women in

2. The ROTATED DISPLAY, sometimes called a "permuted" term display, indexes each word of a compound term in alphabetical sequence. Each term has as many entries as the number of words that comprise it. With the exception of the dates that are listed

as Historical Periods in the Delimiters Display and Roman or Arabic numbers included as parts of terms (**Title IX** or **Executive Order 11246**), all terms in the thesaurus are alphabetized by all words, including conjunctions, prepositions, articles, and possessive forms. This display permits the user to find a term by using any word in the term. **Old boy networks**, for example, will be alphabetized under **networks** and under **boy** as well as under **old**. This display is thus useful for finding all instances of terms in the thesaurus that contain the same word, for example all terms that include the word **employment** (see Figure 3).

FIGURE 3

```
              alternative employment
              barriers to employment   USE   job discrimination
    Comprehensive Employment and Training Act of 1973
                          employment
                          employment agencies
                          employment opportunities
                          employment patterns
                          employment practices
                          employment schedules
                          employment training   USE   job training
                    equal employment opportunity
                    Equal Employment Opportunity Commission
                  federal employment
                household employment
           male dominated employment
                  minority employment
           nontraditional employment
                     paid employment
                part time employment
                     self employment
       sex discrimination in employment
                    state employment
                temporary employment
                   unpaid employment
                    youth employment
```

3. The HIERARCHICAL DISPLAY shows preferred terms with as many as five possible links up to the broadest term for an entry and as many as five possible links down to the narrowest term for an entry. Note that some terms have more than one broad term at the same "level": **history** has two broader terms, **humanities** and **social sciences**. In this display, each broader term is extended and each narrower term indented; each is marked with one or more colons (BT) or periods (NT) to indicate its relationship to the main term (see Figure 4).

FIGURE 4

```
:: mass media
  : electronic media
    television
      . cable television
      . commercial television
      . educational television
      . public television
```

This format will help users to broaden or narrow a search and will lead users further into related concepts. When looking up broader or narrower terms listed under the "point of entry" term, for example, a user will be led to still other related terms in the Alphabetical Display. This Hierarchical Display includes in alphabetical order all preferred terms that are listed in subject groups, even those terms that have no broader or narrower terms listed. This display, however, does not include delimiters like National and Regional Descriptors or Cultural and Political Movements that are not also listed in subject groups. These terms are logically grouped in the Delimiters Display.

It should also be noted that in some instances, we have bent or avoided building literal hierarchies: including both **male circumcision** and **female circumcision** in a hierarchy under "circumcision" and, in turn, under **surgical procedures**, for example, distorts significant differences in both implications and practice between the two procedures.

4. The SUBJECT GROUP DISPLAY alphabetizes main terms within each of the eleven subject groups:

Communications
Print and electronic mass media; journalism; publishing; telecommunications; information science and theory, including libraries; public relations and information; dissemination; propaganda.

Economics and Employment
Economic theory, systems, and conditions; finance, including pension and insurance; business and industry, including agriculture; institutional/organizational/management theory and practice; employment/labor/careers, including homemaking and volunteerism; income/pay equity; workplace.

Education
Nursery and day care programs; primary and secondary education; vocational, professional, and religious education; higher education; continuing, adult, and extension education; career counseling; students; faculty; administration; curricula; boards and governance; funding, including financial aid, and public and private support to education; research methods.

History and Social Change
Women's history; women's movements; history of social change; feminist theory; historiography; lesbian studies.

International Women
Women in development, including urban/rural migration; multinational labor force; women's role in liberation struggles; women in other cultures; human rights.

Language, Literature, Religion, and Philosophy
Linguistics; semiotics; literature, including autobiography, biography, diaries, memoirs, and letters; literary criticism; women's spirituality; religion; theology; mythology; philosophy; ethics.

Law, Government, and Public Policy
Law and legislation, including regulations and enforcement; legal rights; crime, prisons, and punishment; military and defense; politics; political science and theory; economic and social policies and services, including welfare, day care, and housing; international relations.

Natural Sciences and Health
Biological sciences, including biology, botany, chemistry, physiology, zoology, and genetics; health sciences, including medicine, dentistry, nursing, and pharmacology; wellness, including mental health and nutrition; home economics; athletics; sexuality; birth control and abortion; pregnancy and childbirth.

Science and Technology
Physical and earth sciences; environmental sciences, including antinuclear movement; engineering; technology and impact of technology; computer science; mathematics.

Social Sciences and Culture
Psychology; sociology; anthropology; ethnic and interdisciplinary studies, including race, class, and gender studies; demography; stereotyping and perceptual bias; violence against women and children; sex roles; socialization; institutions; marriage and the family; kinship; life cycles; life styles; clothing and social entertaining.

Visual and Performing Arts
Theater; visual arts; photography; dance; mime; music; film; stage entertaining; architecture and interior design; fashion design; folk and domestic arts; art theory, technique, and criticism; museums and galleries; performance spaces.

5. The USE/DO NOT USE DISPLAY lists preferred terms and "do not use" terms, alphabetizing first by preferred terms with references to "do not use" terms, then by "do not use" terms with references to preferred terms.

This display combines several different categories of preferred and "do not use" terms that are grouped for convenience. It suggests alternatives for sexist terms (girl watching USE **street harassment**); terms with feminine prefixes and suffixes that imply male norms (stewardesses USE **flight attendants** or actresses USE **actors**); other terms that contain embedded biases (unwed mothers USE **single mothers**, working women USE **women working outside the home** or **wage earning women**); as well as terms that attempt to avoid euphemism (**armed forces** instead of armed services); terms labeled "preferred" to select from among several synonyms for purposes of simplifying indexing (movies USE **films**, babies USE **infants**); and terms that lead to and from alternative spellings and acronyms (theatre USE **theater**, ERA USE **equal rights amendment**). For consistency and ease in using groupings like the Laws and Regulations list in the Delimiters Display, we have opted to retain spelled-out versions of all acronyms.

6. The DELIMITERS DISPLAY includes generic search terms or proper nouns, often common to several subject groups, that can be used to "delimit," narrow, or refine an online search strategy or standardize a manual filing system. Although all delimiters but historical dates are listed in the Alphabetical and Rotated Displays, we have opted to group these descriptors in a separate display to provide easier access. Key search words like **bibliographies, transcripts, questionnaires, French, Afro American, Medieval Period, expressionism, Title IX,** and **Vietnam War**, for example, are listed alphabetically within logical categories:

> Age Levels
> Cultural and Political Movements
> Education Levels
> Ethnic, Racial, and Religious Descriptors
> Historical Periods
> Laws and Regulations
> National and Regional Descriptors
> Types and Forms of Materials

We expect users to combine these delimiter terms with other terms in the Alphabetical Display as part of any controlled vocabulary, but with some exceptions we have not cross-referenced many of the delimiter terms to other terms in the Alphabetical Display. Nor does the Delimiters Display include all possible terms in any given category. Most delimiter groupings are meant to suggest classifications and other relevant concepts, not be all-inclusive. We expect that users will add terms, even additional categories, to the Delimiters Display to meet their needs for indexing or searching specialized collections. (American history archives, for example, will obviously have to include many more terms describing key periods and movements in the United States, and international collections will need to expand the list of national descriptors.)

With some modifications, the age and education lists use the ERIC Educational/Age Level Descriptors. For period delimiters, we adopted a dual system. For dates before 1800, we have used century designators in addition to some of the more commonly accepted period terms (**Middle Ages**). For dates after 1800, we have used decade breakdowns and some more common designations (**Industrial Revolution**) but have not included the extensive list of date-specific proper names—political administrations, for example, or Supreme Court decisions—that users can supply themselves in searching computerized databases, in indexing a book, or in setting up manual filing systems.

Form of Entry

Since the thesaurus uses language relating primarily if not exclusively to women, we have seldom used the words **woman** and **women** or their synonyms or derivatives in combination with other terms except where the concept would be incomplete or ambiguous without it or where the concept describes an emerging field or area of interest that users want to highlight as its own "entity." (We list **women in development** and **women's athletics, mass media** and **women's media**, for example, but do not list "women in the media"). Persons working with collections that are not exclusive to women are encouraged to assign terms for women as well as terms for men where each is applicable. The objective should be to maintain a balance, free of biases and assumed norms that prefixes, suffixes, and adjectival identifiers often connote. We have included the two terms **women in** and **women and** for the purposes of suggesting consistency of use as well as cross-references for these terms in combination.

We have also tried to avoid using suffixes like *-ess* and *-ette* that assume male norms and instead refer users to a sex-neutral term like **flight attendants** or suggest reclaiming a "traditionally male" term for both sexes (hostesses USE **hosts**). Where the *-ess* form is needed for historical reference, we have included the descriptor "historical" in parentheses with the term, as in **seamstresses (historical)**. In some instances, where women have only recently been accepted into a traditionally male-dominated occupation or profession, we have opted to keep terms like **clergywomen, congresswomen,** or **assemblywomen**. Women who hold these positions often refer to themselves with these titles to underscore women's emerging opportunities. In other instances (**chair**, for example, or **actor** or **host**), there appears to be movement toward more gender-neutral usage.

Each preferred term represents a single concept expressed in one or several words, for example, **abortion, abortion clinics, abortion laws.**

Wherever possible we have used single-word terms, and we expect users will combine terms for their own use. Double delimiters like "bibliographies of bibliographies" or "guides to periodicals" should be postcoordinated from the single-entry delimiters we have included: **bibliographies** and **guides** and **periodicals**.

Multiword terms are used to describe a specialized concept (for example, **consciousness raising**) and are expressed in their natural word order: **day care centers** rather than "centers, day care."

In most instances we have used noun forms, including verb or adjective forms only if a concept could not be expressed in noun form (for example, **desex**). Adjectives are used with a noun only when they describe or limit that noun as part of a specialized concept, for example, **sexual preference**.

The singular is used for processes (**listening**), attributes (**fertility**), and unique things and genres (**menstruation** or **poetry**); the plural is used only for classes of things (**festivals**). In some instances, the singular form will be listed in a subject group as a genre (**film**) and the plural form will be included in the Delimiters Display as a type of material (**films**).

We have included few proper nouns. Most of them are listed as Historical Periods, Cultural and Political Movements, or Laws and Regulations in the Delimiters Display. The few exceptions to these guidelines are terms like **Marxism** or **Freudianism** that, although technically proper nouns, function as larger concepts. We expect that users will assign proper nouns as needed to describe materials for manual or online use.

Minimal punctuation is used. The exception is apostrophes where needed for clarity to mark possessive forms. Users who plan to use the thesaurus terms with computerized systems should be aware that some search and retrieval software will not accept or ignore apostrophes or other punctuation, and thus they will need to strip all punctuation before assigning terms.

Occupation classifications build on U.S. Department of Labor, U.S. Census titles, and ERIC hierarchies but have been revised and expanded to include groupings that more accurately reflect the ways in which the terms are used in women's centers and collections. Terms included in the hierarchical display under **education occupations** and **health care occupations**, for example, cut across professional levels. We have also attempted to avoid the implicit bias in terms like "unskilled workers" and have chosen to use terms like **workers** or **laborers** that are less class-biased and demeaning. There are obviously trade-offs between standardization, descriptive usefulness, and unbiased language.

Subject groups and delimiters groups are designated in the main alphabetical list. If a term is included in more than one group, the additional groups will be listed.

Slang terms are designated as such in scope notes. Quotation marks used in a scope note indicate slang or informal use of a term. Quotation marks also sometimes indicate bias, pejorative uses of a term, or simply embedded assumptions of a male norm (as in "master" list).

One final note about forms of entry: these guidelines were selected because they follow most of the ANSI standards and also because they are especially appropriate for electronic retrieval systems. Users can list as many terms as needed to describe the item, given the space limitations of the record format. When using the thesaurus to create manual indexing terms, file folders, or other category labels, however, users may want to employ techniques appropriate to the particular medium and are encouraged to do so. When setting up file folders, for example, it may be more straightforward to use dashes (**abortion clinics—Maryland**) or reverse order to keep files alphabetized by the key word in a term.

Cross-References

A final summary of the cross-references in the Alphabetical Display may be helpful: these cross-references guide the searcher from a term used as a starting point to (1) a more general (broader) or a more specific (narrower) term (BT or NT); (2) a related term (RT) describing another aspect of the subject; and (3) the preferred term for the concept as it is used in the thesaurus, if a preferred term is indicated (USE/UF). Given our objective of "leading" users into the language, rather than repeat lists of all related terms at each relevant entry, we list several related terms that are meant to suggest synonyms that a user can look up. A user will thus be led into still other dimensions that broaden possible perspectives on a concept. Looking up **clitoris**, for example, a user will be referred to **clitoridectomy** and **female circumcision** as well as to **genitals** and **orgasm**. Looking up **orgasm**, the user will be referred to **masturbation, sex counseling, nonorgasmic women**, and **sexual satisfaction**. Looking up **female circumcision**, in turn, the user will be referred to other related terms like **chastity belts, genital mutilation, infibulation, initiation rites,** and **tribal customs**. With few exceptions, RTs do not refer to opposites.

Abbreviations and cross-references:

SN (SCOPE NOTE) is a brief definition that describes specialized or less familiar meanings of a term being used.

ethic of care
SN *Moral stance placing value on caring and responsibility in relationships rather than on abstract rights and rules.*

NT (NARROW TERM) refers to a term that is narrower or more specialized in concept than the entry term and should be consulted if a user wants more specific information. Terms indented under NTs in the Hierarchical Display are still narrower terms linked to their respective broader terms.

eating disorders
NT anorexia nervosa
    bulimia

domestic violence
NT marital violence

BT (BROAD TERM) refers to a term that is broader or more general in concept than the entry term.

bulimia
BT eating disorders

domestic violence
BT violence

RT (RELATED TERM) refers to a term that describes another concept related to the entry term.

abortion rights
RT   prochoice

domestic violence
RT   crimes against women
     crisis intervention

USE refers to the preferred term for that concept. As described earlier, in some instances we have indicated a USE term that reduces bias in a concept or reflects the most frequent ways of referring to the concept. In other instances, however, the preferred term was selected from among equals in an attempt to provide some guidance for simplifying indexing and filing systems. Even with a preferred term indicated, however, we felt it was important to include as many UF terms as possible since these provide ways into the language for many users. All UF terms as well as USE terms are listed in the Alphabetical Display.

unwed mothers
USE   **single mothers**

family violence
USE   **domestic violence**

UF (USE FOR) refers to other forms or synonyms of an entry that are not the preferred term for the concept.

single mothers
UF   unwed mothers

domestic violence
UF   family violence

Thesaurus Subject Groups

Communications
*Donna Allen, *Media Report to Women*
Sarah Pritchard, Library of Congress
Sarah Sherman, Northwestern
   University Library

Economics and Employment
*Carol Falcione, Graduate School of
   Business Administration Library,
   New York University

*Group Coordinator

Harriett Harper, Women's Bureau, Department of Labor

Heidi Hartmann, National Academy of Sciences

Gurley Turner, Catalyst

Elizabeth Vetter, Scientific Manpower Commission

Education

Lynn Barnett, ERIC Clearinghouse on Higher Education at The George Washington University

Jean Campbell, Center for Continuing Education for Women, University of Michigan

*Renee Feinberg, Brooklyn College Library

History and Social Change

Esther Katz, Institute for Research in History

Cheryl Kern-Simirenko, Syracuse University Library

*Susan E. Searing, Office of the Women's Studies Librarian, The University of Wisconsin System

International Women

Jacqueline Marie, University of California Library, Santa Cruz

Martita Midence and Vicki Semler, International Women's Tribune Centre

*Karen White, International Center for Research on Women

Language, Literature, Religion, and Philosophy

*Patricia M. King, The Arthur and Elizabeth Schlesinger Library, Radcliffe College

Ruth Perry, Program in Women's Studies, Massachusetts Institute of Technology

Law, Government, and Public Policy

*Sara Rix, The Women's Research and Education Institute, Congressional Caucus for Women's Issues

Sarah Watstein, Hunter College Library

Natural Sciences and Health

Belita Cowan, National Women's Health Network

Evelyn Fox Keller, Northeastern University

Kay Rodgers, Library of Congress

M. Elizabeth Tidball, Department of Physiology, George Washington University Medical Center

*Helen Zimmerberg, Biology Library, Princeton University

Science and Technology

Michelle Aldrich, Office of Opportunities in Science, American Association for the Advancement of Science

Joan Callanam, National Research Council

*Wendy Culotta, California State University Library, Long Beach

Barbara Sloat, Women in Science Program, Center for Continuing Education for Women, University of Michigan

Elizabeth Stage, Lawrence Hall of Science, University of California, Berkeley

Social Sciences and Culture

Anne Colby, The Henry R. Murray Research Center, Radcliffe College

*Earnstein Dukes, Center for Research
on Women, Memphis State University
Pat Padala, Center for Continuing
Education for Women, University of
Michigan
Karen Sacks, Business and Professional
Women's Foundation
Beth Stafford, University Library,
University of Illinois at
Urbana-Champaign

Visual and Performing Arts
Jane Gottlieb, The Juilliard School
Library
*Janet Kaplan, National Institute for
Women in the Visual Arts, Moore
College of Art
Elizabeth Wood, musicologist

Thesaurus Task Force

*Mary Ellen S. Capek, National Council
for Research on Women
Anne Colby, The Henry R. Murray
Center, Radcliffe College
Earnstein Dukes, Center for Research
on Women, Memphis State University
Heidi Hartmann, National Academy of
Sciences
Janet Kaplan, National Institute for
Women in the Visual Arts, Moore
College of Art
Esther Katz, Institute for Research in
History
Patricia M. King, The Arthur and
Elizabeth Schlesinger Library,
Radcliffe College

Janie Kritzman, Barnard College
Joan Marshall, Brooklyn College
Barbara Parker, University of Tennessee
Sarah M. Pritchard, Library of
Congress
Susan E. Searing, Office of the Women's
Studies Librarian, The University of
Wisconsin System
Cynthia Secor, Higher Education
Resources Services (HERS),
Mid-America
*Cheryl A. Sloan, Business and
Professional Women's Foundation
Gurley Turner, Catalyst
Sara Whaley, *Women's Studies
Abstracts,* Rush Publishing Company

Original Lists Combined to Form the Thesaurus

Archives of American Minority Cultures
Barnard College Women's Center
Business and Professional Women's Foundation
California State University, Hayward—Women's Studies
Catalyst
Cornell University, Trade Union Women's Studies, Materials Center (books and vertical
files)
Department of Labor, Women's Bureau

Equity Policy Center
Federation of Organizations of Professional Women
Higher Education Resources Services (HERS), Mid-America
Indiana University, Women's Studies Program
International Center for Research on Women
Lesbian Periodicals Index
Memphis State University, Center for Research on Women
National Association for Women Deans, Administrators, and Counselors—Center for Archival Collections
National Institute for Women in the Visual Arts, Moore College of Art
National Organization for Women Library/Resource Center
Project on the Status and Education of Women, Association of American Colleges
Radcliffe College, The Henry A. Murray Research Center
Radcliffe College, The Arthur and Elizabeth Schlesinger Library
Rutgers University, Eagleton Institute of Politics, Center for the American Woman and Politics
Seattle Office for Women's Rights
Smith College, Sophia Smith Collection, Women's History Archive
Southwest Institute for Research on Women
University of California, Berkeley—Center for the Study, Education, and Advancement of Women
University of Colorado, Boulder—Women's Studies Program Curriculum Design Project
University of Delaware, Women's Studies Program
University of Missouri, Columbia—Women's Studies Program
University of Oklahoma, Women's Studies Program
University of Pittsburgh, School of Library and Information Science
The University of Wisconsin System, Office of the Women's Studies Librarian
West Coast Lesbian Collections
Women's Educational Equity Communications Network
Women's Institute for Freedom of the Press
The Women's Research and Education Institute, Congressional Caucus for Women's Issues

Thesaurus Test Sites

U.S.

American Library Association, Committee on the Status of Women in Librarianship
The Business and Professional Women's Foundation
California State University, University Library and Learning Resources
Educational Resources Information Center (ERIC), Clearinghouse on Higher Education
Girls Clubs of America, Inc., National Resource Center
Harvard University, Harvard Divinity School

Hunter College Library
Kappa Alpha Theta Fraternity
Kitchen Table (Women of Color) Press
Lesbian Herstory Archives, Lesbian Herstory Educational Foundation
Louisiana State University, School of Library and Information Science
Media Report to Women
Memphis State University, Center for Research on Women
Michigan State University, Department of Sociology
Northwestern University Library, Women's Collection
Princeton University Biology Library
Princeton University Firestone Library
Radcliffe College, The Arthur and Elizabeth Schlesinger Library
Rutgers University, Eagleton Institute, Center for the American Woman and Politics
Signs: Journal of Women in Culture and Society
Smith College Library
State University of New York, Buffalo, School of Information and Library Studies
State University of New York, College at Plattsburgh, Women's Studies Program
Texas Women's University Library, Texas Women's University
University of Arizona Library
University of California, Berkeley, Asian American Studies Library
University of California, Berkeley, Chicano Periodical Index
University of California, Berkeley, Native American Studies Library
University of California, Irvine, Main Library—History Thesaurus Project
University of California, Los Angeles, Chicano Studies Research Center
University of California, Los Angeles, Institute for Social Science Research
University of Illinois at Urbana-Champaign, College of Medicine
University of Illinois at Urbana-Champaign, University Library
The University of Wisconsin–LaCrosse, Institute for Women's Studies
The University of Wisconsin System Library, Office of the Women's Studies Librarian
Vassar College Library
Womanbooks
Women & Language
Women's Medical College of Pennsylvania, Archives and Special Collections on Women
Women's Poetry Index
Women's Studies Abstracts

International

Canadian Women's Indexing Group, Canada
University of Waterloo, The Library, Canada
Programa de Información para la Mujer, Fundación Acción Ya, Costa Rica
Centro de Investigación para la Acción Femenina, Dominican Republic

Equal Opportunities Commission, England
United Nations Economic Commission for Africa, African Training and Research Centre,
    Ethiopia
Research Unit on Women's Studies, S.N.D.T. Women's University, India
ISIS International, Italy
National Women's Education Centre, Japan
International Organization of Consumers Unions, Regional Office for Asia and the Pacific,
    Malaysia
Rijksuniversiteit Utrecht, Interfacultaire werkgroep vrouwenstudies, The Netherlands
University of Leiden, Research and Documentation Centre, Women and Autonomy, The
    Netherlands
broadsheet, the feminist magazine, New Zealand
New Zealand Committee on Women
Centro Flora Tristan, Women's Documentation Centre, Peru
United Nations Economic and Social Commission for Asia and the Pacific, Thailand
Technische Universität Berlin, West Germany

Selected Bibliography

Berman, Sanford, and James P. Danky, eds. *Alternative Library Literature, 1984/1985: A Biennial Anthology.* Jefferson, NC: McFarland & Company, Inc., 1987.

Bunch, Charlotte. *Passionate Politics: Feminist Theory in Action—Essays 1968–1986.* New York: St. Martin's Press, 1987.

Daly, Mary. *Gyn/Ecology: The Metaethics of Radical Feminism.* Boston: Beacon Press, 1978.

Dickstein, Ruth, Vicki Mills, and Ellen Waite, eds. *Women: In LC's Terms.* Phoenix, AZ: Oryx Press, 1987.

Feminist Periodicals: A Current Listing of Contents. 1981– . [Published quarterly. University of Wisconsin Women's Studies Librarian, 112A Memorial Library, 728 State Street, Madison, WI 53706.]

Feminist Studies. 1972– . [Published three times a year. Women's Studies Program, University of Maryland, College Park, MD 20742.]

Gelfand, Elissa D., and Virginia Thorndike Hules. *French Feminist Criticism: Women, Language, and Literature: An Annotated Bibliography.* New York: Garland, 1985.

Grahn, Judy. *Another Mother Tongue: Gay Words, Gay World.* Boston: Beacon Press, 1984.

Green, Rayna. *American Indian Women: A Contextual Bibliography.* Indianapolis: Indiana University Press, 1983.

Harding, Sandra, and Merrill B. Hintikka, eds. *Discovering Reality: Feminist Perspectives on Epistemology, Metaphysics, Methodology, and Philosophy.* Hingham, MA: Kluwer Boston, 1983.

Henley, Nancy M. *Body Politics: Power, Sex, and Nonverbal Communication.* Englewood Cliffs, NJ: Prentice-Hall, 1977.

Hildenbrand, Suzanne. "Women's Studies Online: Promoting Visibility." *RQ:* 63–74 (Fall 1986).

Hill, Alette Olin. *Mother Tongue, Father Time: A Decade of Linguistic Revolt.* Bloomington: Indiana University Press, 1986.

Hooks, Bell. *Feminist Theory: From Margin to Center.* Boston: South End Press, 1984.

Hull, Gloria T., Patricia Bell Scott, and Barbara Smith, eds. *All the Women Are White, All the Blacks Are Men, But Some of Us Are Brave: Black Women's Studies.* Old Westbury, NY: Feminist Press, 1982.

Keohane, Nannerl, Michelle Rosaldo, and Barbara C. Gelpi, eds. *Feminist Theory: A Critique of Ideology.* Chicago: University of Chicago Press, 1982.

Kramarae, Cheris. *Women and Men Speaking: Frameworks for Analysis.* Rowley, MA: Newbury House, 1981.

Kramarae, Cheris, and Paula A. Treichler, eds. *A Feminist Dictionary.* Boston: Pandora Press, 1986.

Lennert, Midge, and Norma Willson, eds. *A Woman's New World Dictionary.* Lomita, CA: 51% Publications. [Pamphlet in Special Collections, Northwestern University Library, Evanston, IL.]

Loeb, Catherine R., Susan E. Searing, and Esther Stineman. *Women's Studies: A Recommended Core Bibliography 1980–1985.* Littleton, CO: Libraries Unlimited, 1987.

Maggio, Rosalie. *The Nonsexist Word Finder: A Dictionary of Gender-Free Usage.* Phoenix, AZ: Oryx Press, 1987.

Marshall, Joan K. *On Equal Terms: A Thesaurus for Nonsexist Indexing and Cataloging.* New York: Neal-Schuman, 1977.

McConnell-Ginet, Sally, Ruth Borker, and Nelly Furman. *Women and Language in Literature and Society.* New York: Praeger, 1980.

Media Report to Women. 1972– . [Published bimonthly. Women's Institute for Freedom of the Press, 3306 Ross Place, N.W., Washington, DC 20008.]

Miller, Casey, and Kate Swift. *The Handbook of Nonsexist Writing: For Writers, Editors, and Speakers.* New York: Harper & Row, 1980. [Revised edition forthcoming 1988.]

Minnich, Elizabeth. "Conceptual Errors Across the Curriculum: Towards a Transformation of the Tradition." Working Papers Series. Memphis, TN: Center for Research on Women, Memphis State University, 1986.

Moraga, Cherríe, and Gloria Anzaldúa, eds. *This Bridge Called My Back: Writings by Radical Women of Color.* 2nd ed. New York: Kitchen Table (Women of Color) Press, 1983.

Pritchard, Sarah M. "Developing Criteria for Database Evaluation: The Example of Women's Studies." In *Evaluation of Reference Services,* Bill Katz and Ruth Fraley, eds. New York: Heyworth Press, 1984.

Resources for Feminist Research/Documentation sur la recherche féministe. 1972– . [Published quarterly. Ontario Institute for Studies in Education, 252 Bloor Street West, Toronto, Ontario M5S 1V6, Canada.]

Rich, Adrienne. *The Dream of a Common Language: Poems 1974–1977.* New York: W. W. Norton, 1978.

———. *On Lies, Secrets, and Silence: Selected Prose 1966–1978.* New York: W. W. Norton, 1979.

Russ, Joanna. *How to Suppress Women's Writing.* Austin: University of Texas Press, 1983.

Sage: A Scholarly Journal on Black Women. 1984– . [Published semiannually. P.O. Box 42741, Atlanta, GA 30311-0741.]

Seager, Joni, and Ann Olson. *Women in the World: An International Atlas.* New York: Simon and Schuster, 1986.

Searing, Susan E. *Introduction to Library Research in Women's Studies.* Boulder, CO: Westview Press, 1985.

Sherman, Julia A., and Evelyn Torton Beck, eds. *The Prism of Sex: Essays in the Sociology of Knowledge.* Madison, WI: University of Wisconsin Press, 1979.

Signs: Journal of Women in Culture and Society. 1975– . [Published quarterly. The University of Chicago Press, Journals Division, P.O. Box 37005, Chicago, IL 60637.]

Smith, Barbara, ed. *Home Girls: A Black Feminist Anthology.* New York: Kitchen Table (Women of Color) Press, 1983.

Spender, Dale. *Man Made Language.* 2nd ed. Boston: Routledge & Kegan Paul, 1985.

Stimpson, Catharine R., with Nina Kressner Cobb. *Women's Studies in the United States: A Report to the Ford Foundation.* New York: Ford Foundation, 1986.

Stineman, Esther, with Catherine Loeb. *Women's Studies: A Recommended Core Bibliography.* Littleton, CO: Libraries Unlimited, 1979.

Thorne, Barrie, and Nancy Henley, eds. *Language and Sex: Difference and Dominance.* Rowley, MA: Newbury House, 1975.

Thorne, Barrie, Cheris Kramarae, and Nancy Henley, eds. *Language, Gender, and Society.* Rowley, MA: Newbury House, 1983.

Todasco, Ruth, ed. *An Intelligent Woman's Guide to Dirty Words.* Chicago: Loop Center YWCA, 1973.

Tuttle, Lisa. *Encyclopedia of Feminism.* New York: Facts on File, 1986.

Vetterling-Braggin, Mary, ed. *Sexist Language: A Modern Philosophical Analysis.* Totowa, NJ: Rowman and Littlefield, 1981.

Walker, Barbara G. *The Women's Encyclopedia of Myths and Secrets.* New York: Harper & Row, 1983.

Wittig, Monique, and Sande Zeig. *Lesbian Peoples: Material for a Dictionary.* New York: Avon, 1979.

Women & Language. 1975– . [Published two–three times annually. University of Illinois at Urbana-Champaign, 244 Lincoln Hall, 702 South Wright Street, Urbana, IL 61801.]

Women's Studies International Forum. 1978– . [Published bimonthly. Pergamon Press, Maxwell House, Fairview Park, Elmsford, NY 10523.]

Women's Studies Quarterly. 1982– . [Published quarterly. The Feminist Press at the City University of New York, 311 East 94th Street, New York, NY 10128.]

ALPHABETICAL
DISPLAY

MAIN TERM ⟶ **pay equity**

SCOPE NOTE ⟶ SN *Basing compensation on education, skills, effort, training, and responsibility rather than nonrelevant classifications of sex, age, racial or ethnic background, or other discriminatory classifications.* ⟩ USAGE DEFINITION

SUBJECT GROUPS ⟶ SG Economics and Employment
Law, Government, and Public Policy

BROADER TERM ⟶ BT equity

NARROWER TERMS ⟶ NT comparable worth
equal pay for equal work

RELATED TERMS ⟶ RT back pay
careers
economic equity
equal pay
Federal Equitable Pay Practices Act of
1987
labor legislation
low pay
occupational sex segregation
sexual division of labor
wage discrimination
wage gap
wages

ability
SG   Education
NT   academic ability
artistic ability
math ability
nonverbal ability
verbal ability
RT   aptitude
motivation

ableism
SN   *Includes concepts of bias, stereotyping,
and discrimination against people
with physical or mental disabilities.*
SG   History and Social Change
Natural Sciences and Health
Social Sciences and Culture
RT   ageism
classism
developmental disabilities
differently abled
disabled
discrimination against the disabled
doubly disadvantaged
equal access
racism
sexism
stereotyping

abnormal psychology
SG   Social Sciences and Culture
BT   psychology

abolition
SG   History and Social Change
RT   manumission
slavery
social movements
underground railroad

aboriginals
USE   **indigenous**

abortifacient agents
SG   Natural Sciences and Health
RT   abortion
drugs

abortion
SG   History and Social Change
Law, Government, and Public Policy
Natural Sciences and Health
NT   criminal abortion
induced abortion
spontaneous abortion
therapeutic abortion
RT   abortifacient agents
abortion movement
antiabortion movement
attitudes
contraception
dilatation and curettage
fetuses
hospitals
laws
medical ethics
miscarriage
population control
pregnancy prevention
religious law
reproductive freedom
unwanted pregnancy
viability

abortion clinics
SG   Law, Government, and Public Policy
Natural Sciences and Health
UF   abortion mills
BT   clinics
RT   abortion counseling
hospitals
terrorism

abortion counseling
SG   Education
Natural Sciences and Health
Social Sciences and Culture
BT   counseling
RT   abortion clinics
abortion rights
sex education

abortion laws
SG   Law, Government, and Public Policy
BT   laws

(*cont.*)

---

abortion laws (*cont.*)
RT antiabortion movement
criminal abortion
ethics
Medicaid
prochoice
religious sanctions
values

abortion mills
USE **abortion clinics**

abortion movement
SG History and Social Change
DG Cultural and Political Movements
UF prochoice movement
BT social movements
RT abortion
antiabortion movement
prochoice
reproductive freedom
reproductive rights
women's rights

abortion rights
SG Law, Government, and Public Policy
BT rights
RT abortion counseling
freedom of choice
Medicaid
prochoice

absentee fathers
SG Social Sciences and Culture
BT fathers
RT fatherless families
paternity
runaway fathers

absentee mothers
SG Social Sciences and Culture
BT mothers
RT motherless families
runaway mothers

absenteeism
SG Economics and Employment
(*cont.*)

absenteeism (*cont.*)
RT alcohol abuse
employee records
family responsibility
occupational health and safety
school attendance
sick children
work attitudes

abstention
SG Social Sciences and Culture
RT discipline
substance abuse

abstinence
SG Language, Literature, Religion, and
Philosophy
Natural Sciences and Health
Social Sciences and Culture
NT sexual abstinence
RT chastity
discipline
religious practices
self control
substance abuse
vows of chastity

abstract expressionism
DG Cultural and Political Movements

abstract reasoning
SG Language, Literature, Religion, and
Philosophy
Social Sciences and Culture
BT cognitive processes
RT intelligence
intuition
logic
moral reasoning
philosophy
problem solving
psychological testing

abstracts
DG Types and Forms of Materials

UF=Use for   BT=Broader term   NT=Narrower term   RT=Related term

abuse

SG   Social Sciences and Culture
NT   child abuse
     elder abuse
     emotional abuse
     physical abuse
     sexual abuse
     spouse abuse
     substance abuse
     verbal abuse
RT   assault
     crimes
     violence

academia

SG   Education
RT   academic disciplines
     alma mater
     education occupations
     higher education

academic ability

SG   Education
BT   ability
RT   academic achievement
     intelligence
     learning motivation

academic achievement

SG   Education
BT   achievement
RT   academic ability
     academic aptitude
     academic aspirations
     academic awards
     academic failure
     attitudes
     empowerment
     intelligence
     school counseling
     student motivation

academic aptitude

SG   Education
BT   aptitude
RT   academic achievement
     academic aspirations

(cont.)

academic aptitude *(cont.)*

RT   school counseling
     student motivation

academic aspirations

SG   Education
BT   aspirations
RT   academic achievement
     academic aptitude
     educational objectives

academic awards

SG   Education
BT   awards
RT   academic achievement
     degrees
     success

academic degrees
USE **degrees**

academic disciplines

SG   Education
RT   academia

academic enrichment

SG   Education
RT   tutoring

academic failure

SG   Education
BT   failure
RT   academic achievement
     anxiety
     fear of failure
     motivation
     school counseling

academic freedom

SG   Education
BT   freedoms
RT   equal opportunity
     tenure

academic rank

SG   Education
BT   rank

(cont.)

academic rank (*cont.*)
RT   faculty
     professional recognition
     teaching
     tenure
     tenure track

academic standards
SG   Education
BT   standards
RT   accreditation
     admissions criteria
     certification
     licensing

academies
SG   Education
BT   educational facilities
NT   military academies

access
USE   **equal access**

accidental death
SG   Natural Sciences and Health
BT   death
RT   accidents
     insurance
     mortality rates

accidents
SG   Natural Sciences and Health
NT   home accidents
     traffic accidents
RT   accidental death
     hazards
     household hazards
     insurance
     mortality
     prevention
     reconstructive surgery
     victims
     violence

accountants
SG   Economics and Employment
BT   financial occupations

(cont.)

accountants (*cont.*)
BT   professional occupations
RT   accounting

accounting
SG   Economics and Employment
RT   accountants

accreditation
SG   Education
RT   academic standards
     certification
     continuing education units
     education
     educational facilities
     higher education
     licensing

acculturation
SG   Social Sciences and Culture
RT   assimilation patterns
     cultural identity
     culture
     immigrants
     immigration
     majority culture
     socialization

achievement
SG   Education
     Social Sciences and Culture
NT   academic achievement
     overachievement
     underachievement
RT   adults
     approval need
     aptitude
     birth order
     careers
     education
     fear of failure
     fear of success
     motivation
     parents
     success

---

achievement motivation
  USE **achievement need**

achievement need
  SG Education
       Social Sciences and Culture
  UF achievement motivation
  BT psychological needs
  RT birth order
       ego
       psychological testing
       status

acne
  SG Natural Sciences and Health
  RT body image
       complexion
       puberty
       skin

acoustics
  SG Science and Technology
       Visual and Performing Arts
  RT architecture
       instrument makers
       music

acquaintance rape
  SG Social Sciences and Culture
  BT rape
  NT date rape
  RT domestic rape
       sexual intimidation
       social attitudes

acquired immune deficiency syndrome
  SG History and Social Change
       Natural Sciences and Health
       Social Sciences and Culture
  UF AIDS
  BT communicable diseases
       sexually transmitted diseases
  RT blood tests
       chemotherapy
       drug abuse
       epidemiology
       gay men
                                    (*cont.*)

acquired immune deficiency syndrome
  (*cont.*)
  RT safe sex
       sexual behavior

acronyms
  DG Types and Forms of Materials

acting
  SG Communications
       Visual and Performing Arts
  RT actors
       film
       performances
       theater

activism
  SG History and Social Change
       Social Sciences and Culture
  NT political activism
  RT change agents
       community organizers
       militance
       nonviolence
       organizing
       resistance
       social change
       social movements
       woman power

activists
  SG Social Sciences and Culture
  NT political activists
  RT advocacy
       advocates
       burnout
       change agents
       liberation struggles
       radicals
       reformers
       social movements

activities
  SG History and Social Change
       Social Sciences and Culture
  NT campaigns
       celebrations
                                    (*cont.*)

activities (*cont.*)
- NT conferences
  - conventions
  - educational activities
  - exhibitions
  - expositions
  - extracurricular activities
  - festivals
  - forums
  - fund raising events
  - hearings
  - leisure activities
  - mass actions
  - meetings
  - panels
  - parades
  - performances
  - protest actions
  - readings
  - retreats
  - revivals
  - roasts
  - shows
  - social activities
  - symposia
  - testimonials
  - workshops
- RT programs

actors
- SG Communications
  - Economics and Employment
  - Visual and Performing Arts
- UF actresses
- BT arts, entertainment, and media
  - occupations
- NT aspiring actors
- RT acting
  - casting
  - performers

actresses
- USE **actors**

actresses (historical)
- SG Communications
  - Visual and Performing Arts

(cont.)

actresses (historical) (*cont.*)
- BT women
- RT films
  - vaudeville

acts
- DG Types and Forms of Materials

actuarials
- SG Economics and Employment
- RT life expectancy
  - life insurance
  - statistics

ad feminam
- SN *Appeal to prejudice or feelings; assumes split between feelings and reason.*
- SG Communications
  - Social Sciences and Culture
- RT ad hominem
  - arguments
  - dichotomy
  - prejudice
  - trashing

ad hominem
- SN *Appeal to prejudice or feelings; assumes split between feelings and reason.*
- SG Communications
- RT ad feminam

Adam
- SG Language, Literature, Religion, and Philosophy
- RT creation myths
  - Eve
  - Garden of Eden
  - Lilith
  - paradise
  - religious symbols

addiction
- SG Natural Sciences and Health
- NT drug addiction
- RT compulsive behavior

(cont.)

UF=Use for   BT=Broader term   NT=Narrower term   RT=Related term

addiction (*cont.*)
  RT dependent behavior
      diet pills
      drug use
      fetal alcohol syndrome
      gambling
      substance abuse
      withdrawal

adjustment
  SG Social Sciences and Culture
  NT emotional adjustment
      marital adjustment
      psychological adjustment
      social adjustment
  RT change
      conflict
      coping strategies
      counseling
      empty nest
      equilibrium
      stress

administration
  SG Economics and Employment
  RT administrators
      bureaucracy
      collaboration
      governance
      hierarchy
      management practices
      managerial occupations

administrative assistants
  SG Economics and Employment
  UF girl Fridays
  BT administrative support occupations
      female intensive occupations

administrative costs
  SG Economics and Employment
      Education
  BT costs
  RT budgeting

administrative support occupations
  SG Economics and Employment
                 (*cont.*)

administrative support occupations (*cont.*)
  BT occupations
  NT administrative assistants
      clerical occupations
      data processors
      operations researchers
      supervisors
  RT office work
      pink collar workers
      support staff

administrators
  SG Economics and Employment
      Education
  BT managerial occupations
  NT college administrators
  RT administration
      affirmative action

admissions
  SG Education
  NT open door admissions
  RT equal access
      higher education
      letters of recommendation
      student recruitment

admissions criteria
  SG Education
  BT criteria
  RT academic standards
      open door admissions
      references
      student quotas
      student recruitment
      testing

adolescence
  SG Social Sciences and Culture
  RT age of consent
      child development
      childhood
      history of children
      life cycles
      puberty
      rites of passage
      teenagers

adolescent pregnancy
USE **teenage pregnancy**

adolescents
- SG Education
  Social Sciences and Culture
- DG Age Levels
- BT teenagers

adopted children
- SG Social Sciences and Culture
- BT children
- RT adoption
  adoptive parents
  birth parents
  foster families
  records confidentiality

adoption
- SG Social Sciences and Culture
- NT international adoption
  interracial adoption
- RT adopted children
  adoptive parents
  birth parents
  child care leave
  foster children
  foster homes
  infertility
  legal guardians
  single parents
  teenage mothers
  unwanted pregnancy

adoptive parents
- SG Law, Government, and Public Policy
  Social Sciences and Culture
- BT parents
- RT adopted children
  adoption
  birth parents
  stepparents

adornment
- SG Social Sciences and Culture
- RT body image
  jewelry

(cont.)

adornment *(cont.)*
- RT makeup
  perfume
  tattoos
  tribal markings

adult basic education
- SG Education
- DG Education Levels
- BT basic education
  elementary education
- RT high school equivalency programs

adult child relationships
- SG Social Sciences and Culture
- BT relationships
- NT parent child relationships
- RT family relationships

adult development
- SG Social Sciences and Culture
- BT individual development
- RT autonomy
  completion complex
  life cycles
  lifelong learning
  midlife crisis

adult education
- SG Education
- BT education
- RT adult learning
  adult literacy
  adult students
  adults
  continuing education
  lifelong learning
  nonformal education

adult illiteracy
- SG Education
- BT illiteracy
- RT employment opportunities
  high school equivalency programs
  job training
  nondegree programs
  nonformal education

UF=Use for   BT=Broader term   NT=Narrower term   RT=Related term

adult learning
SG   Education
BT   learning
RT   adult education
      adult literacy
      adults
      competence
      learning motivation

adult literacy
SG   Education
BT   literacy
RT   adult education
      adult learning
      adults
      bilingualism
      high school equivalency programs

adult students
SG   Education
UF   mature students
      older students
BT   students
RT   adult education
      continuing education
      part time students
      reentry students
      reentry women

adultery
USE   **extramarital affairs**

adults
SG   Social Sciences and Culture
DG   Age Levels
NT   middle aged adults
      old old adults
      older adults
      young adults
RT   achievement
      adult education
      adult learning
      adult literacy
      life cycles
      maturity
      passages

advanced degrees
USE   **graduate degrees**

adventurers
SG   Economics and Employment
      History and Social Change
      International Women
RT   explorers
      pirates

advertisements
SG   Communications
DG   Types and Forms of Materials
RT   advertising
      personal columns
      propaganda

advertising
SG   Communications
RT   advertisements
      advertising industry
      arts, entertainment, and media
         occupations
      body image
      commercial sex
      commercials
      consumption
      free enterprise
      images of women
      marketing and sales occupations
      popular culture
      publicity
      semiotics

advertising industry
SG   Communications
      Economics and Employment
BT   industries
RT   advertising
      arts, entertainment, and media
         occupations
      market research
      marketing and sales occupations
      mass media

advice columns

SG Communications
      Language, Literature, Religion, and
        Philosophy
BT columns
RT advice shows
    gossip
    journalism
    newspapers
    personal columns
    sex education
    sex manuals
    women's pages

advice shows

SG Communications
      Education
      Natural Sciences and Health
BT shows
RT advice columns
    sex education
    talk shows
    television

advocacy

SG Education
      History and Social Change
      Law, Government, and Public Policy
RT activists
    advocacy groups
    lobbying
    political activism
    services
    social action
    social change

advocacy groups

SN *Groups that work for social change,*
    usually organized around defined
    sets of issues.
SG Education
      History and Social Change
      Law, Government, and Public Policy
BT groups
RT advocacy
    advocates
    change agents

(cont.)

advocacy groups *(cont.)*

RT feminist organizations
    lobbying
    social action
    social change
    special interest groups

advocates

SG Education
      History and Social Change
      Law, Government, and Public Policy
NT consumer advocates
    health advocates
    legal advocates
    peace advocates
RT activists
    advocacy groups
    change agents
    political activists
    reformers
    rights
    social movements

aerobic exercise

SG Natural Sciences and Health
UF aerobics
BT exercise
RT athletics
    body image
    dance
    stress (physical)
    upper body strength

aerobics

USE **aerobic exercise**

aerospace engineering

SG Economics and Employment
      Science and Technology
BT engineering

aestheticism

DG Cultural and Political Movements

UF=Use for   BT=Broader term   NT=Narrower term   RT=Related term

aesthetics

SG   Language, Literature, Religion, and
         Philosophy
        Visual and Performing Arts
RT   criticism
     literature
     performing arts
     philosophy
     visual arts

AFDC

USE **Aid to Families With Dependent Children**

affection

SG   Social Sciences and Culture
BT   psychological needs
RT   alienation of affection
     emotions
     forms of affection
     relationships

affiliation

SG   Social Sciences and Culture
RT   clubs
     community
     empowerment
     groups
     psychological needs

affirmative action

SG   Economics and Employment
     Law, Government, and Public Policy
RT   administrators
     affirmative action hiring
     Civil Rights Restoration Act of 1987
     desegregation
     desegregation methods
     discrimination
     Education Amendments of 1972
     Education Amendments of 1985
     educators
     Equal Employment Opportunity
       Commission
     equal opportunity
     equal rights
     Executive Order 11246
     higher education

(cont.)

affirmative action *(cont.)*

RT   industries
     laws
     lawsuits
     quotas
     reforms
     sex discrimination
     sex discrimination in education
     tokenism
     women in

affirmative action hiring

SG   Economics and Employment
     History and Social Change
BT   hiring policy
RT   affirmative action
     business
     consent orders
     early retirement
     employment
     enforcement
     executive recruitment
     higher education
     industries
     job advertisements
     job candidates
     job discrimination
     laws
     lawsuits
     quotas
     search committees
     sex discrimination in employment

affirmative action officers

SG   Economics and Employment
     Education
     History and Social Change
BT   education occupations
     female intensive occupations
RT   personnel management

affirmative action suits

SG   Economics and Employment
     Education
     History and Social Change
     Law, Government, and Public Policy
BT   lawsuits

(cont.)

affirmative action suits (*cont.*)
RT discrimination laws
investigations
job discrimination
legal settlements

affluence
SG Economics and Employment
RT wealth

Afghan
DG National and Regional Descriptors
BT Asian

African
DG National and Regional Descriptors
NT Algerian
Angolan
Botswanan
Burundian
Cameroonian
Chadian
Egyptian
Ethiopian
Gambian
Ghanaian
Guinean
Ivory Coaster
Kenyan
Liberian
Libyan
Malian
Mauritanian
Moroccan
Namibian
Nigerian
Nigerois
Senegalese
Sierra Leonean
Somalian
South African
Sudanese
Tanzanian
Togan
Tunisian
Ugandan
Upper Voltan

(*cont.*)

African (*cont.*)
NT Zairean
Zambian
Zimbabwean

African studies
SG Education
International Women
Social Sciences and Culture
BT area studies

Afro American
DG Ethnic, Racial, and Religious
Descriptors

Afro American studies
SG Education
History and Social Change
Social Sciences and Culture
UF Black American studies
Black studies
BT ethnic studies
NT Black women's studies
RT Black movement

Afro Caribbean
DG Ethnic, Racial, and Religious
Descriptors

Afros
SG Social Sciences and Culture
BT hair styles

after school day care centers
SG Education
BT day care centers
RT child development
mothers working outside the home

after school programs
SG Education
BT programs
RT child welfare
day care
extracurricular activities
latchkey children
working parents

age

SG Education
Social Sciences and Culture
NT childbearing age
maternal age
middle age
retirement age
RT social stratification

age discrimination

SG Economics and Employment
Law, Government, and Public Policy
BT discrimination
RT Age Discrimination Act of 1975
ageism
aging
displaced homemakers
gray power
human rights violations
laws
older adults
oppression
senior citizens

Age Discrimination Act of 1975

DG Laws and Regulations
RT age discrimination

age of consent

SG Law, Government, and Public Policy
Social Sciences and Culture
RT adolescence
defloration
informed consent
puberty
rites of passage
teenage marriage

age stereotypes

SG Social Sciences and Culture
BT stereotypes
RT ageism
attitudes
gray power

aged

USE **older adults**

ageism

SN *Includes concepts of bias, stereotyping, and discrimination against older adults.*
SG History and Social Change
Social Sciences and Culture
RT ableism
age discrimination
age stereotypes
bias
classism
doubly disadvantaged
gray power
older adults
racism
sexism
social attitudes
stereotyping

agencies

SG Economics and Employment
Law, Government, and Public Policy
BT organizations
NT employment agencies
federal agencies
government agencies
intelligence agencies
modeling agencies
private agencies
public agencies
social agencies
RT social change
social services
social work
welfare programs

agents

SG Economics and Employment
BT female intensive occupations
service occupations
NT airline reservation agents
insurance agents
real estate agents
travel agents

aggression

USE **aggressive behavior**

SN=Scope note   SG=Subject group   DG=Delimiters group   USE=Use

aggressive behavior
- SG   Social Sciences and Culture
- UF   aggression
- BT   behavior
- RT   conflict
  corporate takeovers
  dominance
  feuds
  militarism
  patriarchy
  perceptual bias
  social relations
  street harassment
  trashing
  violence
  war

aging
- SG   Natural Sciences and Health
- RT   age discrimination
  attitudes
  elder abuse
  geriatrics
  gerontology
  gray power
  hormones
  housing
  images of women
  insurance
  life cycles
  life expectancy
  life span
  Medicare
  nursing homes
  nutrition
  older adults
  osteoporosis
  right to die

agnosticism
- DG   Cultural and Political Movements

agoraphobia
- SN   *Fear of open places.*
- SG   Natural Sciences and Health
- BT   phobias
- RT   isolation

(cont.)

agoraphobia *(cont.)*
- RT   private sphere

agreements
- DG   Types and Forms of Materials

agribusiness
- SN   *Business combining farm production operations, manufacture and distribution of farm equipment, and processing, storage, and distribution of farm commodities.*
- SG   Economics and Employment
  International Women
- BT   business
- RT   agricultural economics
  agricultural industry
  agriculture
  farms
  migrant workers
  rural poverty

agricultural economics
- SG   Economics and Employment
- BT   economics
- RT   agribusiness
  agriculture

agricultural extension
- SG   Education
  International Women
- RT   animatrices rurales
  community education
  continuing education
  county government
  extension work
  farms
  information services
  rural development

agricultural, fishing, and forestry occupations
- SG   Economics and Employment
- BT   occupations
- NT   braceros
  development specialists
  divers

(cont.)

agricultural, fishing, and forestry occupations (*cont.*)
- NT   extension workers
  - farm workers
  - farmers
  - fishers
  - gardeners
  - lumber cutters
  - migrant workers
  - ranch hands
- RT   agriculture
  - chemical industry
  - food industry
  - horticulture
  - multinational labor force
  - tobacco industry

agricultural industry
- SG   Economics and Employment
- BT   industries
- RT   agribusiness
  - agriculture

agriculture
- SG   Economics and Employment
- NT   subsistence agriculture
- RT   agribusiness
  - agricultural economics
  - agricultural industry
  - agricultural, fishing, and forestry occupations
  - domestic food production
  - farms
  - land use
  - migrant workers
  - occupations
  - technology

aid
- SG   Economics and Employment
  - International Women
  - Law, Government, and Public Policy
- NT   federal aid
  - financial aid
  - foreign aid
  - state aid
- RT   public assistance

Aid to Families with Dependent Children
- DG   Laws and Regulations
- UF   AFDC
- RT   children living in poverty
  - women living in poverty

AIDS
USE **acquired immune deficiency syndrome**

air pollution
- SG   Science and Technology
- BT   pollution
- RT   conservation
  - corporate liability
  - corporate responsibility
  - environmental health

air transportation
- SG   Science and Technology
- UF   airlines
- BT   transportation
- RT   aviation

airline reservation agents
- SG   Economics and Employment
- BT   agents

airline stewardesses
USE **flight attendants**

airlines
USE **air transportation**

Alaskan Indian
- DG   Ethnic, Racial, and Religious Descriptors

Alaskan Native
- DG   Ethnic, Racial, and Religious Descriptors

Albanian
- DG   National and Regional Descriptors
- BT   European

albums
    DG Types and Forms of Materials

alcohol abuse
    SG Natural Sciences and Health
    BT substance abuse
    RT absenteeism
        blood tests
        drinking
        drug rehabilitation
        fetal alcohol syndrome
        prenatal influences

alcoholism
    SG Natural Sciences and Health
    BT diseases
    RT codependency
        counseling
        drinking
        drinking prohibition
        fetal alcohol syndrome
        substance abuse

Aleut
    DG Ethnic, Racial, and Religious
        Descriptors

Algerian
    DG National and Regional Descriptors
    BT African

alienation
    SG Social Sciences and Culture
    BT emotions
    NT job alienation
        work alienation
    RT community
        delinquent behavior
        depression
        isolation
        objectification

alienation of affection
    SG Law, Government, and Public Policy
        Social Sciences and Culture
    RT affection
        divorce

aliens
    USE **immigrants**

alimony
    SG Economics and Employment
        Law, Government, and Public Policy
    RT child support
        child welfare
        divorce laws
        financial arrangements
        income
        legal settlements
        marriage and family law
        palimony
        spouse support

all volunteer military force
    SG Law, Government, and Public Policy
    BT armed forces
    RT military draft
        military personnel

all women ensembles
    SG Visual and Performing Arts
    RT women's music

allegory
    SG Language, Literature, Religion, and
        Philosophy
    BT figurative language
    RT drama
        fables
        folk literature
        mythology
        religious language
        religious literature
        symbols

alliances
    SG History and Social Change
        Social Sciences and Culture
    BT organizations
    RT coalitions
        networks

alma mater
    SG Education

(cont.)

---

alma mater (*cont.*)
- BT images of women
- RT academia
  - old boy networks

almanacs
- DG Types and Forms of Materials

aloofness
- SG Social Sciences and Culture
- BT attitudes

alternative employment
- SG Economics and Employment
  - Education
- BT employment
- RT career choice
  - electronic cottage
  - entrepreneurs
  - nontraditional employment
  - occupational patterns

alternative programs
- SG Education
  - Law, Government, and Public Policy
- BT programs
- RT antisocial behavior
  - at risk populations
  - dropouts
  - halfway houses
  - juvenile justice system
  - nondegree programs
  - restitution

alternative schools
- SG Education
- BT schools
- RT community education
  - dropouts
  - free schools
  - nontraditional education
  - open door admissions

alternative spaces
- SN *New concepts of space for exhibiting women's art.*
- SG Visual and Performing Arts

(*cont.*)

alternative spaces (*cont.*)
- BT space
- RT art shows
  - galleries
  - museums
  - one woman art shows
  - women's art

alternative work arrangements
- SG Economics and Employment
- RT cottage industry
  - work

altruism
- SG Language, Literature, Religion, and Philosophy
- DG Cultural and Political Movements
- RT humanitarianism
  - philanthropy
  - values
  - volunteer work

alumnae
- SN *Use to refer to female alumnae.*
- SG Education
- RT alumnae/i
  - alumni
  - alumni/ae
  - collegiate athletics
  - educational programs
  - higher education
  - old girl networks
  - women's colleges

alumnae/i
- SN *Use to refer to mixed sex alumnae/i if majority are women.*
- SG Education
- RT alumnae
  - alumni
  - coeducation

alumni
- SN *Use to refer to male alumni.*
- SG Education
- RT alumnae
  - alumnae/i

(*cont.*)

SN=Scope note   SG=Subject group   DG=Delimiters group   USE=Use

alumni (*cont.*)
  RT   alumni/ae
       coeducation
       collegiate athletics
       educational programs
       higher education
       old boy networks

alumni/ae
  SN   *Use to refer to mixed sex alumni/ae if*
       majority are men.
  SG   Education
  RT   alumnae
       alumni

amateur athletics
  SG   Communications
       Education
       Natural Sciences and Health
  BT   athletics
  RT   collegiate athletics
       Olympic Games

amazons
  SN   *Slang, used to denote strong women.*
       In Greek mythology, a race of wo-
       men warriors.
  SG   History and Social Change
  BT   images of women
       women
  RT   female societies
       lesbians
       mythology
       viragos

ambiguity
  SG   Language, Literature, Religion, and
       Philosophy
  BT   figurative language
  RT   literary theory

ambition
  SG   Economics and Employment
       Social Sciences and Culture
  RT   competitive behavior
       initiative
       professional recognition
                                    (*cont.*)

ambition (*cont.*)
  RT   upward mobility

amenorrhea
  SG   Natural Sciences and Health
  BT   menstrual disorders
  RT   drugs
       menarche
       menstruation

Amerasian
  DG   Ethnic, Racial, and Religious
       Descriptors

American Indian
  DG   Ethnic, Racial, and Religious
       Descriptors
  UF   Native American

American Indian studies
  SG   Education
       Social Sciences and Culture
  UF   Native American studies
  BT   ethnic studies

American studies
  SG   Education
       Language, Literature, Religion, and
       Philosophy
       Social Sciences and Culture
  BT   area studies
  RT   humanities

amniocentesis
  SG   Natural Sciences and Health
  BT   medical procedures
  RT   birth defects
       childbearing age
       childbirth
       fetal monitoring
       genetic counseling
       genetic defects
       late childbearing
       sex determination
       ultrasound

---

anal sex
SG Natural Sciences and Health
BT sexual behavior
RT sodomy

analytical psychology
SG Social Sciences and Culture
BT psychology

anarcha feminism
SN *International feminist critique of feminist movement that emerged in late 1970s, attempting to restore early tenets of feminism like decentralization and absence of dogma.*
SG History and Social Change
      International Women
DG Cultural and Political Movements
BT feminism

anarchism
DG Cultural and Political Movements

anarchy
DG Cultural and Political Movements

anatomy
SG Natural Sciences and Health
BT biological sciences
RT body image

ancestor spirits
SG Language, Literature, Religion, and Philosophy
BT spirits
RT ancestors

ancestors
SG Language, Literature, Religion, and Philosophy
      Social Sciences and Culture
RT ancestor spirits
      families
      family history

anchors
SG Communications
      Economics and Employment
BT arts, entertainment, and media occupations
RT television personalities

androcentrism
SG History and Social Change
DG Cultural and Political Movements
RT male chauvinism
      male norms
      misogyny
      patriarchal religion
      patriarchy
      phallocentrism
      sexism

androgens
SG Natural Sciences and Health
BT sex hormones
NT testosterone
RT sexual dysfunction

androgyny
SN *Possessing both traditionally masculine and traditionally feminine traits.*
SG History and Social Change
RT hermaphrodites
      personality traits
      sexual identity
      unisex

anecdotes
DG Types and Forms of Materials

anemia
SG Natural Sciences and Health
BT diseases
NT iron deficiency anemia
RT fatigue
      pregnancy

anesthesia
SG Natural Sciences and Health
NT general anesthesia
      local anesthesia

(cont.)

SN=Scope note   SG=Subject group   DG=Delimiters group   USE=Use

anesthesia (cont.)

NT   obstetrical anesthesia
RT   drugs
hypnotism
prenatal influences
surgical procedures

anesthesiologists

SG   Economics and Employment
Natural Sciences and Health
BT   health care occupations
RT   physicians

angel in the house

SN   *Image of woman as self-sacrificing, always putting others' wishes and
needs above her own.*
SG   Language, Literature, Religion, and
Philosophy
Social Sciences and Culture
BT   images of women
RT   cult of true womanhood
domestic code
domesticity
homemaking
momism
mother syndrome
purity
self denial
superwoman syndrome

angels

SG   Language, Literature, Religion, and
Philosophy
BT   images of girls
images of women
RT   religion
religious art
religious language
religious symbols
sacred ideology

anger

SG   Social Sciences and Culture
BT   emotions
NT   rage
RT   conflict resolution

(cont.)

anger (cont.)

RT   hostility
violence

Anglo American

DG   Ethnic, Racial, and Religious
Descriptors

Anglo Saxon

DG   Ethnic, Racial, and Religious
Descriptors

Angolan

DG   National and Regional Descriptors
BT   African

angora

SG   Social Sciences and Culture
RT   clothing
images of women

anima

SN   *Traditional feminine principle as de-
fined in Jungian psychology.*
SG   History and Social Change
Social Sciences and Culture
RT   animus
feminine principle

animal behavior

SG   Natural Sciences and Health
BT   behavior
NT   grooming behavior
RT   bestiality
bonding
boundary markers
conditioning
ethology
instincts
social sciences
sociobiology
territoriality

animal caretakers

SG   Economics and Employment
Natural Sciences and Health
BT   health care occupations

(cont.)

UF = Use for   BT = Broader term   NT = Narrower term   RT = Related term

animal caretakers (*cont.*)
BT   laboratory assistants
RT   veterinarians

animals
SN   *Use of a more specific term is recommended.*
SG   Natural Sciences and Health
NT   laboratory animals
RT   pets

animation
SG   Visual and Performing Arts
BT   media arts

animatrices rurales
SN   *Women extension workers in French-speaking countries.*
SG   International Women
BT   extension workers
RT   agricultural extension
      farm workers
      farms
      gramsevika
      workers

animus
SN   *Traditional masculine principle as defined in Jungian psychology.*
SG   History and Social Change
      Social Sciences and Culture
RT   anima

ankh
SN   *Women's symbol—Egyptian hieroglyph representing womb; a knotted sign symbolizing protection.*
SG   Language, Literature, Religion, and Philosophy
      Social Sciences and Culture
RT   symbols
      uterus
      women's culture

anlu
SN   *West Cameroon women's social action that punishes offending man with ritual dance and incantation.*
SG   Law, Government, and Public Policy
      Social Sciences and Culture
RT   matriarchy
      woman power

annals
DG   Types and Forms of Materials

anniversaries
SG   Social Sciences and Culture
RT   celebrations
      marriage

annotations
DG   Types and Forms of Materials

announcements
DG   Types and Forms of Materials

announcers
SG   Communications
      Economics and Employment
BT   arts, entertainment, and media occupations
RT   broadcasters
      radio
      television

annual reports
DG   Types and Forms of Materials
BT   reports

annulment
SG   Law, Government, and Public Policy
      Social Sciences and Culture
RT   divorce laws
      marriage contracts
      religious law

anonymous
SG Language, Literature, Religion, and
Philosophy
Social Sciences and Culture
Visual and Performing Arts
RT art
invisibility
literature
philanthropy
pseudonyms
silence

anorexia nervosa
SG Natural Sciences and Health
BT eating disorders
RT body image
fasting

antebellum
DG Historical Periods

antenuptial contracts
USE **prenuptial agreements**

anthologies
DG Types and Forms of Materials

anthropologists
SG Economics and Employment
Social Sciences and Culture
BT social scientists
RT archaeologists

anthropology
SG Social Sciences and Culture
BT social sciences
NT archaeology
cultural anthropology
economic anthropology
ethnography
ethnology
medical anthropology
political anthropology
RT anthropometry
cross cultural studies
culture
human evolution

(*cont.*)

anthropology (*cont.*)
RT social environment
social geography
societies
zoology

anthropometry
SG Natural Sciences and Health
Social Sciences and Culture
RT anthropology
measurement

anthropomorphism
SG Language, Literature, Religion, and
Philosophy
Social Sciences and Culture
DG Cultural and Political Movements
RT belief systems
fairy tales

anti ERA movement
SG History and Social Change
Law, Government, and Public Policy
DG Cultural and Political Movements
BT social movements
RT conservatives

antiabortion movement
SG History and Social Change
DG Cultural and Political Movements
UF antichoice
prolife
right to life
BT social movements
RT abortion
abortion laws
abortion movement
conservatives
moral majority
prochoice
religious sanctions

antiapartheid movement
SG Economics and Employment
History and Social Change
DG Cultural and Political Movements
BT social movements

(*cont.*)

UF=Use for   BT=Broader term   NT=Narrower term   RT=Related term

antiapartheid movement (*cont.*)

RT   Black power movement
     civil rights movements
     divestiture

antichoice
USE **antiabortion movement**

antidepressant drugs

SG   Natural Sciences and Health
BT   psychotropic drugs
RT   depression
     drug addiction
     mental disorders
     prescription drugs

antidiscrimination laws
USE **discrimination laws**

antifeminism

SG   History and Social Change
     Law, Government, and Public Policy
     Social Sciences and Culture
DG   Cultural and Political Movements
RT   conservatives
     right wing organizations
     social movements

antiilliteracy movements

SG   Education
     International Women
DG   Cultural and Political Movements
BT   social movements
RT   illiteracy

antilynching campaign

SG   History and Social Change
     Law, Government, and Public Policy
BT   social movements
RT   lynching

antinuclear movement

SG   History and Social Change
     International Women
     Science and Technology
DG   Cultural and Political Movements
BT   social movements

(*cont.*)

antinuclear movement (*cont.*)

RT   antiwar movement
     nuclear disarmament
     nuclear warfare
     peace advocates
     peace movements

antiques

SG   Visual and Performing Arts
RT   furniture
     material culture

antiquity

DG   Historical Periods

antisemitism

SG   History and Social Change
     Language, Literature, Religion, and
       Philosophy
     Social Sciences and Culture
DG   Cultural and Political Movements
RT   discrimination
     genocide
     holocaust
     prejudice
     racial discrimination

antisepsis

SN   *Disinfection and sterilization.*
SG   Natural Sciences and Health
RT   diseases
     medical procedures
     physical health

antisocial behavior

SG   Social Sciences and Culture
BT   behavior
RT   alternative programs
     juvenile delinquency
     social development
     sociopathology

antisuffrage movement

SG   History and Social Change
DG   Cultural and Political Movements
BT   social movements
RT   suffragists

antithesis
SG Language, Literature, Religion, and
     Philosophy
BT figurative language
RT dichotomy

antitrust legislation
SG Economics and Employment
     Law, Government, and Public Policy
BT legislation
RT cartels
    corporate takeovers
    monopolies

antiwar movement
SN *Use to refer to organized opposition
    against US Vietnam War.*
SG History and Social Change
DG Cultural and Political Movements
BT peace movements
RT antinuclear movement
    conscientious objection
    demonstrations
    peace
    peace advocates
    warfare

anxiety
SG Social Sciences and Culture
BT emotions
RT academic failure
    dysphoria
    fear of failure
    personality traits
    separation

apartheid
SG International Women
     Law, Government, and Public Policy
DG Cultural and Political Movements
RT colonialism
    discrimination
    human rights violations
    liberation struggles
    multinational corporations
    racial discrimination
    third world

apathy
SG Social Sciences and Culture
BT emotions
RT boredom
    depression
    isolation

aphrodisiacs
SG Natural Sciences and Health
BT sexual aids
RT arousal
    love potions
    orgasm
    sexual excitement

Appalachian
DG National and Regional Descriptors
BT United States

appearance
SG Social Sciences and Culture
NT physical appearance
RT beauty
    body image
    clothing
    coiffures
    complexion
    cosmetic surgery
    face lifts
    facism
    fashion
    lookism
    wigs

appendices
DG Types and Forms of Materials

appetite depressants
SG Natural Sciences and Health
NT diet pills
RT diets
    eating disorders

appetite disorders
USE **eating disorders**

UF=Use for   BT=Broader term   NT=Narrower term   RT=Related term

applications

SG Economics and Employment
     Education

RT letters of recommendation

applied linguistics

SG Language, Literature, Religion, and
     Philosophy

BT linguistics

applied mathematics

SG Science and Technology

BT mathematics

applied research

SG Social Sciences and Culture

BT research

RT research methods
    scholars

appointed officials

SG Economics and Employment
     Law, Government, and Public Policy

BT legal and political occupations
    officials

RT government appointments
    judicial appointments
    political office
    politics
    women in politics

appointive positions
USE **government appointments**

apprenticeships

SG Economics and Employment
     Education
     Visual and Performing Arts

BT on the job training

RT intern programs
    mentors
    novices

appropriate technology

SN *Simple, low-cost techniques and tools
    that help increase productivity in
    agriculture and household tasks.*
                 (cont.)

appropriate technology *(cont.)*

SG International Women
     Science and Technology

BT technology

RT technology development

appropriations

SG Law, Government, and Public Policy

RT block grants
    budgeting
    Congress
    federal budget
    federal regulations
    federal taxes
    federally sponsored research
    fund raising
    funding
    government
    legislation
    military budget
    monetary policy
    social policy
    sponsored research
    transit systems
    transportation subsidies

approval need

SG Social Sciences and Culture

BT psychological needs

RT achievement

aptitude

SG Social Sciences and Culture

NT academic aptitude
    language aptitude
    vocational aptitude

RT ability
    achievement
    intelligence
    learning
    motivation
    students

aptitude tests

SG Education
     Social Sciences and Culture

BT testing

                 (cont.)

aptitude tests (*cont.*)
RT measurement
     norms

Arab
DG Ethnic, Racial, and Religious
     Descriptors

arbitration
SG Economics and Employment
     Law, Government, and Public Policy
RT conflict resolution
     contracts
     labor disputes
     labor law reform
     strikes
     unions

archaeologists
SG Economics and Employment
     History and Social Change
     Social Sciences and Culture
BT social scientists
RT anthropologists

archaeology
SG Social Sciences and Culture
BT anthropology
RT culture
     fossil hominids

archery
SG Natural Sciences and Health
BT sports

architects
SG Economics and Employment
     Visual and Performing Arts
BT professional occupations
NT landscape architects
RT urban planners

architecture
SG Visual and Performing Arts
BT visual arts
RT acoustics
     barrier free access

(*cont.*)

architecture (*cont.*)
RT ergonomics
     house design
     housing
     life styles
     work space

archives
DG Types and Forms of Materials

area studies
SG Education
     International Women
     Social Sciences and Culture
BT interdisciplinary studies
NT African studies
     American studies
     Asian studies
     Latin American studies
     Near Eastern studies
     regional studies
     Slavic studies

Argentine
DG National and Regional Descriptors
BT Latin American

arguments
SG Social Sciences and Culture
RT ad feminam
     blame
     communication styles
     compromise
     domestic relations
     listening
     negotiation
     personal relationships

Armageddon
SG Language, Literature, Religion, and
     Philosophy
RT end time thinking
     the religious right

armament
USE **militarism**

armed forces
SG Economics and Employment
UF armed services
military services
BT military
NT all volunteer military force
RT militarism

armed services
USE **armed forces**

Armenian
DG Ethnic, Racial, and Religious
Descriptors

arms control
SG History and Social Change
Law, Government, and Public Policy
RT disarmament
peace movements

arousal
SG Natural Sciences and Health
UF erogenous zones
RT aphrodisiacs
bodies
breasts
clitoris
erotica
eroticism
foreplay
G spot
orgasm
pheromones
sexual attraction
sexual behavior
sexual excitement

arranged marriage
SG Social Sciences and Culture
BT marriage

arson
SG Law, Government, and Public Policy
BT property crimes
RT fire prevention
insurance

(cont.)

arson (*cont.*)
RT insurance fraud

art
SG Visual and Performing Arts
NT body art
children's art
commercial art
cunt art
electronic art
erotic art
folk art
multimedia art
naive art
performance art
political art
primitive art
public art
religious art
tribal art
women's art
RT anonymous
arts
illustration
imagery
performing arts
popular culture
shows
the nude
visual arts

art conservation
SG Visual and Performing Arts
BT conservation
RT art history
museums
visual arts

art criticism
SG Visual and Performing Arts
BT criticism

art exhibits
USE **art shows**

art history

SG   History and Social Change
       Visual and Performing Arts
BT   history
RT   art conservation
     canon

art matronage

SN   *Feminist term for art support and influence by women.*
SG   Visual and Performing Arts
RT   philanthropy
     women's art

art music

SG   Visual and Performing Arts
UF   classical music
     concert music
BT   music

art preservation

SG   Visual and Performing Arts
BT   preservation
RT   curators

art shows

SG   Communications
       Visual and Performing Arts
UF   art exhibits
BT   shows
NT   one woman art shows
RT   alternative spaces
     exhibitions
     galleries

art symbols

SG   Visual and Performing Arts
BT   symbols
RT   cult of the virgin
     iconography

art theory

SG   Visual and Performing Arts
BT   theory

art therapy

SG   Natural Sciences and Health
       Visual and Performing Arts
BT   therapy
RT   mental disorders
     psychodrama

articles

DG   Types and Forms of Materials

artifacts

DG   Types and Forms of Materials

artificial insemination

SG   Natural Sciences and Health
BT   insemination
     reproductive technologies
RT   birth parents
     childbearing
     conception
     donors
     infertility
     self insemination
     single mothers
     sperm banks
     surrogate fathers
     surrogate mothers

artificial intelligence

SG   Science and Technology
BT   intelligence
RT   computers
     programming languages
     technology development

artisans

SG   Economics and Employment
       Visual and Performing Arts
UF   craftsmen
BT   arts, entertainment, and media
     occupations
RT   culture work

artistic ability

SG   Education
       Visual and Performing Arts
BT   ability

(cont.)

UF = Use for   BT = Broader term   NT = Narrower term   RT = Related term

artistic ability (*cont.*)
RT   talent

artists
SG   Communications
Economics and Employment
Language, Literature, Religion, and
Philosophy
Visual and Performing Arts
BT   arts, entertainment, and media
occupations
professional occupations
RT   culture work
models
writers

artists' books
SG   Language, Literature, Religion, and
Philosophy
Visual and Performing Arts
DG   Types and Forms of Materials
BT   books
RT   visual diaries

arts
SG   Language, Literature, Religion, and
Philosophy
Social Sciences and Culture
Visual and Performing Arts
NT   media arts
performing arts
visual arts
RT   art
arts, entertainment, and media
occupations
humanities
literature
women's art

arts and crafts movement
SN   *Turn of the century art movement involving significant numbers of women.*
DG   Cultural and Political Movements

**arts, entertainment, and media
occupations**
SG   Communications
Economics and Employment
Language, Literature, Religion, and
Philosophy
Visual and Performing Arts
BT   occupations
NT   actors
anchors
announcers
artisans
artists
authors
broadcasters
bullfighters
camera operators
cartoonists
circus performers
coaches
columnists
comedians
commentators
composers
conductors
copywriters
craftspersons
critics
dancers
designers
disk jockeys
drafters
dramatists
editors
entertainers
essayists
film directors
film producers
geishas
glassmakers
hostesses (historical)
hosts
illustrators
impersonators
instrument makers
jewelry makers
jockeys

(*cont.*)

SN=Scope note   SG=Subject group   DG=Delimiters group   USE=Use

arts, entertainment, and media occupations (*cont.*)

NT journalists
lyricists
models
musicians
novelists
orators
painters
performers
photographers
playwrights
poets
printers
printmakers
professional athletes
public relations specialists
publishers
reporters
reviewers
sculptors
singers
sports officials
sportscasters
strippers
television personalities
writers

RT advertising
advertising industry
arts
communications industry
entertainment industry
mass media
motion picture industry
music industry
professional occupations
public relations
publishing industry
sports

arts organizations

SG Visual and Performing Arts
BT organizations
RT nonprofit organizations

asbestos

SG Natural Sciences and Health

(*cont.*)

asbestos (*cont.*)

RT carcinogens
health hazards

asceticism

SG Language, Literature, Religion, and Philosophy
DG Cultural and Political Movements
RT celibacy
discipline
monasticism
purity
religious practices
self control
self denial
spirituality
vows of chastity

Asian

DG National and Regional Descriptors
NT Afghan
Bangladeshi
Burmese
Cambodian
Chinese
Filipino
Indian
Indochinese
Indonesian
Japanese
Korean
Laotian
Malaysian
Mongolian
Nepalese
Pakistani
Sri Lankan
Taiwanese
Thai
Tibetan
Vietnamese

Asian American

DG Ethnic, Racial, and Religious Descriptors
NT Asian Pacific American

Asian American studies
- SG Education
  - History and Social Change
  - Social Sciences and Culture
- BT ethnic studies

Asian Pacific
- DG Ethnic, Racial, and Religious
  - Descriptors

Asian Pacific American
- DG Ethnic, Racial, and Religious
  - Descriptors
- BT Asian American

Asian studies
- SG Education
  - International Women
  - Social Sciences and Culture
- UF Oriental studies
- BT area studies
- RT ethnic studies

aspirations
- SG Economics and Employment
  - Social Sciences and Culture
- NT academic aspirations
  - parental aspirations
  - political aspirations
- RT dreams
  - fear of failure
  - fear of success
  - social mobility

aspiring actors
- SG Visual and Performing Arts
- UF starlets
- BT actors

assault
- SG Law, Government, and Public Policy
  - Social Sciences and Culture
- NT sexual assault
- RT abuse
  - rage
  - violence

assemblymen
- SG Law, Government, and Public Policy
- BT elected officials
  - men
- RT state government

assemblywomen
- SG Law, Government, and Public Policy
- BT elected officials
  - women
- RT state government

assertive behavior
- SG Social Sciences and Culture
- UF assertiveness
- BT behavior
- RT assertiveness training
  - initiative
  - learned helplessness
  - personality traits

assertiveness
- USE **assertive behavior**

assertiveness training
- SG Social Sciences and Culture
- BT training
- RT assertive behavior
  - dependent behavior
  - learned helplessness
  - passive behavior

assessment
- SG Economics and Employment
  - Education
- NT quality assessment
- RT diagnoses
  - evaluation criteria
  - testing

assessments
- DG Types and Forms of Materials

assimilation patterns
- SG Social Sciences and Culture
- RT acculturation
  - cultural identity

(cont.)

assimilation patterns (*cont.*)
  RT   immigrants

assistance programs
  SG   Economics and Employment
       Education
       Law, Government, and Public Policy
  BT   programs
  NT   dependent care assistance programs
       federal assistance programs
       state assistance programs

assistantships
  SG   Education
  BT   student financial aid
  RT   fellowships
       internships
       postdoctoral fellowships
       scholarships

associate degrees
  SG   Education
  BT   degrees

associations
  SG   History and Social Change
       Social Sciences and Culture
  BT   organizations

assumable mortgages
  SG   Economics and Employment
  BT   mortgages
  RT   credit
       real estate

astrology
  SG   Language, Literature, Religion, and
       Philosophy
       Social Sciences and Culture
  RT   folk culture
       fortune telling
       seers

astronautics
  USE **space sciences**

astronauts
  SG   Economics and Employment
       Science and Technology
  BT   scientific and technical occupations
  RT   space sciences

astronomers
  SG   Economics and Employment
       Science and Technology
  BT   scientists
  RT   space sciences

astronomy
  SG   Science and Technology
  BT   physical sciences
  RT   space sciences

at risk populations
  SG   Education
       Law, Government, and Public Policy
  RT   alternative programs
       children living in poverty
       diseases
       economically disadvantaged
       juvenile justice system
       juvenile offenders
       life expectancy
       mortality rates
       older women
       pregnant students
       suicide
       teenage mothers
       women living in poverty

atheism
  DG   Cultural and Political Movements

athletes
  SG   Communications
       Economics and Employment
       Education
       Natural Sciences and Health
  NT   professional athletes
  RT   athletics

athletics
  SN   *See* **sports** *for more specific listings.*
                                          (*cont.*)

athletics (*cont.*)
- SG Communications
  - Education
  - Natural Sciences and Health
  - Social Sciences and Culture
- NT amateur athletics
  - collegiate athletics
  - professional athletics
  - women's athletics
- RT aerobic exercise
  - athletes
  - body building
  - brassieres
  - coaches
  - comparable worth
  - competitive behavior
  - contact sports
  - eligibility
  - equal opportunity
  - exercise
  - hormones
  - intramurals
  - locker rooms
  - marathons
  - martial arts
  - physical education
  - physical fitness
  - recreation
  - sports
  - sports awards
  - sports journalism
  - sports officials
  - stress (physical)
  - student recruitment
  - team playing
  - upper body strength

atlases
- DG Types and Forms of Materials
- BT reference books
- RT geography

attachment
- SG Social Sciences and Culture
- RT bonding
  - commitment
  - emotional adjustment

(*cont.*)

attachment (*cont.*)
- RT individual development
  - security

attendants
- SG Economics and Employment
- BT female intensive occupations
  - service occupations

attention
- SG Social Sciences and Culture
- NT selective attention
- RT boredom
  - cognitive processes
  - learning disabilities

attitude change
- SG Social Sciences and Culture
- BT change
- RT attitudes
  - cognitive behavior modification
  - discrimination

attitudes
- SG Social Sciences and Culture
- NT aloofness
  - bigotry
  - family attitudes
  - judicial attitudes
  - occupational attitudes
  - optimism
  - parental attitudes
  - pessimism
  - politeness
  - primness
  - social attitudes
  - stubbornness
  - supervisor attitudes
  - trust
  - work attitudes
- RT abortion
  - academic achievement
  - age stereotypes
  - aging
  - attitude change
  - behavior
  - breast feeding

(*cont.*)

SN=Scope note   SG=Subject group   DG=Delimiters group   USE=Us

attitudes (*cont.*)
RT   complexion
     consciousness
     conservatives
     deviant behavior
     diagnoses
     discrimination
     homosexuality
     hypochondria
     iconoclasts
     images of women
     manners
     marital status
     myths
     norms
     perceptual bias
     premarital relations
     priorities
     racial and ethnic differences
     rebellious behavior
     self concept
     sexual liberation
     single fathers
     single mothers
     skin color
     social behavior
     spinsters
     stereotypes
     stereotyping
     stress (physical)
     uncleanliness
     welfare mothers

attorneys
USE **lawyers**

audiotapes
DG Types and Forms of Materials
BT tapes

auditory perception
SG Natural Sciences and Health
BT perception
RT deafness
     hearing

aunts
SG Social Sciences and Culture
NT maiden aunts
RT extended families
     family structure

Australian
DG National and Regional Descriptors
BT Pacific

Austrian
DG National and Regional Descriptors
BT European

auteur theory
USE **auteurism**

auteurism
SN *Theory that a film, despite the involvement of many individuals, derives its identity from one person, the director.*
SG Visual and Performing Arts
DG Cultural and Political Movements
UF auteur theory
RT film

authoritarian child rearing practices
SG Social Sciences and Culture
BT child rearing practices

authoritarian personality
SG Social Sciences and Culture
BT personality
RT authoritarianism
     personality traits

authoritarianism
SG Law, Government, and Public Policy
     Social Sciences and Culture
DG Cultural and Political Movements
RT authoritarian personality

authority
SG Social Sciences and Culture
RT experts
     influence

(*cont.*)

F=Use for   BT=Broader term   NT=Narrower term   RT=Related term

authority (*cont.*)
  RT leadership
      leadership skills
      officials
      power

authors
  SG Communications
      Economics and Employment
      Language, Literature, Religion, and
        Philosophy
      Visual and Performing Arts
  BT arts, entertainment, and media
      occupations
  RT culture work
      publishing industry
      storytelling
      writers
      writing

autism
  SG Natural Sciences and Health
  BT mental disorders

autobiographies
  DG Types and Forms of Materials

autobiography
  SG Language, Literature, Religion, and
      Philosophy
  BT nonfiction
  RT biography
      diaries
      histories
      journals
      letters
      memoirs
      oral history
      oral literature

autoeroticism
  USE **masturbation**

automation
  SG Science and Technology
  RT business
      ergonomics
                (*cont.*)

automation (*cont.*)
  RT industries
      labor
      machinery
      technology
      technology development
      word processing

automobile insurance
  SG Economics and Employment
  UF car insurance
  BT insurance
  RT no fault insurance
      traffic accidents

automobile repair
  SG Economics and Employment
  UF car repair
  RT business

autonomy
  SG Social Sciences and Culture
  RT adult development
      control
      maturity
      power
      security
      self help
      sisterhood

auxiliaries
  SG Social Sciences and Culture
  UF ladies' auxiliaries
  BT organizations
  RT clubs
      male norms
      voluntary organizations

avant garde
  DG Cultural and Political Movements

aversion therapy
  SG Natural Sciences and Health
  BT therapy

aviation
  SG Science and Technology
                (*cont.*)

SN=Scope note   SG=Subject group   DG=Delimiters group   USE=Us

aviation (*cont.*)
- RT   air transportation
  flight attendants
  industries
  military
  pilots

aviatrices
- USE **pilots**

avoidance behavior
- SG   Social Sciences and Culture
- BT   behavior
- NT   computer avoidance
  math avoidance
  science avoidance
- RT   fear of failure
  fear of success

awards
- SG   Economics and Employment
  Education
- NT   academic awards
  professional awards
  sports awards
- RT   funding
  prizes

babies
- USE **infants**

babysitters
- SG   Economics and Employment
  Social Sciences and Culture
- BT   child care workers

babysitting
- SG   Economics and Employment
  Social Sciences and Culture
- BT   child care

bachelors
- SG   Social Sciences and Culture
- BT   men
- RT   life styles
  marital status
  old maids

(*cont.*)

bachelors (*cont.*)
- RT   single men
  single parents

bachelors' degrees
- SG   Education
- BT   undergraduate degrees

back pay
- SG   Economics and Employment
  Law, Government, and Public Policy
- BT   wages
- RT   comparable worth
  court cases
  discrimination
  Equal Employment Opportunity
  Commission
  income
  legal settlements
  pay equity

backlash
- SG   History and Social Change
- RT   social change
  social movements
  tipping

bag ladies
- USE **homeless women**

bakers
- SG   Economics and Employment
- BT   food preparation occupations

balance of payments
- SG   Economics and Employment
  International Women
  Law, Government, and Public Policy
- RT   exchange rate
  global economy
  international trade policy
  monetary policy

balancing work and family life
- SG   Social Sciences and Culture
- RT   career break
  career family conflict

(*cont.*)

---

balancing work and family life *(cont.)*

RT careers
     coparenting
     corporate responsibility
     day care
     day care centers
     divorce
     domestic roles
     dual roles
     families
     flexible career patterns
     interrole conflict
     mothers working outside the home
     single mothers
     superwoman syndrome
     working parents

balding

USE **hair loss**

ballads

SG Language, Literature, Religion, and
     Philosophy
     Visual and Performing Arts

BT poetry
     songs
RT chivalry
     folk literature
     narratives
     oral history
     oral literature

ballet

SG Visual and Performing Arts
BT dance

balls

USE **testicles**

Bangladeshi

DG National and Regional Descriptors
BT Asian

bangs

SG Social Sciences and Culture
BT hair styles

bank tellers

SG Economics and Employment
BT clerical occupations
     female intensive occupations

bankers

SG Economics and Employment
BT financial occupations

banking industry

SG Economics and Employment
BT industries
RT financial occupations

banks

SG Economics and Employment
BT organizations
NT multinational banks
RT finance
     financiers
     stock exchanges

banners

DG Types and Forms of Materials

baptism

SG Language, Literature, Religion, and
     Philosophy
BT sacraments
RT purification rites
     rebirth

barmaids

USE **cocktail servers**

Barbadan

DG National and Regional Descriptors
BT West Indian

barbers

SG Economics and Employment
BT service occupations

baronesses

SG International Women
     Law, Government, and Public Policy
BT images of women

(cont.)

SN=Scope note   SG=Subject group   DG=Delimiters group   USE=Us

baronesses (*cont.*)
BT titles (nobility)
women

Baroque Period
DG Historical Periods

barren
USE **infertility**

barrier free access
SG Law, Government, and Public Policy
RT architecture
disabilities
disabled
education
housing
transportation

barriers to employment
USE **job discrimination**

barristers
SG Economics and Employment
Law, Government, and Public Policy
BT lawyers

bartenders
SG Economics and Employment
BT service occupations

barter
SG Economics and Employment
RT exchange theory
money

bas mitzvah
USE **bat mitzvah**

bas reliefs
SG Visual and Performing Arts
BT sculpture

basal body temperature
SG Natural Sciences and Health
RT infertility
ovulation

(*cont.*)

basal body temperature (*cont.*)
RT rhythm method

baseball
SG Natural Sciences and Health
BT sports

basic education
SG Education
BT education
NT adult basic education
RT basic skills
literacy

basic human needs
SN *Needs such as adequate nutrition, shelter, health, water and sanitation, which must be satisfied before poverty can be eliminated.*
SG Economics and Employment
International Women
BT human needs
RT class discrimination
food
health
inequality
living conditions
living standards
low income families
minimum income
poverty
quality of life
retirement
sanitation
third world
water

basic skills
SG Education
BT skills
RT basic education
language skills
literacy
mathematics
tutoring

basketball
SG Natural Sciences and Health
BT sports

basketry
SG Visual and Performing Arts
BT craft arts

bastards
SN *Slang.*
SG Law, Government, and Public Policy
Social Sciences and Culture
RT illegitimacy
inheritance customs
legitimization of children

bat mitzvah
SG Language, Literature, Religion, and
Philosophy
UF bas mitzvah
BT rites

bathing suits
SG Social Sciences and Culture
BT clothing
NT bikinis
RT pinups

battered women
SG Law, Government, and Public Policy
Social Sciences and Culture
BT women
RT crimes against women
crisis shelters
domestic violence
marital violence
violence
wife abuse

battlefields
SG Law, Government, and Public Policy
RT military combat
women in the military

beadwork
SG Visual and Performing Arts
BT craft arts

beauticians
SG Economics and Employment
BT female intensive occupations
service occupations
RT beauty parlors
cosmetologists
hairdressers

beauty
SG History and Social Change
Social Sciences and Culture
RT appearance
beauty standards
male norms

beauty contests
SG History and Social Change
RT beauty queens
beauty standards
images of women

beauty parlors
SG Economics and Employment
Social Sciences and Culture
RT beauticians
cosmetologists
hair styles
networks
support systems

beauty queens
SG Social Sciences and Culture
BT images of women
women
RT beauty contests

beauty standards
SG History and Social Change
Social Sciences and Culture
BT standards
RT beauty
beauty contests
blondes
body hair
body image
body odor
cosmetics

(cont.)

SN=Scope note   SG=Subject group   DG=Delimiters group   USE=Use

beauty standards (*cont.*)

  RT deodorants
      facism
      fat liberation
      glamour
      hair
      images of women
      lookism
      makeup
      older women
      stereotyping

bedrooms

  SG Social Sciences and Culture
  BT rooms
  RT boudoirs
      privacy

Beguinism

  SN *Ascetic and philanthropic communities of women in Netherlands in 13th century.*
  SG History and Social Change
  DG Cultural and Political Movements
  RT communities
      women's culture

behavior

  SN *Use of a more specific term is recommended.*
  SG Social Sciences and Culture
  NT aggressive behavior
      animal behavior
      antisocial behavior
      assertive behavior
      avoidance behavior
      competitive behavior
      compliant behavior
      compulsive behavior
      conforming behavior
      consumer behavior
      deferential behavior
      delinquent behavior
      dependent behavior
      destructive behavior
      deviant behavior
      group behavior

(*cont.*)

behavior (*cont.*)

  NT health behavior
      help seeking behavior
      helping behavior
      learned behavior
      manipulative behavior
      nonconforming behavior
      nonjudgmental behavior
      nonverbal behavior
      organizational behavior
      parental behavior
      passive behavior
      psychosexual behavior
      risk taking behavior
      selfish behavior
      sex role behavior
      sexual behavior
      social behavior
      submissive behavior
      voting behavior
  RT attitudes
      behavior change
      behavior modification
      manners
      self concept

behavior change

  SG Social Sciences and Culture
  BT change
  RT behavior
      behavior modification
      biofeedback
      change agents
      counseling

behavior modification

  SG Social Sciences and Culture
  NT cognitive behavior modification
  RT behavior
      behavior change
      biofeedback
      conditioning
      coping strategies
      stress

behavioral objectives

  SG Social Sciences and Culture

(*cont.*)

behavioral objectives (cont.)
BT   objectives

behavioral research
SG   Social Sciences and Culture
BT   social science research

behavioral sciences
USE **social sciences**

behaviorism
DG   Cultural and Political Movements

Belgian
DG   National and Regional Descriptors
BT   European

belief systems
SG   Language, Literature, Religion, and
     Philosophy
RT   anthropomorphism
cosmology
creation myths
cult of the virgin
faith
iconoclasts
ideology
myths
religions
religious beliefs
religious experience
sacred ideology
sex/gender systems
spiritualism
theology
trust
world views

bellboys
USE **bellhops**

bellhops
SG   Economics and Employment
UF   bellboys
BT   service occupations

benefits
SG   Economics and Employment
NT   dependent benefits
educational benefits
employee benefits
flexible benefits
fringe benefits
maternity benefits
paternity benefits
retirement benefits
supplementary benefits
veteran benefits
RT   child care
corporate policy
employer supported day care
parental leave
perquisites
seniority
wages

benign tumors
SG   Natural Sciences and Health
BT   tumors
RT   breasts
cysts
ovaries

bereavement
SG   Social Sciences and Culture
RT   death
emotional adjustment
grief
last rites

bestiality
SG   Natural Sciences and Health
RT   animal behavior
sexual behavior

betrothal
SG   Language, Literature, Religion, and
     Philosophy
     Social Sciences and Culture
RT   child marriage
engagement
marriage proposals

betrothed

SG   Social Sciences and Culture
RT   courtship customs
     engagement

bias

SG   Social Sciences and Culture
NT   gender bias
     perceptual bias
     race bias
     research bias
     social bias
     test bias
     textbook bias
RT   ageism
     blind review
     class discrimination
     discrimination
     equal access
     intelligence tests
     norms
     older adults
     prejudice
     press coverage
     research design
     social perception
     stereotyping
     supervisor attitudes
     television

biblical literature

USE **religious literature**

bibliographies

DG   Types and Forms of Materials

bicultural education

SG   Education
BT   education

biculturalism

SG   History and Social Change
     Social Sciences and Culture
RT   bilingualism
     diversity
     pluralism
     women's culture

bicycling

SG   Natural Sciences and Health
BT   sports

bigamy

SG   Law, Government, and Public Policy
     Social Sciences and Culture
RT   cowives
     marriage
     marriage contracts
     polygamy

bigotry

SG   Social Sciences and Culture
BT   attitudes
RT   discriminatory practices

bikinis

SG   Social Sciences and Culture
BT   bathing suits

bilineal kinship

SG   Social Sciences and Culture
BT   kinship

bilingual education

SG   Education
BT   education

bilingualism

SG   Education
     Language, Literature, Religion, and
     Philosophy
RT   adult literacy
     biculturalism
     language
     language skills
     mother tongue
     social dialects
     women's language

bills

DG   Types and Forms of Materials

binge purge syndrome

USE **bulimia**

UF = Use for   BT = Broader term   NT = Narrower term   RT = Related term

biobibliographies
DG Types and Forms of Materials

biochemistry
SG Natural Sciences and Health
BT biological sciences

bioethics
SG Language, Literature, Religion, and
     Philosophy
     Natural Sciences and Health
BT ethics
RT cloning
     genetic engineering
     genetics
     in vitro fertilization
     reproductive technologies
     sterilization
     women's rights

biofeedback
SG Natural Sciences and Health
BT feedback
RT behavior change
     behavior modification
     conditioning
     stress

biographies
DG Types and Forms of Materials

biography
SG Language, Literature, Religion, and
     Philosophy
BT nonfiction
RT autobiography
     diaries
     hagiography
     journals
     letters
     memoirs

biological clock
SG Natural Sciences and Health
RT childbearing
     childbearing age
     delayed parenthood

(cont.)

biological clock *(cont.)*
RT late childbearing
     sleep

biological determinism
SG Language, Literature, Religion, and
     Philosophy
     Natural Sciences and Health
DG Cultural and Political Movements
RT sex/gender systems

biological fathers
USE **birth fathers**

biological influences
SG Natural Sciences and Health
BT influences
RT environment
     heredity

biological mothers
USE **birth mothers**

biological parents
USE **birth parents**

biological sciences
SG Natural Sciences and Health
UF life sciences
BT natural sciences
NT anatomy
     biochemistry
     biology
     botany
     ecology
     embryology
     ethology
     genetics
     physiology
     sociobiology
     zoology
RT reproductive technologies
     science

biological warfare
SG Natural Sciences and Health
     Social Sciences and Culture

(cont.)

SN=Scope note   SG=Subject group   DG=Delimiters group   USE=Use

biological warfare (*cont.*)
UF   chemical warfare
BT   warfare

biologism
SG   History and Social Change
     Natural Sciences and Health
     Social Sciences and Culture
RT   essentialism
     sex/gender systems

biologists
SG   Economics and Employment
     Natural Sciences and Health
BT   scientists

biology
SG   Natural Sciences and Health
BT   biological sciences

biopsy
SG   Natural Sciences and Health
BT   medical procedures
RT   cancer
     cysts
     tumors

birth
USE   **childbirth**

birth attendants
USE   **midwives**

birth certificates
SG   Natural Sciences and Health
BT   legal documents
RT   lineage
     names
     single parents

birth control
SG   Natural Sciences and Health
NT   sterilization
RT   contraception
     family planning
     pregnancy prevention
     sexual abstinence

(*cont.*)

birth control (*cont.*)
RT   spermicides

birth control methods
USE   **contraception**

birth control pills
USE   **oral contraceptives**

birth defects
SG   Natural Sciences and Health
UF   congenital anomalies
RT   amniocentesis
     chromosome disorders
     disabilities
     drugs
     genetic counseling
     smoking
     substance abuse

birth fathers
SG   Law, Government, and Public Policy
     Natural Sciences and Health
     Social Sciences and Culture
UF   biological fathers
BT   fathers
RT   fathering
     surrogate fathers
     unwanted pregnancy

birth mothers
SG   Law, Government, and Public Policy
     Natural Sciences and Health
     Social Sciences and Culture
UF   biological mothers
BT   mothers
RT   surrogate mothers
     unwanted pregnancy

birth name
SG   Language, Literature, Religion, and
     Philosophy
     Social Sciences and Culture
UF   maiden name
BT   surnames
RT   hyphenated names
     matronymy

(*cont.*)

UF=Use for   BT=Broader term   NT=Narrower term   RT=Related term

birth name (*cont.*)
- RT name rights
     naming
     patronymy
     self concept
     slave name
     wives

birth order
- SG Social Sciences and Culture
- RT achievement
     achievement need
     family structure
     personality traits
     sibling influence
     siblings

birth parents
- SG Law, Government, and Public Policy
     Natural Sciences and Health
     Social Sciences and Culture
- UF biological parents
- BT parents
- RT adopted children
     adoption
     adoptive parents
     artificial insemination
     stepparents
     surrogate mothers

birth rates
- SG Economics and Employment
     Social Sciences and Culture
- BT vital statistics
- RT infant mortality

birthing
- SG Natural Sciences and Health
- RT birthing centers
     childbirth
     home birth

birthing centers
- SG Natural Sciences and Health
- BT centers
- RT birthing
     birthing rooms

(*cont.*)

birthing centers (*cont.*)
- RT delivery rooms
     maternity wards
     natural childbirth
     rooming in

birthing rooms
- SG Natural Sciences and Health
- BT rooms
- RT birthing centers
     delivery rooms
     labor (childbirth)
     maternity wards

bisexuality
- SG Social Sciences and Culture
- BT sexuality
- RT gay men
     hermaphrodites
     homoeroticism
     homosexuality
     lesbians
     straights

bitches
- SN *Slang.*
- SG Social Sciences and Culture
- BT images of women

bitterness
- SG Social Sciences and Culture
- BT emotions
- RT custody
     lawsuits
     romantic love

Black
- DG Ethnic, Racial, and Religious Descriptors
- UF Negro

Black American studies
- USE **Afro American studies**

Black colleges
- SG Education
- UF historically Black colleges

(*cont.*)

Black colleges (*cont.*)
BT colleges
RT normal schools

Black feminism
SG History and Social Change
International Women
DG Cultural and Political Movements
BT feminism
RT womanism

black markets
SG Economics and Employment
International Women
Law, Government, and Public Policy
BT markets
RT dual economy
global economy
informal economy
organized crime
street vendors

Black movement
SG History and Social Change
DG Cultural and Political Movements
BT social movements
NT Black power movement
RT Afro American studies
civil rights movements

Black Muslim
DG Ethnic, Racial, and Religious
Descriptors

Black power movement
SG History and Social Change
DG Cultural and Political Movements
BT Black movement
RT antiapartheid movement
protest actions

Black studies
USE **Afro American studies**

Black women's studies
SG Education
History and Social Change
Social Sciences and Culture
BT Afro American studies
women's studies
RT womanism
womanist writing

blame
SG Social Sciences and Culture
NT self blame
RT arguments
blame allocation
blaming the victim

blame allocation
SG Social Sciences and Culture
RT blame

blaming the victim
SG Economics and Employment
Education
Law, Government, and Public Policy
Social Sciences and Culture
RT blame
discrimination
incest victims
institutional racism
institutional sexism
paranoia
rape fantasies
rape victims
self concept
victimization
victims

blended families
SG Social Sciences and Culture
BT families
RT first husbands
first wives
gay stepfathers
lesbian stepmothers
remarriage
stepchildren
stepparents

blind dates

SG   Social Sciences and Culture
BT   dating
RT   dating customs
     matchmakers
     personal columns

blind review

SN   *Process designed to reduce the chance for bias by removing author's name before soliciting evaluations of work.*
SG   Education
     Social Sciences and Culture
RT   bias
     equal access
     evaluation
     job candidates
     reviewers
     social construction of reality
     tenure

blindness

SG   Natural Sciences and Health
BT   visual impairments
RT   braille
     disabilities

block grants

SG   Law, Government, and Public Policy
BT   grants
RT   appropriations
     federal aid

blockbusting

SG   Law, Government, and Public Policy
BT   discriminatory practices
RT   housing discrimination

blondes

SG   Social Sciences and Culture
BT   images of girls
     images of women
RT   beauty standards

blood

SG   Natural Sciences and Health
     Social Sciences and Culture
(cont.)

blood *(cont.)*

BT   bodies
RT   body image
     donors
     images of women
     menstrual taboos
     menstruation
     purification rites
     purity
     Rh factor
     rites
     taboos

blood tests

SG   Natural Sciences and Health
BT   tests
RT   acquired immune deficiency syndrome
     alcohol abuse
     diseases
     drug tests
     genetic screening
     marriage licenses
     privacy
     Rh factor

bloomers

SG   History and Social Change
BT   clothing
RT   dress reform

blue babies

SG   Natural Sciences and Health
BT   infants
RT   infant mortality
     Rh factor

blue collar workers

SG   Economics and Employment
BT   workers
RT   classism
     manufacturing occupations
     working class

blues

SG   Visual and Performing Arts
BT   music
RT   spirituals

bluestockings

SN *Term used to denigrate intellectual or literary women in late eighteenth, nineteenth centuries who participated in and later formed their own salons that provided alternatives for women's intellectual and cultural growth.*

SG History and Social Change
BT images of women
RT intellectuals

boarding schools

SG Education
BT schools
RT preparatory schools

boards

SG Economics and Employment
   Education
   Social Sciences and Culture
BT organizations
NT boards of directors
   governing boards

boards of directors

SG Economics and Employment
   Law, Government, and Public Policy
BT boards
RT chairpersons
   corporate policy
   corporate responsibility
   governance
   governing boards
   management
   power

boards of governors

USE **governing boards**

boards of regents

USE **governing boards**

boards of trustees

USE **governing boards**

boat operators

SG Economics and Employment
   Science and Technology
BT operators
   transportation occupations

bodies

SG Natural Sciences and Health
NT blood
   brain
   breasts
   buttocks
   cervical mucus
   cervix
   faces
   genitals
   glands
   hair
   hips
   hormones
   legs
   nervous system
   ovaries
   oviducts
   ovum
   perspiration
   skin
   sperm
   vagina
RT arousal
   body art
   body building
   body image
   body language
   body politics
   ejaculation
   images of women
   menstruation
   mind/body split
   physical fitness
   prostheses

body art

SG Visual and Performing Arts
BT art
RT bodies
   makeup

(cont.)

body art (*cont.*)
  RT tribal markings

body building
    SG Natural Sciences and Health
  RT athletics
      bodies

body hair
    SG Natural Sciences and Health
  BT hair
  RT beauty standards
      body image
      hirsutism

body image
    SG Natural Sciences and Health
          Social Sciences and Culture
  BT image
  RT acne
      adornment
      advertising
      aerobic exercise
      anatomy
      anorexia nervosa
      appearance
      beauty standards
      blood
      bodies
      body hair
      body odor
      brassieres
      breast prostheses
      breasts
      buttocks
      cellulite
      cosmetic surgery
      deodorants
      dieting
      diets
      eating disorders
      exercise
      eyeglasses
      face lifts
      fat liberation
      fat oppression
      girdles
                        (*cont.*)

body image (*cont.*)
  RT hair loss
      hair removal
      hair styles
      images of women
      mastectomy
      menstruation
      nudity
      obesity
      padding
      perspiration
      plastic surgery
      prostheses
      purification rites
      sexual attraction
      skin
      thinness
      trimness
      weight perception
      wigs
      wrinkles

body language
    SG Social Sciences and Culture
  BT nonverbal language
  RT bodies
      body politics
      boundary markers
      communication
      cultural influences
      gestures
      group dynamics
      kinesics
      microinequities
      nonverbal communication

body odor
    SG Natural Sciences and Health
  RT beauty standards
      body image
      personal hygiene
      perspiration

body politics
    SG History and Social Change
          Social Sciences and Culture
  BT sexual politics
                    (*cont.*)

        SN=Scope note   SG=Subject group   DG=Delimiters group   USE=Use

body politics (*cont.*)
  RT   bodies
       body language
       kinesics
       nonverbal communication
       personal relationships
       personal space
       power
       sex discrimination

Bolivian
  DG   National and Regional Descriptors
  BT   Latin American

bolshevism
  DG   Cultural and Political Movements

bomfog
  SN   *Journalists' acronym: Brotherhood of Man; Fatherhood of God.*
  SG   Communications
  RT   male norms

bondage
  SG   Natural Sciences and Health
       Social Sciences and Culture
  RT   exploitation
       sadomasochism
       sexual behavior
       sexual slavery

bonding
  SG   History and Social Change
       Natural Sciences and Health
       Social Sciences and Culture
  NT   female bonding
       male bonding
  RT   animal behavior
       attachment
       child development
       childbirth
       early experience
       fathers
       female friendships
       infants
       male friendships
       maternal love

(*cont.*)

bonding (*cont.*)
  RT   mothers
       relationships
       union

book clubs
  SG   Communications
       Language, Literature, Religion, and Philosophy
  BT   clubs
  RT   publishing industry

book conservation
  SG   Communications
       Visual and Performing Arts
  BT   conservation

book lists
  DG   Types and Forms of Materials

book reviews
  DG   Types and Forms of Materials
  BT   reviews

book stores
  SG   Communications
       History and Social Change
  RT   publishing industry
       women's media

bookbinders
  SG   Economics and Employment
  BT   printing workers

bookkeepers
  SG   Economics and Employment
  BT   clerical occupations
       female intensive occupations

booklets
  DG   Types and Forms of Materials

bookplates
  DG   Types and Forms of Materials

books
  DG   Types and Forms of Materials

(*cont.*)

---

books (*cont.*)
NT artists' books
cookbooks
handbooks
reference books

boredom
SG Social Sciences and Culture
BT emotions
RT apathy
attention
frustration

botany
SG Natural Sciences and Health
BT biological sciences

Botswanan
DG National and Regional Descriptors
BT African

bottle feeding
SG Natural Sciences and Health
RT breast feeding
infant formula

boudoirs
SG Social Sciences and Culture
BT rooms
RT bedrooms

boundary markers
SG Social Sciences and Culture
RT animal behavior
body language

bouquets
SG Social Sciences and Culture
BT flowers

bourgeoisie
SG Economics and Employment
Social Sciences and Culture
RT class

bowling
SG Natural Sciences and Health
(*cont.*)

bowling (*cont.*)
BT sports

boy preference of parents
SG Natural Sciences and Health
Social Sciences and Culture
RT girl preference of parents
infanticide
sex preselection
sex selection

boycotts
SG Economics and Employment
Education
History and Social Change
Law, Government, and Public Policy
BT protest actions
NT economic boycotts
RT demonstrations
sanctions
social movements

boys
SN *Use **boys** to refer to male children under eighteen years of age.*
SG Natural Sciences and Health
Social Sciences and Culture
BT children

braceros
SG International Women
BT agricultural, fishing, and forestry occupations
RT immigration policy
workers

braids
SG Social Sciences and Culture
BT hair styles

braille
SG Communications
Language, Literature, Religion, and Philosophy
BT written language
RT blindness
communication
(*cont.*)

SN=Scope note   SG=Subject group   DG=Delimiters group   USE=Use

braille (*cont.*)

RT disabilities
      equal access
      language skills
      sign language

brain

SG Natural Sciences and Health
BT bodies
RT individual development
      mind
      nervous system
      physiology

brainwashing

SG Communications
RT indoctrination
      propaganda

brassieres

SG History and Social Change
      Natural Sciences and Health
BT clothing
RT athletics
      body image
      breast prostheses
      dress reform
      girdles
      padding

Brazilian

DG National and Regional Descriptors
BT Latin American

breadwinners

USE **householders**

breakfasts

SG History and Social Change
      Social Sciences and Culture
BT social activities

breast cancer

SG Natural Sciences and Health
BT cancer
RT chemotherapy
      mastectomy

(*cont.*)

breast cancer (*cont.*)

RT radiation therapy

breast diseases

SG Natural Sciences and Health
BT diseases
RT breast implants
      breasts
      cancer
      cysts
      fibrocystic disease
      mammography
      thermography
      tumors

breast examination

SG Natural Sciences and Health
BT physical examination
NT breast self examination
RT disease prevention
      mammography
      prevention
      self examination
      thermography

breast feeding

SG Natural Sciences and Health
RT attitudes
      bottle feeding
      breast pumps
      colostrum
      expressing milk
      infant formula
      lactation
      mother's milk
      nom de lait
      wet nurses

breast implants

SG Natural Sciences and Health
RT breast diseases
      breasts
      reconstructive surgery

breast prostheses

SG Natural Sciences and Health
BT prostheses

(*cont.*)

---

breast prostheses (*cont.*)
RT   body image
      brassieres
      mastectomy
      reconstructive surgery

breast pumps
SG   Natural Sciences and Health
RT   breast feeding
      expressing milk

breast self examination
SG   Natural Sciences and Health
BT   breast examination
RT   health seeking behavior
      self help

breasts
SG   Natural Sciences and Health
BT   bodies
RT   arousal
      benign tumors
      body image
      breast diseases
      breast implants
      cleavage
      fibrocystic disease
      mammary glands
      mastectomy
      reconstructive surgery
      sex objects
      sexual fantasies

bricklayers
SG   Economics and Employment
BT   construction occupations

bride burning
SN   *Outlawed (Asian) Indian practice of
      in-laws or husbands murdering bride
      for dowry.*
SG   Social Sciences and Culture
BT   murder
RT   dowry
      dowry deaths
      gynocide
      suttee

bride price
SG   Economics and Employment
      Social Sciences and Culture
RT   dowry

brides
SG   Social Sciences and Culture
BT   images of women
      women
NT   child brides
      mail order brides
RT   grooms
      wedding ceremonies

bridesmaids
SG   Social Sciences and Culture
RT   wedding ceremonies

bridewealth
USE **dowry**

broadcasters
SG   Communications
      Economics and Employment
BT   arts, entertainment, and media
      occupations
RT   announcers
      broadcasts
      radio
      television
      television personalities

broadcasts
SG   Communications
RT   broadcasters
      mass media
      shows

broadsides
DG   Types and Forms of Materials

brochures
DG   Types and Forms of Materials

broken home
USE **single parent families**

brothels
SG   Law, Government, and Public Policy
     Social Sciences and Culture
BT   facilities
RT   prostitution

brother sister incest
SG   Social Sciences and Culture
BT   incest

brotherhood of man
USE **humanity**

brothers
SG   Social Sciences and Culture
BT   men
RT   extended families
     families
     family structure
     siblings
     sisters

brothers in law
SG   Social Sciences and Culture
BT   in laws
RT   families

brunches
SG   History and Social Change
     Social Sciences and Culture
BT   social activities

Brunhilde
SG   Social Sciences and Culture
     Visual and Performing Arts
BT   images of women

Buddhism
DG   Cultural and Political Movements

Buddhist
DG   Ethnic, Racial, and Religious
     Descriptors

budget cuts
SG   Economics and Employment
     Law, Government, and Public Policy
                              (*cont.*)

budget cuts (*cont.*)
RT   cost benefit analysis
     federal budget
     impact on women
     social policy

budget deficits
SG   Economics and Employment
     Law, Government, and Public Policy
BT   deficits
RT   federal budget
     federal taxes
     military budget
     social policy

budget process
SG   Economics and Employment
     Law, Government, and Public Policy
BT   process
RT   budgets
     priorities

budgeting
SG   Economics and Employment
     Law, Government, and Public Policy
RT   administrative costs
     appropriations
     Congress
     costs
     families
     family finances
     family income
     government
     grants
     household economics
     income

budgets
SG   Economics and Employment
     Law, Government, and Public Policy
DG   Types and Forms of Materials
RT   budget process
     debt
     depreciation

building industry
USE **construction industry**

built environment
- SG Science and Technology
  Social Sciences and Culture
- BT environment
- RT ecology
  ergonomics
  technology

Bulgarian
- DG National and Regional Descriptors
- BT European

bulimia
- SG Natural Sciences and Health
- UF binge purge syndrome
- BT eating disorders

bulletins
- DG Types and Forms of Materials

bullfighters
- SG Economics and Employment
- BT arts, entertainment, and media
  occupations

bumper stickers
- DG Types and Forms of Materials

bundling
- SG Social Sciences and Culture
- BT courtship customs

bureaucracy
- SG Law, Government, and Public Policy
- RT administration
  government
  hierarchy
  management
  management styles
  organizations
  power structure

bureaus
- SG History and Social Change
  Social Sciences and Culture
- BT organizations

burglaries
- SG Law, Government, and Public Policy
- BT property crimes

burial
- SG Language, Literature, Religion, and
  Philosophy
- RT funeral rites

burlesque
- SG Language, Literature, Religion, and
  Philosophy
- RT drama
  humor
  jokes
  satire

Burmese
- DG National and Regional Descriptors
- BT Asian

burnout
- SN *Numbness and sense of disengagement that results from the stress of confronting emotionally draining, often prejudicial, situations that are difficult to improve or change.*
- SG Economics and Employment
  Social Sciences and Culture
- RT activists
  careers
  change agents
  fatigue
  occupational stress
  parenting
  teaching

Burundian
- DG National and Regional Descriptors
- BT African

bus drivers
- SG Economics and Employment
  Science and Technology
- BT drivers

busboys
USE **waiters' assistants**

business
SG Economics and Employment
NT agribusiness
family owned business
home based business
minority owned business
small business
women owned business
RT affirmative action hiring
automation
automobile repair
corporations
discrimination
enterprises
industries
market research
multinational corporations
occupations
power

business correspondence
SG Communications
Economics and Employment
BT correspondence

business ethics
SG Economics and Employment
Language, Literature, Religion, and
Philosophy
BT ethics
RT corporate responsibility
military trade
public interest

business ownership
SG Economics and Employment
RT entrepreneurs
merchants
minority owned business
women owned business

business security
SG Economics and Employment
BT security

businesses
SG Economics and Employment
BT organizations
RT companies

businessmen
SG Economics and Employment
BT businesspeople
men

businesspeople
SG Economics and Employment
NT businessmen
businesswomen

businesswomen
SG Economics and Employment
BT businesspeople
women
RT career feminism
glass ceiling
institutional discrimination
women owned business

busing
SG Education
Law, Government, and Public Policy
BT desegregation methods
RT racial discrimination
school desegregation

butch
SN *Slang; stereotype of "traditional"
male, dominant role in lesbian relationship.*
SG History and Social Change
RT femme
gender roles
lesbians
sex role stereotyping

butchers
SG Economics and Employment
BT food preparation occupations

UF=Use for   BT=Broader term   NT=Narrower term   RT=Related term   57

butt lifts
USE **cosmetic surgery**

buttocks
SG Natural Sciences and Health
BT bodies
RT body image
liposuction surgery
sex objects
sexual fantasies

buttons
DG Types and Forms of Materials

bylaws
DG Types and Forms of Materials

Byzantine Period
DG Historical Periods

cabinetmakers
SG Economics and Employment
BT construction occupations

cable television
SG Communications
BT television
RT pornography

caesarian section
SG Natural Sciences and Health
BT surgical procedures
RT childbirth
natural childbirth

caffeine
SG Natural Sciences and Health
BT stimulants
RT substance abuse

Cajun
DG Ethnic, Racial, and Religious
Descriptors

calcium deficiency
SG Natural Sciences and Health
RT osteoporosis

calendars
DG Types and Forms of Materials

Calvinism
DG Cultural and Political Movements

Cambodian
DG National and Regional Descriptors
BT Asian

Cambodian American
DG Ethnic, Racial, and Religious
Descriptors

camera operators
SG Economics and Employment
Visual and Performing Arts
UF cameramen
BT arts, entertainment, and media
occupations
operators

cameramen
USE **camera operators**
USE **photographers**

Cameroonian
DG National and Regional Descriptors
BT African

camp followers
SG Social Sciences and Culture
RT prostitutes

campaigns
SG History and Social Change
Social Sciences and Culture
BT activities
NT election campaigns

campus safety
USE **campus security**

SN=Scope note   SG=Subject group   DG=Delimiters group   USE=Use

campus security
SG Education
UF campus safety
BT security

Canadian
DG National and Regional Descriptors
BT North American

Canadian Indian studies
SG Education
International Women
Social Sciences and Culture
BT ethnic studies

cancer
SG Natural Sciences and Health
Science and Technology
BT diseases
NT breast cancer
cervical cancer
RT biopsy
breast diseases
carcinogens
chemotherapy
hospices
industries
lymph glands
malignant tumors
mammography
Pap smear
prostheses
smoking
surgical procedures
women's health movement

candidates
SN *Use of a more specific term is recom-
mended.*
SG Economics and Employment
Law, Government, and Public Policy
NT job candidates
political candidates

canoeing
SG Natural Sciences and Health
BT sports

canon
SG Language, Literature, Religion, and
Philosophy
Visual and Performing Arts
NT literary canon
RT art history
circular reasoning
criticism
invisibility
music history
norms
perceptual bias
quality assessment
women in

canon law
USE **religious law**

canonization
SG Language, Literature, Religion, and
Philosophy
RT holy men
holy women
martyrdom
martyrs
miracles
religion
religious practices
saints
virgins

capital
SG Economics and Employment
NT human capital
seed capital
venture capital
RT credit
debt
family finances
financial resources
investments
investors
small business
wealth
wealth distribution

capital punishment
  USE **death penalty**

capitalism
  DG Cultural and Political Movements
  RT free enterprise
      markets

capitalist economic development models
  SG International Women
  BT economic development models

car insurance
  USE **automobile insurance**

car pools
  SG Social Sciences and Culture
  RT support systems
      transportation

car repair
  USE **automobile repair**

carcinogens
  SG Natural Sciences and Health
  RT asbestos
      cancer
      hazardous waste
      industrial hazards

cardiovascular diseases
  SG Natural Sciences and Health
  BT diseases
  NT heart disease

care
  SG Natural Sciences and Health
      Social Sciences and Culture
  NT community care
      day care
      dependent care
      health care
  RT caregivers
      ethic of care
      responsibility

career awareness
  SG Education
  RT career choice
      career counseling
      career feminism
      career planning

career break
  SG Economics and Employment
      Social Sciences and Culture
  RT balancing work and family life

career change
  SG Economics and Employment
  BT change
  NT midcareer change
  RT career counseling
      faculty retrenchment

career choice
  SG Economics and Employment
  UF occupational choice
      vocational choice
  RT alternative employment
      career awareness
      career counseling
      career planning
      female intensive occupations
      male intensive occupations
      sex differences

career counseling
  SG Education
      Economics and Employment
  UF career guidance
  BT counseling
  RT career awareness
      career change
      career choice
      career interest inventories
      career mapping
      career opportunities
      career planning
      career satisfaction

career education
  SG Education

(cont.)

career education (*cont.*)
  BT   education

career family conflict
  SG   Social Sciences and Culture
  BT   conflict
  RT   balancing work and family life
        families
        geographic mobility

career feminism
  SN   *Label applied to attitudes of women*
        who acknowledge importance of
        achieving personal goals, equal ac-
        cess to jobs, pay equity, and impor-
        tance of networks.
  SG   Economics and Employment
        History and Social Change
  BT   feminism
  RT   businesswomen
        career awareness
        careers
        consciousness raising
        dressing for success
        equal pay
        mainstream feminism

career girls
  USE **wage earning women**

career guidance
  USE **career counseling**

career interest inventories
  SG   Education
  BT   testing
  RT   career counseling

career ladders
  SG   Economics and Employment
        Education
  BT   occupational mobility
  RT   flexible career patterns
        promotions
        upward mobility

career mapping
  SG   Economics and Employment
        Education
  RT   career counseling
        career planning
        flexible career patterns

career mobility
  USE **occupational mobility**

career opportunities
  SG   Economics and Employment
        Education
  BT   opportunities
  RT   career counseling
        geographic mobility

career planning
  SG   Economics and Employment
        Education
  BT   planning
  RT   career awareness
        career choice
        career counseling
        career mapping
        career strategies
        careers
        interviews
        resumes

career satisfaction
  SG   Economics and Employment
  BT   satisfaction
  RT   career counseling
        professional recognition
        vocational aptitude

career strategies
  SG   Economics and Employment
        Education
  BT   strategies
  RT   career planning

careers
  SG   Economics and Employment
  NT   dual careers
        home based careers

(*cont.*)

careers (*cont.*)

NT second careers
RT achievement
    balancing work and family life
    burnout
    career feminism
    career planning
    certification
    dependent care
    economic value of women's work
    flexible career patterns
    male intensive occupations
    occupational options
    occupational roles
    occupations
    pay equity
    records confidentiality
    voluntary organizations
    volunteer work
    workers

caregivers

SG Natural Sciences and Health
    Social Sciences and Culture
UF caretakers
BT female intensive occupations
NT primary caregivers
RT care
    day care
    dependent care
    economic value of women's work
    ethic of care
    forms of affection
    mothers
    nurses
    nursing homes

caretakers
USE **caregivers**

Caribbean

DG National and Regional Descriptors
BT Latin American

Caribbean American

DG Ethnic, Racial, and Religious
    Descriptors

caricatures

SG Communications
RT cartoons
    humor
    parody

carpenters

SG Economics and Employment
BT construction occupations

cartels

SG Economics and Employment
BT organizations
RT antitrust legislation
    monopolies
    multinational corporations

Cartesianism

DG Cultural and Political Movements

cartoonists

SG Communications
    Economics and Employment
    Visual and Performing Arts
BT arts, entertainment, and media
    occupations

cartoons

SG Communications
    Visual and Performing Arts
DG Types and Forms of Materials
BT visual arts
RT caricatures
    comic strips
    humor
    images of women
    parody

case studies

SG Education
    Social Sciences and Culture
DG Types and Forms of Materials
BT research methods

caseworkers
USE **social workers**

SN=Scope note   SG=Subject group   DG=Delimiters group   USE=Use

cassettes
DG Types and Forms of Materials
BT tapes

caste
SG Economics and Employment
International Women
Social Sciences and Culture
RT class
intercaste marriage
pariahs
socioeconomic status
untouchables

casting
SG Visual and Performing Arts
NT colorblind casting
cross cultural casting
RT actors
ethnic diversity
films
theater

castrating females
SG History and Social Change
BT images of women
RT vagina dentata

castration
SG Natural Sciences and Health
RT castration complex
eunuchs
female circumcision
genital mutilation

castration complex
SN *Fear of castration on a physical or psychological level.*
SG Natural Sciences and Health
BT complexes
RT castration

catalogs
DG Types and Forms of Materials

cathartic therapy
SG Social Sciences and Culture

(*cont.*)

cathartic therapy (*cont.*)
BT therapy
NT psychodrama

cathedrals
SG Language, Literature, Religion, and
Philosophy
Visual and Performing Arts
BT religious facilities

cathode ray tubes
USE **video display terminals**

Catholic
DG Ethnic, Racial, and Religious
Descriptors

Catholicism
DG Cultural and Political Movements

Caucasian
DG Ethnic, Racial, and Religious
Descriptors
UF White man

caucuses
SG History and Social Change
Social Sciences and Culture
BT organizations

causal factors
USE **influences**

celebrations
SG Language, Literature, Religion, and
Philosophy
Social Sciences and Culture
BT activities
RT anniversaries
ceremonies
festivals
rites
traditions

UF=Use for   BT=Broader term   NT=Narrower term   RT=Related term

celibacy

SG   Language, Literature, Religion, and
Philosophy
Social Sciences and Culture

RT   asceticism
monasticism
religion
religious orders
religious practices
sexual abstinence
sexual behavior
virginity
vows of chastity

cellulite

SG   Natural Sciences and Health

RT   body image
fat liberation

censorship

SG   Communications

RT   free speech
freedom of speech
freedom of the press
mass media
pornography
sanctions

census

SG   History and Social Change
Law, Government, and Public Policy

RT   demographic measurements
households
housing
posslq
status

censuses

DG   Types and Forms of Materials

centers

SG   History and Social Change
Social Sciences and Culture

BT   facilities

NT   birthing centers
crisis centers
day care centers

(cont.)

centers (*cont.*)

NT   information and referral centers
neighborhood health centers
training centers
women's centers

Central American

DG   National and Regional Descriptors

BT   Latin American

NT   Costa Rican
Guatemalan
Honduran
Nicaraguan
Panamanian
Salvadoran

ceramics

SG   Visual and Performing Arts

BT   craft arts

RT   pottery

ceremonies

SG   Language, Literature, Religion, and
Philosophy

NT   graduation ceremonies
marriage ceremonies
wedding ceremonies

RT   celebrations
faith communities
religious practices
rites
traditions
tribal markings
worship

certification

SG   Education

RT   academic standards
accreditation
careers
credentials
day care centers
education
health care facilities
job standards

cervical cancer
    SG Natural Sciences and Health
  BT cancer
  RT cervix
      diethylstilbestrol
      Pap smear

cervical caps
    SG Natural Sciences and Health
  BT contraception
  RT cervix
      diaphragms

cervical mucus
    SG Natural Sciences and Health
  BT bodies
  RT cervix
      contraception
      ovulation
      rhythm method

cervix
    SG Natural Sciences and Health
  BT bodies
  RT cervical cancer
      cervical caps
      cervical mucus
      Pap smear

CETA
  USE **Comprehensive Employment and Training Act of 1973**

Chadian
  DG National and Regional Descriptors
  BT African

chador
    SN *Dress worn by women in Muslim society that includes veil covering the face.*
    SG International Women
  BT clothing
  RT customs
      domestic code
      private sphere
      veiling of women

(cont.)

chador *(cont.)*
  RT veils

chairpersons
    SG Economics and Employment
          Education
  BT education occupations
      volunteer occupations
  RT boards of directors

chamber music
    SG Visual and Performing Arts
  BT music

chambermaids
  USE **hotel workers**

change
    SG History and Social Change
          Social Sciences and Culture
  NT attitude change
      behavior change
      career change
      sex change
      social change
  RT adjustment
      child rearing practices
      education
      marriage

change agents
    SG History and Social Change
  RT activism
      activists
      advocacy groups
      advocates
      behavior change
      burnout
      militance
      organizing
      radicals
      social change
      volunteers

change of life
  USE **menopause**

channeling
- SG Language, Literature, Religion, and Philosophy
- BT spiritual communication
- RT mediums
  - spirituality
  - trances

chanteuses
- SG Visual and Performing Arts
- BT singers

chants
- SG Language, Literature, Religion, and Philosophy
  - Visual and Performing Arts
- BT religious music

chaperones
- SG Social Sciences and Culture
- RT dating customs
  - parenting
  - responsibility
  - surrogates

chapters
- DG Types and Forms of Materials

charisma
- SG Social Sciences and Culture
- RT influence
  - leadership
  - leadership skills
  - personality traits
  - social skills

charitable work
- SG Economics and Employment
  - History and Social Change
- BT work
- RT charities
  - moral reform
  - philanthropy
  - social welfare
  - volunteer work

charities
- SG Economics and Employment
  - History and Social Change
- BT nonprofit organizations
- RT charitable work
  - donors
  - foundations
  - philanthropists
  - philanthropy
  - private voluntary organizations
  - voluntary organizations

charity balls
- SG Economics and Employment
  - Social Sciences and Culture
- BT dances
  - fund raising events

charts
- DG Types and Forms of Materials
- NT flowcharts

charwomen
- USE **janitors**

chastity
- SG Language, Literature, Religion, and Philosophy
  - Social Sciences and Culture
- RT abstinence
  - virginity
  - vows of chastity

chastity belts
- SG Social Sciences and Culture
- RT female circumcision
  - infibulation

chattels
- SG History and Social Change
  - Social Sciences and Culture
- BT images of women
- RT guardians
  - slaves

chauvinism
- SG History and Social Change

(cont.)

SN=Scope note   SG=Subject group   DG=Delimiters group   USE=Us

chauvinism (*cont.*)
NT female chauvinism
   male chauvinism
RT misogyny

cheerleaders
SG Economics and Employment
   Education
BT images of girls
   images of women

cheesecake
SN *Slang; photographs of scantily clad women.*
SG Social Sciences and Culture
RT images of women
   pinups
   pornography

chefs
SG Economics and Employment
   Natural Sciences and Health
BT food preparation occupations

chemical dependency
USE **drug addiction**

chemical engineering
SG Economics and Employment
   Science and Technology
BT engineering

chemical industry
SG Economics and Employment
BT industries
RT agricultural, fishing, and forestry
      occupations
   hazardous waste
   industrial hazards
   scientific and technical occupations

chemical warfare
USE **biological warfare**

chemistry
SG Natural Sciences and Health
BT physical sciences

chemists
SG Economics and Employment
   Science and Technology
BT scientists

chemotherapy
SG Natural Sciences and Health
BT medical procedures
   therapy
RT acquired immune deficiency syndrome
   breast cancer
   cancer
   clinical trials
   malignant tumors
   wigs

Chicana
DG Ethnic, Racial, and Religious
      Descriptors

Chicana studies
SG Education
   History and Social Change
   International Women
   Social Sciences and Culture
BT Latina studies
RT women's studies

chief executives
SG Economics and Employment
BT executives
RT leadership

child abuse
SG Social Sciences and Culture
UF child molesting
BT abuse
RT child day care centers
   child labor
   child marriage
   child neglect
   children's rights
   crimes against children
   incest
   juvenile prostitution
   physical abuse
   sexual abuse

(*cont.*)

child abuse (*cont.*)
RT   violence
     violence against children

child birth
USE **childbirth**

child brides
     SG   Social Sciences and Culture
BT   brides
RT   child labor
     child marriage

child care
     SG   Education
          Social Sciences and Culture
BT   dependent care
NT   babysitting
     infant care
RT   benefits
     child care licensing
     day care
     dependent benefits
     dependent children
     diaper services
     economic value of women's work
     elderly care
     home based work
     mothers working outside the home
     nannies
     playgroups
     welfare reform
     wives working outside the home

child care leave
     SG   Economics and Employment
          Law, Government, and Public Policy
          Social Sciences and Culture
RT   adoption
     corporate policy
     flexible career patterns
     maternity benefits
     maternity leave
     parental leave
     working parents

child care licensing
     SG   Law, Government, and Public Policy
BT   licensing
RT   child care
     day care
     dependent care

child care policy
     SG   Law, Government, and Public Policy
BT   policy
RT   valuing children

child care workers
     SG   Economics and Employment
          Social Sciences and Culture
BT   female intensive occupations
     service occupations
     workers
NT   babysitters
     governesses
     nannies
     wet nurses
RT   foster parents
     homemaking
     household workers
     mothers

child custody
     SG   Law, Government, and Public Policy
          Social Sciences and Culture
BT   custody
NT   shared custody
RT   child support
     divorce laws
     financial arrangements
     gay fathers
     kidnapping
     lesbian mothers
     marriage and family law
     restraining orders

child day care centers
     SG   Education
          Social Sciences and Culture
BT   day care centers
RT   child abuse

child development

SG Social Sciences and Culture
BT individual development
NT infant development
RT adolescence
after school day care centers
bonding
child welfare
childhood
day care centers
play
toys

child labor

SG Law, Government, and Public Policy
Social Sciences and Culture
BT labor
RT child abuse
child brides
children's rights
history of children
labor legislation
migrant workers

child marriage

SG Social Sciences and Culture
BT marriage
RT betrothal
child abuse
child brides
dowry
early childbearing

child molesting

USE **child abuse**

child neglect

SG Law, Government, and Public Policy
Social Sciences and Culture
RT child abuse
child welfare

child pornography

SG Economics and Employment
Social Sciences and Culture
BT pornography
RT violence against children

child psychology

SG Social Sciences and Culture
BT psychology
RT developmental psychology

child rearing practices

SG Social Sciences and Culture
NT authoritarian child rearing practices
nonsexist child rearing practices
permissive child rearing practices
RT change
couples with children
culture
families
family influence
gay men
history of children
lesbians
parenting
single parent families
single parents
social class

child support

SG Law, Government, and Public Policy
Social Sciences and Culture
RT alimony
child custody
Child Support Enforcement Amendments
of 1984
children living in poverty
desertion
divorce laws
financial arrangements
legal settlements
marriage and family law
paternity
paternity suits
women living in poverty

Child Support Enforcement Amendments of 1984

DG Laws and Regulations
RT child support

child welfare

SG Social Sciences and Culture

(cont.)

UF=Use for   BT=Broader term   NT=Narrower term   RT=Related term

child welfare (*cont.*)

BT welfare
RT after school programs
  alimony
  child development
  child neglect

childbearing

SG Natural Sciences and Health
NT early childbearing
  late childbearing
RT artificial insemination
  biological clock
  childbirth
  contraception
  maternity
  planned parenthood

childbearing age

SG Natural Sciences and Health
BT age
RT amniocentesis
  biological clock
  parenthood
  teenage pregnancy

childbed fever

USE **puerperal fever**

childbirth

SG Natural Sciences and Health
UF birth
  child birth
  delivery
NT labor (childbirth)
  natural childbirth
  premature childbirth
RT amniocentesis
  birthing
  bonding
  caesarian section
  childbearing
  conception
  culture
  delivery rooms
  episiotomy
  fertility

(*cont.*)

childbirth (*cont.*)

RT fetal monitoring
  home birth
  infant mortality
  maternity leave
  maternity wards
  midwives
  multiple births
  obstetrical anesthesia
  parenthood
  parents
  postpartum depression
  pregnancy
  stillbirth
  stress (physical)
  twins
  umbilical cord

childbirth training

SG Natural Sciences and Health
BT training
RT midwifery
  natural childbirth
  patient doctor relationships

childfree marriage

SG Social Sciences and Culture
BT marriage
RT childless couples
  contraception
  couples
  life styles

childhood

SG Social Sciences and Culture
RT adolescence
  child development
  life cycles
  valuing children

childless couples

SG Natural Sciences and Health
BT couples
RT childfree marriage
  family planning
  infertility
  life styles

(*cont.*)

childless couples *(cont.)*
RT reproductive technologies

childlessness
    SG Social Sciences and Culture
RT infertility
       life styles

children
    SG Education
          Social Sciences and Culture
    DG Age Levels
NT adopted children
       boys
       children living in poverty
       dependent children
       foster children
       girls
       grandchildren
       latchkey children
       school age children
       sick children
       stepchildren
       young children
RT children's art
       family size
       friendships
       gay men
       history of children
       illegitimacy
       lesbians
       military dependents
       names
       nurturing
       parents
       play
       runaways
       single parents
       stereotyping
       surnames
       teenagers
       valuing children

children living in poverty
    SG Economics and Employment
          Social Sciences and Culture
BT children

(cont.)

children living in poverty *(cont.)*
    RT Aid to Families with Dependent Children
        at risk populations
        child support
        community property laws
        divorce
        divorce laws
        economic equity
        economically disadvantaged
        National School Lunch Act Amendments
          of 1982
        poverty
        single parent families
        women living in poverty
        Women, Infants, and Children Nutrition
          Program

children's art
    SG Visual and Performing Arts
    BT art
    RT children
        children's culture

children's culture
    SG History and Social Change
          Social Sciences and Culture
    BT culture
    RT children's art
        children's groups
        images of girls
        play

children's groups
    SG Education
          Social Sciences and Culture
    BT groups
    RT children's culture
        play

children's literature
    SG Communications
          Language, Literature, Religion, and
          Philosophy
    BT literature
    RT desex
        fables
        fairy tales

(cont.)

---

children's literature (*cont.*)
> RT fantasies
> illustration
> images of girls
> myths
> sex role stereotyping

children's music
> SG Visual and Performing Arts
> BT music
> RT nursery songs

children's relationships
> SG Social Sciences and Culture
> BT relationships

children's rights
> SG Law, Government, and Public Policy
> BT rights
> RT child abuse
> child labor
> custody
> family courts

Chilean
> DG National and Regional Descriptors
> BT Latin American

china painting
> SG Visual and Performing Arts
> BT craft arts

Chinese
> DG National and Regional Descriptors
> BT Asian

Chinese American
> DG Ethnic, Racial, and Religious
> Descriptors

chiropodists
> SG Natural Sciences and Health
> BT health care occupations
> professional occupations

chiropractors
> SG Natural Sciences and Health
> (*cont.*)

chiropractors (*cont.*)
> BT health care occupations
> professional occupations

chivalry
> SG History and Social Change
> Language, Literature, Religion, and
> Philosophy
> RT ballads
> courtly love
> ideal woman
> images of women
> male chauvinism
> social values
> troubadours

choirs
> SG Language, Literature, Religion, and
> Philosophy
> Visual and Performing Arts
> RT choral music
> choruses

choral music
> SG Visual and Performing Arts
> BT vocal music
> RT choirs
> choruses

chorus dancers
> SG Visual and Performing Arts
> UF chorus girls
> BT dancers

chorus girls
> USE **chorus dancers**

chorus lines
> SG Visual and Performing Arts
> RT dances

choruses
> SG Visual and Performing Arts
> RT choirs
> choral music

Christian
 DG Ethnic, Racial, and Religious
      Descriptors

Christianity
 DG Cultural and Political Movements

chromosome disorders
 SG Natural Sciences and Health
 BT disorders
 RT birth defects
      genetic determinants
      genetic screening

chronicles
 SG Language, Literature, Religion, and
      Philosophy
 BT nonfiction
 RT histories
      oral history

chronologies
 DG Types and Forms of Materials

church music
 USE **religious music**

church work
 SG Economics and Employment
      Language, Literature, Religion, and
      Philosophy
 BT work
 RT ecumenism
      faith communities
      missionary societies
      religion
      social movements
      social welfare

churches
 SG Language, Literature, Religion, and
      Philosophy
 BT religious facilities
 NT house churches
      storefront churches
 RT congregations
      faith communities

(cont.)

churches *(cont.)*
 RT patriarchal religion

cigarettes
 USE **smoking**

Cinderella
 SG Language, Literature, Religion, and
      Philosophy
 BT images of girls
      images of women
 RT fairy tales
      romantic love

cinema
 USE **film**

cinematography
 USE **film**

circles
 SG History and Social Change
      Social Sciences and Culture
 BT organizations

circular reasoning
 SG Language, Literature, Religion, and
      Philosophy
 BT conceptual errors
 RT canon
      norms
      quality assessment
      stereotyping

circus performers
 SG Communications
      Economics and Employment
      Visual and Performing Arts
 BT arts, entertainment, and media
      occupations

citizen groups
 SG Law, Government, and Public Policy
      Social Sciences and Culture
 BT groups
 RT political action
      political leaders

(cont.)

citizen groups (*cont.*)
- RT   social action

citizenship
- SG   Law, Government, and Public Policy
- BT   politics
- RT   civic education
  community responsibility
  immigration
  immigration policy
  jury duty
  naturalization
  political participation
  suffrage
  the state

city government
- SG   Law, Government, and Public Policy
- UF   municipal government
- BT   government
- RT   politics

city planning
- USE **urban planning**

civic education
- SG   Education
  Law, Government, and Public Policy
- BT   education
- RT   citizenship

civil disobedience
- SG   History and Social Change
  International Women
  Law, Government, and Public Policy
- BT   protest actions
- RT   curfew
  sanctions
  social action
  violence

civil engineering
- SG   Economics and Employment
  Science and Technology
- BT   engineering

civil law
- SG   Law, Government, and Public Policy
- BT   law
- RT   court cases
  court decisions

civil lawsuits
- SG   Law, Government, and Public Policy
- BT   lawsuits
- RT   courts

civil liberties
- SG   Law, Government, and Public Policy
- NT   civil rights
  due process
  freedom of assembly
  freedom of speech
  freedom of worship

civil religion
- SN   *Religious or religious-like regard for selected civic values and traditions.*
- SG   Language, Literature, Religion, and Philosophy
  Law, Government, and Public Policy
- BT   religion
- RT   nationalism
  patriotism
  religious pluralism
  secularization
  separation of church and state
  state religion

civil rights
- SN   *See also Delimiters Display: Laws and Regulations.*
- SG   History and Social Change
  International Women
  Law, Government, and Public Policy
- BT   civil liberties
  rights
- RT   Civil Rights Act of 1964
  Civil Rights Restoration Act of 1987
  constitution
  freedom of assembly
  freedom of speech
  freedom of the press

(*cont.*)

civil rights (*cont.*)
- RT   freedom of worship
    - human rights
    - internment
    - involuntary sterilization
    - political repression
    - racial equality
    - suffrage movements

Civil Rights Act of 1964
- DG   Laws and Regulations
- RT   civil rights

civil rights commissions
- SG   History and Social Change
    - Law, Government, and Public Policy
- BT   commissions
- RT   discrimination

civil rights legislation
- SG   Law, Government, and Public Policy
- BT   legislation
- RT   civil rights movements
    - discrimination
    - lawsuits

civil rights movements
- SG   History and Social Change
- DG   Cultural and Political Movements
- BT   social movements
- RT   antiapartheid movement
    - Black movement
    - civil rights legislation
    - nonviolence
    - protest actions
    - voter registration

Civil Rights Restoration Act of 1987
- DG   Laws and Regulations
- RT   affirmative action
    - civil rights
    - Title IX (Education)

civil service
- SG   Economics and Employment
    - Law, Government, and Public Policy
- RT   (*cont.*)

civil service (*cont.*)
- RT   Civil Service Spouse Retirement Equity
    - Act
    - federal employment
    - foreign service
    - government workers

Civil Service Spouse Retirement Equity Act
- DG   Laws and Regulations
- RT   civil service

Civil War
- DG   Historical Periods

civility
- SG   Social Sciences and Culture
- RT   manners
    - politeness

clamydia
- SG   Natural Sciences and Health
- BT   sexually transmitted diseases

clans
- SG   Social Sciences and Culture
- BT   organizations
- RT   extended families

class
- SG   Economics and Employment
    - Social Sciences and Culture
- NT   class division
    - economic class
    - ethclass
    - lower class
    - middle class
    - social class
    - socioeconomic class
    - upper class
    - working class
- RT   bourgeoisie
    - caste
    - class formation
    - class identity
    - class ideology
    - classless society

(*cont.*)

UF = Use for   BT = Broader term   NT = Narrower term   RT = Related term

class (*cont.*)
RT cultural status
privilege
proletariat
race, class, and gender studies
social structure
socioeconomic status
stratification
wealth distribution

class action suits
SG Law, Government, and Public Policy
BT lawsuits
RT discrimination

class consciousness
SG History and Social Change
International Women
Social Sciences and Culture
RT class differences
labor movement
social class

class differences
SG History and Social Change
Social Sciences and Culture
BT differences
RT class consciousness
social class
socioeconomic status

class discrimination
SG Economics and Employment
History and Social Change
Social Sciences and Culture
BT discrimination
RT basic human needs
bias
classism
human rights violations
oppression
poverty
stereotyping

class division
SG Economics and Employment
Social Sciences and Culture
(*cont.*)

class division (*cont.*)
BT class
RT class formation
socioeconomic conditions
status

class formation
SG Social Sciences and Culture
RT class
class division
sex/gender systems
social construction of gender

class identity
SG Economics and Employment
Social Sciences and Culture
BT identity
RT class
community
income
wealth

class ideology
SG Economics and Employment
Law, Government, and Public Policy
Social Sciences and Culture
BT ideology
RT class

classes
SG History and Social Change
Social Sciences and Culture
BT educational activities

classical conditioning
SG Social Sciences and Culture
BT conditioning

classical economics
SG Economics and Employment
BT economics

classical music
USE **art music**

Classical Period
DG Historical Periods

SN=Scope note   SG=Subject group   DG=Delimiters group   USE=Use

classicism
- DG Cultural and Political Movements

classism
- SN *Includes concepts of bias, stereotyping, and discrimination on the basis of socioeconomic status or background.*
- SG History and Social Change
  Social Sciences and Culture
- RT ableism
  ageism
  blue collar workers
  class discrimination
  dual economy
  lower class
  middle class
  racism
  sexism
  social attitudes
  social class
  social stratification
  stereotyping
  untouchables
  upper class
  working class

classless society
- SG Economics and Employment
  Social Sciences and Culture
- BT society
- RT class
  socioeconomic status
  utopias

cleaners
- SG Economics and Employment
- UF cleaning women
- NT housecleaners
  janitors
- RT cleaning

cleaning
- SG Economics and Employment
  Social Sciences and Culture
- RT cleaners
  household labor

cleaning women
- USE **cleaners**

cleanliness
- SG Language, Literature, Religion, and Philosophy
  Natural Sciences and Health
- RT hygiene
  purity

cleavage
- SG Natural Sciences and Health
- RT breasts
  images of women

clergy
- SG Economics and Employment
  Language, Literature, Religion, and Philosophy
- BT religious workers
- NT clergymen
  clergywomen
  ministers
  mullahs
  priestesses
  priests
  rabbis
- RT ordination
  preaching
  religious orders
  seminaries
  women religious
  women's ordination

clergymen
- SG Economics and Employment
  Language, Literature, Religion, and Philosophy
- BT clergy
  men

clergywomen
- SG Economics and Employment
  Language, Literature, Religion, and Philosophy
- BT clergy
  women religious

UF=Use for BT=Broader term NT=Narrower term RT=Related term

clerical occupations
- SG Economics and Employment
- BT administrative support occupations
- NT bank tellers
  bookkeepers
  clerks
  computer equipment operators
  data entry operators
  mail carriers
  receptionists
  secretaries
  stenographers
  telephone operators
  typists
- RT data processing

clerks
- SG Economics and Employment
  Law, Government, and Public Policy
- BT clerical occupations
  female intensive occupations

cliches
- SG Language, Literature, Religion, and
  Philosophy
- RT jargon
  language
  old wives' tales
  perceptual bias
  proverbs

climacteric
- SG Natural Sciences and Health
- RT menopause

clinical psychology
- SG Social Sciences and Culture
- BT psychology

clinical trials
- SN *Testing of drugs.*
- SG Natural Sciences and Health
- RT chemotherapy
  drug dumping
  drug side effects
  informed consent
  pharmaceutical industry

clinics
- SG History and Social Change
  Natural Sciences and Health
  Social Sciences and Culture
- BT facilities
- NT abortion clinics
- RT community health services
  health care facilities

clippings
- DG Types and Forms of Materials

cliques
- SG Social Sciences and Culture
- RT factions

clitoral orgasm
- SG Natural Sciences and Health
- BT orgasm

clitoridectomy
- SG History and Social Change
- BT female circumcision
- RT clitoris
  genital mutilation

clitoris
- SG Natural Sciences and Health
- BT genitals
- RT arousal
  clitoridectomy
  female circumcision
  orgasm

cloning
- SG Natural Sciences and Health
- BT reproductive technologies
- RT bioethics
  genetic engineering
  in vitro fertilization

closeted lesbians
- SG History and Social Change
  Social Sciences and Culture
- BT lesbians
- RT coming out

clothes
USE **clothing**

clothing

SG Natural Sciences and Health
Social Sciences and Culture
Visual and Performing Arts
UF clothes
dress
NT bathing suits
bloomers
brassieres
chador
high heeled shoes
hosiery
lingerie
pants
protective clothing
purses
skirts
tank tops
tee shirts
underwear
veils
RT angora
appearance
dress codes
dress reform
dressing for success
fashion
hemlines
images of women
textile industry

clothing workers

SG Economics and Employment
UF needleworkers
BT female intensive occupations
manufacturing occupations
workers
NT dressmakers
knitting machine operators
milliners
seamstresses (historical)
sewers
sewing machine operators
tailors

(cont.)

clothing workers *(cont.)*

RT dressmaking
garment industry
needlework
textile industry

club women

SG Social Sciences and Culture
BT women
RT social clubs
volunteers

clubs

SG History and Social Change
BT organizations
NT book clubs
garden clubs
night clubs
private clubs
social clubs
RT affiliation
auxiliaries
discrimination
social activities
tea rooms

coaches

SG Economics and Employment
Education
BT arts, entertainment, and media
occupations
education occupations
RT athletics
professional sports

coal miners

SG Economics and Employment
Science and Technology
BT craft occupations
RT extractive industry

coalition politics

SG History and Social Change
BT politics
RT women's groups
women's organizations

UF=Use for   BT=Broader term   NT=Narrower term   RT=Related term

coalitions
- SG History and Social Change
  Social Sciences and Culture
- BT organizations
- RT alliances

coat check girls
- USE **coat checkers**

coat checkers
- SG Economics and Employment
- UF coat check girls
- BT female intensive occupations
  service occupations

cocaine
- SG Natural Sciences and Health
- BT narcotic drugs
- RT drug abuse

cocktail parties
- SG History and Social Change
  Social Sciences and Culture
- BT parties

cocktail servers
- SG Economics and Employment
- UF barmaids
- BT service occupations

codependency
- SG Natural Sciences and Health
  Social Sciences and Culture
- RT alcoholism
  counseling
  dependent behavior
  drug addiction
  personal relationships
  substance abuse

codes
- DG Types and Forms of Materials

codices
- DG Types and Forms of Materials

coeds
- USE **college students**

coeducation
- SG Education
- BT education
- RT alumnae/i
  alumni
  single sex environments

coffee klatches
- SG Social Sciences and Culture
- BT social activities

cognition
- SG Social Sciences and Culture
- RT cognitive processes
  sensation

cognitive behavior modification
- SG Social Sciences and Culture
- BT behavior modification
- RT attitude change

cognitive development
- SG Social Sciences and Culture
- BT individual development
- NT intellectual development
  perceptual development

cognitive dissonance
- SG Social Sciences and Culture
- RT cognitive processes
  conceptual errors
  consciousness
  intuition
  norms
  perceptual bias

cognitive processes
- SG Social Sciences and Culture
- NT abstract reasoning
  creative thinking
  decision making
  logical thinking
  memory
  perception

(cont.)

cognitive processes (*cont.*)
NT problem solving
RT attention
cognition
cognitive dissonance
consciousness
intelligence
intelligence tests
intuition
learning
literacy
mind
rationality
reason
subjective knowledge

cognitive science
SG Social Sciences and Culture
BT science
RT philosophy
psychology

cohabitation
SG Social Sciences and Culture
UF living together
RT common law marriage
divorce
living arrangements
posslq

cohort analysis
SG Science and Technology
Social Sciences and Culture
BT research methods
RT cohorts
statistics

cohorts
SG Education
Social Sciences and Culture
BT groups
RT cohort analysis

coiffures
SG Social Sciences and Culture
RT appearance
hair

(*cont.*)

coiffures (*cont.*)
RT hair styles
wigs

coins
SG Visual and Performing Arts
RT images of women
money

coitus
USE **sexual intercourse**

coitus interruptus
SG Natural Sciences and Health
BT contraception
RT pregnancy
sexual behavior

collaboration
SG History and Social Change
RT administration
feminist methods
group process
leadership
leadership skills
management styles
management theory
organizational theory
social skills
social values
women's organizations

collaborative theater
SG Visual and Performing Arts
BT theater

collage
SG Visual and Performing Arts
BT visual arts
NT femmage

collections
DG Types and Forms of Materials

collective bargaining
SG Economics and Employment
RT contracts

(*cont.*)

UF=Use for   BT=Broader term   NT=Narrower term   RT=Related term

collective bargaining (*cont.*)
  RT   unions

collective behavior
  USE **group behavior**

collective farms
      SG   International Women
  BT   collectives
       farms
  RT   third world

collectives
      SG   History and Social Change
  BT   organizations
  NT   collective farms
  RT   communes
       cooperatives
       kibbutzim
       life styles
       management practices
       support systems

college administrators
      SG   Economics and Employment
           Education
  BT   administrators

college credits
      SG   Education
  BT   credits

college presidents
      SG   Economics and Employment
           Education
  BT   education occupations
  RT   presidential spouses

college students
      SG   Education
  UF   coeds
  BT   students
  NT   women college students

colleges
      SG   Education
  BT   educational facilities
                                        (*cont.*)

colleges (*cont.*)
  NT   Black colleges
       community colleges
       junior colleges
       private colleges
       public colleges
       single sex colleges
       two year colleges
  RT   higher education
       universities

collegiate athletics
      SG   Communications
           Education
           Natural Sciences and Health
  BT   athletics
  RT   alumnae
       alumni
       amateur athletics
       financial aid
       media coverage
       sports
       women's athletics

colloquia
      SG   History and Social Change
           Social Sciences and Culture
  BT   educational activities

Colombian
      DG   National and Regional Descriptors
  BT   Latin American

Colonial Period
      DG   Historical Periods

colonialism
      SG   History and Social Change
           International Women
           Law, Government, and Public Policy
      DG   Cultural and Political Movements
  UF   imperialism
  NT   neocolonialism
  RT   apartheid
       cultural imperialism
       decolonization
       developing nations
                                        (*cont.*)

colonialism (*cont.*)

RT economic development models
exploitation
fifth world
fourth world
genocide
indigenous populations
majority culture
markets
missionaries
multinational corporations
nationalism
patriarchy
plantations
third world

color perception

SG Natural Sciences and Health
BT perception

colorblind casting

SG Visual and Performing Arts
BT casting

colorists

SG Economics and Employment
BT cosmetologists

colostrum

SG Natural Sciences and Health
RT breast feeding

columnists

SG Communications
Economics and Employment
BT arts, entertainment, and media
occupations

columns

SG Communications
DG Types and Forms of Materials
NT advice columns
personal columns

comedians

SG Communications
Economics and Employment
Visual and Performing Arts
UF comediennes
BT arts, entertainment, and media
occupations

comediennes
USE **comedians**

comedy

SG Language, Literature, Religion, and
Philosophy
BT drama
NT farce
skits
RT humor
jokes
parody
satire

comic strips

SG Communications
Visual and Performing Arts
DG Types and Forms of Materials
BT visual arts
RT cartoons
Wonder Woman

coming out

SN *The act of publically revealing one's
homosexuality.*
SG History and Social Change
RT closeted lesbians
homosexuality

commentaries

DG Types and Forms of Materials

commentators

SG Communications
Economics and Employment
BT arts, entertainment, and media
occupations

commercial art
> SG   Visual and Performing Arts
> BT   art
> NT   graphics
>   illustration
>   typography
> RT   design
>   fashion
>   fashion photography
>   visual arts

commercial credit
> SG   Economics and Employment
> BT   credit
> RT   small business

commercial sex
> SG   Economics and Employment
>   Social Sciences and Culture
> BT   sex
> RT   advertising
>   mass media
>   massage parlors
>   sex industry
>   sex tourism
>   sexual equality
>   sexual exploitation

commercial television
> SG   Communications
> BT   television

commercials
> SG   Communications
> NT   radio commercials
>   television commercials
> RT   advertising
>   radio
>   television

commissions
> SG   History and Social Change
> BT   organizations
> NT   civil rights commissions
>   commissions on the status of women
>   equal opportunities commissions
>   human relations commissions
> *(cont.)*

commissions *(cont.)*
> RT   investigations
>   local government

commissions on the status of women
> SG   History and Social Change
>   Law, Government, and Public Policy
> BT   commissions

commitment
> SG   Social Sciences and Culture
> RT   attachment
>   families
>   loyalty
>   relationships
>   social behavior
>   values

committees
> SG   History and Social Change
>   Social Sciences and Culture
> BT   organizations
> NT   political action committees
>   search committees
> RT   task forces

common law marriage
> SG   Social Sciences and Culture
> BT   marriage
> RT   cohabitation
>   marriage customs

communal families
> SG   Social Sciences and Culture
> BT   communal groups
>   families
> RT   life styles

communal groups
> SG   Social Sciences and Culture
> BT   groups
> NT   communal families
> RT   communes
>   community

communes

SG History and Social Change
    Social Sciences and Culture
BT organizations
NT kibbutzim
    village communes
RT collectives
    communal groups
    communities
    housing
    life styles

communicable diseases

SG Natural Sciences and Health
BT diseases
NT acquired immune deficiency syndrome
    sexually transmitted diseases
RT pregnancy
    prevention
    treatment

communication

SG Communications
    Language, Literature, Religion, and
      Philosophy
    Social Sciences and Culture
NT interpersonal communication
    nonverbal communication
    verbal communication
RT body language
    braille
    communication styles
    feedback
    language
    language skills
    listening
    sign language
    synchrony
    talk
    writing

communication satellites

SG Communications
    Science and Technology
BT satellites
RT communications equity
    equal access

(cont.)

communication satellites (cont.)

RT satellite communications
    technology development
    telecommunications

communication styles

SG Language, Literature, Religion, and
      Philosophy
    Social Sciences and Culture
RT arguments
    communication
    consensus building
    female male relationships
    social skills

communications

SN *Science and technology of the trans-
    mission and reception of informa-
    tion.*
SG Communications
NT telecommunications
RT information sciences
    mass media
    satellites
    technology

communications equity

SG Communications
    History and Social Change
BT equity
RT communication satellites
    media stereotyping
    women's media

communications industry

SG Communications
BT industries
RT arts, entertainment, and media
    occupations
    mass media
    women's media

communism

SG Law, Government, and Public Policy
DG Cultural and Political Movements
BT political systems
RT democracy

UF=Use for   BT=Broader term   NT=Narrower term   RT=Related term

communist economic development models
- SG International Women
- BT economic development models

Communist Party
- SG Law, Government, and Public Policy
- BT political parties

communities
- SG History and Social Change
  Social Sciences and Culture
- NT faith communities
  lesbian communities
  utopian communities
- RT Beguinism
  communes
  community
  environmental racism
  ethnic neighborhoods
  households
  life styles
  neighborhoods
  organizations
  suburbs
  urban areas

community
- SG Social Sciences and Culture
- RT affiliation
  alienation
  class identity
  communal groups
  communities
  consensus
  extended families
  groups
  home life
  life styles
  matriarchy
  retreats
  social structure
  social values
  society
  state formation
  support systems
  utopias

(cont.)

community *(cont.)*
- RT women's culture

community action
- SG History and Social Change
  Law, Government, and Public Policy
  Social Sciences and Culture
- RT community responsibility
  protest actions
  social action

community affairs
- USE **public affairs**

community care
- SG Natural Sciences and Health
  Social Sciences and Culture
- BT care
- RT community health services
  dependent care

community colleges
- SG Education
- BT colleges
- RT junior colleges
  two year colleges

community development
- SG Economics and Employment
  Social Sciences and Culture
- BT development
- RT neighborhoods
  urban renewal

community education
- SG Education
- BT education
- RT agricultural extension
  alternative schools
  continuing education

community health services
- SG Natural Sciences and Health
- BT health care services
- RT clinics
  community care

(cont.)

community health services (cont.)

RT health care
health care facilities
temporary housing

community organizers

SG Economics and Employment
History and Social Change
Social Sciences and Culture
BT service occupations
volunteer occupations
RT activism

community problems

SG Social Sciences and Culture
BT problems
RT community responsibility
crimes
educational facilities
housing
property crimes
taxes

community property laws

SG Economics and Employment
Law, Government, and Public Policy
BT laws
RT children living in poverty
divorce laws
financial arrangements
legal settlements
marital property reform
marriage and family law
women living in poverty

community relations

SG Communications
Economics and Employment
BT relationships
RT corporate policy
public relations
voluntary organizations

community responsibility

SG Law, Government, and Public Policy
Social Sciences and Culture
BT responsibility

(cont.)

community responsibility (cont.)

RT citizenship
community action
community problems
educational facilities
political action

community schools

SG Education
BT schools

commuter marriage

SG Social Sciences and Culture
UF long distance marriage
BT marriage
RT dual career families

commuting students

SG Education
BT students

compact disks

DG Types and Forms of Materials
BT disks

companies

SG History and Social Change
Social Sciences and Culture
BT organizations
RT businesses

companionate marriage

SG Social Sciences and Culture
BT marriage

comparable worth

SN *Paying employees equal compensation
for jobs of comparable but different
skills, effort, responsibility, and
working conditions.*
SG Economics and Employment
Law, Government, and Public Policy
BT pay equity
RT athletics
back pay
economic value of women's work
equal pay

(cont.)

---

comparable worth (*cont.*)
- RT equal pay for equal work
  - equity
  - fairness
  - job evaluation
  - occupational sex segregation
  - pink collar workers
  - sports
  - wage discrimination
  - wage gap

comparative psychology
- SG Social Sciences and Culture
- BT psychology

comparative religion
- SG Language, Literature, Religion, and Philosophy
- BT cross cultural studies
- RT ecumenism
  - ethnic studies
  - history of religion
  - religion

compendiums
- DG Types and Forms of Materials

compensation packages
- SG Economics and Employment
- RT employee benefits
  - perquisites
  - wages

compensatory education
- SG Education
- BT education

competence
- SG Education
- NT minimum competencies
- RT adult learning
  - competency based tests
  - life skills
  - performance

competency based tests
- SG Education

(*cont.*)

competency based tests (*cont.*)
- BT testing
- RT competence
  - psychological testing

competitive behavior
- SG Social Sciences and Culture
- BT behavior
- RT ambition
  - athletics
  - confrontation
  - games
  - norms

compilations
- DG Types and Forms of Materials

completion complex
- SN *Ironic label for concern that a woman is incomplete without a man.*
- SG Social Sciences and Culture
- BT complexes
- RT adult development
  - compulsory heterosexuality
  - couples
  - old maids
  - spinsters

complexes
- SN *Use of a more specific term is recommended.*
- SG Natural Sciences and Health
  - Social Sciences and Culture
- NT castration complex
  - completion complex
  - Electra complex
  - Oedipus complex
- RT disorders
  - neuroses

complexion
- SG Natural Sciences and Health
- RT acne
  - appearance
  - attitudes
  - faces
  - skin

(*cont.*)

complexion (*cont.*)
RT   skin color

compliant behavior
SG   Social Sciences and Culture
BT   behavior
RT   conditioning
learned helplessness

compliments
SG   Social Sciences and Culture
RT   flirtation
manners
positive reinforcement

composers
SG   Economics and Employment
Visual and Performing Arts
BT   arts, entertainment, and media
occupations

compositions
DG   Types and Forms of Materials

compositors
SG   Communications
Economics and Employment
BT   printing workers
RT   typesetters

Comprehensive Employment and Training Act of 1973
DG   Laws and Regulations
UF   CETA
RT   job training

compressed workweek
SG   Economics and Employment
RT   recreation
work hours

compromise
SG   Law, Government, and Public Policy
Social Sciences and Culture
RT   arguments
consensus
mediation

(*cont.*)

compromise (*cont.*)
RT   negotiation

compulsions
USE   **compulsive behavior**

compulsive behavior
SG   Social Sciences and Culture
UF   compulsions
BT   behavior
NT   hypersexuality
RT   addiction
obsessive compulsive disorders

compulsive sexuality
USE   **hypersexuality**

compulsory education
SG   Education
BT   education

compulsory heterosexuality
SG   Natural Sciences and Health
Social Sciences and Culture
BT   heterosexuality
RT   completion complex
female sexuality
gay/straight split
heterosexism
homophobia
homosexuality
lesbianism
majority culture
male bonding
male norms
sex stereotypes
straights

compulsory sterilization
USE   **involuntary sterilization**

computer anxiety
USE   **computer avoidance**

computer art
USE   **electronic art**

---

computer avoidance
SG Science and Technology
UF computer anxiety
BT avoidance behavior
RT computer literacy

computer equipment operators
SG Economics and Employment
BT clerical occupations
operators

computer equity
SN *Equal access to computer instruction
and resources.*
SG Science and Technology
BT equity
RT computers
equal access

computer games
SG Communications
Education
Science and Technology
BT video games

computer literacy
SN *Familiarity with fundamentals of computers, sometimes used to describe
basic knowledge of hardware and
programming.*
SG Science and Technology
BT literacy
RT computer avoidance
computers
employment opportunities
equal access
male intensive occupations

computer music
SG Visual and Performing Arts
BT music
RT electronic music

computer programmers
SG Economics and Employment
Science and Technology
BT scientific and technical occupations
(cont.)

computer programmers *(cont.)*
RT operations researchers
systems analysts

computer programming
SG Science and Technology
RT programming languages

computer programs
DG Types and Forms of Materials

computer science
SG Science and Technology
BT information sciences
RT computers
library science
technology
technology development
telecommunications

computer searches
USE **information retrieval services**

computer security
SG Science and Technology
BT security
RT confidentiality

computer terminals
SG Communications
Science and Technology
BT computers
RT electronic cottage
telecommuting
video display terminals

computers
SG Communications
NT computer terminals
RT artificial intelligence
computer equity
computer literacy
computer science
electronics industry
programming languages

concentration camps
SG History and Social Change
Law, Government, and Public Policy
RT genocide
internment

ncept papers
DG Types and Forms of Materials
BT papers

conception
SG Natural Sciences and Health
RT artificial insemination
childbirth
contraception
embryos
in vitro fertilization
pregnancy
religious law
reproduction
sexual intercourse
viability

onceptual errors
SG Language, Literature, Religion, and
Philosophy
NT circular reasoning
faulty generalization
RT cognitive dissonance
discrimination
false dichotomies
false generics
logic
mind/body split
norms
objectivity
patriarchal language
perceptual bias
phallogocentrism
social construction of reality
stereotypes

oncert music
USE **art music**

oncerts
SG Visual and Performing Arts
(cont.)

concerts (*cont.*)
RT performing arts

concordances
DG Types and Forms of Materials

concubinage
SG Social Sciences and Culture
RT courtesans
female sexual slavery
geishas
harems
mistresses
odalisques
prostitutes
sexual slavery

concubines
SG International Women
Social Sciences and Culture
BT images of women
women

concupiscence
USE **lust**

conditioning
SG Natural Sciences and Health
Social Sciences and Culture
UF psychological conditioning
NT classical conditioning
operant conditioning
social conditioning
RT animal behavior
behavior modification
biofeedback
compliant behavior
learned helplessness
learning
paranoia
personality disorders
reinforcement
smiling

conditions
SN *Use of a more specific term is recommended.*
(cont.)

---

conditions (*cont.*)
- SG Social Sciences and Culture
- NT factory conditions
  industrial conditions
  living conditions
  rural conditions
  working conditions

condoms
- SG Natural Sciences and Health
- BT contraception
- RT disease prevention
  safe sex

conductors
- SG Economics and Employment
  Visual and Performing Arts
- BT arts, entertainment, and media
  occupations

confederations
- SG History and Social Change
  Social Sciences and Culture
- BT organizations

conferences
- SG History and Social Change
  Social Sciences and Culture
- BT activities
- NT teleconferences
- RT conventions
  meetings
  panels
  sessions
  workshops

confession
- SG Language, Literature, Religion, and
  Philosophy
- BT sacraments
- RT sin

confidentiality
- SG Communications
- NT records confidentiality
- RT computer security
  counseling

(*cont.*)

confidentiality (*cont.*)
- RT employee records
  lawyer client relationships
  legal services
  medical records
  patient doctor relationships
  privacy
  records
  school records
  therapy

confirmation
- SG Language, Literature, Religion, and
  Philosophy
- BT sacraments

conflict
- SG Social Sciences and Culture
- NT career family conflict
  conflict of interest
  culture conflict
  family conflict
  marital conflict
  role conflict
  social conflict
- RT adjustment
  aggressive behavior
  conflict resolution
  counseling
  satisfaction

conflict of interest
- SG Economics and Employment
  Language, Literature, Religion, and
  Philosophy
  Law, Government, and Public Policy
- BT conflict
- RT ethics
  morality

conflict resolution
- SG Economics and Employment
  Law, Government, and Public Policy
  Social Sciences and Culture
- RT anger
  arbitration
  conflict

(*cont.*)

SN=Scope note SG=Subject group DG=Delimiters group USE=Us

conflict resolution (*cont.*)
RT   confrontation
     counseling
     mediation
     negotiation

conforming behavior
SG   Social Sciences and Culture
UF   conformity
BT   behavior
RT   norms
     organizations
     personality traits

conformity
USE **conforming behavior**

confrontation
SG   Social Sciences and Culture
RT   competitive behavior
     conflict resolution

congenital anomalies
USE **birth defects**

congregations
SG   Language, Literature, Religion, and
       Philosophy
BT   religious groups
RT   churches
     faith communities
     mosques
     synagogues
     temples

Congress
SG   Law, Government, and Public Policy
NT   House of Representatives
     Senate
RT   appropriations
     budgeting
     constitution
     federal budget
     federal legislation

congresses
SG   History and Social Change
     Social Sciences and Culture
BT   organizations

congressional hearings
SG   Law, Government, and Public Policy
BT   hearings

congressmen
SG   Economics and Employment
     Law, Government, and Public Policy
BT   men
     representatives

congresswomen
SG   Economics and Employment
     Law, Government, and Public Policy
BT   representatives
     women

consanguinity
SG   Social Sciences and Culture
RT   kinship

conscientious objection
SG   History and Social Change
RT   antiwar movement
     draft resistance
     military draft
     nonviolence
     pacifism
     peace movements

consciousness
SG   Social Sciences and Culture
NT   false consciousness
RT   attitudes
     cognitive dissonance
     cognitive processes
     consciousness raising
     mind
     protofeminism

consciousness raising
SG   History and Social Change
RT   career feminism

(*cont.*)

UF=Use for   BT=Broader term   NT=Narrower term   RT=Related term

consciousness raising (*cont.*)

RT consciousness
   discrimination
   false consciousness
   feminist movement
   sensitivity training
   woman power

consciousness raising groups

SG History and Social Change
BT groups
RT race relations
   sensitivity training
   women's groups

consensual union

SG Law, Government, and Public Policy
   Social Sciences and Culture
BT union
RT marriage

consensus

SG Economics and Employment
   History and Social Change
NT consensus building
RT community
   compromise
   feminist methods

consensus building

SG History and Social Change
   Law, Government, and Public Policy
BT consensus
RT communication styles
   group process
   leadership skills

consent
   USE **informed consent**

consent orders

SG History and Social Change
   Law, Government, and Public Policy
RT affirmative action hiring
   enforcement
   lawsuits

conservation

SG Science and Technology
   Visual and Performing Arts
NT art conservation
   book conservation
   energy conservation
   soil conservation
RT air pollution
   environment
   mineral resources
   natural resources
   pollution

conservatism

DG Cultural and Political Movements

conservative movement

SG History and Social Change
DG Cultural and Political Movements
BT social movements
RT conservatives
   religious movements
   right wing organizations
   separate spheres
   the religious right

conservatives

SG Law, Government, and Public Policy
RT anti ERA movement
   antiabortion movement
   antifeminism
   attitudes
   conservative movement
   liberals
   moral majority
   political parties
   social movements

conservatories

SG Visual and Performing Arts
BT educational facilities

consortia

SG History and Social Change
   Social Sciences and Culture
BT organizations

constitution

SG History and Social Change
Law, Government, and Public Policy
RT civil rights
Congress
equal rights legislation
legal system

constitutions

DG Types and Forms of Materials

construction industry

SG Economics and Employment
Science and Technology
UF building industry
BT industries
RT construction occupations
laborers

construction occupations

SG Economics and Employment
BT craft occupations
NT bricklayers
cabinetmakers
carpenters
construction workers
electricians
glaziers
heavy equipment operators
housepainters
inspectors
paperhangers
plasterers
plumbers
roofers
woodworkers
RT construction industry
laborers
male intensive occupations
manufacturing industry

construction workers

SG Economics and Employment
BT construction occupations
workers
RT machine operators

consultants

SN *Use of a more specific term is recommended.*
SG Economics and Employment
Education
BT professional occupations

consumer advocates

SG Economics and Employment
BT advocates
RT consumer power
consumer protection

consumer behavior

SG Economics and Employment
Social Sciences and Culture
BT behavior
RT market research

consumer credit

SG Economics and Employment
BT credit
RT consumer information
equal credit

consumer economy

SG Economics and Employment
BT economy
RT consumption
upward mobility

consumer health organizations

SG Economics and Employment
Natural Sciences and Health
BT organizations
RT health advocates

consumer information

SG Economics and Employment
BT information
RT consumer credit
consumer problems
consumer protection
consumerism

consumer installment loans

SG Economics and Employment

(cont.)

UF=Use for   BT=Broader term   NT=Narrower term   RT=Related term

consumer installment loans (*cont.*)
BT loans

consumer power
SG Economics and Employment
BT power
RT consumer advocates
consumer protection
economic power

consumer problems
SG Economics and Employment
BT problems
RT consumer information
consumer protection
consumerism

consumer protection
SG Economics and Employment
Law, Government, and Public Policy
RT consumer advocates
consumer information
consumer power
consumer problems
consumerism

consumerism
SG Economics and Employment
Social Sciences and Culture
DG Cultural and Political Movements
RT consumer information
consumer problems
consumer protection
consumers
consumption
game shows
queen for a day
upward mobility

consumers
SG Economics and Employment
RT consumerism

consumption
SG Economics and Employment
Social Sciences and Culture
RT advertising

(*cont.*)

consumption (*cont.*)
RT consumer economy
consumerism
markets
values

contact dykes
SN *Slang; used to describe members of an informal nationwide network of lesbians.*
SG History and Social Change
BT lesbians
RT lesbian communities

contact sports
SG Education
Natural Sciences and Health
BT sports
RT athletics

contacts
SG Economics and Employment
RT job hunting
mentors
networks
search committees

content analysis
SG Education
Social Sciences and Culture
BT research methods

contextual analysis
SG Education
Language, Literature, Religion, and Philosophy
Social Sciences and Culture
BT research methods

continuing education
SG Education
BT education
RT adult education
adult students
agricultural extension
community education
correspondence courses

(*cont.*)

SN=Scope note   SG=Subject group   DG=Delimiters group   USE=Use

continuing education (*cont.*)
RT credits
    educational benefits
    external degree programs
    nonformal education
    reentry students

continuing education units
SG Education
BT credits
RT accreditation

contraception
SG Natural Sciences and Health
UF birth control methods
NT cervical caps
    coitus interruptus
    condoms
    diaphragms
    injectable contraceptives
    intrauterine devices
    oral contraceptives
    rhythm method
    spermicides
RT abortion
    birth control
    cervical mucus
    childbearing
    childfree marriage
    conception
    family planning
    family size
    planned parenthood
    population control
    pregnancy
    pregnancy prevention
    religious law
    sterilization

contract compliance
SG Economics and Employment
    Education
    Law, Government, and Public Policy
RT contracts
    enforcement
    lawsuits

contract renewal
SG Economics and Employment
    Education
RT tenure
    unions

contracts
SG Economics and Employment
    Law, Government, and Public Policy
DG Types and Forms of Materials
BT legal documents
NT labor contracts
    marriage contracts
RT arbitration
    collective bargaining
    contract compliance
    mediation
    negotiation
    strikes
    unions

control
SG Social Sciences and Culture
NT self control
    social control
RT autonomy
    dominance
    influence
    locus of control
    power

conventional mortgages
SG Economics and Employment
BT mortgages
RT real estate

conventions
SG History and Social Change
    Social Sciences and Culture
BT activities
NT political conventions
RT conferences

convents
SG Language, Literature, Religion, and
    Philosophy
BT religious facilities

(*cont.*)

UF=Use for   BT=Broader term   NT=Narrower term   RT=Related term

convents (*cont.*)

RT holy women
    meditation
    monasticism
    novitiates
    nuns
    religion
    religious music
    religious orders
    single sex environments
    women religious

conversation

SG Language, Literature, Religion, and
    Philosophy
BT verbal communication
RT discourse
    gossip
    language
    sign language
    talk

cookbooks

DG Types and Forms of Materials
BT books

cooking

SG Economics and Employment
    Natural Sciences and Health
RT domestic food production
    food
    food industry
    food preparation
    food preparation occupations
    herbs
    nutrition
    recipes

cooks

SG Economics and Employment
    Natural Sciences and Health
BT female intensive occupations
    food preparation occupations

cooperative education

SG Education
BT education

cooperatives

SG History and Social Change
BT organizations
NT health cooperatives
RT collectives

coordinators

SG Economics and Employment
    Education
    History and Social Change
BT education occupations
    managerial occupations

coparenting

SG Social Sciences and Culture
BT parenting
RT balancing work and family life
    homemakers
    mothers working outside the home
    shared custody

coping strategies

SG Social Sciences and Culture
BT strategies
RT adjustment
    behavior modification
    frustration
    humor
    mental health
    self help
    stress
    support systems

copulation

USE **sexual intercourse**

copyright laws

SG Communications
    Law, Government, and Public Policy
BT laws
RT patents

copywriters

SG Communications
    Economics and Employment
BT arts, entertainment, and media
    occupations

(*cont.*)

copywriters (*cont.*)
RT journalism
    publishing industry
    writers

core curriculum
SG Education
BT curriculum

corporate day care centers
SG Economics and Employment
    Social Sciences and Culture
BT day care centers
NT workplace nurseries
RT employer supported day care

corporate husbands
USE **corporate spouses**

corporate law
SG Economics and Employment
    Law, Government, and Public Policy
BT law

corporate liability
SG Economics and Employment
BT liability
RT air pollution
    corporate responsibility
    drug dumping
    enforcement
    hazardous waste
    intrauterine devices

corporate policy
SG Economics and Employment
    International Women
UF industrial policy
BT policy
NT corporate relocation policy
    foreign investment policy
    hiring policy
    multinational corporation policy
RT benefits
    boards of directors
    child care leave
    community relations

(*cont.*)

corporate policy (*cont.*)
RT dependent care
    dependent care assistance programs
    employer supported day care
    laissez faire
    management
    parental leave
    sexual harassment

corporate relocation policy
SG Economics and Employment
BT corporate policy
RT dual career couples
    dual career families
    dual careers
    relocation

corporate responsibility
SG Economics and Employment
    History and Social Change
BT responsibility
RT air pollution
    balancing work and family life
    boards of directors
    business ethics
    corporate liability
    divestiture
    investments
    management
    sexual harassment
    water pollution

corporate spouses
SG Economics and Employment
    Social Sciences and Culture
UF corporate husbands
    corporate wives
    executive spouses
BT spouses
RT female intensive occupations

corporate takeovers
SG Economics and Employment
RT aggressive behavior
    antitrust legislation
    mergers
    monopolies

(*cont.*)

UF=Use for   BT=Broader term   NT=Narrower term   RT=Related term

corporate takeovers (*cont.*)
RT   multinational corporations

corporate wives
USE **corporate spouses**

corporations
SG   Economics and Employment
BT   organizations
NT   monopolies
     multinational corporations
     networks (media)
RT   business
     industries
     mergers
     military trade
     power structure

correctional facilities
USE **prisons**

correctional officers
SG   Economics and Employment
     Law, Government, and Public Policy
BT   protective service occupations
NT   parole officers
     probation officers
RT   prison workers

correctional rehabilitation
SG   Law, Government, and Public Policy
BT   rehabilitation
RT   criminals
     judiciary system
     juvenile justice system
     recidivism

correspondence
SG   Communications
     Language, Literature, Religion, and
        Philosophy
NT   business correspondence
     personal correspondence
RT   l'ecriture feminine
     letters
     verbal communication
     writing

correspondence courses
SG   Education
RT   continuing education

correspondents
SG   Communications
     Economics and Employment
BT   journalists

corruption
SG   Law, Government, and Public Policy
RT   selfish behavior
     white collar crime

corsages
SG   Social Sciences and Culture
BT   flowers

corsets
SG   History and Social Change
     Natural Sciences and Health
BT   lingerie
RT   dress reform
     girdles
     ritual disfigurement

cosmetic surgery
SG   Natural Sciences and Health
UF   butt lifts
     nose jobs
     tummy tucks
BT   surgery
RT   appearance
     body image
     plastic surgery
     reconstructive surgery

cosmetics
SG   Natural Sciences and Health
RT   beauty standards
     cosmetology
     makeup
     perfume
     skin color

cosmetologists
SG   Economics and Employment
(*cont.*)

SN=Scope note   SG=Subject group   DG=Delimiters group   USE=Use

cosmetologists *(cont.)*
  BT   female intensive occupations
       service occupations
  NT   colorists
       manicurists
       pedicurists
  RT   beauticians
       beauty parlors

cosmetology
  SG   Economics and Employment
       Social Sciences and Culture
  RT   cosmetics

cosmology
  SG   Language, Literature, Religion, and
       Philosophy
  RT   belief systems
       devil
       mythology
       sacred ideology
       theology
       world views

cost benefit analysis
  SG   Economics and Employment
  BT   research methods
  RT   budget cuts
       economies of scale
       planning

cost of living
  SG   Economics and Employment
  RT   costs
       inflation
       poverty

Costa Rican
  DG   National and Regional Descriptors
  BT   Central American

costs
  SG   Economics and Employment
  NT   administrative costs
       educational costs
       health care costs
       housing costs

(cont.)

costs *(cont.)*
  RT   budgeting
       cost of living

costume design
  SG   Visual and Performing Arts
  BT   design

cotillions
  SG   Social Sciences and Culture
  BT   dances
  RT   debutantes

cottage industry
  SG   Economics and Employment
  BT   industries
  RT   alternative work arrangements
       home based business
       home based work
       home based workers
       income generation
       informal sector
       outwork
       part time employment
       piecework
       small business
       technology development
       telecommuting

councils
  SG   History and Social Change
       Social Sciences and Culture
  BT   organizations

counseling
  SG   Social Sciences and Culture
  NT   abortion counseling
       career counseling
       economic counseling
       family counseling
       genetic counseling
       group counseling
       individual counseling
       marriage counseling
       occupational counseling
       school counseling
       sex counseling

(cont.)

UF=Use for   BT=Broader term   NT=Narrower term   RT=Related term

counseling (*cont.*)

RT adjustment
   alcoholism
   behavior change
   codependency
   confidentiality
   conflict
   conflict resolution
   empty nest
   mental health
   personality problems
   rape victims
   stress
   testing
   violence

counselors

SG Economics and Employment
   Education
   Social Sciences and Culture
BT education occupations
   female intensive occupations
   professional occupations

Counter Reformation

DG Historical Periods
BT Reformation

counterculture

SN *Cultural styles and traditions developed as alternatives to dominant culture.*
SG Social Sciences and Culture
BT culture
RT cults
   life styles

countertransference

SG Social Sciences and Culture
BT transference

countesses

SG International Women
   Law, Government, and Public Policy
BT images of women
   titles (nobility)
   women

country music

SG Visual and Performing Arts
BT popular music

county courts

SG Law, Government, and Public Policy
BT courts

county government

SG Law, Government, and Public Policy
BT government
RT agricultural extension

couples

SG Social Sciences and Culture
NT childless couples
   couples with children
   dual career couples
   gay couples
   married couples
RT childfree marriage
   completion complex
   dual roles
   families
   gay men
   lesbians
   life styles
   relationships

couples with children

SG Social Sciences and Culture
BT couples
RT child rearing practices
   families
   nuclear families

coups

SG History and Social Change
   International Women
   Law, Government, and Public Policy
RT military
   protest actions
   revolutionary movements

courage

SG Language, Literature, Religion, and
   Philosophy

(*cont.*)

courage (*cont.*)
RT   integrity
     women of valor

course evaluation
SG   Education
BT   evaluation

course objectives
SG   Education
BT   objectives
RT   teaching

court cases
SG   Law, Government, and Public Policy
RT   back pay
     civil law
     courts
     discrimination
     Equal Employment Opportunity
        Commission

court decisions
SG   Law, Government, and Public Policy
RT   civil law
     courts
     criminal law
     enforcement
     judicial process

courtesans
SG   Social Sciences and Culture
BT   images of women
     women
RT   concubinage
     geishas
     mistresses
     prostitutes

courtly love
SG   Language, Literature, Religion, and
        Philosophy
BT   love
RT   chivalry
     cult of the virgin
     ideal woman
     romance
                                    (*cont.*)

courtly love (*cont.*)
RT   romances
     troubadours

courtroom transcripts
DG   Types and Forms of Materials

courts
SG   Law, Government, and Public Policy
NT   county courts
     family courts
     federal courts
     juvenile courts
     state courts
     Supreme Court
RT   civil lawsuits
     court cases
     court decisions

courtship customs
SG   Social Sciences and Culture
BT   customs
NT   bundling
     marriage proposals
RT   betrothed
     dating
     marriage customs
     showers

cousins
SG   Social Sciences and Culture
RT   extended families
     family structure

covens
SG   Language, Literature, Religion, and
        Philosophy
BT   religious groups
RT   witches

coverture
SN   *Legal status of a married woman; liter-*
        ally a covering, shelter, concealment,
        or disguise.
SG   Law, Government, and Public Policy
     Social Sciences and Culture
RT   marriage

cowboys
USE **ranch hands**

cowgirls
USE **ranch hands**

cowives
SN *Two wives of same spouse.*
SG   Social Sciences and Culture
BT   wives
RT   bigamy
     polygamy
     polygyny

coyness
SG   Social Sciences and Culture
RT   flirtation
     images of women

the Craft
USE **witchcraft**

craft artists
SG   Visual and Performing Arts
UF   craftsmen
NT   potters
     weavers

craft arts
SG   Visual and Performing Arts
UF   crafts
     handicrafts
BT   visual arts
NT   basketry
     beadwork
     ceramics
     china painting
     doll making
     flower painting
     knitting
     lace making
     needlework
     pottery
     puppetry
     quilting
     rug hooking
     spinning

(cont.)

craft arts *(cont.)*
NT   tapestry
     textile making
     weaving
RT   handmade
     instrument makers
     painting
     sewing
     woodworkers

craft occupations
SG   Economics and Employment
     Science and Technology
BT   occupations
NT   coal miners
     construction occupations
     engravers
     machinists
     mechanics
     repairers
     sign painters
     technicians
     tool and die makers
     watchmakers
     welders
RT   scientific and technical occupations
     trades
     working class

crafts
USE **craft arts**

craftsmen
USE **artisans**
    craft artists
    craftspersons

craftspersons
SG   Economics and Employment
     Visual and Performing Arts
UF   craftsmen
BT   arts, entertainment, and media
     occupations

creation myths
SG   Language, Literature, Religion, and
     Philosophy

(cont.)

creation myths (*cont.*)
- BT mythology
- RT Adam
  belief systems
  devil
  earth mother
  Eve
  evolution
  images of women
  Lilith
  paradise

creative thinking
- SG Language, Literature, Religion, and
  Philosophy
  Social Sciences and Culture
- BT cognitive processes
- RT daydreams
  dreams
  fantasies
  imagination
  intuition

creative writing
- SG Language, Literature, Religion, and
  Philosophy
- BT writing
- RT fiction
  imagination
  intuition
  literature

creativity
- SG Social Sciences and Culture
  Visual and Performing Arts
- BT psychological needs
- RT imagination
  intelligence
  personality traits
  talent

creches
- SG Education
  Social Sciences and Culture
- BT nurseries

credentials
- SG Economics and Employment
  Education
- RT certification
  degrees

credit
- SG Economics and Employment
- NT commercial credit
  consumer credit
  equal credit
  tuition tax credit
  utility credit
- RT assumable mortgages
  capital
  divorce
  eligibility
  financial management
  homeowners
  seed capital

credit by examination
- SG Education
- BT credits
- RT nontraditional education

credit for experience
- SG Education
- UF prior learning
- BT credits
- RT experience
  nontraditional education

credit fraud
- SG Economics and Employment
  Law, Government, and Public Policy
- BT fraud

credits
- SG Education
- NT college credits
  continuing education units
  credit by examination
  credit for experience
- RT continuing education

Creole
    DG   Ethnic, Racial, and Religious
            Descriptors

crew
    SG   Natural Sciences and Health
    BT   sports

crib death
    USE **sudden infant death syndrome**

cricket
    SG   Natural Sciences and Health
    BT   sports

crime
    SG   Law, Government, and Public Policy
    NT   organized crime
            white collar crime
    RT   crimes

crime prevention
    SG   Law, Government, and Public Policy
    BT   prevention
    RT   crimes
            property crimes

crime victims
    SG   Law, Government, and Public Policy
    BT   victims
    RT   crimes against children
            crimes against the elderly
            crimes against women

crimes
    SG   Law, Government, and Public Policy
    NT   crimes against children
            crimes against the elderly
            crimes against women
            crimes of honor
            crimes of passion
            property crimes
            sex crimes
            victimless crimes
            war crimes
    RT   abuse
            community problems

(cont.)

crimes *(cont.)*
    RT   crime
            crime prevention
            criminals
            crisis centers
            individual counseling
            investigations
            juvenile delinquency
            murder
            murderers
            survivors
            victims
            violence

crimes against children
    SG   Law, Government, and Public Policy
    BT   crimes
    RT   child abuse
            crime victims
            incest
            rape

crimes against the elderly
    SG   Law, Government, and Public Policy
    BT   crimes
    RT   crime victims
            elder abuse
            older adults

crimes against women
    SG   Law, Government, and Public Policy
    BT   crimes
    RT   battered women
            crime victims
            domestic violence
            dowry deaths
            rape
            rape crisis centers
            rape victims

crimes of honor
    SG   Law, Government, and Public Policy
    BT   crimes
    RT   crimes of passion
            machismo
            violence against women

crimes of passion

SG Law, Government, and Public Policy
BT crimes
RT crimes of honor
jealousy
passion
violence against women

criminal abortion

SG Law, Government, and Public Policy
BT abortion
RT abortion laws
judicial attitudes

criminal justice

SG Law, Government, and Public Policy
BT justice
RT juvenile justice system
legal system

criminal law

SG Law, Government, and Public Policy
BT law
RT court decisions
death penalty
judiciary system
juries

criminal lawsuits

SG Law, Government, and Public Policy
BT lawsuits
RT judiciary system

criminals

SG Law, Government, and Public Policy
UF offenders
NT rapists
RT correctional rehabilitation
crimes
juvenile offenders
outlaws
prisoners

criminology

SG Education
Law, Government, and Public Policy
BT social sciences

crisis centers

SG History and Social Change
Social Sciences and Culture
BT centers
NT rape crisis centers
RT crimes
family counseling
hot lines
substance abuse
victim services
women's shelters

crisis intervention

SG Social Sciences and Culture
RT domestic violence
family conflict
family counseling
hot lines
marital conflict
women's shelters

crisis shelters

SG Social Sciences and Culture
BT shelters
temporary housing
RT battered women

criteria

SG Education
NT admissions criteria
evaluation criteria
RT norms
standards

critical mass

SN *Sufficient numbers of a non-majority group necessary before change can occur in an institution or structure.*
SG Education
Social Sciences and Culture
RT diversity
employment opportunities
ethnic diversity
gender diversity
organizational behavior
racial diversity
tipping

(cont.)

critical mass (*cont.*)
- RT women in

criticism
- SG Language, Literature, Religion, and Philosophy
- Visual and Performing Arts
- NT art criticism
- dance criticism
- feminist criticism
- film criticism
- gynocriticism
- literary criticism
- music criticism
- phallic criticism
- psychoanalytic criticism
- theater criticism
- RT aesthetics
- canon
- critics
- feminist theory
- feminist writing
- fiction
- hermeneutics
- humanities
- intellectuals
- literature
- methods
- research methods
- reviewers
- structuralism
- theory
- writing

critics
- SG Communications
- Economics and Employment
- Language, Literature, Religion, and Philosophy
- Visual and Performing Arts
- BT arts, entertainment, and media occupations
- RT criticism
- writers

crocheting
- SG Visual and Performing Arts

(*cont.*)

crocheting (*cont.*)
- BT needlework

crones
- SG Language, Literature, Religion, and Philosophy
- BT images of women
- women
- RT healers
- medicine women
- older women
- wisdom
- witches

cross cultural casting
- SG Visual and Performing Arts
- BT casting

cross cultural feminism
- SG History and Social Change
- International Women
- DG Cultural and Political Movements
- BT feminism
- RT international women's movement

cross cultural research
- SG International Women
- Social Sciences and Culture
- BT research
- RT cross cultural studies

cross cultural studies
- SG Education
- History and Social Change
- International Women
- Social Sciences and Culture
- BT interdisciplinary studies
- NT comparative religion
- RT anthropology
- cross cultural research
- ethnic studies
- humanities
- interracial relations
- regional studies
- social science research
- social sciences
- women's studies

cross dressing

SN *Dressing in clothing of the opposite sex.*

SG Social Sciences and Culture

UF drag

RT female impersonators
male impersonators
transsexuality
transvestites

cross sex identity

SG Social Sciences and Culture

BT sexual identity

RT female impersonators
gender identity
male impersonators

CRT

USE **video display terminals**

cruising

SN *Slang; looking for brief, uncommitted sexual encounters.*

SG History and Social Change

RT life styles

crying

SG Natural Sciences and Health
Social Sciences and Culture

RT emotions
mourning

crystal ball gazing

SG Language, Literature, Religion, and Philosophy
Social Sciences and Culture

BT fortune telling

Cuban

DG National and Regional Descriptors

BT West Indian

Cuban American

DG Ethnic, Racial, and Religious Descriptors

cubism

DG Cultural and Political Movements

cult of the virgin

SN *Veneration of the Virgin in Western and non-Western culture and Christianity.*

SG Language, Literature, Religion, and Philosophy
Visual and Performing Arts

RT art symbols
belief systems
courtly love
goddess worship
images of girls
images of women
immaculate conception
madonna
marianismo
miracles
religious art
religious practices
Virgin Mary

cult of true womanhood

SN *A trend in late nineteenth century American culture that elevated and exaggerated the importance of women as wives, mothers, and homemakers.*

SG History and Social Change
Social Sciences and Culture

RT angel in the house
domestic code
domesticity
feminine mystique
ideal woman
images of women
mother syndrome
private sphere
separate spheres
womanhood

cults

SG Language, Literature, Religion, and Philosophy

RT counterculture

(cont.)

cults (*cont.*)
RT mediums
     religion
     religions
     religious groups
     secret societies
     sects
     subculture

cultural anthropology
SG Social Sciences and Culture
BT anthropology

cultural constraints
SG History and Social Change
     Social Sciences and Culture
RT norms
     organizations
     social attitudes

cultural feminism
SN *Theory and movement emphasizing strong alternative women's culture; often outspoken against authority and leadership.*
SG History and Social Change
     International Women
DG Cultural and Political Movements
BT feminism
RT lesbian culture
     spirituality
     womanist writing

cultural groups
SG International Women
     Social Sciences and Culture
BT groups
RT social class

cultural heritage
SG International Women
     Social Sciences and Culture
RT culture
     family history
     family recipes
     opportunities

cultural identity
SG International Women
     Social Sciences and Culture
BT identity
RT acculturation
     assimilation patterns

cultural imperialism
SG History and Social Change
     International Women
     Law, Government, and Public Policy
DG Cultural and Political Movements
RT colonialism
     developed nations
     third world

cultural influences
SG International Women
     Social Sciences and Culture
BT influences
RT body language
     dominant culture
     majority culture
     minority experience
     sex/gender systems
     socialization

cultural sadism
SN *Sexual violence against women built into existing social structures and life styles by practices and images that define sexual violence as "normal" behavior.*
SG Communications
     Social Sciences and Culture
BT sadism
RT images of women
     pornography
     sexual violence
     violence against women

cultural status
SG Social Sciences and Culture
BT status
RT class

culture

   SG International Women
         Social Sciences and Culture
  NT children's culture
      counterculture
      dominant culture
      folk culture
      gay culture
      majority culture
      material culture
      popular culture
      subculture
      women's culture
  RT acculturation
      anthropology
      archaeology
      child rearing practices
      childbirth
      cultural heritage
      dialects
      families
      family structure
      language
      matriarchy
      patriarchy
      racial and ethnic differences
      religion
      social class
      social sciences
      societies
      symbolism

culture conflict

   SG International Women
         Social Sciences and Culture
  BT conflict
  RT desegregation
      integration

culture work

  SN *A redefinition of art from a political*
      point of view that defines the artist
      as a worker.
  SG Language, Literature, Religion, and
      Philosophy
      Visual and Performing Arts
  BT work

(cont.)

culture work (*cont.*)

  RT artisans
      artists
      authors
      intellectuals
      political art

cunnilingus

   SG Natural Sciences and Health
  BT oral sex

cunning

   SG Social Sciences and Culture
  RT images of women
      manipulative behavior

cunt art

   SG Visual and Performing Arts
  BT art

cunts

   SN *Slang.*
   SG Social Sciences and Culture
  BT images of women

curators

   SG Communications
        Economics and Employment
        Visual and Performing Arts
  RT art preservation
      libraries
      museums
      preservation

curfew

   SG Law, Government, and Public Policy
  RT civil disobedience
      punishment
      sanctions

curiosity

   SG Education
  BT emotions
  RT imagination
      learning

---

curlers
- SG   Social Sciences and Culture
- RT   hair styles

curls
- SG   Social Sciences and Culture
- BT   hair styles

curricula
- DG   Types and Forms of Materials

curriculum
- SG   Education
- NT   core curriculum
       hidden curriculum
       nonsexist curriculum
- RT   pedagogy

curriculum guides
- DG   Types and Forms of Materials
- BT   guides

curriculum integration
- SN   *Integrating new scholarship on and by people of different social classes and cultures, different ethnic and racial groups, and different gender and sexual preferences into the traditional curriculum.*
- SG   Education
- UF   curriculum transformation
- BT   integration
- RT   education
       mainstreaming
       scholarship

curriculum transformation
- USE   **curriculum integration**

custodial parents
- SG   Law, Government, and Public Policy
       Social Sciences and Culture
- BT   parents
- RT   custody
       visitation rights

custody
- SG   Social Sciences and Culture
- NT   child custody
- RT   bitterness
       children's rights
       custodial parents
       custody decrees
       divorce
       family courts
       gay fathers
       grandparents
       lesbian mothers
       paternity
       single fathers
       single mothers
       stepparents
       visitation rights

custody decrees
- SG   Law, Government, and Public Policy
- BT   legal documents
- RT   custody

customs
- SG   Social Sciences and Culture
- NT   courtship customs
       dating customs
       inheritance customs
       marriage customs
       taboos
       tribal customs
- RT   chador
       manners
       rites
       societies
       traditions

Cypriot
- DG   National and Regional Descriptors
- BT   Middle Eastern

cysts
- SG   Natural Sciences and Health
- RT   benign tumors
       biopsy
       breast diseases

Czechoslovakian
DG National and Regional Descriptors
BT European

D and C
USE **dilatation and curettage**

dadaism
DG Cultural and Political Movements

dames
SG International Women
Law, Government, and Public Policy
BT images of women
titles (nobility)
women

dance
SG Visual and Performing Arts
BT performing arts
NT ballet
experimental dance
folk dance
modern dance
sacred dance
RT aerobic exercise
dances
multimedia art
performances

dance criticism
SG Visual and Performing Arts
BT criticism

dancers
SG Economics and Employment
Natural Sciences and Health
Visual and Performing Arts
BT arts, entertainment, and media
occupations
NT chorus dancers

dances
SG Social Sciences and Culture
Visual and Performing Arts
BT social activities
NT charity balls

dances (*cont.*)
NT cotillions
mixers
proms
society balls
RT chorus lines
dance
dating customs

Danish
DG National and Regional Descriptors
BT Scandinavian

Darwinism
DG Cultural and Political Movements

data
DG Types and Forms of Materials

data analysis
SG Education
Natural Sciences and Health
Science and Technology
Social Sciences and Culture
NT statistical analysis
RT forecasting
data processing
research methods

data collection
SG Education
Natural Sciences and Health
Science and Technology
Social Sciences and Culture
NT sampling
RT information processing
research design
research methods

data entry operators
SG Economics and Employment
UF keypunch operators
BT clerical occupations
female intensive occupations
operators
RT word processing

(*cont.*)

UF=Use for   BT=Broader term   NT=Narrower term   RT=Related term

data processing

    SG Economics and Employment

RT clerical occupations

       data analysis

       information processing

       information retrieval services

data processors

    SG Economics and Employment

       Science and Technology

BT administrative support occupations

       female intensive occupations

data sets

    DG Types and Forms of Materials

date rape

    SG Social Sciences and Culture

BT acquaintance rape

RT dating

       sexual intimidation

       women college students

dating

    SG Social Sciences and Culture

BT social activities

NT blind dates

RT courtship customs

       date rape

       dating customs

       personal relationships

dating customs

    SG Social Sciences and Culture

BT customs

RT blind dates

       chaperones

       dances

       dating

       dating services

       dutch treat

       engagement

       personal columns

dating services

    SG Social Sciences and Culture

BT services

(cont.)

dating services (*cont.*)

RT dating customs

daughter right

    SG History and Social Change

       Natural Sciences and Health

       Social Sciences and Culture

RT female bonding

       mother daughter relationships

       mother right

       sisterhood

daughters

    SG Social Sciences and Culture

BT women

RT families

       father daughter relationships

       mother daughter relationships

       mothers

       socialization

daughters in law

    SG Social Sciences and Culture

BT in laws

RT families

       mother daughter relationships

day care

    SG Education

       Law, Government, and Public Policy

       Social Sciences and Culture

BT care

NT employer supported day care

RT after school programs

       balancing work and family life

       caregivers

       child care

       child care licensing

       day care centers

       dependent benefits

       dependent care

       elderly care

       licensing

       mothers working outside the home

day care centers

    SG   Education
          Law, Government, and Public Policy
          Social Sciences and Culture
    BT centers
    NT after school day care centers
         child day care centers
         corporate day care centers
         drop in day care centers
         elderly day care centers
    RT balancing work and family life
         certification
         child development
         day care
         head start programs
         licensing
         mothers working outside the home
         nurseries
         nursery schools
         support systems

daydreams

    SG   Social Sciences and Culture
    BT dreams
    RT creative thinking
         fantasies
         imagination

deaconesses

    USE **deacons**

deacons

    SG   Economics and Employment
          Language, Literature, Religion, and
            Philosophy
    UF deaconesses
    BT laity
    RT religious workers

deafness

    SG   Natural Sciences and Health
    BT hearing impairments
    RT auditory perception
         hearing aids
         sign language

deans

    SG Economics and Employment
         Education
    BT education occupations

death

    SG Social Sciences and Culture
    NT accidental death
        dowry deaths
        premature death
    RT bereavement
        death and dying
        death certificates
        emotional adjustment
        euthanasia
        funeral rites
        grief
        hospices
        infant mortality
        last rites
        life insurance
        maternal mortality
        morbidity
        mortality
        mortality rates
        mortuary science
        mourning
        obituaries
        property settlements
        reincarnation
        religious beliefs
        suicide
        terminal illness
        widowers
        widows

death and dying

    SG Natural Sciences and Health
         Social Sciences and Culture
    RT death
        funeral rites
        hospices
        last rites
        mourning
        premature death
        terminal illness

---

death certificates
  SG Law, Government, and Public Policy
        Natural Sciences and Health
  BT legal documents
  RT death

death notices
  USE **obituaries**

death penalty
  SG Language, Literature, Religion, and
        Philosophy
        Law, Government, and Public Policy
  UF capital punishment
  RT criminal law
        ethics

debt
  SG Economics and Employment
        Law, Government, and Public Policy
  RT budgets
        capital
        divorce

debutantes
  SG Language, Literature, Religion, and
        Philosophy
        Social Sciences and Culture
  BT images of girls
        images of women
  RT cotillions

decision making
  SG Economics and Employment
        Social Sciences and Culture
  BT cognitive processes

declarations
  DG Types and Forms of Materials

declining neighborhoods
  SG Law, Government, and Public Policy
        Social Sciences and Culture
  BT neighborhoods
  NT slums
  RT demographic measurements

decolonization
  SG International Women
        Law, Government, and Public Policy
  RT colonialism
        liberation struggles

deconstruction
  SN *Contemporary philosophical and criti-*
        cal movement that analyzes events
        and texts as constructs of linguistic
        systems.
  SG History and Social Change
        Language, Literature, Religion, and
        Philosophy
        Visual and Performing Arts
  DG Cultural and Political Movements
  RT hermeneutics
        literary criticism
        literary theory
        phallogocentrism
        poststructuralism

decorative arts
  SN *Art form often associated with the*
        domestic and devalued as minor by
        traditional art history.
  SG Visual and Performing Arts
  BT visual arts
  RT design
        domestic arts
        fashion
        flower arranging
        furniture
        interior design
        painting
        rooms

defamation
  SG Law, Government, and Public Policy
  RT libel
        reputations

defense mechanisms
  SG Social Sciences and Culture
  BT psychological factors
  NT denial
        projection

(cont.)

defense mechanisms (*cont.*)
RT repression
    self defense
    transference

deferential behavior
SG Social Sciences and Culture
BT behavior
RT passive behavior

deficits
SG Economics and Employment
    Law, Government, and Public Policy
NT budget deficits
RT federal budget
    monetary policy

defloration
SG Natural Sciences and Health
RT age of consent
    virginity

degrees
SG Education
UF academic degrees
NT associate degrees
    graduate degrees
    honorary degrees
    professional degrees
    undergraduate degrees
RT academic awards
    credentials
    diplomas
    graduation ceremonies

deindustrialization
SG Economics and Employment
    International Women
    Science and Technology
RT industrialization
    modernization

deinstitutionalization
SG Law, Government, and Public Policy
    Natural Sciences and Health
RT disabled
    halfway houses

(*cont.*)

deinstitutionalization (*cont.*)
RT health care policy
    homeless
    insanity
    mainstreaming
    mental disorders
    mental health treatment
    mental hospitals
    schizophrenia

deism
DG Cultural and Political Movements

deity
SG Language, Literature, Religion, and
    Philosophy
RT divinity
    God the father
    goddesses
    gods
    mother goddess
    Mother/Father God
    paradise
    religion
    sacred texts
    worship

delayed parenthood
SG Natural Sciences and Health
    Social Sciences and Culture
BT parenthood
RT biological clock
    late childbearing
    life styles

delegates
SG Law, Government, and Public Policy
RT political parties
    selection procedures

delinquent behavior
SG Social Sciences and Culture
BT behavior
RT alienation
    family responsibility
    juvenile delinquency
    restitution

UF=Use for   BT=Broader term   NT=Narrower term   RT=Related term

deliverers

    SG Economics and Employment
  UF delivery boys
        deliverymen
  BT service occupations

delivery

  USE **childbirth**

delivery boys

  USE **deliverers**

delivery rooms

    SG Natural Sciences and Health
  BT rooms
  RT birthing centers
        birthing rooms
        childbirth
        home birth
        hospitals

deliverymen

  USE **deliverers**

democracy

    SG Law, Government, and Public Policy
    DG Cultural and Political Movements
  BT political systems
  RT communism
        freedom
        freedom of speech
        government
        majority rule
        pluralism
        political representation
        protest actions
        religious pluralism
        socialism

Democratic Party

    SG Law, Government, and Public Policy
  BT political parties

democratic socialism

    DG Cultural and Political Movements
  BT political systems
        socialism

demographic measurements

    SG Economics and Employment
         Social Sciences and Culture
  UF demographics
  BT measurements
  NT population characteristics
        population decline
        population distribution
        population growth
        vital statistics
  RT census
        declining neighborhoods
        enrollment
        epidemiology
        geography
        morbidity
        population planning
        research methods
        social class

demographic transition

    SG International Women
         Social Sciences and Culture
  RT migration

demographics

  USE **demographic measurements**

demography

    SG Social Sciences and Culture
  BT social sciences
  RT population distribution

demonstrations

    SG History and Social Change
  BT protest actions
  RT antiwar movement
        boycotts
        marches
        pickets
        sit ins
        social movements

den mothers

    SG Social Sciences and Culture
  BT images of women
        mothers

enial
SG Social Sciences and Culture
BT defense mechanisms

ental hygienists
SG Economics and Employment
Natural Sciences and Health
BT female intensive occupations
health care occupations

entistry
SG Economics and Employment
Natural Sciences and Health
BT medical sciences
RT dentists

entists
SG Economics and Employment
Natural Sciences and Health
BT health care occupations
professional occupations
RT dentistry

eodorants
SG Natural Sciences and Health
RT beauty standards
body image
personal hygiene
perspiration

epartments
SG Education
Social Sciences and Culture
BT organizations

pendency
USE **dependent behavior**

pendent behavior
SG Social Sciences and Culture
UF dependency
BT behavior
RT addiction
assertiveness training
codependency
learned helplessness
subordination
(cont.)

dependent behavior *(cont.)*
RT withdrawal

dependent benefits
SG Economics and Employment
BT benefits
RT child care
day care
insurance

dependent care
SG Economics and Employment
Law, Government, and Public Policy
Natural Sciences and Health
Social Sciences and Culture
BT care
NT child care
elderly care
RT careers
caregivers
child care licensing
community care
corporate policy
day care
dependent care assistance programs
Dependent Care Tax Credit
families
insurance
living alone
parenting
primary caregivers
responsibility
sick children

dependent care assistance programs
SG Economics and Employment
Social Sciences and Culture
BT assistance programs
RT corporate policy
dependent care

Dependent Care Tax Credit
DG Laws and Regulations
RT dependent care

dependent children
SG Social Sciences and Culture
(cont.)

dependent children (*cont.*)
BT children
RT child care
      dependents

dependents
SG Social Sciences and Culture
RT dependent children
      elderly care
      spouses

depilation
USE **hair removal**

depilatories
SG Natural Sciences and Health
RT hair removal

Depo Provera
SN *Depo-medroxy progesterone acetate
      (DMPA); a long-acting synthetic
      hormone used as an injectable con-
      traceptive.*
SG Natural Sciences and Health
BT injectable contraceptives
RT drug dumping

depreciation
SG Economics and Employment
RT budgets
      value

depression
SG Natural Sciences and Health
BT mental disorders
NT involuntary depression
      postpartum depression
RT alienation
      antidepressant drugs
      apathy
      dysphoria
      empty nest
      learned helplessness
      suicide

deprivation
SG Social Sciences and Culture
(*cont.*)

deprivation (*cont.*)
RT food
      sleep

depth perception
SG Natural Sciences and Health
BT perception

DES
USE **diethylstilbestrol**

descriptive linguistics
SG Language, Literature, Religion, and
      Philosophy
BT linguistics

descriptive writing
SG Language, Literature, Religion, and
      Philosophy
BT writing
RT nonfiction

desegregation
SG Education
      Law, Government, and Public Policy
NT school desegregation
RT affirmative action
      culture conflict
      discriminatory practices
      integration
      segregation

desegregation methods
SG Education
      Law, Government, and Public Policy
BT methods
NT busing
RT affirmative action
      discriminatory practices
      equal access
      integration

desertion
SG Economics and Employment
      Social Sciences and Culture
RT child support
      runaway husbands
(*cont.*)

desertion (*cont.*)
- RT runaway wives

desex
- SN *To remove sexist connotations.*
- SG Communications
  - Education
  - History and Social Change
- RT children's literature
  - linguistic sexism
  - nonsexist language
  - sexist language
  - textbooks

design
- SG Visual and Performing Arts
- NT costume design
  - experimental design
  - fashion design
  - graphic design
  - house design
  - interior design
  - textile design
- RT commercial art
  - decorative arts
  - fashion
  - furniture
  - visual arts

designers
- SG Communications
  - Economics and Employment
  - Visual and Performing Arts
- BT arts, entertainment, and media occupations
- RT textile industry

desirable neighborhoods
- SG Law, Government, and Public Policy
  - Social Sciences and Culture
- BT neighborhoods

desire
- SG Natural Sciences and Health
- BT emotions
- NT sexual desire
- RT love

(*cont.*)

desire (*cont.*)
- RT passion
  - sexuality

deskilling
- SN *Breaking down a job into its smallest parts and thereby devaluing the work.*
- SG Economics and Employment
- RT devaluation
  - low pay
  - piecework

despair
- SG Social Sciences and Culture
- BT emotions

despotism
- DG Cultural and Political Movements
- NT enlightened despotism

destructive behavior
- SG Social Sciences and Culture
- BT behavior
- NT self destructive behavior

detectives
- SG Economics and Employment
  - Law, Government, and Public Policy
- BT protective service occupations

determinism
- DG Cultural and Political Movements

devaluation
- SG Economics and Employment
- RT deskilling
  - economic value of women's work
  - homemakers
  - household labor

developed countries
- USE **developed nations**

developed nations
- SG International Women
- UF developed countries

(*cont.*)

UF=Use for   BT=Broader term   NT=Narrower term   RT=Related term

developed nations (*cont.*)

RT   cultural imperialism
     technology transfer

developing countries
USE **developing nations**

developing nations

SG   International Women
UF   developing countries
     underdeveloped nations
RT   colonialism
     development
     drug dumping
     foreign aid policy
     foreign investment policy
     global assembly lines
     impact on women
     income generation
     international division of labor
     modernization
     nationalism
     oil industry
     technology transfer
     third world
     water

development

SN   *Use of a more specific term is recom-
     mended.*
SG   Economics and Employment
     International Women
     Natural Sciences and Health
NT   community development
     economic development
     employee development
     individual development
     job development
     language development
     organizational development
     professional development
     rural development
     technology development
     urban development
RT   developing nations
     development studies
     economic growth

(*cont.*)

development (*cont.*)

RT   women in development

development specialists

SG   Economics and Employment
     International Women
BT   agricultural, fishing, and forestry
     occupations
     financial occupations
RT   development studies

development studies

SG   Education
     International Women
     Social Sciences and Culture
BT   interdisciplinary studies
RT   development
     development specialists
     impact on children
     impact on women
     women in development

developmental disabilities

SG   Natural Sciences and Health
BT   disabilities
RT   ableism
     individual development

developmental psychology

SG   Social Sciences and Culture
BT   psychology
RT   child psychology

deviance
USE **deviant behavior**

deviant behavior

SG   Social Sciences and Culture
UF   deviance
BT   behavior
RT   attitudes
     sociopathology
     stereotypes

devil

SG   Language, Literature, Religion, and
     Philosophy

(*cont.*)

devil (*cont.*)

RT cosmology
creation myths
evil
Garden of Eden
images of women
religious symbols
sin
temptation
witchcraft

diabetes

SG Natural Sciences and Health
UF sugar diabetes
BT diseases
RT pregnancy

diagnoses

SG Natural Sciences and Health
Social Sciences and Culture
RT assessment
attitudes
discrimination
medical procedures
mental disorders
mental health treatment
standards
stereotyping

diagrams

DG Types and Forms of Materials

dialects

SG Language, Literature, Religion, and
Philosophy
NT social dialects
RT culture
discrimination
language
speech
talk

diaper services

SG Social Sciences and Culture
BT domestic services
RT child care

diaphragms

SG Natural Sciences and Health
BT contraception
RT cervical caps
spermicides

diaries

SG Language, Literature, Religion, and
Philosophy
DG Types and Forms of Materials
BT nonfiction
NT visual diaries
RT autobiography
biography
histories
journals
letters
memoirs
personal narratives

dichotomy

SG Language, Literature, Religion, and
Philosophy
NT false dichotomies
RT ad feminam
antithesis
dualism

dictionaries

DG Types and Forms of Materials
BT reference books

diet pills

SG Natural Sciences and Health
BT appetite depressants
RT addiction
diets
drugs
eating disorders
substance abuse

diet therapy

SG Natural Sciences and Health
BT therapy
RT obesity

dietetics
- SG Natural Sciences and Health
- RT dieticians
- nutrition

diethylstilbestrol
- SN *Synthetic form of estrogen prescribed as preventive for miscarriage and for other hormonal conditions; linked to cancer in mothers and their children.*
- SG Natural Sciences and Health
- UF DES
- morning after pill
- RT cervical cancer
- drugs
- estrogens
- miscarriage

dieticians
- SG Economics and Employment
- Natural Sciences and Health
- BT female intensive occupations
- health care occupations
- professional occupations
- RT dietetics
- food preparation
- food preparation occupations

dieting
- SG Natural Sciences and Health
- UF slimming
- RT body image
- diets
- discipline
- eating disorders
- fads
- thinness
- trimness

diets
- SG Natural Sciences and Health
- RT appetite depressants
- body image
- diet pills
- dieting
- diuretics
- fasting

(cont.)

diets (cont.)
- RT nutrition
- physical fitness
- weight perception

differences
- SG Education
- Social Sciences and Culture
- NT class differences
- gender differences
- learning differences
- racial and ethnic differences
- sex differences
- social differences
- RT differently abled

differently abled
- SG Natural Sciences and Health
- RT ableism
- differences
- disabled

diffusion
- SG Social Sciences and Culture
- RT information dissemination
- innovation

digests
- DG Types and Forms of Materials

dilatation and curettage
- SG Natural Sciences and Health
- UF D and C
- BT surgical procedures
- RT abortion

dinners
- SG History and Social Change
- Social Sciences and Culture
- BT social activities

diplomacy
- SG International Women
- Law, Government, and Public Policy
- UF statesmanship
- RT diplomats
- disarmament

(cont.)

SN=Scope note   SG=Subject group   DG=Delimiters group   USE=Us

diplomacy *(cont.)*
RT social skills

diplomas
SG Education
RT degrees

diplomats
SG Economics and Employment
International Women
Law, Government, and Public Policy
UF statesmen
BT legal and political occupations
RT diplomacy
foreign service

directions
DG Types and Forms of Materials

directories
DG Types and Forms of Materials

directors
SG Economics and Employment
BT volunteer occupations

directors (film)
USE **film directors**

disabilities
SG Natural Sciences and Health
NT developmental disabilities
hearing impairments
learning disabilities
mental retardation
pregnancy disability
visual impairments
RT barrier free access
birth defects
blindness
braille
disabled
mentally handicapped
rights of the disabled
sign language

disability discrimination
USE **discrimination against the disabled**

disability insurance
SG Economics and Employment
Natural Sciences and Health
BT insurance
RT maternity leave
Retirement and Disability System
Authorization
sick leave

disabled
SG Natural Sciences and Health
UF handicapped
RT ableism
barrier free access
deinstitutionalization
differently abled
disabilities
disadvantaged
equal access
hearing impairments
mainstreaming
mentally handicapped
visual impairments

disadvantaged
SG Economics and Employment
NT doubly disadvantaged
economically disadvantaged
educationally disadvantaged
socially disadvantaged
RT disabled
social class
socioeconomic conditions

disadvantaged groups
SG Economics and Employment
History and Social Change
Social Sciences and Culture
BT groups
RT discrimination
doubly disadvantaged
oppression

disarmament
SG Law, Government, and Public Policy
NT nuclear disarmament
RT arms control
diplomacy
peace movements
warfare

discipline
SG Language, Literature, Religion, and
Philosophy
Social Sciences and Culture
RT abstention
abstinence
asceticism
dieting
punishment
self control
self denial

disclosure laws
SG Law, Government, and Public Policy
BT laws

discographies
DG Types and Forms of Materials

discourse
SG Language, Literature, Religion, and
Philosophy
RT conversation
figurative language
language skills
orators
oratory
rhetoric
sociolinguistics
speech
storytelling
talk

discrimination
SG Social Sciences and Culture
UF social discrimination
NT age discrimination
class discrimination
discrimination against the disabled
(cont.)

discrimination *(cont.)*
NT double discrimination
housing discrimination
institutional discrimination
job discrimination
microinequities
pregnancy discrimination
racial discrimination
religious discrimination
reverse discrimination
sex discrimination
structural discrimination
wage discrimination
RT affirmative action
antisemitism
apartheid
attitude change
attitudes
back pay
bias
blaming the victim
business
civil rights commissions
civil rights legislation
class action suits
clubs
conceptual errors
consciousness raising
court cases
diagnoses
dialects
disadvantaged groups
discrimination laws
discriminatory practices
diversity
double bind
double standard
doubly disadvantaged
economic value of women's work
Equal Employment Opportunity
Commission
ethnic intimidation
executive recruitment
false consciousness
federally sponsored research
gatekeeping
gay rights
(cont.)

SN=Scope note   SG=Subject group   DG=Delimiters group   USE=Use

discrimination (*cont.*)

RT   gender bias
      grievance procedures
      heterosexism
      heterosexual privilege
      homophobia
      illegitimacy
      industries
      inequality
      insurance
      majority culture
      male norms
      nepotism
      oppression
      pariahs
      patriarchal language
      patriarchy
      pension benefits
      political oppression
      poll tax
      prejudice
      private clubs
      purdah
      race bias
      racial and ethnic differences
      racial equality
      segregation
      separate spheres
      sexual equality
      silence
      skin color
      social bias
      stereotyping
      stratification
      tenure
      voter registration
      women in

discrimination against the disabled

SG   Education
      History and Social Change
      Law, Government, and Public Policy
      Natural Sciences and Health
UF   disability discrimination
BT   discrimination
RT   ableism

discrimination laws

SN   *See also Delimiters Display: Laws and Regulations.*
SG   Law, Government, and Public Policy
UF   antidiscrimination laws
BT   laws
RT   affirmative action suits
      discrimination
      enforcement
      entitlement programs

discriminatory language

SG   Language, Literature, Religion, and Philosophy
BT   language
NT   sexist language
RT   false generics
      God the father
      perceptual bias
      racial stereotypes
      stereotypes

discriminatory legislation

SG   Law, Government, and Public Policy
BT   legislation

discriminatory practices

SG   Law, Government, and Public Policy
NT   blockbusting
      glass ceiling
      redlining
      segregation
      steering
RT   bigotry
      desegregation
      desegregation methods
      discrimination
      wage gap

discussion groups

SG   History and Social Change
      Social Sciences and Culture
BT   educational activities
      groups
RT   raps

---

disease prevention
- SG   Natural Sciences and Health
- BT   prevention
- RT   breast examination
  - condoms
  - mammography
  - Pap smear
  - sanitation
  - wellness

diseases
- SG   Natural Sciences and Health
- NT   alcoholism
  - anemia
  - breast diseases
  - cancer
  - cardiovascular diseases
  - communicable diseases
  - diabetes
  - drug addiction
  - fetal alcohol syndrome
  - fibrocystic disease
  - hereditary diseases
  - hypertension
  - iatrogenic disease
  - measles
  - occupational diseases
  - osteoporosis
  - puerperal fever
  - rubella
  - sickle cell anemia
  - sudden infant death syndrome
  - toxic shock syndrome
- RT   antisepsis
  - at risk populations
  - blood tests
  - disorders
  - drugs
  - illness
  - morbidity
  - prevention
  - psychosomatic disorders
  - stress (physical)
  - therapy
  - vaginal infections

dishwashers
- SG   Economics and Employment
- BT   service occupations

disinformation
- SG   Communications
  - Law, Government, and Public Policy
- RT   indoctrination
  - information dissemination
  - propaganda
  - public information
  - right to know legislation

disk jockeys
- SG   Communications
  - Economics and Employment
  - Visual and Performing Arts
- BT   arts, entertainment, and media
  - occupations

diskettes
- USE **disks**

disks
- DG   Types and Forms of Materials
- UF   diskettes
- NT   compact disks
  - laser disks
  - videodisks

disorders
- SG   Natural Sciences and Health
- NT   chromosome disorders
  - eating disorders
  - gynecologic disorders
  - mental disorders
  - obsessive compulsive disorders
  - personality disorders
  - premenstrual tension
  - psychosomatic disorders
- RT   complexes
  - diseases

displaced homemakers
- SG   Social Sciences and Culture
- BT   homemakers
- RT   age discrimination

(cont.)

displaced homemakers (*cont.*)
RT economic equity
      employment
      job layoffs
      labor force
      reentry women
      women in transition

dissent
SG History and Social Change
RT protest actions
      social movements

dissertations
DG Types and Forms of Materials

distributive justice
SG Law, Government, and Public Policy
BT justice

diuretics
SG Natural Sciences and Health
BT drugs
RT diets
      hypertension
      menstrual cycle

divers
SG Economics and Employment
      Science and Technology
BT agricultural, fishing, and forestry
      occupations

diversity
SG History and Social Change
      Social Sciences and Culture
NT ethnic diversity
      gender diversity
      racial diversity
RT biculturalism
      critical mass
      discrimination
      dominant culture
      equality
      global feminism
      mixed economy
      pluralism

(*cont.*)

diversity (*cont.*)
RT racial and ethnic differences
      stereotyping

divestiture
SG Economics and Employment
      History and Social Change
RT antiapartheid movement
      corporate responsibility

divine kingship
SG Language, Literature, Religion, and
      Philosophy
      Law, Government, and Public Policy
RT God the father
      male norms

divining
SG Language, Literature, Religion, and
      Philosophy
      Science and Technology
      Social Sciences and Culture
BT spiritual communication

divinity
SG Language, Literature, Religion, and
      Philosophy
RT deity
      God the father
      goddesses
      gods
      mother goddess
      Mother/Father God
      paradise
      religion
      theology
      worship

division of labor
SG Economics and Employment
NT household division of labor
      international division of labor
      sexual division of labor
RT domestic arrangements
      domestic code
      economic value of women's work
      parenting

(*cont.*)

division of labor (*cont.*)

RT   shared parenting

divorce

SG   Social Sciences and Culture
NT   no fault divorce
RT   alienation of affection
balancing work and family life
children living in poverty
cohabitation
credit
custody
debt
divorce laws
domestic arrangements
emotional adjustment
families
family conflict
family courts
female headed households
financial arrangements
first husbands
first wives
former spouses
husbands
in laws
marital status
marriage
marriage customs
religious law
remarriage
separation
spinsters
stepfathers
stepmothers
wives
women in transition
women living in poverty

divorce decrees

SG   Law, Government, and Public Policy
BT   legal documents

divorce laws

SG   Law, Government, and Public Policy
BT   laws
RT   alimony

(*cont.*)

divorce laws (*cont.*)

RT   annulment
child custody
child support
children living in poverty
community property laws
divorce
domicile rights
economic equity
legal cruelty
marital property reform
marriage and family law
no fault divorce
palimony
prenuptial agreements
property settlements
restraining orders
women living in poverty

divorce rates

SG   Economics and Employment
       Social Sciences and Culture
BT   vital statistics
RT   marriage rates

docents

SG   Economics and Employment
       Visual and Performing Arts
BT   volunteers
RT   museums

doctor patient relationships

USE   **patient doctor relationships**

doctoral degrees

SG   Education
BT   graduate degrees

doctors

USE   **physicians**

documentaries

SG   Communications
       Visual and Performing Arts
BT   film
RT   interviews
television

(*cont.*)

documentaries *(cont.)*
RT   videos

documentation
DG   Types and Forms of Materials

documents
SG   History and Social Change
      Language, Literature, Religion, and
      Philosophy
DG   Types and Forms of Materials
NT   government documents
      legal documents
RT   records

dogma
SG   Language, Literature, Religion, and
      Philosophy
RT   freedom of worship
      immaculate conception
      incarnation
      missionaries
      religion
      religious beliefs
      sacred ideology
      theology

dogmatism
SG   Language, Literature, Religion, and
      Philosophy
      Social Sciences and Culture
RT   fundamentalism
      heresies
      myths
      personality traits
      religious repression
      theology

doll making
SG   Visual and Performing Arts
BT   craft arts

dolls
SG   Social Sciences and Culture
RT   sex stereotypes
      tomboys
      toys

domestic arrangements
SG   Social Sciences and Culture
RT   division of labor
      divorce
      families

domestic arts
SG   Social Sciences and Culture
      Visual and Performing Arts
RT   decorative arts
      home economics
      homemaking

domestic code
SN   *Statement of household ethics and*
      management, found in biblical and
      classical writings, wherein wives are
      expected to be subject to their hus-
      bands, slaves to their masters, and
      children to their parents.
SG   History and Social Change
      Language, Literature, Religion, and
      Philosophy
      Social Sciences and Culture
RT   angel in the house
      chador
      cult of true womanhood
      division of labor
      domestic values
      domesticity
      feminine mystique
      marriage customs
      norms
      private sphere
      veiling of women

domestic food production
SG   Economics and Employment
      International Women
RT   agriculture
      cooking
      economic value of women's work
      subsistence agriculture

domestic labor
USE   **household labor**

---

domestic rape

SG   Social Sciences and Culture
UF   marital rape
     spouse rape
     wife rape
BT   rape
RT   acquaintance rape
     marital violence

domestic relations

SG   Social Sciences and Culture
BT   relationships
RT   arguments
     living arrangements
     marriage and family law

domestic rites

SG   Language, Literature, Religion, and
     Philosophy
BT   rites
RT   earth mother
     worship

domestic roles

SG   Social Sciences and Culture
BT   roles
RT   balancing work and family life
     families

domestic services

SG   Social Sciences and Culture
BT   services
NT   diaper services
     homemaker service
RT   economic value of women's work
     household labor
     household workers

domestic values

SG   Language, Literature, Religion, and
     Philosophy
     Social Sciences and Culture
BT   values
RT   domestic code

domestic violence

SG   Social Sciences and Culture

(cont.)

domestic violence *(cont.)*

UF   family violence
     household violence
BT   violence
NT   marital violence
RT   battered women
     crimes against women
     crisis intervention
     family conflict
     Family Violence Prevention and Services
        Act
     incest
     restraining orders
     women's shelters

domesticity

SG   Social Sciences and Culture
RT   angel in the house
     cult of true womanhood
     domestic code
     home life
     private sphere

domestics

USE **household workers**

domicile rights

SG   Law, Government, and Public Policy
BT   rights
RT   divorce laws
     marriage and family law

dominance

SG   Social Sciences and Culture
RT   aggressive behavior
     control
     experts
     intimidation
     mergers
     sexual behavior
     social behavior

dominant culture

SG   Social Sciences and Culture
BT   culture
RT   cultural influences
     diversity

(cont.)

dominant culture (*cont.*)

RT majority culture

Dominican

DG National and Regional Descriptors

BT West Indian

donors

SG Natural Sciences and Health
Social Sciences and Culture

RT artificial insemination
blood
charities
genetic screening
in kind contributions
in vitro fertilization
philanthropists
sperm banks
surrogate fathers
surrogate mothers

dormitories

SG Education

BT student housing

RT housemothers

double bind

SN *"Catch-22" faced by people of color,
women, and other oppressed groups
whose selectivity sets them apart and
makes acceptance in established
structures difficult.*

SG Education
Social Sciences and Culture

RT discrimination
doubly disadvantaged

double discrimination

SG History and Social Change
Social Sciences and Culture

BT discrimination

RT doubly disadvantaged
minority experience
racism
sexism

double standard

SN *A code of morals that applies different
and more restrictive standards to
women's behavior than to men's
behavior.*

SG Social Sciences and Culture

RT discrimination
male standards
morality
sex role behavior
sexual relationships

doubly disadvantaged

SG History and Social Change
Social Sciences and Culture

BT disadvantaged

RT ableism
ageism
disadvantaged groups
discrimination
double bind
double discrimination
homophobia
race bias
racism
sexism
stereotyping

dowry

SG History and Social Change
International Women

UF bridewealth

RT bride burning
bride price
child marriage
dowry deaths
inheritance customs
marriage contracts
prenuptial agreements

dowry deaths

SG International Women
Social Sciences and Culture

BT death

RT bride burning
crimes against women
dowry

(*cont.*)

UF=Use for   BT=Broader term   NT=Narrower term   RT=Related term

dowry deaths (*cont.*)
RT   marriage

draft
USE   **military draft**

draft resistance
SG   History and Social Change
BT   resistance
RT   conscientious objection
     military draft

drafters
SG   Economics and Employment
     Visual and Performing Arts
UF   draftsmen
BT   arts, entertainment, and media
     occupations

drafts
DG   Types and Forms of Materials

draftsmen
USE   **drafters**

drag
USE   **cross dressing**

drama
SG   Language, Literature, Religion, and
     Philosophy
     Visual and Performing Arts
BT   literature
     theater
NT   comedy
     tragedy
RT   allegory
     burlesque
     farce
     heroes
     irony
     parody
     plays
     playwrights
     rites
     scripts

dramatists
SG   Economics and Employment
     Language, Literature, Religion, and
     Philosophy
     Visual and Performing Arts
BT   arts, entertainment, and media
     occupations

drawing
SG   Visual and Performing Arts
BT   visual arts

drawings
DG   Types and Forms of Materials

dreams
SG   Language, Literature, Religion, and
     Philosophy
     Natural Sciences and Health
     Social Sciences and Culture
     Visual and Performing Arts
NT   daydreams
RT   aspirations
     creative thinking
     fantasies
     psychotherapy
     sleep
     subconscious
     visions

dress
USE   **clothing**

dress codes
SG   Economics and Employment
     Education
RT   clothing
     dress reform
     dressing for success
     stereotypes

dress reform
SG   History and Social Change
BT   reforms
RT   bloomers
     brassieres
     clothing

(*cont.*)

dress reform (*cont.*)

RT corsets
dress codes
pants

dressing for success

SG Economics and Employment
Social Sciences and Culture
RT career feminism
clothing
dress codes

dressmakers

SG Economics and Employment
Visual and Performing Arts
BT clothing workers
RT sewers
tailors

dressmaking

SG Economics and Employment
RT clothing workers

drinking

SG Natural Sciences and Health
RT alcohol abuse
alcoholism

drinking prohibition

SG Law, Government, and Public Policy
Social Sciences and Culture
BT social prohibitions
RT alcoholism
temperance movement

drivers

SG Economics and Employment
Science and Technology
BT transportation occupations
NT bus drivers
taxi drivers
truck drivers

drop in day care centers

SG Social Sciences and Culture
BT day care centers

dropouts

SG Education
RT alternative programs
alternative schools

drug abuse

SG Natural Sciences and Health
BT substance abuse
RT acquired immune deficiency syndrome
cocaine
drug addiction
drug rehabilitation
drug tests
drug use
drugs
heroin
marijuana
prenatal influences
prescription drugs

drug addiction

SG Natural Sciences and Health
UF chemical dependency
BT addiction
diseases
RT antidepressant drugs
codependency
drug abuse
drug side effects
drugs
narcotic drugs
prescription drugs
substance abuse

drug dumping

SN *Multinational pharmaceutical corporate
practice of marketing in developing
countries drugs and devices declared
unsafe in developed countries.*
SG International Women
Natural Sciences and Health
BT multinational corporation policy
RT clinical trials
corporate liability
depo provera
developing nations
drugs

(*cont.*)

---

drug dumping (*cont.*)
RT ethics

drug industry
USE **pharmaceutical industry**

drug overdoses
SG Natural Sciences and Health
RT narcotic drugs

drug rehabilitation
SG Education
    Natural Sciences and Health
BT rehabilitation
RT alcohol abuse
    drug abuse
    substance abuse

drug side effects
SG Natural Sciences and Health
RT clinical trials
    drug addiction
    drugs

drug tests
SG Natural Sciences and Health
BT tests
RT blood tests
    drug abuse
    professional sports

drug therapy
SG Natural Sciences and Health
BT therapy
RT electroconvulsive therapy
    mental health treatment
    psychopharmacology

drug use
SG Natural Sciences and Health
RT addiction
    drug abuse

drugs
SG Natural Sciences and Health
NT diuretics
    fertility drugs
(*cont.*)

drugs (*cont.*)
NT narcotic drugs
    nonprescription drugs
    oral contraceptives
    prescription drugs
    psychotropic drugs
RT abortifacient agents
    amenorrhea
    anesthesia
    birth defects
    diet pills
    diethylstilbestrol
    diseases
    drug abuse
    drug addiction
    drug dumping
    drug side effects
    induced labor
    informed consent
    placebos
    prenatal influences
    substance abuse
    suicide
    therapy

dual career couples
SG Economics and Employment
    Social Sciences and Culture
UF two career couples
BT couples
RT corporate relocation policy
    household division of labor
    marriage tax
    married couples
    relocation
    working parents

dual career families
SN *Use where emphasis is on career;*
    where emphasis is on income, use
    two income families .
SG Economics and Employment
    Social Sciences and Culture
UF two career families
BT families
RT commuter marriage
    corporate relocation policy
(*cont.*)

SN=Scope note   SG=Subject group   DG=Delimiters group   USE=Use

dual career families (*cont.*)
- RT household division of labor
  marriage tax
  married couples
  relocation
  two income families

dual careers
- SG Economics and Employment
  Social Sciences and Culture
- BT careers
- RT corporate relocation policy

dual economy
- SN *Coexistence within same economy of rich and poor sectors marked by increasing divergence of resources and skills.*
- SG Economics and Employment
  International Women
- RT black markets
  classism
  equal access
  global economy
  informal sector
  inherited wealth
  poverty
  street vendors
  wealth

dual roles
- SG Social Sciences and Culture
- BT multiple roles
- RT balancing work and family life
  couples

dual worker families
- USE **two income families**

dualism
- SG Language, Literature, Religion, and Philosophy
- DG Cultural and Political Movements
- RT dichotomy
  evil
  mind/body split
  objectification

(*cont.*)

dualism (*cont.*)
- RT phallogocentrism
  philosophy
  separate spheres
  theology

duchesses
- SG International Women
  Law, Government, and Public Policy
- BT images of women
  titles (nobility)
  women

due process
- SG Law, Government, and Public Policy
- BT civil liberties
- RT fairness
  freedom of speech
  judicial process
  justice

Dutch
- DG National and Regional Descriptors
- BT European

dutch treat
- SN *Custom of each individual paying her or his own way on a date or other social occasion.*
- SG Economics and Employment
  Social Sciences and Culture
- RT dating customs

dybbuks
- SG Language, Literature, Religion, and Philosophy
- BT evil spirits

dykes
- USE **lesbians**

dysmenorrhea
- SG Natural Sciences and Health
- BT menstrual disorders
- RT menstruation

---

dysphoria

SG Natural Sciences and Health
RT anxiety
    depression

early childbearing

SG Natural Sciences and Health
BT childbearing
RT child marriage
    maternal age
    maternal and infant welfare
    teenage mothers
    teenage pregnancy

early childhood education

SG Education
DG Education Levels
BT education
NT preschool education
    primary education

early experience

SG Social Sciences and Culture
BT experience
RT bonding

early retirement

SG Economics and Employment
BT retirement
RT affirmative action hiring
    retirement age
    retirement benefits

earned income

SG Economics and Employment
BT income

earnings

SG Economics and Employment
RT profits

earnings gap

USE **wage gap**

earnings sharing

SG Economics and Employment
    Law, Government, and Public Policy
                                    (*cont.*)

earnings sharing (*cont.*)

RT economic equity
    Social Security

earth mother

SG Language, Literature, Religion, and
    Philosophy
BT images of women
    mothers
RT creation myths
    domestic rites
    goddesses
    mother goddess
    mother nature
    myths
    nature

earth sciences

SG Science and Technology
BT physical sciences
NT geology
    oceanography
RT science

East German

DG National and Regional Descriptors
BT European

Eastern

DG National and Regional Descriptors
BT United States

eating disorders

SG Natural Sciences and Health
UF appetite disorders
BT disorders
NT anorexia nervosa
    bulimia
RT appetite depressants
    body image
    diet pills
    dieting
    food
    individual counseling
    mental disorders
    nutrition
    obesity
                                    (*cont.*)

eating disorders (*cont.*)
RT starvation
    thinness
    weight perception

eclecticism
DG Cultural and Political Movements

ecofeminism
SN *Feminist theory emphasizing inter-*
    dependence of all living things, the
    relationship of social oppression and
    ecological domination.
SG History and Social Change
BT feminism
RT ecology
    female spirituality
    mother earth
    spirituality

ecological factors
SG Science and Technology
BT influences
RT environment
    nature

ecology
SG Science and Technology
BT biological sciences
RT built environment
    ecofeminism
    environmental health
    environmental movement
    environmental sciences
    nature

econometrics
SG Economics and Employment
RT economic indicators
    economics
    forecasting
    mathematical models
    statistics
    unemployment rates

economic anthropology
SG Economics and Employment
    Social Sciences and Culture
BT anthropology
RT economics

economic boycotts
SG Economics and Employment
BT boycotts
RT economic sanctions
    social movements

economic class
SG Economics and Employment
    Social Sciences and Culture
BT class
RT socioeconomic class

economic counseling
SG Economics and Employment
BT counseling

economic depression
SG Economics and Employment
RT inflation

economic development
SG Economics and Employment
    International Women
BT development
RT economic development theory
    economic policy
    foreign aid
    fourth world
    small business
    third world
    underdevelopment

economic development models
SG Economics and Employment
    International Women
NT capitalist economic development models
    communist economic development models
    Marxist economic development models
    socialist economic development models
RT colonialism
    economic development theory

(cont.)

UF=Use for   BT=Broader term   NT=Narrower term   RT=Related term   139

economic development models *(cont.)*
RT   impact on women
      political economic systems
      third world

economic development theory
SG Economics and Employment
      International Women
BT economic theory
RT economic development
      economic development models

economic equity
SG Economics and Employment
      Law, Government, and Public Policy
BT equity
RT children living in poverty
      displaced homemakers
      divorce laws
      earnings sharing
      Economic Equity Act of 1987
      pay equity
      wealth distribution
      women living in poverty

Economic Equity Act of 1987
DG Laws and Regulations
RT economic equity

economic factors
SG Economics and Employment
BT influences

economic geography
SG Economics and Employment
      Social Sciences and Culture
BT geography
RT economics

economic growth
SG Economics and Employment
RT development
      global economy

economic history
SG Economics and Employment
      History and Social Change

(cont.)

economic history *(cont.)*
BT history
RT economics

economic indicators
SG Economics and Employment
BT socioeconomic indicators
RT econometrics

economic policy
SG Economics and Employment
BT policy
RT economic development

economic power
SG Economics and Employment
BT power
RT consumer power
      influence
      military trade
      spending

Economic Recovery Tax Act of 1981
DG Laws and Regulations
RT tax reform

economic refugees
SG Economics and Employment
BT refugees

economic sanctions
SG International Women
      Law, Government, and Public Policy
BT sanctions
RT economic boycotts
      social movements

economic status
SG Economics and Employment
      Law, Government, and Public Policy
      Social Sciences and Culture
BT status
RT prestige

economic structure
SG Economics and Employment
      Social Sciences and Culture

(cont.)

economic structure (*cont.*)

RT economic value of women's work
  social structure
  socioeconomic status

economic theory

SG Economics and Employment
  Law, Government, and Public Policy
BT theory
NT economic development theory
RT feminist theory

economic trends

SG Economics and Employment
BT trends
RT equilibrium

economic value of women's work

SG Economics and Employment
RT careers
  caregivers
  child care
  comparable worth
  devaluation
  discrimination
  division of labor
  domestic food production
  domestic services
  economic structure
  equal pay
  equal pay for equal work
  female intensive occupations
  home economics
  homemakers
  household employment
  household labor
  housework
  human capital
  human resources
  impact on women
  labor theory of value
  Marxist feminism
  momism
  pin money
  pink collar workers
  professional sports
  prostitution

(*cont.*)

economic value of women's work (*cont.*)

RT public sphere
  sexual division of labor
  unpaid employment
  unpaid household labor
  value
  valuing children
  wage gap
  wages for housework
  wives
  women in development

economically disadvantaged

SG Economics and Employment
BT disadvantaged
RT at risk populations
  children living in poverty
  homeless
  poverty
  welfare
  women living in poverty

economics

SG Economics and Employment
  Law, Government, and Public Policy
  Social Sciences and Culture
BT social sciences
NT agricultural economics
  classical economics
  health economics
  macroeconomics
  microeconomics
  neoclassical economics
  welfare economics
RT econometrics
  economic anthropology
  economic geography
  economic history
  public sphere

economies of scale

SG Economics and Employment
RT cost benefit analysis

economists

SG Economics and Employment
BT financial occupations

(*cont.*)

economists *(cont.)*
  BT   social scientists

economy
  SG   Economics and Employment
  NT   consumer economy
       global economy
       mixed economy
       underground economy
  RT   federal budget
       international trade policy
       military budget
       productivity

l'ecriture feminine
  SN   *Term used by French feminists and*
       others to refer to women's writing
       that breaks new ground for women's
       imagination and use of language.
  SG   Language, Literature, Religion, and
       Philosophy
  RT   correspondence
       female authored texts
       feminist criticism
       feminist writing

ectogenesis
  USE **in vitro fertilization**

ectopic pregnancy
  SG   Natural Sciences and Health
  BT   pregnancy
  RT   fallopian tubes
       spontaneous abortion

Ecuadoran
  DG   National and Regional Descriptors
  BT   Latin American

ecumenism
  SG   Language, Literature, Religion, and
       Philosophy
  DG   Cultural and Political Movements
  RT   church work
       comparative religion
       freedom of worship
       religious pluralism

editions
  DG   Types and Forms of Materials

editorials
  SG   Communications
  DG   Types and Forms of Materials
  RT   freedom of the press
       journalism
       newspapers

editors
  SG   Communications
       Economics and Employment
       Language, Literature, Religion, and
       Philosophy
  BT   arts, entertainment, and media
       occupations
  RT   journalists
       publishers
       publishing industry
       reporters
       writers

education
  SN   *See also Delimiters Display: Education*
       Levels.
  SG   Education
  NT   adult education
       basic education
       bicultural education
       bilingual education
       career education
       civic education
       coeducation
       community education
       compensatory education
       compulsory education
       continuing education
       cooperative education
       early childhood education
       elementary secondary education
       family education
       health education
       inservice education
       medical education
       nondegree education
       nonformal education

(cont.)

education (*cont.*)

NT   nontraditional education
nursing education
physical education
postsecondary education
private education
professional education
progressive education
public education
religious education
remedial education
sex education
single sex education
special education
teacher education
technical education
vocational education

RT   accreditation
achievement
barrier free access
certification
change
curriculum integration
educational attainment
educational benefits
educational equity
educational psychology
equal access
individual development
lifelong learning
racial discrimination
records confidentiality
scholars
schools
sexism
teenage fathers
teenage mothers

Education Amendments of 1972

DG   Laws and Regulations
RT   affirmative action

Education Amendments of 1985

DG   Laws and Regulations
RT   affirmative action

education occupations

SG   Economics and Employment
      Education
BT   occupations
NT   affirmative action officers
chairpersons
coaches
college presidents
coordinators
counselors
deans
educators
faculty
home economists
housemothers
humanists
laboratory assistants
librarians
library workers
principals
professors
provosts
research assistants
researchers
scholars
school personnel
scientists
social scientists
superintendents
teacher aides
teachers
teaching assistants
vice presidents

RT   academia
presidential spouses
professional occupations

educational activities

SG   Education
      History and Social Change
      Social Sciences and Culture
BT   activities
NT   classes
colloquia
discussion groups
lectures
seminars

(*cont.*)

UF=Use for   BT=Broader term   NT=Narrower term   RT=Related term

educational activities (*cont.*)

NT study groups
      teach ins
RT panels
      symposia
      workshops

educational attainment

SG Education
RT education
      school attendance

educational benefits

SG Economics and Employment
      Education
BT benefits
RT continuing education
      education
      educational opportunities
      educational subsidies

educational costs

SG Education
UF educational financing
BT costs
RT student financial aid
      student loans
      tuition tax credit

educational equity

SG Education
      Law, Government, and Public Policy
BT equity
RT education
      racial equality
      sexual equality
      Women's Educational Equity Act

educational facilities

SG Education
BT facilities
NT academies
      colleges
      conservatories
      elderhostel
      kindergarten
      libraries

(*cont.*)

educational facilities (*cont.*)

NT schools
      seminaries
      universities
RT accreditation
      community problems
      community responsibility
      taxes

educational financing

USE **educational costs**

educational legislation

SG Education
      Law, Government, and Public Policy
BT legislation
RT sex discrimination in education

educational methods

SG Education
BT methods

educational objectives

SG Education
BT objectives
RT academic aspirations

educational opportunities

SG Education
BT opportunities
NT equal educational opportunity
RT educational benefits
      educationally disadvantaged
      nonsexist curriculum
      race equity
      school attendance
      school counseling
      sex discrimination in education
      sex equity
      sexual equality

educational policy

SG Education
      Law, Government, and Public Policy
BT policy

educational programs
   SG Education
BT programs
NT external degree programs
    Head Start programs
    high school equivalency programs
    nondegree programs
RT alumnae
    alumni
    nontraditional education

educational psychology
   SG Education
      Social Sciences and Culture
BT psychology
RT education

educational reform
   SG Education
BT reforms
RT financial aid
    nonsexist curriculum
    student financial aid

educational subsidies
   SG Education
      Law, Government, and Public Policy
BT subsidies
RT educational benefits
    student financial aid

educational television
   SG Education
BT television
RT public television

educationally disadvantaged
   SG Education
BT disadvantaged
RT educational opportunities
    special education

educators
   SG Economics and Employment
      Education
BT education occupations
    female intensive occupations

(cont.)

educators *(cont.)*
RT affirmative action
    mentors

EEOC
   USE **Equal Employment Opportunity
       Commission**

efficiency
   SG Economics and Employment
      Social Sciences and Culture
RT evaluation criteria
    time management
    time use studies
    work incentives
    work styles

egalitarian families
   SG Social Sciences and Culture
BT families
RT equality

ego
   SG Natural Sciences and Health
      Social Sciences and Culture
RT achievement need
    identity
    individual development
    mind
    narcissism
    power
    pride
    self concept

Egyptian
   DG National and Regional Descriptors
BT African

ejaculation
   SG Natural Sciences and Health
RT bodies
    impotence
    oral sex
    sperm

elder abuse
   SG Social Sciences and Culture

(cont.)

UF=Use for   BT=Broader term   NT=Narrower term   RT=Related term

elder abuse (*cont.*)

BT abuse
RT aging
   crimes against the elderly
   violence

elderhostel

SG Education
BT educational facilities
RT lifelong learning
   older adults

elderly
USE **older adults**

elderly care

SG Social Sciences and Culture
BT dependent care
RT child care
   day care
   dependents
   older adults
   senior citizens

elderly day care centers

SG Social Sciences and Culture
UF respite care
BT day care centers

elderly households

SG Economics and Employment
   Social Sciences and Culture
BT households
RT home health care
   older adults

elected officials

SG Economics and Employment
   Law, Government, and Public Policy
UF politicians
BT legal and political occupations
   officials
NT assemblymen
   assemblywomen
   governors
   mayors
   representatives
(*cont.*)

elected officials (*cont.*)

NT senators
RT gender gap
   legislatures
   political aspirations
   political office
   politics

election campaigns

SG Law, Government, and Public Policy
UF political campaigns
BT campaigns
RT political candidates

elections

SG Law, Government, and Public Policy
RT political candidates
   politics
   presidential office
   vice presidential office

Electra complex

SG Social Sciences and Culture
BT complexes
RT female Oedipus complex
   Oedipus complex

electric utilities

SG Law, Government, and Public Policy
   Science and Technology
BT utilities

electrical engineering

SG Science and Technology
BT engineering

electricians

SG Economics and Employment
   Science and Technology
BT construction occupations

electroconvulsive therapy

SG Natural Sciences and Health
   Social Sciences and Culture
UF shock therapy
BT therapy
RT drug therapy

electrolysis
SG   Natural Sciences and Health
RT   hair removal

electronic art
SG   Visual and Performing Arts
UF   computer art
BT   art
　　media arts

electronic cottage
SG   Communications
　　Economics and Employment
　　Social Sciences and Culture
RT   alternative employment
　　computer terminals
　　home based work
　　telecommuting

electronic mail
SG   Communications
DG   Types and Forms of Materials
RT   telecommunications
　　teleconferencing

electronic media
SG   Communications
BT   mass media
NT   radio
　　television
RT   industries
　　news services
　　print media
　　telecommunications

electronic music
SG   Visual and Performing Arts
BT   music
RT   computer music

electronics industry
SG   Economics and Employment
　　Science and Technology
BT   industries
RT   computers
　　scientific and technical occupations

elegies
SG   Language, Literature, Religion, and
　　Philosophy
BT   poetry

elementary education
SG   Education
DG   Education Levels
BT   elementary secondary education
NT   adult basic education
　　intermediate grades
　　primary education

elementary schools
SG   Education
BT   schools

elementary secondary education
SG   Education
DG   Education Levels
BT   education
NT   elementary education
　　secondary education

eligibility
SG   Economics and Employment
RT   athletics
　　credit
　　financial aid
　　insurance
　　military draft
　　services
　　voting

elites
SG   Social Sciences and Culture
RT   upper class

Elizabethan Period
DG   Historical Periods

emancipation
SG   Social Sciences and Culture
RT   slavery

embroidery
SG   Visual and Performing Arts

(cont.)

embroidery (*cont.*)
  BT needlework
  RT samplers

embryo transfer
      SG Natural Sciences and Health
  BT reproductive technologies
  RT fertilization
      in vitro fertilization
      infertility
      surrogate mothers

embryology
      SG Natural Sciences and Health
  BT biological sciences
  RT reproductive technologies

embryos
      SG Natural Sciences and Health
  RT conception
      fetuses
      pregnancy

emergency medical services
      SG Natural Sciences and Health
  BT health care services
  RT hospitals

emmenagogues
  USE **menstruation inducing agents**

emotional abuse
      SG Natural Sciences and Health
          Social Sciences and Culture
  BT abuse
  RT emotional problems

emotional adjustment
      SG Social Sciences and Culture
  BT adjustment
  RT attachment
      bereavement
      death
      divorce
      emotional problems
      emotions
      grief
                                      (*cont.*)

emotional adjustment (*cont.*)
  RT mastectomy

emotional development
      SG Social Sciences and Culture
  BT individual development
  RT maturity

emotional experience
      SG Social Sciences and Culture
  BT experience
  RT emotions

emotional problems
      SG Social Sciences and Culture
  BT problems
  RT emotional abuse
      emotional adjustment
      emotions

emotionalism
      SG Social Sciences and Culture
  RT images of women

emotions
      SG Natural Sciences and Health
          Social Sciences and Culture
  UF feelings
  NT alienation
      anger
      anxiety
      apathy
      bitterness
      boredom
      curiosity
      desire
      despair
      empathy
      fear
      frustration
      greed
      grief
      guilt
      happiness
      hate
      hostility
      jealousy
                                      (*cont.*)

emotions (*cont.*)
NT joy
    loneliness
    love
    lust
    passion
    pleasure
    rage
    sadness
    sympathy
    trust
    vulnerability
RT affection
    crying
    emotional adjustment
    emotional experience
    emotional problems
    forms of affection
    human needs
    instincts
    optimism
    personal relationships
    pessimism
    sensitivity
    sex

empathy
SG Social Sciences and Culture
BT emotions
RT human interest
    listening
    sensitivity
    synchrony

employed mothers
USE **mothers working outside the home**

employee benefits
SG Economics and Employment
BT benefits
RT compensation packages
    employees
    employer supported day care
    fringe benefits
    health insurance
    life insurance
    maternity benefits
                                    (*cont.*)

employee benefits (*cont.*)
RT paternity benefits
    pension benefits
    perquisites

employee development
SG Economics and Employment
BT development
RT equal access
    job training
    mentors
    motivation
    performance appraisal

employee records
SG Economics and Employment
BT records
RT absenteeism
    confidentiality
    records confidentiality

employees
SG Economics and Employment
RT employee benefits
    employers
    performance appraisal

employer supported day care
SG Economics and Employment
    Education
    Social Sciences and Culture
BT day care
RT benefits
    corporate day care centers
    corporate policy
    employee benefits
    valuing children

employers
SG Economics and Employment
RT employees
    management

employment
SG Economics and Employment
NT alternative employment
    federal employment
                                    (*cont.*)

employment (*cont.*)
- NT household employment
  - male dominated employment
  - minority employment
  - nontraditional employment
  - paid employment
  - part time employment
  - self employment
  - state employment
  - temporary employment
  - underemployment
  - unpaid employment
  - youth employment
- RT affirmative action hiring
  - displaced homemakers
  - employment opportunities
  - entrepreneurs
  - equal access
  - flexible career patterns
  - hiring policy
  - job recruitment
  - job sharing
  - labor
  - labor force
  - nepotism
  - occupational health and safety
  - occupational mobility
  - occupations
  - older women
  - promotions
  - racial discrimination
  - references
  - sex segregation
  - sexism
  - turnover rates
  - wage earning women
  - work
  - work hours
  - work reentry

employment agencies
- SG Economics and Employment
- BT agencies
- RT job recruitment
  - outplacement

employment opportunities
- SG Economics and Employment
- BT opportunities
- NT equal employment opportunity
- RT adult illiteracy
  - computer literacy
  - critical mass
  - employment
  - executive recruitment
  - job ghettos
  - job market
  - right to work
  - rural poverty

employment patterns
- SG Economics and Employment
- RT occupational patterns

employment practices
- SG Economics and Employment
- NT hiring policy
  - job descriptions
  - job recruitment
  - promotions
- RT job ghettos

employment schedules
- SG Economics and Employment
- BT schedules
- NT flexible work schedules
- RT shift work
  - work hours

employment training
- USE **job training**

empowerment
- SG International Women
  - Social Sciences and Culture
- RT a room of one's own
  - academic achievement
  - affiliation
  - lack of confidence
  - leadership training
  - listening
  - power
  - social skills

empty nest
SN *Used to describe period in parents'*
lives after children leave home.
SG Social Sciences and Culture
RT adjustment
counseling
depression
life cycles
midlife crisis
parenting

encounter groups
SG Social Sciences and Culture
BT groups
RT sensitivity training

encyclopedias
DG Types and Forms of Materials
BT reference books

end time thinking
SN *The belief that nuclear holocaust is*
inevitable.
SG Language, Literature, Religion, and
Philosophy
Social Sciences and Culture
RT Armageddon
fundamentalism
nuclear warfare
the religious right

endogamy
SG Social Sciences and Culture
BT marriage customs
RT exogamy

endometriosis
SG Natural Sciences and Health
BT menstrual disorders
RT menstruation

endowments
SG Economics and Employment
RT financial aid
fund raising
philanthropy

energy
SG Science and Technology
NT nuclear energy
solar energy
RT technology development

energy conservation
SG Science and Technology
BT conservation
RT house design
natural resources

enforcement
SG History and Social Change
Law, Government, and Public Policy
Science and Technology
RT affirmative action hiring
consent orders
contract compliance
corporate liability
court decisions
discrimination laws
environmental hazards
law enforcement
laws
punishment
regulations
social change

enfranchisement
SG History and Social Change
Law, Government, and Public Policy
RT franchise
suffrage
voting rights

engagement
SG Social Sciences and Culture
RT betrothal
betrothed
dating customs
marriage

engineering
SG Science and Technology
NT aerospace engineering
chemical engineering

(cont.)

UF=Use for   BT=Broader term   NT=Narrower term   RT=Related term

engineering (*cont.*)
- NT civil engineering
     electrical engineering
     mechanical engineering
     nuclear engineering
- RT scientific and technical occupations

engineers
- SG Economics and Employment
     Science and Technology
- BT professional occupations
     scientific and technical occupations

English
- DG National and Regional Descriptors
- BT European

engravers
- SG Economics and Employment
     Science and Technology
     Visual and Performing Arts
- BT craft occupations

engraving
- SG Visual and Performing Arts
- BT visual arts

enlightened despotism
- DG Cultural and Political Movements
- BT despotism

Enlightenment
- DG Historical Periods

enlisted personnel
- SG Law, Government, and Public Policy
- BT personnel
- RT military enlistment
     military recruitment

enrollment
- SG Education
- RT demographic measurements

enterprises
- SG History and Social Change
     Social Sciences and Culture

(*cont.*)

enterprises (*cont.*)
- BT organizations
- RT business

entertainers
- SG Communications
     Economics and Employment
     Visual and Performing Arts
- BT arts, entertainment, and media
     occupations
- RT performers

entertaining
- USE **social entertaining**

entertainment
- SG Visual and Performing Arts
- RT hosts
     jokes
     night clubs
     performances
     professional athletics
     recreation

entertainment industry
- SG Communications
     Economics and Employment
- BT industries
- NT motion picture industry
     music industry
- RT arts, entertainment, and media
     occupations
     media arts

entitlement programs
- SN *See also Delimiters Display: Laws and*
     Regulations.
- SG Education
     Law, Government, and Public Policy
- BT programs
- RT discrimination laws
     equal rights legislation

entrepreneurs
- SG Economics and Employment
- RT alternative employment
     business ownership

(*cont.*)

entrepreneurs (*cont.*)

- RT   employment
  - family owned business
  - small business
  - street vendors
  - women owned business

environment

- SG   Social Sciences and Culture
- NT   built environment
  - family environment
  - permissive environment
  - single sex environments
  - smokefree environments
  - social environment
  - urban environment
- RT   biological influences
  - conservation
  - ecological factors
  - soil conservation

environmental hazards

- SG   Science and Technology
- BT   hazards
- RT   enforcement
  - environmental health

environmental health

- SG   Natural Sciences and Health
- BT   health
- RT   air pollution
  - ecology
  - environmental hazards
  - natural resources
  - water pollution

environmental medicine

- SG   Natural Sciences and Health
- BT   medical sciences

environmental movement

- SG   History and Social Change
  - Science and Technology
- DG   Cultural and Political Movements
- BT   social movements
- RT   ecology
  - environmentalism

environmental racism

- SN   *Phenomenon of hazardous waste sites existing in disproporationate numbers in communities with higher percentages of minority citizens.*
- SG   Science and Technology
- BT   racism
- RT   communities
  - hazardous waste
  - institutional racism

environmental sciences

- SG   Science and Technology
- BT   natural sciences
- RT   ecology

environmentalism

- DG   Cultural and Political Movements
- RT   environmental movement

ephemera

- DG   Types and Forms of Materials

epics

- SG   Language, Literature, Religion, and Philosophy
- BT   poetry
- RT   folk literature
  - heroes
  - heroines (historical)
  - oral tradition

epidemiology

- SG   Natural Sciences and Health
  - Social Sciences and Culture
- RT   acquired immune deficiency syndrome
  - demographic measurements
  - health care
  - public health

epigrams

- SG   Language, Literature, Religion, and Philosophy
- BT   poetry

episiotomy

- SG   Natural Sciences and Health

(*cont.*)

F=Use for   BT=Broader term   NT=Narrower term   RT=Related term   153

episiotomy (*cont.*)
- BT surgical procedures
- RT childbirth
  natural childbirth

epistemology
- SG Language, Literature, Religion, and
  Philosophy
- BT philosophy

epithets
- SG Language, Literature, Religion, and
  Philosophy
- BT figurative language
- RT forms of address

equal access
- SG Law, Government, and Public Policy
- UF access
- RT ableism
  admissions
  bias
  blind review
  braille
  communication satellites
  computer equity
  computer literacy
  desegregation methods
  disabled
  dual economy
  education
  employee development
  employment
  health care
  housing
  real estate
  sports
  technology
  women's media

equal credit
- SG Economics and Employment
- BT credit
- RT consumer credit
  Equal Credit Opportunity Act of 1974

Equal Credit Opportunity Act of 1974
- DG Laws and Regulations
- RT equal credit

equal educational opportunity
- SG Education
  Economics and Employment
- BT educational opportunities
  equal opportunity

equal employment opportunity
- SG Economics and Employment
  Education
- BT employment opportunities
  equal opportunity
- RT job ghettos
  occupational sex segregation
  racial discrimination

Equal Employment Opportunity Commission
- SG Economics and Employment
  History and Social Change
  Law, Government, and Public Policy
- UF EEOC
- BT equal opportunities commissions
- RT affirmative action
  back pay
  court cases
  discrimination

equal opportunities commissions
- SG History and Social Change
  Law, Government, and Public Policy
- BT commissions
- NT Equal Employment Opportunity
  Commission

equal opportunity
- SG Law, Government, and Public Policy
- NT equal educational opportunity
  equal employment opportunity
- RT academic freedom
  affirmative action
  athletics
  freedom
  opportunities

(*cont.*)

equal opportunity (*cont.*)
- RT   rights
-      tokenism

equal pay
- SG   Economics and Employment
- BT   wages
- RT   career feminism
-      comparable worth
-      economic value of women's work
-      equal pay for equal work
-      equal pay legislation
-      pay equity
-      wage gap

equal Pay Act of 1963
- DG   Laws and Regulations
- RT   equal pay legislation

equal Pay Act of 1970 (Great Britain)
- DG   Laws and Regulations
- RT   equal pay legislation

equal pay for equal work
- SN   *Prohibiting discrimination in compensation for jobs of equal skill, effort, responsibility, and working conditions.*
- SG   Economics and Employment
- BT   pay equity
- RT   comparable worth
-      economic value of women's work
-      equal pay
-      wage discrimination
-      wage gap

equal pay legislation
- SG   Economics and Employment
-      Law, Government, and Public Policy
- BT   legislation
- RT   equal pay
-      Equal Pay Act of 1963
-      Equal Pay Act of 1970 (Great Britain)

equal protection under the law
- SG   Law, Government, and Public Policy
- BT   protection

(*cont.*)

equal protection under the law (*cont.*)
- RT   laws

equal rights
- SN   *See also Delimiters Display: Laws and Regulations.*
- SG   Law, Government, and Public Policy
- BT   rights
- RT   affirmative action
-      Equal Rights Amendment
-      human rights

Equal Rights Amendment
- DG   Laws and Regulations
- UF   ERA
- RT   equal rights

equal rights legislation
- SG   History and Social Change
-      Law, Government, and Public Policy
- BT   legislation
- RT   constitution
-      entitlement programs
-      legal status
-      race equity
-      sex equity

equality
- SG   History and Social Change
-      Language, Literature, Religion, and Philosophy
- NT   racial equality
-      sexual equality
- RT   diversity
-      egalitarian families
-      freedom
-      nonsexist language
-      nonsexist literature
-      partners
-      values

equilibrium
- SG   Economics and Employment
- RT   adjustment
-      economic trends
-      tipping

F=Use for   BT=Broader term   NT=Narrower term   RT=Related term

equity
- SN *Fair treatment of all classes of people without regard to gender, class, race, ethnic background, religion, handicap, age, or sexual preference.*
- SG Law, Government, and Public Policy
- NT communications equity
  - computer equity
  - economic equity
  - educational equity
  - pay equity
  - race equity
  - sex equity
- RT comparable worth
  - equity funding
  - fairness
  - justice
  - values

equity funding
- SG Economics and Employment
  - Education
- RT equity
  - federal aid
  - fund raising
  - state aid

ERA
- USE **Equal Rights Amendment**

ergonomics
- SG Science and Technology
- RT architecture
  - automation
  - built environment
  - experimental design
  - house design
  - kitchens
  - labor saving devices
  - occupational health and safety
  - work space

erogenous zones
- USE **arousal**

erotic art
- SG Visual and Performing Arts
  - *(cont.)*

erotic art *(cont.)*
- BT art
  - erotica

erotic literature
- SG Language, Literature, Religion, and Philosophy
- BT erotica
  - literature

erotica
- SG Language, Literature, Religion, and Philosophy
  - Visual and Performing Arts
- NT erotic art
  - erotic literature
- RT arousal
  - fantasies
  - pornography
  - pulp fiction

eroticism
- SG Natural Sciences and Health
- RT arousal
  - pleasure
  - sexual behavior

escorts
- SG Economics and Employment
  - Social Sciences and Culture
- BT service occupations

Eskimo
- DG Ethnic, Racial, and Religious Descriptors

ESP
- USE **extrasensory perception**

essayists
- SG Communications
  - Economics and Employment
  - Language, Literature, Religion, and Philosophy
- BT arts, entertainment, and media occupations

SN=Scope note   SG=Subject group   DG=Delimiters group   USE=Use

essays

    SG Language, Literature, Religion, and
        Philosophy

    DG Types and Forms of Materials

  BT nonfiction

essentialism

    SN *Belief in a unique and superior female
        "essence" that exists beyond cultur-
        al conditioning.*

    SG Language, Literature, Religion, and
        Philosophy
        Natural Sciences and Health
        Social Sciences and Culture

    DG Cultural and Political Movements

  RT biologism
       female chauvinism
       feminine principle
       feminist ethics
       gynarchy

estradiol

    SG Natural Sciences and Health

  RT estrogens

estrogen replacement therapy

    SG Natural Sciences and Health

  BT hormone therapy

  RT menopause
       osteoporosis

estrogens

    SG Natural Sciences and Health

  BT sex hormones

  RT diethylstilbestrol
       estradiol

estrus

    SG Natural Sciences and Health

  RT reproductive cycle

ethclass

    SN *Describes ethnic group and class posi-
        tion overlap.*

    SG Economics and Employment
        Social Sciences and Culture

  BT class

ethic of care

    SN *Moral stance placing value on caring
        and responsibility in relationships
        rather than on abstract rights and
        rules.*

    SG Social Sciences and Culture

  BT moral development

  RT care
       caregivers
       ethics
       feminist ethics
       helping behavior
       love
       male norms
       moral reasoning
       nursing homes
       nurturing
       parenting rewards
       personal relationships
       relationships
       values

ethics

    SG Language, Literature, Religion, and
        Philosophy

  BT philosophy

  NT bioethics
       business ethics
       feminist ethics
       medical ethics
       political ethics
       religious ethics

  RT abortion laws
       conflict of interest
       death penalty
       drug dumping
       ethic of care
       honesty
       humanitarianism
       immorality
       moral reform
       morality
       social values
       trust
       values

Ethiopian
- DG National and Regional Descriptors
- BT African

ethnic comparisons
- USE **racial and ethnic differences**

ethnic diversity
- SG History and Social Change
  Social Sciences and Culture
- BT diversity
- RT casting
  critical mass
  pluralism

ethnic groups
- SN *Use of a more specific term is recommended. See Delimiters Display:
  Ethnic, Racial, and Religious Descriptors for specific ethnic descriptors.*
- SG Social Sciences and Culture
- UF minorities
- BT groups
- RT ethnic studies
  ethnography
  foreign workers
  immigrants
  minority groups
  race
  voting records

ethnic intimidation
- SG History and Social Change
  Law, Government, and Public Policy
  Social Sciences and Culture
- BT intimidation
- RT discrimination
  prejudice
  sexual harassment
  terrorism

ethnic neighborhoods
- SG History and Social Change
  Law, Government, and Public Policy
  Social Sciences and Culture
- BT neighborhoods

(cont.)

ethnic neighborhoods *(cont.)*
- NT ghettos
- RT communities
  households
  redlining
  urban planning

ethnic relations
- SG Social Sciences and Culture
- BT relationships
- RT interracial relations

ethnic studies
- SG Education
  International Women
  Social Sciences and Culture
- UF minority studies
- BT interdisciplinary studies
- NT Afro American studies
  American Indian studies
  Asian American studies
  Canadian Indian studies
  Jewish women's studies
  Latina studies
- RT Asian studies
  comparative religion
  cross cultural studies
  ethnic groups
  ethnomusicology
  immigrants
  mainstreaming
  regional studies
  social studies
  societies
  tribal art
  women's studies

ethnic women
- SN *See Delimiters Display: Ethnic, Racial,
  and Religious Descriptors for more
  specific ethnic descriptors.*
- SG Social Sciences and Culture
- UF minority women
- BT women
- RT immigrants
  women of color

ethnicity
- SG Social Sciences and Culture
- RT minority experience
  - race formation
  - racial and ethnic differences

ethnography
- SG Social Sciences and Culture
- BT anthropology
- RT ethnic groups
  - ethnomusicology
  - social geography

ethnology
- SG Social Sciences and Culture
- BT anthropology

ethnomethodology
- SG Social Sciences and Culture
- RT fieldwork
  - research methods

ethnomusicology
- SG Social Sciences and Culture
  - Visual and Performing Arts
- RT ethnic studies
  - ethnography
  - folk music
  - humanities
  - interdisciplinary studies
  - musicology
  - tribal music

ethologists
- SG Economics and Employment
  - Social Sciences and Culture
- BT scientists

ethology
- SN *Study of animal social behavior.*
- SG Natural Sciences and Health
  - Social Sciences and Culture
- BT biological sciences
  - social sciences
- RT animal behavior
  - sociobiology

etiquette
- SG Language, Literature, Religion, and
  - Philosophy
  - Social Sciences and Culture
- RT manners
  - norms

eucharist
- USE **holy communion**

eugenic sterilization
- SN *Sterilization of groups or classes of*
  - *people considered to be genetically*
  - *"inferior."*
- SG History and Social Change
  - International Women
  - Natural Sciences and Health
- BT sterilization
- RT holocaust
  - mental retardation
  - population control
  - racism

eugenics
- SG History and Social Change
  - Natural Sciences and Health
- RT genetic engineering

eulogies
- SG Language, Literature, Religion, and
  - Philosophy
- DG Types and Forms of Materials
- RT obituaries

eunuchs
- SG History and Social Change
  - Natural Sciences and Health
- RT castration
  - harems

Euro American
- DG Ethnic, Racial, and Religious
  - Descriptors

European
- DG National and Regional Descriptors
- NT Albanian

(*cont.*)

UF = Use for   BT = Broader term   NT = Narrower term   RT = Related term

European (*cont.*)
NT Austrian
    Belgian
    Bulgarian
    Czechoslovakian
    Dutch
    East German
    English
    French
    German
    Greek
    Hungarian
    Irish
    Italian
    Luxembourgian
    Maltese
    Northern Irish
    Polish
    Portuguese
    Rumanian
    Russian
    Scandinavian
    Scotch
    Spanish
    Swiss
    Turkish
    Welsh
    West German
    Yugoslav

euthanasia
SG Social Sciences and Culture
RT death
    medical ethics
    premature death
    religious law
    right to die
    terminal illness

evaluation
SG Social Sciences and Culture
NT course evaluation
    job evaluation
    medical evaluation
    mental evaluation
    personnel evaluation
RT blind review

(*cont.*)

evaluation (*cont.*)
RT feedback

evaluation criteria
SG Education
BT criteria
RT assessment
    efficiency

evaluations
DG Types and Forms of Materials

evangelism
DG Cultural and Political Movements

evangelists
SG Language, Literature, Religion, and
        Philosophy
BT religious workers

Eve
SG Language, Literature, Religion, and
        Philosophy
BT images of women
RT Adam
    creation myths
    Garden of Eden
    Lilith
    religious symbols
    sacred texts
    temptation

eve teasing
SG International Women
        Social Sciences and Culture
RT street harassment
    violence against women

evil
SG Language, Literature, Religion, and
        Philosophy
RT devil
    dualism

evil spirits
SG Language, Literature, Religion, and
        Philosophy

(*cont.*)

SN=Scope note   SG=Subject group   DG=Delimiters group   USE=Use

evil spirits (*cont.*)
- BT spirits
- NT dybbuks
  - incubi
  - succubi

evolution
- SG Natural Sciences and Health
  - Social Sciences and Culture
- NT human evolution
- RT creation myths
  - natural selection

examinations
- DG Types and Forms of Materials
- BT testing

excerpts
- DG Types and Forms of Materials

exchange rate
- SG Economics and Employment
  - International Women
- RT balance of payments
  - international trade policy

exchange students
- SG Education
- BT students
- RT foreign students
  - study abroad

exchange theory
- SG Social Sciences and Culture
- BT theory
- RT barter
  - food for work
  - money

excommunication
- SG Language, Literature, Religion, and
  - Philosophy
- RT religious beliefs
  - religious law
  - religious sanctions

Executive Order 11246
- DG Laws and Regulations
- RT affirmative action

executive recruitment
- SG Economics and Employment
- UF headhunters
- BT job recruitment
- RT affirmative action hiring
  - discrimination
  - employment opportunities
  - executive search firms
  - job hunting
  - job search methods

executive search firms
- SG Economics and Employment
- BT organizations
- RT executive recruitment
  - search committees

executive spouses
- USE **corporate spouses**

executives
- SG Economics and Employment
- BT managerial occupations
- NT chief executives
- RT managers

executors
- SG Economics and Employment
  - Law, Government, and Public Policy
- UF executrixes
- RT guardians
  - inheritance customs
  - wills

executrixes
- USE **executors**

exercise
- SG Natural Sciences and Health
- NT aerobic exercise
  - isometric exercise
- RT athletics
  - body image

(*cont.*)

UF=Use for BT=Broader term NT=Narrower term RT=Related term

exercise *(cont.)*
- RT physical fitness
  - physiology
  - running

exhibitionism
- SG Natural Sciences and Health
- RT sexual behavior

exhibitions
- SG History and Social Change
  - Social Sciences and Culture
- BT activities
- RT art shows

exhusbands
- USE **former husbands**

exile
- SG International Women
  - Social Sciences and Culture
- RT immigration
  - political asylum
  - refugees

existentialism
- DG Cultural and Political Movements

exogamy
- SN *Marriage outside of a specific group.*
- SG Social Sciences and Culture
- BT marriage customs
- RT endogamy

expectations
- SG Social Sciences and Culture
- RT feedback

experience
- SG Social Sciences and Culture
- NT early experience
  - emotional experience
  - gay experience
  - religious experience
  - work experience
- RT credit for experience
  - experiential learning

experiential learning
- SG Education
- BT learning
- RT experience

experimental dance
- SG Visual and Performing Arts
- BT dance

experimental design
- SG Education
  - Natural Sciences and Health
  - Science and Technology
  - Social Sciences and Culture
- BT design
- RT ergonomics

experimental psychology
- SG Social Sciences and Culture
- BT psychology

experimental theater
- SG Visual and Performing Arts
- BT theater

experts
- SG Economics and Employment
  - Education
  - Social Sciences and Culture
- RT authority
  - dominance
  - medical oppression
  - professional occupations
  - professionalism
  - self help
  - sex manuals
  - transference

expiation
- SG Language, Literature, Religion, and
  - Philosophy
- RT sin

exploitation
- SG Social Sciences and Culture
- NT sexual exploitation
- RT bondage

(cont.)

exploitation *(cont.)*
RT colonialism
     fifth world
     fourth world
     juvenile prostitution
     multinational corporations
     oppression
     patriarchy
     pornography
     poverty
     powerlessness
     privilege
     sadomasochism
     sex industry
     sex tourism
     sexual harassment
     slavery
     social class
     third world
     untouchables

explorers
SG Economics and Employment
     International Women
BT professional occupations
RT adventurers

expositions
SG History and Social Change
     Social Sciences and Culture
BT activities

expressing milk
SG Natural Sciences and Health
RT breast feeding
     breast pumps
     lactation

expressionism
DG Cultural and Political Movements

extended care facilities
SG Natural Sciences and Health
BT health care facilities

extended families
SN *Support network of individuals, not
     necessarily blood-related.*
SG Social Sciences and Culture
UF extended kinship network
BT families
RT aunts
     brothers
     clans
     community
     cousins
     family relationships
     family structure
     single women
     support groups
     support systems
     uncles

extended kinship network
USE **extended families**

extension work
SN *Educational and service programs that
     provide information and technical
     assistance to people living in rural or
     developing areas; in nonrural areas,
     also off-campus educational pro-
     grams.*
SG Economics and Employment
     Education
     International Women
BT work
NT home economics extension work
RT agricultural extension
     extension workers

extension workers
SG Economics and Employment
     International Women
BT agricultural, fishing, and forestry
     occupations
     female intensive occupations
     workers
NT animatrices rurales
     gramsevika
RT extension work

---

external degree programs
SG   Education
BT   educational programs
RT   continuing education

extractive industry
SG   Economics and Employment
     Science and Technology
BT   industries
NT   mining industry
     oil industry
RT   coal miners

extracurricular activities
SG   Education
BT   activities
RT   after school programs

extramarital affairs
SG   Social Sciences and Culture
UF   adultery
RT   gigolos
     infidelity
     mistresses

extrasensory perception
SG   Social Sciences and Culture
UF   ESP
BT   perception
RT   intuition
     parapsychology

extroversion
SG   Social Sciences and Culture
RT   introversion
     personality traits

exwives
USE **former wives**

eyeglasses
SG   Natural Sciences and Health
     Social Sciences and Culture
RT   body image
     faces
     vision

Fabianism
DG   Cultural and Political Movements

fables
SG   Language, Literature, Religion, and
     Philosophy
BT   folk literature
RT   allegory
     children's literature
     stories

face lifts
SG   Natural Sciences and Health
RT   appearance
     body image
     skin
     wrinkles

faces
SG   Natural Sciences and Health
     Social Sciences and Culture
BT   bodies
RT   complexion
     eyeglasses
     facism

facilities
SG   Education
     Social Sciences and Culture
NT   brothels
     centers
     clinics
     educational facilities
     foster homes
     halfway houses
     health care facilities
     hostels
     houses
     laboratories
     lodges
     maternity homes
     museums
     offices (facilities)
     prisons
     reformatories
     religious facilities
     seraglios

(*cont.*)

facilities (*cont.*)
- NT shelters
  theaters
- RT institutions
  organizations
  rooms

facism
- SN *Excessive emphasis on traditionally-defined beauty, especially facial features.*
- SG History and Social Change
  Social Sciences and Culture
- RT appearance
  beauty standards
  faces
  lookism

factions
- SG Social Sciences and Culture
- BT groups
- RT cliques
  sects
  special interest groups

factories
- SG Economics and Employment
- RT manufacturing industry
  offshore production plants
  runaway shops
  sweatshops
  textile industry

factory conditions
- SG Economics and Employment
- BT conditions
- RT health hazards

factory workers
- SG Economics and Employment
  Science and Technology
- UF mill girls
- BT manufacturing occupations
  workers
- RT shift work
  working class

faculty
- SG Economics and Employment
  Education
- BT education occupations
  professional occupations
- RT academic rank
  teaching
  teaching assistants
  tenure

faculty retrenchment
- SN *Cutbacks in faculty hiring that sometimes includes removal of existing tenured faculty.*
- SG Education
- RT career change
  forced retirement
  independent scholars
  job retraining
  teachers

fads
- SG Social Sciences and Culture
- RT dieting
  nutrition
  social trends

faghag
- SN *Slang; a heterosexual woman with visible social ties to gay male friends.*
- SG History and Social Change
  Social Sciences and Culture
- RT relationships

failure
- SG Economics and Employment
- NT academic failure
- RT fear of failure
  success

fainting
- SG Natural Sciences and Health
- RT swooning

fair play
- SG Economics and Employment
  Social Sciences and Culture

(*cont.*)

UF=Use for   BT=Broader term   NT=Narrower term   RT=Related term

fair play (*cont.*)
  UF   sportsmanship
  RT   sports

fairness
      SG   Social Sciences and Culture
  RT   comparable worth
       due process
       equity
       values

fairy tales
      SG   Language, Literature, Religion, and
            Philosophy
  BT   folk literature
  RT   anthropomorphism
       children's literature
       Cinderella
       fantasies
       legends
       myths
       romantic love
       stories

faith
      SG   Language, Literature, Religion, and
            Philosophy
  RT   belief systems
       religions

faith communities
      SG   Language, Literature, Religion, and
            Philosophy
  BT   communities
       religious groups
  RT   ceremonies
       church work
       churches
       congregations
       laymen
       laywomen
       monasticism

faith healers
      SG   Language, Literature, Religion, and
            Philosophy
            Natural Sciences and Health
                                            (*cont.*)

faith healers (*cont.*)
  BT   healers
  RT   laying on of hands

Falkland Islander
      DG   National and Regional Descriptors
  BT   Latin American

fallen women
      SG   Language, Literature, Religion, and
            Philosophy
  BT   images of women
       women
  RT   reputations

fallopian tubes
      SG   Natural Sciences and Health
  RT   ectopic pregnancy
       infertility
       sterilization
       tubal ligation

false consciousness
      SN   *Term used by Marxist and socialist*
            feminists to describe erroneous be-
            liefs that keep women from becom-
            ing aware of their oppression in sex-
            ist societies.
      SG   History and Social Change
            Social Sciences and Culture
  BT   consciousness
  RT   consciousness raising
       discrimination
       feminine mystique
       sexual oppression

false dichotomies
      SN   *Traditionally defined splits between*
            body and mind, feeling and thinking,
            private and public spheres, that have
            often worked to the disadvantage of
            nonmainstream groups.
      SG   Language, Literature, Religion, and
            Philosophy
  BT   dichotomy
  NT   mind/body split
  RT   conceptual errors
                                            (*cont.*)

false dichotomies (*cont.*)

RT sex/gender systems

false generics

SG Language, Literature, Religion, and Philosophy

RT conceptual errors

discriminatory language

faulty generalization

gender marking

generic pronouns

God the father

he/man language

invisibility

language

man

masculine pronouns

men

pronoun envy

pronouns

research methods

sexist language

false pregnancy

USE **pseudopregnancy**

falsies

USE **padding**

families

SG Social Sciences and Culture

UF the family

NT blended families

communal families

dual career families

egalitarian families

extended families

fatherless families

foster families

interethnic families

interracial families

interreligious families

low income families

middle class families

motherless families

nuclear families

single parent families

(*cont.*)

families (*cont.*)

NT surrogate families

two income families

upper class families

RT ancestors

balancing work and family life

brothers

brothers in law

budgeting

career family conflict

child rearing practices

commitment

couples

couples with children

culture

daughters

daughters in law

dependent care

divorce

domestic arrangements

domestic roles

family finances

family life

family size

family structure

fathers

fathers in law

female headed households

gay marriage

grandchildren

grandparents

harems

heads of families

home life

households

in laws

incest

infants

life styles

lower class

marriage and family law

middle class

mothers

mothers in law

parent child relationships

single women

sisters

(*cont.*)

families (*cont.*)
- RT   social class
  - social policy
  - social structure
  - sons
  - sons in law
  - status
  - support systems
  - upper class
  - valuing children

the family
USE **families**

Family and Medical Leave Act of 1987
- DG   Laws and Regulations
- RT   parental leave

family attitudes
- SG   Social Sciences and Culture
- BT   attitudes
- RT   family size
  - history of children
  - valuing children

family conflict
- SG   Social Sciences and Culture
- BT   conflict
- RT   crisis intervention
  - divorce
  - domestic violence
  - family counseling
  - family courts
  - family therapy
  - substance abuse

family counseling
- SG   Social Sciences and Culture
- BT   counseling
- RT   crisis centers
  - crisis intervention
  - family conflict
  - family problems
  - family therapy
  - substance abuse

family courts
- SG   Law, Government, and Public Policy
- BT   courts
- RT   children's rights
  - custody
  - divorce
  - family conflict
  - guardians
  - mediation

family economics
- SG   Economics and Employment
  - Social Sciences and Culture
- RT   family finances
  - family income
  - inherited wealth

family education
- SG   Education
  - Social Sciences and Culture
- BT   education
- RT   family therapy

family environment
- SG   Social Sciences and Culture
- BT   environment
- RT   family life
  - family structure

family farms
- SG   Economics and Employment
- BT   farms

family finances
- SG   Economics and Employment
  - Social Sciences and Culture
- BT   finances
- RT   budgeting
  - capital
  - families
  - family economics
  - food stamps
  - household economics
  - income
  - low income families
  - low income households
  - two income families

(*cont.*)

family finances (*cont.*)
RT welfare

family history
SG History and Social Change
BT social history
RT ancestors
cultural heritage
generation gap
traditions

family income
SG Economics and Employment
Social Sciences and Culture
BT income
RT budgeting
family economics

family influence
SG Social Sciences and Culture
BT influence
NT parent influence
sibling influence
RT child rearing practices
family life
family structure
kinship
personality
personality traits

family life
SG Social Sciences and Culture
RT families
family environment
family influence
history of children

family medicine
SG Natural Sciences and Health
UF family practice
BT medical sciences
RT medical education
patient doctor relationships

family mobility
SG Social Sciences and Culture
BT mobility

(*cont.*)

family mobility (*cont.*)
RT military spouses

family owned business
SG Economics and Employment
Social Sciences and Culture
BT business
RT entrepreneurs
nepotism
organized crime
small business
women owned business

family planning
SG Natural Sciences and Health
BT planning
RT birth control
childless couples
contraception
family size
planned parenthood
population control
pregnancy

family policy
SN *See also Delimiters Display: Laws and Regulations.*
SG Law, Government, and Public Policy
Social Sciences and Culture
BT social policy

family practice
USE **family medicine**

family practitioners
SG Natural Sciences and Health
BT health care occupations

family problems
SG Social Sciences and Culture
BT problems
RT family counseling
runaways

family recipes
SG Natural Sciences and Health
Social Sciences and Culture

(*cont.*)

family recipes (*cont.*)
- BT recipes
- RT cultural heritage

family relationships
- SG Social Sciences and Culture
- BT relationships
- NT sibling relationships
- RT adult child relationships
  extended families
  family roles
  life styles

family responsibility
- SG Social Sciences and Culture
- BT responsibility
- RT absenteeism
  delinquent behavior
  sick children

family rights
- SG Law, Government, and Public Policy
  Social Sciences and Culture
- BT rights

family roles
- SG Social Sciences and Culture
- BT roles
- RT family relationships
  sex/gender systems

family size
- SG Social Sciences and Culture
- UF ideal family size
- RT children
  contraception
  families
  family attitudes
  family planning
  family structure
  population control

family structure
- SG Social Sciences and Culture
- RT aunts
  birth order
  brothers

(*cont.*)

family structure (*cont.*)
- RT cousins
  culture
  extended families
  families
  family environment
  family influence
  family size
  grandchildren
  grandparents
  kinship
  matriarchy
  nephews
  nieces
  patriarchy
  sisters
  social class
  social structure
  uncles

family therapy
- SG Natural Sciences and Health
  Social Sciences and Culture
- BT therapy
- RT family conflict
  family counseling
  family education

family violence
- USE **domestic violence**

Family Violence Prevention and Services Act
- DG Laws and Regulations
- RT domestic violence

famine
- SG Economics and Employment
  International Women
  Law, Government, and Public Policy
  Natural Sciences and Health
- RT foreign aid
  hunger
  poverty
  social policy
  starvation
  third world

SN=Scope note   SG=Subject group   DG=Delimiters group   USE=Use

fantasies
SG Language, Literature, Religion, and
      Philosophy
NT rape fantasies
      sexual fantasies
RT children's literature
      creative thinking
      daydreams
      dreams
      erotica
      fairy tales
      imagination
      queen for a day
      sexual behavior

farce
SG Language, Literature, Religion, and
      Philosophy
BT comedy
RT drama
      literature
      satire
      skits

farm workers
SG Economics and Employment
BT agricultural, fishing, and forestry
      occupations
      workers
RT animatrices rurales
      farmers
      farms
      immigrants
      migrant workers

farmers
SG Economics and Employment
BT agricultural, fishing, and forestry
      occupations
RT farm workers
      farms
      rural women

farming
SG Economics and Employment
NT tenant farming
RT farms

(*cont.*)

farming (*cont.*)
RT rural development

farms
SG Economics and Employment
      International Women
NT collective farms
      family farms
RT agribusiness
      agricultural extension
      agriculture
      animatrices rurales
      farm workers
      farmers
      farming
      rural living

fascism
DG Cultural and Political Movements

fashion
SG Social Sciences and Culture
RT appearance
      clothing
      commercial art
      decorative arts
      design
      fashion illustration
      fashion photography
      furniture
      hemlines
      high heeled shoes
      images of women
      lingerie
      lookism
      material culture

fashion design
SG Visual and Performing Arts
BT design

fashion illustration
SG Visual and Performing Arts
BT illustration
RT fashion
      models

---

fashion photography
SG Visual and Performing Arts
BT photography
RT commercial art
fashion
images of women
models

fashion shows
SG Visual and Performing Arts
BT shows

fasting
SG Natural Sciences and Health
BT spiritual communication
RT anorexia nervosa
diets
rites

fat liberation
SG History and Social Change
Natural Sciences and Health
BT liberation
RT beauty standards
body image
cellulite
physical fitness
thinness

fat oppression
SG Natural Sciences and Health
BT oppression
RT body image

father daughter incest
SG Law, Government, and Public Policy
Natural Sciences and Health
Social Sciences and Culture
BT incest

father daughter relationships
SG Social Sciences and Culture
BT female male relationships
parent child relationships
RT daughters
fathers

father son incest
SG Law, Government, and Public Policy
Natural Sciences and Health
Social Sciences and Culture
BT incest

father son relationships
SG Social Sciences and Culture
BT male male relationships
parent child relationships
RT fathers
sons

fatherhood
USE **fathers**
USE **parenthood**

fathering
SG Natural Sciences and Health
Social Sciences and Culture
BT parenting
RT birth fathers
fathers
nurturing
paternity

fatherless families
SG Social Sciences and Culture
BT families
RT absentee fathers
single parent families

fathers
SG Social Sciences and Culture
UF fatherhood
BT men
NT absentee fathers
birth fathers
gay fathers
runaway fathers
single fathers
stepfathers
surrogate fathers
teenage fathers
RT bonding
families
father daughter relationships

(cont.)

fathers (*cont.*)
- RT father son relationships
  - fathering
  - fathers in law
  - gender roles
  - God the father
  - infants
  - lower class
  - male bonding
  - middle class
  - mothers
  - parent child relationships
  - parenthood
  - parents
  - patriarchs
  - patricide
  - priests
  - primary caregivers
  - upper class

fathers (religious)
- USE **priests**

fathers in law
- SG Social Sciences and Culture
- BT in laws
  - men
- RT families
  - fathers

fatigue
- SG Natural Sciences and Health
- RT anemia
  - burnout
  - sleep

faulty generalization
- SG Language, Literature, Religion, and Philosophy
- BT conceptual errors
- RT false generics
  - generic pronouns
  - man

fear
- SG Social Sciences and Culture
- BT emotions

(*cont.*)

fear (*cont.*)
- NT fear of failure
  - fear of success
- RT phobias

fear of failure
- SG Social Sciences and Culture
- BT fear
- RT academic failure
  - achievement
  - anxiety
  - aspirations
  - avoidance behavior
  - failure
  - fear of success
  - impotence
  - lack of confidence
  - risk taking
  - risk taking behavior
  - student motivation
  - success

fear of success
- SG Social Sciences and Culture
- BT fear
- RT achievement
  - aspirations
  - avoidance behavior
  - fear of failure
  - risk taking behavior
  - success
  - underachievement

federal agencies
- SG Law, Government, and Public Policy
- BT agencies

federal aid
- SN *See also Delimiters Display: Laws and Regulations.*
- SG Economics and Employment
  - Education
  - Law, Government, and Public Policy
- BT aid
- RT block grants
  - equity funding
  - federal assistance programs

(*cont.*)

federal aid (*cont.*)
  RT rural development
      state aid
      student loans

federal assistance programs
  SN *See also Delimiters Display: Laws and*
      Regulations.
  SG Economics and Employment
      Law, Government, and Public Policy
  BT assistance programs
  RT federal aid
      food stamps
      Medicare
      public assistance
      work incentive programs

federal budget
  SG Economics and Employment
      Law, Government, and Public Policy
  NT military budget
  RT appropriations
      budget cuts
      budget deficits
      Congress
      deficits
      economy
      federal taxes
      social policy
      taxes

federal courts
  SG Law, Government, and Public Policy
  BT courts

federal employment
  SG Economics and Employment
      Law, Government, and Public Policy
  BT employment
  RT civil service

Federal Equitable Pay Practices Act of 1987
  DG Laws and Regulations
  RT pay equity

federal government
  SG Law, Government, and Public Policy
  BT government

federal legislation
  SG Law, Government, and Public Policy
  BT legislation
  RT Congress
      laws
      reproductive rights

federal regulations
  SG Law, Government, and Public Policy
  BT regulations
  RT appropriations

federal taxes
  SG Law, Government, and Public Policy
  BT taxes
  RT appropriations
      budget deficits
      federal budget

federalism
  DG Cultural and Political Movements

federally sponsored research
  SG Education
      Law, Government, and Public Policy
      Science and Technology
  BT sponsored research
  RT appropriations
      discrimination
      fund raising
      referees

federations
  SG History and Social Change
      Social Sciences and Culture
  BT organizations

feedback
  SG Economics and Employment
  NT biofeedback
  RT communication
      evaluation
      expectations

(*cont.*)

feedback (*cont.*)
- RT listening
  performance
  self confidence

feelings
- USE **emotions**

fellatio
- SG Natural Sciences and Health
- BT oral sex

fellowships
- SG Education
- BT student financial aid
- NT postdoctoral fellowships
- RT assistantships
  internships
  scholarships

female authored texts
- SG Language, Literature, Religion, and
  Philosophy
- BT texts
- RT l'ecriture feminine
  womanist writing
  women's literature

female bonding
- SG History and Social Change
  Natural Sciences and Health
  Social Sciences and Culture
- BT bonding
- RT daughter right
  female female relationships
  sisterhood

female chauvinism
- SG History and Social Change
- BT chauvinism
- RT essentialism
  feminism
  misandry
  separatism
  womanism

female circumcision
- SG Natural Sciences and Health
- NT clitoridectomy
  vulvectomy
- RT castration
  chastity belts
  clitoris
  genital mutilation
  infibulation
  initiation rites
  tribal customs

female dominated careers
- USE **female intensive occupations**

female dominated occupations
- USE **female intensive occupations**

female dominated professions
- USE **female intensive occupations**

female female relationships
- SG Social Sciences and Culture
- UF same sex relationships
- BT personal relationships
- NT female friendships
  lesbian relationships
  mother daughter relationships
- RT female bonding
  old girl networks
  women identified women
  women's networks

female friendships
- SG History and Social Change
  Social Sciences and Culture
- BT female female relationships
  friendships
- RT bonding
  harems
  sisterhood
  women identified women

female headed households
- SG Economics and Employment
  Social Sciences and Culture
- BT households

(*cont.*)

---

female headed households (*cont.*)
- RT   divorce
-      families
-      parent child relationships
-      single mothers
-      single parent families
-      superwoman syndrome

female homosexuality
- USE **lesbianism**

female homosexuals
- USE **lesbians**

female hypersexuality
- SG   Natural Sciences and Health
- UF nymphomania
- BT hypersexuality
- RT male norms

female impersonators
- SG   Social Sciences and Culture
- BT impersonators
- RT cross dressing
-      cross sex identity
-      sexual identity

female intensive occupations
- SG   Economics and Employment
- UF female dominated careers
-      female dominated occupations
-      female dominated professions
-      nontraditional careers
-      nontraditional occupations
-      women intensive careers
-      women intensive occupations
-      women intensive professions
- BT occupations
- NT administrative assistants
-      affirmative action officers
-      agents
-      attendants
-      bank tellers
-      beauticians
-      bookkeepers
-      caregivers
-      child care workers

(cont.)

female intensive occupations (*cont.*)
- NT clerks
-      clothing workers
-      coat checkers
-      cooks
-      cosmetologists
-      counselors
-      data entry operators
-      data processors
-      dental hygienists
-      dieticians
-      educators
-      extension workers
-      flight attendants
-      food service workers
-      fortune tellers
-      geishas
-      hairdressers
-      hat checkers
-      healers
-      health care workers
-      home economists
-      homemakers
-      hostesses (historical)
-      household workers
-      housekeepers
-      housemothers
-      ironers
-      launderers
-      librarians
-      library workers
-      masseuses
-      medicine women
-      midwives
-      milliners
-      models
-      nurse practitioners
-      nurses
-      nutritionists
-      paralegals
-      physical therapists
-      physicians' assistants
-      pink collar workers
-      prostitutes
-      psychics
-      real estate agents
-      receptionists

(cont.)

female intensive occupations (*cont.*)

NT sales personnel
secretaries
seers
social workers
stenographers
strippers
teacher aides
teachers
telephone operators
tour guides
typists
volunteers
women religious
RT career choice
corporate spouses
economic value of women's work
household labor
job ghettos
male intensive occupations
mothers
multinational labor force
occupational sex segregation
piecework
political spouses
sex discrimination in employment
sexual division of labor
unpaid labor force
women in

female male friendships

SG Social Sciences and Culture
UF male female friendships
BT female male relationships
friendships

female male relationships

SG Social Sciences and Culture
UF male female relationships
BT personal relationships
NT father daughter relationships
female male friendships
mother son relationships
RT communication styles
interruptions

female Oedipus complex

SG Natural Sciences and Health
BT Oedipus Complex
RT Electra Complex

female sexual slavery

SG History and Social Change
International Women
BT sexual slavery
RT concubinage
harems
odalisques
prostitution
sexual exploitation

female sexuality

SG Natural Sciences and Health
BT sexuality
RT compulsory heterosexuality
gender identity
images of women
lesbians
masturbation
pleasure
sexual identity

female societies

SG History and Social Change
Social Sciences and Culture
BT societies
RT amazons
lesbian communities
matriarchy
matrilineal kinship

female spirituality

SG Language, Literature, Religion, and
Philosophy
BT spirituality
RT ecofeminism
holy women
mediums
saints
visionaries
witches
women religious

females

SN   *Use the term FEMALE or FEMALES to refer to biologically based references to sex; use WOMAN or WOMEN, GIRL or GIRLS to refer to socially or culturally based references to gender.*

SG   History and Social Change
Natural Sciences and Health
Social Sciences and Culture

RT   women

feminine mystique

SN   *Term coined by Betty Friedan to describe oppressive constraints on American womanhood in the '50s.*

SG   History and Social Change
Social Sciences and Culture

RT   cult of true womanhood
domestic code
false consciousness
feminine principle
images of women
reentry women
the woman question
women working outside the home

feminine principle

SN   *Psychological concept of a universal essence, present to varying extents in both men and women but seen as fundamental in women, that dictates laws of human relationships and inner or spiritual worlds.*

SG   History and Social Change
Language, Literature, Religion, and Philosophy

RT   anima
essentialism
feminine mystique
images of women
stereotyping

femininity

SG   Social Sciences and Culture

RT   femme
masculinity

(cont.)

femininity *(cont.)*

RT   sex role stereotyping
stereotyping
women's roles

feminism

SN   *Theories and practices of political, social, and economic equality of the sexes.*

SG   History and Social Change
International Women

DG   Cultural and Political Movements

NT   anarcha feminism
Black feminism
career feminism
cross cultural feminism
cultural feminism
ecofeminism
first wave feminism
global feminism
lesbian feminism
liberal feminism
mainstream feminism
Marxist feminism
nonaligned feminism
protofeminism
psychoanalytic feminism
radical feminism
socialist feminism
spiritual feminism

RT   female chauvinism
feminist theory
feminists
human rights
male feminists
men's liberation
political theory
separatism
sexual politics
sisterhood
social movements
suffrage
the woman question
woman power
woman's rights
women's liberation
women's movement

(cont.)

feminism (*cont.*)
- RT women's rights

feminist criticism
- SG History and Social Change
  Language, Literature, Religion, and
  Philosophy
- DG Cultural and Political Movements
- BT criticism
- RT feminist scholarship
  feminist theory
  feminist writing
  gynocriticism
  l'ecriture feminine
  texts

feminist ethics
- SG History and Social Change
  Language, Literature, Religion, and
  Philosophy
- BT ethics
- RT essentialism
  ethic of care
  feminist methods
  feminist theory
  moral reform
  nonviolence

feminist methods
- SG History and Social Change
- BT methods
- RT collaboration
  consensus
  feminist ethics
  feminist organizations
  feminist theory
  historiography
  networks
  support systems

feminist movement
- SG History and Social Change
- DG Cultural and Political Movements
- BT social movements
- RT consciousness raising
  women's liberation
  women's movement

feminist music
- SG History and Social Change
  Visual and Performing Arts
- BT music
- RT political music
  protest music
  women's music

feminist organizations
- SG History and Social Change
- BT women's organizations
- RT advocacy groups
  feminist methods
  groups
  health advocates
  political action committees
  social clubs
  social movements
  special interest groups
  women's groups

feminist perspective
- SG History and Social Change
- RT feminist scholarship

feminist publications
- SG Communications
  Language, Literature, Religion, and
  Philosophy
- BT publications
  women's media
- RT women's magazines

feminist scholarship
- SG Education
  History and Social Change
  Language, Literature, Religion, and
  Philosophy
- BT scholarship
- RT feminist criticism
  feminist perspective
  feminist theory
  feminist writing
  gynocriticism
  social policy
  texts

feminist studies

SG Education
History and Social Change
Social Sciences and Culture

BT interdisciplinary studies

RT gender studies
men's studies
women's studies

feminist theology

SG Language, Literature, Religion, and
Philosophy

BT theology

NT thealogy

RT freedom of worship
liberation theology
womanist theology

feminist theory

SG History and Social Change

BT theory

RT criticism
economic theory
feminism
feminist criticism
feminist ethics
feminist methods
feminist scholarship
feminist writing
historiography
humanities
ideology
liberal feminism
Marxist feminism
philosophy
political theory
psychoanalytic feminism
race, class, and gender studies
radical feminism
scholarship
sexual politics
social sciences
socialist feminism
womanism

feminist therapy

SG Natural Sciences and Health

(cont.)

feminist therapy *(cont.)*

BT therapy

feminist writing

SG Communications
Language, Literature, Religion, and
Philosophy

BT writing

RT criticism
feminist criticism
feminist scholarship
feminist theory
l'ecriture feminine
literature
texts
womanist writing
women's literature
women's media

feminists

SG History and Social Change
Language, Literature, Religion, and
Philosophy

NT male feminists

RT feminism
suffragists

feminization of occupations

USE **tipping**

feminization of poverty

USE **pauperization of women**
women living in poverty

feminization of professions

USE **tipping**

femmage

SN *Feminist art form that is pieced together, like collage.*

SG Visual and Performing Arts

BT collage

femme

SN *Slang; describes exaggerated "traditional" feminine characteristics.*

SG History and Social Change

(cont.)

femme (*cont.*)
  RT butch
       femininity
       gender roles
       lesbians
       sex role stereotyping

femmes fatales
  SG Language, Literature, Religion, and
       Philosophy
       Social Sciences and Culture
  BT images of women
  RT temptresses
       vagina dentata

fencing
  SG Natural Sciences and Health
  BT sports

fertility
  SG Natural Sciences and Health
  RT childbirth
       insemination
       ovum
       pregnancy
       sperm

fertility drugs
  SG Natural Sciences and Health
  BT drugs
       reproductive technologies
  RT hormone therapy
       hormones
       infertility
       multiple births
       ovulation

fertility rates
  SG Economics and Employment
       Social Sciences and Culture
  BT vital statistics

fertility rites
  SG Social Sciences and Culture
  BT rites
  RT tribal customs

fertilization
  SG Natural Sciences and Health
  NT in vitro fertilization
  RT embryo transfer
       impregnation
       pregnancy
       reproductive cycle
       sperm banks

festivals
  SG Visual and Performing Arts
  BT activities
  NT film festivals
       music festivals
  RT celebrations
       rites

fetal alcohol syndrome
  SG Natural Sciences and Health
  BT diseases
  RT addiction
       alcohol abuse
       alcoholism
       infants
       prenatal influences

fetal monitoring
  SG Natural Sciences and Health
  BT medical procedures
  RT amniocentesis
       childbirth
       genetic counseling
       ultrasound

fetuses
  SG Natural Sciences and Health
  UF unborn child
  RT abortion
       embryos
       pregnancy
       viability

feudalism
  DG Cultural and Political Movements
  RT titles (nobility)

---

feuds
SG   Social Sciences and Culture
RT   aggressive behavior

fiber art
SG   Visual and Performing Arts
BT   visual arts

fibrocystic disease
SG   Natural Sciences and Health
BT   diseases
RT   breast diseases
breasts
uterus

fiction
SG   Language, Literature, Religion, and
Philosophy
BT   prose
NT   mysteries
novels
pulp fiction
romances
science fiction
short stories
RT   creative writing
criticism
fictional characters
texts

fictional characters
SG   Language, Literature, Religion, and
Philosophy
RT   fiction
heroes
heroines (historical)

field hockey
SG   Natural Sciences and Health
BT   sports

fieldwork
SG   Social Sciences and Culture
RT   ethnomethodology
participant observation
research methods

fifth world
SN   *Label applied to women who, as half
of the population worldwide, are
most often used as cheap labor with
the least control over capital or tech
nology.*
SG   Economics and Employment
History and Social Change
International Women
RT   colonialism
exploitation
fourth world
impact on women
international perspective
maquiladora
multinational labor force
sexual division of labor
third world

figurative language
SG   Language, Literature, Religion, and
Philosophy
UF   figures of speech
BT   language
NT   allegory
ambiguity
antithesis
epithets
imagery
irony
metaphors
puns
RT   discourse
literature
mythology
rhetoric
symbols
writing

figures of speech
USE **figurative language**

files
DG   Types and Forms of Materials

Filipino
DG   National and Regional Descriptors
(*cont.*)

Filipino (*cont.*)
  BT Asian

Filipino American
  DG Ethnic, Racial, and Religious
       Descriptors

film
  SG Visual and Performing Arts
  UF cinema
       cinematography
  BT media arts
  NT documentaries
  RT acting
       auteurism
       film criticism
       films
       incidental music
       motion picture industry
       performing arts
       screenplays
       scripts
       videos
       visual arts

film criticism
  SG Visual and Performing Arts
  BT criticism
  RT film

film directors
  SG Communications
       Economics and Employment
       Visual and Performing Arts
  UF directors (film)
  BT arts, entertainment, and media
       occupations

film festivals
  SG Visual and Performing Arts
  BT festivals
  RT visual arts

film producers
  SG Communications
       Economics and Employment
       Visual and Performing Arts
           (*cont.*)

film producers (*cont.*)
  BT arts, entertainment, and media
       occupations

filmographies
  DG Types and Forms of Materials

films
  SG Visual and Performing Arts
  DG Types and Forms of Materials
  UF motion pictures
       movies
  RT actresses (historical)
       casting
       film

filmstrips
  DG Types and Forms of Materials

finance
  SG Economics and Employment
  RT banks

finances
  SG Economics and Employment
  NT family finances
       personal finances

financial aid
  SG Education
       Law, Government, and Public Policy
  BT aid
  NT student financial aid
  RT collegiate athletics
       educational reform
       eligibility
       endowments
       sports

financial arrangements
  SG Economics and Employment
       Law, Government, and Public Policy
  RT alimony
       child custody
       child support
       community property laws
       divorce
           (*cont.*)

F=Use for   BT=Broader term   NT=Narrower term   RT=Related term

financial arrangements (*cont.*)
- RT palimony
- spouse support

financial management
- SG Economics and Employment
- BT management
- RT credit
- fiscal policy

financial occupations
- SG Economics and Employment
- BT occupations
- NT accountants
- bankers
- development specialists
- economists
- financial planners
- financiers
- insurance adjusters
- insurance examiners
- philanthropists
- stockbrokers
- venture capitalists
- RT banking industry
- investors
- professional occupations

financial planners
- SG Economics and Employment
- BT financial occupations
- RT financial planning

financial planning
- SG Economics and Employment
- BT planning
- RT financial planners
- retirement
- retirement benefits

financial resources
- SG Economics and Employment
- BT resources
- RT capital

financial statements
- DG Types and Forms of Materials

(*cont.*)

financial statements (*cont.*)
- BT statements

financiers
- SG Economics and Employment
- BT financial occupations
- RT banks
- venture capitalists

fine arts
- USE **performing arts**
- **visual arts**

finishing schools
- SG Education
- BT private schools
- RT socialization
- upper class

Finnish
- DG National and Regional Descriptors
- BT Scandinavian

fire fighters
- SG Economics and Employment
- Science and Technology
- UF firemen
- BT protective service occupations

fire prevention
- SG Law, Government, and Public Policy
- BT prevention
- RT arson

firemen
- USE **fire fighters**

firing
- SG Economics and Employment
- RT job layoffs
- unemployment

first husbands
- SG Social Sciences and Culture
- BT husbands
- RT blended families
- divorce

(*cont.*)

first husbands *(cont.)*
RT remarriage

First Ladies
USE **governors' spouses**
presidential spouses

First Ladies (historical)
SG Economics and Employment
BT political spouses
women
RT legal and political occupations

first wave feminism
SN *Term describing nineteenth, early twentieth century women's movement.*
SG History and Social Change
DG Cultural and Political Movements
BT feminism
RT suffrage movements
woman's rights

first wives
SG Social Sciences and Culture
BT wives
RT blended families
divorce
remarriage

fiscal policy
SG Economics and Employment
BT policy
RT financial management

fish sellers
SG Economics and Employment
UF fishwives

fishermen
USE **fishers**

fishers
SG Economics and Employment
UF fishermen
BT agricultural, fishing, and forestry occupations

fishwives
USE **fish sellers**

flexible benefits
SG Economics and Employment
BT benefits

flexible career patterns
SG Economics and Employment
RT balancing work and family life
career ladders
career mapping
careers
child care leave
employment
occupational mobility
occupational options
occupational patterns
parental leave

flexible hours
USE **flexible work schedules**

flexible work schedules
SG Economics and Employment
UF flexible hours
flexitime
BT employment schedules
RT four day workweek
home based work
job sharing
work hours

flexitime
USE **flexible work schedules**

flight attendants
SG Economics and Employment
Science and Technology
UF airline stewardesses
stewardesses
BT female intensive occupations
transportation occupations
RT aviation

flirtation
SG Social Sciences and Culture

(cont.)

UF=Use for   BT=Broader term   NT=Narrower term   RT=Related term

flirtation (*cont.*)
BT sex role behavior
RT compliments
     coyness
     flirts
     images of women
     ingratiation
     relationships
     teases

flirts
     SG Social Sciences and Culture
BT images of women
RT flirtation

flowcharts
     DG Types and Forms of Materials
BT charts

flower arranging
     SG Visual and Performing Arts
RT decorative arts
     garden clubs

flower painting
     SG Visual and Performing Arts
BT craft arts

flowers
     SG Natural Sciences and Health
          Social Sciences and Culture
NT bouquets
     corsages
RT gardens

flyers
     DG Types and Forms of Materials

folk art
     SG Visual and Performing Arts
BT art
RT folk culture
     material culture
     naive art
     samplers

folk culture
     SG Social Sciences and Culture
UF folklore
BT culture
NT old wives' tales
RT astrology
     folk art
     folk dance
     folk healers
     folk literature
     folk music
     legends
     magic
     mythology
     rites
     storytelling
     tarot
     traditions

folk dance
     SG Visual and Performing Arts
BT dance
RT folk culture

folk healers
     SG Economics and Employment
          Language, Literature, Religion, and
               Philosophy
          Natural Sciences and Health
BT healers
RT folk culture
     folk medicine
     laying on of hands
     native healers
     spiritualists

folk literature
     SG Language, Literature, Religion, and
               Philosophy
BT literature
NT fables
     fairy tales
     legends
     mythology
     parables
     proverbs
RT allegory

(*cont.*)

SN=Scope note SG=Subject group DG=Delimiters group USE=Use

folk literature (*cont.*)
RT ballads
    epics
    folk culture
    folklorists
    oral tradition
    popular culture

folk medicine
SN *Treatment of ailments in the home and community using remedies based on experience and knowledge handed down from generation to generation.*
SG Natural Sciences and Health
BT medical sciences
RT folk healers
    healing
    herbal remedies
    holistic medicine
    home remedies
    love potions
    medicine women
    menstruation inducing agents
    remedies

folk music
SG Visual and Performing Arts
BT popular music
RT ethnomusicology
    folk culture
    spirituals

folklore
USE **folk culture**

folklorists
SG Economics and Employment
    Language, Literature, Religion, and Philosophy
    Social Sciences and Culture
RT folk literature
    oral tradition

food
SG Economics and Employment
    Natural Sciences and Health
NT food for work

(*cont.*)

food (*cont.*)
RT basic human needs
    cooking
    deprivation
    eating disorders
    gardens
    hunger
    nutrition

food for work
SN *A development project in which the participants, often women, are paid with food.*
SG Economics and Employment
    International Women
BT food
RT exchange theory
    income generation
    money

food industry
SG Economics and Employment
BT industries
RT agricultural, fishing, and forestry occupations
    cooking
    food preparation occupations

food marketing
SG Economics and Employment
    Social Sciences and Culture
RT household labor

food preparation
SG Natural Sciences and Health
    Social Sciences and Culture
RT cooking
    dieticians

food preparation occupations
SG Economics and Employment
    Natural Sciences and Health
BT service occupations
NT bakers
    butchers
    chefs
    cooks

(*cont.*)

UF = Use for   BT = Broader term   NT = Narrower term   RT = Related term

food preparation occupations (*cont.*)
- RT cooking
  dieticians
  food industry
  homemaking
  mothers

food processing
- SG Economics and Employment
- RT food technology
  hygiene

food service workers
- SG Economics and Employment
- BT female intensive occupations
  service occupations
  workers

food stamps
- SG Law, Government, and Public Policy
  Social Sciences and Culture
- BT stamps
- RT family finances
  federal assistance programs
  poverty
  public assistance
  welfare

food technology
- SG Science and Technology
- BT technology
- RT food processing

foot binding
- SG International Women
  Natural Sciences and Health
- RT private sphere
  ritual disfigurement
  seclusion
  violence against women

football
- SG Natural Sciences and Health
- BT sports

forced retirement
- SG Economics and Employment
  (*cont.*)

forced retirement (*cont.*)
- BT retirement
- RT faculty retrenchment
  reduction in force

forecasting
- SG Economics and Employment
- RT data analysis
  econometrics
  mathematical models

foreign affairs
- USE **international relations**

foreign aid
- SG Economics and Employment
  International Women
  Law, Government, and Public Policy
- BT aid
- RT economic development
  famine
  impact on children
  impact on women
  international relations
  technology development

foreign aid policy
- SG Economics and Employment
  International Women
  Law, Government, and Public Policy
- BT international policy
- RT developing nations
  impact on children
  impact on women
  third world

foreign investment policy
- SG Economics and Employment
  International Women
- BT corporate policy
- RT developing nations
  investments
  multinational corporations
  third world

SN=Scope note   SG=Subject group   DG=Delimiters group   USE=Use

foreign service
 SG International Women
    Law, Government, and Public Policy
 RT civil service
   diplomats
   government workers
   international relations

foreign students
 SG Education
    International Women
 BT students
 RT exchange students

foreign workers
 SG Economics and Employment
    International Women
 BT workers
 RT ethnic groups
   global assembly lines
   maquiladora
   migrant workers
   multinational corporations
   multinational labor force
   offshore production plants
   piecework labor policy

foremen
 USE **supervisors**

foremothers
 SG History and Social Change
 BT mothers
 RT protofeminism
   role models
   suffrage movements
   women's history

foreplay
 SG Natural Sciences and Health
 BT sexual behavior
 RT arousal
   sexual satisfaction

forgiveness
 SG Language, Literature, Religion, and
    Philosophy
            (cont.)

forgiveness *(cont.)*
 RT sin
   values

formalism
 DG Cultural and Political Movements

former husbands
 SG Social Sciences and Culture
 UF exhusbands
 BT former spouses
   husbands

former spouses
 SG Social Sciences and Culture
 BT spouses
 NT former husbands
   former wives
 RT divorce
   friendships
   reconciliation

former wives
 SG Social Sciences and Culture
 UF exwives
 BT former spouses
   wives

forms of address
 SG Language, Literature, Religion, and
    Philosophy
 NT Ms
 RT epithets
   language
   name rights
   names
   naming
   titles

forms of affection
 SG Natural Sciences and Health
    Social Sciences and Culture
 NT hugging
   kissing
   listening
   lovemaking
   touching
            (cont.)

UF=Use for BT=Broader term NT=Narrower term RT=Related term

forms of affection *(cont.)*
RT affection
    caregivers
    emotions
    love
    trust

fortune tellers
SG Economics and Employment
    Social Sciences and Culture
BT female intensive occupations
    service occupations
RT mediums

fortune telling
SG Language, Literature, Religion, and
    Philosophy
    Social Sciences and Culture
NT crystal ball gazing
    Ouija boards
    palm reading
    tarot reading
    tea leaf reading
RT astrology
    seances
    seers
    spiritual communication

forums
SG History and Social Change
    Social Sciences and Culture
BT activities

fossil hominids
SN *Ancestors of humans (pre-sapiens) re-*
    ferred to in evolution studies.
SG Social Sciences and Culture
BT human evolution
RT archaeology

foster children
SG Social Sciences and Culture
BT children
RT adoption
    foster homes
    foster parents

foster families
SG Social Sciences and Culture
BT families
RT adopted children

foster grandparents
SG Social Sciences and Culture
BT grandparents

foster homes
SG Social Sciences and Culture
BT facilities
RT adoption
    foster children
    foster parents

foster parents
SG Economics and Employment
    Social Sciences and Culture
BT parents
RT child care workers
    foster children
    foster homes

foundations
SG Economics and Employment
BT nonprofit organizations
RT charities
    fund raising
    grant proposals
    grants
    philanthropists
    philanthropy
    private voluntary organizations

four day workweek
SG Economics and Employment
RT flexible work schedules

four year colleges
SG Education
DG Education Levels
BT higher education

fourth world
SN *Label applied to poorest nonindustrial-*
    ized countries.

(cont.)

fourth world (*cont.*)
  SG Economics and Employment
       History and Social Change
       International Women
  RT colonialism
       economic development
       exploitation
       fifth world
       international perspective
       markets
       sexual division of labor
       technology transfer
       third world
       underdevelopment

franchise
  SG Economics and Employment
  RT enfranchisement
       suffrage

fraternal twins
  SG Natural Sciences and Health
       Social Sciences and Culture
  BT twins

fraternities
  SG Education
  RT initiation rites
       secret societies
       social organizations
       sororities

fraud
  SG Law, Government, and Public Policy
  NT credit fraud
       insurance fraud
       welfare fraud

free association
  SG Social Sciences and Culture
  RT imagination
       psychotherapy

free enterprise
  SG Economics and Employment
  RT advertising
       capitalism

(*cont.*)

free enterprise (*cont.*)
  RT initiative
       laissez faire
       markets
       multinational corporations
       private sector

free love
  USE **sexual liberation**

free schools
  SG Education
  BT schools
  RT alternative schools

free speech
  SG Communications
       Law, Government, and Public Policy
  BT speech
  RT censorship
       freedom of speech
       freedom of the press
       social movements

free trade zones
  SN *Enclaves within countries that are partially or totally exempt from customs and tax levies and other national laws and decrees.*
  SG Economics and Employment
       International Women
  RT international trade policy
       laissez faire
       markets
       multinational corporations

freedom
  SG History and Social Change
       Law, Government, and Public Policy
  RT democracy
       equal opportunity
       equality
       freedoms
       manumission
       rights
       sanctuaries
       sexual liberation

freedom from oppression
  SG   International Women
       Law, Government, and Public Policy
  RT   oppression
       political oppression

freedom of assembly
  SG   Language, Literature, Religion, and
       Philosophy
       Law, Government, and Public Policy
  BT   civil liberties
  RT   civil rights
       freedoms
       political rights

freedom of choice
  SG   Law, Government, and Public Policy
  RT   abortion rights
       freedoms
       women's rights

freedom of information
  SG   Communications
       Law, Government, and Public Policy
  RT   freedom of the press
       information
       intelligence agencies
       libraries
       right to know legislation

freedom of speech
  SG   Communications
  BT   civil liberties
  RT   censorship
       civil rights
       democracy
       due process
       free speech
       freedom of the press
       freedoms
       political rights
       pornography

freedom of the press
  SG   Communications
       Law, Government, and Public Policy
  RT   censorship

                        (cont.)

freedom of the press *(cont.)*
  RT   civil rights
       editorials
       free speech
       freedom of information
       freedom of speech
       freedoms
       libel
       media coverage
       political rights
       women's media

freedom of worship
  SG   Language, Literature, Religion, and
       Philosophy
       Law, Government, and Public Policy
  UF   religious freedom
  BT   civil liberties
  RT   civil rights
       dogma
       ecumenism
       feminist theology
       freedoms
       political rights
       religious beliefs
       religious pluralism
       religious reforms
       state religion

freedoms
  SG   History and Social Change
       Law, Government, and Public Policy
  NT   academic freedom
       reproductive freedom
       sexual freedom
  RT   freedom
       freedom of assembly
       freedom of choice
       freedom of speech
       freedom of the press
       freedom of worship
       human rights

French
  DG   National and Regional Descriptors
  BT   European

SN=Scope note   SG=Subject group   DG=Delimiters group   USE=Use

French Revolution
DG　Historical Periods

Freudianism
DG　Cultural and Political Movements

friends
SG　Social Sciences and Culture
RT　friendships
　　lovers
　　support systems

friendships
SG　History and Social Change
　　Social Sciences and Culture
BT　personal relationships
NT　female friendships
　　female male friendships
　　male friendships
RT　children
　　former spouses
　　friends
　　love
　　sisterhood

frigidity
USE　**nonorgasmic women**

fringe benefits
SG　Economics and Employment
BT　benefits
RT　employee benefits

frontier life
SG　History and Social Change
RT　homesteading

frustration
SG　Social Sciences and Culture
BT　emotions
RT　boredom
　　coping strategies

fund raising
SG　Economics and Employment
RT　appropriations
　　endowments

(cont.)

fund raising *(cont.)*
RT　equity funding
　　federally sponsored research
　　foundations
　　fund raising events
　　funding
　　grant proposals
　　grants
　　in kind contributions

fund raising events
SG　Economics and Employment
　　History and Social Change
　　Social Sciences and Culture
BT　activities
NT　charity balls
RT　fund raising
　　philanthropy

fundamentalism
SG　Language, Literature, Religion, and
　　　Philosophy
DG　Cultural and Political Movements
RT　dogmatism
　　end time thinking
　　religious beliefs
　　religious movements
　　the religious right

funding
SG　Economics and Employment
NT　grants
　　in kind contributions
RT　appropriations
　　awards
　　fund raising
　　nonprofit organizations
　　philanthropy
　　sponsored research

funeral rites
SG　Social Sciences and Culture
BT　rites
RT　burial
　　death
　　death and dying
　　obituaries

(cont.)

UF=Use for　　BT=Broader term　　NT=Narrower term　　RT=Related term　　　　　　　193

funeral rites (*cont.*)
  RT suttee

furniture
  SG Visual and Performing Arts
  RT antiques
      decorative arts
      design
      fashion
      house design
      material culture

future
  DG Historical Periods

future studies
  SG Education
      Social Sciences and Culture
  BT interdisciplinary studies
  RT futurism

futurism
  SG Education
      Language, Literature, Religion, and
          Philosophy
  DG Cultural and Political Movements
  RT future studies

G spot
  SG Natural Sciences and Health
  RT arousal
      vagina

gallantry
  SG Social Sciences and Culture
  BT manners

galleries
  SG Visual and Performing Arts
  RT alternative spaces
      art shows
      one woman art shows
      salons

Gambian
  DG National and Regional Descriptors
  BT African

gambling
  SG Economics and Employment
      Social Sciences and Culture
  RT addiction
      organized crime
      social prohibitions
      substance abuse

game shows
  SG Communications
  BT shows
  RT consumerism
      television

game theory
  SG Economics and Employment
      Social Sciences and Culture
  BT theory
  RT games

games
  SG Social Sciences and Culture
  NT video games
  RT competitive behavior
      game theory
      leisure

gang rape
  SG Social Sciences and Culture
  BT rape

gangs
  SG Education
      Law, Government, and Public Policy
      Social Sciences and Culture
  RT juvenile delinquency
      peer influence

garden clubs
  SG Social Sciences and Culture
  BT clubs
  RT flower arranging
      gardens

Garden of Eden
  SG Language, Literature, Religion, and
          Philosophy

(*cont.*)

Garden of Eden *(cont.)*
RT Adam
devil
Eve
snakes

gardeners
SG Economics and Employment
Natural Sciences and Health
BT agricultural, fishing, and forestry
occupations

gardens
SG Economics and Employment
Natural Sciences and Health
RT flowers
food
garden clubs

garment industry
SG Economics and Employment
BT industries
NT millinery trade
RT clothing workers

gas utilities
SG Law, Government, and Public Policy
Science and Technology
BT utilities

gatekeeping
SG Economics and Employment
Education
RT discrimination
institutional racism
institutional sexism
presidency

gay couples
SG History and Social Change
Social Sciences and Culture
BT couples
NT gay male couples
lesbian couples
RT gay marriage
relationships

gay culture
SG History and Social Change
Social Sciences and Culture
BT culture
NT gay male culture
lesbian culture
RT gay pride
gays

gay experience
SG History and Social Change
Social Sciences and Culture
BT experience
NT gay male experience
lesbian experience
RT minority experience

gay fathers
SG History and Social Change
Social Sciences and Culture
BT fathers
RT child custody
custody
gay male couples
gay stepfathers
lesbian mothers
parenthood
parenting

gay female culture
USE **lesbian culture**

gay female experience
USE **lesbian experience**

gay literature
SG History and Social Change
Language, Literature, Religion, and
Philosophy
BT literature
NT gay male literature
lesbian literature
RT gay studies

gay male couples
SG History and Social Change
Social Sciences and Culture
(cont.)

gay male couples (*cont.*)
BT gay couples
RT gay fathers
   lesbian couples

gay male culture
SG History and Social Change
   Social Sciences and Culture
BT gay culture
RT gay male experience
   homosexuality
   lesbian culture

gay male experience
SG History and Social Change
   Natural Sciences and Health
   Social Sciences and Culture
BT gay experience
RT gay male culture
   gay pride
   homophile movement
   lesbian experience

gay male literature
SG History and Social Change
   Language, Literature, Religion, and
      Philosophy
BT gay literature

gay male marriage
SG History and Social Change
   Social Sciences and Culture
BT gay marriage
RT lesbian marriage

gay male relationships
SG Natural Sciences and Health
   Social Sciences and Culture
BT gay relationships
   male male relationships

gay males
   USE **gay men**

gay marriage
SG History and Social Change
   Social Sciences and Culture
(*cont.*)

gay marriage (*cont.*)
UF homosexual marriage
BT marriage
NT gay male marriage
   lesbian marriage
RT families
   gay couples

gay men
SG History and Social Change
   Social Sciences and Culture
UF gay males
   male homosexuals
BT gays
   men
RT acquired immune deficiency syndrome
   bisexuality
   child rearing practices
   children
   couples
   heterosexuality
   homophobia
   life styles
   stereotyping

gay pride
SG History and Social Change
   Social Sciences and Culture
BT pride
RT gay culture
   gay male experience
   lesbian experience

gay relationships
SG Natural Sciences and Health
   Social Sciences and Culture
UF homosexual relationships
BT personal relationships
NT gay male relationships
   lesbian relationships

gay rights
SG History and Social Change
   Law, Government, and Public Policy
BT rights
RT discrimination
   homophile movement
(*cont.*)

gay rights (*cont.*)
RT homophobia
lesbians
lesbophobia

gay stepfathers
SG History and Social Change
Social Sciences and Culture
BT stepfathers
RT blended families
gay fathers
lesbian stepmothers
parent child relationships

gay stepmothers
USE **lesbian stepmothers**

gay studies
SG Education
History and Social Change
Social Sciences and Culture
BT interdisciplinary studies
NT lesbian studies
RT gay literature

gay women
USE **lesbians**

gay/straight split
SN *Term used to describe lesbian/hetero-
sexual conflict in early '70s women's
movement.*
SG History and Social Change
Social Sciences and Culture
RT compulsory heterosexuality
lesbian experience
lesbian feminism
lesbian separatism
lesbophobia

gays
SG History and Social Change
Social Sciences and Culture
UF homosexuals
NT gay men
lesbians
RT gay culture

(*cont.*)

gays (*cont.*)
RT homosexuality
passing

gazetteers
DG Types and Forms of Materials

geishas
SG Economics and Employment
International Women
Visual and Performing Arts
BT arts, entertainment, and media
occupations
female intensive occupations
images of women
women
RT concubinage
courtesans
mistresses
prostitutes

gender
SN *Use **gender** for socially or culturally
based references, **sex** for biologically
based references.*
SG History and Social Change
Social Sciences and Culture
RT gender development
gender ideology
race, class, and gender studies
sex
sex/gender systems
social construction of gender
social stratification
socialization
stratification

gender bias
SG History and Social Change
Social Sciences and Culture
BT bias
RT discrimination
sex/gender systems
test bias

UF=Use for   BT=Broader term   NT=Narrower term   RT=Related term

gender development
  SG History and Social Change
      Natural Sciences and Health
  BT individual development
  RT gender
      gender ideology
      men's roles
      sex role development
      sex/gender systems
      social construction of gender
      social organization
      women's roles

gender differences
  SG History and Social Change
      Social Sciences and Culture
  BT differences
  RT sex differences
      sex/gender systems
      stereotypes

gender diversity
  SG History and Social Change
      Social Sciences and Culture
  BT diversity
  RT critical mass
      pluralism

gender gap
  SN *A quantitative difference observed be-*
      tween men's and women's voting
      patterns for particular candidates or
      on particular issues.
  SG History and Social Change
      Law, Government, and Public Policy
  RT elected officials
      opinion polls
      voting behavior
      voting records
      women in politics

gender identity
  SG Natural Sciences and Health
  BT identity
  RT cross sex identity
      female sexuality
      sexual identity

(cont.)

gender identity *(cont.)*
  RT sexual preference
      social construction of gender

gender ideology
  SG History and Social Change
      Social Sciences and Culture
  BT ideology
  RT gender
      gender development
      public sphere
      separate spheres
      sex/gender systems
      social construction of gender
      women's roles

gender marking
  SN *A linguistics term used to describe the*
      presence of female or male designa-
      tions in words.
  SG Language, Literature, Religion, and
      Philosophy
  RT false generics
      invisibility
      language
      linguistic sexism
      male norms
      masculine pronouns
      nonsexist language
      patriarchal language
      sexist language
      sociolinguistics

gender roles
  SG History and Social Change
      Natural Sciences and Health
      Social Sciences and Culture
  BT roles
  RT butch
      fathers
      femme
      household division of labor
      machismo
      sex roles
      sex/gender systems
      sexual politics
      social construction of gender

gender studies
- SG Education
  - History and Social Change
  - Social Sciences and Culture
- BT interdisciplinary studies
- RT feminist studies
  - men's studies
  - race, class, and gender studies
  - women's studies

general anesthesia
- SG Natural Sciences and Health
- BT anesthesia
- RT surgery

generation gap
- SG Social Sciences and Culture
- RT family history

generative grammar
- SG Language, Literature, Religion, and
  - Philosophy
- BT grammar

generic pronouns
- SN *Masculine pronouns (he, him, his)
  traditionally claimed to cover any
  member of a species, female or male,
  as well as to designate specifically
  "male."*
- SG Language, Literature, Religion, and
  - Philosophy
- BT pronouns
- RT false generics
  - faulty generalization
  - invisibility
  - linguistic sexism
  - male norms
  - sexist language

genetic counseling
- SG Natural Sciences and Health
- BT counseling
- RT amniocentesis
  - birth defects
  - fetal monitoring
  - genetic screening

(cont.)

genetic counseling *(cont.)*
- RT inbreeding
  - induced abortion

genetic defects
- SG Natural Sciences and Health
- RT amniocentesis
  - genetic determinants
  - genetic screening
  - hereditary diseases

genetic determinants
- SG Natural Sciences and Health
- RT chromosome disorders
  - genetic defects
  - heredity

genetic engineering
- SG Natural Sciences and Health
- RT bioethics
  - cloning
  - eugenics
  - heredity
  - in vitro fertilization
  - medical procedures
  - reproductive technologies

genetic screening
- SG Natural Sciences and Health
- BT medical procedures
- RT blood tests
  - chromosome disorders
  - donors
  - genetic counseling
  - genetic defects
  - sperm banks

geneticists
- SG Economics and Employment
  - Natural Sciences and Health
- BT scientists

genetics
- SG Natural Sciences and Health
- BT biological sciences
- NT population genetics
- RT bioethics

(cont.)

UF=Use for   BT=Broader term   NT=Narrower term   RT=Related term

genetics (*cont.*)
RT   heredity

genital herpes
SG   Natural Sciences and Health
UF   herpes simplex virus type II
BT   sexually transmitted diseases

genital mutilation
SG   Natural Sciences and Health
RT   castration
    clitoridectomy
    female circumcision
    infibulation
    ritual disfigurement
    vulvectomy

genitalia
USE   **genitals**

genitals
SG   Natural Sciences and Health
UF   genitalia
    private parts
BT   bodies
NT   clitoris
    labia
    penis
    scrotum
    testicles
    vulva
RT   sexual excitement
    vagina

genocide
SG   History and Social Change
    International Women
RT   antisemitism
    colonialism
    concentration camps
    gynocide
    holocaust
    indigenous populations
    murder
    persecution

geographic mobility
SG   Economics and Employment
    History and Social Change
BT   mobility
RT   career family conflict
    career opportunities
    occupational mobility
    relocation

geography
SG   Science and Technology
BT   social sciences
NT   economic geography
    social geography
RT   atlases
    demographic measurements

geologists
SG   Economics and Employment
    Science and Technology
BT   scientists

geology
SG   Science and Technology
BT   earth sciences

geriatrics
SG   Natural Sciences and Health
BT   medical sciences
RT   aging
    gerontology
    older adults
    senior citizens

German
DG   National and Regional Descriptors
BT   European

German measles
USE   **rubella**

gerontology
SG   Social Sciences and Culture
BT   interdisciplinary studies
    social sciences
RT   aging
    geriatrics

SN=Scope note   SG=Subject group   DG=Delimiters group   USE=Use

gestalt therapy
  SG Social Sciences and Culture
  BT therapy

gestation
  USE **pregnancy**

gestation period
  SG Natural Sciences and Health
  RT pregnancy
      pregnancy trimesters

gestures
  SG Language, Literature, Religion, and
      Philosophy
  BT nonverbal communication
  RT body language
      kinesics
      nonverbal language
      semiotics
      sign language
      talk

Ghanaian
  DG National and Regional Descriptors
  BT African

ghettos
  SG Law, Government, and Public Policy
      Social Sciences and Culture
  BT ethnic neighborhoods
  RT inner city
      poverty
      segregation
      slum landlords
      social class
      urban renewal

gigolos
  SG Social Sciences and Culture
  BT service occupations
  RT extramarital affairs
      mistresses

girdles
  SG History and Social Change
      Natural Sciences and Health
                              (*cont.*)

girdles (*cont.*)
  BT lingerie
  RT body image
      brassieres
      corsets
      padding
      ritual disfigurement

girl Fridays
  USE **administrative assistants**

girl preference of parents
  SG Natural Sciences and Health
      Social Sciences and Culture
  RT boy preference of parents
      sex preselection
      sex selection

girl watching
  USE **street harassment**

girls
  SN *Use **girls** to refer to female children
      under eighteen years of age.*
  SG Natural Sciences and Health
      Social Sciences and Culture
  BT children
  RT women

glamour
  SG Social Sciences and Culture
  RT beauty standards

glands
  SG Natural Sciences and Health
  BT bodies
  NT lymph glands
      mammary glands
      pituitary gland
      thyroid gland
  RT hormones

glass ceiling
  SN *Invisible but pervasive career barrier
      encountered by women seeking to
      advance to senior positions.*
  SG Economics and Employment
                              (*cont.*)

UF=Use for   BT=Broader term   NT=Narrower term   RT=Related term

glass ceiling (*cont.*)
- BT discriminatory practices
- RT businesswomen
  - institutional discrimination
  - institutional sexism
  - job discrimination
  - job ghettos
  - promotions

glassmakers
- SG Economics and Employment
  - Visual and Performing Arts
- BT arts, entertainment, and media
  - occupations

glaziers
- SG Economics and Employment
  - Science and Technology
- BT construction occupations

global assembly lines
- SN *Refers to workers in developing countries employed doing light assembly work in multinational plants.*
- SG Economics and Employment
  - International Women
- BT multinational corporation policy
- RT developing nations
  - foreign workers
  - international division of labor
  - piecework labor policy

global economy
- SG Economics and Employment
  - International Women
- BT economy
- RT balance of payments
  - black markets
  - dual economy
  - economic growth
  - global village
  - international division of labor
  - international trade policy
  - multinational corporations
  - multinational labor force

global feminism
- SG History and Social Change
  - International Women
- DG Cultural and Political Movements
- UF international feminism
- BT feminism
- RT diversity
  - International Decade for Women
  - international perspective
  - international women's movement
  - nationality
  - nonaligned feminism

global security
- SG History and Social Change
  - International Women
  - Law, Government, and Public Policy
- BT security
- RT peace movements
  - ratification
  - treaty ratification

global village
- SG International Women
  - Social Sciences and Culture
- RT global economy
  - markets

glossaries
- DG Types and Forms of Materials

glossolalia
- SG Language, Literature, Religion, and
  - Philosophy
- UF speaking in tongues
- BT spiritual communication

gnosticism
- DG Cultural and Political Movements

goals
- USE **objectives**

God the father
- SG Language, Literature, Religion, and
  - Philosophy
- BT gods

(*cont.*)

God the father (*cont.*)

RT deity
    discriminatory language
    divine kingship
    divinity
    false generics
    fathers
    immaculate conception
    male norms
    Mother/Father God
    patriarchal language
    patriarchal religion
    patriarchs
    patronymy
    phallogocentrism
    religion
    religious language

goddess worship

SG Language, Literature, Religion, and
    Philosophy
BT worship
RT cult of the virgin
    goddesses
    spiritual feminism
    thealogy
    wicca

goddesses

SG History and Social Change
    Language, Literature, Religion, and
    Philosophy
BT images of women
NT mother goddess
    Mother/Father God
RT deity
    divinity
    earth mother
    goddess worship
    gods
    matriarchy
    matronymy
    mother earth
    mythology
    pantheon
    religion
    rites

(*cont.*)

goddesses (*cont.*)

RT spirituality
    thealogy
    Virgin Mary
    womanspirit
    worship

gods

SG Language, Literature, Religion, and
    Philosophy
NT God the father
    Mother/Father God
RT deity
    divinity
    goddesses
    mythology
    pantheon
    patriarchy
    patronymy
    religion
    rites
    spirituality
    theology
    worship

golf

SG Natural Sciences and Health
BT sports

gonorrhea

SG Natural Sciences and Health
BT sexually transmitted diseases

gospel music

SG Visual and Performing Arts
BT religious music
RT spirituals

gossip

SG Language, Literature, Religion, and
    Philosophy
BT verbal communication
RT advice columns
    conversation
    grapevine
    language
    talk

Gothic style
DG Cultural and Political Movements

governance
SG Economics and Employment
RT administration
boards of directors
institutional racism
institutional sexism
management

governesses
SG Economics and Employment
Social Sciences and Culture
BT child care workers
women

governing boards
SG Education
UF boards of governors
boards of regents
boards of trustees
school boards
BT boards
RT boards of directors
power
trustees

government
SG Law, Government, and Public Policy
NT city government
county government
federal government
local government
state government
student government
RT appropriations
budgeting
bureaucracy
democracy
organizations
politics
public sector
social structure
state formation
the state

government agencies
SG International Women
Law, Government, and Public Policy
BT agencies

government appointments
SG Law, Government, and Public Policy
UF appointive positions
RT appointed officials
loyalty oaths

government documents
DG Types and Forms of Materials
BT documents

government workers
SG Economics and Employment
Law, Government, and Public Policy
BT legal and political occupations
service occupations
workers
RT civil service
foreign service
mail carriers
public service

governors
SG Economics and Employment
Law, Government, and Public Policy
BT elected officials

governors' spouses
SG Law, Government, and Public Policy
UF First Ladies
BT political spouses
RT legal and political occupations

graciousness
SG Social Sciences and Culture
BT manners

graduate degrees
SG Education
UF advanced degrees
BT degrees
NT doctoral degrees
masters' degrees

(cont.)

SN=Scope note   SG=Subject group   DG=Delimiters group   USE=Use

graduate degrees (*cont.*)
- RT   graduate education
  - postdoctoral fellowships
  - professional education

graduate education
- SG   Education
- DG   Education Levels
- BT   higher education
- RT   graduate degrees

graduation ceremonies
- SG   Education
- BT   ceremonies
- RT   degrees
  - honorary degrees
  - students

graffiti
- DG   Types and Forms of Materials

grammar
- SG   Language, Literature, Religion, and
  - Philosophy
- NT   generative grammar
  - transformational grammar
- RT   language structure

gramsevika
- SN   *Village-level extension workers in rural*
  - *India.*
- SG   Economics and Employment
  - International Women
- BT   extension workers
- RT   animatrices rurales

grandchildren
- SG   Social Sciences and Culture
- BT   children
- NT   granddaughters
  - grandsons
- RT   families
  - family structure
  - grandparents

granddaughters
- SG   Social Sciences and Culture

(*cont.*)

granddaughters (*cont.*)
- BT   grandchildren
  - women

grandfathers
- SG   Social Sciences and Culture
- BT   grandparents
  - men

grandmothers
- SG   Social Sciences and Culture
- BT   grandparents
  - women

grandparents
- SG   Social Sciences and Culture
- NT   foster grandparents
  - grandfathers
  - grandmothers
- RT   custody
  - families
  - family structure
  - grandchildren
  - parenting

grandsons
- SG   Social Sciences and Culture
- BT   grandchildren
  - men

granny midwives
- USE **lay midwives**

grant proposals
- SG   Economics and Employment
- BT   proposals
- RT   foundations
  - fund raising
  - proposal writing
  - referees

grant writing
- USE **proposal writing**

grants
- SG   Education
- BT   funding

(*cont.*)

---

grants (*cont.*)

NT block grants
research grants
tuition grants
RT budgeting
foundations
fund raising
proposal writing
referees
student financial aid

grapevine

SN *Informal communication network involving circles of acquaintances who provide information often faster than formal communication channels.*
SG Communications
Education
RT gossip
information dissemination
old boy networks
old girl networks
organizational behavior

graphic design

SG Visual and Performing Arts
BT design
RT printmaking
sign painters

graphics

SG Communications
Visual and Performing Arts
BT commercial art
visual arts
RT iconography
illustration
printers

graphs

DG Types and Forms of Materials

grass roots

SN *Society at the local level.*
SG History and Social Change
International Women
RT local politics

(*cont.*)

grass roots (*cont.*)

RT organizing
populism
social action
social movements

gray power

SG History and Social Change
Law, Government, and Public Policy
Social Sciences and Culture
BT power
RT age discrimination
age stereotypes
ageism
aging
older adults
senior citizens
Social Security

Great Awakening

DG Historical Periods

Great Depression

DG Historical Periods

greed

SG Language, Literature, Religion, and Philosophy
BT emotions
RT sin

Greek

DG National and Regional Descriptors
BT European

Greek American

DG Ethnic, Racial, and Religious Descriptors

Grenadan

DG National and Regional Descriptors
BT West Indian

grief

SG Social Sciences and Culture
BT emotions
RT bereavement

(*cont.*)

SN=Scope note   SG=Subject group   DG=Delimiters group   USE=Use

grief (*cont.*)

RT death
emotional adjustment
loss
mourning
sadness

grievance procedures

SG Economics and Employment

RT discrimination

grooming behavior

SN *Parasite removal as a sign of hierarchy or sexual favor.*

SG Social Sciences and Culture

BT animal behavior

grooms

SG Social Sciences and Culture

BT men

RT brides
wedding ceremonies

gross income

SG Economics and Employment

BT income

group behavior

SG Natural Sciences and Health
Social Sciences and Culture

UF collective behavior

BT behavior

RT group dynamics
peer influence

group counseling

SG Social Sciences and Culture

BT counseling

group developed theater

SG Visual and Performing Arts

BT theater

group dynamics

SG Social Sciences and Culture

RT body language
group behavior

(*cont.*)

group dynamics (*cont.*)

RT group process
groups
organizations
perceptual bias
rites
stereotyping
synchrony
synergy

group marriage

SG Social Sciences and Culture

BT marriage

group process

SG Social Sciences and Culture

BT process

RT collaboration
consensus building
group dynamics
leadership

group sex

SG Natural Sciences and Health

BT sexual behavior

group therapy

SG Social Sciences and Culture

BT therapy

groups

SG Social Sciences and Culture

NT advocacy groups
children's groups
citizen groups
cohorts
communal groups
consciousness raising groups
cultural groups
disadvantaged groups
discussion groups
encounter groups
ethnic groups
factions
heterogeneous groups
homogeneous groups
minority groups

(*cont.*)

UF=Use for   BT=Broader term   NT=Narrower term   RT=Related term

groups *(cont.)*
- NT   mixed sex groups
  - pressure groups
  - religious groups
  - special interest groups
  - study groups
  - support groups
  - women's groups
- RT   affiliation
  - community
  - feminist organizations
  - group dynamics
  - networks
  - organizations

growth
- USE **physical development**

guaranteed income
- SG   Economics and Employment
- BT   income

guardians
- SG   Social Sciences and Culture
- NT   legal guardians
- RT   chattels
  - executors
  - family courts
  - protection
  - spokespersons
  - wards

guards
- SG   Economics and Employment
- UF   watchmen
- BT   protective service occupations
- NT   security guards

Guatemalan
- DG   National and Regional Descriptors
- BT   Central American

guerrilla warfare
- SG   Law, Government, and Public Policy
- BT   warfare

guidelines
- DG   Types and Forms of Materials

guides
- DG   Types and Forms of Materials
- NT   curriculum guides
  - how to guides

guilt
- SG   Social Sciences and Culture
- BT   emotions
- RT   penance
  - religious practices
  - religious repression
  - self denial
  - sexual behavior
  - sin
  - superego

Guinean
- DG   National and Regional Descriptors
- BT   African

gun control laws
- SG   Law, Government, and Public Policy
- BT   laws
- RT   weapons

Guyanese
- DG   National and Regional Descriptors
- BT   Latin American

gymnastics
- SG   Natural Sciences and Health
- BT   sports

gynarchy
- SN   *Government by women.*
- SG   History and Social Change
  - Social Sciences and Culture
- RT   essentialism
  - lesbian separatism
  - matriarchy

gynecologic disorders
- SG   Natural Sciences and Health
- BT   disorders

(cont.)

gynecologic disorders (*cont.*)
NT menstrual disorders
vaginismus
vaginitis

gynecology
SG Natural Sciences and Health
BT medical sciences

gynocide
SN *Murder of women.*
SG Social Sciences and Culture
BT murder
RT bride burning
genocide
infanticide
suttee
witch burning
witch persecutions

gynocologists
SG Natural Sciences and Health
BT health care occupations

gynocriticism
SN *Study of the history, themes, genres,
and structures of literature by wo-
men; also used to define psychody-
namics of female creativity.*
SG History and Social Change
Language, Literature, Religion, and
Philosophy
DG Cultural and Political Movements
BT criticism
RT feminist criticism
feminist scholarship
literary criticism

Gypsy
DG Ethnic, Racial, and Religious
Descriptors

hagiography
SG Language, Literature, Religion, and
Philosophy
RT biography
holy women

(*cont.*)

hagiography (*cont.*)
RT iconography
religious symbols
saints

haiku
SG Language, Literature, Religion, and
Philosophy
BT poetry

hair
SG Natural Sciences and Health
BT bodies
NT body hair
pubic hair
RT beauty standards
coiffures
hair loss
hormones
wigs

hair dryers
SG Social Sciences and Culture
RT hair styles

hair loss
SG Natural Sciences and Health
UF balding
RT body image
hair
hair styles
wigs

hair removal
SG Natural Sciences and Health
UF depilation
RT body image
depilatories
electrolysis

hair straightening
SG Social Sciences and Culture
RT hair styles

hair styles
SG Social Sciences and Culture
NT Afros

(*cont.*)

UF=Use for   BT=Broader term   NT=Narrower term   RT=Related term

hair styles (*cont.*)

NT bangs
    braids
    curls
    ponytails
RT beauty parlors
    body image
    coiffures
    curlers
    hair dryers
    hair loss
    hair straightening
    hairdressers
    images of girls
    images of women
    permanents

hairdressers

SG Economics and Employment
BT female intensive occupations
    service occupations
RT beauticians
    hair styles

Haitian

DG National and Regional Descriptors
BT West Indian

Haitian American

DG Ethnic, Racial, and Religious
    Descriptors

halfway houses

SG History and Social Change
    Social Sciences and Culture
BT facilities
    houses
    temporary housing
RT alternative programs
    deinstitutionalization
    mainstreaming
    probation
    restitution

hand eye coordination

SG Education
    Natural Sciences and Health

(*cont.*)

hand eye coordination (*cont.*)

BT motor skills
RT reaction times
    sports
    video games

handbooks

DG Types and Forms of Materials
BT books

handicapped

USE **disabled**

handicrafts

USE **craft arts**

handmade

SG Economics and Employment
    Visual and Performing Arts
UF manmade
RT craft arts

happiness

SG Social Sciences and Culture
BT emotions

harems

SG History and Social Change
    International Women
RT concubinage
    eunuchs
    families
    female friendships
    female sexual slavery
    hidjab
    living arrangements
    odalisques
    private sphere
    purdah
    seclusion
    separate spheres
    seraglios
    sex objects
    slavery
    space
    veils

harlots

   SG History and Social Change
        Social Sciences and Culture
BT images of women
RT prostitutes

hat check girls

USE **hat checkers**

hat checkers

   SG Economics and Employment
UF hat check girls
BT female intensive occupations
      service occupations

hate

   SG Social Sciences and Culture
BT emotions
RT prejudice

Hawaiian

   DG National and Regional Descriptors
BT Pacific

hazardous waste

   SG Science and Technology
UF toxic waste
RT carcinogens
      chemical industry
      corporate liability
      environmental racism
      hazards
      health hazards
      industrial hazards
      industries
      pollution

hazards

   SG Economics and Employment
        Natural Sciences and Health
NT environmental hazards
      health hazards
      household hazards
      industrial hazards
      work hazards
RT accidents
      hazardous waste

(cont.)

hazards *(cont.)*

RT right to know legislation
      safety

he/man language

   SN *Term used to describe most blatant*
        forms of linguistic sexism.
   SG Language, Literature, Religion, and
        Philosophy
BT patriarchal language
      sexist language
RT false generics
      linguistic sexism
      masculine pronouns
      pronoun envy

Head Start programs

   SN *Education and welfare programs for 3-*
        to 5-year olds introduced in 1965 by
        the US government.
   SG Education
BT educational programs
RT day care centers
      preschools

headaches

   SG Natural Sciences and Health
NT migraine headaches
      tension headaches

headhunters

USE **executive recruitment**

headmasters

USE **principals**

headmistresses

USE **principals**

heads of families

   SG Economics and Employment
        Social Sciences and Culture
RT families
      householders

heads of households

USE **householders**

---

heads of state

SG Economics and Employment
      International Women
      Law, Government, and Public Policy
BT legal and political occupations

healers

SG Economics and Employment
      Language, Literature, Religion, and
         Philosophy
      Natural Sciences and Health
BT female intensive occupations
      health care occupations
NT faith healers
      folk healers
      native healers
RT crones
      healing
      medicine women
      midwives
      shamans
      wisdom
      witches

healing

SG Language, Literature, Religion, and
         Philosophy
      Natural Sciences and Health
RT folk medicine
      healers
      holistic medicine
      home remedies
      medical sciences
      prayer
      religion
      rites
      salvation
      witchcraft
      women's health movement

health

SG Natural Sciences and Health
NT environmental health
      holistic health
      mental health
      occupational health and safety
      physical health

(cont.)

health *(cont.)*

NT reproductive health
RT basic human needs
      health seeking behavior
      nutrition
      wellness
      women's health movement

health advocates

SG Natural Sciences and Health
BT advocates
NT mental health advocates
RT consumer health organizations
      feminist organizations
      women's health movement

health behavior

SG Natural Sciences and Health
BT behavior
NT health seeking behavior
RT health care utilization
      sexual behavior
      social behavior

health care

SG Natural Sciences and Health
BT care
NT home health care
      medical care
      prenatal care
RT community health services
      epidemiology
      equal access
      health care utilization
      health insurance
      women's health movement

health care costs

SG Natural Sciences and Health
BT costs
RT health care providers
      health insurance

health care delivery

SG Natural Sciences and Health
RT health care legislation
      health care services

(cont.)

SN=Scope note   SG=Subject group   DG=Delimiters group   USE=Use

health care delivery (*cont.*)

- RT   health care utilization
  health cooperatives
  health insurance
  health maintenance organizations
  home health care
  National Health Service (Great Britain)
  public health

health care facilities

- SG   Natural Sciences and Health
- BT   facilities
- NT   extended care facilities
  hospices
  hospitals
  neighborhood health centers
  nursing homes
- RT   certification
  clinics
  community health services
  health cooperatives
  licensing

health care legislation

- SN   *See also Delimiters Display: Laws and Regulations.*
- SG   Law, Government, and Public Policy
  Natural Sciences and Health
- BT   legislation
- RT   health care delivery
  health care policy
  public health

health care occupations

- SG   Natural Sciences and Health
- BT   occupations
- NT   anesthesiologists
  animal caretakers
  chiropodists
  chiropractors
  dental hygienists
  dentists
  dieticians
  family practitioners
  gynocologists
  healers
  health care workers

                                 (*cont.*)

health care occupations (*cont.*)

- NT   medicine women
  midwives
  nurse practitioners
  nurses
  nutritionists
  obstetricians
  optometrists
  paramedics
  pediatricians
  pharmacists
  physicians
  physicians' assistants
  podiatrists
  psychiatrists
  psychologists
  surgeons
  therapists
  veterinarians
- RT   health care providers
  pharmaceutical industry
  professional occupations
  scientific and technical occupations

health care policy

- SG   Natural Sciences and Health
- BT   policy
- RT   deinstitutionalization
  health care legislation
  health maintenance organizations
  socialized medicine

health care providers

- SG   Natural Sciences and Health
- RT   health care costs
  health care occupations
  health care services

health care services

- SG   Natural Sciences and Health
- UF   health services
- BT   services
- NT   community health services
  emergency medical services
  maternal health service
  multicultural health care services
  school health services

                                 (*cont.*)

UF=Use for   BT=Broader term   NT=Narrower term   RT=Related term   213

health care services *(cont.)*

RT   health care delivery
     health care providers
     health maintenance organizations
     home health care

health care utilization

SG   Natural Sciences and Health
RT   health behavior
     health care
     health care delivery

health care workers

SG   Economics and Employment
     Natural Sciences and Health
BT   female intensive occupations
     health care occupations
     workers

health cooperatives

SG   Natural Sciences and Health
BT   cooperatives
RT   health care delivery
     health care facilities

health economics

SG   Economics and Employment
     Natural Sciences and Health
BT   economics
RT   health insurance
     insurance industry
     liability insurance
     pharmaceutical industry

health education

SG   Education
     Natural Sciences and Health
BT   education

health hazards

SG   Natural Sciences and Health
BT   hazards
RT   asbestos
     factory conditions
     hazardous waste
     household hazards
     work hazards

health insurance

SG   Law, Government, and Public Policy
     Natural Sciences and Health
UF   medical insurance
BT   insurance
NT   Medicaid
     Medicare
     national health insurance
RT   employee benefits
     health care
     health care costs
     health care delivery
     health economics
     Health Insurance Continuation
     health maintenance organizations
     medical care
     nursing homes
     preventive medicine
     socialized medicine

Health Insurance Continuation

DG   Laws and Regulations
RT   health insurance

health maintenance organizations

SG   Economics and Employment
     Natural Sciences and Health
UF   HMOs
BT   organizations
RT   health care delivery
     health care policy
     health care services
     health insurance

health seeking behavior

SG   Natural Sciences and Health
BT   health behavior
RT   breast self examination
     health
     holistic health
     preventive medicine
     wellness
     women's health movement

health services

USE **health care services**

hearing
SG Natural Sciences and Health
RT auditory perception

hearing aids
SG Natural Sciences and Health
RT deafness
hearing impairments

hearing impairments
SG Natural Sciences and Health
BT disabilities
NT deafness
RT disabled
hearing aids
sign language

hearings
SG Law, Government, and Public Policy
BT activities
NT congressional hearings
RT testimony

heart disease
SG Natural Sciences and Health
BT cardiovascular diseases
RT hypertension
stress

heavy equipment operators
SG Economics and Employment
Science and Technology
BT construction occupations
operators
transportation occupations

Hegelianism
DG Cultural and Political Movements

Hellenic Period
DG Historical Periods

help seeking behavior
SG Social Sciences and Culture
BT behavior
NT self help

helping behavior
SG Social Sciences and Culture
BT behavior
RT ethic of care

helplessness
USE **learned helplessness**

hemlines
SG Social Sciences and Culture
RT clothing
fashion
miniskirts
skirts

herbal remedies
SG Natural Sciences and Health
BT remedies
RT folk medicine
herbs
holistic medicine
home remedies

herbs
SG Natural Sciences and Health
RT cooking
herbal remedies

hereditary diseases
SG Natural Sciences and Health
BT diseases
RT genetic defects

heredity
SN *Genetic inheritance.*
SG Natural Sciences and Health
RT biological influences
genetic determinants
genetic engineering
genetics

heresies
SG Language, Literature, Religion, and
Philosophy
RT dogmatism
heretics
religious repression

---

heretics
> SG Language, Literature, Religion, and
> Philosophy
> RT heresies
> religious repression
> witches

hermaphrodites
> SG Natural Sciences and Health
> RT androgyny
> bisexuality
> hermaphroditism

hermaphroditism
> SN *Possessing both female and male repro-*
> *ductive organs.*
> SG Natural Sciences and Health
> RT hermaphrodites

hermeneutics
> SG Language, Literature, Religion, and
> Philosophy
> RT criticism
> deconstruction
> theology

heroes
> SG History and Social Change
> Language, Literature, Religion, and
> Philosophy
> Visual and Performing Arts
> UF heroic women
> heroines
> NT women of valor
> RT drama
> epics
> fictional characters
> heroines (historical)
> integrity

heroic women
> USE **heroes**

heroin
> SG Natural Sciences and Health
> BT narcotic drugs
> RT drug abuse

heroines
> USE **heroes**

heroines (historical)
> SG History and Social Change
> Language, Literature, Religion, and
> Philosophy
> BT women
> RT epics
> fictional characters
> heroes
> literature
> mythology
> women of valor
> women's history

herpes simplex virus type II
> USE **genital herpes**

herstory
> SN *Coined term for the history of women*
> *that has been neglected in "tradi-*
> *tional" history.*
> SG History and Social Change
> RT history
> thealogy
> women's history

heterogeneous groups
> SG Education
> Social Sciences and Culture
> BT groups
> NT mixed sex groups

heterosexism
> SG History and Social Change
> Social Sciences and Culture
> RT compulsory heterosexuality
> discrimination
> heterosexual privilege
> homophobia

heterosexual privilege
> SG History and Social Change
> Social Sciences and Culture
> BT privilege
> RT discrimination

> *(cont.)*

heterosexual privilege *(cont.)*
RT heterosexism
    stereotyping

heterosexual relationships
SG Natural Sciences and Health
    Social Sciences and Culture
BT relationships

heterosexuality
SG Social Sciences and Culture
UF heterosexuals
BT sexuality
NT compulsory heterosexuality
RT gay men
    lesbians
    straights

heterosexuals
USE **heterosexuality**

hidden curriculum
SG Education
BT curriculum
RT institutional racism
    institutional sexism

hidjab
SN *Seclusion of women in Islamic culture.*
SG Social Sciences and Culture
RT harems
    private sphere
    purdah
    separate spheres
    veils

hierarchy
SG Economics and Employment
    Social Sciences and Culture
RT administration
    bureaucracy

high blood pressure
USE **hypertension**

high heeled shoes
SG History and Social Change
    Natural Sciences and Health
BT clothing
RT fashion
    physical health
    ritual disfigurement

high priestesses
SG Language, Literature, Religion, and
    Philosophy
BT priestesses

high school equivalency programs
SG Education
DG Education Levels
BT educational programs
    secondary education
RT adult basic education
    adult illiteracy
    adult literacy

high schools
SG Education
DG Education Levels
BT schools
    secondary education
NT junior high schools

higher education
SG Education
DG Education Levels
BT postsecondary education
NT four year colleges
    graduate education
    two year colleges
RT academia
    accreditation
    admissions
    affirmative action
    affirmative action hiring
    alumnae
    alumni
    colleges
    universities

Hindu
DG Ethnic, Racial, and Religious
Descriptors

Hinduism
DG Cultural and Political Movements

hips
SG Natural Sciences and Health
BT bodies

hiring policy
SG Economics and Employment
BT corporate policy
employment practices
NT affirmative action hiring
job advertisements
veteran preference
RT employment
information dissemination
job placement
job recruitment
nominations
quotas
selection procedures

hirsutism
SN *Presence of excessive body and facial
hair.*
SG Natural Sciences and Health
RT body hair

Hispanic
DG Ethnic, Racial, and Religious
Descriptors

Hispanic American
DG Ethnic, Racial, and Religious
Descriptors

Hispanic studies
USE **Latina studies**

historians
SG Economics and Employment
History and Social Change
BT humanists

(cont.)

historians *(cont.)*
BT social scientists

historical linguistics
SG Language, Literature, Religion, and
Philosophy
BT linguistics

historically Black colleges
USE **Black colleges**

histories
SG History and Social Change
Language, Literature, Religion, and
Philosophy
DG Types and Forms of Materials
BT nonfiction
NT life histories
oral history
RT autobiography
chronicles
diaries
history
journals
memoirs

historiography
SN *Study of historical methods.*
SG History and Social Change
BT history
RT feminist methods
feminist theory
research methods

history
SN *See also Delimiters Displays: Historical
Periods, Cultural and Political
Movements.*
SG History and Social Change
BT humanities
social sciences
NT art history
economic history
historiography
history of children
history of religion
history of science

(cont.)

history (cont.)
- NT intellectual history
  - labor history
  - literary history
  - music history
  - oral history
  - social history
  - women's history
- RT herstory
  - histories

history of children
- SG History and Social Change
  - Social Sciences and Culture
- BT history
- RT adolescence
  - child labor
  - child rearing practices
  - children
  - family attitudes
  - family life
  - valuing children

history of religion
- SG History and Social Change
  - Language, Literature, Religion, and
  - Philosophy
- BT history
- RT comparative religion
  - humanities
  - religion

history of science
- SG Science and Technology
- BT history
- RT paradigms

history of women
- USE **women's history**

HMOs
- USE **health maintenance organizations**

hobbies
- SG Social Sciences and Culture
- RT leisure activities
  - retirement

(cont.)

hobbies (cont.)
- RT volunteer work

holistic health
- SG Natural Sciences and Health
- BT health
- RT health seeking behavior

holistic medicine
- SG Natural Sciences and Health
- BT medical sciences
- RT folk medicine
  - healing
  - herbal remedies
  - wellness

holistic music
- SG Visual and Performing Arts
- BT music
- RT music therapy

holocaust
- SG History and Social Change
- RT antisemitism
  - eugenic sterilization
  - genocide

holy communion
- SG Language, Literature, Religion, and
  - Philosophy
- UF eucharist
- BT sacraments
  - spiritual communication

holy matrimony
- SG Language, Literature, Religion, and
  - Philosophy
- BT sacraments
- RT marriage
  - marriage vows

holy men
- SG Language, Literature, Religion, and
  - Philosophy
- BT men
- RT canonization
  - monasticism

(cont.)

UF=Use for   BT=Broader term   NT=Narrower term   RT=Related term

holy men (*cont.*)
- RT religious orders
  - saints
  - shamans
  - spirituality

holy women
- SG Language, Literature, Religion, and Philosophy
- BT women
- RT canonization
  - convents
  - female spirituality
  - hagiography
  - madonna
  - martyrs
  - monasticism
  - priestesses
  - religious orders
  - saints
  - shamans
  - spirituality
  - wisdom
  - witches
  - women religious

home accidents
- SG Social Sciences and Culture
- BT accidents
- RT household hazards
  - insurance

home based business
- SG Economics and Employment
- BT business
- RT cottage industry
  - home based work
  - women owned business

home based careers
- SG Economics and Employment
- BT careers

home based work
- SG Economics and Employment
  - Social Sciences and Culture
- BT work

(*cont.*)

home based work (*cont.*)
- RT child care
  - cottage industry
  - electronic cottage
  - flexible work schedules
  - home based business
  - home based workers
  - piecework
  - piecework labor policy
  - telecommuting

home based workers
- SG Economics and Employment
- BT workers
- RT cottage industry
  - home based work
  - homemakers

home birth
- SG Natural Sciences and Health
- RT birthing
  - childbirth
  - delivery rooms
  - natural childbirth

home economics
- SG Economics and Employment
  - Social Sciences and Culture
- RT domestic arts
  - economic value of women's work

home economics extension work
- SG Economics and Employment
- BT extension work

home economists
- SG Economics and Employment
  - Education
  - Science and Technology
  - Social Sciences and Culture
- BT education occupations
  - female intensive occupations
  - scientific and technical occupations

home health care
- SG Natural Sciences and Health
- BT health care

(*cont.*)

SN=Scope note   SG=Subject group   DG=Delimiters group   USE=Use

home health care (*cont.*)
RT elderly households
      health care delivery
      health care services

home improvement loans
SG Economics and Employment
BT loans
RT homeowners

home labor
USE **household labor**

home life
SG History and Social Change
      Social Sciences and Culture
RT community
      domesticity
      families
      private sphere

home remedies
SG Natural Sciences and Health
BT remedies
RT folk medicine
      healing
      herbal remedies

home schooling
SG Education
RT nonformal education

home study
SG Education
RT independent study

homeless
SG Law, Government, and Public Policy
      Social Sciences and Culture
UF street people
NT homeless men
      homeless women
RT deinstitutionalization
      economically disadvantaged
      housing
      poverty
      shelters

(*cont.*)

homeless (*cont.*)
RT squatters
      temporary housing

homeless men
SG Social Sciences and Culture
BT homeless
      men

homeless women
SG Social Sciences and Culture
UF bag ladies
BT homeless
      women
RT women living in poverty

homemaker rights
SG Law, Government, and Public Policy
BT rights

homemaker service
SG Economics and Employment
BT domestic services

homemakers
SG Social Sciences and Culture
UF house husbands
      house wives
      househusbands
      housewives
BT female intensive occupations
NT displaced homemakers
      visiting homemakers
RT coparenting
      devaluation
      economic value of women's work
      home based workers
      household division of labor
      life styles
      wives working outside the home

homemaking
SG Economics and Employment
      Social Sciences and Culture
RT angel in the house
      child care workers
      domestic arts

(*cont.*)

UF=Use for   BT=Broader term   NT=Narrower term   RT=Related term

homemaking (*cont.*)
- RT food preparation occupations
  household division of labor
  household labor
  houses
  housewares
  labor saving devices
  service occupations
  superwoman syndrome
  unpaid employment

homeowners
- SG Economics and Employment
- RT credit
  home improvement loans
  housing
  mortgages

homes
- USE **housing**

homesteading
- SG Economics and Employment
  Social Sciences and Culture
- RT frontier life
  urban renewal

homicide
- USE **murder**

homilies
- SG Language, Literature, Religion, and
  Philosophy
- RT sermons

homoeroticism
- SN *Heterosexual men's love of other men.*
- SG History and Social Change
  Natural Sciences and Health
  Social Sciences and Culture
- RT bisexuality
  male bonding

homogeneous groups
- SG Education
  Social Sciences and Culture
- BT groups

homophile movement
- SN *Early movement for gay rights, begin-*
  ning in the late 1950s. Term adopted
  first by West Coast organizations to
  deemphasize "sex" in the word
  "homosexuality."
- SG History and Social Change
- DG Cultural and Political Movements
- BT social movements
- RT gay male experience
  gay rights
  lesbian experience

homophobia
- SG History and Social Change
  Natural Sciences and Health
  Social Sciences and Culture
- BT phobias
- NT lesbophobia
- RT compulsory heterosexuality
  discrimination
  doubly disadvantaged
  gay men
  gay rights
  heterosexism
  lesbians
  oppression

homosexual marriage
- USE **gay marriage**

homosexual relationships
- USE **gay relationships**

homosexuality
- SG History and Social Change
  Natural Sciences and Health
  Social Sciences and Culture
- BT sexuality
- NT lesbianism
  male homosexuality
- RT attitudes
  bisexuality
  coming out
  compulsory heterosexuality
  gay male culture
  gays

(*cont.*)

homosexuality (*cont.*)
- RT lesbian culture
- lesbians

homosexuals
- USE **gays**

Honduran
- DG National and Regional Descriptors
- BT Central American

honesty
- SG Language, Literature, Religion, and Philosophy
- RT ethics
- integrity
- lying
- moral reform
- morality
- social reform
- values

honeymoons
- SG Social Sciences and Culture
- RT marriage customs
- wedding nights

honorary degrees
- SG Education
- BT degrees
- RT graduation ceremonies

honorary societies
- SG Education
- BT societies
- RT initiation rites

hookers
- USE **prostitutes**

hormone therapy
- SG Natural Sciences and Health
- BT therapy
- NT estrogen replacement therapy
- RT fertility drugs
- hormones
- osteoporosis

hormones
- SG Natural Sciences and Health
- BT bodies
- NT pituitary hormones
- sex hormones
- RT aging
- athletics
- fertility drugs
- glands
- hair
- hormone therapy
- hysterectomy
- muscular development

horticulture
- SG Natural Sciences and Health
- RT agricultural, fishing, and forestry occupations

hosiery
- SG Social Sciences and Culture
- UF pantyhose
- BT clothing

hospices
- SG Natural Sciences and Health
- BT health care facilities
- RT cancer
- death
- death and dying
- hospitals
- quality of life
- right to die
- terminal illness

hospitals
- SG Natural Sciences and Health
- BT health care facilities
- NT maternity wards
- mental hospitals
- RT abortion
- abortion clinics
- delivery rooms
- emergency medical services
- hospices

UF=Use for   BT=Broader term   NT=Narrower term   RT=Related term

hostels
- SG Law, Government, and Public Policy
- BT facilities
  temporary housing
- RT housing

hostesses
- USE **hosts**

hostesses (historical)
- SG Economics and Employment
  Social Sciences and Culture
- BT arts, entertainment, and media
  occupations
  female intensive occupations
  women
- RT hosts

hostility
- SG Social Sciences and Culture
- BT emotions
- RT anger

hosts
- SG Communications
  Economics and Employment
  Social Sciences and Culture
  Visual and Performing Arts
- UF hostesses
- BT arts, entertainment, and media
  occupations
- RT entertainment
  hostesses (historical)
  manners
  master of ceremonies
  social activities
  social skills
  spouses
  television personalities

hosts (media)
- USE **television personalities**

hot flashes
- SG Natural Sciences and Health
- RT menopause

hot lines
- SG Communications
- RT crisis centers
  crisis intervention
  support systems
  telephones

hotel workers
- SG Economics and Employment
- UF chambermaids
- BT service occupations
  workers
- RT housekeeping services

house churches
- SG Language, Literature, Religion, and
  Philosophy
- BT churches

house design
- SG Social Sciences and Culture
- BT design
- RT architecture
  energy conservation
  ergonomics
  furniture
  houses
  labor saving devices

house husbands
- USE **homemakers**

House of Representatives
- SG Law, Government, and Public Policy
- BT Congress

house wives
- USE **homemakers**

housecleaners
- SG Economics and Employment
  Social Sciences and Culture
- BT cleaners
  household workers

housecleaning

    SG Economics and Employment
           Social Sciences and Culture
  BT household labor

household division of labor

    SG Economics and Employment
           Social Sciences and Culture
  BT division of labor
  RT dual career couples
       dual career families
       gender roles
       homemakers
       homemaking
       household labor
       marriage contracts
       sexual division of labor
       two income families
       wives working outside the home

household economics

    SG Economics and Employment
  RT budgeting
       family finances
       two income families

household employment

    SG Economics and Employment
  BT employment
  RT economic value of women's work
       household labor
       household workers

household hazards

    SG Natural Sciences and Health
           Social Sciences and Culture
  BT hazards
  RT accidents
       health hazards
       home accidents
       households

household labor

    SG Economics and Employment
  UF domestic labor
       home labor
  BT labor

(cont.)

household labor *(cont.)*

  NT housecleaning
       unpaid household labor
  RT cleaning
       devaluation
       domestic services
       economic value of women's work
       female intensive occupations
       food marketing
       homemaking
       household division of labor
       household employment
       household workers
       housework
       ironing
       kitchens
       laundry
       service occupations
       wages for housework

household violence

  USE **domestic violence**

household workers

    SG Economics and Employment
           Social Sciences and Culture
  UF domestics
       maids
       servants
  BT female intensive occupations
       service occupations
       workers
  NT housecleaners
  RT child care workers
       domestic services
       household employment
       household labor
       housekeeping services

householders

    SG Economics and Employment
           Social Sciences and Culture
  UF breadwinners
       heads of households
  RT heads of families
       households

(cont.)

UF=Use for   BT=Broader term   NT=Narrower term   RT=Related term

householders (*cont.*)
RT   single parent families

households
SG   Economics and Employment
      Social Sciences and Culture
NT   elderly households
      female headed households
      low income households
RT   census
      communities
      ethnic neighborhoods
      families
      household hazards
      householders
      posslq
      singles

househusbands
USE **homemakers**

housekeepers
SG   Economics and Employment
      Social Sciences and Culture
BT   female intensive occupations
      service occupations

housekeeping services
SG   Economics and Employment
BT   services
RT   hotel workers
      household workers

housemothers
SG   Economics and Employment
      Education
BT   education occupations
      female intensive occupations
      mothers
RT   dormitories

housepainters
SG   Economics and Employment
BT   construction occupations

houses
SG   Social Sciences and Culture
BT   facilities

(*cont.*)

houses (*cont.*)
NT   halfway houses
RT   homemaking
      house design
      neighborhoods
      rooms

housewares
SG   Social Sciences and Culture
RT   homemaking
      labor saving devices

housewives
USE **homemakers**

housework
SG   Economics and Employment
      Social Sciences and Culture
RT   economic value of women's work
      household labor

housing
SG   Economics and Employment
      International Women
      Law, Government, and Public Policy
UF   homes
NT   public housing
      segregated housing
      student housing
      temporary housing
RT   aging
      architecture
      barrier free access
      census
      communes
      community problems
      equal access
      homeless
      homeowners
      hostels
      housing costs
      housing discrimination
      inner city
      landlords
      life styles
      property taxes
      racial discrimination

(*cont.*)

SN=Scope note   SG=Subject group   DG=Delimiters group   USE=Use

housing (*cont.*)
RT redlining
    rent
    space

housing costs
SG Economics and Employment
    Law, Government, and Public Policy
    Social Sciences and Culture
BT costs
RT housing
    housing subsidies

housing discrimination
SG Law, Government, and Public Policy
    Social Sciences and Culture
BT discrimination
RT blockbusting
    housing
    single mothers

housing subsidies
SG Economics and Employment
    Law, Government, and Public Policy
    Social Sciences and Culture
BT subsidies
RT housing costs

how to guides
DG Types and Forms of Materials
BT guides

hugging
SG Natural Sciences and Health
    Social Sciences and Culture
BT forms of affection

human capital
SG Economics and Employment
BT capital
RT economic value of women's work
    human resources
    multinational labor force

human evolution
SG Social Sciences and Culture
BT evolution

(*cont.*)

human evolution (*cont.*)
NT fossil hominids
RT anthropology
    social sciences

human interest
SG Social Sciences and Culture
RT empathy

human needs
SG History and Social Change
    Social Sciences and Culture
NT basic human needs
    psychological needs
RT emotions
    personal relationships
    security

human relations
SG Social Sciences and Culture
BT relationships
RT public relations

human relations commissions
SG History and Social Change
    Law, Government, and Public Policy
BT commissions

human resources
SG Economics and Employment
    Social Sciences and Culture
UF manpower
BT resources
NT labor force
    labor supply
RT economic value of women's work
    human capital

human rights
SG History and Social Change
    Law, Government, and Public Policy
BT rights
RT civil rights
    equal rights
    feminism
    freedoms
    human rights violations

(*cont.*)

UF=Use for   BT=Broader term   NT=Narrower term   RT=Related term

human rights (*cont.*)

RT   sanctuaries

human rights violations

SG   International Women
      Law, Government, and Public Policy

RT   age discrimination
      apartheid
      class discrimination
      human rights
      persecution
      political oppression
      political prisoners
      prisoners
      racial discrimination
      refugees
      sanctions
      sex discrimination
      tyranny

human services

SG   Social Sciences and Culture

BT   services

NT   social services

humanism

DG   Cultural and Political Movements

humanists

SG   Economics and Employment
      Education
      Language, Literature, Religion, and
        Philosophy

BT   education occupations

NT   historians
      philosophers

humanitarianism

SG   Language, Literature, Religion, and
      Philosophy

DG   Cultural and Political Movements

RT   altruism
      ethics
      moral reform
      social reform
      social values

humanities

SG   Education
      Language, Literature, Religion, and
        Philosophy

NT   history
      linguistics
      literature
      musicology
      philosophy
      theology

RT   American studies
      arts
      criticism
      cross cultural studies
      ethnomusicology
      feminist theory
      history of religion
      interdisciplinary studies
      media arts
      performing arts
      social science research
      social sciences
      writing

humanity

SG   History and Social Change
      Social Sciences and Culture

UF   brotherhood of man
      mankind

RT   man

humor

SG   Language, Literature, Religion, and
        Philosophy
      Visual and Performing Arts

RT   burlesque
      caricatures
      cartoons
      comedy
      coping strategies
      images of women
      irony
      jokes
      laughter
      mental health
      parody
      personality traits

(*cont.*)

humor (*cont.*)
RT   puns
     satire
     sense of humor
     slapstick

Hungarian
DG   National and Regional Descriptors
BT   European

hunger
SG   International Women
     Natural Sciences and Health
RT   famine
     food
     malnutrition
     poverty
     third world

husband abuse
SG   Social Sciences and Culture
BT   spouse abuse

husbands
SG   Social Sciences and Culture
UF   married men
BT   men
     spouses
NT   first husbands
     former husbands
     runaway husbands
RT   divorce
     polyandry
     wives

hygiene
SG   Natural Sciences and Health
NT   industrial hygiene
     personal hygiene
RT   cleanliness
     food processing
     sanitation

hymen
SG   Natural Sciences and Health
UF   maidenhead
BT   vagina

(*cont.*)

hymen (*cont.*)
RT   virginity

hymenoplasty
SN   *Surgical operation to restore hymen.*
SG   Natural Sciences and Health
RT   virginity

hymns
SG   Visual and Performing Arts
BT   religious music
RT   images of women
     lyrics
     religious language

hypersexuality
SG   Natural Sciences and Health
UF   compulsive sexuality
BT   compulsive behavior
     sexuality
NT   female hypersexuality
     male hypersexuality
RT   promiscuity
     sexual behavior

hypertension
SG   Natural Sciences and Health
UF   high blood pressure
BT   diseases
RT   diuretics
     heart disease
     stress

hyphenated names
SG   Language, Literature, Religion, and
     Philosophy
BT   names
RT   birth name
     matronymy
     name rights
     patronymy
     surnames

hypnotism
SG   Natural Sciences and Health
RT   anesthesia
     psychotherapy

(*cont.*)

UF=Use for   BT=Broader term   NT=Narrower term   RT=Related term   229

hypnotism (*cont.*)
- RT   subconscious

hypochondria
- SG   Natural Sciences and Health
- RT   attitudes
-      psychosomatic disorders
-      self concept

hysterectomy
- SG   Natural Sciences and Health
- BT   surgical procedures
- RT   hormones
-      malignant tumors
-      oophorectomy

hysteria
- SG   Natural Sciences and Health
- BT   mental disorders
- RT   images of women

iatrogenic disease
- SN   *Doctor-introduced disease.*
- SG   Natural Sciences and Health
- BT   diseases

ice hockey
- SG   Natural Sciences and Health
- BT   sports

ice skating
- SG   Natural Sciences and Health
- BT   sports

Icelandic
- DG   National and Regional Descriptors
- BT   Scandinavian

iconoclasts
- SG   Social Sciences and Culture
- RT   attitudes
-      belief systems
-      nonconforming behavior

iconography
- SG   Language, Literature, Religion, and
-      Philosophy
-      Visual and Performing Arts
- RT   art symbols
-      graphics
-      hagiography
-      icons
-      images of women
-      madonna
-      music
-      performing arts
-      popular culture
-      religious art
-      symbols
-      visual arts

icons
- SG   Language, Literature, Religion, and
-      Philosophy
- RT   iconography
-      nonverbal language
-      semiotics
-      sign language
-      symbols

ideal family size
- USE   **family size**

ideal woman
- SG   History and Social Change
- BT   images of women
- RT   chivalry
-      courtly love
-      cult of true womanhood
-      pedestals
-      perfection
-      romance
-      sex role stereotyping
-      virgins

idealism
- DG   Cultural and Political Movements
- RT   morality
-      purists

identical twins

SG Natural Sciences and Health
Social Sciences and Culture
BT twins

identity

SG Natural Sciences and Health
Social Sciences and Culture
NT class identity
cultural identity
gender identity
sexual identity
social identity
RT ego
identity crisis
individual development
kinship
self concept
socialization

identity crisis

SG Natural Sciences and Health
Social Sciences and Culture
RT identity
loss of self

ideology

SG Language, Literature, Religion, and
Philosophy
Law, Government, and Public Policy
NT class ideology
gender ideology
political ideology
sacred ideology
RT belief systems
feminist theory
mothering

illegal aliens

USE **illegal immigrants**

illegal immigrants

SG International Women
Law, Government, and Public Policy
UF illegal aliens
BT immigrants
RT immigration quotas

(*cont.*)

illegal immigrants (*cont.*)

RT migrant workers
undocumented workers

illegitimacy

SG Social Sciences and Culture
RT bastards
children
discrimination
legitimization of children
single fathers
single mothers
social attitudes

illiteracy

SG Education
International Women
Language, Literature, Religion, and
Philosophy
NT adult illiteracy
RT antiilliteracy movements
literacy
oral history
poverty

illness

SG Natural Sciences and Health
NT terminal illness
RT diseases
psychosomatic disorders
stress
wellness

illustration

SG Communications
Language, Literature, Religion, and
Philosophy
BT commercial art
NT fashion illustration
RT art
children's literature
graphics

illustrators

SG Communications
Economics and Employment
Visual and Performing Arts

(*cont.*)

---

illustrators (*cont.*)

- BT arts, entertainment, and media
       occupations
- RT sign painters

image

- SG Communications
      History and Social Change
- NT body image
- RT images of women
      norms
      popular culture
      role models
      roles
      social attitudes
      social class
      social status
      social values
      status

imagery

- SG Communications
      Language, Literature, Religion, and
        Philosophy
      Visual and Performing Arts
- BT figurative language
- RT art

images of girls

- SG Communications
      History and Social Change
      Language, Literature, Religion, and
        Philosophy
      Social Sciences and Culture
      Visual and Performing Arts
- NT angels
      blondes
      cheerleaders
      Cinderella
      debutantes
      Orphan Annie
      sissies
      sisters
      tomboys
      virgins
      waifs
- RT children's culture

(*cont.*)

images of girls (*cont.*)

- RT children's literature
      cult of the virgin
      hair styles
      images of women
      innocence
      invisibility
      lesbians
      media portrayal
      music videos
      purity
      sex role stereotyping
      stereotyping
      textbooks

images of women

- SG Communications
      History and Social Change
      Language, Literature, Religion, and
        Philosophy
      Social Sciences and Culture
      Visual and Performing Arts
- NT alma mater
      amazons
      angel in the house
      angels
      baronesses
      beauty queens
      bitches
      blondes
      bluestockings
      brides
      Brunhilde
      castrating females
      chattels
      cheerleaders
      Cinderella
      concubines
      countesses
      courtesans
      crones
      cunts
      dames
      debutantes
      den mothers
      duchesses
      earth mother

(*cont.*)

images of women (cont.)

NT Eve
      fallen women
      femmes fatales
      flirts
      geishas
      goddesses
      harlots
      ideal woman
      instigators
      ladies (historical)
      ladies (nobility)
      Lilith
      Lolita
      madonna
      mammies
      manipulators
      mannequins
      mermaids
      mother earth
      mother nature
      mothers in law
      nags
      nuns
      nurturers
      odalisques
      old maids
      princesses
      prostitutes
      queen for a day
      queens
      scolds
      seductresses
      sirens
      sisters
      Snow White
      sphinx
      spinsters
      Statue of Liberty
      stepmothers
      strumpets
      succubi
      superwoman
      teases
      temptresses
      vagina dentata
      vampires

(cont.)

images of women (cont.)

NT vamps
      viragos
      Virgin Mary
      virgins
      waifs
      widows
      witches
      woman the gatherer
      Wonder Woman
RT advertising
      aging
      angora
      attitudes
      beauty contests
      beauty standards
      blood
      bodies
      body image
      cartoons
      cheesecake
      chivalry
      cleavage
      clothing
      coins
      coyness
      creation myths
      cult of the virgin
      cult of true womanhood
      cultural sadism
      cunning
      devil
      emotionalism
      fashion
      fashion photography
      female sexuality
      feminine mystique
      feminine principle
      flirtation
      hair styles
      humor
      hymns
      hysteria
      iconography
      image
      images of girls
      ingratiation

(cont.)

images of women (*cont.*)

  RT innocence
       invisibility
       lesbians
       lingerie
       literature
       lyrics
       makeup
       manners
       mass media
       maternal love
       media portrayal
       modesty
       mother syndrome
       motion picture industry
       music videos
       mythology
       nervousness
       old wives' tales
       original sin
       paternity suits
       pedestals
       pinups
       pornography
       puns
       purity
       rock and roll
       romantic love
       sex objects
       sex role stereotyping
       sex stereotypes
       soap operas
       stamps
       stereotypes
       stereotyping
       superwoman syndrome
       television commercials
       television personalities
       the nude
       violence in the media
       voluptuousness
       wealth
       wigs
       womanhood
       women

imagination

  SG Language, Literature, Religion, and
       Philosophy
  RT creative thinking
       creative writing
       creativity
       curiosity
       daydreams
       fantasies
       free association
       initiative
       integrity
       intuition
       risk taking
       sexual fantasies

immaculate conception

  SG Language, Literature, Religion, and
       Philosophy
  BT religious beliefs
  RT cult of the virgin
       dogma
       God the father
       madonna
       purity
       sacred ideology
       virgin birth
       Virgin Mary

immigrants

  SG International Women
  UF aliens
  NT illegal immigrants
  RT acculturation
       assimilation patterns
       ethnic groups
       ethnic studies
       ethnic women
       farm workers
       nationality
       pioneers
       refugees
       women of color

immigration

  SG Law, Government, and Public Policy
  RT acculturation

(cont.)

immigration *(cont.)*

RT citizenship
    exile
    migration patterns
    naturalization

immigration policy

SG International Women
    Law, Government, and Public Policy
BT international policy
RT braceros
    citizenship
    migrant workers
    undocumented workers

immigration quotas

SG Law, Government, and Public Policy
BT quotas
RT illegal immigrants

immorality

SG Language, Literature, Religion, and
    Philosophy
    Law, Government, and Public Policy
    Social Sciences and Culture
RT ethics
    judicial attitudes
    moral reform
    sin
    social attitudes
    social reform

impact on children

SN *Refers to both need and criteria for
    measuring and evaluating effects of
    economic, social, and political poli-
    cies on children's lives.*
SG Economics and Employment
    International Women
    Law, Government, and Public Policy
    Social Sciences and Culture
RT development studies
    foreign aid
    foreign aid policy
    impact on women
    valuing children

impact on women

SN *Refers to both need and criteria for
    measuring and evaluating effects of
    economic, social, and political poli-
    cies on women's lives.*
SG Economics and Employment
    International Women
    Law, Government, and Public Policy
    Social Sciences and Culture
RT budget cuts
    developing nations
    development studies
    economic development models
    economic value of women's work
    fifth world
    foreign aid
    foreign aid policy
    impact on children
    technology
    women in development

imperialism

USE **colonialism**

impersonators

SG Social Sciences and Culture
BT arts, entertainment, and media
    occupations
NT female impersonators
    male impersonators

impotence

SG Natural Sciences and Health
BT sexual dysfunction
RT ejaculation
    fear of failure
    intimacy
    sex counseling

impoverishment of women

SG Economics and Employment
    International Women
    Social Sciences and Culture
RT women living in poverty

---

impregnation

SG Language, Literature, Religion, and
   Philosophy
   Natural Sciences and Health
RT fertilization
   virgin birth

impressionism

DG Cultural and Political Movements

improvisation

SG Visual and Performing Arts
BT theater

impurity

SG Language, Literature, Religion, and
   Philosophy
RT purification rites

in kind contributions

SG Economics and Employment
BT funding
RT donors
   fund raising
   philanthropy
   volunteer work

in laws

SG Social Sciences and Culture
NT brothers in law
   daughters in law
   fathers in law
   mothers in law
   sisters in law
   sons in law
RT divorce
   families
   parents

in vitro fertilization

SG Law, Government, and Public Policy
   Natural Sciences and Health
UF ectogenesis
   test tube babies
BT fertilization
   reproductive technologies
RT bioethics

(cont.)

in vitro fertilization *(cont.)*

RT cloning
   conception
   donors
   embryo transfer
   genetic engineering
   infants
   infertility

inbreeding

SG Natural Sciences and Health
RT genetic counseling

incarceration

SG Law, Government, and Public Policy
RT prisons

incarnation

SG Language, Literature, Religion, and
   Philosophy
BT religious beliefs
RT dogma
   religion
   theology

incentives

SG Economics and Employment
NT monetary incentives
   tax incentives
   work incentives

incest

SG Law, Government, and Public Policy
   Natural Sciences and Health
   Social Sciences and Culture
NT brother sister incest
   father daughter incest
   father son incest
   mother daughter incest
   mother son incest
RT child abuse
   crimes against children
   domestic violence
   families
   incest victims
   parent child relationships
   rape

(cont.)

incest (*cont.*)
RT　sex crimes
　　sexual violence

incest victims
　　SG　Law, Government, and Public Policy
　　　　Natural Sciences and Health
　　　　Social Sciences and Culture
BT　victims
RT　blaming the victim
　　incest
　　self concept
　　sexual abuse
　　therapy
　　victim services

incidental music
　　SG　Visual and Performing Arts
BT　music
RT　film
　　multimedia art
　　musical theater
　　radio

income
　　SG　Economics and Employment
NT　earned income
　　family income
　　gross income
　　guaranteed income
　　minimum income
　　net income
　　transfer income
RT　alimony
　　back pay
　　budgeting
　　class identity
　　family finances
　　income distribution
　　low income families
　　low income households
　　paid employment
　　pension benefits
　　social class
　　Social Security
　　two income families
　　wages

(*cont.*)

income (*cont.*)
RT　wealth

income distribution
　　SG　Economics and Employment
RT　income
　　wealth distribution

income generation
　　SN　*Activities that produce an income; fre-*
　　　　quently used to describe activities in
　　　　developing countries that produce in-
　　　　come for women.
　　SG　Economics and Employment
　　　　International Women
RT　cottage industry
　　developing nations
　　food for work
　　small business

income tax
　　SG　Economics and Employment
　　　　Law, Government, and Public Policy
BT　taxes
RT　minimum income

incubi
　　SG　Language, Literature, Religion, and
　　　　Philosophy
BT　evil spirits

independence
　　SG　Law, Government, and Public Policy
RT　living alone
　　self concept
　　self determination
　　self help

independent scholars
　　SN　*Persons without institutional faculty or*
　　　　research affiliations, usually em-
　　　　ployed outside academia.
　　SG　Education
UF　unaffiliated scholars
BT　scholars
RT　faculty retrenchment

UF=Use for　　BT=Broader term　　NT=Narrower term　　RT=Related term

237

independent study
> SG   Education
> RT   home study

indexes
> DG   Types and Forms of Materials

Indian
> DG   National and Regional Descriptors
> BT   Asian

indigenous
> DG   Ethnic, Racial, and Religious
>   Descriptors
> UF   aboriginals

indigenous populations
> SG   International Women
>   Social Sciences and Culture
> RT   colonialism
>   genocide
>   native healers
>   pioneers

individual counseling
> SG   Social Sciences and Culture
> BT   counseling
> RT   crimes
>   eating disorders
>   substance abuse
>   victims

individual development
> SG   Social Sciences and Culture
> UF   personal development
> BT   development
> NT   adult development
>   child development
>   cognitive development
>   emotional development
>   gender development
>   language development
>   moral development
>   personality development
>   physical development
>   sex role development
>   skill development

(cont.)

individual development (*cont.*)
> NT   social development
> RT   attachment
>   brain
>   developmental disabilities
>   education
>   ego
>   identity
>   personal management
>   self concept
>   socialization
>   twins

individualism
> SG   Social Sciences and Culture

individuality
> SG   Social Sciences and Culture

Indochinese
> DG   National and Regional Descriptors
> BT   Asian

Indochinese American
> DG   Ethnic, Racial, and Religious
>   Descriptors

indoctrination
> SG   Communications
> RT   brainwashing
>   disinformation
>   propaganda

Indonesian
> DG   National and Regional Descriptors
> BT   Asian

induced abortion
> SG   Natural Sciences and Health
> BT   abortion
> RT   genetic counseling

induced labor
> SG   Natural Sciences and Health
> BT   labor (childbirth)
> RT   drugs

---

industrial classification
 SG Economics and Employment
 RT industries
  occupational status
  occupations

industrial conditions
 SG Economics and Employment
  Science and Technology
 BT conditions

industrial hazards
 SG Science and Technology
 BT hazards
 RT carcinogens
  chemical industry
  hazardous waste
  industries
  nuclear energy
  occupational health and safety

industrial hygiene
 SG Economics and Employment
  Natural Sciences and Health
 BT hygiene
 RT occupational health and safety

industrial policy
 USE **corporate policy**

industrial psychology
 SG Economics and Employment
  Social Sciences and Culture
 BT psychology

industrial relations
 SG Economics and Employment
 BT relationships
 RT labor contracts
  labor relations
  management theory

Industrial Revolution
 DG Historical Periods

industrialization
 SG Economics and Employment
  History and Social Change
  Science and Technology
 RT deindustrialization
  technology
  technology development

industries
 SG Economics and Employment
  Science and Technology
 NT advertising industry
  agricultural industry
  banking industry
  chemical industry
  communications industry
  construction industry
  cottage industry
  electronics industry
  entertainment industry
  extractive industry
  food industry
  garment industry
  insurance industry
  manufacturing industry
  mining industry
  personal service industry
  pharmaceutical industry
  professional and related services industry
  publishing industry
  retail trade industry
  sex industry
  textile industry
  tobacco industry
  transportation industry
  wholesale trade industry
 RT affirmative action
  affirmative action hiring
  automation
  aviation
  business
  cancer
  corporations
  discrimination
  electronic media
  hazardous waste
  industrial classification

          (cont.)

industries (*cont.*)
- RT industrial hazards
  insurance
  machinery
  multinational corporations
  occupations
  print media
  technology development

inequality
- SG Law, Government, and Public Policy
- RT basic human needs
  discrimination
  living standards
  wealth distribution

infant care
- SG Economics and Employment
  Law, Government, and Public Policy
  Social Sciences and Culture
- BT child care

infant development
- SG Social Sciences and Culture
- BT child development
  postnatal period

infant formula
- SG International Women
  Natural Sciences and Health
- RT bottle feeding
  breast feeding
  milk substitutes
  multinational corporations

infant mortality
- SG Natural Sciences and Health
- BT mortality
- NT stillbirth
- RT birth rates
  blue babies
  childbirth
  death
  maternal and infant welfare
  poverty
  premature childbirth
  premature infants

(*cont.*)

infant mortality (*cont.*)
- RT prenatal care
  sudden infant death syndrome

infanticide
- SG History and Social Change
- BT murder
- RT boy preference of parents
  gynocide
  population control
  poverty

infants
- SG Natural Sciences and Health
  Social Sciences and Culture
- DG Age Levels
- UF babies
- BT young children
- NT blue babies
  premature infants
- RT bonding
  families
  fathers
  fetal alcohol syndrome
  in vitro fertilization
  maternal and infant welfare
  mothers
  nurturing
  parenting
  postnatal period
  sudden infant death syndrome

infertility
- SG Natural Sciences and Health
- UF barren
- RT adoption
  artificial insemination
  basal body temperature
  childless couples
  childlessness
  embryo transfer
  fallopian tubes
  fertility drugs
  in vitro fertilization
  reproductive technologies
  sterility
  surrogate fathers

(*cont.*)

infertility *(cont.)*
    RT surrogate mothers

infibulation
    SG Natural Sciences and Health
    RT chastity belts
         female circumcision
         genital mutilation

infidelity
    SG Social Sciences and Culture
    RT extramarital affairs

inflation
    SG Economics and Employment
    RT cost of living
         economic depression
         interest rates
         recession

influence
    SN *Use to describe influence of individual(s) on others; use **influences** to describe external influences on individual(s).*
    SG Law, Government, and Public Policy
         Social Sciences and Culture
    NT family influence
         peer influence
         political influence
    RT authority
         charisma
         control
         economic power
         leadership roles
         leadership skills
         nonviolence
         political power
         power

influences
    SN *Use to describe external influences on individual(s); use **influence** to describe influence of individual(s) on others.*
                       (cont.)

influences *(cont.)*
    SG Natural Sciences and Health
         Science and Technology
         Social Sciences and Culture
    UF causal factors
    NT biological influences
         cultural influences
         ecological factors
         economic factors
         performance factors
         prenatal influences
         racial factors
         religious influences
         social influences
    RT social class
         social environment

informal economy
    SG Economics and Employment
         International Women
    BT informal sector
    RT black markets

informal education
    USE **nonformal education**

informal language
    SG Language, Literature, Religion, and Philosophy
    BT language
    NT slang

informal sector
    SN *Economic activities that are insecure, generate low incomes, do not provide full-time employment, and are not subject to government regulations.*
    SG Economics and Employment
         International Women
    NT informal economy
    RT cottage industry
         dual economy
         street vendors
         third world
         underground economy

information

SN   *Use of a more specific term is recommended.*
SG   Communications
NT   consumer information
     public information
RT   freedom of information
     information processing
     right to know legislation

information and referral centers

SG   Communications
BT   centers
RT   information services
     libraries

information dissemination

SG   Communications
RT   diffusion
     disinformation
     grapevine
     hiring policy
     innovation
     job recruitment
     networks

information processing

SG   Communications
     Education
BT   information services
RT   data collection
     data processing
     information

information retrieval

SG   Communications
BT   information services
RT   libraries

information retrieval services

SG   Communications
UF   computer searches
BT   information services
RT   data processing

information sciences

SG   Science and Technology

(*cont.*)

information sciences (*cont.*)

NT   computer science
     library science
RT   communications
     information scientists
     information services
     information theory
     mass media
     science
     technology

information scientists

SG   Economics and Employment
     Science and Technology
BT   professional occupations
     scientific and technical occupations
RT   information sciences
     librarians
     scientists

information services

SN   *Use to describe a broad range of services that provide information to clients or the general public, such as libraries, referral centers, document delivery, and fee-based consultants.*
SG   Communications
BT   services
NT   information processing
     information retrieval
     information retrieval services
     information storage
     news services
RT   agricultural extension
     information and referral centers
     information sciences
     libraries

information storage

SG   Communications
BT   information services

information theory

SG   Communications
     Science and Technology
BT   theory
RT   information sciences

informed consent
SG Natural Sciences and Health
UF consent
RT age of consent
clinical trials
drugs
sterilization
surgical procedures

ingratiation
SG Social Sciences and Culture
RT flirtation
images of women

inheritance customs
SG Social Sciences and Culture
BT customs
RT bastards
dowry
executors
inherited wealth
land rights
legitimacy
legitimization of children
matrilineal societies
money
titles (nobility)

inheritance rights
SG Law, Government, and Public Policy
BT rights
RT inherited wealth
marital property reform

inherited wealth
SG Economics and Employment
History and Social Change
BT wealth
RT dual economy
family economics
inheritance customs
inheritance rights
upper class

initiation rites
SG Language, Literature, Religion, and
Philosophy
Social Sciences and Culture
(cont.)

initiation rites (cont.)
BT rites
RT female circumcision
fraternities
honorary societies
novitiates
rites of passage
secret societies
sororities
tribal customs

initiative
SG Social Sciences and Culture
RT ambition
assertive behavior
free enterprise
imagination
job rewards
motivation

injectable contraceptives
SG Natural Sciences and Health
BT contraception
NT Depo Provera

inner city
SG Law, Government, and Public Policy
Social Sciences and Culture
BT urban areas
RT ghettos
housing
neighborhoods
poverty
redlining
slums
urban renewal

innocence
SG Social Sciences and Culture
RT images of girls
images of women
purity

innovation
SG Science and Technology
Social Sciences and Culture
RT diffusion
(cont.)

innovation (*cont.*)

RT   information dissemination

insanity

SG   Natural Sciences and Health
       Social Sciences and Culture

RT   deinstitutionalization
       mental disorders
       sanity

insemination

SG   Natural Sciences and Health

NT   artificial insemination
       self insemination

RT   fertility
       pregnancy
       reproductive technologies
       sexual intercourse
       surrogate mothers

inservice education

SG   Education

BT   education

RT   on the job training
       teacher education

inspectors

SG   Economics and Employment
       Law, Government, and Public Policy

BT   construction occupations

instigators

SG   Social Sciences and Culture

BT   images of women

RT   rebellious behavior

instincts

SG   Natural Sciences and Health

RT   animal behavior
       emotions
       intuition
       learned behavior

institutes

SG   History and Social Change
       Social Sciences and Culture

BT   organizations

institutional discrimination

SG   Economics and Employment
       History and Social Change

BT   discrimination

NT   institutional racism
       institutional sexism

RT   businesswomen
       glass ceiling
       microinequities
       organizations

institutional racism

SG   Education
       History and Social Change
       Law, Government, and Public Policy
       Social Sciences and Culture

BT   institutional discrimination
       racism

RT   blaming the victim
       environmental racism
       gatekeeping
       governance
       hidden curriculum
       occupational stress
       structural discrimination

institutional sexism

SG   Education
       History and Social Change
       Law, Government, and Public Policy
       Social Sciences and Culture

BT   institutional discrimination
       sexism

RT   blaming the victim
       gatekeeping
       glass ceiling
       governance
       hidden curriculum
       occupational stress
       structural discrimination

institutions

SN   *Use of a more specific term is recom-*
       mended.

(*cont.*)

---

institutions (*cont.*)
> SG Education
> History and Social Change
> Law, Government, and Public Policy
> Social Sciences and Culture

BT organizations
RT facilities

instructions
> DG Types and Forms of Materials

instrument makers
> SG Economics and Employment
> Visual and Performing Arts

BT arts, entertainment, and media
> occupations

RT acoustics
> craft arts

instrumental music
> SG Visual and Performing Arts

BT music

insurance
> SG Economics and Employment
> Law, Government, and Public Policy

NT automobile insurance
> disability insurance
> health insurance
> liability insurance
> life insurance
> no fault insurance
> unemployment insurance

RT accidental death
> accidents
> aging
> arson
> dependent benefits
> dependent care
> discrimination
> eligibility
> home accidents
> industries
> insurance adjusters
> insurance examiners
> intrauterine devices
> liability

(*cont.*)

insurance (*cont.*)
> RT limited liability
> value

insurance adjusters
> SG Economics and Employment

BT financial occupations
RT insurance

insurance agents
> SG Economics and Employment

BT agents
> marketing and sales occupations

insurance examiners
> SG Economics and Employment

BT financial occupations
RT insurance

insurance fraud
> SG Law, Government, and Public Policy

BT fraud
RT arson

insurance industry
> SG Economics and Employment

BT industries
RT health economics

insured loans
> SG Economics and Employment

BT loans

integration
> SG History and Social Change
> Law, Government, and Public Policy

NT curriculum integration
> school integration

RT culture conflict
> desegregation
> desegregation methods
> mainstreaming

integrity
> SG Language, Literature, Religion, and
> Philosophy

RT courage

(*cont.*)

UF=Use for   BT=Broader term   NT=Narrower term   RT=Related term

integrity (cont.)

RT heroes
    honesty
    imagination
    moral reform
    morality
    social reform
    values

intellectual development

SG Social Sciences and Culture
BT cognitive development
RT intellectuals

intellectual history

SG History and Social Change
BT history

intellectuals

SG Education
    Social Sciences and Culture
RT bluestockings
    criticism
    culture work
    intellectual development

intelligence

SG Education
NT artificial intelligence
RT abstract reasoning
    academic ability
    academic achievement
    aptitude
    cognitive processes
    creativity
    learning
    reinforcement
    self confidence
    testing

intelligence agencies

SG Communications
    Law, Government, and Public Policy
BT agencies
RT freedom of information

intelligence tests

SG Education
BT testing
RT bias
    cognitive processes
    psychological testing

intercaste marriage

SG International Women
    Social Sciences and Culture
BT marriage
RT caste
    untouchables

interdisciplinary studies

SG Education
    History and Social Change
    Social Sciences and Culture
NT area studies
    cross cultural studies
    development studies
    ethnic studies
    feminist studies
    future studies
    gay studies
    gender studies
    gerontology
    men's studies
    race, class, and gender studies
    women's studies
RT ethnomusicology
    humanities
    natural sciences
    research bias
    research methods
    scholarship
    social science research
    social sciences
    women in development

interest rates

SG Economics and Employment
BT socioeconomic indicators
NT prime interest rate
RT inflation
    mortgages

interethnic families
SG Social Sciences and Culture
BT families

interfaith marriage
SG Social Sciences and Culture
BT marriage

interior design
SG Visual and Performing Arts
BT design
RT decorative arts
    kitchens

intermediate grades
SG Education
DG Education Levels
BT elementary education

intern programs
SG Education
    Economics and Employment
BT programs
RT apprenticeships
    internships

international adoption
SG International Women
    Social Sciences and Culture
BT adoption

international affairs
USE **international relations**

International Decade for Women
SG History and Social Change
    International Women
    Law, Government, and Public Policy
RT global feminism

international division of labor
SN *Refers to women being slotted into low wage, low status jobs in developing countries.*
SG Economics and Employment
    International Women
BT division of labor
(cont.)

international division of labor *(cont.)*
RT developing nations
    global assembly lines
    global economy
    piecework labor policy
    sexual division of labor

international feminism
USE **global feminism**

international marriage
SG International Women
    Social Sciences and Culture
BT marriage
RT interracial marriage
    nationality

international perspective
SG History and Social Change
    International Women
RT fifth world
    fourth world
    global feminism
    international women's movement
    third world

international policy
SG Economics and Employment
    International Women
    Law, Government, and Public Policy
BT policy
NT foreign aid policy
    immigration policy
    international trade policy
RT international relations

international relations
SG International Women
    Law, Government, and Public Policy
UF foreign affairs
    international affairs
BT relationships
RT foreign aid
    foreign service
    international policy
    nationality
    politics

---

international trade policy
- SG International Women
  Law, Government, and Public Policy
- BT international policy
- RT balance of payments
  economy
  exchange rate
  free trade zones
  global economy
  laissez faire
  markets
  multinational corporations

international women's movement
- SG History and Social Change
  International Women
- DG Cultural and Political Movements
- BT women's movement
- RT cross cultural feminism
  global feminism
  international perspective

internment
- SG History and Social Change
  Law, Government, and Public Policy
- RT civil rights
  concentration camps
  prisons

internships
- SG Education
  Economics and Employment
- RT assistantships
  fellowships
  intern programs
  medical education
  on the job training
  residency programs
  scholarships
  student financial aid

interpersonal communication
- SG Social Sciences and Culture
- BT communication
- RT interruptions
  language
  listening

(cont.)

interpersonal communication *(cont.)*
- RT talk

interpersonal relationships
- USE **personal relationships**

interpreters
- SG Economics and Employment
  International Women
  Law, Government, and Public Policy
- BT legal and political occupations
- RT translators

interracial adoption
- SG Law, Government, and Public Policy
  Social Sciences and Culture
- BT adoption
- RT interracial families

interracial families
- SG Social Sciences and Culture
- BT families
- RT interracial adoption
  norms

interracial marriage
- SG Social Sciences and Culture
- BT marriage
- RT international marriage
  miscegenation

interracial relations
- SG History and Social Change
  Social Sciences and Culture
- BT relationships
- RT cross cultural studies
  ethnic relations

interreligious families
- SG Social Sciences and Culture
- BT families

interrole conflict
- SG Social Sciences and Culture
- BT role conflict
- RT balancing work and family life
  multiple roles

SN=Scope note SG=Subject group DG=Delimiters group USE=Use

interruptions
- SG Language, Literature, Religion, and
   Philosophy
   Social Sciences and Culture
- RT female male relationships
   interpersonal communication
   patriarchal language
   sexist language
   sociolinguistics
   talk

interviewers
- SG Communications
   Social Sciences and Culture
- RT journalists
   research methods

interviewing
- SG Social Sciences and Culture
- BT research methods

interviews
- SG Communications
   Education
   Social Sciences and Culture
- DG Types and Forms of Materials
- RT career planning
   documentaries
   oral history
   resumes
   social science research

intimacy
- SG Social Sciences and Culture
- BT psychological needs
- RT impotence
   nonorgasmic women
   relationships
   self disclosure

intimidation
- SG Social Sciences and Culture
- NT ethnic intimidation
   sexual intimidation
- RT dominance

intramurals
- SG Education
- RT athletics
   sports

intrauterine devices
- SG Natural Sciences and Health
- UF IUDs
- BT contraception
- RT corporate liability
   insurance
   wicking

introversion
- SG Social Sciences and Culture
- RT extroversion
   personality traits

intuition
- SG Social Sciences and Culture
- BT knowledge
- RT abstract reasoning
   cognitive dissonance
   cognitive processes
   creative thinking
   creative writing
   extrasensory perception
   imagination
   instincts
   logical thinking
   mysticism
   perception skills
   problem solving

Inuit
- DG Ethnic, Racial, and Religious
   Descriptors

inventions
- SG Science and Technology
- RT patents
   technology development

inventors
- SG Economics and Employment
   Science and Technology
- BT scientific and technical occupations

UF=Use for   BT=Broader term   NT=Narrower term   RT=Related term

investigations
- SG Economics and Employment
  History and Social Change
  Law, Government, and Public Policy
- RT affirmative action suits
  commissions
  crimes

investigative journalism
- SG Communications
- BT journalism

investments
- SG Economics and Employment
- RT capital
  corporate responsibility
  foreign investment policy
  stock exchanges

investors
- SG Economics and Employment
- RT capital
  financial occupations

invisibility
- SG History and Social Change
  Language, Literature, Religion, and
    Philosophy
  Social Sciences and Culture
  Visual and Performing Arts
- RT anonymous
  canon
  false generics
  gender marking
  generic pronouns
  images of girls
  images of women
  jargon
  literary canon
  patronymy
  pseudonyms
  silence
  women in
  women's culture

involuntary depression
- SG Natural Sciences and Health
  (cont.)

involuntary depression *(cont.)*
- BT depression

involuntary sterilization
- SG Natural Sciences and Health
- UF compulsory sterilization
- BT sterilization
- RT civil rights

Iranian
- DG National and Regional Descriptors
- BT Middle Eastern

Iraqi
- DG National and Regional Descriptors
- BT Middle Eastern

Irish
- DG National and Regional Descriptors
- BT European

iron deficiency anemia
- SG Natural Sciences and Health
- BT anemia

ironers
- SG Economics and Employment
- BT female intensive occupations
  service occupations
- RT launderers

ironing
- SG Economics and Employment
  Social Sciences and Culture
- RT household labor

irony
- SG Language, Literature, Religion, and
    Philosophy
- BT figurative language
- RT drama
  humor
  jokes
  satire
  tragedy

irrationalism
DG Cultural and Political Movements

irrigation
SG Language, Literature, Religion, and
    Philosophy
    Science and Technology
RT water

Islam
DG Cultural and Political Movements

isolation
SG Language, Literature, Religion, and
    Philosophy
RT agoraphobia
    alienation
    apathy

isolationism
DG Cultural and Political Movements

isometric exercise
SG Natural Sciences and Health
BT exercise

Israeli
DG National and Regional Descriptors
BT Middle Eastern

Italian
DG National and Regional Descriptors
BT European

Italian American
DG Ethnic, Racial, and Religious
    Descriptors

IUDs
USE **intrauterine devices**

Ivory Coaster
DG National and Regional Descriptors
BT African

jails
USE **prisons**

Jamaican
DG National and Regional Descriptors
BT West Indian

janitors
SG Economics and Employment
UF charwomen
BT cleaners
    service occupations

Japanese
DG National and Regional Descriptors
BT Asian

Japanese American
DG Ethnic, Racial, and Religious
    Descriptors

jargon
SG Language, Literature, Religion, and
    Philosophy
RT cliches
    invisibility
    language
    talk

jazz
SG Visual and Performing Arts
BT music

jazz musicians
SG Economics and Employment
    Visual and Performing Arts
BT musicians

jealousy
SG Social Sciences and Culture
BT emotions
RT crimes of passion
    possessiveness

jewelry
SG Visual and Performing Arts
NT rings
RT adornment
    metal art
    pierced ears

UF = Use for   BT = Broader term   NT = Narrower term   RT = Related term

jewelry makers
SG Economics and Employment
     Visual and Performing Arts
BT arts, entertainment, and media
     occupations

Jewish
DG Ethnic, Racial, and Religious
     Descriptors

Jewish women's studies
SG Education
     Language, Literature, Religion, and
     Philosophy
BT ethnic studies
     women's studies

job advertisements
SG Economics and Employment
BT hiring policy
RT affirmative action hiring
     job hunting
     job recruitment
     job search methods

job alienation
SG Economics and Employment
BT alienation
RT job satisfaction
     work alienation

job candidates
SG Economics and Employment
BT candidates
RT affirmative action hiring
     blind review
     search committees

job counseling
USE **occupational counseling**

job descriptions
SG Economics and Employment
BT employment practices

job development
SG Economics and Employment
     Education
BT development
RT job skills
     motivation
     training

job discrimination
SG Economics and Employment
     History and Social Change
UF barriers to employment
BT discrimination
RT affirmative action hiring
     affirmative action suits
     glass ceiling
     job standards
     racism
     sex discrimination in employment

job evaluation
SG Economics and Employment
BT evaluation
RT comparable worth
     job standards

job ghettos
SG Economics and Employment
RT employment opportunities
     employment practices
     equal employment opportunity
     female intensive occupations
     glass ceiling
     race equity
     sex equity
     sex segregation

job hunting
SG Economics and Employment
UF job search
RT contacts
     executive recruitment
     job advertisements
     job market
     networks
     nominations
     work reentry

job layoffs
- SG Economics and Employment
- RT displaced homemakers
  firing
  job security
  reduction in force
  unemployment

job market
- SG Economics and Employment
- RT employment opportunities
  job hunting

job mobility
- USE **occupational mobility**

job performance
- SG Economics and Employment
- BT performance
- RT performance appraisal
  personnel evaluation

job placement
- SG Economics and Employment
- RT hiring policy
  outplacement

job recruitment
- SG Economics and Employment
- UF personnel recruitment
- BT employment practices
- NT executive recruitment
- RT employment
  employment agencies
  hiring policy
  information dissemination
  job advertisements
  networks
  search committees

job responsibility
- SG Economics and Employment
- RT job rewards
  occupational stress
  perquisites

job retraining
- SG Economics and Employment
  Education
- RT faculty retrenchment
  job training
  outplacement
  technology

job rewards
- SG Economics and Employment
- RT initiative
  job responsibility
  job satisfaction
  risk taking

job satisfaction
- SG Economics and Employment
- BT satisfaction
- RT job alienation
  job rewards
  turnover rates
  vocational aptitude

job search
- USE **job hunting**

job search methods
- SG Economics and Employment
- BT methods
- RT executive recruitment
  job advertisements
  networks

job security
- SG Economics and Employment
- BT security
- RT job layoffs
  reduction in force
  tenure

job segregation
- USE **occupational segregation**

job sharing
- SG Economics and Employment
- UF work sharing
- BT part time employment

(cont.)

UF=Use for   BT=Broader term   NT=Narrower term   RT=Related term   253

job sharing (*cont.*)
- RT employment
  flexible work schedules

job skills
- SG Economics and Employment
- BT skills
- RT job development
  vocational aptitude

job standards
- SG Economics and Employment
- BT standards
- RT certification
  job discrimination
  job evaluation
  occupational sex segregation
  stereotypes

job stress
- USE **occupational stress**

job training
- SG Education
  Economics and Employment
- UF employment training
  occupational training
- BT training
- NT on the job training
- RT adult illiteracy
  Comprehensive Employment and Training
    Act of 1973
  employee development
  job retraining
  Job Training Partnership Act
  performance appraisal

Job Training Partnership Act
- DG Laws and Regulations
- RT job training

jobs
- USE **occupations**

jockeys
- SG Economics and Employment
  Natural Sciences and Health

  (cont.)

jockeys (*cont.*)
- BT arts, entertainment, and media
  occupations

jogging
- USE **running**

johns
- SG Social Sciences and Culture
- RT prostitutes

joint custody
- USE **shared custody**

jokes
- SG Communications
  Language, Literature, Religion, and
    Philosophy
- RT burlesque
  comedy
  entertainment
  humor
  irony
  puns
  satire
  sense of humor
  slapstick
  stereotypes

journalism
- SG Communications
- NT investigative journalism
  photojournalism
  sports journalism
- RT advice columns
  copywriters
  editorials
  mass media
  press coverage
  public relations
  science reporting
  women's media
  women's pages
  writing

SN=Scope note   SG=Subject group   DG=Delimiters group   USE=Use

journalists

SG Communications
     Economics and Employment
BT arts, entertainment, and media
     occupations
NT correspondents
RT editors
     interviewers
     reporters
     writers

journals

SG Language, Literature, Religion, and
     Philosophy
DG Types and Forms of Materials
BT nonfiction
RT autobiography
     biography
     diaries
     histories
     letters
     memoirs
     narratives
     personal narratives

journals (periodicals)

DG Types and Forms of Materials
BT periodicals

joy

SG Social Sciences and Culture
BT emotions
RT pleasure

Judaism

DG Cultural and Political Movements

judges

SG Economics and Employment
     Law, Government, and Public Policy
BT legal and political occupations
     professional occupations
RT legal system
     officials

judicial appointments

SG Law, Government, and Public Policy
(cont.)

judicial appointments (cont.)

RT appointed officials
     legal and political occupations

judicial attitudes

SG Law, Government, and Public Policy
BT attitudes
RT criminal abortion
     immorality

judicial process

SG Law, Government, and Public Policy
BT process
RT court decisions
     due process
     lawsuits
     legal system

judiciary

SG Law, Government, and Public Policy
BT legal system

judiciary system

SG Law, Government, and Public Policy
RT correctional rehabilitation
     criminal law
     criminal lawsuits
     prisoners

judo

SG Natural Sciences and Health
BT martial arts
     sports

Jungianism

DG Cultural and Political Movements

junior colleges

SG Education
BT colleges
RT community colleges

junior high schools

SG Education
DG Education Levels
BT high schools

juries

    SG Law, Government, and Public Policy
  RT criminal law
      jurors
      trials (courtroom)

jurors

    SG Economics and Employment
          Law, Government, and Public Policy
  RT juries
      legal system

jury duty

    SG Law, Government, and Public Policy
  RT citizenship
      responsibility

justice

    SG Law, Government, and Public Policy
  NT criminal justice
      distributive justice
  RT due process
      equity
      values

juvenile courts

    SG Law, Government, and Public Policy
  BT courts
      juvenile justice system

juvenile delinquency

    SG Law, Government, and Public Policy
          Social Sciences and Culture
  RT antisocial behavior
      crimes
      delinquent behavior
      gangs
      juvenile offenders
      rebellious behavior

juvenile justice system

    SG Law, Government, and Public Policy
  BT legal system
  NT juvenile courts
  RT alternative programs
      at risk populations
      correctional rehabilitation

(cont.)

juvenile justice system *(cont.)*

  RT criminal justice
      juvenile offenders
      reformatories
      restitution

juvenile offenders

    SG Law, Government, and Public Policy
          Social Sciences and Culture
  RT at risk populations
      criminals
      juvenile delinquency
      juvenile justice system

juvenile prostitution

    SG Law, Government, and Public Policy
          Social Sciences and Culture
  BT prostitution
  RT child abuse
      exploitation
      pornography
      runaways

Kantianism

    DG Cultural and Political Movements

karate

    SG Natural Sciences and Health
  BT martial arts
      sports

keening

    SG Language, Literature, Religion, and
          Philosophy
  BT mourning

Kenyan

    DG National and Regional Descriptors
  BT African

keypunch operators

    USE **data entry operators**

kibbutzim

    SG Social Sciences and Culture
  BT communes
  RT collectives

(cont.)

kibbutzim (*cont.*)
RT life styles

kidnapping
SG Law, Government, and Public Policy
RT child custody

kindergarten
SG Education
BT educational facilities
RT primary education

kinesics
SG Language, Literature, Religion, and
Philosophy
Social Sciences and Culture
RT body language
body politics
gestures
language
nonverbal language

kinesthetic perception
SG Social Sciences and Culture
BT perception

kinship
SG Social Sciences and Culture
NT bilineal kinship
matrilineal kinship
patrilineal kinship
unilineal kinship
RT consanguinity
family influence
family structure
identity
lineage
names
surnames
totemism

kissing
SG Social Sciences and Culture
BT forms of affection

kitchens
SG History and Social Change
Social Sciences and Culture
BT rooms
RT ergonomics
household labor
interior design
labor saving devices
separate spheres

knitting
SG Visual and Performing Arts
BT craft arts
needlework

knitting machine operators
SG Economics and Employment
BT clothing workers
machine operators

knowledge
SG Education
Language, Literature, Religion, and
Philosophy
NT intuition
subjective knowledge

Korean
DG National and Regional Descriptors
BT Asian

Korean American
DG Ethnic, Racial, and Religious
Descriptors

Korean War
DG Historical Periods

labels
SG History and Social Change
RT names
sexist language
stereotyping
surnames

labia
SG Natural Sciences and Health
(*cont.*)

UF = Use for   BT = Broader term   NT = Narrower term   RT = Related term

labia (*cont.*)
BT   genitals

labor
SG   Economics and Employment
NT   child labor
     household labor
     manual labor
RT   automation
     employment
     labor unions
     political parties
     work

labor (childbirth)
SG   Natural Sciences and Health
BT   childbirth
NT   induced labor
RT   birthing rooms
     labor coaching
     natural childbirth
     pain

labor coaching
SG   Natural Sciences and Health
RT   labor (childbirth)
     natural childbirth

labor contracts
SG   Economics and Employment
BT   contracts
RT   industrial relations
     labor disputes
     mediation
     negotiation
     unions

labor disputes
SG   Economics and Employment
     Law, Government, and Public Policy
RT   arbitration
     labor contracts
     mediation
     strikes
     unfair labor practices
     unions

labor force
SG   Economics and Employment
UF   manpower
     work force
BT   human resources
NT   multinational labor force
     unpaid labor force
RT   displaced homemakers
     employment
     labor force participation
     occupations
     reentry women

labor force participation
SG   Economics and Employment
RT   labor force
     labor supply
     labor turnover
     work history

labor force rates
SG   Economics and Employment
BT   labor force statistics

labor force statistics
SG   Economics and Employment
NT   labor force rates

labor history
SG   History and Social Change
BT   history
RT   labor movement
     labor unions

labor law reform
SG   Law, Government, and Public Policy
BT   reforms
RT   arbitration
     labor legislation
     labor movement

labor laws
USE **labor legislation**

labor legislation
SG   Law, Government, and Public Policy
UF   labor laws

(*cont.*)

labor legislation (*cont.*)
- BT legislation
- RT child labor
  - labor law reform
  - pay equity
  - racial discrimination
  - sex discrimination in employment

labor market
- SG Economics and Employment
- RT occupations

labor movement
- SG History and Social Change
- DG Cultural and Political Movements
- BT social movements
- RT class consciousness
  - labor history
  - labor law reform
  - labor unions
  - untouchables

labor policy
- SG Economics and Employment
  - Law, Government, and Public Policy
- BT policy
- NT piecework labor policy
- RT labor theory of value

labor relations
- SG Economics and Employment
- BT relationships
- RT industrial relations

labor saving devices
- SG Economics and Employment
  - Social Sciences and Culture
- RT ergonomics
  - homemaking
  - house design
  - housewares
  - kitchens

labor supply
- SG Economics and Employment
- BT human resources
- RT labor force participation

(*cont.*)

labor supply (*cont.*)
- RT multinational labor force
  - occupations

labor theory of value
- SG Economics and Employment
- BT theory
- RT economic value of women's work
  - labor policy

labor turnover
- SG Economics and Employment
- RT labor force participation

labor unions
- SG Economics and Employment
- BT unions
- RT labor
  - labor history
  - labor movement
  - occupations
  - organizing
  - union membership
  - workplace

laboratories
- SG Education
  - History and Social Change
  - Social Sciences and Culture
- BT facilities
- RT laboratory assistants
  - sponsored research

laboratory animals
- SG Natural Sciences and Health
- BT animals
- RT research

laboratory assistants
- SG Education
  - Natural Sciences and Health
- BT education occupations
- NT animal caretakers
- RT laboratories

UF=Use for   BT=Broader term   NT=Narrower term   RT=Related term

laborers
SG Economics and Employment
Science and Technology
UF unskilled laborers
BT workers
RT construction industry
construction occupations
manufacturing occupations

lace making
SG Economics and Employment
Social Sciences and Culture
BT craft arts

lack of confidence
SG Social Sciences and Culture
RT empowerment
fear of failure
nervousness
self concept

lacrosse
SG Natural Sciences and Health
BT sports

lactation
SG Natural Sciences and Health
RT breast feeding
expressing milk

lactose intolerance
SG Natural Sciences and Health
RT milk substitutes

ladies
USE **women**

ladies (historical)
SG History and Social Change
Social Sciences and Culture
BT images of women
women

ladies (nobility)
SG International Women
Law, Government, and Public Policy
BT images of women
(cont.)

ladies (nobility) (cont.)
BT titles (nobility)
women

ladies' aid societies
SG History and Social Change
Social Sciences and Culture
BT societies

ladies' auxiliaries
USE **auxiliaries**

laissez faire
SG Economics and Employment
International Women
Law, Government, and Public Policy
RT corporate policy
free enterprise
free trade zones
international trade policy

laity
SG Language, Literature, Religion, and
Philosophy
UF laypeople
NT deacons
laymen
laywomen
RT religious workers
volunteers

land reform
SG International Women
BT reforms
RT land use
peasants
property rights

land rights
SG Law, Government, and Public Policy
BT rights
RT inheritance customs
marital property reform
property ownership

land settlement
SG International Women
(cont.)

land settlement (*cont.*)
- UF resettlement
- NT rural resettlement
- RT pioneers

land tenure
- SG Economics and Employment
      International Women
- RT property rights

land use
- SG Economics and Employment
      International Women
- RT agriculture
      land reform

land use technology
- SG Science and Technology
- BT technology

landlords
- SG Economics and Employment
      Law, Government, and Public Policy
      Social Sciences and Culture
- NT slum landlords
- RT housing
      rent

landscape architects
- SG Economics and Employment
      Visual and Performing Arts
- BT architects

language
- SG Language, Literature, Religion, and
      Philosophy
- NT discriminatory language
      figurative language
      informal language
      nonsexist language
      nonverbal language
      patriarchal language
      programming languages
      religious language
      sign language
      women's language
      written language

(*cont.*)

language (*cont.*)
- RT bilingualism
      cliches
      communication
      conversation
      culture
      dialects
      false generics
      forms of address
      gender marking
      gossip
      interpersonal communication
      jargon
      kinesics
      language aptitude
      language skills
      language structure
      lies
      linguistics
      literacy
      mother tongue
      nonverbal ability
      profanity
      racial and ethnic differences
      racism
      sexism
      slang
      sociolinguistics
      speech
      stereotyping
      storytelling
      symbols
      talk

language aptitude
- SG Education
      Language, Literature, Religion, and
      Philosophy
- BT aptitude
- RT language
      language skills
      verbal ability

language development
- SG Education
      Language, Literature, Religion, and
      Philosophy

(*cont.*)

UF=Use for   BT=Broader term   NT=Narrower term   RT=Related term

language development (*cont.*)
- BT development
      individual development
- NT verbal development
- RT linguistics

language skills
- SG Education
      Language, Literature, Religion, and
      Philosophy
- BT skills
- RT basic skills
      bilingualism
      braille
      communication
      discourse
      language
      language aptitude
      reading
      sign language
      social dialects
      women's language
      writing

language structure
- SG Language, Literature, Religion, and
      Philosophy
- RT grammar
      language
      masculine pronouns
      programming languages
      transformational grammar
      written language

Laotian
- DG National and Regional Descriptors
- BT Asian

larceny
- SG Law, Government, and Public Policy
- BT property crimes

large cities
- USE **urban areas**

laser disks
- DG Types and Forms of Materials
                                    (*cont.*)

laser disks (*cont.*)
- BT disks

last rites
- SG Language, Literature, Religion, and
      Philosophy
- BT sacraments
- RT bereavement
      death
      death and dying

latchkey children
- SG Education
      Social Sciences and Culture
- BT children
- RT after school programs
      working parents

late childbearing
- SG Natural Sciences and Health
- BT childbearing
- RT amniocentesis
      biological clock
      delayed parenthood
      maternal age
      planned parenthood

lateral dominance
- SN *Functional supremacy of one side of
      the brain, left or right, over the oth-
      er.*
- SG Natural Sciences and Health
- RT learning disabilities
      math ability
      psychology
      sex differences

Latin American
- DG National and Regional Descriptors
- UF South American
- NT Argentine
      Bolivian
      Brazilian
      Caribbean
      Central American
      Chilean
      Colombian
                                    (*cont.*)

Latin American (*cont.*)
- NT Ecuadoran
  - Falkland Islander
  - Guyanese
  - Mexican
  - Paraguayan
  - Peruvian
  - Surinamese
  - Uruguayan
  - Venezuelan
  - West Indian

Latin American studies
- SG Education
  - International Women
  - Social Sciences and Culture
- BT area studies

Latina
- DG Ethnic, Racial, and Religious
  - Descriptors

Latina studies
- SG Education
  - History and Social Change
  - International Women
  - Social Sciences and Culture
- UF Hispanic studies
- BT ethnic studies
  - women's studies
- NT Chicana studies

laughter
- SG Social Sciences and Culture
- RT humor
  - smiling

launderers
- SG Economics and Employment
- UF laundresses
  - washerwomen
- BT female intensive occupations
  - service occupations
- RT ironers

laundresses
- USE **launderers**

laundry
- SG Economics and Employment
  - Social Sciences and Culture
- RT household labor

law
- SN *See also Delimiters Display: Laws and*
  - *Regulations.*
- SG Law, Government, and Public Policy
- NT civil law
  - corporate law
  - criminal law
  - marriage and family law
  - religious law
- RT laws
  - legal and political occupations
  - legislation

law enforcement
- SG Law, Government, and Public Policy
- RT enforcement
  - police officers

laws
- SN *See also Delimiters Display: Laws and*
  - *Regulations.*
- SG Law, Government, and Public Policy
- NT abortion laws
  - community property laws
  - copyright laws
  - disclosure laws
  - discrimination laws
  - divorce laws
  - gun control laws
  - property laws
  - tax laws
- RT abortion
  - affirmative action
  - affirmative action hiring
  - age discrimination
  - enforcement
  - equal protection under the law
  - federal legislation
  - law
  - legislation
  - licensing
  - marriage

(*cont.*)

UF=Use for   BT=Broader term   NT=Narrower term   RT=Related term

laws (*cont.*)
RT rights
social prohibitions
taxes

lawsuits
SG Law, Government, and Public Policy
UF litigation
suits
NT affirmative action suits
civil lawsuits
class action suits
criminal lawsuits
paternity suits
RT affirmative action
affirmative action hiring
bitterness
civil rights legislation
consent orders
contract compliance
judicial process
libel

lawyer client relationships
SG Law, Government, and Public Policy
Social Sciences and Culture
BT relationships
RT confidentiality

lawyers
SG Economics and Employment
Law, Government, and Public Policy
UF attorneys
BT legal and political occupations
professional occupations
NT barristers
RT legal system

lay midwives
SG Economics and Employment
Natural Sciences and Health
UF granny midwives
BT midwives

laying on of hands
SG Language, Literature, Religion, and
Philosophy
Natural Sciences and Health
RT faith healers
folk healers

laymen
SG Language, Literature, Religion, and
Philosophy
BT laity
men
RT faith communities

laypeople
USE **laity**

laywomen
SG Language, Literature, Religion, and
Philosophy
BT laity
women
RT faith communities
patriarchal religion
women religious

leadership
SG History and Social Change
NT student leadership
RT authority
charisma
chief executives
collaboration
group process
management styles
organizations
political leaders
power
presidency

leadership roles
SG Economics and Employment
Law, Government, and Public Policy
Social Sciences and Culture
BT roles
RT influence
perceptual bias

(*cont.*)

leadership roles (*cont.*)
RT socialization

leadership skills
SG Economics and Employment
BT skills
RT authority
charisma
collaboration
consensus building
influence
power

leadership training
SG Economics and Employment
BT training
RT empowerment
mentors

leagues
SG History and Social Change
Social Sciences and Culture
BT organizations

learned behavior
SG Social Sciences and Culture
BT behavior
RT instincts
mother syndrome
parenting

learned helplessness
SG History and Social Change
Social Sciences and Culture
UF helplessness
RT assertive behavior
assertiveness training
compliant behavior
conditioning
dependent behavior
depression
obedience
oppression
passive behavior
powerlessness
social conditioning
socialization

(*cont.*)

learned helplessness (*cont.*)
RT submissive behavior
victimization
withdrawal

learning
SG Education
NT adult learning
experiential learning
lifelong learning
RT aptitude
cognitive processes
conditioning
curiosity
intelligence
reinforcement

learning differences
SG Education
BT differences

learning disabilities
SG Natural Sciences and Health
BT disabilities
RT attention
lateral dominance
mental retardation

learning motivation
SG Education
BT motivation
RT academic ability
adult learning

Lebanese
DG National and Regional Descriptors
BT Middle Eastern

lectures
SG History and Social Change
Social Sciences and Culture
BT educational activities

ledgers
DG Types and Forms of Materials

---

left wing organizations
SG History and Social Change
Social Sciences and Culture
BT organizations
RT new left
radicals

legal advocates
SG Law, Government, and Public Policy
BT advocates

legal aid services
SG Law, Government, and Public Policy
BT legal services

legal and political occupations
SG Economics and Employment
Law, Government, and Public Policy
BT occupations
NT appointed officials
diplomats
elected officials
government workers
heads of state
interpreters
judges
lawyers
legislators
magistrates
mediators
military personnel
negotiators
presidents
prime ministers
public officials
vice presidents
RT first ladies (historical)
governors' spouses
judicial appointments
law
political spouses
presidential spouses
professional occupations
protective service occupations
volunteer occupations
women in politics

legal briefs
DG Types and Forms of Materials
BT legal documents

legal cruelty
SG Law, Government, and Public Policy
RT divorce laws

legal documents
SG Law, Government, and Public Policy
DG Types and Forms of Materials
BT documents
NT birth certificates
contracts
custody decrees
death certificates
divorce decrees
legal briefs
licenses
property settlements
restraining orders
separation agreements
wills
working papers

legal guardians
SG Law, Government, and Public Policy
BT guardians
surrogates
RT adoption

legal responsibility
SG Law, Government, and Public Policy
BT responsibility

legal services
SG Law, Government, and Public Policy
BT services
social services
NT legal aid services
RT confidentiality

legal settlements
SG Law, Government, and Public Policy
RT affirmative action suits
alimony
back pay

(cont.)

SN=Scope note   SG=Subject group   DG=Delimiters group   USE=Use

legal settlements (*cont.*)
- RT child support
  community property laws
  poverty
  spouse support

legal status
- SG Law, Government, and Public Policy
- BT status
- RT equal rights legislation

legal system
- SG Law, Government, and Public Policy
- NT judiciary
  juvenile justice system
- RT constitution
  criminal justice
  judges
  judicial process
  jurors
  lawyers
  legislatures
  organizations
  restitution
  trials (courtroom)

legends
- SG Language, Literature, Religion, and
  Philosophy
- BT folk literature
- RT fairy tales
  folk culture
  mythology
  oral history
  oral literature
  oral tradition
  romances
  stories

legislation
- SN *See also Delimiters Display: Laws and
  Regulations.*
- SG Law, Government, and Public Policy
- NT antitrust legislation
  civil rights legislation
  discriminatory legislation
  educational legislation

(*cont.*)

legislation (*cont.*)
- NT equal pay legislation
  equal rights legislation
  federal legislation
  health care legislation
  labor legislation
  local legislation
  minimum wage legislation
  protective legislation
  right to know legislation
  social legislation
  state legislation
- RT appropriations
  law
  laws
  legislators
  policy making
  reforms

legislators
- SG Economics and Employment
  Law, Government, and Public Policy
- BT legal and political occupations
- RT legislation

legislatures
- SG Law, Government, and Public Policy
- BT organizations
- RT elected officials
  legal system
  women in politics

legitimacy
- SG Law, Government, and Public Policy
  Social Sciences and Culture
- RT inheritance customs
  legitimization of children

legitimization of children
- SG Law, Government, and Public Policy
  Social Sciences and Culture
- RT bastards
  illegitimacy
  inheritance customs
  legitimacy

UF=Use for   BT=Broader term   NT=Narrower term   RT=Related term

legs

SG Natural Sciences and Health
BT bodies

leisure

SG Social Sciences and Culture
RT games
recreation
relaxation
vacations

leisure activities

SG Social Sciences and Culture
BT activities
RT hobbies

Leninism

DG Cultural and Political Movements

lesbian communities

SG History and Social Change
Social Sciences and Culture
BT communities
RT contact dykes
female societies
lesbian culture
lesbian feminism
lesbian separatism
lesbians

lesbian couples

SG History and Social Change
Social Sciences and Culture
BT gay couples
RT gay male couples
lesbian marriage
lesbian mothers
relationships

lesbian culture

SG History and Social Change
Social Sciences and Culture
UF gay female culture
BT gay culture
women's culture
RT cultural feminism
gay male culture

(cont.)

lesbian culture *(cont.)*

RT homosexuality
lesbian communities
lesbian feminism
lesbianism
lesbians

lesbian experience

SG History and Social Change
Social Sciences and Culture
UF gay female experience
BT gay experience
RT gay male experience
gay pride
gay/straight split
homophile movement
lesbians

lesbian feminism

SG History and Social Change
International Women
DG Cultural and Political Movements
BT feminism
RT gay/straight split
lesbian communities
lesbian culture
lesbian movement
lesbianism

lesbian literature

SG History and Social Change
Language, Literature, Religion, and
Philosophy
BT gay literature
women's literature
RT lesbian studies

lesbian marriage

SG History and Social Change
Social Sciences and Culture
BT gay marriage
RT gay male marriage
lesbian couples
lesbians

lesbian mothers

- SG History and Social Change
  Social Sciences and Culture
- BT mothers
- RT child custody
  custody
  gay fathers
  lesbian couples
  lesbian stepmothers
  lesbians
  parenthood
  parenting

lesbian movement

- SG History and Social Change
- DG Cultural and Political Movements
- BT social movements
- RT lesbian feminism
  lesbians

lesbian relationships

- SG Natural Sciences and Health
  Social Sciences and Culture
- BT female female relationships
  gay relationships

lesbian separatism

- SG History and Social Change
- DG Cultural and Political Movements
- BT separatism
- RT gay/straight split
  gynarchy
  lesbian communities
  life styles

lesbian stepmothers

- SG Social Sciences and Culture
- UF gay stepmothers
- BT stepmothers
- RT blended families
  gay stepfathers
  lesbian mothers
  parent child relationships

lesbian studies

- SG Education
  History and Social Change
  Social Sciences and Culture
- BT gay studies
- RT lesbian literature
  lesbians

lesbianism

- SN *Moves beyond women's relationships to include cultures of women-identified women.*
- SG History and Social Change
- DG Cultural and Political Movements
- UF female homosexuality
- BT homosexuality
- RT compulsory heterosexuality
  lesbian culture
  lesbian feminism
  lesbians
  women identified women

lesbians

- SG History and Social Change
  Social Sciences and Culture
- UF dykes
  female homosexuals
  gay women
- BT gays
  women
- NT closeted lesbians
  contact dykes
- RT amazons
  bisexuality
  butch
  child rearing practices
  children
  couples
  female sexuality
  femme
  gay rights
  heterosexuality
  homophobia
  homosexuality
  images of girls
  images of women
  lesbian communities

(cont.)

lesbians *(cont.)*

RT lesbian culture
      lesbian experience
      lesbian marriage
      lesbian mothers
      lesbian movement
      lesbian studies
      lesbianism
      lesbophobia
      life styles
      passing
      stereotyping
      tribadism
      women identified women

lesbophobia

SG History and Social Change
      Natural Sciences and Health
      Social Sciences and Culture
BT homophobia
RT gay rights
      gay/straight split
      lesbians

lesson plans

DG Types and Forms of Materials
BT plans

letter writers

SG Language, Literature, Religion, and
      Philosophy
RT pen pals

letters

SG Language, Literature, Religion, and
      Philosophy
DG Types and Forms of Materials
BT nonfiction
RT autobiography
      biography
      correspondence
      diaries
      journals
      literature
      memoirs
      personal correspondence

letters of recommendation

SG Education
      Economics and Employment
RT admissions
      applications
      occupational mobility

levirate

SN *Marriage of a widow to the brother or*
      heir of her deceased husband.
SG Social Sciences and Culture
BT marriage customs

liability

SG Economics and Employment
      Law, Government, and Public Policy
NT corporate liability
      limited liability
RT insurance
      no fault insurance

liability insurance

SG Economics and Employment
BT insurance
RT health economics
      limited liability
      midwives

libel

SG Communications
      Law, Government, and Public Policy
RT defamation
      freedom of the press
      lawsuits

liberal feminism

SN *Feminist theory that advocates legal*
      reforms without requiring more radi-
      cal alterations in basic social, eco-
      nomic, and political institutions.
SG History and Social Change
      International Women
DG Cultural and Political Movements
BT feminism
RT feminist theory
      mainstream feminism

liberalism
- DG Cultural and Political Movements

liberals
- SG Law, Government, and Public Policy
- RT conservatives
  political parties

liberation
- SG History and Social Change
- NT fat liberation
  men's liberation
  sexual liberation
  women's liberation
- RT liberation struggles
  liberation theology
  oppression
  social movements

liberation struggles
- SG International Women
- BT struggles
- RT activists
  apartheid
  decolonization
  liberation
  resistance
  revolution
  slavery

liberation theology
- SG Language, Literature, Religion, and
  Philosophy
- BT theology
- RT feminist theology
  liberation
  moral reform
  social reform

Liberian
- DG National and Regional Descriptors
- BT African

Libertarian Party
- SG Law, Government, and Public Policy
- BT political parties

libertarianism
- DG Cultural and Political Movements

libido
- USE **sex drive**

librarians
- SG Communications
  Economics and Employment
- BT education occupations
  female intensive occupations
  professional occupations
- RT information scientists

libraries
- SG Communications
  Education
- BT educational facilities
- RT curators
  freedom of information
  information and referral centers
  information retrieval
  information services

library science
- SG Communications
- BT information sciences
- RT computer science
  preservation

library workers
- SG Communications
  Economics and Employment
  Education
- BT education occupations
  female intensive occupations
  workers

librettos
- SG Language, Literature, Religion, and
  Philosophy
  Visual and Performing Arts
- DG Types and Forms of Materials
- RT lyrics
  musical theater
  opera
  scores

Libyan
  DG National and Regional Descriptors
  BT African

licenses
  SG Law, Government, and Public Policy
  DG Types and Forms of Materials
  BT legal documents
  NT marriage licenses

licensing
  SG Communications
      Economics and Employment
      Law, Government, and Public Policy
  NT child care licensing
  RT academic standards
      accreditation
      day care
      day care centers
      health care facilities
      laws
      midwives
      patents
      regulations

lieder
  SG Visual and Performing Arts
  BT songs

lies
  SG Language, Literature, Religion, and
      Philosophy
  RT language
      lying

life cycles
  SG Natural Sciences and Health
      Social Sciences and Culture
  RT adolescence
      adult development
      adults
      aging
      childhood
      empty nest
      life expectancy
      life span
      menopause
                                    (cont.)

life cycles (cont.)
  RT middle age
      midlife crisis
      older adults
      passages
      transitions

life expectancy
  SG Social Sciences and Culture
  RT actuarials
      aging
      at risk populations
      life cycles
      life insurance
      life span
      mortality
      mortality rates

life histories
  SG History and Social Change
      Social Sciences and Culture
  DG Types and Forms of Materials
  BT histories
  RT oral history

life insurance
  SG Economics and Employment
  BT insurance
  RT actuarials
      death
      employee benefits
      life expectancy

life sciences
  USE **biological sciences**

life skills
  SG Education
      Natural Sciences and Health
  BT skills
  RT competence
      survival strategies

life span
  SG Natural Sciences and Health
      Social Sciences and Culture
  RT aging
                                    (cont.)

SN=Scope note   SG=Subject group   DG=Delimiters group   USE=Use

life span (*cont.*)
RT   life cycles
     life expectancy
     mortality

life styles
SG   Social Sciences and Culture
RT   architecture
     bachelors
     childfree marriage
     childless couples
     childlessness
     collectives
     communal families
     communes
     communities
     community
     counterculture
     couples
     cruising
     delayed parenthood
     families
     family relationships
     gay men
     homemakers
     housing
     kibbutzim
     lesbian separatism
     lesbians
     living arrangements
     marriage
     monogamy
     nudity
     posslq
     rural living
     separatism
     singles
     social class
     social differences
     space
     spinsters
     stress
     subculture
     utopias

lifelong learning
SG   Education

(cont.)

lifelong learning (*cont.*)
BT   learning
RT   adult development
     adult education
     education
     elderhostel
     older adults

Lilith
SG   Language, Literature, Religion, and
     Philosophy
BT   images of women
RT   Adam
     creation myths
     Eve
     religious symbols

limericks
SG   Language, Literature, Religion, and
     Philosophy
BT   poetry

limited liability
SG   Economics and Employment
BT   liability
RT   insurance
     liability insurance

lineage
SG   Social Sciences and Culture
RT   birth certificates
     kinship
     matriarchy

lingerie
SG   History and Social Change
     Social Sciences and Culture
BT   clothing
NT   corsets
     girdles
RT   fashion
     images of women
     sexual aids
     underwear

linguistic sexism

SG   Language, Literature, Religion, and
     Philosophy
     Social Sciences and Culture
BT   sexism
RT   desex
    gender marking
    generic pronouns
    he/man language
    male norms
    nonsexist language
    old maids
    patriarchal language
    prefixes
    semantics
    spinsters
    verbal abuse

linguistics

SG   Language, Literature, Religion, and
     Philosophy
BT   humanities
NT   applied linguistics
    descriptive linguistics
    historical linguistics
    morphology
    phonology
    psycholinguistics
    semantics
    sociolinguistics
    structural linguistics
    syntax
RT   language
    language development
    semiotics

liposuction surgery

SN   *Plastic surgery technique for removal
    of fatty tissue, such as in the abdo-
    men or buttocks.*
SG   Natural Sciences and Health
UF   suction lipectomy
BT   plastic surgery
RT   buttocks

listening

SG   Language, Literature, Religion, and
     Philosophy
     Social Sciences and Culture
BT   forms of affection
RT   arguments
    communication
    empathy
    empowerment
    feedback
    interpersonal communication
    oral tradition
    relationships
    social skills

lists

DG   Types and Forms of Materials

literacy

SG   Education
    International Women
    Language, Literature, Religion, and
     Philosophy
NT   adult literacy
    computer literacy
RT   basic education
    basic skills
    cognitive processes
    illiteracy
    language
    literacy campaigns
    oral history
    reading
    writing

literacy campaigns

SG   Education
    International Women
RT   literacy

literary arts

USE **literature**

literary canon

SG   History and Social Change
    Language, Literature, Religion, and
     Philosophy

(cont.)

literary canon (*cont.*)
BT   canon
RT   invisibility
      literary criticism
      male norms
      perceptual bias
      phallic criticism
      women's history
      women's literature

literary criticism
SG   Language, Literature, Religion, and
      Philosophy
BT   criticism
RT   deconstruction
      gynocriticism
      literary canon

literary genres
USE **literature**

literary history
SG   History and Social Change
      Language, Literature, Religion, and
      Philosophy
BT   history
RT   literature

literary symbols
SG   Language, Literature, Religion, and
      Philosophy
BT   symbols
RT   literature

literary theory
SG   Language, Literature, Religion, and
      Philosophy
BT   theory
RT   ambiguity
      deconstruction

literature
SG   Language, Literature, Religion, and
      Philosophy
UF   literary arts
      literary genres
BT   humanities

(*cont.*)

literature (*cont.*)
NT   children's literature
      drama
      erotic literature
      folk literature
      gay literature
      nonsexist literature
      oral literature
      poetry
      prose
      religious literature
      travel literature
      utopian literature
      women's literature
RT   aesthetics
      anonymous
      arts
      creative writing
      criticism
      farce
      feminist writing
      figurative language
      heroines (historical)
      images of women
      letters
      literary history
      literary symbols
      media arts
      mythology
      oratory
      performing arts
      popular culture
      pseudonyms
      public speaking
      satire
      skits
      speeches
      stream of consciousness
      writing

litigation
USE **lawsuits**

liturgies
SG   Language, Literature, Religion, and
      Philosophy
RT   rites

UF=Use for   BT=Broader term   NT=Narrower term   RT=Related term

living alone
SG   Social Sciences and Culture
RT   dependent care
independence
living arrangements
loneliness
solitude
support systems

living arrangements
SG   Social Sciences and Culture
RT   cohabitation
domestic relations
harems
life styles
living alone
marriage
marriage customs
relationships
space

living conditions
SG   Social Sciences and Culture
BT   conditions
RT   basic human needs
women living in poverty

living standards
SG   Economics and Employment
UF   standards of living
BT   standards
RT   basic human needs
inequality
poverty
quality of life
social class
socioeconomic conditions
socioeconomic indicators
upper class
wealth
women living in poverty

living together
USE **cohabitation**

loans
SG   Economics and Employment
Education
NT   consumer installment loans
home improvement loans
insured loans
student loans
RT   scholarships
student financial aid

lobbying
SG   History and Social Change
Law, Government, and Public Policy
RT   advocacy
advocacy groups
political action committees
political activism
pressure groups
special interest groups

local anesthesia
SG   Natural Sciences and Health
BT   anesthesia

local government
SG   Law, Government, and Public Policy
BT   government
RT   commissions

local legislation
SG   Law, Government, and Public Policy
BT   legislation

local politics
SG   Law, Government, and Public Policy
BT   politics
RT   grass roots

locker rooms
SG   Education
Social Sciences and Culture
BT   rooms
RT   athletics
male bonding
old boy networks
sports

locus of control

SN *Center of responsibility for control of an individual's behavior; can be defined as as internal or external to an individual.*

SG Social Sciences and Culture

BT psychological factors

RT control
power
self control

lodges

SG History and Social Change
Social Sciences and Culture

BT facilities

logic

SG Language, Literature, Religion, and Philosophy

BT philosophy

RT abstract reasoning
conceptual errors
logical thinking
problem solving

logical thinking

SG Language, Literature, Religion, and Philosophy
Social Sciences and Culture

BT cognitive processes

RT intuition
logic

logs

DG Types and Forms of Materials

Lolita

SG Language, Literature, Religion, and Philosophy

BT images of women

loneliness

SG Social Sciences and Culture

BT emotions

RT living alone
personal columns
solitude

(cont.)

loneliness *(cont.)*

RT unrequited love

long distance marriage
USE **commuter marriage**

long term memory

SG Social Sciences and Culture

BT memory

longshore workers

SG Economics and Employment

UF longshoremen
stevedores

BT workers

longshoremen
USE **longshore workers**

lookism

SN *Discrimination on the basis of physical looks.*

SG History and Social Change

RT appearance
beauty standards
facism
fashion

loss

SG Social Sciences and Culture

RT grief
mourning

loss of self

SG Natural Sciences and Health
Social Sciences and Culture

RT identity crisis
self denial

love

SG Language, Literature, Religion, and Philosophy
Social Sciences and Culture

BT emotions

NT courtly love
maternal love
romantic love

(cont.)

UF=Use for   BT=Broader term   NT=Narrower term   RT=Related term

love (cont.)
- NT unrequited love
- RT desire
    ethic of care
    forms of affection
    friendships
    nurturing
    parenting rewards
    passion
    romance

love potions
- SG Natural Sciences and Health
    Social Sciences and Culture
- RT aphrodisiacs
    folk medicine

lovemaking
- SG Social Sciences and Culture
- BT forms of affection
- RT sex
    sexual behavior

lovers
- SG Social Sciences and Culture
- RT friends
    personal relationships
    significant others

low income families
- SG Economics and Employment
    Social Sciences and Culture
- BT families
- RT basic human needs
    family finances
    income
    low pay
    moonlighting

low income households
- SG Economics and Employment
    Social Sciences and Culture
- BT households
- RT family finances
    income

low pay
- SG Economics and Employment
- BT wages
- RT deskilling
    low income families
    pay equity
    poverty
    wage gap

lower class
- SG Economics and Employment
    Social Sciences and Culture
- BT class
- RT classism
    families
    fathers
    maternal and infant welfare
    mothers
    poverty
    women living in poverty

loyalty
- SG Language, Literature, Religion, and
    Philosophy
- RT commitment
    values

loyalty oaths
- SG Law, Government, and Public Policy
- RT government appointments

lubricants
- SG Natural Sciences and Health
- RT sexual aids

lullabies
- SG Visual and Performing Arts
- BT songs
- RT nursery songs

lumber cutters
- SG Economics and Employment
- UF lumbermen
- BT agricultural, fishing, and forestry
    occupations

SN = Scope note   SG = Subject group   DG = Delimiters group   USE = Use

lumbermen
USE **lumber cutters**

lunches
SG   History and Social Change
     Social Sciences and Culture
BT   social activities

lust
SG   Social Sciences and Culture
UF   concupiscence
BT   emotions

Luxembourgian
DG   National and Regional Descriptors
BT   European

lying
SG   Language, Literature, Religion, and
     Philosophy
     Social Sciences and Culture
RT   honesty
     lies
     social values

lymph glands
SG   Natural Sciences and Health
BT   glands
RT   cancer

lynching
SG   History and Social Change
     Social Sciences and Culture
BT   violence
RT   antilynching campaign
     racial discrimination
     racism
     rape
     slave rape

lyric poetry
SG   Language, Literature, Religion, and
     Philosophy
BT   poetry
RT   troubadours

lyricists
SG   Economics and Employment
     Visual and Performing Arts
BT   arts, entertainment, and media
     occupations

lyrics
SG   Visual and Performing Arts
RT   hymns
     images of women
     librettos
     music
     performing arts
     poetry

machine operators
SG   Economics and Employment
BT   operators
NT   knitting machine operators
     sewing machine operators
RT   construction workers

machinery
SG   Science and Technology
RT   automation
     industries

machinists
SG   Economics and Employment
     Science and Technology
BT   craft occupations

machismo
SG   History and Social Change
     Social Sciences and Culture
RT   crimes of honor
     gender roles
     male chauvinism
     marianismo
     sex stereotypes
     sexism
     war

macroeconomics
SG   Economics and Employment
BT   economics

UF=Use for   BT=Broader term   NT=Narrower term   RT=Related term   279

madonna

   SG Language, Literature, Religion, and
       Philosophy
       Visual and Performing Arts
BT images of women
RT cult of the virgin
     holy women
     iconography
     immaculate conception
     religious art
     religious symbols
     sacred ideology
     virgin birth
     Virgin Mary

madrigals

   SG Visual and Performing Arts
BT vocal music

magazines

   SG Communications
   DG Types and Forms of Materials
BT periodicals
NT women's magazines

magic

   SG Visual and Performing Arts
RT folk culture
     witchcraft

magistrates

   SG Economics and Employment
       Law, Government, and Public Policy
BT legal and political occupations

magnetic tapes

   DG Types and Forms of Materials
BT tapes

maiden aunts

   SG Social Sciences and Culture
BT aunts
RT old maids
     spinsters

maiden name

   USE **birth name**

maidenhead

   USE **hymen**

maids

   USE **household workers**

mail carriers

   SG Economics and Employment
BT clerical occupations
RT government workers

mail order brides

   SG Social Sciences and Culture
BT brides
RT personal columns

mainstream feminism

   SG History and Social Change
   DG Cultural and Political Movements
BT feminism
RT career feminism
     liberal feminism

mainstreaming

   SG History and Social Change
       Social Sciences and Culture
RT curriculum integration
     deinstitutionalization
     disabled
     ethnic studies
     halfway houses
     integration
     racial and ethnic differences
     women's studies

majority culture

   SG International Women
       Social Sciences and Culture
BT culture
RT acculturation
     colonialism
     compulsory heterosexuality
     cultural influences
     discrimination
     dominant culture
     minority experience
     passing

(cont.)

majority culture (*cont.*)
RT socialization
    stereotyping

majority rule
SG Law, Government, and Public Policy
RT democracy
    pluralism

makeup
SG Visual and Performing Arts
RT adornment
    beauty standards
    body art
    cosmetics
    images of women
    tribal markings

Malaysian
DG National and Regional Descriptors
BT Asian

male bonding
SG History and Social Change
    Natural Sciences and Health
    Social Sciences and Culture
BT bonding
RT compulsory heterosexuality
    fathers
    homoeroticism
    locker rooms
    male friendships
    male male relationships
    male norms
    old boy networks

male chauvinism
SG History and Social Change
UF male chauvinist pig
    MCP
BT chauvinism
RT androcentrism
    chivalry
    machismo
    male norms
    sexism

male chauvinist pig
USE **male chauvinism**

male circumcision
SG Natural Sciences and Health
    Social Sciences and Culture
BT surgical procedures
RT penis
    rites

male dominated careers
USE **male dominated employment**

male dominated employment
SG Economics and Employment
UF male dominated careers
BT employment
RT male intensive occupations
    nontraditional employment

male female friendships
USE **female male friendships**

male female relationships
USE **female male relationships**

male feminists
SG History and Social Change
BT feminists
RT feminism
    men's liberation
    men's studies

male friendships
SG History and Social Change
    Social Sciences and Culture
BT friendships
    male male relationships
RT bonding
    male bonding

male homosexuality
SG History and Social Change
    Natural Sciences and Health
BT homosexuality

male homosexuals
USE **gay men**

male hypersexuality
SG Natural Sciences and Health
BT hypersexuality

male impersonators
SG Social Sciences and Culture
BT impersonators
RT cross dressing
cross sex identity

male intensive occupations
SG Economics and Employment
UF nontraditional careers
nontraditional occupations
BT occupations
RT career choice
careers
computer literacy
construction occupations
female intensive occupations
male dominated employment
occupational sex segregation
physical strength
sex discrimination in employment
women in

male male relationships
SG Social Sciences and Culture
UF same sex relationships
BT personal relationships
NT father son relationships
gay male relationships
male friendships
RT male bonding
old boy networks

male norms
SG History and Social Change
Social Sciences and Culture
BT norms
RT androcentrism
auxiliaries
beauty
bomfog

male norms *(cont.)*
RT compulsory heterosexuality
discrimination
divine kingship
ethic of care
female hypersexuality
gender marking
generic pronouns
God the father
linguistic sexism
literary canon
male bonding
male chauvinism
male standards
marginality
objectification
objectivity
patriarchal language
patriarchy
phallocentrism
phallogocentrism
pronoun envy
religious language
scientific method
social construction of reality
women's culture
women's language

male pregnancy
SG Natural Sciences and Health
BT pregnancy
RT sympathetic pregnancy
womb envy

male sexuality
SG Natural Sciences and Health
BT sexuality

male standards
SG Social Sciences and Culture
BT standards
RT double standard
male norms

(cont.)

males
- SN *Use the term **male** or **males** to refer to biologically based references to sex; use the term **man** or **men** , **boy** or **boys** to refer to socially or culturally based references to gender.*
- SG History and Social Change
  Natural Sciences and Health
  Social Sciences and Culture
- RT men

male nurses
- USE **nurses**

Malian
- DG National and Regional Descriptors
- BT African

malignant tumors
- SG Natural Sciences and Health
- BT tumors
- RT cancer
  chemotherapy
  hysterectomy
  radiation therapy
  surgical procedures

malnutrition
- SG International Women
  Natural Sciences and Health
- RT hunger
  nutrition
  pica
  poverty
  starvation

Maltese
- DG National and Regional Descriptors
- BT European

Malthusianism
- DG Cultural and Political Movements

mammary glands
- SG Natural Sciences and Health
- BT glands
- RT breasts

mammies
- SN *Slang; Black women, usually slaves, who served as nurses, often surrogate mothers, to White children in the south (US).*
- SG Economics and Employment
  History and Social Change
- BT images of women
- RT slavery
  wet nurses

mammography
- SG Natural Sciences and Health
- BT medical procedures
- RT breast diseases
  breast examination
  cancer
  disease prevention

man
- SN *Use to refer to an adult male; use **humanity** to refer to women and men collectively.*
- SG History and Social Change
  Language, Literature, Religion, and Philosophy
  Social Sciences and Culture
- RT false generics
  faulty generalization
  humanity

man hours
- USE **work hours**

man the hunter
- SG Social Sciences and Culture
- RT men's roles
  sex role stereotyping
  woman the gatherer

management
- SG Economics and Employment
- NT financial management
  money management
  personal management
  personnel management
  time management

(cont.)

UF = Use for   BT = Broader term   NT = Narrower term   RT = Related term

management (*cont.*)
- NT water management
- RT boards of directors
  - bureaucracy
  - corporate policy
  - corporate responsibility
  - employers
  - governance
  - organizational psychology
  - power

management practices
- SG Economics and Employment
- RT administration
  - collectives
  - management theory

management styles
- SG Economics and Employment
- BT work styles
- RT bureaucracy
  - collaboration
  - leadership
  - management techniques
  - organizational psychology

management techniques
- SG Economics and Employment
- RT management styles
  - team playing

management theory
- SG Economics and Employment
- BT theory
- RT collaboration
  - industrial relations
  - management practices

management training
- SG Economics and Employment
- BT training

managerial occupations
- SG Economics and Employment
- BT occupations
- NT administrators
  - coordinators

(*cont.*)

managerial occupations (*cont.*)
- NT executives
  - managers
  - presidents
  - underwriters
  - vice presidents
- RT administration
  - professional occupations

managers
- SG Economics and Employment
- BT managerial occupations
- NT middle managers
- RT executives

manicurists
- SG Economics and Employment
  - Natural Sciences and Health
- BT cosmetologists

manipulative behavior
- SG Social Sciences and Culture
- BT behavior
- RT cunning

manipulators
- SG Social Sciences and Culture
- BT images of women

mankind
- USE **humanity**

manmade
- USE **handmade**
  - **manufactured**

mannequins
- SG Economics and Employment
  - Social Sciences and Culture
- BT images of women
- RT models

manners
- SG Social Sciences and Culture
- BT social behavior
- NT gallantry
  - graciousness

(*cont.*)

manners (*cont.*)
RT attitudes
behavior
civility
compliments
customs
etiquette
hosts
images of women
mores
politeness
tea pouring

manpower
USE **human resources**
labor force
personnel

manual labor
SG Economics and Employment
BT labor
RT workers

manuals
DG Types and Forms of Materials
NT sex manuals

manufactured
SG Economics and Employment
UF manmade

manufacturers
SG Economics and Employment
BT manufacturing occupations

manufacturing industry
SG Economics and Employment
BT industries
RT construction occupations
factories
manufacturing occupations

manufacturing occupations
SG Economics and Employment
Science and Technology
BT occupations
NT clothing workers

(*cont.*)

manufacturing occupations (*cont.*)
NT factory workers
manufacturers
metalworkers
printing workers
steelworkers
RT blue collar workers
laborers
manufacturing industry
sewing
textile industry

manumission
SG History and Social Change
International Women
Social Sciences and Culture
RT abolition
freedom
slavery
underground railroad

manuscripts
DG Types and Forms of Materials

maps
DG Types and Forms of Materials

maquiladora
SN *Plants in Third World countries that*
assemble materials and then ship
them back to the US or Europe for
further assembly or distribution.
This term is used across cultures.
SG International Women
RT fifth world
foreign workers
multinational corporations
offshore production plants

marathons
SG Natural Sciences and Health
RT athletics
running

marches
SG History and Social Change
BT protest actions

(*cont.*)

UF=Use for   BT=Broader term   NT=Narrower term   RT=Related term

marches (*cont.*)
RT demonstrations
parades

marginality
SG Social Sciences and Culture
RT male norms

marianismo
SN *Coined term that defines the flip side*
*of **machismo** ; describes belief in*
feminine spiritual superiority.
SG Language, Literature, Religion, and
Philosophy
Social Sciences and Culture
RT cult of the virgin
machismo

marijuana
SG Natural Sciences and Health
BT narcotic drugs
RT drug abuse
smoking
social attitudes

marital adjustment
SG Social Sciences and Culture
BT adjustment
RT marital conflict
marital satisfaction
marital stability
marriage counseling

marital conflict
SG Social Sciences and Culture
BT conflict
RT crisis intervention
marital adjustment
marriage counseling
sexual dysfunction

marital property reform
SG Economics and Employment
Law, Government, and Public Policy
Social Sciences and Culture
BT reforms
RT community property laws
(*cont.*)

marital property reform (*cont.*)
RT divorce laws
inheritance rights
land rights
marriage and family law

marital rape
USE **domestic rape**

marital roles
SG Social Sciences and Culture
BT roles

marital satisfaction
SG Social Sciences and Culture
BT satisfaction
RT marital adjustment
marriage counseling

marital stability
SG Social Sciences and Culture
RT marital adjustment
marriage counseling

marital status
SG Social Sciences and Culture
BT status
RT attitudes
bachelors
divorce
marriage
Ms
separation
spinsters

marital violence
SG Social Sciences and Culture
BT domestic violence
RT battered women
domestic rape
spouse abuse
wife abuse

market research
SG Economics and Employment
BT social science research
RT advertising industry
(*cont.*)

market research (cont.)

RT business
     consumer behavior
     markets

marketing and sales occupations

SG Economics and Employment
BT occupations
NT insurance agents
     merchandisers
     real estate agents
     sales personnel
     stockbrokers
     vendors
RT advertising
     advertising industry
     public relations

markets

SG Economics and Employment
NT black markets
RT capitalism
     colonialism
     consumption
     fourth world
     free enterprise
     free trade zones
     global village
     international trade policy
     market research
     third world

marriage

SG Social Sciences and Culture
UF matrimony
NT arranged marriage
     child marriage
     childfree marriage
     common law marriage
     commuter marriage
     companionate marriage
     gay marriage
     group marriage
     intercaste marriage
     interfaith marriage
     international marriage
     interracial marriage

(cont.)

marriage (cont.)

NT marriage by proxy
     posthumous marriage
     remarriage
     teenage marriage
     trial marriage
RT anniversaries
     bigamy
     change
     consensual union
     coverture
     divorce
     dowry deaths
     engagement
     holy matrimony
     laws
     life styles
     living arrangements
     marital status
     marriage contracts
     marriage counseling
     marriage customs
     married couples
     married students
     monogamy
     relationships
     spouses
     union
     uxoriousness
     virginity
     wedding ceremonies

marriage and family law

SG Law, Government, and Public Policy
BT law
RT alimony
     child custody
     child support
     community property laws
     divorce laws
     domestic relations
     domicile rights
     families
     marital property reform
     spouse support

---

marriage by proxy
SG Social Sciences and Culture
BT marriage

marriage ceremonies
SG Language, Literature, Religion, and Philosophy
BT ceremonies
RT marriage vows

marriage contracts
SG Social Sciences and Culture
BT contracts
NT prenuptial agreements
RT annulment
     bigamy
     dowry
     household division of labor
     marriage

marriage counseling
SG Social Sciences and Culture
BT counseling
RT marital adjustment
     marital conflict
     marital satisfaction
     marital stability
     marriage

marriage customs
SG Social Sciences and Culture
BT customs
NT endogamy
     exogamy
     levirate
     polyandry
     polygamy
     sororate
RT common law marriage
     courtship customs
     divorce
     domestic code
     honeymoons
     living arrangements
     marriage
     matchmakers

(cont.)

marriage customs *(cont.)*
RT uxorial rights
     wedding nights

marriage licenses
SG Law, Government, and Public Policy
BT licenses
RT blood tests
     wedding ceremonies

marriage proposals
SG Social Sciences and Culture
BT courtship customs
RT betrothal

marriage rates
SG Economics and Employment
     Social Sciences and Culture
BT vital statistics
RT divorce rates

marriage tax
SG Economics and Employment
     Social Sciences and Culture
RT dual career couples
     dual career families
     taxes

marriage vows
SG Language, Literature, Religion, and Philosophy
BT vows
RT holy matrimony
     marriage ceremonies
     obedience

married couples
SG Social Sciences and Culture
BT couples
RT dual career couples
     dual career families
     marriage
     spouses

married men
USE **husbands**

married students

SG Education
BT students
RT marriage

married women
USE **wives**

martial arts

SG Education
    Natural Sciences and Health
    Social Sciences and Culture
NT judo
    karate
RT athletics
    self defense

martyrdom

SG Language, Literature, Religion, and
    Philosophy
RT canonization
    saints

martyrs

SG History and Social Change
    Language, Literature, Religion, and
    Philosophy
RT canonization
    holy women
    religion
    saints
    self denial
    witch burning
    witches

Marxism

DG Cultural and Political Movements

Marxist economic development models

SG International Women
BT economic development models

Marxist feminism

SN *Feminist theory that emphasizes class
    analysis from a feminist perspective,
    with women assigned class on the
    basis of work they do within the*
                      (*cont.*)

Marxist feminism (*cont.*)

    *economy, not on basis of husband's
    or father's relation to means of pro-
    duction.*
SG History and Social Change
    International Women
DG Cultural and Political Movements
BT feminism
RT economic value of women's work
    feminist theory
    socialist feminism

masculine pronouns

SG Language, Literature, Religion, and
    Philosophy
BT pronouns
RT false generics
    gender marking
    he/man language
    language structure
    sexist language

masculinity

SG Social Sciences and Culture
RT femininity
    men's roles
    sex role stereotyping

masochism

SG Natural Sciences and Health
RT sadism
    sadomasochism
    sexual behavior
    violence

mass actions

SG History and Social Change
    Social Sciences and Culture
BT activities
NT rallies
RT protest actions

mass media

SG Communications
UF media
NT electronic media
    print media

                      (*cont.*)

UF=Use for   BT=Broader term   NT=Narrower term   RT=Related term

mass media (*cont.*)
NT   women's media
RT   advertising industry
     arts, entertainment, and media
       occupations
     broadcasts
     censorship
     commercial sex
     communications
     communications industry
     images of women
     information sciences
     journalism
     media arts
     news services
     popular culture
     professional sports
     propaganda
     publishing industry

massage
SG   Natural Sciences and Health
UF   massage therapy
RT   relaxation
     stress

massage parlors
SG   Social Sciences and Culture
RT   commercial sex
     prostitution

massage therapy
USE **massage**

masseuses
SG   Natural Sciences and Health
BT   female intensive occupations

mastectomy
SG   Natural Sciences and Health
BT   surgical procedures
RT   body image
     breast cancer
     breast prostheses
     breasts
     emotional adjustment
     reconstructive surgery

master of ceremonies
SG   Visual and Performing Arts
UF   mistress of ceremonies
RT   hosts

masters' degrees
SG   Education
BT   graduate degrees

masturbation
SG   Natural Sciences and Health
UF   autoeroticism
BT   sexual behavior
RT   female sexuality
     orgasm
     sexual satisfaction

matchmakers
SG   Social Sciences and Culture
RT   blind dates
     marriage customs

material culture
SG   History and Social Change
BT   culture
RT   antiques
     fashion
     folk art
     furniture
     popular culture
     tribal art

materialism
DG   Cultural and Political Movements

maternal age
SG   Natural Sciences and Health
BT   age
RT   early childbearing
     late childbearing
     teenage pregnancy

maternal and infant welfare
SG   Natural Sciences and Health
     Social Sciences and Culture
BT   welfare
RT   early childbearing

(*cont.*)

maternal and infant welfare (*cont.*)

RT infant mortality
 infants
 lower class
 maternal mortality
 middle class
 nutrition
 prenatal care
 teenage pregnancy
 upper class
 working class

maternal health service

 SN *Prenatal and postnatal care.*
 SG Natural Sciences and Health
BT health care services

maternal love

 SG Natural Sciences and Health
  Social Sciences and Culture
BT love
RT bonding
 images of women
 mother syndrome
 mothering
 self sacrifice

maternal mortality

 SG Natural Sciences and Health
BT mortality
RT death
 maternal and infant welfare
 prenatal care

maternity

 SG Natural Sciences and Health
RT childbearing
 nurturance
 paternity

maternity benefits

 SG Economics and Employment
BT benefits
RT child care leave
 employee benefits
 maternity rights

maternity homes

 SG Natural Sciences and Health
  Social Sciences and Culture
BT facilities
RT teenage pregnancy

maternity leave

 SG Economics and Employment
  Law, Government, and Public Policy
  Social Sciences and Culture
BT parental leave
RT child care leave
 childbirth
 disability insurance
 maternity rights
 parenthood
 pregnancy leave

maternity rights

 SG Economics and Employment
  Law, Government, and Public Policy
  Natural Sciences and Health
BT rights
RT maternity benefits
 maternity leave
 parental rights

maternity wards

 SG Natural Sciences and Health
BT hospitals
RT birthing centers
 birthing rooms
 childbirth
 rooming in

math

 USE **mathematics**

math ability

 SG Education
  Science and Technology
BT ability
RT lateral dominance
 math avoidance
 math confidence
 mathematics
 testing

---

math anxiety
USE **math avoidance**

math avoidance
SG   Education
UF   math anxiety
BT   avoidance behavior
RT   math ability

math confidence
SN   *Strategy for teaching mathematics by building the confidence of students who have avoided math.*
SG   Education
RT   math ability

mathematical models
SG   Science and Technology
      Social Sciences and Culture
RT   econometrics
      forecasting
      models (paradigms)

mathematicians
SG   Economics and Employment
      Science and Technology
BT   professional occupations
      scientific and technical occupations

mathematics
SG   Science and Technology
UF   math
NT   applied mathematics
      statistics
RT   basic skills
      math ability
      natural sciences
      social sciences

matriarchs
SG   Social Sciences and Culture
RT   matriarchy
      patriarchs

matriarchy
SN   *Society that traces descent, often inheritance and other social prerogatives, through the mother.*
SG   Social Sciences and Culture
RT   anlu
      community
      culture
      family structure
      female societies
      goddesses
      gynarchy
      lineage
      matriarchs
      matricentric societies
      matrilineal kinship
      mother right
      patriarchy
      power
      utopias
      women's culture

matricentric societies
SG   History and Social Change
      Social Sciences and Culture
BT   society
RT   matriarchy
      matrilineal societies

matricide
SG   Law, Government, and Public Policy
BT   murder
RT   mothers

matrilineal kinship
SG   Social Sciences and Culture
BT   kinship
RT   female societies
      matriarchy
      matrilineal societies
      matronymy
      mother right

matrilineal societies
SG   Social Sciences and Culture
BT   society
RT   inheritance customs

(cont.)

matrilineal societies (*cont.*)
RT matricentric societies
matrilineal kinship
matrilocal residences

matrilocal residences
SG Social Sciences and Culture
RT matrilineal societies

matrimony
USE **marriage**

matronymy
SN *Naming derived from mother or maternal ancestor.*
SG Language, Literature, Religion, and Philosophy
Social Sciences and Culture
BT naming
RT birth name
goddesses
hyphenated names
matrilineal kinship
Ms
name rights
names
patronymy
surnames

mature students
USE **adult students**

maturity
SG Social Sciences and Culture
RT adults
autonomy
emotional development

Mauritanian
DG National and Regional Descriptors
BT African

mayors
SG Economics and Employment
Law, Government, and Public Policy
BT elected officials

MCP
USE **male chauvinism**

measles
SG Natural Sciences and Health
BT diseases
RT pregnancy
rubella

measurement
SG Education
Social Sciences and Culture
RT anthropometry
aptitude tests
norms
research methods

measurements
DG Types and Forms of Materials
NT demographic measurements

mechanical engineering
SG Science and Technology
BT engineering

mechanics
SG Economics and Employment
Science and Technology
BT craft occupations

media
USE **mass media**

media arts
SG Visual and Performing Arts
BT arts
NT animation
electronic art
film
video art
RT entertainment industry
humanities
literature
mass media
mixed media
motion picture industry
performing arts

(*cont.*)

UF=Use for   BT=Broader term   NT=Narrower term   RT=Related term

media arts (cont.)
RT visual arts

media coverage
SG Communications
NT press coverage
television coverage
RT collegiate athletics
freedom of the press
media reform
professional athletics
women's media

media portrayal
SG Communications
RT images of girls
images of women
media stereotyping
women's media

media reform
SG Communications
BT reforms
RT media coverage
media stereotyping

media stereotyping
SG Communications
BT stereotyping
RT communications equity
media portrayal
media reform
women's media

mediation
SG Law, Government, and Public Policy
Social Sciences and Culture
RT compromise
conflict resolution
contracts
family courts
labor contracts
labor disputes
mediators
reconciliation
strikes
unions

mediators
SG Economics and Employment
Law, Government, and Public Policy
BT legal and political occupations
RT mediation
negotiators

Medicaid
SN *Federal health insurance for people living in poverty.*
SG Law, Government, and Public Policy
Natural Sciences and Health
DG Laws and Regulations
BT health insurance
RT abortion laws
abortion rights
medical care
National Health Service (Great Britain)

medical anthropology
SG Natural Sciences and Health
Social Sciences and Culture
BT anthropology

medical care
SG Natural Sciences and Health
BT health care
RT health insurance
Medicaid
Medicare
national health insurance

medical education
SG Education
Natural Sciences and Health
BT education
RT family medicine
internships
medical ethics
medical sciences
residency programs
sensitivity training

medical ethics
SG Natural Sciences and Health
BT ethics
RT abortion

(cont.)

medical ethics (*cont.*)
- RT   euthanasia
-      medical education

medical evaluation
- SG   Natural Sciences and Health
- BT   evaluation
- NT   physical examination
- RT   medical procedures

medical insurance
- USE   **health insurance**

medical oppression
- SG   Natural Sciences and Health
- BT   oppression
- RT   experts
-      patient doctor relationships

medical procedures
- SG   Natural Sciences and Health
- NT   amniocentesis
-      biopsy
-      chemotherapy
-      fetal monitoring
-      genetic screening
-      mammography
-      Pap smear
-      radiation therapy
-      surgical procedures
-      thermography
-      ultrasound
- RT   antisepsis
-      diagnoses
-      genetic engineering
-      medical evaluation
-      reproductive technologies

medical records
- SG   Natural Sciences and Health
- BT   records
- RT   confidentiality
-      patient doctor relationships
-      records confidentiality

medical sciences
- SG   Natural Sciences and Health

                             (*cont.*)

medical sciences (*cont.*)
- UF   medicine
- NT   dentistry
-      environmental medicine
-      family medicine
-      folk medicine
-      geriatrics
-      gynecology
-      holistic medicine
-      nursing
-      obstetrics
-      pediatrics
-      pharmacology
-      preventive medicine
-      psychiatry
-      surgery
- RT   healing
-      medical education
-      medical sociology
-      natural sciences
-      nursing education
-      optometry
-      social sciences
-      technology development

medical sociology
- SG   Natural Sciences and Health
-        Social Sciences and Culture
- BT   sociology
- RT   medical sciences

Medicare
- SN   *Federal health insurance for the elderly.*
- SG   Law, Government, and Public Policy
-        Natural Sciences and Health
- DG   Laws and Regulations
- BT   health insurance
- RT   aging
-      federal assistance programs
-      medical care
-      national health insurance
-      National Health Service (Great Britain)
-      older adults

medicine
- USE   **medical sciences**

UF=Use for   BT=Broader term   NT=Narrower term   RT=Related term

medicine women
    SG   Natural Sciences and Health
BT female intensive occupations
       health care occupations
       women
RT crones
       folk medicine
       healers
       native healers

Medieval Period
    DG Historical Periods

meditation
    SG   Language, Literature, Religion, and
         Philosophy
BT spiritual communication
RT convents
       monasticism
       prayer
       relaxation
       religious practices
       spirituality
       stress

meditation music
    SG Visual and Performing Arts
BT music

mediums
    SG Language, Literature, Religion, and
         Philosophy
BT religious workers
NT physical mediums
       spiritual mediums
RT channeling
       cults
       female spirituality
       fortune tellers
       salons
       seances
       seers
       spiritualism
       trances
       visionaries

meetings
    SG History and Social Change
         Social Sciences and Culture
BT activities
NT planning meetings
       prayer meetings
RT conferences

memoirs
    SG Language, Literature, Religion, and
         Philosophy
    DG Types and Forms of Materials
BT nonfiction
RT autobiography
       biography
       diaries
       histories
       journals
       letters

memoranda
    DG Types and Forms of Materials

memory
    SG Social Sciences and Culture
BT cognitive processes
NT long term memory
       recall
       recognition
       short term memory
RT oral tradition
       repression

memos
    DG Types and Forms of Materials

men
    SN *Use the term **men** or **man** to refer to*
        socially or culturally based refer-
        ences to gender of adult males,
        ***males** or **male** to refer to biologically*
        based references to sex.
    SG History and Social Change
         Natural Sciences and Health
         Social Sciences and Culture
NT assemblymen
       bachelors

(cont.)

    SN=Scope note   SG=Subject group   DG=Delimiters group   USE=Use

men (*cont.*)
- NT brothers
  - businessmen
  - clergymen
  - congressmen
  - fathers
  - fathers in law
  - gay men
  - grandfathers
  - grandsons
  - grooms
  - holy men
  - homeless men
  - husbands
  - laymen
  - older men
  - ombudsmen
  - single men
  - sons
  - widowers
- RT false generics
  - males

men's liberation
- SG History and Social Change
- BT liberation
- RT feminism
  - male feminists
  - men's movement
  - women's liberation

men's movement
- SN *Organized effort to raise male con-sciousness of gender stereotyping and roles and to provide structures for support.*
- SG History and Social Change
- DG Cultural and Political Movements
- BT social movements
- RT men's liberation

men's roles
- SG History and Social Change
  - Social Sciences and Culture
- BT roles
- RT gender development
  - man the hunter

(*cont.*)

men's roles (*cont.*)
- RT masculinity
  - sex roles
  - sex/gender systems
  - socialization

men's studies
- SG Education
  - History and Social Change
  - Social Sciences and Culture
- BT interdisciplinary studies
- RT feminist studies
  - gender studies
  - male feminists
  - women's studies

menarche
- SN *The first onset of menstruation.*
- SG Natural Sciences and Health
- RT amenorrhea
  - menstruation

menopause
- SG Natural Sciences and Health
- UF change of life
- RT climacteric
  - estrogen replacement therapy
  - hot flashes
  - life cycles
  - menstrual cycle
  - menstruation
  - osteoporosis

menses
- USE **menstruation**

menstrual cycle
- SG Natural Sciences and Health
- RT diuretics
  - menopause
  - menstruation
  - ovulation
  - ovum
  - premenstrual syndrome
  - premenstrual tension
  - reproductive cycle
  - rhythm method

UF=Use for   BT=Broader term   NT=Narrower term   RT=Related term

menstrual disorders
SG   Natural Sciences and Health
BT   gynecologic disorders
NT   amenorrhea
    dysmenorrhea
    endometriosis

menstrual extraction
SG   Natural Sciences and Health
RT   menstruation

menstrual taboos
SG   Language, Literature, Religion, and
    Philosophy
    Natural Sciences and Health
RT   blood

menstruation
SG   Natural Sciences and Health
UF   menses
    period
RT   amenorrhea
    blood
    bodies
    body image
    dysmenorrhea
    endometriosis
    menarche
    menopause
    menstrual cycle
    menstrual extraction
    mikveh
    premenstrual syndrome
    premenstrual tension
    sanitary napkins
    tampons
    toxic shock syndrome

menstruation inducing agents
SG   Natural Sciences and Health
UF   emmenagogues
RT   folk medicine
    prescription drugs

mental disorders
SG   Natural Sciences and Health
UF   mental illness

(cont.)

mental disorders *(cont.)*
BT   disorders
NT   autism
    depression
    hysteria
    neuroses
    phobias
    schizophrenia
RT   antidepressant drugs
    art therapy
    deinstitutionalization
    diagnoses
    eating disorders
    insanity
    music therapy
    narcissism
    paranoia
    repression
    social conditioning
    therapy

mental evaluation
SG   Natural Sciences and Health
BT   evaluation

mental health
SG   Natural Sciences and Health
BT   health
RT   coping strategies
    counseling
    humor
    psychological stress
    wellness

mental health advocates
SG   Natural Sciences and Health
BT   health advocates

mental health issues
SG   Natural Sciences and Health
RT   policy making

mental health treatment
SG   Natural Sciences and Health
BT   treatment
RT   deinstitutionalization
    diagnoses

(cont.)

mental health treatment (*cont.*)
  RT drug therapy
      therapy

mental hospitals
      SG Natural Sciences and Health
  BT hospitals
  RT deinstitutionalization

mental illness
  USE **mental disorders**

mental retardation
      SG Natural Sciences and Health
  BT disabilities
  RT eugenic sterilization
      learning disabilities

mentally handicapped
      SG Education
          Natural Sciences and Health
  RT disabilities
      disabled

mentors
      SN *Experienced individuals who guide, direct, and assist the careers of less experienced proteges in long term, professionally centered relationships.*
      SG Economics and Employment
          Education
  RT apprenticeships
      contacts
      educators
      employee development
      leadership training
      networks
      occupational mobility
      old boy networks
      personal relationships
      professional development
      queen bee syndrome
      role models
      skills
      sponsors
      supervisor attitudes
      wisdom

mercantilism
      DG Cultural and Political Movements

merchandisers
      SG Economics and Employment
  BT marketing and sales occupations

merchants
      SG Economics and Employment
  RT business ownership
      small business

mergers
      SG Economics and Employment
          Education
          Social Sciences and Culture
  RT corporate takeovers
      corporations
      dominance
      monopolies
      single sex environments
      social organizations

mermaids
      SG Language, Literature, Religion, and
          Philosophy
  BT images of women
  RT mythology

metal art
      SG Visual and Performing Arts
  BT visual arts
  RT jewelry
      sculpture

metalworkers
      SG Economics and Employment
          Visual and Performing Arts
  BT manufacturing occupations
      workers

metaphors
      SG Language, Literature, Religion, and
          Philosophy
  BT figurative language

UF=Use for   BT=Broader term   NT=Narrower term   RT=Related term

metaphysics
- SG Language, Literature, Religion, and Philosophy
- BT philosophy
- RT mysticism

meteorologists
- SG Economics and Employment
- UF weathermen
- BT scientists

methodologies
- DG Types and Forms of Materials

methodology
- USE **methods**

methods
- SG Social Sciences and Culture
- UF methodology
  procedures
- NT desegregation methods
  educational methods
  feminist methods
  job search methods
  research methods
- RT criticism

Mexican
- DG National and Regional Descriptors
- BT Latin American

Mexican American
- DG Ethnic, Racial, and Religious Descriptors

microeconomics
- SG Economics and Employment
- BT economics

microfiche
- DG Types and Forms of Materials

microfilm
- DG Types and Forms of Materials

microinequities
- SN *Subtle, often unconscious, gestures or actions that appear too insignificant to be noticed but are actually powerful forms of discrimination.*
- SG Economics and Employment
  Education
- BT discrimination
- RT body language
  institutional discrimination
  sexist language

midcareer change
- SG Economics and Employment
  Education
- BT career change
- RT middle age
  motivation
  second careers

middle age
- SG Social Sciences and Culture
- BT age
- RT life cycles
  midcareer change
  middle aged adults
  midlife
  reentry women

middle aged adults
- SG Education
  Social Sciences and Culture
- DG Age Levels
- BT adults
- RT middle age

Middle Ages
- DG Historical Periods

Middle Atlantic
- DG National and Regional Descriptors
- BT United States

middle class
- SG Economics and Employment
  Social Sciences and Culture
- BT class

(*cont.*)

middle class *(cont.)*
RT   classism
     families
     fathers
     maternal and infant welfare
     mothers
     popular culture

middle class families
SG   Social Sciences and Culture
BT   families

Middle Eastern
DG   National and Regional Descriptors
UF   Near Eastern
NT   Cypriot
     Iranian
     Iraqi
     Israeli
     Lebanese
     Palestinian
     Saudi Arabian
     Sudanese
     Syrian

middle managers
SG   Economics and Employment
BT   managers

middle schools
SG   Education
BT   schools

midlife
SG   Social Sciences and Culture
RT   middle age
     midlife crisis

midlife crisis
SG   Social Sciences and Culture
RT   adult development
     empty nest
     life cycles
     midlife
     popular culture

Midwestern
DG   National and Regional Descriptors
BT   United States

midwifery
SG   International Women
     Natural Sciences and Health
RT   childbirth training
     midwives
     natural childbirth

midwives
SG   Economics and Employment
     International Women
     Natural Sciences and Health
UF   birth attendants
BT   female intensive occupations
     health care occupations
     women
NT   lay midwives
RT   childbirth
     healers
     liability insurance
     licensing
     midwifery
     nurse practitioners

migraine headaches
SG   Natural Sciences and Health
BT   headaches
RT   stress

migrant workers
SG   Economics and Employment
     International Women
UF   regional labor workers
BT   agricultural, fishing, and forestry
     occupations
     workers
RT   agribusiness
     agriculture
     child labor
     farm workers
     foreign workers
     illegal immigrants
     immigration policy
     seasonal migration

UF=Use for   BT=Broader term   NT=Narrower term   RT=Related term

migration

SG International Women
NT rural migration
seasonal migration
urban migration
RT demographic transition
migration patterns
rural resettlement

migration patterns

SG International Women
RT immigration
migration

mikiri

SN *Women's self-rule forum among the African Igbo.*
SG Law, Government, and Public Policy
Social Sciences and Culture
RT women's culture

mikveh

SN *Purification bath in Jewish ritual; used after woman has finished her monthly menstrual cycle.*
SG Language, Literature, Religion, and Philosophy
RT menstruation
purification rites
women's culture

militance

SG History and Social Change
RT activism
change agents
protest actions
resistance
social change
social movements
suffragists

militarism

SG Law, Government, and Public Policy
UF armament
RT aggressive behavior
armed forces
war

military

SG Law, Government, and Public Policy
BT organizations
NT armed forces
RT aviation
coups
military academies
military personnel
military rank
military spouses
military trade
power structure
technology development
veterans
warfare
women in the military

military academies

SG Education
Law, Government, and Public Policy
BT academies
RT military

military budget

SG Economics and Employment
Law, Government, and Public Policy
BT federal budget
RT appropriations
budget deficits
economy
social policy

military combat

SG Law, Government, and Public Policy
RT battlefields
upper body strength
veterans
women in the military

military defense

SG Law, Government, and Public Policy
RT warfare

military dependents

SG Law, Government, and Public Policy
Social Sciences and Culture
NT military spouses

(cont.)

SN=Scope note   SG=Subject group   DG=Delimiters group   USE=Use

military dependents (*cont.*)
  RT children

military draft
  SG Law, Government, and Public Policy
  UF draft
  RT all volunteer military force
      conscientious objection
      draft resistance
      eligibility

military enlistment
  SG Law, Government, and Public Policy
  RT enlisted personnel

military personnel
  SG Economics and Employment
      Law, Government, and Public Policy
  BT legal and political occupations
      personnel
  RT all volunteer military force
      military
      military rank
      spies
      veterans

military rank
  SG Law, Government, and Public Policy
  BT rank
  RT military
      military personnel

military recruitment
  SG Law, Government, and Public Policy
  RT enlisted personnel

military services
  USE **armed forces**

military spouses
  SG Law, Government, and Public Policy
  BT military dependents
      spouses
  RT family mobility
      military
      occupational mobility
                    (*cont.*)

military spouses (*cont.*)
  RT Uniformed Services Former Spouses'
      Protection Act
      women in the military

military trade
  SG Economics and Employment
      Law, Government, and Public Policy
  RT business ethics
      corporations
      economic power
      military
      profits
      weapons

milk
  SG Natural Sciences and Health
  NT milk substitutes

milk substitutes
  SG Natural Sciences and Health
  BT milk
  RT infant formula
      lactose intolerance

mill girls
  USE **factory workers**

millenarian movements
  DG Cultural and Political Movements

millenialism
  DG Cultural and Political Movements

milliners
  SG Economics and Employment
      Visual and Performing Arts
  BT clothing workers
      female intensive occupations

millinery trade
  SG Economics and Employment
  BT garment industry

mime
  SG Visual and Performing Arts
  BT performing arts

UF=Use for   BT=Broader term   NT=Narrower term   RT=Related term

mind
   SG   Language, Literature, Religion, and
         Philosophy
         Natural Sciences and Health
         Social Sciences and Culture
  RT brain
       cognitive processes
       consciousness
       ego
       mind/body split
       subconscious

mind/body split
   SG   Language, Literature, Religion, and
         Philosophy
         Natural Sciences and Health
  BT false dichotomies
  RT bodies
       conceptual errors
       dualism
       mind
       objectification

mineral resources
   SG   Science and Technology
  BT natural resources
  RT conservation

miniatures
   SG   Visual and Performing Arts
  BT visual arts

minimum competencies
   SG   Education
  BT competence

minimum income
   SG   Economics and Employment
  BT income
  RT basic human needs
       income tax
       poverty

minimum wage legislation
   SG   Law, Government, and Public Policy
  BT legislation

mining industry
   SG   Economics and Employment
         Science and Technology
  BT extractive industry
       industries
  RT natural resources

miniskirts
   SG   Social Sciences and Culture
  BT skirts
  RT hemlines

ministers
   SG   Economics and Employment
         Language, Literature, Religion, and
         Philosophy
  BT clergy
  RT women religious

minor parties
   SG   Law, Government, and Public Policy
  UF third parties
  BT political parties

minorities
  USE **ethnic groups**
        people of color

minority employment
   SG   Economics and Employment
  BT employment

minority experience
   SG   History and Social Change
         Social Sciences and Culture
  RT cultural influences
       double discrimination
       ethnicity
       gay experience
       majority culture
       race relations
       racism
       sexism

minority groups
   SG   Social Sciences and Culture
  BT groups

(cont.)

minority groups (*cont.*)
RT ethnic groups

minority owned business
SG Economics and Employment
BT business
RT business ownership
small business
women owned business

minority studies
USE **ethnic studies**

minority women
USE **ethnic women**
women of color

miracles
SG Language, Literature, Religion, and
Philosophy
RT canonization
cult of the virgin
religious beliefs
theology

misandry
SN *Mistrust and hatred of men.*
SG History and Social Change
Social Sciences and Culture
RT female chauvinism

miscarriage
SG Natural Sciences and Health
RT abortion
diethylstilbestrol
pregnancy
spontaneous abortion
therapeutic abortion

miscegenation
SG History and Social Change
Social Sciences and Culture
RT interracial marriage
race relations
slavery

misogyny
SN *Mistrust and hatred of women.*
SG History and Social Change
Language, Literature, Religion, and
Philosophy
RT androcentrism
chauvinism
sexism
sexist language
sexual abuse
vagina dentata
violence against women

missionaries
SG Economics and Employment
Language, Literature, Religion, and
Philosophy
BT religious workers
RT colonialism
dogma
social reform

missionary societies
SG History and Social Change
BT societies
RT church work

mistress of ceremonies
USE **master of ceremonies**

mistresses
SG Social Sciences and Culture
BT women
RT concubinage
courtesans
extramarital affairs
geishas
gigolos

mixed economy
SG Economics and Employment
BT economy
RT diversity

mixed media
SG Visual and Performing Arts
RT media arts

UF=Use for   BT=Broader term   NT=Narrower term   RT=Related term

mixed sex groups

SG   Social Sciences and Culture

BT   groups
     heterogeneous groups

mixers

SG   History and Social Change
     Social Sciences and Culture

BT   dances
     social activities

mobility

SG   History and Social Change
     Social Sciences and Culture

NT   family mobility
     geographic mobility
     occupational mobility
     social mobility
     upward mobility

model programs

SG   Education

BT   programs

modeling agencies

SG   Economics and Employment

BT   agencies
RT   models

models

SN   *Use for occupation. Use ROLE MOD-
      ELS for models of behavior.*

SG   Communications
     Economics and Employment
     Visual and Performing Arts

BT   arts, entertainment, and media
     occupations
     female intensive occupations

RT   artists
     fashion illustration
     fashion photography
     mannequins
     modeling agencies

models (paradigms)

SG   Science and Technology
     Social Sciences and Culture

(cont.)

models (paradigms) *(cont.)*

DG   Types and Forms of Materials

RT   mathematical models
     paradigms
     social construction of reality

modern dance

SG   Visual and Performing Arts

BT   dance

modernism

DG   Cultural and Political Movements

modernization

SG   Economics and Employment
     International Women
     Social Sciences and Culture

RT   deindustrialization
     developing nations
     technology development

modesty

SG   Social Sciences and Culture

RT   images of women

momism

SN   *Idealizing mother's role, defining her
      as central to the family, although
      often without according her social or
      financial recognition in the "out-
      side" world.*

SG   Social Sciences and Culture

RT   angel in the house
     economic value of women's work
     mother syndrome
     private sphere
     supermom

monasteries

SG   Language, Literature, Religion, and
     Philosophy

BT   religious facilities
RT   novitiates

monasticism

SG   Language, Literature, Religion, and
     Philosophy

(cont.)

monasticism (cont.)

DG   Cultural and Political Movements
RT   asceticism
      celibacy
      convents
      faith communities
      holy men
      holy women
      meditation
      nuns
      prayer
      religion
      religious beliefs
      religious orders
      women religious

monetary incentives

SG   Economics and Employment
BT   incentives
RT   money
      perquisites
      upward mobility

monetary policy

SG   Economics and Employment
      Law, Government, and Public Policy
BT   policy
RT   appropriations
      balance of payments
      deficits

money

SG   Economics and Employment
NT   pin money
RT   barter
      coins
      exchange theory
      food for work
      inheritance customs
      monetary incentives
      power
      status
      value
      wages
      wealth

money management

SG   Economics and Employment
BT   management

Mongolian

DG   National and Regional Descriptors
BT   Asian

monogamy

SG   Social Sciences and Culture
RT   life styles
      marriage
      sexual liberation

monographs

DG   Types and Forms of Materials

monopolies

SG   Economics and Employment
BT   corporations
RT   antitrust legislation
      cartels
      corporate takeovers
      mergers
      multinational corporations

monotheism

SG   Language, Literature, Religion, and
      Philosophy
DG   Cultural and Political Movements
RT   patriarchal religion

moonlighting

SG   Economics and Employment
RT   low income families
      part time employment
      two income families

moral development

SG   Language, Literature, Religion, and
      Philosophy
      Social Sciences and Culture
BT   individual development
NT   ethic of care
      moral reasoning
RT   morality
      values

---

moral majority
SG Language, Literature, Religion, and
   Philosophy
   Law, Government, and Public Policy
RT antiabortion movement
   conservatives
   right wing organizations
   the religious right

moral reasoning
SG Language, Literature, Religion, and
   Philosophy
   Social Sciences and Culture
BT moral development
RT abstract reasoning
   ethic of care
   superego

moral reform
SG History and Social Change
   Language, Literature, Religion, and
   Philosophy
BT reforms
RT charitable work
   ethics
   feminist ethics
   honesty
   humanitarianism
   immorality
   integrity
   liberation theology
   morality
   norms
   social history
   social movements
   temperance movement
   values

morality
SG Language, Literature, Religion, and
   Philosophy
UF morals
RT conflict of interest
   double standard
   ethics
   honesty
   idealism

(cont.)

morality *(cont.)*
RT integrity
   moral development
   moral reform
   promiscuity
   public opinion
   religious ethics
   sexual permissiveness
   values

morals
USE **morality**

morbidity
SG Natural Sciences and Health
   Social Sciences and Culture
RT death
   demographic measurements
   diseases

mores
SG Social Sciences and Culture
RT manners
   social behavior
   values

Mormon
DG Ethnic, Racial, and Religious
   Descriptors

Mormonism
DG Cultural and Political Movements

morning after pill
USE **diethylstilbestrol**

Moroccan
DG National and Regional Descriptors
BT African

morphology
SG Language, Literature, Religion, and
   Philosophy
BT linguistics

mortality
SG Natural Sciences and Health

(cont.)

mortality (*cont.*)
- NT infant mortality
      maternal mortality
      occupational mortality
- RT accidents
      death
      life expectancy
      life span
      mortality rates

mortality rates
- SG Economics and Employment
      Social Sciences and Culture
- BT vital statistics
- RT accidental death
      at risk populations
      death
      life expectancy
      mortality
      occupational mortality
      poverty

mortgages
- SG Economics and Employment
- NT assumable mortgages
      conventional mortgages
- RT homeowners
      interest rates
      real estate
      redlining

mortuary science
- SG Natural Sciences and Health
- RT death
      service occupations

Moslem
- USE **Muslim**

mosques
- SG Language, Literature, Religion, and
      Philosophy
- BT religious facilities
- RT congregations

mother daughter incest
- SG Law, Government, and Public Policy
      Natural Sciences and Health
      Social Sciences and Culture
- BT incest

mother daughter relationships
- SG Social Sciences and Culture
- BT female female relationships
      parent child relationships
- RT daughter right
      daughters
      daughters in law
      mother right
      mothers

mother earth
- SG Language, Literature, Religion, and
      Philosophy
      Science and Technology
- BT images of women
- RT ecofeminism
      goddesses
      mother nature
      nature
      rites

mother goddess
- SG Language, Literature, Religion, and
      Philosophy
- BT goddesses
- RT deity
      divinity
      earth mother
      mother nature
      Mother/Father God
      mothers
      priestesses
      religion
      wicca

mother nature
- SG Social Sciences and Culture
- BT images of women
- RT earth mother
      mother earth
      mother goddess

mother right

SN *Term used by J. J. Bachofen and other 19th century matriarchal theorists; current use includes recognition that even matrilineal social structures do not guarantee women significant rights.*

SG History and Social Change
Natural Sciences and Health
Social Sciences and Culture

RT daughter right
matriarchy
matrilineal kinship
mother daughter relationships

mother son incest

SG Law, Government, and Public Policy
Natural Sciences and Health
Social Sciences and Culture

BT incest

mother son relationships

SG Social Sciences and Culture

BT female male relationships
parent child relationships

RT mothers
sons
sons in law

mother superiors

SG Language, Literature, Religion, and Philosophy

BT nuns

mother syndrome

SN *Stereotyped need to be the "perfect" mother: self-sacrificing, always cheerful nurturer who instinctively puts everyone else's demands first.*

SG Social Sciences and Culture

RT angel in the house
cult of true womanhood
images of women
learned behavior
maternal love
momism
mothering

(cont.)

mother syndrome *(cont.)*

RT mothers
myths
perfection
self denial
self sacrifice
stress
supermom
superwoman syndrome

mother tongue

SG Language, Literature, Religion, and Philosophy

RT bilingualism
language
women's language

Mother/Father God

SG Language, Literature, Religion, and Philosophy

BT goddesses
gods

RT deity
divinity
God the Father
mother goddess
thealogy
Virgin Mary

mother's milk

SG Natural Sciences and Health

RT breast feeding
nurturance
nutrition

motherhood

USE **mothers**
parenthood

mothering

SG Natural Sciences and Health
Social Sciences and Culture

BT parenting

RT ideology
maternal love
mother syndrome
mothers

(cont.)

mothering (*cont.*)
  RT role models
      skills

motherless families
      SG Social Sciences and Culture
  BT families
  RT absentee mothers

mothers
      SG Social Sciences and Culture
  UF motherhood
  BT women
  NT absentee mothers
      birth mothers
      den mothers
      earth mother
      foremothers
      housemothers
      lesbian mothers
      mothers in law
      mothers working outside the home
      runaway mothers
      single mothers
      stepmothers
      supermom
      surrogate mothers
      teenage mothers
      wage earning mothers
      welfare mothers
  RT bonding
      caregivers
      child care workers
      daughters
      families
      fathers
      female intensive occupations
      food preparation occupations
      infants
      lower class
      matricide
      middle class
      mother daughter relationships
      mother goddess
      mother son relationships
      mother syndrome
      mothering

(*cont.*)

mothers (*cont.*)
  RT nurturance
      parent child relationships
      parenthood
      parenting
      parents
      primary caregivers
      service occupations
      superwoman syndrome
      upper class
      wisdom

mothers in law
      SG Social Sciences and Culture
  BT images of women
      in laws
      mothers
  RT families

mothers working outside the home
      SG Economics and Employment
          Social Sciences and Culture
  UF employed mothers
      working mothers
  BT mothers
      women working outside the home
  RT after school day care centers
      balancing work and family life
      child care
      coparenting
      day care
      day care centers
      wage earning mothers

motion picture industry
      SG Communications
          Visual and Performing Arts
  BT entertainment industry
  RT arts, entertainment, and media
          occupations
      film
      images of women
      media arts

motion pictures
  USE **films**

UF=Use for   BT=Broader term   NT=Narrower term   RT=Related term

motivation
SG   Natural Sciences and Health
        Social Sciences and Culture
NT   learning motivation
        student motivation
        teacher motivation
RT   ability
        academic failure
        achievement
        aptitude
        employee development
        initiative
        job development
        midcareer change
        nurturing
        opportunities
        positive reinforcement
        promotions
        success
        supervisor attitudes
        work attitudes
        work ethic

motor development
SG   Natural Sciences and Health
BT   physical development
RT   motor skills

motor skills
SG   Natural Sciences and Health
BT   skills
NT   hand eye coordination
RT   motor development

mountaineering
SG   Natural Sciences and Health
BT   sports

mourning
SG   Social Sciences and Culture
NT   keening
        wailing
RT   crying
        death
        death and dying
        grief
        loss

movements
USE **social movements**

movers
SG   Economics and Employment
        Science and Technology
BT   transportation occupations

movies
USE **films**

Ms
SG   History and Social Change
BT   forms of address
RT   marital status
        matronymy
        names
        surnames
        titles

mullahs
SG   Language, Literature, Religion, and
        Philosophy
BT   clergy
RT   priests

multicultural health care services
SG   Natural Sciences and Health
BT   health care services

multimedia art
SG   Visual and Performing Arts
BT   art
RT   dance
        incidental music
        performance art
        performances

multinational banks
SG   Economics and Employment
        International Women
UF   transnational banks
BT   banks
RT   multinational corporations

SN=Scope note   SG=Subject group   DG=Delimiters group   USE=Use

multinational corporation policy

SG International Women
     Law, Government, and Public Policy
BT corporate policy
NT drug dumping
    global assembly lines
    offshore production plants
    piecework labor policy
RT multinational corporations

multinational corporations

SG Economics and Employment
UF transnational corporations
BT corporations
RT apartheid
    business
    cartels
    colonialism
    corporate takeovers
    exploitation
    foreign investment policy
    foreign workers
    free enterprise
    free trade zones
    global economy
    industries
    infant formula
    international trade policy
    maquiladora
    monopolies
    multinational banks
    multinational corporation policy
    multinational labor force
    runaway shops
    third world
    women in development

multinational labor force

SG Economics and Employment
    International Women
BT labor force
RT agricultural, fishing, and forestry
    occupations
    female intensive occupations
    fifth world
    foreign workers
    global economy

(cont.)

multinational labor force *(cont.)*

RT human capital
    labor theory of value
    multinational corporations

multiple births

SG Natural Sciences and Health
UF quadruplets
    quintuplets
    sextuplets
    triplets
RT childbirth
    fertility drugs
    premature infants
    twins

multiple roles

SG Social Sciences and Culture
BT roles
NT dual roles
RT interrole conflict
    superwoman syndrome

municipal government

USE **city government**

municipalities

SG International Women
    Law, Government, and Public Policy
BT urban areas

mural art

SG Visual and Performing Arts
BT visual arts

murder

SG Law, Government, and Public Policy
UF homicide
NT bride burning
    gynocide
    infanticide
    matricide
    patricide
RT crimes
    genocide

murderers

    SG History and Social Change
          Law, Government, and Public Policy
  RT crimes

muscular development

    SG Natural Sciences and Health
  BT physical development
  RT hormones
       upper body strength

museums

    SG Visual and Performing Arts
  BT facilities
  RT alternative spaces
       art conservation
       curators
       docents
       visual arts

music

    SG Visual and Performing Arts
  BT performing arts
  NT art music
       blues
       chamber music
       children's music
       computer music
       electronic music
       feminist music
       holistic music
       incidental music
       instrumental music
       jazz
       meditation music
       orchestral music
       political music
       popular music
       religious music
       salon music
       tribal music
       vocal music
       women's music
  RT acoustics
       iconography
       lyrics
       music criticism

                (*cont.*)

music (*cont.*)

  RT music festivals
       music history
       music industry
       music theory
       music therapy
       music videos
       musical theater
       musicals
       musicians
       musicology
       performances
       popular culture
       scores
       sheet music
       teachers
       vaudeville

music criticism

    SG Visual and Performing Arts
  BT criticism
  RT music

music festivals

    SG Visual and Performing Arts
  BT festivals
  RT music
       women's music

music history

    SG History and Social Change
          Visual and Performing Arts
  BT history
  RT canon
       music

music industry

    SG Communications
          Economics and Employment
          Visual and Performing Arts
  BT entertainment industry
  RT arts, entertainment, and media
       occupations
       music
       performing arts

        SN=Scope note   SG=Subject group   DG=Delimiters group   USE=Use

music theory
SG   Visual and Performing Arts
BT   theory
RT   music

music therapy
SG   Natural Sciences and Health
     Visual and Performing Arts
BT   therapy
RT   holistic music
     mental disorders
     music

music videos
SG   Communications
     Visual and Performing Arts
BT   videos
RT   images of girls
     images of women
     music
     rock and roll
     singers

musical theater
SG   Visual and Performing Arts
BT   theater
RT   incidental music
     librettos
     music
     musicals
     vaudeville

musicals
SG   Visual and Performing Arts
RT   music
     musical theater

musicians
SG   Economics and Employment
     Visual and Performing Arts
BT   arts, entertainment, and media
     occupations
NT   jazz musicians
     troubadours
RT   music
     singers

musicology
SG   Visual and Performing Arts
BT   humanities
RT   ethnomusicology
     music

Muslim
DG   Ethnic, Racial, and Religious
     Descriptors
UF   Moslem

mysteries
SG   Language, Literature, Religion, and
     Philosophy
BT   fiction

mysticism
SG   Language, Literature, Religion, and
     Philosophy
DG   Cultural and Political Movements
RT   intuition
     metaphysics
     prayer
     spirituality
     visionaries
     visions

mythology
SG   History and Social Change
     Language, Literature, Religion, and
     Philosophy
     Social Sciences and Culture
UF   myths (folk culture)
BT   folk literature
NT   creation myths
RT   allegory
     amazons
     cosmology
     figurative language
     folk culture
     goddesses
     gods
     heroines (historical)
     images of women
     legends
     literature
     mermaids

(cont.)

UF=Use for   BT=Broader term   NT=Narrower term   RT=Related term

mythology (*cont.*)
- RT myths
  - oral tradition
  - pantheon
  - romantic love
  - stories

myths
- SG History and Social Change
  - Social Sciences and Culture
- RT attitudes
  - belief systems
  - children's literature
  - dogmatism
  - earth mother
  - fairy tales
  - mother syndrome
  - mythology
  - old wives' tales
  - stereotypes

myths (folk culture)
- USE **mythology**

nags
- SG Social Sciences and Culture
- BT images of women

naive art
- SG Visual and Performing Arts
- BT art
- RT folk art

name rights
- SG Law, Government, and Public Policy
- BT rights
- RT birth name
  - forms of address
  - hyphenated names
  - matronymy
  - names
  - single mothers
  - slave name
  - surnames

names
- SG History and Social Change
  - Language, Literature, Religion, and
    - Philosophy
- NT hyphenated names
  - nom de lait
  - pen name
  - surnames
- RT birth certificates
  - children
  - forms of address
  - kinship
  - labels
  - matronymy
  - Ms
  - name rights
  - naming
  - patronymy
  - pseudonyms
  - semantics
  - sexist language
  - stereotyping
  - titles

Namibian
- DG National and Regional Descriptors
- BT African

naming
- SG Language, Literature, Religion, and
  - Philosophy
- NT matronymy
  - patronymy
- RT birth name
  - forms of address
  - names
  - nonsexist language
  - sexist language
  - titles

nannies
- SG Economics and Employment
  - Social Sciences and Culture
- BT child care workers
- RT child care

narcissism

    SG Social Sciences and Culture

  RT ego

       mental disorders

       selfish behavior

       values

narcotic drugs

    SG Natural Sciences and Health

  UF narcotics

  BT drugs

  NT cocaine

       heroin

       marijuana

  RT drug addiction

       drug overdoses

       therapy

       withdrawal

narcotics

  USE **narcotic drugs**

narratives

    SG Language, Literature, Religion, and

          Philosophy

    DG Types and Forms of Materials

  NT personal narratives

  RT ballads

       journals

       oral history

       prose

       storytelling

       voice

national health insurance

    SG Law, Government, and Public Policy

         Natural Sciences and Health

  BT health insurance

  RT medical care

       Medicare

       socialized medicine

National Health Service (Great Britain)

    SG Law, Government, and Public Policy

         Natural Sciences and Health

    DG Laws and Regulations

  RT health care delivery

                 (*cont.*)

National Health Service (Great Britain)

    (*cont.*)

  RT Medicaid

       Medicare

National School Lunch Act Amendments of 1982

    DG Laws and Regulations

  RT children living in poverty

       nutrition

national security

    SG Law, Government, and Public Policy

  BT security

nationalism

    SG Law, Government, and Public Policy

    DG Cultural and Political Movements

  RT civil religion

       colonialism

       developing nations

       state formation

nationalist movements

    SG History and Social Change

         International Women

         Law, Government, and Public Policy

  BT social movements

  RT revolutionary movements

nationalist revolutions

    SG History and Social Change

         International Women

         Law, Government, and Public Policy

  BT revolution

nationality

    SG International Women

         Law, Government, and Public Policy

  RT global feminism

       immigrants

       international marriage

       international relations

nationalization

    SG Economics and Employment

         Law, Government, and Public Policy

                 (*cont.*)

UF=Use for   BT=Broader term   NT=Narrower term   RT=Related term

nationalization (*cont.*)
- RT   privatization
-      welfare state

Native Alaskan
- DG   Ethnic, Racial, and Religious
-       Descriptors

Native American
- USE **American Indian**

Native American studies
- USE **American Indian studies**

Native Canadian
- DG   Ethnic, Racial, and Religious
-       Descriptors

native healers
- SN   *Indigenous healers in a culture.*
- SG   Language, Literature, Religion, and
-       Philosophy
-       Natural Sciences and Health
- BT   healers
- RT   folk healers
-      indigenous populations
-      medicine women
-      spiritualists

nativistic movements
- DG   Cultural and Political Movements

natural childbirth
- SG   Natural Sciences and Health
- BT   childbirth
- RT   birthing centers
-      caesarian section
-      childbirth training
-      episiotomy
-      home birth
-      labor (childbirth)
-      labor coaching
-      midwifery

natural family planning
- USE **rhythm method**

natural resources
- SG   Science and Technology
- BT   resources
- NT   mineral resources
-      water resources
- RT   conservation
-      energy conservation
-      environmental health
-      mining industry

natural sciences
- SG   Natural Sciences and Health
- NT   biological sciences
-      environmental sciences
-      physical sciences
- RT   interdisciplinary studies
-      mathematics
-      medical sciences
-      research bias
-      science
-      social sciences
-      space sciences
-      veterinary sciences

natural selection
- SG   Natural Sciences and Health
- RT   evolution

naturalism
- DG   Cultural and Political Movements

naturalists
- SG   Economics and Employment
-      Natural Sciences and Health
-      Science and Technology
- BT   scientific and technical occupations

naturalization
- SG   History and Social Change
-      Law, Government, and Public Policy
- RT   citizenship
-      immigration

nature
- SG   Language, Literature, Religion, and
-      Philosophy
-      Science and Technology

                                 (*cont.*)

nature (*cont.*)
RT   earth mother
      ecological factors
      ecology
      mother earth
      spirituality

Nazism
DG   Cultural and Political Movements

Near Eastern
USE **Middle Eastern**

Near Eastern studies
SG   Education
      International Women
      Social Sciences and Culture
BT   area studies

needlepoint
SG   Visual and Performing Arts
BT   needlework

needlework
SG   Visual and Performing Arts
BT   craft arts
NT   crocheting
      embroidery
      knitting
      needlepoint
RT   clothing workers
      quilting
      samplers

needleworkers
USE **clothing workers**

negative reinforcement
SG   Social Sciences and Culture
BT   reinforcement

negotiation
SG   Economics and Employment
      Law, Government, and Public Policy
RT   arguments
      compromise
      conflict resolution

(*cont.*)

negotiation (*cont.*)
RT   contracts
      labor contracts
      negotiators

negotiators
SG   Economics and Employment
      International Women
      Law, Government, and Public Policy
BT   legal and political occupations
RT   mediators
      negotiation
      unions

Negro
USE **Black**

neighborhood health centers
SG   Natural Sciences and Health
BT   centers
      health care facilities

neighborhood preservation
SG   Social Sciences and Culture
BT   preservation

neighborhoods
SG   Law, Government, and Public Policy
      Social Sciences and Culture
NT   declining neighborhoods
      desirable neighborhoods
      ethnic neighborhoods
RT   communities
      community development
      houses
      inner city
      urban areas
      zoning

neoclassical economics
SG   Economics and Employment
BT   economics

neoclassicism
DG   Cultural and Political Movements

---

neocolonialism
DG Cultural and Political Movements
BT colonialism

neoconservatism
DG Cultural and Political Movements

neoorthodoxy
DG Cultural and Political Movements

neophytes
USE **novices**

neoplatonism
DG Cultural and Political Movements

neopositivism
DG Cultural and Political Movements

Nepalese
DG National and Regional Descriptors
BT Asian

nephews
SG Social Sciences and Culture
RT family structure

nepotism
SG Economics and Employment
RT discrimination
employment
family owned business
occupations
promotions

nervous system
SG Natural Sciences and Health
Social Sciences and Culture
BT bodies
RT brain

nervousness
SG Natural Sciences and Health
Social Sciences and Culture
RT images of women
lack of confidence
self concept

net income
SG Economics and Employment
BT income
RT taxes

network ratings
SG Communications
BT ratings
RT networks (media)
program ratings
radio
television

network theory
SG Economics and Employment
BT theory

networking
SG Social Sciences and Culture
RT organizing

networks
SN *Formal and informal channels of communication that provide information
and support.*
SG Education
UF social networks
NT old boy networks
women's networks
RT alliances
beauty parlors
contacts
feminist methods
groups
information dissemination
job hunting
job recruitment
job search methods
mentors
organizations
political power
professional women's groups
search committees
support systems

networks (media)
SG Communications

(*cont.*)

---

networks (media) *(cont.)*
　BT　corporations
　RT　network ratings

neuroses
　SG　Natural Sciences and Health
　　　Social Sciences and Culture
　BT　mental disorders
　RT　complexes
　　　obsessive compulsive disorders

New Deal
　DG　Historical Periods

new girl networks
　USE **old girl networks**

new left
　SN　*Political movement originating in the*
　　　1960s that actively advocates radical
　　　changes in social, political, and edu-
　　　cational policies and practices.
　SG　History and Social Change
　　　Law, Government, and Public Policy
　RT　left wing organizations
　　　radical feminism

New Zealander
　DG　National and Regional Descriptors
　BT　Pacific

news services
　SG　Communications
　UF　press services
　BT　information services
　RT　electronic media
　　　mass media
　　　print media

newsletters
　SG　Communications
　　　History and Social Change
　DG　Types and Forms of Materials
　BT　periodicals

newspapers
　SG　Communications

(cont.)

newspapers *(cont.)*
　DG　Types and Forms of Materials
　BT　periodicals
　RT　advice columns
　　　editorials
　　　women's media
　　　women's pages

Nicaraguan
　DG　National and Regional Descriptors
　BT　Central American

nieces
　SG　Social Sciences and Culture
　RT　family structure

Nigerian
　DG　National and Regional Descriptors
　BT　African

Nigerois
　DG　National and Regional Descriptors
　BT　African

night clubs
　SG　Visual and Performing Arts
　BT　clubs
　RT　entertainment
　　　performers

nihilism
　DG　Cultural and Political Movements

no fault divorce
　SG　Social Sciences and Culture
　BT　divorce
　RT　divorce laws

no fault insurance
　SG　Economics and Employment
　BT　insurance
　RT　automobile insurance
　　　liability

noise pollution
　SG　Science and Technology
　BT　pollution

UF=Use for　BT=Broader term　NT=Narrower term　RT=Related term

nom de lait

SN *"Milk name" given by French mothers to children when they nurse.*

SG Natural Sciences and Health

BT names

RT breast feeding

nominations

SG Economics and Employment
      Law, Government, and Public Policy

RT hiring policy
      job hunting
      officials

nonaligned feminism

SN *Term describing feminism that aspires to be both radical and independent, integrating political, cultural, economic, and spiritual dimensions of women's lives.*

SG History and Social Change

DG Cultural and Political Movements

BT feminism

RT global feminism
      race, class, and gender studies

nonconforming behavior

SG Social Sciences and Culture

BT behavior

RT iconoclasts

noncustodial parents

SG Law, Government, and Public Policy
      Social Sciences and Culture

BT parents

RT visitation rights

nondegree education

SG Education

BT education

RT nondegree programs
      nonformal education

nondegree programs

SG Education

BT educational programs

RT adult illiteracy

(cont.)

nondegree programs *(cont.)*

RT alternative programs
      nondegree education
      nonformal education

nonfiction

SG Language, Literature, Religion, and Philosophy

BT prose

NT autobiography
      biography
      chronicles
      diaries
      essays
      histories
      journals
      letters
      memoirs
      parody
      satire

RT descriptive writing

nonformal education

SG Education

UF informal education

BT education

RT adult education
      adult illiteracy
      continuing education
      home schooling
      nondegree education
      nondegree programs

nongovernmental organizations

SN *Development organizations that are not affiliated with a specific government.*

SG International Women
      Law, Government, and Public Policy

BT nonprofit organizations

NT nongovernmental women's organizations

nongovernmental women's organizations

SG Economics and Employment
      International Women

BT nongovernmental organizations
      women's organizations

nonjudgmental behavior
 SG Social Sciences and Culture
BT behavior

nonorgasmic women
 SG Natural Sciences and Health
UF frigidity
BT women
RT intimacy
  orgasm
  sex counseling
  sexual dysfunction

nonprescription drugs
 SG Natural Sciences and Health
BT drugs
RT pain

nonprofit organizations
 SG Economics and Employment
BT organizations
NT charities
  foundations
  nongovernmental organizations
  voluntary organizations
RT arts organizations
  funding
  tax exempt status

nonsexist child rearing practices
 SG Social Sciences and Culture
BT child rearing practices

nonsexist curriculum
 SG Education
BT curriculum
RT educational opportunities
  educational reform

nonsexist language
 SG Communications
  Language, Literature, Religion, and
   Philosophy
BT language
RT desex
  equality
  gender marking
      (cont.)

nonsexist language *(cont.)*
RT linguistic sexism
  naming
  stereotyping

nonsexist literature
 SG Language, Literature, Religion, and
   Philosophy
BT literature
RT equality
  nonsexist textbooks

nonsexist textbooks
 SG Education
BT textbooks
RT nonsexist literature
  textbook bias

nontraditional careers
 USE **female intensive occupations**
   male intensive occupations

nontraditional education
 SG Education
BT education
RT alternative schools
  credit by examination
  credit for experience
  educational programs
  open door admissions
  teach ins

nontraditional employment
 SG Economics and Employment
BT employment
RT alternative employment
  male dominated employment
  occupational sex segregation
  occupations

nontraditional occupations
 USE **female intensive occupations**
   male intensive occupations

nontraditional work patterns
 SG Economics and Employment
RT occupational patterns

UF=Use for BT=Broader term NT=Narrower term RT=Related term

nonverbal ability
- SG   Education
- BT   ability
- RT   language
    - nonverbal language

nonverbal behavior
- SG   Social Sciences and Culture
- BT   behavior

nonverbal communication
- SG   Social Sciences and Culture
- BT   communication
- NT   gestures
- RT   body language
    - body politics

nonverbal language
- SG   Language, Literature, Religion, and
    - Philosophy
- BT   language
- NT   body language
- RT   gestures
    - icons
    - kinesics
    - nonverbal ability
    - sign language

nonviolence
- SG   History and Social Change
    - Social Sciences and Culture
- RT   activism
    - civil rights movements
    - conscientious objection
    - feminist ethics
    - influence
    - pacifism
    - peace movements
    - social movements
    - struggles

nonwage labor
- USE   **unpaid employment**

normal schools
- SN   *Colleges that trained teachers, histori-*
    - *cally the first opportunity women*
        - *(cont.)*

normal schools (*cont.*)
- *and Blacks had for mass higher edu-*
    - *cation.*
- SG   Education
- BT   schools
- RT   Black colleges
    - teacher education

norms
- SG   Education
- NT   male norms
- RT   aptitude tests
    - attitudes
    - bias
    - canon
    - circular reasoning
    - cognitive dissonance
    - competitive behavior
    - conceptual errors
    - conforming behavior
    - criteria
    - cultural constraints
    - domestic code
    - etiquette
    - image
    - interracial families
    - measurement
    - moral reform
    - objectivity
    - prefixes
    - priorities
    - reinforcement
    - research methods
    - sampling
    - social change
    - social prohibitions
    - standards
    - values

North American
- DG   National and Regional Descriptors
- NT   Canadian
    - United States

North Atlantic
- DG   National and Regional Descriptors
- BT   United States

SN=Scope note   SG=Subject group   DG=Delimiters group   USE=Use

Northeastern
DG National and Regional Descriptors
BT United States

Northern
DG National and Regional Descriptors
BT United States

Northern Irish
DG National and Regional Descriptors
BT European

Northwestern
DG National and Regional Descriptors
BT United States

Norwegian
DG National and Regional Descriptors
BT Scandinavian

nose jobs
USE **cosmetic surgery**

notes
DG Types and Forms of Materials

notices
DG Types and Forms of Materials

novelists
SG Economics and Employment
   Language, Literature, Religion, and
   Philosophy
BT arts, entertainment, and media
   occupations
RT writers

novellas
SG Language, Literature, Religion, and
   Philosophy
BT novels

novels
SG Language, Literature, Religion, and
   Philosophy
DG Types and Forms of Materials
BT fiction

(cont.)

novels *(cont.)*
NT novellas
RT romances

novices
SG Economics and Employment
   Language, Literature, Religion, and
   Philosophy
   Social Sciences and Culture
UF neophytes
RT apprenticeships
   nuns

novitiates
SG Language, Literature, Religion, and
   Philosophy
RT convents
   initiation rites
   monasteries
   nuns
   religious practices
   vows of chastity
   women religious

nuclear disarmament
SG Law, Government, and Public Policy
   Science and Technology
BT disarmament
RT antinuclear movement
   nuclear free zones

nuclear energy
SG Science and Technology
UF nuclear power
BT energy
RT industrial hazards
   technology

nuclear engineering
SG Economics and Employment
   Science and Technology
BT engineering

nuclear families
SG Social Sciences and Culture
BT families
RT couples with children

nuclear free zones
    SG Law, Government, and Public Policy
  RT nuclear disarmament

nuclear power
    USE **nuclear energy**

nuclear warfare
    SG Law, Government, and Public Policy
  BT warfare
  RT antinuclear movement
       end time thinking

the nude
    SN *Recurrent image of women in art.*
    SG Visual and Performing Arts
  RT art
       images of women

nudity
    SG Social Sciences and Culture
  RT body image
       clothes
       life styles

nuns
    SG Economics and Employment
         Language, Literature, Religion, and
           Philosophy
  BT images of women
       women religious
  NT mother superiors
  RT convents
       monasticism
       novices
       novitiates
       vows of chastity
       women's ordination

nurse practitioners
    SG Economics and Employment
         Natural Sciences and Health
  BT female intensive occupations
       health care occupations
  RT midwives
       nurses

nurseries
    SG Education
         Social Sciences and Culture
  NT creches
       workplace nurseries
  RT day care centers

nursery schools
    SG Education
  BT schools
  RT day care centers
       preschool education

nursery songs
    SG Visual and Performing Arts
  BT songs
  RT children's music
       lullabies

nurses
    SG Economics and Employment
         Natural Sciences and Health
  UF male nurses
  BT female intensive occupations
       health care occupations
  NT practical nurses
       registered nurses
       visiting nurses
       vocational nurses
  RT caregivers
       nurse practitioners

nursing
    SG Economics and Employment
         Natural Sciences and Health
  BT medical sciences
  RT nursing education

nursing education
    SG Education
         Natural Sciences and Health
  BT education
  RT medical sciences
       nursing

nursing homes
>   SG   Natural Sciences and Health
> BT   health care facilities
> RT   aging
>   caregivers
>   ethic of care
>   health insurance
>   quality of life
>   right to die

nurturance
>   SG   Natural Sciences and Health
>   Social Sciences and Culture
> RT   maternity
>   mother's milk
>   mothers
>   parenting rewards
>   trust
>   values

nurturers
>   SG   Natural Sciences and Health
>   Social Sciences and Culture
> BT   images of women

nurturing
>   SG   Natural Sciences and Health
>   Social Sciences and Culture
> RT   children
>   ethic of care
>   fathering
>   infants
>   love
>   motivation
>   parenting
>   relationships

nutrition
>   SG   International Women
>   Natural Sciences and Health
> RT   aging
>   cooking
>   dietetics
>   diets
>   eating disorders
>   fads
>   food

(cont.)

nutrition (cont.)
> RT   health
>   malnutrition
>   maternal and infant welfare
>   mother's milk
>   National School Lunch Act Amendments
>   of 1982
>   osteoporosis
>   premature childbirth
>   prenatal care
>   vegetarianism
>   Women, Infants, and Children Nutrition
>   Program

nutritionists
>   SG   Economics and Employment
>   Natural Sciences and Health
> BT   female intensive occupations
>   health care occupations

nymphomania
>   USE **female hypersexuality**

nymphs
>   SG   Language, Literature, Religion, and
>   Philosophy
> BT   women

obedience
>   SG   Social Sciences and Culture
> RT   learned helplessness
>   marriage vows
>   parent child relationships
>   passive behavior
>   power

obesity
>   SG   Natural Sciences and Health
> RT   body image
>   diet therapy
>   eating disorders

obituaries
>   SG   Social Sciences and Culture
>   DG   Types and Forms of Materials
> UF   death notices

(cont.)

UF=Use for   BT=Broader term   NT=Narrower term   RT=Related term

obituaries *(cont.)*
RT   death
     eulogies
     funeral rites

objectification
SN   *Term used to describe process of viewing women as sex objects that exist only in relation to men and male desires.*
SG   History and Social Change
     Social Sciences and Culture
RT   alienation
     dualism
     male norms
     mind/body split
     sex objects
     violence against women

objectives
SG   Social Sciences and Culture
UF   goals
NT   behavioral objectives
     course objectives
     educational objectives
     organizational objectives
     training objectives

objectivity
SG   Science and Technology
     Social Sciences and Culture
RT   conceptual errors
     male norms
     norms
     paradigms
     perceptual bias
     press coverage
     research bias
     research methods
     science
     scientific method
     scientific research
     social construction of reality
     socialization

obscenity
SG   Social Sciences and Culture
(cont.)

obscenity *(cont.)*
RT   pornography

observance
SG   Language, Literature, Religion, and Philosophy
RT   rites

obsessive compulsive disorders
SG   Natural Sciences and Health
     Social Sciences and Culture
BT   disorders
RT   compulsive behavior
     neuroses

obstetrical anesthesia
SG   Natural Sciences and Health
BT   anesthesia
RT   childbirth

obstetricians
SG   Economics and Employment
     Natural Sciences and Health
BT   health care occupations
RT   physicians

obstetrics
SG   Natural Sciences and Health
BT   medical sciences

occupational attitudes
SG   Economics and Employment
UF   occupational perceptions
BT   attitudes

occupational choice
USE **career choice**

occupational counseling
SG   Economics and Employment
UF   job counseling
     vocational counseling
BT   counseling
RT   outplacement

---

occupational diseases
- SG Economics and Employment
  Natural Sciences and Health
- BT diseases

occupational hazards
- USE **work hazards**

occupational health and safety
- SG Economics and Employment
  Natural Sciences and Health
- BT health
  safety
- RT absenteeism
  employment
  ergonomics
  industrial hazards
  industrial hygiene
  occupational stress
  pregnant workers
  protective clothing
  work hazards

occupational mobility
- SG Economics and Employment
- UF career mobility
  job mobility
- BT mobility
- NT career ladders
- RT employment
  flexible career patterns
  geographic mobility
  letters of recommendation
  mentors
  military spouses
  relocation
  turnover rates

occupational mortality
- SG Economics and Employment
- BT mortality
- RT mortality rates

occupational options
- SG Economics and Employment
- RT careers
  flexible career patterns

(cont.)

occupational options *(cont.)*
- RT occupational patterns

occupational patterns
- SG Economics and Employment
  Natural Sciences and Health
- RT alternative employment
  employment patterns
  flexible career patterns
  nontraditional work patterns
  occupational options

occupational perceptions
- USE **occupational attitudes**

occupational roles
- SG Economics and Employment
- BT roles
- RT careers

occupational segregation
- SG Economics and Employment
- UF job segregation
- BT segregation
- NT occupational sex segregation

occupational sex segregation
- SG Economics and Employment
  History and Social Change
  Social Sciences and Culture
- BT occupational segregation
- RT comparable worth
  equal employment opportunity
  female intensive occupations
  job standards
  male intensive occupations
  nontraditional employment
  pay equity
  sexual division of labor
  tipping
  wage gap

occupational status
- SG Economics and Employment
- BT status
- RT industrial classification

occupational stress

SG   Economics and Employment
       Natural Sciences and Health
UF   job stress
BT   stress
RT   burnout
     institutional racism
     institutional sexism
     job responsibility
     occupational health and safety
     turnover rates

occupational therapists

SG   Economics and Employment
       Natural Sciences and Health
BT   therapists

occupational training

USE **job training**

occupational trends

SG   Economics and Employment
BT   trends

occupations

SG   Economics and Employment
UF   jobs
     professions
NT   administrative support occupations
     agricultural, fishing, and forestry
       occupations
     arts, entertainment, and media
       occupations
     craft occupations
     education occupations
     female intensive occupations
     financial occupations
     health care occupations
     legal and political occupations
     male intensive occupations
     managerial occupations
     manufacturing occupations
     marketing and sales occupations
     paraprofessional occupations
     professional occupations
     scientific and technical occupations
     service occupations

(cont.)

occupations *(cont.)*

NT   transportation occupations
     volunteer occupations
RT   agriculture
     business
     careers
     employment
     industrial classification
     industries
     labor force
     labor market
     labor supply
     labor unions
     nepotism
     nontraditional employment
     work
     workers

oceanography

SG   Science and Technology
BT   earth sciences

odalisques

SN   *Female slaves or concubines in a*
      harem.
SG   History and Social Change
      Social Sciences and Culture
BT   images of women
RT   concubinage
     female sexual slavery
     harems
     sex objects

odes

SG   Language, Literature, Religion, and
      Philosophy
BT   poetry

Oedipus complex

SG   Social Sciences and Culture
BT   complexes
NT   female Oedipus complex
RT   Electra complex
     psychoanalysis

offenders

USE **criminals**

office hazards

USE **work hazards**

office parties

SG Economics and Employment
Social Sciences and Culture

BT parties

office work

SG Economics and Employment

BT work

RT administrative support occupations
typewriters

offices (facilities)

SG Economics and Employment
Social Sciences and Culture

BT facilities

RT quality of work life
work hazards

officials

SG Law, Government, and Public Policy

NT appointed officials
elected officials
public officials
sports officials

RT authority
judges
nominations

offshore production plants

SN *Factories or offices in lower wage
countries where work has been
moved from higher wage countries
and generally assigned to women.*

SG Economics and Employment
International Women

BT multinational corporation policy

RT factories
foreign workers
maquiladora
runaway shops
sweatshops

oil industry

SG International Women
Science and Technology

BT extractive industry

RT developing nations

old age

USE **older adults**

old boy networks

SN *Traditional informal male networking
critical for career opportunities and
advancement; important information
is shared, often in social situations.*

SG Economics and Employment
Education
Social Sciences and Culture

BT networks

RT alma mater
alumni
grapevine
locker rooms
male bonding
male male relationships
mentors
old girl networks
private clubs

old girl networks

SG Economics and Employment
Education
History and Social Change
Social Sciences and Culture

UF new girl networks

BT women's networks

RT alumnae
female female relationships
grapevine
old boy networks
professional women's groups

old maids

SN *Slang.*

SG Social Sciences and Culture

BT images of women

RT bachelors
completion complex

(cont.)

---

old maids (*cont.*)
- RT linguistic sexism
      maiden aunts
      spinsters

old old adults
- SG Natural Sciences and Health
      Social Sciences and Culture
- DG Age Levels
- BT adults

old wives' tales
- SG Natural Sciences and Health
      Social Sciences and Culture
- BT folk culture
- RT cliches
      images of women
      myths
      oral tradition

older adults
- SG Social Sciences and Culture
- DG Age Levels
- UF aged
      elderly
      old age
- BT adults
- NT older men
      older women
      senior citizens
- RT age discrimination
      ageism
      aging
      bias
      crimes against the elderly
      elderhostel
      elderly care
      elderly households
      geriatrics
      gray power
      life cycles
      lifelong learning
      Medicare
      second careers
      Social Security
      stereotyping
      test bias

older adults (*cont.*)
- RT women living in poverty

older men
- SG Social Sciences and Culture
- BT men
      older adults

older students
- USE **adult students**

older women
- SG Social Sciences and Culture
- BT older adults
      women
- RT at risk populations
      beauty standards
      crones
      employment
      stereotyping
      wisdom
      women in transition
      women living in poverty

Olympic Games
- SG Education
      Natural Sciences and Health
- RT amateur athletics
      sports

ombudsmen
- SG Economics and Employment
      Law, Government, and Public Policy
- BT men

ombudswomen
- SG Economics and Employment
      Law, Government, and Public Policy
- BT women

on the job training
- SG Economics and Employment
- BT job training
- NT apprenticeships
- RT inservice education
      internships

(*cont.*)

one parent families
  USE **single parent families**

one woman art shows
  SG Visual and Performing Arts
  BT art shows
  RT alternative spaces
      galleries
      women's art

oophorectomy
  SN *Removal of the ovaries.*
  SG Natural Sciences and Health
  UF ovariectomy
  BT surgical procedures
  RT hysterectomy
      ovaries

open door admissions
  SG Education
  BT admissions
  RT admissions criteria
      alternative schools
      nontraditional education

opera
  SG Visual and Performing Arts
  BT vocal music
  RT librettos

opera singers
  SG Economics and Employment
      Visual and Performing Arts
  BT singers

operant conditioning
  SG Social Sciences and Culture
  BT conditioning

operations
  USE **surgical procedures**

operations researchers
  SG Economics and Employment
      Science and Technology
  BT administrative support occupations
  RT computer programmers

operators
  SN *Use of a more specific term is recommended.*
  SG Economics and Employment
  BT workers
  NT boat operators
      camera operators
      computer equipment operators
      data entry operators
      heavy equipment operators
      machine operators
      press operators
      telephone operators

opinion polls
  SG Communications
      Law, Government, and Public Policy
  UF polling
      polls
      public opinion polls
  RT gender gap
      public opinion
      viewer ratings

opportunities
  SG Social Sciences and Culture
  NT career opportunities
      educational opportunities
      employment opportunities
  RT cultural heritage
      equal opportunity
      motivation

oppression
  SG History and Social Change
      International Women
  NT fat oppression
      medical oppression
      political oppression
      sexual oppression
  RT age discrimination
      class discrimination
      disadvantaged groups
      discrimination
      exploitation
      freedom from oppression
      homophobia

                                   (*cont.*)

UF=Use for   BT=Broader term   NT=Narrower term   RT=Related term

oppression (*cont.*)

RT   learned helplessness
    liberation
    powerlessness
    racism
    sexism
    slavery
    social movements
    subordination
    subordination of women
    tyranny

optimism

SG   Social Sciences and Culture
BT   attitudes
RT   emotions
    personality traits

optometrists

SG   Economics and Employment
    Natural Sciences and Health
BT   health care occupations
    professional occupations
RT   optometry

optometry

SG   Natural Sciences and Health
RT   medical sciences
    optometrists

oral communication

USE **verbal communication**

oral contraceptives

SG   Natural Sciences and Health
UF   birth control pills
    the pill
BT   contraception
    drugs

oral histories

DG   Types and Forms of Materials
BT   histories
RT   oral history

oral history

SG   Communications
    Language, Literature, Religion, and
    Philosophy
BT   history
RT   autobiography
    ballads
    chronicles
    histories
    illiteracy
    interviews
    legends
    life histories
    literacy
    narratives
    oral histories
    oral literature
    oral tradition
    personal narratives
    storytelling

oral literature

SG   Communications
    Language, Literature, Religion, and
    Philosophy
BT   literature
RT   autobiography
    ballads
    legends
    oral history
    oral tradition
    storytelling

oral sex

SG   Natural Sciences and Health
BT   sexual behavior
NT   cunnilingus
    fellatio
RT   ejaculation

oral tradition

SG   Communications
    Language, Literature, Religion, and
    Philosophy
BT   traditions
RT   epics
    folk literature

(*cont.*)

oral tradition (*cont.*)
RT folklorists
    legends
    listening
    memory
    mythology
    old wives' tales
    oral history
    oral literature
    orators
    oratory
    proverbs
    storytelling

orators
SG Communications
    Economics and Employment
    Language, Literature, Religion, and
       Philosophy
    Visual and Performing Arts
BT arts, entertainment, and media
    occupations
RT discourse
    oral tradition
    preaching
    public speaking
    rhetoric

oratory
SG Communications
    Language, Literature, Religion, and
       Philosophy
RT discourse
    literature
    oral tradition
    preaching
    public speaking
    rhetoric
    sermons
    speeches

orchestral music
SG Visual and Performing Arts
BT music

ordination
SG Language, Literature, Religion, and
       Philosophy
BT sacraments
NT women's ordination
RT clergy
    priests

organizational behavior
SG Economics and Employment
BT behavior
RT critical mass
    grapevine
    tipping

organizational development
SG Economics and Employment
BT development

organizational objectives
SG Economics and Employment
BT objectives

organizational psychology
SG Economics and Employment
    Social Sciences and Culture
BT psychology
RT management
    management styles
    organizations

organizational theory
SG Economics and Employment
BT theory
RT collaboration
    power
    power structure

organizations ·
SG Economics and Employment
    Social Sciences and Culture
NT agencies
    alliances
    arts organizations
    associations
    auxiliaries
    banks

(*cont.*)

UF=Use for   BT=Broader term   NT=Narrower term   RT=Related term

organizations (*cont.*)

NT boards
    bureaus
    businesses
    cartels
    caucuses
    circles
    clans
    clubs
    coalitions
    collectives
    commissions
    committees
    communes
    companies
    confederations
    congresses
    consortia
    consumer health organizations
    cooperatives
    corporations
    councils
    departments
    enterprises
    executive search firms
    federations
    health maintenance organizations
    institutes
    institutions
    leagues
    left wing organizations
    legislatures
    military
    nonprofit organizations
    parent teacher organizations
    parliaments
    pension funds
    political parties
    religious orders
    right wing organizations
    social organizations
    societies
    stock exchanges
    task forces
    unions
    utilities
    women's organizations

(*cont.*)

organizations (*cont.*)

RT bureaucracy
    communities
    conforming behavior
    cultural constraints
    facilities
    government
    group dynamics
    groups
    institutional discrimination
    leadership
    legal system
    networks
    organizational psychology
    organizing
    programs
    religious groups
    services
    social change
    social organization
    structural discrimination

organized crime

SG Law, Government, and Public Policy
BT crime
RT black markets
    family owned business
    gambling
    prostitution

organizing

SG History and Social Change
RT activism
    change agents
    grass roots
    labor unions
    networking
    organizations
    social movements
    unions
    workplace

orgasm

SG Natural Sciences and Health
NT clitoral orgasm
    vaginal orgasm
RT aphrodisiacs

(*cont.*)

orgasm (*cont.*)
RT arousal
  clitoris
  masturbation
  nonorgasmic women
  sex counseling
  sexual behavior
  sexual satisfaction

Oriental studies
USE **Asian studies**

original sin
  SG Social Sciences and Culture
BT sin
RT images of women
  religion
  temptation

Orphan Annie
  SG Social Sciences and Culture
BT images of girls

orthodoxy
  DG Cultural and Political Movements

osteoporosis
  SG Natural Sciences and Health
BT diseases
RT aging
  calcium deficiency
  estrogen replacement therapy
  hormone therapy
  menopause
  nutrition

Ouija boards
  SG Language, Literature, Religion, and
    Philosophy
    Social Sciences and Culture
BT fortune telling

outlaws
  SG History and Social Change
RT criminals
  pirates
  revolution

outlines
  DG Types and Forms of Materials

outplacement
  SG Economics and Employment
RT employment agencies
  job placement
  job retraining
  occupational counseling
  perquisites
  unemployment

outreach programs
  SG Education
    Social Sciences and Culture
BT programs

Outward Bound programs
  SN *Organized programs of outdoor physi-*
    cal activity intended to increase self-
    esteem and confidence.
  SG Education
BT programs
RT physical endurance
  self concept
  self confidence

outwork
  SG Economics and Employment
RT cottage industry
  piecework

ovariectomy
USE **oophorectomy**

ovaries
  SG Natural Sciences and Health
BT bodies
RT benign tumors
  oophorectomy
  oviducts
  ovulation
  ovum

overachievement
  SG Social Sciences and Culture
BT achievement

(*cont.*)

UF=Use for   BT=Broader term   NT=Narrower term   RT=Related term

overachievement (*cont.*)
RT   supermom
    superwoman syndrome

oviducts
SG   Natural Sciences and Health
BT   bodies
RT   ovaries

ovulation
SG   Natural Sciences and Health
RT   basal body temperature
    cervical mucus
    fertility drugs
    menstrual cycle
    ovaries
    ovum
    reproductive cycle

ovum
SG   Natural Sciences and Health
BT   bodies
RT   fertility
    menstrual cycle
    ovaries
    ovulation
    reproduction
    reproductive cycle
    sperm
    spermicides

Pacific
DG   National and Regional Descriptors
NT   Australian
    Hawaiian
    New Zealander
    Pacific Islander
    Papua New Guinean
    South Pacific
    Tahitian

Pacific Coast
DG   National and Regional Descriptors
BT   United States

Pacific Islander
DG   National and Regional Descriptors
(*cont.*)

Pacific Islander (*cont.*)
BT   Pacific

pacifism
SG   Language, Literature, Religion, and
    Philosophy
    Law, Government, and Public Policy
DG   Cultural and Political Movements
RT   conscientious objection
    nonviolence
    peace
    peace movements

PACs
USE **political action committees**

padding
SG   Social Sciences and Culture
UF   falsies
RT   body image
    brassieres
    girdles

paid employment
SG   Economics and Employment
BT   employment
RT   income
    wage labor

pain
SG   Natural Sciences and Health
RT   labor (childbirth)
    nonprescription drugs
    prescription drugs

painters
SG   Economics and Employment
    Visual and Performing Arts
BT   arts, entertainment, and media
    occupations

painting
SG   Visual and Performing Arts
BT   visual arts
RT   craft arts
    decorative arts

paintings
- DG Types and Forms of Materials

Pakistani
- DG National and Regional Descriptors
- BT Asian

Palestinian
- DG National and Regional Descriptors
- BT Middle Eastern

palimony
- SG Social Sciences and Culture
- RT alimony
  - divorce laws
  - financial arrangements
  - significant others

palm reading
- SG Economics and Employment
  - Language, Literature, Religion, and Philosophy
- UF palmistry
- BT fortune telling
- RT seances
  - seers

palmistry
- USE **palm reading**

pamphlets
- DG Types and Forms of Materials

Panamanian
- DG National and Regional Descriptors
- BT Central American

panels
- SG History and Social Change
  - Social Sciences and Culture
- BT activities
- RT conferences
  - educational activities

pantheism
- DG Cultural and Political Movements

pantheon
- SG Language, Literature, Religion, and Philosophy
- RT goddesses
  - gods
  - mythology

pants
- SG Social Sciences and Culture
- UF trousers
- BT clothing
- RT dress reform

pantyhose
- USE **hosiery**

Pap smear
- SG Natural Sciences and Health
- UF Papanicolaou smear
- BT medical procedures
- RT cancer
  - cervical cancer
  - cervix
  - disease prevention
  - physical examination

Papanicolaou smear
- USE **Pap smear**

paperhangers
- SG Economics and Employment
- BT construction occupations

papers
- DG Types and Forms of Materials
- NT concept papers
  - position papers

Papua New Guinean
- DG National and Regional Descriptors
- BT Pacific

parables
- SG Language, Literature, Religion, and Philosophy
- BT folk literature
- RT stories

UF=Use for   BT=Broader term   NT=Narrower term   RT=Related term

parades

SG History and Social Change
Social Sciences and Culture
BT activities
RT marches

paradigms

SG Science and Technology
Social Sciences and Culture
RT history of science
models (paradigms)
objectivity
social construction of reality
sociology of knowledge

paradise

SG Language, Literature, Religion, and
Philosophy
RT Adam
creation myths
deity
divinity
temptation

Paraguayan

DG National and Regional Descriptors
BT Latin American

paralegal workers

SG Economics and Employment
Law, Government, and Public Policy
BT workers

paralegals

SG Economics and Employment
Law, Government, and Public Policy
BT female intensive occupations
paraprofessional occupations

paramedics

SG Economics and Employment
Natural Sciences and Health
BT health care occupations
paraprofessional occupations

paranoia

SG Natural Sciences and Health
Social Sciences and Culture
RT blaming the victim
conditioning
mental disorders
social construction of reality

paraprofessional occupations

SG Economics and Employment
BT occupations
NT paralegals
paramedics
physicians' assistants
teacher aides
technicians
RT paraprofessionals
professional occupations

paraprofessionals

SG Economics and Employment
Education
Natural Sciences and Health
Science and Technology
RT paraprofessional occupations

parapsychology

SG Natural Sciences and Health
RT extrasensory perception
psychology
social sciences

parent child relationships

SG Social Sciences and Culture
BT adult child relationships
NT father daughter relationships
father son relationships
mother daughter relationships
mother son relationships
RT families
fathers
female headed households
gay stepfathers
incest
lesbian stepmothers
mothers
obedience

(cont.)

parent child relationships *(cont.)*
- RT parenting rewards
  stepparents
  teenagers

parent influence
- SG Social Sciences and Culture
- BT family influence

parent teacher organizations
- SG Education
- BT organizations
- RT volunteer work

parent teacher relationships
- SG Education
- BT relationships

parental aspirations
- SG Social Sciences and Culture
- BT aspirations
- RT parents

parental attitudes
- SG Social Sciences and Culture
- BT attitudes
- RT parents

parental behavior
- SG Social Sciences and Culture
- BT behavior

parental leave
- SG Economics and Employment
  Law, Government, and Public Policy
  Social Sciences and Culture
- NT maternity leave
  paternity leave
- RT benefits
  child care leave
  corporate policy
  Family and Medical Leave Act of 1987
  flexible career patterns
  parental rights
  pregnancy leave
  valuing children

parental rights
- SG Law, Government, and Public Policy
  Natural Sciences and Health
  Social Sciences and Culture
- BT rights
- RT maternity rights
  parental leave
  paternity rights

parenthood
- SG Natural Sciences and Health
  Social Sciences and Culture
- UF fatherhood
  motherhood
- NT delayed parenthood
  planned parenthood
- RT childbearing age
  childbirth
  fathers
  gay fathers
  lesbian mothers
  maternity leave
  mothers
  parenting
  parents
  paternity leave
  single parents

parenting
- SG Natural Sciences and Health
  Social Sciences and Culture
- NT coparenting
  fathering
  mothering
  shared parenting
- RT burnout
  chaperones
  child rearing practices
  dependent care
  division of labor
  empty nest
  gay fathers
  grandparents
  infants
  learned behavior
  lesbian mothers
  mothers

(cont.)

parenting (*cont.*)
RT nurturing
    parenthood
    parents
    primary caregivers
    reconciliation
    shared custody
    stepparents
    teenagers

parenting rewards
SG Natural Sciences and Health
    Social Sciences and Culture
RT ethic of care
    love
    nurturance
    parent child relationships

parents
SG Social Sciences and Culture
NT adoptive parents
    birth parents
    custodial parents
    foster parents
    noncustodial parents
    single parents
    stepparents
    working parents
RT achievement
    childbirth
    children
    fathers
    in laws
    mothers
    parental aspirations
    parental attitudes
    parenthood
    parenting

pariahs
SG International Women
    Social Sciences and Culture
RT caste
    discrimination

parliaments
SG International Women
    Law, Government, and Public Policy
BT organizations

parody
SG Language, Literature, Religion, and
    Philosophy
BT nonfiction
RT caricatures
    cartoons
    comedy
    drama
    humor
    satire

parole officers
SG Economics and Employment
    Law, Government, and Public Policy
BT correctional officers

part time employment
SG Economics and Employment
UF part time work
BT employment
NT job sharing
RT cottage industry
    moonlighting
    substitute teaching

part time students
SG Education
BT students
RT adult students

part time work
USE **part time employment**

parthenogenesis
SN *Nonsexual reproduction; cloning.*
SG Natural Sciences and Health
BT reproduction
RT reproductive technologies

participant observation
SG Social Sciences and Culture
BT research methods

                                        (*cont.*)

participant observation *(cont.)*
  RT   fieldwork

parties
      SG   History and Social Change
           Social Sciences and Culture
  BT   social activities
  NT   cocktail parties
       office parties

partners
      SG   Economics and Employment
           Social Sciences and Culture
  RT   equality
       personal relationships

passages
      SG   Language, Literature, Religion, and
           Philosophy
           Social Sciences and Culture
  RT   adults
       life cycles
       rites of passage

passing
      SN   *Practice by which members of minority*
           or oppressed groups live as members
           of dominant race or culture.
      SG   History and Social Change
  RT   gays
       lesbians
       majority culture
       people of color

passion
      SG   Social Sciences and Culture
  BT   emotions
  RT   crimes of passion
       desire
       love
       romance
       sexual behavior

passive behavior
      SG   Social Sciences and Culture
  BT   behavior
  RT   assertiveness training

                                    (cont.)

passive behavior *(cont.)*
  RT   deferential behavior
       learned helplessness
       obedience
       somnambulism
       spirit possession

patents
      SG   Law, Government, and Public Policy
  RT   copyright laws
       inventions
       licensing
       technology development

paternity
      SG   Natural Sciences and Health
  RT   absentee fathers
       child support
       custody
       fathering
       maternity
       paternity leave
       paternity suits
       responsibility
       teenage fathers

paternity benefits
      SG   Economics and Employment
  BT   benefits
  RT   employee benefits

paternity leave
      SG   Economics and Employment
           Law, Government, and Public Policy
           Social Sciences and Culture
  BT   parental leave
  RT   parenthood
       paternity
       paternity rights

paternity rights
      SG   Law, Government, and Public Policy
           Natural Sciences and Health
           Social Sciences and Culture
  BT   rights
  RT   parental rights
       paternity leave

UF=Use for   BT=Broader term   NT=Narrower term   RT=Related term

paternity suits
- SG   Law, Government, and Public Policy
- BT   lawsuits
- RT   child support
  - images of women
  - paternity

patience
- SG   Language, Literature, Religion, and Philosophy
  - Social Sciences and Culture
- RT   personality traits
  - tolerance

patient doctor relationships
- SG   Natural Sciences and Health
- UF   doctor patient relationships
  - physician patient relationships
- BT   relationships
- RT   childbirth training
  - confidentiality
  - family medicine
  - medical oppression
  - medical records
  - placebos

patriarchal language
- SG   Language, Literature, Religion, and Philosophy
- BT   language
  - sexist language
- NT   he/man language
- RT   conceptual errors
  - discrimination
  - gender marking
  - God the father
  - interruptions
  - linguistic sexism
  - male norms
  - patriarchy
  - phallogocentrism
  - religion
  - religious language

patriarchal religion
- SG   Language, Literature, Religion, and Philosophy

(cont.)

patriarchal religion *(cont.)*
- BT   religion
- RT   androcentrism
  - churches
  - God the father
  - laywomen
  - monotheism
  - patriarchy
  - religious discrimination
  - religious law
  - spiritual feminism
  - theology
  - witch burning
  - women religious
  - women's ordination

patriarchs
- SG   Social Sciences and Culture
- RT   fathers
  - God the father
  - matriarchs

patriarchy
- SG   History and Social Change
  - Social Sciences and Culture
- RT   aggressive behavior
  - androcentrism
  - colonialism
  - culture
  - discrimination
  - exploitation
  - family structure
  - gods
  - male norms
  - matriarchy
  - patriarchal language
  - patriarchal religion
  - phallocentrism
  - power
  - religion
  - sexism
  - theology
  - violence

patricide
- SG   Social Sciences and Culture
- BT   murder

(cont.)

patricide (*cont.*)
  RT fathers

patrilineal kinship
  SG Social Sciences and Culture
  BT kinship
  RT patronymy

patriotism
  SG Language, Literature, Religion, and
        Philosophy
        Law, Government, and Public Policy
  DG Cultural and Political Movements
  RT civil religion
        state religion

patronymy
  SN *Naming derived from father or father's*
        ancestors.
  SG Language, Literature, Religion, and
        Philosophy
  BT naming
  RT birth name
        God the father
        gods
        hyphenated names
        invisibility
        matronymy
        names
        patrilineal kinship
        pseudonyms
        slave name
        surnames

pauperization of women
  SG Economics and Employment
        Social Sciences and Culture
  UF feminization of poverty
  RT women living in poverty

pay
  USE **wages**

pay equity
  SN *Basing compensation on education,*
        skills, effort, training, and responsi-
        bility rather than nonrelevant clas-
                  (*cont.*)

pay equity (*cont.*)
        sifications of sex, age, racial or eth-
        nic background, or other discrimina-
        tory classifications.
  SG Economics and Employment
        Law, Government, and Public Policy
  BT equity
  NT comparable worth
        equal pay for equal work
  RT back pay
        careers
        economic equity
        equal pay
        Federal Equitable Pay Practices Act of
          1987
        labor legislation
        low pay
        occupational sex segregation
        sexual division of labor
        wage discrimination
        wage gap
        wages

peace
  SG History and Social Change
  RT antiwar movement
        pacifism
        peace advocates
        peace camps
        peace movements
        war

peace advocates
  SG History and Social Change
        International Women
        Law, Government, and Public Policy
  BT advocates
  RT antinuclear movement
        antiwar movement
        peace

peace camps
  SG History and Social Change
        Law, Government, and Public Policy
  RT peace

peace movements
　　SG　History and Social Change
　　　　International Women
　　　　Law, Government, and Public Policy
　BT　social movements
　NT　antiwar movement
　RT　antinuclear movement
　　　arms control
　　　conscientious objection
　　　disarmament
　　　global security
　　　nonviolence
　　　pacifism
　　　peace

peasants
　　SG　History and Social Change
　　　　International Women
　　　　Social Sciences and Culture
　RT　land reform
　　　rural poverty

pedagogy
　　SG　Education
　RT　curriculum
　　　teaching

pedestals
　　SG　Social Sciences and Culture
　RT　ideal woman
　　　images of women

pediatricians
　　SG　Natural Sciences and Health
　BT　health care occupations

pediatrics
　　SG　Natural Sciences and Health
　BT　medical sciences

pedicurists
　　SG　Social Sciences and Culture
　BT　cosmetologists

peer influence
　　SG　Social Sciences and Culture
　BT　influence
　　　　　　　　　　　　　　　　　　(cont.)

peer influence (cont.)
　RT　gangs
　　　group behavior
　　　peers
　　　social values

peer relationships
　　SG　Social Sciences and Culture
　BT　relationships
　RT　peers

peeresses
　　SG　International Women
　　　　Law, Government, and Public Policy
　BT　titles (nobility)
　　　women

peers
　　SG　Social Sciences and Culture
　RT　peer influence
　　　peer relationships

pelvic examination
　　SG　Natural Sciences and Health
　BT　physical examination

pen name
　　SG　Language, Literature, Religion, and
　　　　Philosophy
　BT　names

pen pals
　　SG　Language, Literature, Religion, and
　　　　Philosophy
　　　　Social Sciences and Culture
　RT　letter writers

penance
　　SG　Language, Literature, Religion, and
　　　　Philosophy
　RT　guilt
　　　purification rites
　　　sin

penis
　　SG　Natural Sciences and Health
　BT　genitals
　　　　　　　　　　　　　　　　　　(cont.)

penis (*cont.*)
RT   male circumcision
     phallus

penis envy
SN   *Females' alleged sense of inferiority be-*
     cause males have penises and females
     do not.
SG   Social Sciences and Culture
RT   womb envy

pension benefits
SG   Economics and Employment
UF   pensions
BT   retirement benefits
RT   discrimination
     employee benefits
     income
     retirement age

pension funds
SG   Economics and Employment
BT   organizations
RT   Social Security
     unions

pensions
USE **pension benefits**

people of color
SN   *See Delimiters Display: Ethnic, Racial,*
     and Religious Descriptors for more
     specific terms.
SG   Social Sciences and Culture
UF   minorities
NT   women of color
RT   passing
     race
     stereotyping
     voting records

perception
SG   Social Sciences and Culture
BT   cognitive processes
NT   auditory perception
     color perception
     depth perception
                  (*cont.*)

perception (*cont.*)
NT   extrasensory perception
     kinesthetic perception
     self perception
     social perception
     spatial perception
     tactual perception
     visual perception
     weight perception
RT   perception skills
     perceptual bias
     perceptual development

perception skills
SG   Natural Sciences and Health
        Social Sciences and Culture
BT   skills
RT   intuition
     perception

perceptual bias
SG   Social Sciences and Culture
BT   bias
RT   aggressive behavior
     attitudes
     canon
     cliches
     cognitive dissonance
     conceptual errors
     discriminatory language
     group dynamics
     leadership roles
     literary canon
     objectivity
     perception
     prefixes
     research methods
     scientific method
     skin color
     social construction of reality
     stereotyping
     viragos

perceptual development
SG   Social Sciences and Culture
BT   cognitive development
RT   perception

---

perfection
    SG Social Sciences and Culture
RT ideal woman
      mother syndrome
      values

performance
    SG Social Sciences and Culture
NT job performance
RT competence
      feedback
      performance appraisal
      performance factors

performance appraisal
    SG Economics and Employment
BT personnel evaluation
RT employee development
      employees
      job performance
      job training
      performance
      promotions
      standards
      wage increases

performance art
    SG Visual and Performing Arts
BT art
RT multimedia art
      performing arts
      visual arts

performance factors
    SG Social Sciences and Culture
BT influences
RT performance

performance spaces
    SG Visual and Performing Arts
BT space

performances
    SG Communications
      Language, Literature, Religion, and
        Philosophy
      Visual and Performing Arts
                (cont.)

performances *(cont.)*
BT activities
RT acting
      dance
      entertainment
      multimedia art
      music
      performers
      readings

performers
    SG Communications
        Economics and Employment
        Visual and Performing Arts
BT arts, entertainment, and media
      occupations
NT prima donnas
      soloists
RT actors
      entertainers
      night clubs
      performances
      singers

performing arts
    SG Visual and Performing Arts
UF fine arts
BT arts
NT dance
      mime
      music
      theater
RT aesthetics
      art
      concerts
      film
      humanities
      iconography
      literature
      lyrics
      media arts
      music industry
      performance art
      visual arts

perfume
    SG Social Sciences and Culture
                (cont.)

perfume (*cont.*)
RT   adornment
cosmetics
pheromones

period
USE **menstruation**

periodicals
SG   Communications
DG   Types and Forms of Materials
BT   print media
NT   journals (periodicals)
magazines
newsletters
newspapers

permanents
SG   Social Sciences and Culture
RT   hair styles

permissive child rearing practices
SG   Social Sciences and Culture
BT   child rearing practices
RT   permissive environment
teenage pregnancy

permissive environment
SG   Social Sciences and Culture
BT   environment
RT   permissive child rearing practices
sexual behavior

perquisites
SG   Economics and Employment
RT   benefits
compensation packages
employee benefits
job responsibility
monetary incentives
outplacement

persecution
SG   History and Social Change
Social Sciences and Culture
NT   witch persecutions
RT   genocide

(*cont.*)

persecution (*cont.*)
RT   human rights violations
refugees

personal columns
SG   Communications
Social Sciences and Culture
BT   columns
RT   advertisements
advice columns
blind dates
dating customs
loneliness
mail order brides
relationships
single men
single women
stereotypes

personal correspondence
SG   Language, Literature, Religion, and
Philosophy
BT   correspondence
RT   letters

personal development
USE **individual development**

personal finances
SG   Economics and Employment
BT   finances

personal hygiene
SG   Natural Sciences and Health
BT   hygiene
RT   body odor
deodorants

personal management
SG   Economics and Employment
Social Sciences and Culture
BT   management
RT   individual development
time management

UF=Use for   BT=Broader term   NT=Narrower term   RT=Related term

personal narratives

- SG   Language, Literature, Religion, and Philosophy
- DG   Types and Forms of Materials
- BT   narratives
- RT   diaries
     journals
     oral history

personal relationships

- SG   Social Sciences and Culture
- UF   interpersonal relationships
- BT   relationships
- NT   female female relationships
     female male relationships
     friendships
     gay relationships
     male male relationships
- RT   arguments
     body politics
     codependency
     dating
     emotions
     ethic of care
     human needs
     lovers
     mentors
     partners
     politeness
     possessiveness
     rejection
     sensitivity
     social relations
     synchrony
     unrequited love

personal service industry

- SG   Economics and Employment
- BT   industries

personal space

- SG   Social Sciences and Culture
- BT   psychological needs
     space
- RT   body politics
     privacy
     solitude

personal values

- SG   Social Sciences and Culture
- BT   values

personality

- SG   Social Sciences and Culture
- NT   authoritarian personality
- RT   family influence
     personality traits

personality development

- SG   Social Sciences and Culture
- BT   individual development

personality disorders

- SG   Natural Sciences and Health
- BT   disorders
- RT   conditioning
     social conditioning

personality problems

- SG   Social Sciences and Culture
- BT   problems
- RT   counseling

personality tests

- SG   Social Sciences and Culture
- BT   testing
- RT   personality traits
     psychological testing

personality traits

- SG   Social Sciences and Culture
- BT   traits
- RT   androgyny
     anxiety
     assertive behavior
     authoritarian personality
     birth order
     charisma
     conforming behavior
     creativity
     dogmatism
     extroversion
     family influence
     humor
     introversion

(cont.)

personality traits (*cont.*)

RT optimism
    patience
    personality
    personality tests
    pessimism
    self blame
    self control
    self denial
    self esteem
    self sacrifice

personnel

SG Economics and Employment
UF manpower
NT enlisted personnel
    military personnel
    sales personnel
    school personnel

personnel evaluation

SG Economics and Employment
BT evaluation
NT performance appraisal
RT job performance

personnel management

SG Economics and Employment
BT management
RT affirmative action officers

personnel recruitment

USE **job recruitment**

perspiration

SG Natural Sciences and Health
    Social Sciences and Culture
BT bodies
RT body image
    body odor
    deodorants

Peruvian

DG National and Regional Descriptors
BT Latin American

pessimism

SG Social Sciences and Culture
BT attitudes
RT emotions
    personality traits

pets

SG Social Sciences and Culture
RT animals

phallic criticism

SN *Male-normed critical perspectives and methods.*
SG History and Social Change
    Language, Literature, Religion, and Philosophy
DG Cultural and Political Movements
BT criticism
RT literary canon
    phallogocentrism

phallocentrism

SN *Male-centeredness. Cultural traditions that assume male norms.*
SG Language, Literature, Religion, and Philosophy
    Social Sciences and Culture
DG Cultural and Political Movements
NT phallogocentrism
RT androcentrism
    male norms
    patriarchy
    phallus
    sex differences

phallogocentrism

SN *Critical theory asserting that western cultural norms are rooted in male-defined symbol systems.*
SG Language, Literature, Religion, and Philosophy
DG Cultural and Political Movements
BT phallocentrism
RT conceptual errors
    deconstruction
    dualism
    God the father

(*cont.*)

---

phallogocentrism (*cont.*)
- RT male norms
  - patriarchal language
  - phallic criticism
  - phallus
  - sexist language
  - social construction of reality

phallus
- SG Language, Literature, Religion, and
  - Philosophy
  - Natural Sciences and Health
- RT penis
  - phallocentrism
  - phallogocentrism
  - power

pharmaceutical industry
- SG Economics and Employment
  - Natural Sciences and Health
- UF drug industry
- BT industries
- RT clinical trials
  - health care occupations
  - health economics
  - scientific and technical occupations

pharmacists
- SG Economics and Employment
  - Natural Sciences and Health
- BT health care occupations
  - professional occupations

pharmacology
- SG Natural Sciences and Health
- BT medical sciences

phenomenalism
- DG Cultural and Political Movements

phenomenology
- SG Language, Literature, Religion, and
  - Philosophy
- BT philosophy

pheromones
- SN *Normally occurring sexually attractive*
  - *chemicals secreted by both females*
  - *and males.*
- SG Natural Sciences and Health
- RT arousal
  - perfume
  - reproductive technologies
  - sexual attraction
  - sexual behavior

philanderers
- SG History and Social Change
  - Social Sciences and Culture
- RT womanizers

philanthropists
- SG Economics and Employment
  - History and Social Change
- BT financial occupations
- RT charities
  - donors
  - foundations
  - philanthropy
  - upper class

philanthropy
- SG History and Social Change
- RT altruism
  - anonymous
  - art matronage
  - charitable work
  - charities
  - endowments
  - foundations
  - fund raising events
  - funding
  - in kind contributions
  - philanthropists
  - social reform
  - voluntary organizations
  - volunteer work

philosophers
- SG Economics and Employment
  - Language, Literature, Religion, and
  - Philosophy

(*cont.*)

philosophers (*cont.*)
BT   humanists

philosophy
SG   Language, Literature, Religion, and
        Philosophy
BT   humanities
NT   epistemology
        ethics
        logic
        metaphysics
        phenomenology
        political philosophy
        semiotics
RT   abstract reasoning
        aesthetics
        cognitive science
        dualism
        feminist theory
        social values
        values

phobias
SG   Natural Sciences and Health
BT   mental disorders
NT   agoraphobia
        homophobia
RT   fear
        psychotherapy

phonograph records
DG   Types and Forms of Materials

phonology
SG   Language, Literature, Religion, and
        Philosophy
BT   linguistics

photograph albums
DG   Types and Forms of Materials

photographers
SG   Economics and Employment
        Visual and Performing Arts
UF   cameramen
BT   arts, entertainment, and media
        occupations

photographs
DG   Types and Forms of Materials

photography
SG   Visual and Performing Arts
BT   visual arts
NT   fashion photography
RT   photojournalism

photojournalism
SG   Visual and Performing Arts
BT   journalism
RT   photography

phrenology
SG   Language, Literature, Religion, and
        Philosophy
        Social Sciences and Culture
BT   spiritual communication

physical abuse
SG   Social Sciences and Culture
BT   abuse
RT   child abuse
        ritual disfigurement
        sexual assault
        verbal abuse
        victims
        violence

physical appearance
SG   Natural Sciences and Health
        Social Sciences and Culture
BT   appearance

physical development
SG   Natural Sciences and Health
UF   growth
BT   individual development
NT   motor development
        muscular development
        sensory development
RT   pituitary hormones

physical education
SG   Education
        Natural Sciences and Health
(*cont.*)

UF=Use for   BT=Broader term   NT=Narrower term   RT=Related term   353

physical education (*cont.*)
- BT   education
- RT   athletics

physical endurance
- SG   Natural Sciences and Health
- UF   stamina
- BT   physical fitness
- RT   Outward Bound programs
       upper body strength

physical examination
- SG   Natural Sciences and Health
- BT   medical evaluation
- NT   breast examination
       pelvic examination
- RT   Pap smear
       prevention

physical fitness
- SG   Natural Sciences and Health
- BT   physical health
- NT   physical endurance
       physical strength
- RT   athletics
       bodies
       diets
       exercise
       fat liberation
       trimness

physical health
- SG   Natural Sciences and Health
- BT   health
- NT   physical fitness
- RT   antisepsis
       high heeled shoes
       tumors

physical mediums
- SG   Language, Literature, Religion, and
       Philosophy
- BT   mediums

physical sciences
- SG   Science and Technology
- BT   natural sciences

(*cont.*)

physical sciences (*cont.*)
- NT   astronomy
       chemistry
       earth sciences
       physics
       space sciences
- RT   science

physical strength
- SG   Natural Sciences and Health
- BT   physical fitness
- NT   upper body strength
- RT   male intensive occupations

physical therapists
- SG   Economics and Employment
       Natural Sciences and Health
- BT   female intensive occupations
       therapists

physical therapy
- SG   Natural Sciences and Health
- BT   therapy

physician patient relationships
- USE **patient doctor relationships**

physicians
- SG   Economics and Employment
       Natural Sciences and Health
- UF   doctors
- BT   health care occupations
       professional occupations
- RT   anesthesiologists
       obstetricians
       surgeons

physicians' assistants
- SG   Economics and Employment
       Natural Sciences and Health
- BT   female intensive occupations
       health care occupations
       paraprofessional occupations

physicists
- SG   Economics and Employment
       Science and Technology

(*cont.*)

SN=Scope note   SG=Subject group   DG=Delimiters group   USE=Use

physicists (*cont.*)
  BT   scientists

physics
  SG   Science and Technology
  BT   physical sciences

physiological psychology
  SG   Natural Sciences and Health
       Social Sciences and Culture
  BT   psychology

physiologists
  SG   Economics and Employment
       Natural Sciences and Health
  BT   scientific and technical occupations

physiology
  SG   Natural Sciences and Health
  BT   biological sciences
  RT   brain
       exercise

pica
  SN   *Appetite for ice, clay, starch, and other
       nonnutritious substances seen in
       some iron deficient subjects, especial-
       ly in women and children in low in-
       come groups.*
  SG   Natural Sciences and Health
  RT   malnutrition
       poverty

pickets
  SG   History and Social Change
  BT   protest actions
  RT   demonstrations
       strikes

pictures
  DG   Types and Forms of Materials

piecework
  SG   Economics and Employment
       International Women
  BT   work
  RT   cottage industry

                              (*cont.*)

piecework (*cont.*)
  RT   deskilling
       female intensive occupations
       home based work
       outwork
       piecework labor policy
       telecommuting
       third world

piecework labor policy
  SG   Economics and Employment
       International Women
       Law, Government, and Public Policy
  BT   labor policy
       multinational corporation policy
  RT   foreign workers
       global assembly lines
       home based work
       international division of labor
       piecework

pieceworkers
  SG   Economics and Employment
  BT   workers

pierced ears
  SG   Natural Sciences and Health
       Social Sciences and Culture
  RT   jewelry
       ritual disfigurement

the pill
  USE **oral contraceptives**

pilots
  SG   Economics and Employment
       Science and Technology
  UF   aviatrices
  BT   transportation occupations
  RT   aviation

pimps
  SG   Social Sciences and Culture
  RT   prostitutes

---

pin money

SN *In traditional marriage, allowance a husband gives his wife for personal expenses.*

SG Economics and Employment
Social Sciences and Culture

BT money

RT economic value of women's work
wage earning women
women working outside the home

pink collar workers

SN *Women working in women-intensive support occupations.*

SG Economics and Employment

BT female intensive occupations
workers

RT administrative support occupations
comparable worth
economic value of women's work
service occupations
white collar workers

pinups

SG Social Sciences and Culture

RT bathing suits
cheesecake
images of women

pioneers

SG History and Social Change

RT immigrants
indigenous populations
land settlement

pirates

SG History and Social Change

RT adventurers
outlaws

pituitary gland

SG Natural Sciences and Health

BT glands

RT pituitary hormones

pituitary hormones

SG Natural Sciences and Health

BT hormones

RT physical development
pituitary gland

placebos

SG Natural Sciences and Health

RT drugs
patient doctor relationships
research

placenta

SG Natural Sciences and Health

RT pregnancy

planned parenthood

SG Natural Sciences and Health

BT parenthood

RT childbearing
contraception
family planning
late childbearing
sex education

planning

SG Law, Government, and Public Policy

NT career planning
family planning
financial planning
population planning
rural planning
urban planning

RT cost benefit analysis
priorities
retreats
time use studies

planning meetings

SG History and Social Change
Social Sciences and Culture

BT meetings

plans

DG Types and Forms of Materials

NT lesson plans

SN=Scope note   SG=Subject group   DG=Delimiters group   USE=Use

plantations
SG International Women
RT colonialism
    slavery

plasterers
SG Economics and Employment
BT construction occupations

plastic surgery
SG Natural Sciences and Health
BT surgery
NT liposuction surgery
RT body image
    cosmetic surgery
    reconstructive surgery

plates
DG Types and Forms of Materials

Platonism
DG Cultural and Political Movements

play
SG Social Sciences and Culture
RT child development
    children
    children's culture
    children's groups
    toys

playbooks
DG Types and Forms of Materials

playgrounds
SG Education
    Social Sciences and Culture
RT recreation
    sports

playgroups
SG Education
    Social Sciences and Culture
RT child care
    preschool education

plays
SG Language, Literature, Religion, and
       Philosophy
    Visual and Performing Arts
DG Types and Forms of Materials
RT drama
    playwrights
    scripts
    skits
    theater

playwrights
SG Economics and Employment
    Language, Literature, Religion, and
       Philosophy
    Visual and Performing Arts
BT arts, entertainment, and media
       occupations
RT drama
    plays
    scripts
    writers

pleasure
SG Social Sciences and Culture
BT emotions
RT eroticism
    female sexuality
    joy
    satisfaction
    sex
    sexual behavior
    sexual fantasies

plenary sessions
SG History and Social Change
    Social Sciences and Culture
BT sessions

plumbers
SG Economics and Employment
    Science and Technology
BT construction occupations

pluralism

- SG Language, Literature, Religion, and Philosophy
       Law, Government, and Public Policy
- DG Cultural and Political Movements
- NT religious pluralism
- RT biculturalism
     democracy
     diversity
     ethnic diversity
     gender diversity
     majority rule
     populism
     racial diversity

PMS

USE **premenstrual syndrome**

podiatrists

- SG Economics and Employment
     Natural Sciences and Health
- BT health care occupations
     professional occupations

poetry

- SG Language, Literature, Religion, and Philosophy
- BT literature
- NT ballads
     elegies
     epics
     epigrams
     haiku
     limericks
     lyric poetry
     odes
     sonnets
- RT lyrics

poets

- SG Economics and Employment
     Language, Literature, Religion, and Philosophy
     Visual and Performing Arts
- BT arts, entertainment, and media occupations
- RT troubadours

(cont.)

poets *(cont.)*

- RT writers

polemics

- SG Language, Literature, Religion, and Philosophy
     Law, Government, and Public Policy
- RT rhetoric

police officers

- SG Economics and Employment
     Law, Government, and Public Policy
- UF policemen
- BT protective service occupations
- RT law enforcement

policemen

USE **police officers**

policy

- SN *Use of a more specific term is recommended.*
- SG Law, Government, and Public Policy
- NT child care policy
     corporate policy
     economic policy
     educational policy
     fiscal policy
     health care policy
     international policy
     labor policy
     monetary policy
     population policy
     public policy
     social policy
- RT policy making

policy making

- SG Law, Government, and Public Policy
- RT legislation
     mental health issues
     policy
     public policy
     social policy

Polish

- DG National and Regional Descriptors

(cont.)

Polish (*cont.*)
BT European

Polish American
DG Ethnic, Racial, and Religious
Descriptors

politeness
SG Social Sciences and Culture
BT attitudes
RT civility
manners
personal relationships
power

political action
SG Law, Government, and Public Policy
RT citizen groups
community responsibility
political action committees
political participation
protest actions
voting

political action committees
SG Economics and Employment
Law, Government, and Public Policy
UF PACs
BT committees
RT feminist organizations
lobbying
political action
pressure groups
special interest groups

political activism
SG History and Social Change
Law, Government, and Public Policy
BT activism
RT advocacy
lobbying
social action

political activists
SG History and Social Change
Law, Government, and Public Policy
BT activists

(*cont.*)

political activists (*cont.*)
RT advocates

political anthropology
SG Law, Government, and Public Policy
Social Sciences and Culture
BT anthropology
RT political science

political art
SG Visual and Performing Arts
BT art
RT culture work
political music

political aspirations
SG Law, Government, and Public Policy
BT aspirations
RT elected officials
political candidates

political asylum
SG International Women
Law, Government, and Public Policy
RT exile
political oppression

political campaigns
USE **election campaigns**

political candidates
SG Law, Government, and Public Policy
BT candidates
RT election campaigns
elections
political aspirations
political office
women in politics

political conventions
SG Law, Government, and Public Policy
BT conventions

political economic systems
SG History and Social Change
Law, Government, and Public Policy
RT economic development models

political ethics
    SG Law, Government, and Public Policy
  BT ethics

political husbands
  USE **political spouses**

political ideology
    SG Law, Government, and Public Policy
  BT ideology

political influence
    SG Law, Government, and Public Policy
  BT influence

political leaders
    SG Economics and Employment
  UF statesmen
  RT citizen groups
       leadership
       power

political music
    SG Law, Government, and Public Policy
         Visual and Performing Arts
  BT music
  NT protest music
  RT feminist music
       political art

political office
    SG Law, Government, and Public Policy
  RT appointed officials
       elected officials
       political candidates
       women in politics

political oppression
    SG Law, Government, and Public Policy
  BT oppression
  RT discrimination
       freedom from oppression
       human rights violations
       political asylum
       political prisoners
       poll tax
       refugees

political participation
    SG Law, Government, and Public Policy
  RT citizenship
       political action
       voting

political parties
    SG Law, Government, and Public Policy
  UF political party affiliations
  BT organizations
  NT Communist Party
       Democratic Party
       Libertarian Party
       minor parties
       Republican Party
       Socialist Party
  RT conservatives
       delegates
       labor
       liberals
       political philosophy
       politics
       radicals
       voting behavior

political party affiliations
  USE **political parties**

political philosophy
    SG History and Social Change
         Language, Literature, Religion, and
           Philosophy
         Law, Government, and Public Policy
  BT philosophy
  RT political parties
       political theory

political power
    SG Law, Government, and Public Policy
  BT power
  RT influence
       networks

political prisoners
    SG International Women
         Law, Government, and Public Policy
  BT prisoners

(cont.)

political prisoners (*cont.*)
  RT human rights violations
      political oppression
      political repression

political refugees
  SG International Women
      Law, Government, and Public Policy
  BT refugees

political representation
  SG Law, Government, and Public Policy
  BT representation
  RT democracy
      representatives
      voting

political repression
  SG Law, Government, and Public Policy
  BT repression
  RT civil rights
      political prisoners

political rights
  SG Communications
      International Women
      Law, Government, and Public Policy
  BT rights
  RT freedom of assembly
      freedom of speech
      freedom of the press
      freedom of worship

political sanctions
  SG International Women
      Law, Government, and Public Policy
  BT sanctions

political science
  SG Social Sciences and Culture
  BT social sciences
  RT political anthropology
      political theory

political spouses
  SG Law, Government, and Public Policy
      Social Sciences and Culture
                  (*cont.*)

political spouses (*cont.*)
  UF political husbands
      political wives
  BT spouses
  NT First Ladies (historical)
      governors' spouses
      presidential spouses
  RT female intensive occupations
      legal and political occupations

political status
  SG Law, Government, and Public Policy
      Social Sciences and Culture
  BT status

political systems
  SG International Women
      Law, Government, and Public Policy
  NT communism
      democracy
      democratic socialism
      socialism
  RT public sphere
      the state

political theory
  SG History and Social Change
      Law, Government, and Public Policy
  BT theory
  RT feminism
      feminist theory
      political philosophy
      political science
      social sciences

political wives
  USE **political spouses**

politicians
  USE **elected officials**

politics
  SG Law, Government, and Public Policy
  NT citizenship
      coalition politics
      local politics
      sexual politics
                  (*cont.*)

politics (*cont.*)
RT appointed officials
city government
elected officials
elections
government
international relations
political parties
voting behavior
women in politics

poll tax
SG Economics and Employment
History and Social Change
Law, Government, and Public Policy
RT discrimination
political oppression
voting
voting rights

polling
USE **opinion polls**

polls
USE **opinion polls**

pollution
SG Science and Technology
NT air pollution
noise pollution
water pollution
RT conservation
hazardous waste
sewage disposal

polyandry
SN *Having more than one husband.*
SG History and Social Change
Social Sciences and Culture
BT marriage customs
polygamy
RT husbands

polygamy
SN *Having more than one spouse (applies
to either men or women).*
(*cont.*)

polygamy (*cont.*)
SG History and Social Change
Social Sciences and Culture
BT marriage customs
NT polyandry
polygyny
RT bigamy
cowives
spouses

polygyny
SN *Having more than one wife.*
SG History and Social Change
Social Sciences and Culture
BT polygamy
RT cowives
wives

polytheism
DG Cultural and Political Movements

ponytails
SG Social Sciences and Culture
BT hair styles

poor
USE **poverty**

popular culture
SG Communications
Language, Literature, Religion, and
Philosophy
Social Sciences and Culture
BT culture
RT advertising
art
folk literature
iconography
image
literature
mass media
material culture
middle class
midlife crisis
music
soap operas
social trends
(*cont.*)

popular culture (*cont.*)
RT values

popular music
    SG Visual and Performing Arts
BT music
NT country music
    folk music
    rock and roll
RT protest music
    vaudeville

population characteristics
    SG Economics and Employment
    Social Sciences and Culture
BT demographic measurements

population control
    SG International Women
    Natural Sciences and Health
RT abortion
    contraception
    eugenic sterilization
    family planning
    family size
    infanticide
    population planning

population decline
    SG Economics and Employment
    Social Sciences and Culture
BT demographic measurements

population distribution
    SG Economics and Employment
    Social Sciences and Culture
BT demographic measurements
RT demography
    social sciences

population genetics
    SG Natural Sciences and Health
    Social Sciences and Culture
BT genetics

population growth
    SG Economics and Employment
    Social Sciences and Culture
BT demographic measurements
NT zero population growth

population planning
    SG International Women
    Law, Government, and Public Policy
    Natural Sciences and Health
BT planning
RT demographic measurements
    population control
    zero population growth

population policy
    SG International Women
    Law, Government, and Public Policy
    Social Sciences and Culture
BT policy

population trends
    SG Economics and Employment
    Social Sciences and Culture
BT trends

populism
    SG Law, Government, and Public Policy
    DG Cultural and Political Movements
RT grass roots
    pluralism

pornography
    SG Communications
    Law, Government, and Public Policy
    Social Sciences and Culture
NT child pornography
RT cable television
    censorship
    cheesecake
    cultural sadism
    erotica
    exploitation
    freedom of speech
    images of women
    juvenile prostitution
    obscenity

(*cont.*)

pornography (*cont.*)
RT rape fantasies
    sex discrimination
    sex industry
    sexism
    sexual exploitation
    videos
    violence
    violence against women
    violence in the media

portraits
SG Visual and Performing Arts
BT visual arts

Portuguese
DG National and Regional Descriptors
BT European

Portuguese American
DG Ethnic, Racial, and Religious
    Descriptors

position papers
DG Types and Forms of Materials
BT papers

positive reinforcement
SG Social Sciences and Culture
BT reinforcement
RT compliments
    motivation
    student motivation

positivism
DG Cultural and Political Movements

possessiveness
SG Social Sciences and Culture
RT jealousy
    personal relationships

posslq
SN *Census acronym for person of opposite*
    sex sharing living quarters.
SG Social Sciences and Culture
                                                    (*cont.*)

posslq (*cont.*)
RT census
    cohabitation
    households
    life styles
    relationships
    significant others

postdoctoral fellowships
SG Education
BT fellowships
RT assistantships
    graduate degrees

poster art
SG Visual and Performing Arts
BT visual arts

posters
DG Types and Forms of Materials

posthumous marriage
SG Social Sciences and Culture
BT marriage

postindustrial society
SG Economics and Employment
    History and Social Change
    Social Sciences and Culture
BT society
RT urbanization

postmodernism
DG Cultural and Political Movements

postnatal depression
USE **postpartum depression**

postnatal period
SG Natural Sciences and Health
NT infant development
RT infants

postpartum depression
SG Natural Sciences and Health
UF postnatal depression
BT depression
RT childbirth

SN=Scope note   SG=Subject group   DG=Delimiters group   USE=Use

postsecondary education

SG Education
DG Education Levels
BT education
NT higher education

poststructuralism

SN *Mode of literary criticism and thought dating from the 1960s that sees language as a changing system based on differences and absences, not as a paradigm for all other structures.*
SG Language, Literature, Religion, and Philosophy
DG Cultural and Political Movements
RT deconstruction
structuralism

potluck suppers

SG History and Social Change
BT suppers

potters

SG Economics and Employment
Visual and Performing Arts
BT craft artists

pottery

SG Visual and Performing Arts
BT craft arts
RT ceramics

poverty

SG Economics and Employment
Social Sciences and Culture
UF poor
NT rural poverty
RT basic human needs
children living in poverty
class discrimination
cost of living
dual economy
economically disadvantaged
exploitation
famine
food stamps
ghettos

(cont.)

poverty *(cont.)*

RT homeless
hunger
illiteracy
infant mortality
infanticide
inner city
legal settlements
living standards
low pay
lower class
malnutrition
minimum income
mortality rates
pica
social class
social services
starvation
untouchables
vows of poverty
wealth distribution
women living in poverty

power

SN *The ability to mobilize material and human resources; also used for concepts of authority and control.*
SG History and Social Change
NT consumer power
economic power
gray power
political power
woman power
RT authority
autonomy
boards of directors
body politics
business
control
ego
empowerment
governing boards
influence
leadership
leadership skills
locus of control
management

(cont.)

power (*cont.*)
RT matriarchy
money
obedience
organizational theory
patriarchy
phallus
politeness
political leaders
private sphere
sexual harassment

power structure
SG Law, Government, and Public Policy
RT bureaucracy
corporations
military
organizational theory
social structure
upper class

powerlessness
SG History and Social Change
RT exploitation
learned helplessness
oppression

practical nurses
SG Economics and Employment
Natural Sciences and Health
BT nurses

pragmatism
DG Cultural and Political Movements

prayer
SG Language, Literature, Religion, and
Philosophy
BT spiritual communication
RT healing
meditation
monasticism
mysticism
religion
religious experience
religious practices
rites

(*cont.*)

prayer (*cont.*)
RT spirituality

prayer meetings
SG History and Social Change
Social Sciences and Culture
BT meetings
RT revivals

preaching
SG Language, Literature, Religion, and
Philosophy
RT clergy
orators
oratory
prophecy
religious language
rhetoric

predestination
SG Language, Literature, Religion, and
Philosophy
BT religious beliefs

prefixes
SG Language, Literature, Religion, and
Philosophy
RT linguistic sexism
norms
perceptual bias

pregnancy
SG Natural Sciences and Health
UF gestation
NT ectopic pregnancy
male pregnancy
pseudopregnancy
sympathetic pregnancy
teenage pregnancy
tubal pregnancy
unwanted pregnancy
RT anemia
childbirth
coitus interruptus
communicable diseases
conception
contraception

(*cont.*)

pregnancy (*cont.*)
RT diabetes
embryos
family planning
fertility
fertilization
fetuses
gestation period
insemination
measles
miscarriage
placenta
prenatal influences
reproduction
reproductive cycle
rhythm method
sex education
sexually transmitted diseases
sterilization
stress (physical)
toxemia

pregnancy disability
SG Economics and Employment
Natural Sciences and Health
BT disabilities

pregnancy discrimination
SG Economics and Employment
Law, Government, and Public Policy
Natural Sciences and Health
Social Sciences and Culture
BT discrimination
RT Pregnancy Discrimination Act of 1978
pregnant workers
unfair labor practices

Pregnancy Discrimination Act of 1978
SN *Amendment to Title VII of the Civil Rights Act of 1964.*
DG Laws and Regulations
RT pregnancy discrimination

pregnancy leave
SG Economics and Employment
Law, Government, and Public Policy
Social Sciences and Culture
(*cont.*)

pregnancy leave (*cont.*)
RT maternity leave
parental leave

pregnancy prevention
SG Education
Natural Sciences and Health
BT prevention
RT abortion
birth control
contraception
sex education
spermicides

pregnancy trimesters
SG Natural Sciences and Health
RT gestation period

pregnant students
SG Education
BT students
RT at risk populations

pregnant workers
SG Economics and Employment
Natural Sciences and Health
BT workers
RT occupational health and safety
pregnancy discrimination

prehistory
DG Historical Periods

prejudice
SG History and Social Change
RT ad feminam
antisemitism
bias
discrimination
ethnic intimidation
hate
racial discrimination
sex discrimination

premarital relations
SG Social Sciences and Culture
BT sexual relationships
(*cont.*)

UF=Use for   BT=Broader term   NT=Narrower term   RT=Related term

premarital relations (*cont.*)
- RT   attitudes
       sexual behavior

premature childbirth
- SG   Natural Sciences and Health
- BT   childbirth
- RT   infant mortality
       nutrition
       premature infants

premature death
- SG   Social Sciences and Culture
- BT   death
- RT   death and dying
       euthanasia

premature infants
- SG   Natural Sciences and Health
- BT   infants
- RT   infant mortality
       multiple births
       premature childbirth
       sudden infant death syndrome

premenstrual syndrome
- SG   Natural Sciences and Health
- UF   PMS
- RT   menstrual cycle
       menstruation
       premenstrual tension

premenstrual tension
- SG   Natural Sciences and Health
- BT   disorders
- RT   menstrual cycle
       menstruation
       premenstrual syndrome

prenatal care
- SG   Natural Sciences and Health
- BT   health care
- RT   infant mortality
       maternal and infant welfare
       maternal mortality
       nutrition
       stillbirth

prenatal influences
- SG   Natural Sciences and Health
- BT   influences
- RT   alcohol abuse
       anesthesia
       drug abuse
       drugs
       fetal alcohol syndrome
       pregnancy
       substance abuse

prenuptial agreements
- SG   Social Sciences and Culture
- UF   antenuptial contracts
- BT   marriage contracts
- RT   divorce laws
       dowry
       separation

preparatory schools
- SG   Economics and Employment
       Education
- BT   private schools
- RT   boarding schools
       socialization
       upper class

preRaphaelites
- DG   Cultural and Political Movements

preschool children
- SG   Education
       Social Sciences and Culture
- DG   Age Levels
- BT   young children

preschool education
- SG   Education
- DG   Education Levels
- BT   early childhood education
- RT   nursery schools
       playgroups

preschools
- SG   Education
- BT   schools
- RT   head start programs

prevention

prescription drugs
SG Natural Sciences and Health
BT drugs
RT antidepressant drugs
drug abuse
drug addiction
menstruation inducing agents
pain
substance abuse
tranquilizers

preservation
SG Communications
NT art preservation
neighborhood preservation
RT curators
library science

presidency
SG Economics and Employment
Law, Government, and Public Policy
RT gatekeeping
leadership

presidential office
SG Law, Government, and Public Policy
RT elections
presidents
vice presidential office

presidential spouses
SG Law, Government, and Public Policy
UF First Ladies
BT political spouses
RT college presidents
education occupations
legal and political occupations

presidents
SG Economics and Employment
International Women
Law, Government, and Public Policy
BT legal and political occupations
managerial occupations
RT presidential office
vice presidents

the press
USE **print media**

press coverage
SG Communications
History and Social Change
Law, Government, and Public Policy
BT media coverage
RT bias
journalism
objectivity
protest actions
public information
public relations
publicity
women's media

press operators
SG Economics and Employment
UF pressmen
BT operators
printing workers

press services
USE **news services**

pressmen
USE **press operators**

pressure groups
SG Law, Government, and Public Policy
BT groups
RT lobbying
political action committees

prestige
SG Economics and Employment
Social Sciences and Culture
RT economic status
privilege
socioeconomic status
status
wealth

prevention
SG Law, Government, and Public Policy
Natural Sciences and Health
(cont.)

UF=Use for   BT=Broader term   NT=Narrower term   RT=Related term   369

prevention (*cont.*)

NT crime prevention
disease prevention
fire prevention
pregnancy prevention
rape prevention

RT accidents
breast examination
communicable diseases
diseases
physical examination
preventive medicine
violence

preventive medicine

SG Natural Sciences and Health

BT medical sciences

RT health insurance
health seeking behavior
prevention

pride

SG Social Sciences and Culture

NT gay pride

RT ego
self concept
self confidence
self esteem
sin

priestesses

SG Language, Literature, Religion, and
Philosophy

BT clergy
women religious

NT high priestesses

RT holy women
mother goddess
shamans

priests

SG Economics and Employment
Language, Literature, Religion, and
Philosophy

UF fathers (religious)

BT clergy

RT fathers

(*cont.*)

priests (*cont.*)

RT mullahs
ordination
rabbis
shamans
women religious
women's ordination

prima donnas

SG Social Sciences and Culture

BT performers

primary caregivers

SG Natural Sciences and Health
Social Sciences and Culture

BT caregivers

RT dependent care
fathers
mothers
parenting
sex role development
socialization

primary education

SG Education

DG Education Levels

BT early childhood education
elementary education

RT kindergarten

primary schools

SG Education

BT schools

primate studies

SG Education
Natural Sciences and Health
Social Sciences and Culture

BT zoology

prime interest rate

SG Economics and Employment

BT interest rates

prime ministers

SG Economics and Employment
International Women

(*cont.*)

prime ministers (*cont.*)
BT legal and political occupations

primitive art
SG Visual and Performing Arts
BT art

primitivism
DG Cultural and Political Movements

primness
SG Social Sciences and Culture
BT attitudes

princesses
SG International Women
  Law, Government, and Public Policy
BT images of women
  titles (nobility)
  women

principals
SG Economics and Employment
  Education
UF headmasters
  headmistresses
BT education occupations

print media
SG Communications
UF the press
BT mass media
NT periodicals
  publications
RT electronic media
  industries
  news services

printers
SG Communications
  Economics and Employment
  Language, Literature, Religion, and
    Philosophy
  Visual and Performing Arts
BT arts, entertainment, and media
  occupations
  printing workers

(*cont.*)

printers (*cont.*)
RT graphics
  publishing industry

printing workers
SG Communications
  Economics and Employment
BT manufacturing occupations
  workers
NT bookbinders
  compositors
  press operators
  printers
  typesetters

printmakers
SG Economics and Employment
  Visual and Performing Arts
BT arts, entertainment, and media
  occupations

printmaking
SG Visual and Performing Arts
BT visual arts
RT graphic design

prints
DG Types and Forms of Materials

prior learning
USE **credit for experience**

priorities
SG Economics and Employment
  Social Sciences and Culture
RT attitudes
  budget process
  norms
  planning
  values

prison workers
SG Economics and Employment
  Law, Government, and Public Policy
BT protective service occupations
  workers
RT correctional officers

UF=Use for   BT=Broader term   NT=Narrower term   RT=Related term

prisoners

    SG Law, Government, and Public Policy
NT political prisoners
     prisoners of war
RT criminals
     human rights violations
     judiciary system
     probation

prisoners of war

    SG Law, Government, and Public Policy
BT prisoners
RT veterans

prisons

    SG Law, Government, and Public Policy
UF correctional facilities
     jails
BT facilities
RT incarceration
     internment
     recidivism
     reformatories
     rehabilitation
     sentencing

privacy

    SG Communications
     Law, Government, and Public Policy
     Natural Sciences and Health
     Social Sciences and Culture
RT a room of one's own
     bedrooms
     blood tests
     confidentiality
     personal space
     relationships
     solitude

privacy rights

    SG Law, Government, and Public Policy
BT rights

private agencies

    SG Law, Government, and Public Policy
BT agencies

private clubs

    SG History and Social Change
BT clubs
RT discrimination
     old boy networks
     taxes

private colleges

    SG Education
BT colleges
RT public colleges

private education

    SG Education
BT education
RT public education

private parts

    USE **genitals**

private schools

    SG Education
BT schools
NT finishing schools
     preparatory schools
RT religious education
     religious schools

private sector

    SG Economics and Employment
RT free enterprise
     privatization
     public sector

private sphere

    SN *Assumption that society is divided into male and female spheres, women's sphere private and domestic, men's sphere public.*
    SG History and Social Change
     Law, Government, and Public Policy
     Social Sciences and Culture
BT separate spheres
RT agoraphobia
     chador
     cult of true womanhood
     domestic code

(cont.)

private sphere (*cont.*)
RT domesticity
foot binding
harems
hidjab
home life
momism
power
public sphere
sacred space
seclusion
space
the woman question
unpaid household labor

private voluntary organizations
SG Economics and Employment
International Women
BT voluntary organizations
RT charities
foundations

privatization
SG Economics and Employment
Law, Government, and Public Policy
RT nationalization
private sector
property ownership

privilege
SG Economics and Employment
Social Sciences and Culture
NT heterosexual privilege
RT class
exploitation
prestige
socioeconomic status
wealth

prizes
SG Education
RT awards
professional awards

probation
SG Education
Law, Government, and Public Policy
(*cont.*)

probation (*cont.*)
RT halfway houses
prisoners
work release programs

probation officers
SG Economics and Employment
Education
Law, Government, and Public Policy
BT correctional officers

problem solving
SG Education
Science and Technology
BT cognitive processes
RT abstract reasoning
intuition
logic

problems
SG Social Sciences and Culture
NT community problems
consumer problems
emotional problems
family problems
personality problems
research problems
sexual problems
social problems

procedures
USE **methods**

proceedings
DG Types and Forms of Materials

process
SN *Use of a more specific term is recommended.*
SG Law, Government, and Public Policy
Social Sciences and Culture
NT budget process
group process
judicial process

processes
DG Types and Forms of Materials

---

prochoice

SN *In the strictest sense, the belief in the right of a woman to choose to have an abortion.*

SG   Law, Government, and Public Policy

UF   right to choose

RT   abortion laws
abortion movement
abortion rights
antiabortion movement
reproductive rights

prochoice movement

USE **abortion movement**

procreation

SG   Language, Literature, Religion, and Philosophy
Natural Sciences and Health

RT   religious beliefs

productivity

SG   Economics and Employment

RT   economy

profanity

SG   Language, Literature, Religion, and Philosophy

RT   language

professional and related services industry

SG   Economics and Employment

BT   industries

professional athletes

SG   Communications
Economics and Employment

BT   arts, entertainment, and media occupations
athletes

RT   professional athletics
sports

professional athletics

SG   Communications
Economics and Employment
Natural Sciences and Health

BT   athletics

RT   entertainment
media coverage
professional athletes
sports

professional awards

SG   Economics and Employment

BT   awards
professional recognition

RT   prizes

professional degrees

SG   Education

BT   degrees

professional development

SG   Economics and Employment

BT   development

RT   mentors
role models

professional education

SG   Education

BT   education

RT   graduate degrees

professional occupations

SG   Economics and Employment

BT   occupations

NT   accountants
architects
artists
chiropodists
chiropractors
consultants
counselors
dentists
dieticians
engineers
explorers
faculty
information scientists

(cont.)

professional occupations (*cont.*)
- NT   judges
  lawyers
  librarians
  mathematicians
  optometrists
  pharmacists
  physicians
  podiatrists
  psychologists
  registered nurses
  religious workers
  researchers
  scientists
  social scientists
  social workers
  statisticians
  systems analysts
  teachers
  therapists
  veterinarians
  writers
- RT   arts, entertainment, and media
  occupations
  education occupations
  experts
  financial occupations
  health care occupations
  legal and political occupations
  managerial occupations
  paraprofessional occupations
  professionalism
  scientific and technical occupations

professional recognition
- SG   Economics and Employment
  Education
- NT   professional awards
- RT   academic rank
  ambition
  career satisfaction

professional sports
- SN   *See SPORTS for list of specific sports.*
- SG   Communications
  Economics and Employment
- BT   sports

(*cont.*)

professional sports (*cont.*)
- RT   coaches
  drug tests
  economic value of women's work
  mass media
  sports journalism

professional status
- SG   Social Sciences and Culture
- BT   status

professional women's groups
- SG   Economics and Employment
  History and Social Change
- BT   women's groups
- RT   networks
  old girl networks

professionalism
- SG   Economics and Employment
- RT   experts
  professional occupations

professions
- USE   **occupations**

professors
- SG   Economics and Employment
  Education
- BT   education occupations

profits
- SG   Economics and Employment
- RT   earnings
  military trade
  sex industry
  stock options
  structural unemployment

progesterone
- SG   Natural Sciences and Health
- BT   progestins

progestins
- SG   Natural Sciences and Health
- BT   sex hormones
- NT   progesterone

UF=Use for   BT=Broader term   NT=Narrower term   RT=Related term

program ratings

    SG Communications
BT ratings
RT network ratings
      radio
      television

programming languages

    SG Language, Literature, Religion, and
        Philosophy
        Science and Technology
BT language
RT artificial intelligence
      computer programming
      computers
      language structure

programs

    SN *Use of a more specific term is recom-*
        mended.
    SG Education
NT after school programs
      alternative programs
      assistance programs
      educational programs
      entitlement programs
      intern programs
      model programs
      outreach programs
      Outward Bound programs
      public policy programs
      residency programs
      welfare programs
      work incentive programs
      work release programs
RT activities
      organizations

progress

    SG History and Social Change
RT social change
      social values

progressive education

    SG Education
BT education

Progressive Period

    DG Historical Periods

progressivism

    DG Cultural and Political Movements

Prohibition

    DG Historical Periods

projection

    SG Social Sciences and Culture
BT defense mechanisms

proletariat

    SG Economics and Employment
        Social Sciences and Culture
RT class
      working class

prolife

    USE **antiabortion movement**

promiscuity

    SG Social Sciences and Culture
RT hypersexuality
      morality
      relationships
      sexual behavior
      social attitudes

promotions

    SG Economics and Employment
BT employment practices
RT career ladders
      employment
      glass ceiling
      motivation
      nepotism
      performance appraisal
      tenure

proms

    SG Social Sciences and Culture
BT dances

pronoun envy

SG Language, Literature, Religion, and
Philosophy
RT false generics
he/man language
male norms
pronouns

pronouns

SG Language, Literature, Religion, and
Philosophy
NT generic pronouns
masculine pronouns
RT false generics
pronoun envy

proofs

DG Types and Forms of Materials

propaganda

SG Communications
Law, Government, and Public Policy
RT advertisements
brainwashing
disinformation
indoctrination
mass media
public opinion
rhetoric

property confiscation

SG International Women
Law, Government, and Public Policy
RT property laws
property ownership

property crimes

SG Law, Government, and Public Policy
BT crimes
NT arson
burglaries
larceny
shoplifting
vandalism
RT community problems
crime prevention

property laws

SG Law, Government, and Public Policy
BT laws
RT property confiscation

property ownership

SG Social Sciences and Culture
RT land rights
privatization
property confiscation

property rights

SG Law, Government, and Public Policy
BT rights
RT land reform
land tenure

property settlements

SG Law, Government, and Public Policy
BT legal documents
RT death
divorce laws
separation

property taxes

SG Economics and Employment
Law, Government, and Public Policy
BT state taxes
taxes
RT housing

prophecy

SG Language, Literature, Religion, and
Philosophy
RT preaching
religious beliefs
religious practices
rites
seers
visions

prophets

SG Language, Literature, Religion, and
Philosophy
BT religious workers
RT visionaries

proposal writing

SG Communications
Education
Language, Literature, Religion, and
Philosophy
UF grant writing
BT writing
RT grant proposals
grants

proposals

DG Types and Forms of Materials
NT grant proposals

proprietary schools

SG Education
BT schools

prose

SG Language, Literature, Religion, and
Philosophy
BT literature
NT fiction
nonfiction
RT narratives
voice

prostheses

SG Natural Sciences and Health
NT breast prostheses
RT bodies
body image
cancer
psychological adjustment

prostitutes

SG Economics and Employment
International Women
Social Sciences and Culture
UF hookers
whores
BT female intensive occupations
images of women
service occupations
RT camp followers
concubinage
courtesans

(cont.)

prostitutes *(cont.)*

RT geishas
harlots
johns
pimps
sex tourism
sexual exploitation
sexually transmitted diseases

prostitution

SG Social Sciences and Culture
NT juvenile prostitution
RT brothels
economic value of women's work
female sexual slavery
massage parlors
organized crime
sex tourism
sexual exploitation
sexually transmitted diseases
state regulations
tricks
violence against women

protection

SG Social Sciences and Culture
NT equal protection under the law
RT guardians

protective clothing

SG Economics and Employment
Natural Sciences and Health
BT clothing
RT occupational health and safety

protective legislation

SG Law, Government, and Public Policy
BT legislation

protective service occupations

SG Economics and Employment
Law, Government, and Public Policy
BT service occupations
NT correctional officers
detectives
fire fighters
guards

(cont.)

SN=Scope note   SG=Subject group   DG=Delimiters group   USE=Use

protective service occupations (*cont.*)
NT police officers
    prison workers
    sheriffs
RT legal and political occupations

protest
SG History and Social Change
    Social Sciences and Culture
RT protest actions
    rebellious behavior

protest actions
SG Communications
    Education
    History and Social Change
UF protests
BT activities
NT boycotts
    civil disobedience
    demonstrations
    marches
    pickets
    rebellions
    riots
    sit ins
    strikes
RT Black power movement
    civil rights movements
    community action
    coups
    democracy
    dissent
    mass actions
    militance
    political action
    press coverage
    protest
    resistance
    sanctions
    social action
    social movements
    struggles
    teach ins
    terrorism
    violence

protest music
SG History and Social Change
    Visual and Performing Arts
BT political music
RT feminist music
    popular music
    spirituals

Protestant
DG Ethnic, Racial, and Religious
    Descriptors

Protestantism
DG Cultural and Political Movements

protests
USE **protest actions**

protofeminism
SN *Term used to describe feminist con-*
    sciousness and actions that existed
    before feminism was defined as a
    movement or theory.
SG History and Social Change
DG Cultural and Political Movements
BT feminism
RT consciousness
    foremothers
    sexual oppression
    suffrage movements
    woman's rights
    women's history
    women's rights

proverbs
SG Language, Literature, Religion, and
    Philosophy
BT folk literature
RT cliches
    oral tradition
    samplers

provosts
SG Economics and Employment
    Education
BT education occupations

pseudonyms
- SG Language, Literature, Religion, and Philosophy
- RT anonymous
  invisibility
  literature
  names
  patronymy

pseudopregnancy
- SG Natural Sciences and Health
- UF false pregnancy
- BT pregnancy

psychiatrists
- SG Economics and Employment
  Natural Sciences and Health
- BT health care occupations
- RT psychotherapy

psychiatry
- SG Natural Sciences and Health
- BT medical sciences

psychic readings
- SG Language, Literature, Religion, and Philosophy
- BT spiritual communication
- RT psychics

psychics
- SG Economics and Employment
  Language, Literature, Religion, and Philosophy
  Natural Sciences and Health
- BT female intensive occupations
- RT psychic readings
  seances
  seers
  visionaries

psychoanalysis
- SG Natural Sciences and Health
- RT Oedipus Complex
  psychotherapy
  therapy
  transference

psychoanalytic criticism
- SG History and Social Change
  Language, Literature, Religion, and Philosophy
- DG Cultural and Political Movements
- BT criticism

psychoanalytic feminism
- SN *Feminist critical theory using aspects of psychoanalytic theory to explain gender development.*
- SG History and Social Change
  International Women
- DG Cultural and Political Movements
- BT feminism
- RT feminist theory

psychodrama
- SG Social Sciences and Culture
- BT cathartic therapy
- RT art therapy

psycholinguistics
- SG Language, Literature, Religion, and Philosophy
- BT linguistics
- RT psychology
  social sciences

psychological adjustment
- SG Social Sciences and Culture
- BT adjustment
- RT prostheses

psychological conditioning
- USE **conditioning**

psychological factors
- SG Social Sciences and Culture
- NT defense mechanisms
  locus of control
- RT psychological needs

psychological needs
- SG Social Sciences and Culture
- BT human needs
- NT achievement need

(cont.)

SN=Scope note   SG=Subject group   DG=Delimiters group   USE=Use

psychological needs (*cont.*)

NT   affection
      approval need
      creativity
      intimacy
      personal space
      self actualization
      self concept
      self esteem
      self respect
      self sufficiency
RT   affiliation
      psychological factors

psychological repression

SG   Law, Government, and Public Policy
      Social Sciences and Culture
BT   repression

psychological stress

SG   Social Sciences and Culture
BT   stress
RT   mental health

psychological testing

SG   Social Sciences and Culture
UF   psychological tests
BT   testing
RT   abstract reasoning
      achievement need
      competency based tests
      intelligence tests
      personality tests
      test bias

psychological tests

USE **psychological testing**

psychologists

SG   Economics and Employment
      Social Sciences and Culture
BT   health care occupations
      professional occupations
      social scientists
RT   psychotherapy

psychology

SG   Social Sciences and Culture
BT   social sciences
NT   abnormal psychology
      analytical psychology
      child psychology
      clinical psychology
      comparative psychology
      developmental psychology
      educational psychology
      experimental psychology
      industrial psychology
      organizational psychology
      physiological psychology
      social psychology
RT   cognitive science
      lateral dominance
      parapsychology
      psycholinguistics
      sociolinguistics

psychometry

SG   Language, Literature, Religion, and
      Philosophy
      Social Sciences and Culture
BT   spiritual communication

psychopharmacology

SG   Natural Sciences and Health
      Social Sciences and Culture
RT   drug therapy

psychosexual behavior

SG   Social Sciences and Culture
BT   behavior

psychosomatic disorders

SG   Natural Sciences and Health
BT   disorders
RT   diseases
      hypochondria
      illness
      stress

psychosurgery

SG   Natural Sciences and Health
BT   surgery

UF=Use for   BT=Broader term   NT=Narrower term   RT=Related term

psychotherapists

SG Economics and Employment
Natural Sciences and Health
BT therapists
RT psychotherapy

psychotherapy

SG Social Sciences and Culture
BT therapy
RT dreams
free association
hypnotism
phobias
psychiatrists
psychoanalysis
psychologists
psychotherapists
social workers
stream of consciousness
tranquilizers

psychotropic drugs

SG Natural Sciences and Health
BT drugs
NT antidepressant drugs
tranquilizers

puberty

SG Natural Sciences and Health
RT acne
adolescence
age of consent

pubic hair

SG Natural Sciences and Health
BT hair

public accommodations

SG Law, Government, and Public Policy
RT public housing
public transportation

public affairs

SG Economics and Employment
Law, Government, and Public Policy
UF community affairs
RT public information

public agencies

SG Law, Government, and Public Policy
BT agencies
NT state agencies

public art

SG Communications
Visual and Performing Arts
BT art

public assistance

SG Law, Government, and Public Policy
Social Sciences and Culture
RT aid
federal assistance programs
food stamps
state assistance programs
support systems
welfare

public colleges

SG Education
BT colleges
RT private colleges
public schools

public education

SG Education
BT education
RT private education

public health

SG Law, Government, and Public Policy
RT epidemiology
health care delivery
health care legislation
Public Health Service Act
sewage disposal

Public Health Service Act

DG Laws and Regulations
RT public health

public housing

SG Law, Government, and Public Policy
UF subsidized housing
BT housing

(cont.)

SN=Scope note   SG=Subject group   DG=Delimiters group   USE=Use

public housing (*cont.*)
RT   public accommodations

public information
SG   Communications
Science and Technology
BT   information
RT   disinformation
press coverage
public affairs
right to know legislation

public interest
SG   Communications
Law, Government, and Public Policy
Social Sciences and Culture
RT   business ethics

public officials
SG   Economics and Employment
Law, Government, and Public Policy
BT   legal and political occupations
officials

public opinion
SG   Communications
Law, Government, and Public Policy
RT   morality
opinion polls
propaganda
ratings
stereotyping
viewer ratings

public opinion polls
USE **opinion polls**

public policy
SG   Law, Government, and Public Policy
BT   policy
RT   policy making
public policy programs
social issues
social policy

public policy programs
SG   Law, Government, and Public Policy
(*cont.*)

public policy programs (*cont.*)
BT   programs
RT   public policy

public radio
SG   Communications
BT   radio

public relations
SG   Economics and Employment
Communications
BT   relationships
RT   arts, entertainment, and media
occupations
community relations
human relations
journalism
marketing and sales occupations
press coverage
publicity

public relations specialists
SG   Communications
Economics and Employment
BT   arts, entertainment, and media
occupations

public schools
SG   Education
BT   schools
RT   public colleges

public sector
SG   Economics and Employment
Law, Government, and Public Policy
RT   government
private sector

public service
SG   Economics and Employment
Law, Government, and Public Policy
Social Sciences and Culture
RT   government workers
voluntary organizations

public speaking
SG   Communications
(*cont.*)

UF=Use for   BT=Broader term   NT=Narrower term   RT=Related term

public speaking (*cont.*)
- RT literature
  - orators
  - oratory
  - speeches

public sphere
- SN *Assumption that society is divided into male and female spheres, women's sphere private and domestic, men's sphere public.*
- SG History and Social Change
  - Law, Government, and Public Policy
  - Social Sciences and Culture
- BT separate spheres
- RT economic value of women's work
  - economics
  - gender ideology
  - political systems
  - private sphere
  - sex roles
  - space

public television
- SG Communications
- BT television
- RT educational television

public transportation
- SG Science and Technology
- BT transportation
- RT public accommodations

public utilities
- SG Law, Government, and Public Policy
  - Science and Technology
- BT utilities

public welfare
- SG Law, Government, and Public Policy
  - Social Sciences and Culture
- BT welfare

publications
- SG Communications
- BT print media
- NT feminist publications

(cont.)

publications (*cont.*)
- RT publishing industry

publicity
- SG Communications
  - History and Social Change
  - Law, Government, and Public Policy
- RT advertising
  - press coverage
  - public relations

publishers
- SG Communications
  - Economics and Employment
  - Language, Literature, Religion, and Philosophy
- BT arts, entertainment, and media occupations
- RT editors

publishing industry
- SG Economics and Employment
  - Communications
- BT industries
- RT arts, entertainment, and media occupations
  - authors
  - book clubs
  - book stores
  - copywriters
  - editors
  - mass media
  - printers
  - publications

puerperal fever
- SG Natural Sciences and Health
- UF childbed fever
- BT diseases

Puerto Rican
- DG Ethnic, Racial, and Religious Descriptors

pulp fiction
- SG Language, Literature, Religion, and Philosophy

(cont.)

pulp fiction (*cont.*)
BT fiction
RT erotica
   romances
   short stories
   soap operas

punishment
SG Law, Government, and Public Policy
   Social Sciences and Culture
RT curfew
   discipline
   enforcement
   reinforcement
   sanctions
   sentencing
   shunning

puns
SG Language, Literature, Religion, and
   Philosophy
BT figurative language
RT humor
   images of women
   jokes

puppetry
SG Visual and Performing Arts
BT craft arts

purdah
SN *Hindu practice of secluding women;
   literally a curtain or veil used to
   screen women from men.*
SG International Women
   Social Sciences and Culture
RT discrimination
   harems
   hidjab
   seclusion
   separate spheres
   veiling of women
   veils

purification rites
SG Language, Literature, Religion, and
   Philosophy

(*cont.*)

purification rites (*cont.*)
BT rites
RT baptism
   blood
   body image
   impurity
   mikveh
   penance
   self concept
   spirituality

purists
SG Language, Literature, Religion, and
   Philosophy
   Social Sciences and Culture
RT idealism

puritanism
DG Cultural and Political Movements

purity
SG Language, Literature, Religion, and
   Philosophy
   Social Sciences and Culture
RT angel in the house
   asceticism
   blood
   cleanliness
   images of girls
   images of women
   immaculate conception
   innocence
   virginity
   virgins
   vows of chastity

purses
SG Social Sciences and Culture
BT clothing

puzzles
DG Types and Forms of Materials

quadruplets
USE **multiple births**

qualitative analysis
SG   Education
     Social Sciences and Culture
BT   research methods

quality assessment
SG   Social Sciences and Culture
BT   assessment
RT   canon
     circular reasoning

quality of life
SG   Natural Sciences and Health
     Social Sciences and Culture
NT   quality of work life
RT   basic human needs
     hospices
     living standards
     nursing homes
     right to die
     technology
     values

quality of work life
SG   Economics and Employment
BT   quality of life
RT   offices (facilities)
     unfair labor practices
     work space

quantitative analysis
SG   Education
     Social Sciences and Culture
BT   research methods
RT   statistical analysis

queen bee syndrome
SN   *Stereotype of successful woman seen as
     refusing to share information or as-
     sist career advancement of other as-
     piring women.*
SG   Economics and Employment
RT   mentors
     stereotypes
     women's networks

queen for a day
SG   Communications
     Social Sciences and Culture
BT   images of women
RT   consumerism
     fantasies

queens
SG   International Women
     Law, Government, and Public Policy
BT   images of women
     titles (nobility)
     women
RT   royalty

questionnaires
DG   Types and Forms of Materials

quilting
SG   Visual and Performing Arts
UF   quilts
BT   craft arts
RT   needlework

quilts
USE **quilting**

quintuplets
USE **multiple births**

quotas
SG   Economics and Employment
     Law, Government, and Public Policy
NT   immigration quotas
     student quotas
RT   affirmative action
     affirmative action hiring
     hiring policy
     women in

quotations
DG   Types and Forms of Materials

rabbis
SG   Economics and Employment
     Language, Literature, Religion, and
     Philosophy
                                    (cont.)

rabbis (*cont.*)
BT   clergy
RT   priests

race
SN   *See Delimiters Display: Ethnic, Racial,*
     and Religious Descriptors for specif-
     ic racial and ethnic descriptors.
SG   Social Sciences and Culture
RT   ethnic groups
     people of color
     race, class, and gender studies
     racism
     stratification
     women of color

race bias
SG   History and Social Change
     Social Sciences and Culture
BT   bias
RT   discrimination
     doubly disadvantaged
     racism
     test bias

race, class, and gender studies
SN   *Emerging interdisciplinary area of*
     study that attempts to integrate un-
     derstanding of the complex current
     and historical forces affecting eco-
     nomic, political, and social status of
     women and men.
SG   Education
     History and Social Change
     Social Sciences and Culture
BT   interdisciplinary studies
RT   class
     feminist theory
     gender
     gender studies
     nonaligned feminism
     race
     research
     sex/gender systems
     social class

race equity
SN   *Use to refer to policies of fair treat-*
     *ment; use **racial equality** to refer to*
     broader social and personal concept
     of equality.
SG   Economics and Employment
     Education
     History and Social Change
     Law, Government, and Public Policy
BT   equity
RT   educational opportunities
     equal rights legislation
     job ghettos
     racial equality

race formation
SG   Social Sciences and Culture
RT   ethnicity
     social construction of gender
     social construction of reality

race relations
SG   Social Sciences and Culture
BT   relationships
RT   consciousness raising groups
     minority experience
     miscegenation

racial and ethnic differences
SG   Social Sciences and Culture
UF   ethnic comparisons
     racial comparisons
BT   differences
RT   attitudes
     culture
     discrimination
     diversity
     ethnicity
     language
     mainstreaming
     skin color
     social differences
     test bias

racial comparisons
USE **racial and ethnic differences**

UF = Use for   BT = Broader term   NT = Narrower term   RT = Related term   387

racial discrimination

    SG History and Social Change
          Social Sciences and Culture
BT discrimination
RT antisemitism
    apartheid
    busing
    education
    employment
    equal employment opportunity
    housing
    human rights violations
    labor legislation
    lynching
    prejudice
    racial stratification
    racism
    redlining
    segregation
    textbook bias
    unfair labor practices

racial diversity

    SG Social Sciences and Culture
BT diversity
RT critical mass
    pluralism

racial equality

    SG History and Social Change
          Language, Literature, Religion, and
            Philosophy
BT equality
RT civil rights
    discrimination
    educational equity
    race equity
    racism
    social reform
    textbooks

racial factors

    SG Social Sciences and Culture
BT influences

racial stereotypes

    SG Social Sciences and Culture

(cont.)

racial stereotypes *(cont.)*

BT stereotypes
RT discriminatory language

racial stratification

    SG History and Social Change
          Social Sciences and Culture
BT social stratification
RT racial discrimination
    social class

racism

    SG History and Social Change
          Social Sciences and Culture
NT environmental racism
    institutional racism
RT ableism
    ageism
    classism
    double discrimination
    doubly disadvantaged
    eugenic sterilization
    job discrimination
    language
    lynching
    minority experience
    oppression
    race
    race bias
    racial discrimination
    racial equality
    sexism
    stereotyping

racist rape

    SG Social Sciences and Culture
BT rape
RT slave rape

raconteurs

    SG Language, Literature, Religion, and
            Philosophy
          Social Sciences and Culture
RT storytelling

racquetball

    SG Natural Sciences and Health

(cont.)

racquetball (*cont.*)
- BT sports

radiation therapy
- SG Natural Sciences and Health
- BT medical procedures
  therapy
- RT breast cancer
  malignant tumors

radical feminism
- SN *Feminist theory that describes women as a "sex class" whose oppression sustains existing economic, social, political, and psychological systems; asserts that change possible only through concerted experiments and broad-based movements.*
- SG History and Social Change
  International Women
- DG Cultural and Political Movements
- BT feminism
- RT feminist theory
  new left
  radicals

radicalism
- DG Cultural and Political Movements

radicals
- SG History and Social Change
- RT activists
  change agents
  left wing organizations
  political parties
  radical feminism

radio
- SG Communications
- BT electronic media
- NT public radio
- RT announcers
  broadcasters
  commercials
  incidental music
  network ratings
  program ratings

(*cont.*)

radio (*cont.*)
- RT radio commercials
  ratings
  soap operas
  talk shows

radio commercials
- SG Communications
- BT commercials
- RT radio

rage
- SG Social Sciences and Culture
- BT anger
  emotions
- RT assault

rail transportation
- SG Science and Technology
- BT transportation

railroad workers
- SG Economics and Employment
  Science and Technology
- BT transportation occupations
  workers
- NT train conductors

rallies
- SG History and Social Change
  Social Sciences and Culture
- BT mass actions

ranch hands
- SG Economics and Employment
- UF cowboys
  cowgirls
- BT agricultural, fishing, and forestry occupations

random sampling
- SG Science and Technology
  Social Sciences and Culture
- BT sampling
- RT research methods
  statistics

UF=Use for   BT=Broader term   NT=Narrower term   RT=Related term

rank
  SG   Education
NT   academic rank
     military rank
RT   seniority
     titles
     titles (nobility)

rape
  SG   Social Sciences and Culture
BT   sexual violence
NT   acquaintance rape
     domestic rape
     gang rape
     racist rape
     slave rape
RT   crimes against children
     crimes against women
     incest
     lynching
     sex crimes
     slavery
     violence
     violence against women

rape crisis centers
  SG   Social Sciences and Culture
BT   crisis centers
RT   crimes against women
     rape prevention

rape fantasies
  SG   Social Sciences and Culture
BT   fantasies
RT   blaming the victim
     pornography

rape prevention
  SG   Social Sciences and Culture
BT   prevention
RT   rape crisis centers

rape victims
  SG   Social Sciences and Culture
BT   victims
RT   blaming the victim
     counseling

(cont.)

rape victims *(cont.)*
RT   crimes against women
     rapists

rapists
  SG   Social Sciences and Culture
BT   criminals
RT   rape victims

raps
  SG   History and Social Change
       Social Sciences and Culture
RT   discussion groups

ratification
  SG   Law, Government, and Public Policy
NT   treaty ratification
RT   global security

ratings
  SG   Communications
NT   network ratings
     program ratings
     viewer ratings
RT   public opinion
     radio
     television

rationalism
  DG   Cultural and Political Movements

rationality
  SG   Language, Literature, Religion, and
       Philosophy
RT   cognitive processes

reaction times
  SG   Natural Sciences and Health
RT   hand eye coordination

reading
  SG   Education
RT   language skills
     literacy

SN=Scope note   SG=Subject group   DG=Delimiters group   USE=Use

readings
    SG History and Social Change
         Social Sciences and Culture
  BT activities
  RT performances

real estate
    SG Economics and Employment
  RT assumable mortgages
      conventional mortgages
      equal access
      mortgages

real estate agents
    SG Economics and Employment
  BT agents
      female intensive occupations
      marketing and sales occupations

realism
    DG Cultural and Political Movements
  NT social realism

reason
    SG Language, Literature, Religion, and
         Philosophy
  RT cognitive processes

rebellions
    SG History and Social Change
  BT protest actions
  RT resistance
      revolution
      social movements

rebellious behavior
    SG Social Sciences and Culture
  RT attitudes
      instigators
      juvenile delinquency
      protest
      social conditioning

rebirth
    SG Language, Literature, Religion, and
         Philosophy
  BT religious beliefs

(cont.)

rebirth *(cont.)*
  RT baptism

recall
    SG Social Sciences and Culture
  BT memory

receptionists
    SG Communications
         Economics and Employment
  BT clerical occupations
      female intensive occupations

receptions
    SG History and Social Change
         Social Sciences and Culture
  BT social activities

recession
    SG Economics and Employment
  RT inflation

recidivism
    SG Law, Government, and Public Policy
  RT correctional rehabilitation
      prisons

recipes
    SG Social Sciences and Culture
  NT family recipes
  RT cooking

recognition
    SG Social Sciences and Culture
  BT memory

reconciliation
    SG Social Sciences and Culture
  RT former spouses
      mediation
      parenting
      tolerance

Reconstruction
    DG Historical Periods

UF=Use for   BT=Broader term   NT=Narrower term   RT=Related term

reconstructive surgery

- SG   Natural Sciences and Health
- BT   surgery
- RT   accidents
  - breast implants
  - breast prostheses
  - breasts
  - cosmetic surgery
  - mastectomy
  - plastic surgery

record albums

- DG   Types and Forms of Materials

records

- SG   Economics and Employment
  - Education
  - Law, Government, and Public Policy
  - Natural Sciences and Health
- DG   Types and Forms of Materials
- NT   employee records
  - medical records
  - school records
  - voting records
- RT   confidentiality
  - documents

records confidentiality

- SG   Communications
  - Law, Government, and Public Policy
- BT   confidentiality
- RT   adopted children
  - careers
  - education
  - employee records
  - medical records
  - school records

recreation

- SG   Social Sciences and Culture
- RT   athletics
  - compressed workweek
  - entertainment
  - leisure
  - playgrounds
  - relaxation

redlining

- SG   Law, Government, and Public Policy
- BT   discriminatory practices
- RT   ethnic neighborhoods
  - housing
  - inner city
  - mortgages
  - racial discrimination

reduction in force

- SG   Economics and Employment
- UF   RIF
- RT   forced retirement
  - job layoffs
  - job security

reel to reel tapes

- DG   Types and Forms of Materials
- BT   tapes

reentry students

- SG   Economics and Employment
  - Education
- BT   students
- RT   adult students
  - continuing education
  - women college students

reentry women

- SG   Economics and Employment
  - Education
  - Social Sciences and Culture
- UF   returning women
- BT   women
- RT   adult students
  - displaced homemakers
  - feminine mystique
  - labor force
  - middle age
  - women college students
  - women in transition

referees

- SN   *Those who evaluate proposals and journal articles.*
- SG   Education
- RT   federally sponsored research

(cont.)

     SN=Scope note   SG=Subject group   DG=Delimiters group   USE=Use

referees (*cont.*)
  RT   grant proposals
       grants
       references

reference books
  DG   Types and Forms of Materials
  BT   books
  NT   atlases
       dictionaries
       encyclopedias
       thesauri

references
  SG   Economics and Employment
       Education
  RT   admissions criteria
       employment
       referees
       tenure

referenda
  DG   Types and Forms of Materials

Reformation
  DG   Historical Periods
  NT   Counter Reformation

reformatories
  SG   Law, Government, and Public Policy
  BT   facilities
  RT   juvenile justice system
       prisons

reformers
  SG   History and Social Change
  RT   activists
       advocates
       reforms
       social movements
       suffragists

reforms
  SG   Law, Government, and Public Policy
  NT   dress reform
       educational reform
       labor law reform
                                    (*cont.*)

reforms (*cont.*)
  NT   land reform
       marital property reform
       media reform
       moral reform
       religious reforms
       social reform
       welfare reform
  RT   affirmative action
       legislation
       reformers

refugees
  SG   International Women
       Law, Government, and Public Policy
  NT   economic refugees
       political refugees
       religious refugees
  RT   exile
       human rights violations
       immigrants
       persecution
       political oppression
       sanctuaries

regional labor workers
  USE **migrant workers**

regional studies
  SG   Education
       International Women
       Social Sciences and Culture
  BT   area studies
  RT   cross cultural studies
       ethnic studies

registered nurses
  SG   Economics and Employment
       Natural Sciences and Health
  BT   nurses
       professional occupations

regulations
  SG   Communications
       Law, Government, and Public Policy
  NT   federal regulations
       state regulations
                                    (*cont.*)

UF=Use for   BT=Broader term   NT=Narrower term   RT=Related term   393

regulations (*cont.*)
- RT enforcement
  licensing
  sponsored research

rehabilitation
- SG Natural Sciences and Health
- NT correctional rehabilitation
  drug rehabilitation
  vocational rehabilitation
- RT prisons
  restitution

reincarnation
- SG Language, Literature, Religion, and
  Philosophy
- BT religious beliefs
- RT death

reinforcement
- SG Social Sciences and Culture
- NT negative reinforcement
  positive reinforcement
- RT conditioning
  intelligence
  learning
  norms
  punishment

rejection
- SG Social Sciences and Culture
- RT personal relationships
  self concept

relationships
- SG Social Sciences and Culture
- NT adult child relationships
  children's relationships
  community relations
  domestic relations
  ethnic relations
  family relationships
  heterosexual relationships
  human relations
  industrial relations
  international relations
  interracial relations

(*cont.*)

relationships (*cont.*)
- NT labor relations
  lawyer client relationships
  parent teacher relationships
  patient doctor relationships
  peer relationships
  personal relationships
  public relations
  race relations
  sexual relationships
  social relations
  teacher student relationships
- RT affection
  bonding
  commitment
  couples
  ethic of care
  faghag
  flirtation
  gay couples
  intimacy
  lesbian couples
  listening
  living arrangements
  marriage
  nurturing
  personal columns
  posslq
  privacy
  promiscuity
  self disclosure
  women identified women

relativism
- DG Cultural and Political Movements

relaxation
- SG Social Sciences and Culture
- RT leisure
  massage
  meditation
  recreation

religion
- SG Language, Literature, Religion, and
  Philosophy
- NT civil religion

(*cont.*)

religion (*cont.*)
- NT patriarchal religion
- state religion
- RT angels
- canonization
- celibacy
- church work
- comparative religion
- convents
- cults
- culture
- deity
- divinity
- dogma
- God the father
- goddesses
- gods
- healing
- history of religion
- incarnation
- martyrs
- monasticism
- mother goddess
- original sin
- patriarchal language
- patriarchy
- prayer
- sacred ideology
- sacred space
- saints
- salvation
- sects
- separation of church and state
- sin
- spiritualism
- spirituality
- thealogy
- theology
- wicca
- women's ordination

religions
- SG Language, Literature, Religion, and Philosophy
- RT belief systems
- cults
- faith

(*cont.*)

religions (*cont.*)
- RT sects
- spiritualism

religious art
- SG Visual and Performing Arts
- BT art
- RT angels
- cult of the virgin
- iconography
- madonna
- religious symbols

religious beliefs
- SG Language, Literature, Religion, and Philosophy
- NT immaculate conception
- incarnation
- predestination
- rebirth
- reincarnation
- salvation
- sin
- RT belief systems
- death
- dogma
- excommunication
- freedom of worship
- fundamentalism
- miracles
- monasticism
- procreation
- prophecy
- sacred ideology
- separation of church and state
- theology

religious discrimination
- SG Social Sciences and Culture
- BT discrimination
- RT patriarchal religion

religious education
- SG Education
- Language, Literature, Religion, and Philosophy
- BT education

(*cont.*)

religious education (*cont.*)
RT private schools
    religious schools

religious ethics
SG Language, Literature, Religion, and
    Philosophy
BT ethics
RT morality
    values

religious experience
SG Language, Literature, Religion, and
    Philosophy
BT experience
RT belief systems
    prayer
    rites
    spiritualism

religious facilities
SG Language, Literature, Religion, and
    Philosophy
BT facilities
NT cathedrals
    churches
    convents
    monasteries
    mosques
    synagogues
    temples
RT religious groups
    sacred space

religious freedom
USE **freedom of worship**

religious groups
SG Language, Literature, Religion, and
    Philosophy
BT groups
NT congregations
    covens
    faith communities
    sects
RT cults
    organizations

(*cont.*)

religious groups (*cont.*)
RT religious facilities
    spiritual communication

religious influences
SG Language, Literature, Religion, and
    Philosophy
BT influences

religious language
SG Language, Literature, Religion, and
    Philosophy
BT language
RT allegory
    angels
    God the father
    hymns
    male norms
    patriarchal language
    preaching
    sacred texts
    sermons

religious law
SG Language, Literature, Religion, and
    Philosophy
UF canon law
BT law
RT abortion
    annulment
    conception
    contraception
    divorce
    euthanasia
    excommunication
    patriarchal religion
    viability

religious literature
SG Language, Literature, Religion, and
    Philosophy
UF biblical literature
BT literature
RT allegory

SN=Scope note   SG=Subject group   DG=Delimiters group   USE=Use

religious movements

- SG Language, Literature, Religion, and
  Philosophy
- BT social movements
- RT conservative movement
  fundamentalism
  religious reforms

religious music

- SG Language, Literature, Religion, and
  Philosophy
  Visual and Performing Arts
- UF church music
  sacred music
- BT music
  spiritual communication
- NT chants
  gospel music
  hymns
  spirituals
- RT convents
  rites

religious orders

- SG Language, Literature, Religion, and
  Philosophy
- BT organizations
- RT celibacy
  clergy
  convents
  holy men
  holy women
  monasticism
  sexual abstinence
  vows of chastity
  vows of obedience
  vows of poverty
  vows of silence
  women religious
  women's ordination

religious pluralism

- SG Language, Literature, Religion, and
  Philosophy
  Law, Government, and Public Policy
- DG Cultural and Political Movements
- BT pluralism

(cont.)

religious pluralism *(cont.)*

- RT civil religion
  democracy
  ecumenism
  freedom of worship
  religious reforms
  separation of church and state

religious practices

- SG Language, Literature, Religion, and
  Philosophy
- RT abstinence
  asceticism
  canonization
  celibacy
  ceremonies
  cult of the virgin
  guilt
  meditation
  novitiates
  prayer
  prophecy
  revivals
  rites
  sects

religious reforms

- SG Language, Literature, Religion, and
  Philosophy
- BT reforms
- RT freedom of worship
  religious movements
  religious pluralism
  separation of church and state

religious refugees

- SG International Women
  Language, Literature, Religion, and
  Philosophy
- BT refugees
- RT witches

religious repression

- SG Language, Literature, Religion, and
  Philosophy
  Law, Government, and Public Policy
- BT repression

(cont.)

UF=Use for   BT=Broader term   NT=Narrower term   RT=Related term

religious repression (*cont.*)
- RT dogmatism
- guilt
- heresies
- heretics
- reproductive technologies
- self denial
- witch burning
- witch persecutions

the religious right
- SG Language, Literature, Religion, and
- Philosophy
- Law, Government, and Public Policy
- RT Armageddon
- conservative movement
- end time thinking
- fundamentalism
- moral majority
- right wing organizations

religious sanctions
- SG International Women
- Language, Literature, Religion, and
- Philosophy
- Law, Government, and Public Policy
- BT sanctions
- RT abortion laws
- antiabortion movement
- excommunication

religious schools
- SG Education
- BT schools
- RT private schools
- religious education

religious symbols
- SG Language, Literature, Religion, and
- Philosophy
- BT symbols
- RT Adam
- angels
- devil
- Eve
- hagiography
- Lilith

(*cont.*)

religious symbols (*cont.*)
- RT madonna
- religious art

religious traditions
- SG Language, Literature, Religion, and
- Philosophy
- BT traditions
- RT rites

religious values
- SG Language, Literature, Religion, and
- Philosophy
- BT values

religious workers
- SG Economics and Employment
- Language, Literature, Religion, and
- Philosophy
- BT professional occupations
- workers
- NT clergy
- evangelists
- mediums
- missionaries
- prophets
- seers
- spirit guides
- spiritualists
- women religious
- RT deacons
- laity
- shamans

relocation
- SG Economics and Employment
- International Women
- RT corporate relocation policy
- dual career couples
- dual career families
- geographic mobility
- occupational mobility

remarriage
- SG Social Sciences and Culture
- BT marriage
- RT blended families

(*cont.*)

SN=Scope note   SG=Subject group   DG=Delimiters group   USE=Use

remarriage (*cont.*)
RT divorce
  first husbands
  first wives
  stepchildren
  stepparents

remedial education
  SG Education
BT education

remedies
  SG Natural Sciences and Health
NT herbal remedies
  home remedies
RT folk medicine

Renaissance
  DG Historical Periods

renewable energy sources
  SG Science and Technology
NT solar energy

rent
  SG Economics and Employment
RT housing
  landlords

repairers
  SG Economics and Employment
    Science and Technology
UF repairmen
BT craft occupations

repairmen
  USE **repairers**

reporters
  SG Communications
    Economics and Employment
BT arts, entertainment, and media
    occupations
NT weather reporters
RT editors
  journalists
  writers

reports
  DG Types and Forms of Materials
NT annual reports
  status reports

representation
  SG Law, Government, and Public Policy
NT political representation

representatives
  SG Economics and Employment
    Law, Government, and Public Policy
BT elected officials
NT congressmen
  congresswomen
RT political representation

repression
  SG Social Sciences and Culture
NT political repression
  psychological repression
  religious repression
  sexual repression
RT defense mechanisms
  memory
  mental disorders
  ulcers

reprints
  DG Types and Forms of Materials

reproduction
  SG Natural Sciences and Health
NT parthenogenesis
RT conception
  ovum
  pregnancy
  sperm

reproductive cycle
  SG Natural Sciences and Health
RT estrus
  fertilization
  menstrual cycle
  ovulation
  ovum
  pregnancy

(*cont.*)

UF=Use for   BT=Broader term   NT=Narrower term   RT=Related term

reproductive cycle (*cont.*)
RT rhythm method
    sperm

reproductive freedom
SG History and Social Change
    Law, Government, and Public Policy
    Natural Sciences and Health
BT freedoms
RT abortion .
    abortion movement
    reproductive rights

reproductive hazards at work
SG Economics and Employment
    Natural Sciences and Health
BT work hazards
RT technology

reproductive health
SG Natural Sciences and Health
BT health

reproductive rights
SG History and Social Change
    Law, Government, and Public Policy
BT rights
RT abortion movement
    federal legislation
    prochoice
    reproductive freedom
    state legislation

reproductive technologies
SG Natural Sciences and Health
    Science and Technology
BT technology
NT artificial insemination
    cloning
    embryo transfer
    fertility drugs
    in vitro fertilization
    sperm banks
RT bioethics
    biological sciences
    childless couples
    embryology

(*cont.*)

reproductive technologies (*cont.*)
RT genetic engineering
    infertility
    insemination
    medical procedures
    parthenogenesis
    pheromones
    religious repression
    self insemination
    sex determination
    sex preselection
    sex selection
    surrogate mothers
    viability

Republican Party
SG Law, Government, and Public Policy
BT political parties

reputations
SG Social Sciences and Culture
RT defamation
    fallen women
    social attitudes

research
SG Education
    Natural Sciences and Health
    Science and Technology
    Social Sciences and Culture
NT applied research
    cross cultural research
    scientific research
    social science research
    sponsored research
RT laboratory animals
    placebos
    race, class, and gender studies
    research methods
    scholarship

research assistants
SG Economics and Employment
    Education
    Natural Sciences and Health
    Science and Technology
    Social Sciences and Culture

(*cont.*)

SN=Scope note   SG=Subject group   DG=Delimiters group   USE=Use

research assistants (*cont.*)
   BT education occupations

research bias
   SG Education
         Natural Sciences and Health
         Science and Technology
         Social Sciences and Culture
   BT bias
   RT interdisciplinary studies
        natural sciences
        objectivity
        scientific research
        social construction of reality
        social science research
        social sciences
        sponsored research
        testing

research design
   SG Education
         Natural Sciences and Health
         Science and Technology
         Social Sciences and Culture
   RT bias
        data collection

research grants
   SG Economics and Employment
         Education
   BT grants

research methods
   SG Education
         Natural Sciences and Health
         Science and Technology
         Social Sciences and Culture
   BT methods
   NT case studies
        cohort analysis
        content analysis
        contextual analysis
        cost benefit analysis
        interviewing
        participant observation
        qualitative analysis
        quantitative analysis
(*cont.*)

research methods (*cont.*)
   RT applied research
        criticism
        data analysis
        data collection
        demographic measurements
        ethnomethodology
        false generics
        fieldwork
        historiography
        interdisciplinary studies
        interviewers
        measurement
        norms
        objectivity
        perceptual bias
        random sampling
        research
        sampling
        tests

research problems
   SG Education
         Natural Sciences and Health
         Science and Technology
         Social Sciences and Culture
   BT problems

researchers
   SG Economics and Employment
         Education
         Natural Sciences and Health
         Science and Technology
         Social Sciences and Culture
   BT education occupations
        professional occupations

resettlement
   USE **land settlement**

residence halls
   SG Education
   BT student housing

residency programs
   SG Education
         Natural Sciences and Health
(*cont.*)

residency programs (*cont.*)
BT programs
RT internships
    medical education

residential security
SG Social Sciences and Culture
BT security

resistance
SG History and Social Change
    Law, Government, and Public Policy
NT draft resistance
RT activism
    liberation struggles
    militance
    protest actions
    rebellions
    revolution
    social movements

resources
SG Science and Technology
NT financial resources
    human resources
    natural resources

respite care
USE **elderly day care centers**

responsibility
SG Social Sciences and Culture
NT community responsibility
    corporate responsibility
    family responsibility
    legal responsibility
RT care
    chaperones
    dependent care
    jury duty
    paternity

restitution
SG Economics and Employment
    Law, Government, and Public Policy
RT alternative programs
    delinquent behavior
(cont.)

restitution (*cont.*)
RT halfway houses
    juvenile justice system
    legal system
    rehabilitation
    work release programs

restraining orders
SG Law, Government, and Public Policy
BT legal documents
RT child custody
    divorce laws
    domestic violence

resumes
SG Economics and Employment
RT career planning
    interviews

retail trade
SG Economics and Employment
BT trades
RT retail trade industry

retail trade industry
SG Economics and Employment
BT industries
RT retail trade

retirement
SG Economics and Employment
NT early retirement
    forced retirement
RT basic human needs
    financial planning
    hobbies
    Retirement and Disability System
      Authorization
    retirement benefits
    Retirement Equity Act of 1984
    Social Security

retirement age
SG Economics and Employment
    Social Sciences and Culture
BT age
RT early retirement
(cont.)

retirement age (*cont.*)
RT   pension benefits

Retirement and Disability System Authorization
SN *Foreign Service Act of 1980.*
DG Laws and Regulations
RT   disability insurance
      retirement

retirement benefits
SG Economics and Employment
BT   benefits
NT   pension benefits
RT   early retirement
      financial planning
      retirement
      Social Security

Retirement Equity Act of 1984
DG Laws and Regulations
RT   retirement

retreats
SG History and Social Change
      Language, Literature, Religion, and
        Philosophy
      Social Sciences and Culture
BT   activities
RT   community
      planning

returning women
USE **reentry women**

reverse discrimination
SG Social Sciences and Culture
BT   discrimination

reviewers
SG Communications
      Economics and Employment
      Language, Literature, Religion, and
        Philosophy
      Visual and Performing Arts
BT   arts, entertainment, and media
      occupations
                              (*cont.*)

reviewers (*cont.*)
RT   blind review
      criticism

reviews
DG Types and Forms of Materials
NT   book reviews

revisionism
DG Cultural and Political Movements

revivals
SG History and Social Change
      Social Sciences and Culture
BT   activities
RT   prayer meetings
      religious practices

revolution
SG History and Social Change
NT   nationalist revolutions
      sexual revolution
      socialist revolutions
RT   liberation struggles
      outlaws
      rebellions
      resistance
      revolutionary movements

revolutionary movements
SN *See also Delimiters Displays: Cultural
      and Political Movements, Historical
      Periods.*
SG History and Social Change
      International Women
      Law, Government, and Public Policy
BT   social movements
RT   coups
      nationalist movements
      revolution
      struggles

Revolutionary War
DG Historical Periods

Rh factor
SG Natural Sciences and Health
                              (*cont.*)

UF=Use for   BT=Broader term   NT=Narrower term   RT=Related term

Rh factor (*cont.*)
UF rhesus factor
RT blood
 blood tests
 blue babies
 Rh incompatibility

Rh incompatibility
SG Natural Sciences and Health
RT Rh factor

rhesus factor
USE **Rh factor**

rhetoric
SG Education
 Language, Literature, Religion, and
  Philosophy
 Law, Government, and Public Policy
RT discourse
 figurative language
 orators
 oratory
 polemics
 preaching
 propaganda

rhythm method
SG Natural Sciences and Health
UF natural family planning
BT contraception
RT basal body temperature
 cervical mucus
 menstrual cycle
 pregnancy
 reproductive cycle
 sexual abstinence

RIF
USE **reduction in force**

right to choose
USE **prochoice**

right to die
SG Law, Government, and Public Policy
 Natural Sciences and Health
 Social Sciences and Culture
BT rights
RT aging
 euthanasia
 hospices
 nursing homes
 quality of life
 terminal illness

right to know legislation
SG Law, Government, and Public Policy
BT legislation
RT disinformation
 freedom of information
 hazards
 information
 public information
 rights

right to life
USE **antiabortion movement**

right to work
SG Economics and Employment
 International Women
BT rights
RT employment opportunities

right wing organizations
SG History and Social Change
 Law, Government, and Public Policy
BT organizations
RT antifeminism
 conservative movement
 moral majority
 the religious right

rights
SN *Use of a more specific term is recom-
  mended.*
SG History and Social Change
 Law, Government, and Public Policy
 Natural Sciences and Health
NT abortion rights

(*cont.*)

SN=Scope note   SG=Subject group   DG=Delimiters group   USE=Use

rights *(cont.)*

NT	children's rights
	civil rights
	domicile rights
	equal rights
	family rights
	gay rights
	homemaker rights
	human rights
	inheritance rights
	land rights
	maternity rights
	name rights
	parental rights
	paternity rights
	political rights
	privacy rights
	property rights
	reproductive rights
	right to die
	right to work
	rights of the disabled
	uxorial rights
	visitation rights
	voting rights
	welfare rights
	woman's rights
	women's rights
RT	advocates
	equal opportunity
	freedom
	laws
	right to know legislation

rights of the disabled

SG	Education
	Law, Government, and Public Policy
	Natural Sciences and Health
BT	rights
RT	disabilities

rights of women

USE **women's rights**

rings

SG	Social Sciences and Culture
BT	jewelry

(cont.)

rings *(cont.)*

NT	wedding rings
RT	symbols

riots

SG	History and Social Change
	Law, Government, and Public Policy
BT	protest actions
RT	violence

risk taking

SG	Social Sciences and Culture
RT	fear of failure
	imagination
	job rewards
	risks

risk taking behavior

SG	Social Sciences and Culture
BT	behavior
RT	fear of failure
	fear of success
	risks

risks

SG	Social Sciences and Culture
RT	risk taking
	risk taking behavior

rites

SG	Language, Literature, Religion, and Philosophy
UF	rituals
BT	spiritual communication
NT	bat mitzvah
	domestic rites
	fertility rites
	funeral rites
	initiation rites
	purification rites
	rites of passage
	sacraments
	votive rites
RT	blood
	celebrations
	ceremonies
	customs

(cont.)

UF=Use for   BT=Broader term   NT=Narrower term   RT=Related term

rites (*cont.*)
RT drama
 fasting
 festivals
 folk culture
 goddesses
 gods
 group dynamics
 healing
 liturgies
 male circumcision
 mother earth
 observance
 prayer
 prophecy
 religious experience
 religious music
 religious practices
 religious traditions
 romantic love
 sacred dance
 sacred space
 sects
 solstice
 totemism
 traditions
 tribal markings
 tribal music
 tshiwila
 uzr
 wedding ceremonies
 worship

rites of passage
 SG Language, Literature, Religion, and
  Philosophy
  Social Sciences and Culture
 BT rites
 RT adolescence
 age of consent
 initiation rites
 passages
 transitions

ritual disfigurement
 SG Social Sciences and Culture
 RT corsets
  (*cont.*)

ritual disfigurement (*cont.*)
 RT foot binding
 genital mutilation
 girdles
 high heeled shoes
 physical abuse
 pierced ears
 tribal markings
 veiling of women

rituals
 USE **rites**

road workers
 SG Economics and Employment
 BT transportation occupations
 workers

roasts
 SG Communications
 BT activities

rock and roll
 SG Visual and Performing Arts
 BT popular music
 RT images of women
 music videos

rococo style
 DG Cultural and Political Movements

role conflict
 SG Social Sciences and Culture
 BT conflict
 NT interrole conflict

role expectations
 SG Social Sciences and Culture
 RT roles

role models
 SG Economics and Employment
  Social Sciences and Culture
 RT foremothers
 image
 mentors
 mothering
  (*cont.*)

SN=Scope note   SG=Subject group   DG=Delimiters group   USE=Use

role models (*cont.*)
- RT professional development

role reversal
- SG Social Sciences and Culture
- RT roles

roles
- SG History and Social Change
  Social Sciences and Culture
- NT domestic roles
  family roles
  gender roles
  leadership roles
  marital roles
  men's roles
  multiple roles
  occupational roles
  sex roles
  women's roles
- RT image
  role expectations
  role reversal
  sex/gender systems
  socialization
  stereotyping

roller skating
- SG Natural Sciences and Health
- BT sports

Roman Catholic
- DG Ethnic, Racial, and Religious
  Descriptors

Roman Catholicism
- DG Cultural and Political Movements

romance
- SG Social Sciences and Culture
- RT courtly love
  ideal woman
  love
  passion
  romances
  romantic love
  unrequited love

romances
- SG Language, Literature, Religion, and
  Philosophy
- BT fiction
- RT courtly love
  legends
  novels
  pulp fiction
  romance
  soap operas
  troubadours

Romanesque
- DG Cultural and Political Movements

romantic love
- SG Social Sciences and Culture
- BT love
- RT bitterness
  Cinderella
  fairy tales
  images of women
  mythology
  rites
  romance

Romantic Period
- DG Historical Periods

romanticism
- DG Cultural and Political Movements

roofers
- SG Economics and Employment
- BT construction occupations

a room of one's own
- SG History and Social Change
  Social Sciences and Culture
- BT rooms
- RT empowerment
  privacy

rooming in
- SN *Mother's having immediate and un-
  scheduled access to newborn infant.*
- SG Natural Sciences and Health

(*cont.*)

UF=Use for   BT=Broader term   NT=Narrower term   RT=Related term

rooming in (*cont.*)
  RT birthing centers
       maternity wards

rooms
  SG Social Sciences and Culture
  NT a room of one's own
       bedrooms
       birthing rooms
       boudoirs
       delivery rooms
       kitchens
       locker rooms
  RT decorative arts
       facilities
       houses

royalty
  SG Social Sciences and Culture
  RT queens
       titles (nobility)

rubella
  SG Natural Sciences and Health
  UF German measles
       three day measles
  BT diseases
  RT measles

rug hooking
  SG Visual and Performing Arts
  BT craft arts

Rumanian
  DG National and Regional Descriptors
  BT European

runaway fathers
  SG Law, Government, and Public Policy
       Social Sciences and Culture
  BT fathers
  RT absentee fathers

runaway husbands
  SG Law, Government, and Public Policy
       Social Sciences and Culture
  BT husbands

(*cont.*)

runaway husbands (*cont.*)
  RT desertion

runaway mothers
  SG Law, Government, and Public Policy
       Social Sciences and Culture
  BT mothers
  RT absentee mothers

runaway shops
  SN *Production plants that leave a country
       to gain special advantages, such as
       lower wages, or to avoid disadvan-
       tages, such as unionization of the la-
       bor force.*
  SG Economics and Employment
       International Women
  RT factories
       multinational corporations
       offshore production plants

runaway wives
  SG Law, Government, and Public Policy
       Social Sciences and Culture
  BT wives
  RT desertion

runaways
  SG Law, Government, and Public Policy
       Social Sciences and Culture
  RT children
       family problems
       juvenile prostitution
       teenagers

running
  SG Natural Sciences and Health
  UF jogging
  BT sports
  RT exercise
       marathons

rural areas
  SG International Women
       Social Sciences and Culture
  RT rural development
       suburbs

rural conditions
  SG   International Women
       Social Sciences and Culture
  BT   conditions
  RT   rural development

rural development
  SN   *Strategies designed to improve the eco-*
       nomic and social life of the rural
       poor.
  SG   Economics and Employment
       International Women
  BT   development
  RT   agricultural extension
       farming
       federal aid
       rural areas
       rural conditions
       rural planning
       rural poverty

rural living
  SG   International Women
       Social Sciences and Culture
  RT   farms
       life styles

rural migration
  SG   International Women
       Social Sciences and Culture
  BT   migration

rural planning
  SG   Economics and Employment
       International Women
       Law, Government, and Public Policy
       Social Sciences and Culture
  BT   planning
  RT   rural development
       zoning

rural poverty
  SG   Economics and Employment
       International Women
       Social Sciences and Culture
  BT   poverty
  RT   agribusiness
                                    (*cont.*)

rural poverty (*cont.*)
  RT   employment opportunities
       peasants
       rural development
       subsistence agriculture

rural resettlement
  SG   International Women
       Law, Government, and Public Policy
       Social Sciences and Culture
  BT   land settlement
  RT   migration

rural women
  SG   Economics and Employment
       International Women
       Social Sciences and Culture
  BT   women
  RT   farmers

Russian
  DG   National and Regional Descriptors
  BT   European

sacraments
  SG   Language, Literature, Religion, and
       Philosophy
  BT   rites
  NT   baptism
       confession
       confirmation
       holy communion
       holy matrimony
       last rites
       ordination

sacred dance
  SG   Language, Literature, Religion, and
       Philosophy
       Social Sciences and Culture
  BT   dance
       spiritual communication
  RT   rites

sacred ideology
  SG   Language, Literature, Religion, and
       Philosophy
                                    (*cont.*)

UF=Use for   BT=Broader term   NT=Narrower term   RT=Related term   409

sacred ideology (*cont.*)
- BT   ideology
- RT   angels
     belief systems
     cosmology
     dogma
     immaculate conception
     madonna
     religion
     religious beliefs

sacred music
- USE **religious music**

sacred space
- SG   History and Social Change
     Language, Literature, Religion, and
        Philosophy
     Social Sciences and Culture
- BT   space
- RT   private sphere
     religion
     religious facilities
     rites

sacred texts
- SG   Language, Literature, Religion, and
        Philosophy
- BT   texts
- RT   deity
     Eve
     religious language

sacrifice
- SG   Language, Literature, Religion, and
        Philosophy
     Social Sciences and Culture
- BT   spiritual communication

sadism
- SG   Natural Sciences and Health
- NT   cultural sadism
- RT   masochism
     sadomasochism
     sexual behavior

sadness
- SG   Social Sciences and Culture
- BT   emotions
- RT   grief

sadomasochism
- SG   Natural Sciences and Health
- RT   bondage
     exploitation
     masochism
     sadism
     sexual behavior

safe sex
- SG   Law, Government, and Public Policy
     Social Sciences and Culture
- BT   sex
- RT   acquired immune deficiency syndrome
     condoms
     sexually transmitted diseases

safety
- SG   Natural Sciences and Health
- NT   occupational health and safety
- RT   hazards

sailing
- SG   Natural Sciences and Health
- BT   sports

saints
- SG   Language, Literature, Religion, and
        Philosophy
- RT   canonization
     female spirituality
     hagiography
     holy men
     holy women
     martyrdom
     martyrs
     religion
     spirituality
     virgins
     witches

salaries
- USE **wages**

---

sales personnel
SG Economics and Employment
BT female intensive occupations
marketing and sales occupations
personnel
NT salesmen
saleswomen

sales taxes
SG Economics and Employment
Law, Government, and Public Policy
BT state taxes

salesgirls
USE **saleswomen**

salesmen
SG Economics and Employment
BT sales personnel

saleswomen
SG Economics and Employment
UF salesgirls
BT sales personnel

salon music
SG Visual and Performing Arts
BT music

salons
SG Language, Literature, Religion, and
Philosophy
Visual and Performing Arts
RT galleries
mediums

Salvadoran
DG National and Regional Descriptors
BT Central American

salvation
SG Language, Literature, Religion, and
Philosophy
BT religious beliefs
RT healing
religion
sin

salvation (*cont.*)
RT theology

same sex relationships
USE **female female relationships**
male male relationships

Samoan American
DG Ethnic, Racial, and Religious
Descriptors

samplers
SG Visual and Performing Arts
RT embroidery
folk art
needlework
proverbs

samples
DG Types and Forms of Materials

sampling
SG Education
Natural Sciences and Health
Science and Technology
Social Sciences and Culture
BT data collection
NT random sampling
RT norms
research methods

sanctions
SG International Women
Law, Government, and Public Policy
NT economic sanctions
political sanctions
religious sanctions
RT boycotts
censorship
civil disobedience
curfew
human rights violations
protest actions
punishment

(*cont.*)

---

sanctuaries
  SG History and Social Change
     Social Sciences and Culture
  RT freedom
     human rights
     refugees

sanitary napkins
  SG Natural Sciences and Health
  RT menstruation
     tampons

sanitation
  SN *The promotion of hygiene and preven-*
     tion of disease by maintenance of
     sanitary conditions.
  SG International Women
     Natural Sciences and Health
  RT basic human needs
     disease prevention
     hygiene
     sewage disposal
     water management

sanitation workers
  SG Economics and Employment
  BT service occupations
     workers

sanity
  SG Social Sciences and Culture
  RT insanity

satellite communications
  SG Communications
     Science and Technology
  RT communication satellites
     telecommunications
     teleconferencing

satellites
  SG Communications
  NT communication satellites
  RT communications
     telecommunications

satire
  SG Communications
     Language, Literature, Religion, and
        Philosophy
     Visual and Performing Arts
  BT nonfiction
  RT burlesque
     comedy
     farce
     humor
     irony
     jokes
     literature
     parody
     slapstick

satisfaction
  SG Social Sciences and Culture
  NT career satisfaction
     job satisfaction
     marital satisfaction
     sexual satisfaction
  RT conflict
     pleasure

Saudi Arabian
  DG National and Regional Descriptors
  BT Middle Eastern

scales
  DG Types and Forms of Materials

Scandinavian
  DG National and Regional Descriptors
  BT European
  NT Danish
     Finnish
     Icelandic
     Norwegian
     Swedish

schedules
  SG Economics and Employment
  NT employment schedules
     school schedules

schizophrenia
SG   Natural Sciences and Health
BT   mental disorders
RT   deinstitutionalization

scholars
SG   Economics and Employment
     Education
BT   education occupations
NT   independent scholars
     visiting scholars
RT   applied research
     education
     teaching

scholarship
SG   Education
NT   feminist scholarship
RT   curriculum integration
     feminist theory
     interdisciplinary studies
     research

scholarships
SG   Education
BT   student financial aid
RT   assistantships
     fellowships
     internships
     loans

school age children
SG   Education
     Social Sciences and Culture
DG   Age Levels
BT   children

school attendance
SG   Education
RT   absenteeism
     educational attainment
     educational opportunities
     schools

school boards
USE **governing boards**

school counseling
SG   Education
BT   counseling
RT   academic achievement
     academic aptitude
     academic failure
     educational opportunities

school desegregation
SG   Education
BT   desegregation
RT   busing
     school integration
     school segregation

school health services
SG   Education
     Natural Sciences and Health
BT   health care services

school integration
SG   Education
BT   integration
RT   school desegregation

school personnel
SG   Economics and Employment
     Education
BT   education occupations
     personnel

school records
SG   Education
BT   records
RT   confidentiality
     records confidentiality

school schedules
SG   Economics and Employment
     Education
BT   schedules

school segregation
SG   Education
BT   segregation
RT   school desegregation

UF=Use for   BT=Broader term   NT=Narrower term   RT=Related term

schools

- SG Education
- BT educational facilities
- NT alternative schools
      boarding schools
      community schools
      elementary schools
      free schools
      high schools
      middle schools
      normal schools
      nursery schools
      preschools
      primary schools
      private schools
      proprietary schools
      public schools
      religious schools
      secondary schools
      single sex schools
- RT education
      school attendance

science

- SN *Use of a more specific term is recommended.*
- SG Natural Sciences and Health
      Science and Technology
- NT cognitive science
- RT biological sciences
      earth sciences
      information sciences
      natural sciences
      objectivity
      physical sciences
      social sciences

science anxiety

- USE **science avoidance**

science avoidance

- SG Education
- UF science anxiety
- BT avoidance behavior

science fiction

- SG Language, Literature, Religion, and
      Philosophy
- BT fiction

science reporting

- SG Communications
      Science and Technology
- RT journalism
      technical writing

scientific and technical occupations

- SG Economics and Employment
      Natural Sciences and Health
      Science and Technology
- BT occupations
- NT astronauts
      computer programmers
      engineers
      home economists
      information scientists
      inventors
      mathematicians
      naturalists
      physiologists
      scientists
      statisticians
      systems analysts
- RT chemical industry
      craft occupations
      electronics industry
      engineering
      health care occupations
      pharmaceutical industry
      professional occupations
      women in science

scientific method

- SG Natural Sciences and Health
      Science and Technology
- RT male norms
      objectivity
      perceptual bias

scientific research

- SG Education
      Science and Technology

(cont.)

scientific research (*cont.*)
BT research
RT objectivity
    research bias

scientists
SG Economics and Employment
    Natural Sciences and Health
    Science and Technology
BT education occupations
    professional occupations
    scientific and technical occupations
NT astronomers
    biologists
    chemists
    ethologists
    geneticists
    geologists
    meteorologists
    physicists
    sociobiologists
RT information scientists
    social scientists

scientology
DG Cultural and Political Movements

scolds
SG Social Sciences and Culture
BT images of women

scores
SG Visual and Performing Arts
DG Types and Forms of Materials
RT librettos
    music

Scotch
DG National and Regional Descriptors
BT European

screenplays
SG Visual and Performing Arts
RT film
    scripts

scripts
SG Language, Literature, Religion, and
    Philosophy
    Visual and Performing Arts
DG Types and Forms of Materials
RT drama
    film
    plays
    playwrights
    screenplays

scrotum
SG Natural Sciences and Health
BT genitals

sculptors
SG Economics and Employment
    Visual and Performing Arts
BT arts, entertainment, and media
    occupations

sculpture
SG Visual and Performing Arts
BT visual arts
NT bas reliefs
    soft sculpture
RT metal art
    statues

seafarers
SG Economics and Employment
    Science and Technology
BT transportation occupations

seamstresses
USE **tailors**

seamstresses (historical)
SN *Use TAILORS, except when describing historically women intensive occupations.*
SG Economics and Employment
BT clothing workers
    women

seances

SG Language, Literature, Religion, and
 Philosophy
RT fortune telling
 mediums
 palm reading
 psychics
 seers
 spiritualism
 trances

search committees

SG Economics and Employment
 Education
BT committees
RT affirmative action hiring
 contacts
 executive search firms
 job candidates
 job recruitment
 networks
 selection procedures

seasonal migration

SN *A process whereby migrants go season-*
 ally to another part of their own or
 a neighboring country.
SG Economics and Employment
 International Women
 Social Sciences and Culture
BT migration
RT migrant workers

seclusion

SG History and Social Change
 International Women
 Social Sciences and Culture
RT foot binding
 harems
 private sphere
 purdah
 veiling of women

second careers

SG Economics and Employment
BT careers
RT midcareer change

(cont.)

second careers *(cont.)*

RT older adults
 transitions

secondary education

SG Education
DG Education Levels
BT elementary secondary education
NT high school equivalency programs
 high schools

secondary schools

SG Education
BT schools

secret societies

SG Social Sciences and Culture
BT societies
RT cults
 fraternities
 initiation rites
 sororities

secretaries

SG Economics and Employment
BT clerical occupations
 female intensive occupations
RT word processing

sects

SG Language, Literature, Religion, and
 Philosophy
BT religious groups
RT cults
 factions
 religion
 religions
 religious practices
 rites

secularism

DG Cultural and Political Movements

secularization

SG Language, Literature, Religion, and
 Philosophy
 Social Sciences and Culture

(cont.)

SN=Scope note   SG=Subject group   DG=Delimiters group   USE=Use

secularization (*cont.*)
RT civil religion

security
SG Law, Government, and Public Policy
NT business security
campus security
computer security
global security
job security
national security
residential security
RT attachment
autonomy
human needs

security guards
SG Economics and Employment
Law, Government, and Public Policy
BT guards

seduction
SG Language, Literature, Religion, and
Philosophy
Social Sciences and Culture
RT sexual behavior
temptresses

seductresses
SG History and Social Change
Language, Literature, Religion, and
Philosophy
Social Sciences and Culture
BT images of women

seed capital
SG Economics and Employment
BT capital
RT credit

seers
SG Economics and Employment
Language, Literature, Religion, and
Philosophy
BT female intensive occupations
religious workers
RT astrology

(*cont.*)

seers (*cont.*)
RT fortune telling
mediums
palm reading
prophecy
psychics
seances
shamans
visionaries
visions

segregated housing
SG Law, Government, and Public Policy
Social Sciences and Culture
BT housing
RT segregation

segregation
SG Social Sciences and Culture
BT discriminatory practices
NT occupational segregation
school segregation
sex segregation
RT desegregation
discrimination
ghettos
racial discrimination
segregated housing

selection procedures
SG Economics and Employment
Education
RT delegates
hiring policy
search committees

selective attention
SG Social Sciences and Culture
BT attention

self actualization
SG Social Sciences and Culture
BT psychological needs

self blame
SG Social Sciences and Culture
BT blame

(*cont.*)

UF=Use for   BT=Broader term   NT=Narrower term   RT=Related term

self blame (*cont.*)
- RT   personality traits
-      self concept

self concept
- SG   Social Sciences and Culture
- UF   self image
- BT   psychological needs
- RT   attitudes
-      behavior
-      birth name
-      blaming the victim
-      ego
-      hypochondria
-      identity
-      incest victims
-      independence
-      individual development
-      lack of confidence
-      nervousness
-      Outward Bound programs
-      pride
-      purification rites
-      rejection
-      self blame
-      self confidence
-      self understanding
-      slave name

self confidence
- SG   Social Sciences and Culture
- RT   feedback
-      intelligence
-      Outward Bound programs
-      pride
-      self concept
-      self determination

self control
- SG   Social Sciences and Culture
- BT   control
- RT   abstinence
-      asceticism
-      discipline
-      locus of control
-      personality traits
-      self denial

self defense
- SG   Social Sciences and Culture
- RT   defense mechanisms
-      martial arts

self denial
- SG   Language, Literature, Religion, and
-        Philosophy
-      Social Sciences and Culture
- RT   angel in the house
-      asceticism
-      discipline
-      guilt
-      loss of self
-      martyrs
-      mother syndrome
-      personality traits
-      religious repression
-      self control
-      sin

self destructive behavior
- SG   Social Sciences and Culture
- BT   destructive behavior

self determination
- SG   Social Sciences and Culture
- RT   independence
-      self confidence

self disclosure
- SG   Social Sciences and Culture
- RT   intimacy
-      relationships

self employed
- USE **self employment**

self employment
- SG   Economics and Employment
- UF   self employed
- BT   employment

self esteem
- SG   Social Sciences and Culture
- BT   psychological needs
- RT   personality traits

(*cont.*)

self esteem (*cont.*)
 RT   pride

self examination
 SG   Natural Sciences and Health
 RT   breast examination
      speculums

self help
 SG   Social Sciences and Culture
 BT   help seeking behavior
 RT   autonomy
      breast self examination
      coping strategies
      experts
      independence
      self insemination
      self sufficiency
      speculums

self image
 USE **self concept**

self insemination
 SN   *Self-administered artificial insemina-*
      tion.
 SG   Natural Sciences and Health
 BT   insemination
 RT   artificial insemination
      reproductive technologies
      self help
      single mothers

self perception
 SG   Natural Sciences and Health
      Social Sciences and Culture
 BT   perception

self respect
 SG   Social Sciences and Culture
 BT   psychological needs

self sacrifice
 SG   Social Sciences and Culture
 RT   maternal love
      mother syndrome
      personality traits

                              (*cont.*)

self sacrifice (*cont.*)
 RT   subjugation
      superwoman syndrome

self sufficiency
 SG   Social Sciences and Culture
 BT   psychological needs
 RT   self help

self understanding
 SG   Social Sciences and Culture
 RT   self concept

selfish behavior
 SG   Social Sciences and Culture
 BT   behavior
 RT   corruption
      narcissism

semantics
 SG   Language, Literature, Religion, and
      Philosophy
 BT   linguistics
 RT   linguistic sexism
      names

seminaries
 SG   Education
      Language, Literature, Religion, and
      Philosophy
 BT   educational facilities
 RT   clergy

seminars
 SG   History and Social Change
      Social Sciences and Culture
 BT   educational activities

semiotics
 SG   Language, Literature, Religion, and
      Philosophy
 BT   philosophy
 RT   advertising
      gestures
      icons
      linguistics

Senate
SG Law, Government, and Public Policy
BT Congress

senators
SG Economics and Employment
    Law, Government, and Public Policy
BT elected officials

Senegalese
DG National and Regional Descriptors
BT African

senior citizens
SG Social Sciences and Culture
BT older adults
RT age discrimination
    elderly care
    geriatrics
    gray power
    Social Security

seniority
SG Economics and Employment
RT benefits
    rank

sensation
SG Social Sciences and Culture
RT cognition

sense of humor
SG Natural Sciences and Health
RT humor
    jokes

sensitivity
SG Social Sciences and Culture
RT emotions
    empathy
    personal relationships

sensitivity training
SG History and Social Change
BT training
RT consciousness raising
    consciousness raising groups

(cont.)

sensitivity training (cont.)
RT encounter groups
    medical education

sensory development
SG Natural Sciences and Health
BT physical development

sensuality
SG Social Sciences and Culture
RT sexual behavior
    sexuality

sentencing
SG Law, Government, and Public Policy
RT prisons
    punishment
    trials (courtroom)

separate spheres
SN *Assumption that society is divided into male and female spheres, women's sphere private and domestic, men's sphere public.*
SG History and Social Change
    Law, Government, and Public Policy
    Social Sciences and Culture
NT private sphere
    public sphere
RT conservative movement
    cult of true womanhood
    discrimination
    dualism
    gender ideology
    harems
    hidjab
    kitchens
    purdah
    sex role stereotyping
    sex segregation
    sexual division of labor
    social organization

separation
SG Social Sciences and Culture
RT anxiety
    divorce

(cont.)

separation (*cont.*)
- RT marital status
  prenuptial agreements
  property settlements

separation agreements
- SG Law, Government, and Public Policy
- BT legal documents

separation of church and state
- SG Language, Literature, Religion, and
  Philosophy
  Law, Government, and Public Policy
- RT civil religion
  religion
  religious beliefs
  religious pluralism
  religious reforms
  state religion

separatism
- SG History and Social Change
- DG Cultural and Political Movements
- NT lesbian separatism
- RT female chauvinism
  feminism
  life styles

seraglios
- SG History and Social Change
  Social Sciences and Culture
- BT facilities
- RT harems

serials
- SG Communications
- DG Types and Forms of Materials

series
- DG Types and Forms of Materials

sermons
- SG Language, Literature, Religion, and
  Philosophy
- RT homilies
  oratory
  religious language

servants
- USE **household workers**

service occupations
- SG Economics and Employment
- BT occupations
- NT agents
  attendants
  barbers
  bartenders
  beauticians
  bellhops
  child care workers
  cleaners
  coat checkers
  cocktail servers
  community organizers
  cosmetologists
  deliverers
  dishwashers
  escorts
  food preparation occupations
  food service workers
  fortune tellers
  gigolos
  government workers
  hairdressers
  hat checkers
  hotel workers
  household workers
  housekeepers
  ironers
  launderers
  prostitutes
  protective service occupations
  sanitation workers
  tour guides
  ushers
  visiting homemakers
  volunteers
  waiters
  waiters' assistants
- RT homemaking
  household labor
  mortuary science
  mothers
  pink collar workers

---

services

SN *Use of a more specific term is recommended.*

SG Social Sciences and Culture

NT dating services
domestic services
health care services
housekeeping services
human services
information services
legal services

RT advocacy
eligibility
organizations

sessions

SG History and Social Change
Social Sciences and Culture

NT plenary sessions

RT conferences

sewage disposal

SG Natural Sciences and Health

RT pollution
public health
sanitation

sewers

SG Economics and Employment

BT clothing workers

RT dressmakers

sewing

SG Economics and Employment
Social Sciences and Culture

RT craft arts
manufacturing occupations

sewing machine operators

SG Economics and Employment
Visual and Performing Arts

BT clothing workers
machine operators

sex

SN *Use of a more specific term is recommended.*

(cont.)

sex *(cont.)*

SG Natural Sciences and Health
Social Sciences and Culture

NT commercial sex
safe sex

RT emotions
gender
lovemaking
pleasure
sex/gender systems
sexual behavior
sexual intercourse
sexuality
wedding nights

sex change

SG Natural Sciences and Health

BT change

RT sex reversal

sex counseling

SG Natural Sciences and Health
Social Sciences and Culture

UF sex therapy
sexual counseling

BT counseling

RT impotence
nonorgasmic women
orgasm
sexual aids
sexual behavior
sexual dysfunction
sexual problems
sexual satisfaction

sex crimes

SG Law, Government, and Public Policy

UF sex offenses

BT crimes

RT incest
rape
sexual violence
sodomy
victims
violence against women

sex determination
SG Natural Sciences and Health
RT amniocentesis
reproductive technologies
sex selection

sex differences
SG Natural Sciences and Health
BT differences
RT career choice
gender differences
lateral dominance
phallocentrism
sexual dimorphism

sex discrimination
SG History and Social Change
Social Sciences and Culture
BT discrimination
NT sex discrimination in education
sex discrimination in employment
RT affirmative action
body politics
human rights violations
pornography
prejudice
sex segregation
sexism
sexual harassment
subordination of women
unfair labor practices

sex discrimination in education
SG Education
History and Social Change
BT sex discrimination
RT affirmative action
educational legislation
educational opportunities

sex discrimination in employment
SG Economics and Employment
Social Sciences and Culture
BT sex discrimination
RT affirmative action hiring
female intensive occupations
job discrimination

(cont.)

sex discrimination in employment *(cont.)*
RT labor legislation
male intensive occupations

sex drive
SG Natural Sciences and Health
UF libido
RT sexual behavior
sexuality

sex education
SG Natural Sciences and Health
BT education
RT abortion counseling
advice columns
advice shows
planned parenthood
pregnancy
pregnancy prevention
teenage pregnancy

sex equality
USE **sexual equality**

sex equity
SN *Use to refer to policies of fair treatment; use **sexual equality** to refer to broader social and personal concept of equality.*
SG Economics and Employment
Education
History and Social Change
Law, Government, and Public Policy
UF sexual equity
BT equity
RT educational opportunities
equal rights legislation
job ghettos
sexual equality

sex hormones
SG Natural Sciences and Health
BT hormones
NT androgens
estrogens
progestins

UF=Use for   BT=Broader term   NT=Narrower term   RT=Related term

sex identity
    USE **sexual identity**

sex industry
    SG   Economics and Employment
          International Women
          Social Sciences and Culture
  BT   industries
  RT   commercial sex
      exploitation
      pornography
      profits
      sex tourism

sex manuals
    SG   Natural Sciences and Health
    DG   Types and Forms of Materials
  BT   manuals
  RT   advice columns
      experts

sex objects
    SG   Social Sciences and Culture
  RT   breasts
      buttocks
      harems
      images of women
      objectification
      odalisques

sex offenses
    USE **sex crimes**

sex preselection
    SG   Natural Sciences and Health
  BT   sex selection
  RT   boy preference of parents
      girl preference of parents
      reproductive technologies

sex ratio
    SG   Social Sciences and Culture
  BT   vital statistics
  RT   sex selection

sex reversal
    SG   Natural Sciences and Health
                  (cont.)

sex reversal *(cont.)*
  RT   sex change

sex role behavior
    SG   Social Sciences and Culture
  BT   behavior
  NT   flirtation
  RT   double standard

sex role development
    SG   Social Sciences and Culture
  BT   individual development
  RT   gender development
      primary caregivers
      sex roles

sex role identification
    USE **sexual identity**

sex role stereotyping
    SG   Social Sciences and Culture
  BT   stereotyping
  RT   butch
      children's literature
      femininity
      femme
      ideal woman
      images of girls
      images of women
      man the hunter
      masculinity
      separate spheres
      sex roles
      textbooks
      tomboys
      woman the gatherer
      women's roles

sex roles
    SG   Social Sciences and Culture
  BT   roles
  RT   gender roles
      men's roles
      public sphere
      sex role development
      sex role stereotyping
      sex/gender systems
                  (cont.)

sex roles (*cont.*)
  RT sexual politics
      social construction of gender
      socialization

sex segregation
  SG Education
      History and Social Change
      Social Sciences and Culture
  BT segregation
  RT employment
      job ghettos
      separate spheres
      sex discrimination

sex selection
  SG Natural Sciences and Health
      Social Sciences and Culture
  NT sex preselection
  RT boy preference of parents
      girl preference of parents
      reproductive technologies
      sex determination
      sex ratio

sex stereotypes
  SG Social Sciences and Culture
  BT stereotypes
  RT compulsory heterosexuality
      dolls
      images of women
      machismo

sex therapy
  USE **sex counseling**

sex tourism
  SN *Packaged tours, especially in Asian
      countries, that include prostitutes as
      part of the arrangement.*
  SG International Women
  UF traffic in women
  RT commercial sex
      exploitation
      prostitutes
      prostitution
      sex industry

(*cont.*)

sex tourism (*cont.*)
  RT sexual exploitation

sex/gender systems
  SN *Term used to describe ways society
      transforms biological sexuality into
      products of human activity.*
  SG History and Social Change
      Social Sciences and Culture
  RT belief systems
      biological determinism
      biologism
      class formation
      cultural influences
      false dichotomies
      family roles
      gender
      gender bias
      gender development
      gender differences
      gender ideology
      gender roles
      men's roles
      race, class, and gender studies
      roles
      sex
      sex roles
      sexual division of labor
      social construction of gender
      stereotypes
      stereotyping
      unisex

sexism
  SG History and Social Change
      Social Sciences and Culture
  NT institutional sexism
      linguistic sexism
  RT ableism
      ageism
      androcentrism
      classism
      double discrimination
      doubly disadvantaged
      education
      employment
      language

(*cont.*)

UF=Use for   BT=Broader term   NT=Narrower term   RT=Related term

sexism (*cont.*)
RT   machismo
        male chauvinism
        minority experience
        misogyny
        oppression
        patriarchy
        pornography
        racism
        sex discrimination
        sexist language
        sexual oppression
        stereotyping

sexist language
SG   Language, Literature, Religion, and
        Philosophy
BT   discriminatory language
NT   he/man language
        patriarchal language
RT   desex
        false generics
        gender marking
        generic pronouns
        interruptions
        labels
        masculine pronouns
        microinequities
        misogyny
        names
        naming
        phallogocentrism
        sexism
        sexual oppression
        titles

sextuplets
USE   **multiple births**

sexual abstinence
SG   Natural Sciences and Health
        Social Sciences and Culture
BT   abstinence
RT   birth control
        celibacy
        religious orders
        rhythm method

                        (*cont.*)

sexual abstinence (*cont.*)
RT   virginity

sexual abuse
SG   Social Sciences and Culture
BT   abuse
RT   child abuse
        incest victims
        misogyny
        sexual violence
        violence

sexual aids
SG   Natural Sciences and Health
NT   aphrodisiacs
        vibrators
RT   lingerie
        lubricants
        sex counseling
        sexual behavior
        sexual dysfunction
        sexual problems

sexual assault
SG   Social Sciences and Culture
BT   assault
        sexual violence
RT   physical abuse

sexual attraction
SG   Natural Sciences and Health
        Social Sciences and Culture
RT   arousal
        body image
        pheromones
        sexual behavior

sexual behavior
SG   Natural Sciences and Health
UF   sexual practices
BT   behavior
NT   anal sex
        foreplay
        group sex
        masturbation
        oral sex
        sexual intercourse

                        (*cont.*)

sexual behavior (*cont.*)
- NT tribadism
- RT acquired immune deficiency syndrome
  - arousal
  - bestiality
  - bondage
  - celibacy
  - coitus interruptus
  - dominance
  - eroticism
  - exhibitionism
  - fantasies
  - guilt
  - health behavior
  - hypersexuality
  - lovemaking
  - masochism
  - orgasm
  - passion
  - permissive environment
  - pheromones
  - pleasure
  - premarital relations
  - promiscuity
  - sadism
  - sadomasochism
  - seduction
  - sensuality
  - sex
  - sex counseling
  - sex drive
  - sexual aids
  - sexual attraction
  - sexual dysfunction
  - sexual excitement
  - sexual fantasies
  - sexual satisfaction
  - sexual violence
  - sin
  - sodomy
  - taboos
  - touching

sexual counseling
- USE **sex counseling**

sexual desire
- SG Natural Sciences and Health
- BT desire
- RT sexual excitement

sexual dimorphism
- SN *Differences in physical characteristics due to sex.*
- SG Natural Sciences and Health
- RT sex differences

sexual division of labor
- SG Economics and Employment
- BT division of labor
- RT economic value of women's work
  - female intensive occupations
  - fifth world
  - fourth world
  - household division of labor
  - international division of labor
  - occupational sex segregation
  - pay equity
  - separate spheres
  - sex/gender systems

sexual dysfunction
- SG Natural Sciences and Health
- NT impotence
- RT androgens
  - marital conflict
  - nonorgasmic women
  - sex counseling
  - sexual aids
  - sexual behavior
  - sexual satisfaction

sexual equality
- SN *Use to refer to broad social and personal concept of equality; use* **sex equity** *to refer to policies of fair treatment.*
- SG History and Social Change
  - Language, Literature, Religion, and Philosophy
- UF sex equality
- BT equality
- RT commercial sex

(*cont.*)

sexual equality (*cont.*)
RT discrimination
    educational equity
    educational opportunities
    sex equity
    social reform

sexual equity
USE **sex equity**

sexual excitement
SG Natural Sciences and Health
RT aphrodisiacs
    arousal
    genitals
    sexual behavior
    sexual desire

sexual exploitation
SG Social Sciences and Culture
BT exploitation
RT commercial sex
    female sexual slavery
    pornography
    prostitutes
    prostitution
    sex tourism
    sexual oppression

sexual fantasies
SG Social Sciences and Culture
BT fantasies
RT breasts
    buttocks
    imagination
    pleasure
    sexual behavior

sexual freedom
SG History and Social Change
    Social Sciences and Culture
BT freedoms
RT sexual preference

sexual harassment
SG Economics and Employment
    Education
    Law, Government, and Public Policy
NT street harassment
RT corporate policy
    corporate responsibility
    ethnic intimidation
    exploitation
    power
    sex discrimination
    sexual intimidation

sexual identity
SG Natural Sciences and Health
    Social Sciences and Culture
UF sex identity
    sex role identification
BT identity
NT cross sex identity
RT androgyny
    female impersonators
    female sexuality
    gender identity
    sexual preference
    sexuality

sexual intercourse
SG Natural Sciences and Health
UF coitus
    copulation
BT sexual behavior
RT conception
    insemination
    sex

sexual intimidation
SG Social Sciences and Culture
BT intimidation
RT acquaintance rape
    date rape
    sexual harassment

sexual liberation
SG History and Social Change
    Social Sciences and Culture
UF free love

(*cont.*)

sexual liberation (*cont.*)
  BT liberation
  RT attitudes
     freedom
     monogamy
     sexual revolution
     values

sexual oppression
     SG History and Social Change
        Social Sciences and Culture
  BT oppression
  RT false consciousness
     protofeminism
     sexism
     sexist language
     sexual exploitation
     sexual slavery

sexual permissiveness
     SG Social Sciences and Culture
  RT morality

sexual politics
     SG History and Social Change
        Social Sciences and Culture
  BT politics
  NT body politics
  RT feminism
     feminist theory
     gender roles
     sex roles
     womanism

sexual practices
  USE **sexual behavior**

sexual preference
     SG Natural Sciences and Health
  RT gender identity
     sexual freedom
     sexual identity

sexual problems
     SG Natural Sciences and Health
  BT problems
  RT sex counseling

(cont.)

sexual problems (*cont.*)
  RT sexual aids

sexual relationships
     SG Natural Sciences and Health
        Social Sciences and Culture
  BT relationships
  NT premarital relations
  RT double standard

sexual repression
     SG Natural Sciences and Health
  BT repression

sexual revolution
     SG History and Social Change
  BT revolution
  RT sexual liberation
     social change

sexual satisfaction
     SG Natural Sciences and Health
  BT satisfaction
  RT foreplay
     masturbation
     orgasm
     sex counseling
     sexual behavior
     sexual dysfunction

sexual slavery
     SG Social Sciences and Culture
  BT slavery
  NT female sexual slavery
  RT bondage
     concubinage
     sexual oppression

sexual stratification
     SG Social Sciences and Culture
  BT social stratification

sexual violence
     SG Law, Government, and Public Policy
        Natural Sciences and Health
        Social Sciences and Culture
  BT violence

(cont.)

sexual violence (*cont.*)
- NT   rape
      sexual assault
- RT   cultural sadism
      incest
      sex crimes
      sexual abuse
      sexual behavior
      sodomy

sexuality
- SG   Natural Sciences and Health
- NT   bisexuality
      female sexuality
      heterosexuality
      homosexuality
      hypersexuality
      male sexuality
      transsexuality
- RT   desire
      sensuality
      sex
      sex drive
      sexual identity

sexually transmitted diseases
- SG   Natural Sciences and Health
- UF   VD
      venereal diseases
- BT   communicable diseases
- NT   acquired immune deficiency syndrome
      clamydia
      genital herpes
      gonorrhea
      syphilis
- RT   pregnancy
      prostitutes
      prostitution
      safe sex

shamans
- SG   Language, Literature, Religion, and
         Philosophy
       Social Sciences and Culture
- RT   healers
      holy men
      holy women

(*cont.*)

shamans (*cont.*)
- RT   priestesses
      priests
      religious workers
      seers
      visionaries
      wisdom

shared custody
- SG   Social Sciences and Culture
- UF   joint custody
- BT   child custody
- RT   coparenting
      parenting

shared parenting
- SG   Natural Sciences and Health
       Social Sciences and Culture
- BT   parenting
- RT   division of labor

sheet music
- SG   Visual and Performing Arts
- DG   Types and Forms of Materials
- RT   music

shelters
- SG   History and Social Change
       Social Sciences and Culture
- BT   facilities
- NT   crisis shelters
      women's shelters
- RT   homeless

sheriffs
- SG   Economics and Employment
       Law, Government, and Public Policy
- BT   protective service occupations

shift work
- SG   Economics and Employment
- BT   work
      work hours
- RT   employment schedules
      factory workers

SN=Scope note   SG=Subject group   DG=Delimiters group   USE=Use

shock therapy
USE **electroconvulsive therapy**

shoplifting
SG Law, Government, and Public Policy
BT property crimes

short stories
SG Language, Literature, Religion, and
Philosophy
BT fiction
RT pulp fiction
stories

short term memory
SG Social Sciences and Culture
BT memory

showers
SN *Engagement parties.*
SG Social Sciences and Culture
RT courtship customs

shows
SG Communications
BT activities
NT advice shows
art shows
fashion shows
game shows
talk shows
RT art
broadcasts
television
theater

shunning
SG Language, Literature, Religion, and
Philosophy
Social Sciences and Culture
RT punishment

sibling influence
SG Social Sciences and Culture
BT family influence
RT birth order

sibling relationships
SG Social Sciences and Culture
BT family relationships

siblings
SG Social Sciences and Culture
RT birth order
brothers
sisters

sick children
SG Natural Sciences and Health
BT children
RT absenteeism
dependent care
family responsibility
sick leave

sick leave
SG Economics and Employment
Natural Sciences and Health
RT disability insurance
sick children

sickle cell anemia
SG Natural Sciences and Health
BT diseases

Sierra Leonean
DG National and Regional Descriptors
BT African

sign language
SG Communications
Language, Literature, Religion, and
Philosophy
BT language
RT braille
communication
conversation
deafness
disabilities
gestures
hearing impairments
icons
language skills
nonverbal language

(*cont.*)

---

sign language (*cont.*)

RT   talk

sign painters

SG   Communications
     Economics and Employment
     Visual and Performing Arts

BT   craft occupations

RT   graphic design
     illustrators

significant others

SG   Social Sciences and Culture

RT   lovers
     palimony
     posslq
     spouses

silence

SG   Language, Literature, Religion, and
     Philosophy
     Social Sciences and Culture

RT   anonymous
     discrimination
     invisibility

sin

SG   Language, Literature, Religion, and
     Philosophy

BT   religious beliefs

NT   original sin

RT   confession
     devil
     expiation
     forgiveness
     greed
     guilt
     immorality
     penance
     pride
     religion
     salvation
     self denial
     sexual behavior

singers

SG   Communications
     Economics and Employment
     Visual and Performing Arts

BT   arts, entertainment, and media
     occupations

NT   chanteuses
     opera singers
     torch singers

RT   music videos
     musicians
     performers

single fathers

SG   Social Sciences and Culture

UF   unmarried fathers

BT   fathers
     single parents

RT   attitudes
     custody
     illegitimacy
     single mothers

single men

SG   Social Sciences and Culture

UF   unmarried men

BT   men

RT   bachelors
     personal columns

single mothers

SG   Social Sciences and Culture

UF   unmarried mothers
     unwed mothers

BT   mothers
     single parents

RT   artificial insemination
     attitudes
     balancing work and family life
     custody
     female headed households
     housing discrimination
     illegitimacy
     name rights
     self insemination
     single fathers
     teenage pregnancy

single parent families

SG   Social Sciences and Culture
UF   broken home
     one parent families
BT   families
RT   child rearing practices
     children living in poverty
     fatherless families
     female headed households
     householders
     women living in poverty

single parents

SG   Social Sciences and Culture
BT   parents
NT   single fathers
     single mothers
RT   adoption
     bachelors
     birth certificates
     child rearing practices
     children
     parenthood
     spinsters

single sex colleges

SG   Education
BT   colleges
NT   women's colleges
RT   single sex environments

single sex education

SG   Education
BT   education
RT   single sex schools

single sex environments

SG   Education
     Social Sciences and Culture
BT   environment
RT   coeducation
     convents
     mergers
     single sex colleges
     single sex schools

single sex schools

SG   Education
BT   schools
RT   single sex education
     single sex environments

single women

SG   Social Sciences and Culture
UF   unmarried women
BT   women
RT   extended families
     families
     personal columns
     spinsters
     support systems

singles

SG   Social Sciences and Culture
RT   households
     life styles
     taxes

sirens

SG   History and Social Change
     Language, Literature, Religion, and
        Philosophy
BT   images of women

sissies

SG   Social Sciences and Culture
BT   images of girls

sisterhood

SN   *Solidarity of women.*
SG   History and Social Change
RT   autonomy
     daughter right
     female bonding
     female friendships
     feminism
     friendships
     woman power
     womanism
     women identified women

sisters

SG   Social Sciences and Culture

(cont.)

UF=Use for   BT=Broader term   NT=Narrower term   RT=Related term

sisters (*cont.*)
- BT images of girls
  - images of women
  - women
- RT brothers
  - families
  - family structure
  - siblings

sisters in law
- SG Social Sciences and Culture
- BT in laws

sit ins
- SG History and Social Change
- BT protest actions
- RT demonstrations
  - social movements

skepticism
- DG Cultural and Political Movements

sketches
- DG Types and Forms of Materials

skiing
- SG Natural Sciences and Health
- BT sports

skill development
- SG Economics and Employment
  - Education
- BT individual development
- RT social skills

skill training
- SG Economics and Employment
  - Education
- BT training
- RT trades

skilled trades
- SG Economics and Employment
- BT trades

skills
- SG Social Sciences and Culture
  - (*cont.*)

skills (*cont.*)
- NT basic skills
  - job skills
  - language skills
  - leadership skills
  - life skills
  - motor skills
  - perception skills
  - social skills
  - spatial skills
- RT mentors
  - mothering

skin
- SG Natural Sciences and Health
- BT bodies
- RT acne
  - body image
  - complexion
  - face lifts
  - wrinkles

skin color
- SG Social Sciences and Culture
- RT attitudes
  - complexion
  - cosmetics
  - discrimination
  - perceptual bias
  - racial and ethnic differences

skirts
- SG Social Sciences and Culture
- BT clothing
- NT miniskirts
- RT hemlines

skits
- SG Language, Literature, Religion, and
  - Philosophy
  - Visual and Performing Arts
- BT comedy
- RT farce
  - literature
  - plays

slang

SG Language, Literature, Religion, and
Philosophy
BT informal language
RT language

slapstick

SG Language, Literature, Religion, and
Philosophy
RT humor
jokes
satire

slave name

SG History and Social Change
Language, Literature, Religion, and
Philosophy
BT surnames
RT birth name
name rights
patronymy
self concept
slavery

slave rape

SG History and Social Change
Social Sciences and Culture
BT rape
RT lynching
racist rape
slavery
violence against women

slave songs

SG History and Social Change
Visual and Performing Arts
BT songs
RT spirituals

slavery

SG History and Social Change
NT sexual slavery
white slavery
RT abolition
emancipation
exploitation
harems

(cont.)

slavery *(cont.)*

RT liberation struggles
mammies
manumission
miscegenation
oppression
plantations
rape
slave name
slave rape
underground railroad

slaves

SG History and Social Change
RT chattels

Slavic

DG Ethnic, Racial, and Religious
Descriptors

Slavic studies

SG Education
International Women
Social Sciences and Culture
BT area studies

sleep

SG Social Sciences and Culture
RT biological clock
deprivation
dreams
fatigue

slide collections

DG Types and Forms of Materials

slide registries

DG Types and Forms of Materials

slide tapes

DG Types and Forms of Materials

slides

DG Types and Forms of Materials

slimming

USE **dieting**

slogans
DG Types and Forms of Materials

slum landlords
SG Law, Government, and Public Policy
BT landlords
RT ghettos
    slums

slums
SG International Women
BT declining neighborhoods
RT inner city
    slum landlords
    squatters

small business
SN *Includes small manufacturing firms and informal activities, such as handicrafts.*
SG Economics and Employment
    International Women
BT business
RT capital
    commercial credit
    cottage industry
    economic development
    entrepreneurs
    family owned business
    income generation
    merchants
    minority owned business
    women owned business

smiling
SG Social Sciences and Culture
RT conditioning
    laughter
    social skills

smokefree environments
SG Natural Sciences and Health
BT environment
RT smoking
    smoking prohibition

smoking
SG Natural Sciences and Health
UF cigarettes
RT birth defects
    cancer
    marijuana
    smokefree environments
    tobacco

smoking prohibition
SG Law, Government, and Public Policy
    Social Sciences and Culture
BT social prohibitions
RT smokefree environments

snakes
SG Language, Literature, Religion, and Philosophy
RT Garden of Eden
    temptation

Snow White
SG Language, Literature, Religion, and Philosophy
BT images of women

soap operas
SG Communications
RT images of women
    popular culture
    pulp fiction
    radio
    romances
    television

soccer
SG Natural Sciences and Health
BT sports

social action
SG History and Social Change
RT advocacy
    advocacy groups
    citizen groups
    civil disobedience
    community action
    grass roots

(cont.)

social action (*cont.*)
- RT political activism
  - protest actions
  - social change
  - social movements
  - social reform

social activities
- SG History and Social Change
  - Social Sciences and Culture
- BT activities
- NT breakfasts
  - brunches
  - coffee klatches
  - dances
  - dating
  - dinners
  - lunches
  - parties
  - receptions
  - suppers
  - teas
- RT clubs
  - hosts

social adjustment
- SG Social Sciences and Culture
- BT adjustment

social agencies
- SG Law, Government, and Public Policy
  - Social Sciences and Culture
- BT agencies
- NT welfare agencies

social attitudes
- SG Social Sciences and Culture
- BT attitudes
- RT acquaintance rape
  - ageism
  - classism
  - cultural constraints
  - illegitimacy
  - image
  - immorality
  - marijuana
  - promiscuity

(cont.)

social attitudes (*cont.*)
- RT reputations
  - social values

social behavior
- SG Social Sciences and Culture
- BT behavior
- NT manners
- RT attitudes
  - commitment
  - dominance
  - health behavior
  - mores
  - values

social bias
- SG Social Sciences and Culture
- BT bias
- RT discrimination

social change
- SN *See also Delimiters Displays: Cultural and Political Movements, Historical Periods.*
- SG History and Social Change
- BT change
- RT activism
  - advocacy
  - advocacy groups
  - agencies
  - backlash
  - change agents
  - enforcement
  - militance
  - norms
  - organizations
  - progress
  - sexual revolution
  - social action
  - social movements
  - social reform
  - social trends
  - social values
  - strikes
  - struggles
  - suffrage movements
  - volunteer work

(cont.)

UF=Use for   BT=Broader term   NT=Narrower term   RT=Related term

social change (*cont.*)
RT women's media

social characteristics
SG Social Sciences and Culture
RT social values

social class
SG Economics and Employment
    Social Sciences and Culture
BT class
RT child rearing practices
    class consciousness
    class differences
    classism
    cultural groups
    culture
    demographic measurements
    disadvantaged
    exploitation
    families
    family structure
    ghettos
    image
    income
    influences
    life styles
    living standards
    poverty
    race, class, and gender studies
    racial stratification
    social clubs
    social indicators
    social mobility
    social status
    social stratification
    social structure
    social values
    society
    socioeconomic status
    status
    test bias
    unemployment
    volunteer work
    volunteers
    wealth
    workers

social clubs
SG History and Social Change
BT clubs
RT club women
    feminist organizations
    social class
    social organizations
    women's groups

social conditioning
SG Social Sciences and Culture
BT conditioning
RT learned helplessness
    mental disorders
    personality disorders
    rebellious behavior

social conflict
SG Social Sciences and Culture
BT conflict

social construction of gender
SG History and Social Change
    Social Sciences and Culture
BT social construction of reality
RT class formation
    gender
    gender development
    gender identity
    gender ideology
    gender roles
    race formation
    sex roles
    sex/gender systems
    social organization

social construction of reality
SG History and Social Change
    Science and Technology
    Social Sciences and Culture
NT social construction of gender
RT blind review
    conceptual errors
    male norms
    models (paradigms)
    objectivity
    paradigms

(*cont.*)

social construction of reality (cont.)

RT paranoia
    perceptual bias
    phallogocentrism
    race formation
    research bias
    sociology of knowledge

social control

SG Social Sciences and Culture
BT control

social Darwinism

DG Cultural and Political Movements

social development

SG Education
    Social Sciences and Culture
BT individual development
RT antisocial behavior
    social skills

social dialects

SG Language, Literature, Religion, and
    Philosophy
BT dialects
RT bilingualism
    language skills
    sociolinguistics
    women's language

social differences

SG Social Sciences and Culture
BT differences
RT life styles
    racial and ethnic differences

social discrimination
USE **discrimination**

social entertaining

SG Communications
    Social Sciences and Culture
UF entertaining
RT tea pouring

social environment

SG Social Sciences and Culture
BT environment
RT anthropology
    influences
    social sciences

social geography

SG Social Sciences and Culture
BT geography
RT anthropology
    ethnography
    sociology

social history

SG History and Social Change
BT history
NT family history
RT moral reform

social identity

SG Social Sciences and Culture
BT identity

social indicators

SG Economics and Employment
    Social Sciences and Culture
BT socioeconomic indicators
RT social class

social influences

SG Social Sciences and Culture
BT influences
RT social values

social issues

SG History and Social Change
    Law, Government, and Public Policy
RT public policy
    social movements
    social policy

social learning
USE **socialization**

social legislation

SG Law, Government, and Public Policy
(cont.)

---

social legislation (*cont.*)

BT legislation
RT social policy
    women in politics

social mobility

SG History and Social Change
    Social Sciences and Culture
BT mobility
RT aspirations
    social class

social movements

SN *Organized efforts to create formal and
    informal structures that provide
    broad-based support for an idea, be-
    lief, or issue. See also Delimiters
    Displays: Cultural and Political
    Movements, Historical Periods.*
SG History and Social Change
UF movements
NT abortion movement
    anti ERA movement
    antiabortion movement
    antiapartheid movement
    antiilliteracy movements
    antilynching campaign
    antinuclear movement
    antisuffrage movement
    Black movement
    civil rights movements
    conservative movement
    environmental movement
    feminist movement
    homophile movement
    labor movement
    lesbian movement
    men's movement
    nationalist movements
    peace movements
    religious movements
    revolutionary movements
    suffrage movements
    temperance movement
    women's movement
    youth movement
RT abolition

(*cont.*)

social movements (*cont.*)

RT activism
    activists
    advocates
    antifeminism
    backlash
    boycotts
    church work
    conservatives
    demonstrations
    dissent
    economic boycotts
    economic sanctions
    feminism
    feminist organizations
    free speech
    grass roots
    liberation
    militance
    moral reform
    nonviolence
    oppression
    organizing
    protest actions
    rebellions
    reformers
    resistance
    sit ins
    social action
    social change
    social issues
    social reform
    struggles

social networks
USE **networks**

social organization

SG Social Sciences and Culture
RT gender development
    organizations
    separate spheres
    social construction of gender
    social structure
    social values
    societies
    structural discrimination

SN=Scope note   SG=Subject group   DG=Delimiters group   USE=Use

social organizations
SG   Social Sciences and Culture
BT   organizations
RT   fraternities
mergers
social clubs
sororities

social perception
SG   Social Sciences and Culture
BT   perception
RT   bias

social policy
SG   History and Social Change
Law, Government, and Public Policy
Social Sciences and Culture
BT   policy
NT   family policy
RT   appropriations
budget cuts
budget deficits
families
famine
federal budget
feminist scholarship
military budget
policy making
public policy
social issues
social legislation
social science research
social services
socialized medicine
welfare programs
welfare reform
welfare state
welfare system

social problems
SG   Social Sciences and Culture
BT   problems
RT   values

social prohibitions
SG   History and Social Change
Social Sciences and Culture
(cont.)

social prohibitions *(cont.)*
NT   drinking prohibition
smoking prohibition
RT   gambling
laws
norms

social psychology
SG   Social Sciences and Culture
BT   psychology

social realism
DG   Cultural and Political Movements
BT   realism

social reform
SG   History and Social Change
Language, Literature, Religion, and
Philosophy
BT   reforms
RT   honesty
humanitarianism
immorality
integrity
liberation theology
missionaries
philanthropy
racial equality
sexual equality
social action
social change
social movements
social welfare

social relations
SG   Social Sciences and Culture
BT   relationships
RT   aggressive behavior
personal relationships

social science research
SG   Social Sciences and Culture
BT   research
NT   behavioral research
market research
RT   cross cultural studies
humanities
(cont.)

UF=Use for   BT=Broader term   NT=Narrower term   RT=Related term   441

social science research (*cont.*)
RT interdisciplinary studies
    interviews
    research bias
    social policy
    social sciences
    socioeconomic indicators

social sciences
SG Social Sciences and Culture
UF behavioral sciences
NT anthropology
    criminology
    demography
    economics
    ethology
    geography
    gerontology
    history
    political science
    psychology
    social studies
    sociobiology
    sociology
RT animal behavior
    cross cultural studies
    culture
    feminist theory
    human evolution
    humanities
    interdisciplinary studies
    mathematics
    medical sciences
    natural sciences
    parapsychology
    political theory
    population distribution
    psycholinguistics
    research bias
    science
    social environment
    social science research
    societies
    sociolinguistics
    zoology

social scientists
SG Economics and Employment
    Education
    Social Sciences and Culture
BT education occupations
    professional occupations
NT anthropologists
    archaeologists
    economists
    historians
    psychologists
    sociologists
    urban planners
RT scientists

Social Security
SG Law, Government, and Public Policy
    Social Sciences and Culture
DG Laws and Regulations
RT earnings sharing
    gray power
    income
    older adults
    pension funds
    retirement
    retirement benefits
    senior citizens
    supplementary benefits
    welfare state

social services
SG Social Sciences and Culture
BT human services
NT legal services
    victim services
    youth services
RT agencies
    poverty
    social policy
    social work
    voluntary organizations
    welfare

social skills
SG Social Sciences and Culture
BT skills
RT charisma

(*cont.*)

social skills (*cont.*)
- RT collaboration
- communication styles
- diplomacy
- empowerment
- hosts
- listening
- skill development
- smiling
- social development

social status
- SG Social Sciences and Culture
- BT status
- RT image
- social class
- wealth

social stratification
- SG Social Sciences and Culture
- BT stratification
- NT racial stratification
- sexual stratification
- RT age
- classism
- gender
- social class
- social structure

social structure
- SG Social Sciences and Culture
- UF social system
- RT class
- community
- economic structure
- families
- family structure
- government
- power structure
- social class
- social organization
- social stratification
- socioeconomic status
- volunteer work

social studies
- SG Education
- Social Sciences and Culture
- BT social sciences
- RT ethnic studies

social support systems
- USE **support systems**

social system
- USE **social structure**

social trends
- SG History and Social Change
- Social Sciences and Culture
- BT trends
- RT fads
- popular culture
- social change

social values
- SG Social Sciences and Culture
- BT values
- RT chivalry
- collaboration
- community
- ethics
- humanitarianism
- image
- lying
- peer influence
- philosophy
- progress
- social attitudes
- social change
- social characteristics
- social class
- social influences
- social organization
- trust

social welfare
- SG History and Social Change
- Social Sciences and Culture
- BT welfare
- RT charitable work
- church work

(cont.)

social welfare (*cont.*)
RT   social reform

social work
SG   Economics and Employment
       Social Sciences and Culture
BT   work
RT   agencies
       social services

social workers
SG   Economics and Employment
UF   caseworkers
BT   female intensive occupations
       professional occupations
       workers
RT   psychotherapy

socialism
SG   Law, Government, and Public Policy
DG   Cultural and Political Movements
BT   political systems
NT   democratic socialism
       utopian socialism
RT   democracy

socialist economic development models
SG   International Women
BT   economic development models

socialist feminism
SN   *Feminist theory emphasizing structural
       discrimination in economic, political,
       and social systems that perpetuate
       inequality.*
SG   History and Social Change
       International Women
DG   Cultural and Political Movements
BT   feminism
RT   feminist theory
       Marxist feminism

Socialist Party
SG   Law, Government, and Public Policy
BT   political parties

socialist revolutions
SG   History and Social Change
       International Women
       Law, Government, and Public Policy
BT   revolution

socialization
SG   Social Sciences and Culture
UF   social learning
RT   acculturation
       cultural influences
       daughters
       finishing schools
       gender
       identity
       individual development
       leadership roles
       learned helplessness
       majority culture
       men's roles
       objectivity
       preparatory schools
       primary caregivers
       roles
       sex roles
       sons
       team playing
       upper class
       women's roles

socialized medicine
SG   Economics and Employment
       Law, Government, and Public Policy
       Natural Sciences and Health
RT   health care policy
       health insurance
       national health insurance
       social policy

socially disadvantaged
SG   Economics and Employment
       Social Sciences and Culture
BT   disadvantaged

societies
SG   Social Sciences and Culture
BT   organizations

                                                                        (*cont.*)

societies (*cont.*)

NT female societies
    honorary societies
    ladies' aid societies
    missionary societies
    secret societies
RT anthropology
    culture
    customs
    ethnic studies
    social organization
    social sciences

society

SG History and Social Change
    Social Sciences and Culture
NT classless society
    matricentric societies
    matrilineal societies
    postindustrial society
    stateless societies
RT community
    social class
    state formation

society balls

SG Economics and Employment
    Social Sciences and Culture
BT dances

sociobiologists

SG Natural Sciences and Health
    Social Sciences and Culture
BT scientists

sociobiology

SG Natural Sciences and Health
    Social Sciences and Culture
BT biological sciences
    social sciences
RT animal behavior
    ethology

socioeconomic class

SG Economics and Employment
    Social Sciences and Culture
BT class

(*cont.*)

socioeconomic class (*cont.*)

RT economic class
    titles (nobility)

socioeconomic conditions

SG Economics and Employment
    Social Sciences and Culture
RT class division
    disadvantaged
    living standards
    socioeconomic status

socioeconomic indicators

SG Economics and Employment
    Social Sciences and Culture
NT economic indicators
    interest rates
    social indicators
    unemployment rates
    urban indicators
RT living standards
    social science research

socioeconomic status

SG Economics and Employment
    Social Sciences and Culture
BT status
RT caste
    class
    class differences
    classless society
    economic structure
    prestige
    privilege
    social class
    social structure
    socioeconomic conditions
    wealth distribution

sociolinguistics

SG Language, Literature, Religion, and
    Philosophy
BT linguistics
RT discourse
    gender marking
    interruptions
    language

(*cont.*)

UF=Use for   BT=Broader term   NT=Narrower term   RT=Related term

sociolinguistics (*cont.*)
RT psychology
    social dialects
    social sciences

sociologists
    SG Economics and Employment
        Social Sciences and Culture
BT social scientists

sociology
    SG Social Sciences and Culture
BT social sciences
NT medical sociology
    sociology of knowledge
RT social geography

sociology of knowledge
    SG Social Sciences and Culture
BT sociology
RT paradigms
    social construction of reality

sociopathology
    SG Social Sciences and Culture
RT antisocial behavior
    deviant behavior

sodomy
    SG Natural Sciences and Health
RT anal sex
    sex crimes
    sexual behavior
    sexual violence

soft sculpture
    SG Visual and Performing Arts
BT sculpture

softball
    SG Natural Sciences and Health
BT sports

software
    DG Types and Forms of Materials

soil conservation
    SG Science and Technology
BT conservation
RT environment

solar energy
    SG Science and Technology
BT energy
    renewable energy sources

solitude
    SG Social Sciences and Culture
RT living alone
    loneliness
    personal space
    privacy

soloists
    SG Visual and Performing Arts
BT performers

solstice
    SG History and Social Change
        Language, Literature, Religion, and
        Philosophy
RT rites

Somalian
    DG National and Regional Descriptors
BT African

somnambulism
    SG Natural Sciences and Health
        Social Sciences and Culture
RT passive behavior
    spirit possession

songs
    SG Visual and Performing Arts
BT vocal music
NT ballads
    lieder
    lullabies
    nursery songs
    slave songs

sonnets
    SG Language, Literature, Religion, and
            Philosophy
  BT poetry

sons
    SG Social Sciences and Culture
  BT men
  RT families
       father son relationships
       mother son relationships
       socialization

sons in law
    SG Social Sciences and Culture
  BT in laws
  RT families
       mother son relationships

sororal twins
    SG Natural Sciences and Health
          Social Sciences and Culture
  BT twins

sororate
    SN *Marriage of one man to two or more
         sisters, usually successively.*
    SG Social Sciences and Culture
  BT marriage customs

sororities
    SG Education
         History and Social Change
  BT women's organizations
  RT fraternities
       initiation rites
       secret societies
       social organizations
       women college students

South African
    DG National and Regional Descriptors
  BT African

South American
    USE **Latin American**

South Atlantic
    DG National and Regional Descriptors
  BT United States

South Pacific
    DG National and Regional Descriptors
  BT Pacific

Southern
    DG National and Regional Descriptors
  BT United States

Southwestern
    DG National and Regional Descriptors
  BT United States

space
    SG Social Sciences and Culture
  NT alternative spaces
       performance spaces
       personal space
       sacred space
  RT harems
       housing
       life styles
       living arrangements
       private sphere
       public sphere
       time
       work space

space sciences
    SG Science and Technology
  UF astronautics
  BT physical sciences
  RT astronauts
       astronomers
       astronomy
       natural sciences

Spanish
    DG National and Regional Descriptors
  BT European

Spanish American
    DG Ethnic, Racial, and Religious
         Descriptors

---

spatial perception
  SG Natural Sciences and Health
BT perception

spatial skills
  SG Natural Sciences and Health
BT skills

speaking in tongues
  USE **glossolalia**

special education
  SG Education
BT education
RT educationally disadvantaged

special interest groups
  SG Law, Government, and Public Policy
BT groups
RT advocacy groups
    factions
    feminist organizations
    lobbying
    political action committees

speculums
  SG Natural Sciences and Health
RT self examination
    self help
    uterus

speech
  SG Natural Sciences and Health
NT free speech
RT dialects
    discourse
    language

speech therapists
  SG Economics and Employment
      Natural Sciences and Health
BT therapists

speeches
  SG Communications
  DG Types and Forms of Materials
RT literature

(cont.)

speeches *(cont.)*
RT oratory
    public speaking

spending
  SG Economics and Employment
RT economic power

sperm
  SG Natural Sciences and Health
BT bodies
RT ejaculation
    fertility
    ovum
    reproduction
    reproductive cycle
    sperm banks
    sterility

sperm banks
  SG Natural Sciences and Health
BT reproductive technologies
RT artificial insemination
    donors
    fertilization
    genetic screening
    sperm

spermicides
  SG Natural Sciences and Health
BT contraception
RT birth control
    diaphragms
    ovum
    pregnancy prevention

sphinx
  SG Language, Literature, Religion, and
      Philosophy
      Visual and Performing Arts
BT images of women

spies
  SG Economics and Employment
      International Women
      Law, Government, and Public Policy
RT military personnel

spinning
    SG   Visual and Performing Arts
    BT   craft arts

spinsters
    SG   Social Sciences and Culture
    BT   images of women
         women
    RT   attitudes
         completion complex
         divorce
         life styles
         linguistic sexism
         maiden aunts
         marital status
         old maids
         single parents
         single women

spirit guides
    SG   Language, Literature, Religion, and
         Philosophy
    BT   religious workers

spirit possession
    SG   Language, Literature, Religion, and
         Philosophy
    RT   passive behavior
         somnambulism

spirits
    SG   Language, Literature, Religion, and
         Philosophy
    NT   ancestor spirits
         evil spirits

spiritual communication
    SG   Language, Literature, Religion, and
         Philosophy
    NT   channeling
         divining
         fasting
         glossolalia
         holy communion
         meditation
         phrenology
         prayer

(cont.)

spiritual communication (*cont.*)
    NT   psychic readings
         psychometry
         religious music
         rites
         sacred dance
         sacrifice
         trances
    RT   fortune telling
         religious groups
         spiritualism

spiritual feminism
    SG   History and Social Change
         Language, Literature, Religion, and
            Philosophy
    DG   Cultural and Political Movements
    BT   feminism
    RT   goddess worship
         patriarchal religion
         spirituality
         thealogy
         wicca
         witchcraft
         womanism
         womanspirit
         women religious

spiritual mediums
    SG   Language, Literature, Religion, and
         Philosophy
    BT   mediums

spiritualism
    SG   Language, Literature, Religion, and
         Philosophy
    DG   Cultural and Political Movements
    RT   belief systems
         mediums
         religion
         religions
         religious experience
         seances
         spiritual communication
         trances

---

spiritualists
  SG Language, Literature, Religion, and
       Philosophy
  BT religious workers
  RT folk healers
      native healers

spirituality
  SG Language, Literature, Religion, and
       Philosophy
  NT female spirituality
  RT asceticism
      channeling
      cultural feminism
      ecofeminism
      goddesses
      gods
      holy men
      holy women
      meditation
      mysticism
      nature
      prayer
      purification rites
      religion
      saints
      spiritual feminism
      tarot
      wicca

spirituals
  SG Visual and Performing Arts
  BT religious music
  RT blues
      folk music
      gospel music
      protest music
      slave songs

spokesmen
  USE **spokespersons**

spokespersons
  SG Communications
      Economics and Employment
      Law, Government, and Public Policy
  UF spokesmen
                                          (cont.)

spokespersons *(cont.)*
  RT guardians

sponsored research
  SG Education
      Law, Government, and Public Policy
  BT research
  NT federally sponsored research
      state sponsored research
  RT appropriations
      funding
      laboratories
      regulations
      research bias

sponsors
  SN *Professional superiors who provide spe-*
      cific recommendations, introductions,
      and opportunities for job advance-
      ment.
  SG Education
  RT mentors

spontaneous abortion
  SG Natural Sciences and Health
  BT abortion
  RT ectopic pregnancy
      miscarriage

sports
  SG Communications
      Education
      Natural Sciences and Health
  NT archery
      baseball
      basketball
      bicycling
      bowling
      canoeing
      contact sports
      crew
      cricket
      fencing
      field hockey
      football
      golf
      gymnastics
                                          (cont.)

sports (*cont.*)
- NT   ice hockey
  - ice skating
  - judo
  - karate
  - lacrosse
  - mountaineering
  - professional sports
  - racquetball
  - roller skating
  - running
  - sailing
  - skiing
  - soccer
  - softball
  - squash
  - swimming
  - tennis
  - track and field
  - volleyball
  - weight lifting
  - wrestling
- RT   arts, entertainment, and media occupations
  - athletics
  - collegiate athletics
  - comparable worth
  - equal access
  - fair play
  - financial aid
  - hand eye coordination
  - intramurals
  - locker rooms
  - Olympic Games
  - playgrounds
  - professional athletes
  - professional athletics
  - sports enthusiasts
  - testosterone

sports awards
- SG   Natural Sciences and Health
  - Social Sciences and Culture
- BT   awards
- RT   athletics

sports enthusiasts
- SG   Communications
  - Social Sciences and Culture
- UF   sportsmen
- RT   sports

sports journalism
- SG   Communications
- BT   journalism
- RT   athletics
  - professional sports

sports officials
- SG   Economics and Employment
  - Natural Sciences and Health
- BT   arts, entertainment, and media occupations
  - officials
- RT   athletics

sportscasters
- SG   Communications
  - Economics and Employment
- BT   arts, entertainment, and media occupations

sportsmanship
- USE   **fair play**

sportsmen
- USE   **sports enthusiasts**

spouse abuse
- SG   Social Sciences and Culture
- BT   abuse
- NT   husband abuse
  - wife abuse
- RT   marital violence
  - women's shelters

spouse rape
- USE   **domestic rape**

spouse support
- SG   Economics and Employment
  - Law, Government, and Public Policy
  - Social Sciences and Culture

(*cont.*)

UF=Use for   BT=Broader term   NT=Narrower term   RT=Related term   451

spouse support (*cont.*)
- RT alimony
  - financial arrangements
  - legal settlements
  - marriage and family law

spouses
- SG Social Sciences and Culture
- NT corporate spouses
  - former spouses
  - husbands
  - military spouses
  - political spouses
  - wives
- RT dependents
  - hosts
  - marriage
  - married couples
  - polygamy
  - significant others

spreadsheets
- DG Types and Forms of Materials

squash
- SG Natural Sciences and Health
- BT sports

squatters
- SG Social Sciences and Culture
- RT homeless
  - slums
  - temporary housing

Sri Lankan
- DG National and Regional Descriptors
- BT Asian

staff
- SG Economics and Employment
- NT support staff

stamina
- USE **physical endurance**

stamps
- SG Visual and Performing Arts

(*cont.*)

stamps (*cont.*)
- NT food stamps
- RT images of women

standardized tests
- SG Education
- BT testing

standards
- SG Economics and Employment
  - Education
  - Social Sciences and Culture
- NT academic standards
  - beauty standards
  - job standards
  - living standards
  - male standards
- RT criteria
  - diagnoses
  - norms
  - performance appraisal
  - values

standards of living
- USE **living standards**

starlets
- USE **aspiring actors**

starvation
- SG International Women
  - Natural Sciences and Health
- RT eating disorders
  - famine
  - malnutrition
  - poverty

the state
- SG History and Social Change
  - Law, Government, and Public Policy
- RT citizenship
  - government
  - political systems
  - state formation

state agencies
- SG Law, Government, and Public Policy

(*cont.*)

state agencies *(cont.)*
- BT   public agencies
- RT   states

state aid
- SG   Economics and Employment
     Education
     Law, Government, and Public Policy
- BT   aid
- RT   equity funding
     federal aid

state assistance programs
- SG   Economics and Employment
     Law, Government, and Public Policy
- BT   assistance programs
- RT   public assistance

state courts
- SG   Law, Government, and Public Policy
- BT   courts
- RT   states

state employment
- SG   Economics and Employment
     Law, Government, and Public Policy
- BT   employment

state formation
- SN   *Dynamics of political, social, and historical processes by which small territories or units gradually form or become integrated into a single nation or sovereign entity.*
- SG   International Women
     Law, Government, and Public Policy
     Social Sciences and Culture
- RT   community
     government
     nationalism
     society
     the state

state government
- SG   Law, Government, and Public Policy
- BT   government
- RT   assemblymen

(cont.)

state government *(cont.)*
- RT   assemblywomen
     states

state legislation
- SG   Law, Government, and Public Policy
- BT   legislation
- RT   reproductive rights
     states

state regulations
- SG   Law, Government, and Public Policy
- BT   regulations
- RT   prostitution
     states

state religion
- SG   Language, Literature, Religion, and
     Philosophy
     Law, Government, and Public Policy
- BT   religion
- RT   civil religion
     freedom of worship
     patriotism
     separation of church and state

state sponsored research
- SG   Education
     International Women
     Law, Government, and Public Policy
     Science and Technology
- BT   sponsored research

state taxes
- SG   Law, Government, and Public Policy
- BT   taxes
- NT   property taxes
     sales taxes
- RT   states

stateless societies
- SG   Law, Government, and Public Policy
     Social Sciences and Culture
- BT   society
- RT   utopias

statements

DG Types and Forms of Materials
NT financial statements

states

SG Law, Government, and Public Policy
RT state agencies
state courts
state government
state legislation
state regulations
state taxes

statesmanship
USE **diplomacy**

statesmen
USE **diplomats**
political leaders

statistical analysis

SG Education
Natural Sciences and Health
Science and Technology
Social Sciences and Culture
BT data analysis
RT quantitative analysis

statisticians

SG Economics and Employment
Science and Technology
BT professional occupations
scientific and technical occupations

statistics

SG Science and Technology
BT mathematics
RT actuarials
cohort analysis
econometrics
random sampling

Statue of Liberty

SG History and Social Change
BT images of women

statues

SG Visual and Performing Arts
DG Types and Forms of Materials
RT sculpture

status

SG Social Sciences and Culture
NT cultural status
economic status
legal status
marital status
occupational status
political status
professional status
social status
socioeconomic status
status of women
tax exempt status
RT achievement need
census
class division
families
image
money
prestige
social class
upward mobility

status of women

SG History and Social Change
Social Sciences and Culture
BT status

status reports

DG Types and Forms of Materials
BT reports

statutes

DG Types and Forms of Materials

steelworkers

SG Economics and Employment
BT manufacturing occupations
workers

steering

SG Law, Government, and Public Policy
(cont.)

SN=Scope note   SG=Subject group   DG=Delimiters group   USE=Use

steering (*cont.*)
BT   discriminatory practices

stenographers
SG   Economics and Employment
BT   clerical occupations
     female intensive occupations

stepchildren
SG   Natural Sciences and Health
     Social Sciences and Culture
BT   children
RT   blended families
     remarriage
     stepparents

stepfathers
SG   Social Sciences and Culture
BT   fathers
NT   gay stepfathers
RT   divorce
     stepparents

stepmothers
SG   Social Sciences and Culture
BT   images of women
     mothers
NT   lesbian stepmothers
RT   divorce
     stepparents
     stereotyping

stepparents
SG   Social Sciences and Culture
BT   parents
RT   adoptive parents
     birth parents
     blended families
     custody
     parent child relationships
     parenting
     remarriage
     stepchildren
     stepfathers
     stepmothers

stereotypes
SG   Social Sciences and Culture
NT   age stereotypes
     racial stereotypes
     sex stereotypes
RT   attitudes
     conceptual errors
     deviant behavior
     discriminatory language
     dress codes
     gender differences
     images of women
     job standards
     jokes
     myths
     personal columns
     queen bee syndrome
     sex/gender systems
     stereotyping

stereotyping
SG   Social Sciences and Culture
NT   media stereotyping
     sex role stereotyping
RT   ableism
     ageism
     attitudes
     beauty standards
     bias
     children
     circular reasoning
     class discrimination
     classism
     diagnoses
     discrimination
     diversity
     doubly disadvantaged
     feminine principle
     femininity
     gay men
     group dynamics
     heterosexual privilege
     images of girls
     images of women
     labels
     language
     lesbians

(*cont.*)

UF = Use for   BT = Broader term   NT = Narrower term   RT = Related term

stereotyping (*cont.*)
- RT majority culture
  - names
  - nonsexist language
  - older adults
  - older women
  - people of color
  - perceptual bias
  - public opinion
  - racism
  - roles
  - sex/gender systems
  - sexism
  - stepmothers
  - stereotypes
  - stigmas
  - straights
  - surnames
  - welfare mothers
  - women of color

sterility
- SG Natural Sciences and Health
- RT infertility
  - sperm
  - sterilization
  - surrogate fathers
  - testosterone

sterilization
- SG Natural Sciences and Health
- BT birth control
- NT eugenic sterilization
  - involuntary sterilization
- RT bioethics
  - contraception
  - fallopian tubes
  - informed consent
  - pregnancy
  - sterility
  - tubal ligation
  - vasectomy

sterilization reversal
- SG Natural Sciences and Health
- NT tubal ligation reversal
  - vasectomy reversal

stevedores
- USE **longshore workers**

stewardesses
- USE **flight attendants**

stigmas
- SG Social Sciences and Culture
- RT stereotyping
  - taboos

stillbirth
- SG Natural Sciences and Health
- BT infant mortality
- RT childbirth
  - prenatal care

stimulants
- SG Natural Sciences and Health
  - Social Sciences and Culture
- NT caffeine
- RT substance abuse

stock exchanges
- SG Economics and Employment
- BT organizations
- RT banks
  - investments

stock markets
- SG Economics and Employment
- RT stockbrokers

stock options
- SG Economics and Employment
- RT profits

stockbrokers
- SG Economics and Employment
- BT financial occupations
  - marketing and sales occupations
- RT stock markets

storefront churches
- SG Language, Literature, Religion, and Philosophy
- BT churches

stories
>SG Language, Literature, Religion, and
>   Philosophy
>DG Types and Forms of Materials
RT fables
>fairy tales
>legends
>mythology
>parables
>short stories
>storytelling

storytelling
>SG Communications
>   Language, Literature, Religion, and
>   Philosophy
RT authors
>discourse
>folk culture
>language
>narratives
>oral history
>oral literature
>oral tradition
>raconteurs
>stories

straights
>SN *Slang; those with a preference for
>   heterosexual intimacies.*
>SG History and Social Change
>   Social Sciences and Culture
RT bisexuality
>compulsory heterosexuality
>heterosexuality
>stereotyping

strategies
>SG Social Sciences and Culture
NT career strategies
>coping strategies
>survival strategies

stratification
>SG Social Sciences and Culture
NT social stratification
RT class
>discrimination

(cont.)

stratification *(cont.)*
RT gender
>race

stream of consciousness
>SG Language, Literature, Religion, and
>   Philosophy
>   Natural Sciences and Health
>   Social Sciences and Culture
RT literature
>psychotherapy

street harassment
>SG Social Sciences and Culture
UF girl watching
>wolfing
BT sexual harassment
RT aggressive behavior
>eve teasing
>verbal abuse
>violence against women

street people
USE **homeless**

street theater
>SG Visual and Performing Arts
BT theater

street vendors
>SG Economics and Employment
>   International Women
BT vendors
RT black markets
>dual economy
>entrepreneurs
>informal sector

stress
>SG Natural Sciences and Health
NT occupational stress
>psychological stress
RT adjustment
>behavior modification
>biofeedback
>coping strategies
>counseling

(cont.)

UF=Use for BT=Broader term NT=Narrower term RT=Related term

stress (*cont.*)

RT heart disease
  hypertension
  illness
  life styles
  massage
  meditation
  migraine headaches
  mother syndrome
  psychosomatic disorders
  superwoman syndrome
  tension headaches
  ulcers
  vacations

stress (physical)

SG Natural Sciences and Health
RT aerobic exercise
  athletics
  attitudes
  childbirth
  diseases
  pregnancy

strikes

SG History and Social Change
  Law, Government, and Public Policy
BT protest actions
RT arbitration
  contracts
  labor disputes
  mediation
  pickets
  social change
  unemployment
  unions

strippers

SG Economics and Employment
  Visual and Performing Arts
BT arts, entertainment, and media
  occupations
  female intensive occupations

structural discrimination

SG History and Social Change
  Social Sciences and Culture
(*cont.*)

structural discrimination (*cont.*)

BT discrimination
RT institutional racism
  institutional sexism
  organizations
  social organization

structural linguistics

SG Language, Literature, Religion, and
  Philosophy
BT linguistics

structural unemployment

SN *Unemployment related to basic shifts
  in the economy, such as the emer-
  gence of new industries and the effects of automation; difficult to control, long-term, and persistent.*
SG Economics and Employment
  Social Sciences and Culture
BT unemployment
RT profits

structuralism

SG Language, Literature, Religion, and
  Philosophy
DG Cultural and Political Movements
RT criticism
  poststructuralism

struggles

SG History and Social Change
NT liberation struggles
RT nonviolence
  protest actions
  revolutionary movements
  social change
  social movements

strumpets

SG History and Social Change
  Social Sciences and Culture
BT images of women

stubbornness

SG Social Sciences and Culture
BT attitudes

---

student aid
 USE **student financial aid**

student financial aid
 SG Education
 UF student aid
 BT financial aid
 NT assistantships
   fellowships
   scholarships
 RT educational costs
   educational reform
   educational subsidies
   grants
   internships
   loans
   student loans
   tuition grants

student government
 SG Education
 BT government

student housing
 SG Education
   Law, Government, and Public Policy
 BT housing
 NT dormitories
   residence halls

student leadership
 SG Education
 BT leadership

student loans
 SG Education
 BT loans
 RT educational costs
   federal aid
   student financial aid

student motivation
 SG Education
 BT motivation
 RT academic achievement
   academic aptitude
   fear of failure

(*cont.*)

student motivation (*cont.*)
 RT positive reinforcement
   students

student quotas
 SG Education
 BT quotas
 RT admissions criteria

student recruitment
 SG Education
 RT admissions
   admissions criteria
   athletics

students
 SG Education
 NT adult students
   college students
   commuting students
   exchange students
   foreign students
   married students
   part time students
   pregnant students
   reentry students
   transfer students
 RT aptitude
   graduation ceremonies
   student motivation

studies
 DG Types and Forms of Materials

study abroad
 SG Education
 RT exchange students

study groups
 SG History and Social Change
   Social Sciences and Culture
 BT educational activities
   groups

subconscious
 SG Natural Sciences and Health
   Social Sciences and Culture

(*cont.*)

subconscious (*cont.*)
RT dreams
hypnotism
mind
unconscious

subculture
SG Social Sciences and Culture
BT culture
RT cults
life styles

subject headings
DG Types and Forms of Materials

subjective knowledge
SG Education
Language, Literature, Religion, and
Philosophy
Social Sciences and Culture
BT knowledge
RT cognitive processes

subjectivism
DG Cultural and Political Movements

subjugation
SG Social Sciences and Culture
RT self sacrifice

submissive behavior
SG Social Sciences and Culture
BT behavior
RT learned helplessness

subordination
SG History and Social Change
Social Sciences and Culture
NT subordination of women
RT dependent behavior
oppression

subordination of women
SG History and Social Change
Social Sciences and Culture
BT subordination
RT oppression

(cont.)

subordination of women (*cont.*)
RT sex discrimination

subsidies
SG Law, Government, and Public Policy
NT educational subsidies
housing subsidies
transportation subsidies

subsidized housing
USE **public housing**

subsistence agriculture
SG Economics and Employment
International Women
BT agriculture
RT domestic food production
rural poverty

substance abuse
SG Natural Sciences and Health
BT abuse
NT alcohol abuse
drug abuse
RT abstention
abstinence
addiction
alcoholism
birth defects
caffeine
codependency
crisis centers
diet pills
drug addiction
drug rehabilitation
drugs
family conflict
family counseling
gambling
individual counseling
prenatal influences
prescription drugs
stimulants
therapy
tranquilizers
withdrawal

SN=Scope note   SG=Subject group   DG=Delimiters group   USE=Use

substitute teaching
SG   Education
BT   teaching
RT   part time employment

suburbs
SG   Social Sciences and Culture
RT   communities
rural areas
urban areas

subway workers
SG   Economics and Employment
BT   transportation occupations
NT   train conductors

success
SG   Social Sciences and Culture
RT   academic awards
achievement
failure
fear of failure
fear of success
motivation

succubi
SG   Language, Literature, Religion, and Philosophy
BT   evil spirits
images of women

suction lipectomy
USE **liposuction surgery**

Sudanese
DG   National and Regional Descriptors
BT   African
Middle Eastern

sudden infant death syndrome
SG   Natural Sciences and Health
UF   crib death
BT   diseases
RT   infant mortality
infants
premature infants

suffrage
SG   History and Social Change
Law, Government, and Public Policy
RT   citizenship
enfranchisement
feminism
franchise
the woman question
voting rights
woman's rights

suffrage movements
SG   History and Social Change
DG   Cultural and Political Movements
BT   social movements
RT   civil rights
first wave feminism
foremothers
protofeminism
social change
women's history
women's movement

suffragettes
USE **suffragists**

suffragists
SG   History and Social Change
UF   suffragettes
RT   antisuffrage movement
feminists
militance
reformers

sugar diabetes
USE **diabetes**

suicide
SG   Social Sciences and Culture
NT   suttee
RT   at risk populations
death
depression
drugs

suits
USE **lawsuits**

UF=Use for   BT=Broader term   NT=Narrower term   RT=Related term   461

summaries
- DG   Types and Forms of Materials

superego
- SG   Social Sciences and Culture
- RT   guilt
      moral reasoning
      values

superintendents
- SG   Economics and Employment
      Education
- BT   education occupations

supermom
- SG   Economics and Employment
      Social Sciences and Culture
- BT   mothers
- RT   momism
      mother syndrome
      overachievement
      superwoman syndrome

superstitions
- SG   Language, Literature, Religion, and
      Philosophy
- RT   vampires

supervisor attitudes
- SG   Economics and Employment
- BT   attitudes
- RT   bias
      mentors
      motivation

supervisors
- SG   Economics and Employment
- UF   foremen
- BT   administrative support occupations

superwoman
- SG   Economics and Employment
      History and Social Change
- BT   images of women

superwoman syndrome
- SN   *The need to excel in multiple roles as*
      mother, wife, and full-time worker.
- SG   Economics and Employment
      History and Social Change
      Social Sciences and Culture
- RT   angel in the house
      balancing work and family life
      female headed households
      homemaking
      images of women
      mother syndrome
      mothers
      multiple roles
      overachievement
      self sacrifice
      stress
      supermom
      workaholics

suppers
- SG   History and Social Change
      Social Sciences and Culture
- BT   social activities
- NT   potluck suppers

supplementary benefits
- SG   Economics and Employment
- BT   benefits
- RT   Social Security
      welfare

support groups
- SG   History and Social Change
- BT   groups
- RT   extended families
      support systems

support staff
- SG   Economics and Employment
- BT   staff
- RT   administrative support occupations

support systems
- SN   *Networks of emotional, social, and*
      material support, both formal and
      informal.

(cont.)

support systems (*cont.*)
    SG Social Sciences and Culture
UF social support systems
RT beauty parlors
     car pools
     collectives
     community
     coping strategies
     day care centers
     extended families
     families
     feminist methods
     friends
     hot lines
     living alone
     networks
     public assistance
     single women
     support groups
     women identified women
     women's groups
     working parents

Supreme Court
    SG Law, Government, and Public Policy
BT courts

surgeons
    SG Economics and Employment
        Natural Sciences and Health
BT health care occupations
RT physicians

surgery
    SG Natural Sciences and Health
BT medical sciences
NT cosmetic surgery
     plastic surgery
     psychosurgery
     reconstructive surgery
RT general anesthesia

surgical procedures
    SG Natural Sciences and Health
UF operations
BT medical procedures
NT caesarian section

                      (*cont.*)

surgical procedures (*cont.*)
    NT dilatation and curettage
        episiotomy
        hysterectomy
        male circumcision
        mastectomy
        oophorectomy
        tubal ligation
        vasectomy
    RT anesthesia
        cancer
        informed consent
        malignant tumors
        tumors

Surinamese
    DG National and Regional Descriptors
    BT Latin American

surnames
    SG Social Sciences and Culture
    BT names
    NT birth name
        slave name
    RT children
        hyphenated names
        kinship
        labels
        matronymy
        Ms
        name rights
        patronymy
        stereotyping

surrealism
    DG Cultural and Political Movements

surrogate families
    SG Social Sciences and Culture
    BT families
        surrogates

surrogate fathers
    SG Social Sciences and Culture
    BT fathers
        surrogates
    RT artificial insemination

                      (*cont.*)

UF = Use for   BT = Broader term   NT = Narrower term   RT = Related term

surrogate fathers (cont.)
RT birth fathers
     donors
     infertility
     sterility

surrogate mothers
SG Social Sciences and Culture
BT mothers
     surrogates
RT artificial insemination
     birth mothers
     birth parents
     donors
     embryo transfer
     infertility
     insemination
     reproductive technologies

surrogates
SG Social Sciences and Culture
NT legal guardians
     surrogate families
     surrogate fathers
     surrogate mothers
RT chaperones

surveys
DG Types and Forms of Materials

survival strategies
SG Social Sciences and Culture
BT strategies
RT life skills

survivors
SG Law, Government, and Public Policy
RT crimes

suttee
SN *Historic Hindu rite of widow suicide by burning alive on husband's funeral pyre.*
SG International Women
     Language, Literature, Religion, and Philosophy
BT suicide

(cont.)

suttee (cont.)
RT bride burning
     funeral rites
     gynocide
     widows

sweatshops
SG Economics and Employment
RT factories
     offshore production plants
     unfair labor practices

Swedish
DG National and Regional Descriptors
BT Scandinavian

swimming
SG Natural Sciences and Health
BT sports

Swiss
DG National and Regional Descriptors
BT European

swooning
SG Natural Sciences and Health
RT fainting

syllabi
DG Types and Forms of Materials

symbolism
SG Language, Literature, Religion, and Philosophy
     Social Sciences and Culture
     Visual and Performing Arts
DG Cultural and Political Movements
RT culture
     values

symbols
SG Language, Literature, Religion, and Philosophy
     Social Sciences and Culture
     Visual and Performing Arts
NT art symbols
     literary symbols
     religious symbols

(cont.)

symbols (*cont.*)
RT allegory
ankh
figurative language
iconography
icons
language
rings
tribal markings

sympathetic pregnancy
SG Natural Sciences and Health
BT pregnancy
RT male pregnancy

sympathy
SG Natural Sciences and Health
Social Sciences and Culture
BT emotions

symposia
SG History and Social Change
Social Sciences and Culture
BT activities
RT educational activities

synagogues
SG Language, Literature, Religion, and
Philosophy
BT religious facilities
RT congregations

synchrony
SN *Moving together in harmony; used to
describe interactional patterns between people or in groups.*
SG Natural Sciences and Health
RT communication
empathy
group dynamics
personal relationships

synergy
SN *Used to describe the experience of energy among individuals or in a
group where the whole is greater
than the sum of its parts.*
SG Social Sciences and Culture
RT group dynamics

synopses
DG Types and Forms of Materials

syntax
SG Language, Literature, Religion, and
Philosophy
BT linguistics

syphilis
SG Natural Sciences and Health
BT sexually transmitted diseases

Syrian
DG National and Regional Descriptors
BT Middle Eastern

systems analysts
SG Economics and Employment
Science and Technology
BT professional occupations
scientific and technical occupations
RT computer programmers

systems theory
SG Social Sciences and Culture
BT theory

tables
DG Types and Forms of Materials

taboos
SG Social Sciences and Culture
BT customs
RT blood
sexual behavior
stigmas
uncleanliness

tactual perception
   SG Social Sciences and Culture
BT perception

Tahitian
   DG National and Regional Descriptors
BT Pacific

tailors
   SG Economics and Employment
       Visual and Performing Arts
UF seamstresses
BT clothing workers
RT dressmakers

Taiwanese
   DG National and Regional Descriptors
BT Asian

talent
   SG Education
       Visual and Performing Arts
RT artistic ability
     creativity

talk
   SG Language, Literature, Religion, and
       Philosophy
BT verbal communication
RT communication
     conversation
     dialects
     discourse
     gestures
     gossip
     interpersonal communication
     interruptions
     jargon
     language
     sign language
     verbal ability

talk shows
   SG Communications
BT shows
RT advice shows
     radio

(cont.)

talk shows *(cont.)*
RT television

tampons
   SG Natural Sciences and Health
RT menstruation
     sanitary napkins
     toxic shock syndrome

tank tops
   SG Social Sciences and Culture
BT clothing

Tanzanian
   DG National and Regional Descriptors
BT African

tapes
   DG Types and Forms of Materials
NT audiotapes
     cassettes
     magnetic tapes
     reel to reel tapes
     videotapes

tapestry
   SG Visual and Performing Arts
BT craft arts

tarot
   SG Language, Literature, Religion, and
       Philosophy
       Social Sciences and Culture
RT folk culture
     spirituality
     tarot reading

tarot reading
   SG Language, Literature, Religion, and
       Philosophy
       Social Sciences and Culture
BT fortune telling
RT tarot

task forces
   SG History and Social Change
       Social Sciences and Culture

(cont.)

SN = Scope note   SG = Subject group   DG = Delimiters group   USE = Use

task forces (*cont.*)
  BT organizations
  RT committees

tattoos
     SG Social Sciences and Culture
  RT adornment

tax exempt status
     SG Law, Government, and Public Policy
  BT status
  RT nonprofit organizations
        taxes
        voluntary organizations

tax incentives
     SG Economics and Employment
        Law, Government, and Public Policy
  BT incentives
  RT taxes

tax laws
     SG Economics and Employment
        Law, Government, and Public Policy
  BT laws
  RT taxes

tax reform
     SG Economics and Employment
        Law, Government, and Public Policy
  RT Economic Recovery Tax Act of 1981
        Tax Reform Act of 1985

Tax Reform Act of 1985
     DG Laws and Regulations
  RT tax reform

taxation
     SG Economics and Employment
        Law, Government, and Public Policy
  RT taxes

taxes
     SG Law, Government, and Public Policy
  NT federal taxes
        income tax
        property taxes
                     (*cont.*)

taxes (*cont.*)
  NT state taxes
  RT community problems
        educational facilities
        federal budget
        laws
        marriage tax
        net income
        private clubs
        singles
        tax exempt status
        tax incentives
        tax laws
        taxation
        tuition tax credit

taxi drivers
     SG Economics and Employment
  BT drivers

tea leaf reading
     SG Language, Literature, Religion, and
        Philosophy
        Social Sciences and Culture
  BT fortune telling

tea pouring
     SG Economics and Employment
        Social Sciences and Culture
  RT manners
        social entertaining
        teas

tea rooms
     SG Social Sciences and Culture
  RT clubs

teach ins
     SG Education
        History and Social Change
  BT educational activities
  RT nontraditional education
        protest actions

teacher aides
     SG Economics and Employment
        Education
                     (*cont.*)

---

teacher aides (cont.)
- BT education occupations
  female intensive occupations
  paraprofessional occupations

teacher education
- SG Education
- UF teacher training
- BT education
- RT inservice education
  normal schools

teacher motivation
- SG Education
- BT motivation

teacher student relationships
- SG Education
- BT relationships

teacher training
- USE **teacher education**

teachers
- SG Economics and Employment
  Education
- BT education occupations
  female intensive occupations
  professional occupations
- RT faculty retrenchment
  music
  tenure

teaching
- SG Education
- NT substitute teaching
- RT academic rank
  burnout
  course objectives
  faculty
  pedagogy
  scholars

teaching assistants
- SG Education
- BT education occupations
- RT faculty

team playing
- SG Economics and Employment
  Education
- RT athletics
  management techniques
  socialization

teas
- SG History and Social Change
  Social Sciences and Culture
- BT social activities
- RT tea pouring

teases
- SG Social Sciences and Culture
- BT images of women
- RT flirtation

technical assistance
- SG Economics and Employment
  International Women
  Science and Technology
- RT technology transfer

technical education
- SG Education
- BT education

technical writing
- SG Language, Literature, Religion, and
  Philosophy
- BT writing
- RT science reporting

technicians
- SG Economics and Employment
  Natural Sciences and Health
  Science and Technology
- BT craft occupations
  paraprofessional occupations

technology
- SG Science and Technology
- NT appropriate technology
  food technology
  land use technology
  reproductive technologies

(cont.)

technology (*cont.*)

RT agriculture
automation
built environment
communications
computer science
equal access
impact on women
industrialization
information sciences
job retraining
nuclear energy
quality of life
reproductive hazards at work

technology development

SG Science and Technology

BT development

RT appropriate technology
artificial intelligence
automation
communication satellites
computer science
cottage industry
energy
foreign aid
industrialization
industries
inventions
medical sciences
military
modernization
patents
technology transfer
telecommunications
telecommuting
underdevelopment

technology transfer

SN *Process whereby a group or agency in the developed world shares technical knowledge and resources with a group or agency in the developing world.*

SG International Women

RT developed nations
developing nations

(*cont.*)

technology transfer (*cont.*)

RT fourth world
technical assistance
technology development
third world

tee shirts

SG Social Sciences and Culture

BT clothing

teenage fathers

SG Social Sciences and Culture

BT fathers

RT education
paternity
teenage marriage
teenage pregnancy

teenage marriage

SG Social Sciences and Culture

BT marriage

RT age of consent
teenage fathers
teenage mothers
teenage pregnancy

teenage mothers

SG Social Sciences and Culture

BT mothers

RT adoption
at risk populations
early childbearing
education
teenage marriage
teenage pregnancy
unwanted pregnancy
women living in poverty

teenage pregnancy

SG Natural Sciences and Health

UF adolescent pregnancy

BT pregnancy

RT childbearing age
early childbearing
maternal age
maternal and infant welfare
maternity homes

(*cont.*)

UF = Use for   BT = Broader term   NT = Narrower term   RT = Related term

teenage pregnancy (*cont.*)
- RT permissive child rearing practices
  sex education
  single mothers
  teenage fathers
  teenage marriage
  teenage mothers

teenagers
- SG Social Sciences and Culture
- DG Age Levels
- NT adolescents
- RT adolescence
  children
  parent child relationships
  parenting
  runaways

telecommunications
- SG Communications
  Science and Technology
- BT communications
- RT communication satellites
  computer science
  electronic mail
  electronic media
  satellite communications
  satellites
  technology development
  teleconferencing

telecommuting
- SN *Using a computer and telecommunica-*
  tions equipment to work at home.
- SG Economics and Employment
  Science and Technology
- RT computer terminals
  cottage industry
  electronic cottage
  home based work
  piecework
  technology development

teleconferences
- SG History and Social Change
  Social Sciences and Culture
- BT conferences

(*cont.*)

teleconferences (*cont.*)
- RT teleconferencing

teleconferencing
- SG Communications
- RT electronic mail
  satellite communications
  telecommunications
  teleconferences

telephone operators
- SG Communications
  Economics and Employment
- BT clerical occupations
  female intensive occupations
  operators

telephones
- SG Communications
  Science and Technology
- RT hot lines

television
- SG Communications
- BT electronic media
- NT cable television
  commercial television
  educational television
  public television
- RT advice shows
  announcers
  bias
  broadcasters
  commercials
  documentaries
  game shows
  network ratings
  program ratings
  ratings
  shows
  soap operas
  talk shows
  television personalities
  videos
  violence

television commercials
SG Communications
BT commercials
RT images of women

television coverage
SG Communications
BT media coverage

television personalities
SG Communications
    Economics and Employment
UF hosts (media)
BT arts, entertainment, and media
    occupations
RT anchors
    broadcasters
    hosts
    images of women
    television

temperance movement
SG History and Social Change
    Language, Literature, Religion, and
    Philosophy
DG Cultural and Political Movements
BT social movements
RT drinking prohibition
    moral reform

temples
SG Language, Literature, Religion, and
    Philosophy
BT religious facilities
RT congregations

temporary employment
SG Economics and Employment
BT employment

temporary housing
SG Law, Government, and Public Policy
    Social Sciences and Culture
BT housing
NT crisis shelters
    halfway houses
    hostels
(cont.)

temporary housing (cont.)
RT community health services
    homeless
    squatters

temporary workers
SG Economics and Employment
UF temps
BT workers

temps
USE **temporary workers**

temptation
SG Language, Literature, Religion, and
    Philosophy
RT devil
    Eve
    original sin
    paradise
    snakes

temptresses
SG History and Social Change
    Language, Literature, Religion, and
    Philosophy
    Social Sciences and Culture
BT images of women
RT femmes fatales
    seduction

tenant farming
SG Economics and Employment
BT farming

tennis
SG Natural Sciences and Health
BT sports

tension headaches
SG Natural Sciences and Health
BT headaches
RT stress

tenure
SG Economics and Employment
    Education
(cont.)

UF=Use for   BT=Broader term   NT=Narrower term   RT=Related term

tenure (*cont.*)
- RT   academic freedom
  - academic rank
  - blind review
  - contract renewal
  - discrimination
  - faculty
  - job security
  - promotions
  - references
  - teachers
  - tenure track

tenure track
- SG   Education
- RT   academic rank
  - tenure

terminal illness
- SG   Natural Sciences and Health
  - Social Sciences and Culture
- BT   illness
- RT   death
  - death and dying
  - euthanasia
  - hospices
  - right to die

territoriality
- SG   Social Sciences and Culture
- RT   animal behavior

terrorism
- SG   International Women
  - Law, Government, and Public Policy
- RT   abortion clinics
  - ethnic intimidation
  - protest actions
  - terrorists
  - violence

terrorists
- SG   International Women
  - Law, Government, and Public Policy
- RT   terrorism

test bias
- SG   Education
- BT   bias
- RT   gender bias
  - older adults
  - psychological testing
  - race bias
  - racial and ethnic differences
  - social class
  - testing

test tube babies
- USE **in vitro fertilization**

testicles
- SG   Natural Sciences and Health
- UF   balls
- BT   genitals

testimonials
- DG   Types and Forms of Materials
- BT   activities

testimony
- SG   Law, Government, and Public Policy
- RT   hearings

testing
- SG   Education
  - Social Sciences and Culture
- UF   tests and measurements
- NT   aptitude tests
  - career interest inventories
  - competency based tests
  - examinations
  - intelligence tests
  - personality tests
  - psychological testing
  - standardized tests
- RT   admissions criteria
  - assessment
  - counseling
  - intelligence
  - math ability
  - research bias
  - test bias
  - tests

testosterone
  SG Natural Sciences and Health
  BT androgens
  RT sports
      sterility

tests
  SG Natural Sciences and Health
      Science and Technology
      Social Sciences and Culture
  DG Types and Forms of Materials
  NT blood tests
      drug tests
      virginity tests
  RT research methods
      testing

tests and measurements
  USE **testing**

textbook bias
  SG Education
  BT bias
  RT nonsexist textbooks
      racial discrimination

textbooks
  SG Education
  NT nonsexist textbooks
  RT desex
      images of girls
      racial equality
      sex role stereotyping

textile design
  SG Visual and Performing Arts
  BT design

textile industry
  SG Economics and Employment
  BT industries
  RT clothing
      clothing workers
      designers
      factories
      manufacturing occupations

textile making
  SG Visual and Performing Arts
  BT craft arts

texts
  SG Language, Literature, Religion, and
      Philosophy
  NT female authored texts
      sacred texts
  RT feminist criticism
      feminist scholarship
      feminist writing
      fiction
      womanist writing

Thai
  DG National and Regional Descriptors
  BT Asian

Thai American
  DG Ethnic, Racial, and Religious
      Descriptors

thealogy
  SN *Coined term referring to woman-cen-*
      tered theology.
  SG Language, Literature, Religion, and
      Philosophy
  BT feminist theology
  RT goddess worship
      goddesses
      herstory
      Mother/Father God
      religion
      spiritual feminism
      theology
      wicca
      witchcraft
      womanist theology

theater
  SG Visual and Performing Arts
  UF theater arts
      theatre
  BT performing arts
  NT collaborative theater
      drama

(cont.)

UF=Use for   BT=Broader term   NT=Narrower term   RT=Related term

theater (*cont.*)

NT   experimental theater
     group developed theater
     improvisation
     musical theater
     street theater
     vaudeville

RT   acting
     casting
     plays
     shows

theater arts
   USE **theater**

theater criticism

SG   Visual and Performing Arts
BT   criticism

theaters

SG   History and Social Change
     Social Sciences and Culture
BT   facilities

theatre
   USE **theater**

theism

DG   Cultural and Political Movements

theology

SG   Language, Literature, Religion, and
     Philosophy
BT   humanities
NT   feminist theology
     liberation theology
     womanist theology
RT   belief systems
     cosmology
     divinity
     dogma
     dogmatism
     dualism
     gods
     hermeneutics
     incarnation
     miracles

(cont.)

theology (*cont.*)

RT   patriarchal religion
     patriarchy
     religion
     religious beliefs
     salvation
     thealogy

theory

SN   *Use of a more specific term is recom-*
     mended.
SG   Social Sciences and Culture
NT   art theory
     economic theory
     exchange theory
     feminist theory
     game theory
     information theory
     labor theory of value
     literary theory
     management theory
     music theory
     network theory
     organizational theory
     political theory
     systems theory
RT   criticism

therapeutic abortion

SG   Natural Sciences and Health
BT   abortion
RT   miscarriage

therapists

SG   Economics and Employment
     Natural Sciences and Health
     Social Sciences and Culture
BT   health care occupations
     professional occupations
NT   occupational therapists
     physical therapists
     psychotherapists
     speech therapists

therapy

SG   Natural Sciences and Health
     Social Sciences and Culture

(cont.)

SN=Scope note   SG=Subject group   DG=Delimiters group   USE=Use

therapy (*cont.*)
- NT art therapy
  - aversion therapy
  - cathartic therapy
  - chemotherapy
  - diet therapy
  - drug therapy
  - electroconvulsive therapy
  - family therapy
  - feminist therapy
  - gestalt therapy
  - group therapy
  - hormone therapy
  - music therapy
  - physical therapy
  - psychotherapy
  - radiation therapy
- RT confidentiality
  - diseases
  - drugs
  - incest victims
  - mental disorders
  - mental health treatment
  - narcotic drugs
  - psychoanalysis
  - substance abuse
  - tumors

thermography
- SG Natural Sciences and Health
- BT medical procedures
- RT breast diseases
  - breast examination

thesauri
- DG Types and Forms of Materials
- BT reference books

theses
- DG Types and Forms of Materials

thinness
- SG Natural Sciences and Health
  - Social Sciences and Culture
- RT body image
  - dieting
  - eating disorders

(*cont.*)

thinness (*cont.*)
- RT fat liberation
  - trimness

third parties
- USE **minor parties**

third world
- SG Economics and Employment
  - International Women
  - Law, Government, and Public Policy
- RT apartheid
  - basic human needs
  - collective farms
  - colonialism
  - cultural imperialism
  - developing nations
  - economic development
  - economic development models
  - exploitation
  - famine
  - fifth world
  - foreign aid policy
  - foreign investment policy
  - fourth world
  - hunger
  - informal sector
  - international perspective
  - markets
  - multinational corporations
  - piecework
  - technology transfer
  - water
  - women in development

three day measles
- USE **rubella**

thyroid gland
- SG Natural Sciences and Health
- BT glands

Tibetan
- DG National and Regional Descriptors
- BT Asian

---

time
- SG   Social Sciences and Culture
- RT   space
  time management

time management
- SG   Economics and Employment
- BT   management
- RT   efficiency
  personal management
  time

time use studies
- SG   Economics and Employment
  Education
- RT   efficiency
  planning

tipping
- SN   *Used to describe point at which status and salaries fall as larger numbers of women or minorities enter a profession or occupation.*
- SG   Economics and Employment
- UF   feminization of occupations
  feminization of professions
- RT   backlash
  critical mass
  equilibrium
  occupational sex segregation
  organizational behavior
  women in

Title IV (Civil Rights)
- SN   *Civil Rights Act of 1974*
- DG   Laws and Regulations

Title IX (Education)
- SN   *Education Amendments of 1972*
- DG   Laws and Regulations
- RT   Civil Rights Restoration Act of 1987
  women's athletics

Title VI (Civil Rights)
- SN· *Civil Rights Act of 1964*
- DG   Laws and Regulations

Title VII (Civil Rights)
- SN   *Civil Rights Act of 1964*
- DG   Laws and Regulations

Title VII (Public Health)
- SN   *Public Health Service Act*
- DG   Laws and Regulations

Title VIII (Public Health)
- SN   *Public Health Service Act*
- DG   Laws and Regulations

Title X (Public Health)
- SN   *Public Health Service Act*
- DG   Laws and Regulations

Title XX (Dependent Care)
- SN   *Social Security Act of 1974.*
- DG   Laws and Regulations

titles
- SG   Language, Literature, Religion, and Philosophy
- RT   forms of address
  Ms
  names
  naming
  rank
  sexist language

titles (nobility)
- SG   International Women
  Law, Government, and Public Policy
- NT   baronesses
  countesses
  dames
  duchesses
  ladies (nobility)
  peeresses
  princesses
  queens
- RT   feudalism
  inheritance customs
  rank
  royalty
  socioeconomic class
  upper class

(cont.)

titles (nobility) *(cont.)*
RT wealth

tobacco
SG Economics and Employment
RT smoking

tobacco industry
SG Economics and Employment
BT industries
RT agricultural, fishing, and forestry
     occupations

Togan
DG National and Regional Descriptors
BT African

tokenism
SG Economics and Employment
     History and Social Change
RT affirmative action
     equal opportunity

tolerance
SG Language, Literature, Religion, and
     Philosophy
RT patience
     reconciliation
     values

tomboys
SG Social Sciences and Culture
BT images of girls
RT dolls
     sex role stereotyping

tombstones
DG Types and Forms of Materials

tool and die makers
SG Economics and Employment
     Science and Technology
BT craft occupations

torch singers
SG Visual and Performing Arts
BT singers

totalitarianism
DG Cultural and Political Movements

totemism
SG Language, Literature, Religion, and
     Philosophy
     Social Sciences and Culture
RT kinship
     rites
     worship

touching
SG Social Sciences and Culture
BT forms of affection
RT sexual behavior

tour guides
SG Economics and Employment
BT female intensive occupations
     service occupations

toxemia
SG Natural Sciences and Health
RT pregnancy

toxic shock syndrome
SG Natural Sciences and Health
BT diseases
RT menstruation
     tampons

toxic waste
USE **hazardous waste**

toys
SG Social Sciences and Culture
RT child development
     dolls
     play

track and field
SG Natural Sciences and Health
BT sports

trade unions
SG Economics and Employment
BT unions

UF=Use for   BT=Broader term   NT=Narrower term   RT=Related term

trades
> SG Economics and Employment
> NT retail trade
>   skilled trades
> RT craft occupations
>   skill training
>   unions

traditional warfare
> SG Law, Government, and Public Policy
> BT warfare

traditionalism
> DG Cultural and Political Movements

traditions
> SG Language, Literature, Religion, and
>   Philosophy
>   Social Sciences and Culture
> NT oral tradition
>   religious traditions
> RT celebrations
>   ceremonies
>   customs
>   family history
>   folk culture
>   rites

traffic accidents
> SG Economics and Employment
> BT accidents
> RT automobile insurance

traffic in women
> USE **sex tourism**

tragedy
> SG Language, Literature, Religion, and
>   Philosophy
> BT drama
> RT irony

train conductors
> SG Economics and Employment
>   Science and Technology
> BT railroad workers
>   subway workers

trainers
> SG Economics and Employment
> RT training

training
> SG Economics and Employment
>   Education
> NT assertiveness training
>   childbirth training
>   job training
>   leadership training
>   management training
>   sensitivity training
>   skill training
> RT job development
>   trainers
>   welfare reform

training centers
> SG Education
> BT centers

training objectives
> SG Education
>   Social Sciences and Culture
> BT objectives

traits
> SG Social Sciences and Culture
> NT personality traits

trances
> SG Language, Literature, Religion, and
>   Philosophy
> BT spiritual communication
> RT channeling
>   mediums
>   seances
>   spiritualism

tranquilizers
> SG Natural Sciences and Health
> BT psychotropic drugs
> RT prescription drugs
>   psychotherapy
>   substance abuse

SN=Scope note   SG=Subject group   DG=Delimiters group   USE=Use

transcendentalism
> DG Cultural and Political Movements

transcripts
> DG Types and Forms of Materials

transfer income
> SG Economics and Employment
>   Law, Government, and Public Policy
> BT income

transfer students
> SG Education
> BT students

transference
> SG Social Sciences and Culture
> NT countertransference
> RT defense mechanisms
>   experts
>   psychoanalysis

transformational grammar
> SG Language, Literature, Religion, and
>   Philosophy
> BT grammar
> RT language structure

transit systems
> SG Law, Government, and Public Policy
> RT appropriations
>   transportation

transitions
> SG Language, Literature, Religion, and
>   Philosophy
>   Social Sciences and Culture
> RT life cycles
>   rites of passage
>   second careers

translations
> DG Types and Forms of Materials

translators
> SG Economics and Employment
>   Language, Literature, Religion, and
>   Philosophy
> BT writers
> RT interpreters

transnational banks
> USE **multinational banks**

transnational corporations
> USE **multinational corporations**

transportation
> SG Science and Technology
> NT air transportation
>   public transportation
>   rail transportation
> RT barrier free access
>   car pools
>   transit systems

transportation industry
> SG Economics and Employment
> BT industries

transportation occupations
> SG Economics and Employment
> BT occupations
> NT boat operators
>   drivers
>   flight attendants
>   heavy equipment operators
>   movers
>   pilots
>   railroad workers
>   road workers
>   seafarers
>   subway workers

transportation subsidies
> SG Law, Government, and Public Policy
> BT subsidies
> RT appropriations

transsexualism
> USE **transsexuality**

UF=Use for   BT=Broader term   NT=Narrower term   RT=Related term   479

transsexuality
- SG Natural Sciences and Health
- UF transsexualism
  - transsexuals
- BT sexuality
- RT cross dressing

transsexuals
- USE **transsexuality**

transvestites
- SG Natural Sciences and Health
- RT cross dressing

trashing
- SN *Politically motivated, destructive criticism or character assassination, often in the guise of honest conflict.*
- SG History and Social Change
  - Social Sciences and Culture
- RT ad feminam
  - aggressive behavior

travel agents
- SG Economics and Employment
- BT agents

travel literature
- SG Language, Literature, Religion, and Philosophy
- BT literature

travelogues
- DG Types and Forms of Materials

treaties
- DG Types and Forms of Materials

treatises
- DG Types and Forms of Materials

treatment
- SG Natural Sciences and Health
- NT mental health treatment
- RT communicable diseases

treatments
- DG Types and Forms of Materials

treaty ratification
- SG Law, Government, and Public Policy
- BT ratification
- RT global security

trends
- SG Economics and Employment
  - Social Sciences and Culture
- NT economic trends
  - occupational trends
  - population trends
  - social trends

trial marriage
- SG Social Sciences and Culture
- BT marriage

trials (courtroom)
- SG Law, Government, and Public Policy
- RT juries
  - legal system
  - sentencing

tribadism
- SG Natural Sciences and Health
- BT sexual behavior
- RT lesbians

tribal art
- SG Visual and Performing Arts
- BT art
- RT ethnic studies
  - material culture
  - tribal music

tribal customs
- SG Social Sciences and Culture
- BT customs
- RT female circumcision
  - fertility rites
  - initiation rites
  - tribal markings

tribal markings
- SG International Women
- Social Sciences and Culture
- RT adornment
- body art
- ceremonies
- makeup
- rites
- ritual disfigurement
- symbols
- tribal customs

tribal music
- SG Visual and Performing Arts
- BT music
- RT ethnomusicology
- rites
- tribal art

tricks
- SN *Slang.*
- SG Social Sciences and Culture
- RT prostitution

trimness
- SG Natural Sciences and Health
- RT body image
- dieting
- physical fitness
- thinness

Trinidadian
- DG National and Regional Descriptors
- BT West Indian

triplets
- USE **multiple births**

Trotskyism
- DG Cultural and Political Movements

troubadours
- SG History and Social Change
- Language, Literature, Religion, and
- Philosophy
- Visual and Performing Arts
- BT musicians

(cont.)

troubadours *(cont.)*
- RT chivalry
- courtly love
- lyric poetry
- poets
- romances

trousers
- USE **pants**

truck drivers
- SG Economics and Employment
- BT drivers

trust
- SG Language, Literature, Religion, and
- Philosophy
- Natural Sciences and Health
- Social Sciences and Culture
- BT attitudes
- emotions
- RT belief systems
- ethics
- forms of affection
- nurturance
- social values

trustees
- SG Economics and Employment
- Education
- BT volunteer occupations
- RT governing boards

tshiwila
- SN *African rite—performed in Angola, Zambia, and Zaire—for mature women affirming dignity of women among women.*
- SG Social Sciences and Culture
- RT rites
- women's culture

tubal ligation
- SG Natural Sciences and Health
- UF tube tying
- BT surgical procedures
- RT fallopian tubes

(cont.)

---

tubal ligation (*cont.*)
  RT   sterilization

tubal ligation reversal
  SG   Natural Sciences and Health
  BT   sterilization reversal

tubal pregnancy
  SG   Natural Sciences and Health
  BT   pregnancy

tube tying
  USE **tubal ligation**

tuition grants
  SG   Education
  BT   grants
  RT   student financial aid

tuition tax credit
  SG   Education
  BT   credit
  RT   educational costs
       taxes

tummy tucks
  USE **cosmetic surgery**

tumors
  SG   Natural Sciences and Health
  NT   benign tumors
       malignant tumors
  RT   biopsy
       breast diseases
       physical health
       surgical procedures
       therapy

Tunisian
  DG   National and Regional Descriptors
  BT   African

Turkish
  DG   National and Regional Descriptors
  BT   European

turnover rates
  SG   Economics and Employment
  RT   employment
       job satisfaction
       occupational mobility
       occupational stress

tutoring
  SG   Education
  RT   academic enrichment
       basic skills

twins
  SG   Natural Sciences and Health
       Social Sciences and Culture
  NT   fraternal twins
       identical twins
       sororal twins
  RT   childbirth
       individual development
       multiple births

two career couples
  USE **dual career couples**

two career families
  USE **dual career families**

two income families
  SN   *Use where emphasis is on income;*
       where emphasis is on career, use
       dual career families .
  SG   Economics and Employment
       Social Sciences and Culture
  UF   dual worker families
  BT   families
  RT   dual career families
       family finances
       household division of labor
       household economics
       income
       moonlighting

two year colleges
  SG   Education
  DG   Education Levels
  BT   colleges

(*cont.*)

---

two year colleges (*cont.*)
- BT   higher education
- RT   community colleges

typesetters
- SG   Communications
      Economics and Employment
- BT   printing workers
- RT   compositors

typewriters
- SG   Communications
      Economics and Employment
      Science and Technology
- RT   office work
      word processing

typists
- SG   Economics and Employment
- BT   clerical occupations
      female intensive occupations

typography
- SG   Visual and Performing Arts
- BT   commercial art

tyranny
- SG   History and Social Change
      Law, Government, and Public Policy
- RT   human rights violations
      oppression

Ugandan
- DG   National and Regional Descriptors
- BT   African

ulcers
- SG   Natural Sciences and Health
- RT   repression
      stress

ultrasound
- SG   Natural Sciences and Health
- BT   medical procedures
- RT   amniocentesis
      fetal monitoring

umbilical cord
- SG   Natural Sciences and Health
- RT   childbirth

unaffiliated scholars
- USE **independent scholars**

unborn child
- USE **fetuses**

uncleanliness
- SG   Language, Literature, Religion, and
      Philosophy
      Natural Sciences and Health
- RT   attitudes
      taboos

uncles
- SG   Social Sciences and Culture
- RT   extended families
      family structure

unconscious
- SG   Social Sciences and Culture
- RT   subconscious

underachievement
- SG   Education
      Social Sciences and Culture
- BT   achievement
- RT   fear of success

underdeveloped nations
- USE **developing nations**

underdevelopment
- SG   Economics and Employment
      International Women
- RT   economic development
      fourth world
      technology development

underemployment
- SG   Economics and Employment
- BT   employment
- RT   unemployment

---

undergraduate degrees
SG   Education
BT   degrees
NT   bachelors' degrees

underground economy
SG   Economics and Employment
BT   economy
RT   informal sector

underground railroad
SG   History and Social Change
RT   abolition
     manumission
     slavery

underwear
SG   Social Sciences and Culture
BT   clothing
RT   lingerie

underwriters
SG   Economics and Employment
BT   managerial occupations

undocumented workers
SG   Economics and Employment
     International Women
BT   workers
RT   illegal immigrants
     immigration policy

unemployed
USE **unemployment**

unemployment
SG   Economics and Employment
UF   unemployed
NT   structural unemployment
     youth unemployment
RT   firing
     job layoffs
     outplacement
     social class
     strikes
     underemployment
     workers

unemployment compensation
SG   Economics and Employment
RT   unemployment insurance

unemployment insurance
SG   Economics and Employment
BT   insurance
RT   unemployment compensation

unemployment rates
SG   Economics and Employment
BT   socioeconomic indicators
RT   econometrics

unfair labor practices
SG   Economics and Employment
RT   labor disputes
     pregnancy discrimination
     quality of work life
     racial discrimination
     sex discrimination
     sweatshops
     work hazards

Uniformed Services Former Spouses' Protection Act
DG   Laws and Regulations
RT   military spouses

unilineal kinship
SG   Social Sciences and Culture
BT   kinship

union
SG   Language, Literature, Religion, and Philosophy
NT   consensual union
RT   bonding
     marriage

union membership
SG   Economics and Employment
     History and Social Change
RT   labor unions
     unions

unions
- SG Economics and Employment
- BT organizations
- NT labor unions
  trade unions
- RT arbitration
  collective bargaining
  contract renewal
  contracts
  labor contracts
  labor disputes
  mediation
  negotiators
  organizing
  pension funds
  strikes
  trades
  union membership
  workplace

unisex
- SG Social Sciences and Culture
- RT androgyny
  sex/gender systems

United States
- DG National and Regional Descriptors
- BT North American
- NT Appalachian
  Eastern
  Middle Atlantic
  Midwestern
  North Atlantic
  Northeastern
  Northern
  Northwestern
  Pacific Coast
  South Atlantic
  Southern
  Southwestern
  Western

universities
- SG Education
- BT educational facilities
- RT colleges

(cont.)

universities *(cont.)*
- RT higher education

unmarried fathers
USE **single fathers**

unmarried men
USE **single men**

unmarried mothers
USE **single mothers**

unmarried women
USE **single women**

unpaid employment
- SG Economics and Employment
- UF nonwage labor
- BT employment
- NT unpaid household labor
- RT economic value of women's work
  homemaking
  unpaid labor force
  valuing children
  volunteer work

unpaid household labor
- SG Economics and Employment
  International Women
- BT household labor
  unpaid employment
  unpaid labor force
- RT economic value of women's work
  private sphere

unpaid labor force
- SG Economics and Employment
- BT labor force
- NT unpaid household labor
- RT female intensive occupations
  unpaid employment
  wage labor

unrequited love
- SG Language, Literature, Religion, and
  Philosophy
  Social Sciences and Culture

(cont.)

unrequited love (*cont.*)
- BT   love
- RT   loneliness
  - personal relationships
  - romance

unskilled laborers
- USE **laborers**

unskilled workers
- USE **workers**

untouchables
- SG   International Women
  - Social Sciences and Culture
- RT   caste
  - classism
  - exploitation
  - intercaste marriage
  - labor movement
  - poverty

unwanted pregnancy
- SG   Natural Sciences and Health
- BT   pregnancy
- RT   abortion
  - adoption
  - birth fathers
  - birth mothers
  - teenage mothers

unwed mothers
- USE **single mothers**

upper body strength
- SG   Natural Sciences and Health
- BT   physical strength
- RT   aerobic exercise
  - athletics
  - military combat
  - muscular development
  - physical endurance

upper class
- SG   Economics and Employment
  - Social Sciences and Culture
- BT   class

(*cont.*)

upper class (*cont.*)
- RT   classism
  - elites
  - families
  - fathers
  - finishing schools
  - inherited wealth
  - living standards
  - maternal and infant welfare
  - mothers
  - philanthropists
  - power structure
  - preparatory schools
  - socialization
  - titles (nobility)
  - volunteers

upper class families
- SG   Social Sciences and Culture
- BT   families

Upper Voltan
- DG   National and Regional Descriptors
- BT   African

upward mobility
- SG   Social Sciences and Culture
- BT   mobility
- RT   ambition
  - career ladders
  - consumer economy
  - consumerism
  - monetary incentives
  - status

urban areas
- SG   International Women
  - Social Sciences and Culture
- UF   large cities
- NT   inner city
  - municipalities
- RT   communities
  - neighborhoods
  - suburbs

urban development

SN *Policies and programs designed to improve the economic and social life of the urban poor.*

SG International Women
Law, Government, and Public Policy

BT development

RT urban environment

urban environment

SG Science and Technology
Social Sciences and Culture

BT environment

RT urban development
urban planning

urban indicators

SG Economics and Employment
Social Sciences and Culture

BT socioeconomic indicators

urban migration

SG International Women
Social Sciences and Culture

BT migration

RT urbanization

urban planners

SG Economics and Employment
Law, Government, and Public Policy

BT social scientists

RT architects

urban planning

SG Law, Government, and Public Policy

UF city planning

BT planning

RT ethnic neighborhoods
urban environment
urban renewal
urbanization
zoning

urban renewal

SG International Women
Law, Government, and Public Policy

RT community development

(cont.)

urban renewal *(cont.)*

RT ghettos
homesteading
inner city
urban planning

urbanization

SG Social Sciences and Culture

RT postindustrial society
urban migration
urban planning

Uruguayan

DG National and Regional Descriptors

BT Latin American

usherettes

USE **ushers**

ushers

SG Economics and Employment

UF usherettes

BT service occupations

uterus

SG Natural Sciences and Health

UF womb

RT ankh
fibrocystic disease
speculums

utilitarianism

DG Cultural and Political Movements

utilities

SG Law, Government, and Public Policy
Science and Technology

BT organizations

NT electric utilities
gas utilities
public utilities
water utilities

utility credit

SG Law, Government, and Public Policy
Science and Technology

BT credit

UF=Use for   BT=Broader term   NT=Narrower term   RT=Related term

utopian communities
- SG Language, Literature, Religion, and Philosophy
  Social Sciences and Culture
- BT communities
- RT utopias

utopian literature
- SG Language, Literature, Religion, and Philosophy
- BT literature

utopian socialism
- DG Cultural and Political Movements
- BT socialism

utopianism
- DG Cultural and Political Movements

utopias
- SG History and Social Change
- RT classless society
  community
  life styles
  matriarchy
  stateless societies
  utopian communities

uxorial rights
- SN *Rights of a man to a woman's property and person.*
- SG Law, Government, and Public Policy
- BT rights
- RT marriage customs

uxoriousness
- SN *Term used to describe what is seen to be a man's excessive fondness of or submission to his wife.*
- SG Social Sciences and Culture
- RT marriage

uzr
- SN *Islamic ritual for airing discontent.*
- SG Social Sciences and Culture
- RT rites

vacations
- SG Economics and Employment
  Social Sciences and Culture
- RT leisure
  stress

vagina
- SG Natural Sciences and Health
- BT bodies
- NT hymen
- RT G spot
  genitals
  vaginal infections

vagina dentata
- SN *Image of "toothed vagina"; used as symbol of men's fear of sex with women.*
- SG Social Sciences and Culture
- BT images of women
- RT castrating females
  femmes fatales
  misogyny
  vampires

vaginal infections
- SG Natural Sciences and Health
- RT diseases
  vagina

vaginal orgasm
- SG Natural Sciences and Health
- BT orgasm

vaginismus
- SN *Painful spasm of the vagina.*
- SG Natural Sciences and Health
- BT gynecologic disorders

vaginitis
- SG Natural Sciences and Health
- BT gynecologic disorders

value
- SG Economics and Employment
- RT depreciation
  economic value of women's work

(cont.)

value (*cont.*)
RT insurance
money

value systems
SG Language, Literature, Religion, and
Philosophy
RT values

values
SG Language, Literature, Religion, and
Philosophy
Social Sciences and Culture
NT domestic values
personal values
religious values
social values
RT abortion laws
altruism
commitment
consumption
equality
equity
ethic of care
ethics
fairness
forgiveness
honesty
integrity
justice
loyalty
moral development
moral reform
morality
mores
narcissism
norms
nurturance
perfection
philosophy
popular culture
priorities
quality of life
religious ethics
sexual liberation
social behavior
social problems
(*cont.*)

values (*cont.*)
RT standards
superego
symbolism
tolerance
value systems
valuing children

valuing children
SG Law, Government, and Public Policy
Social Sciences and Culture
RT child care policy
childhood
children
economic value of women's work
employer supported day care
families
family attitudes
history of children
impact on children
parental leave
unpaid employment
values

vampires
SG Language, Literature, Religion, and
Philosophy
BT images of women
RT superstitions
vagina dentata

vamps
SG History and Social Change
Visual and Performing Arts
BT images of women

vandalism
SG Law, Government, and Public Policy
BT property crimes

vasectomy
SG Natural Sciences and Health
BT surgical procedures
RT sterilization

vasectomy reversal
SG Natural Sciences and Health
(*cont.*)

UF=Use for   BT=Broader term   NT=Narrower term   RT=Related term

vasectomy reversal (*cont.*)
BT   sterilization reversal

vaudeville
SG   Visual and Performing Arts
BT   theater
RT   actresses (historical)
     music
     musical theater
     popular music

VD
USE **sexually transmitted diseases**

VDT
USE **video display terminals**

vegetarianism
SG   Natural Sciences and Health
RT   nutrition

veiling of women
SG   International Women
     Social Sciences and Culture
RT   chador
     domestic code
     purdah
     ritual disfigurement
     seclusion
     veils

veils
SG   Social Sciences and Culture
BT   clothing
RT   chador
     harems
     hidjab
     purdah
     veiling of women

vendors
SG   Economics and Employment
     International Women
BT   marketing and sales occupations
NT   street vendors

venereal diseases
USE **sexually transmitted diseases**

Venezuelan
DG   National and Regional Descriptors
BT   Latin American

venture capital
SG   Economics and Employment
BT   capital

venture capitalists
SG   Economics and Employment
BT   financial occupations
RT   financiers

verbal ability
SG   Education
BT   ability
RT   language aptitude
     talk
     verbal communication

verbal abuse
SG   Language, Literature, Religion, and
     Philosophy
BT   abuse
RT   linguistic sexism
     physical abuse
     street harassment
     violence

verbal communication
SG   Language, Literature, Religion, and
     Philosophy
UF   oral communication
BT   communication
NT   conversation
     gossip
     talk
RT   correspondence
     verbal ability

verbal development
SG   Language, Literature, Religion, and
     Philosophy
     Social Sciences and Culture

(*cont.*)

verbal development (*cont.*)
  BT language development

veteran benefits
  SG Economics and Employment
  BT benefits

veteran preference
  SG Economics and Employment
      Law, Government, and Public Policy
  BT hiring policy

veterans
  SG Economics and Employment
      Law, Government, and Public Policy
  RT military
      military combat
      military personnel
      prisoners of war

veterinarians
  SG Economics and Employment
      Natural Sciences and Health
  BT health care occupations
      professional occupations
  RT animal caretakers

veterinary sciences
  SG Natural Sciences and Health
  RT natural sciences

viability
  SN *Ability of fetus to live outside mother's womb.*
  SG Natural Sciences and Health
  RT abortion
      conception
      fetuses
      religious law
      reproductive technologies

vibrators
  SG Natural Sciences and Health
  BT sexual aids

vice presidential office
  SG Law, Government, and Public Policy
                              (*cont.*)

vice presidential office (*cont.*)
  RT elections
      presidential office

vice presidents
  SG Economics and Employment
      Education
      International Women
      Law, Government, and Public Policy
  BT education occupations
      legal and political occupations
      managerial occupations
  RT presidents

victim services
  SG Law, Government, and Public Policy
      Social Sciences and Culture
  BT social services
  RT crisis centers
      incest victims

victimization
  SG Law, Government, and Public Policy
      Social Sciences and Culture
  RT blaming the victim
      learned helplessness
      victims

victimless crimes
  SG Law, Government, and Public Policy
  BT crimes

victims
  SG Language, Literature, Religion, and
      Philosophy
      Social Sciences and Culture
  NT crime victims
      incest victims
      rape victims
  RT accidents
      blaming the victim
      crimes
      individual counseling
      physical abuse
      sex crimes
      victimization
      violence

UF=Use for   BT=Broader term   NT=Narrower term   RT=Related term

Victorian Period
DG Historical Periods

video art
SG Visual and Performing Arts
BT media arts

video display terminals
SG Communications
     Economics and Employment
     Science and Technology
UF cathode ray tubes
     CRT
     VDT
RT computer terminals
     word processing
     work hazards

video games
SG Communications
     Education
     Social Sciences and Culture
BT games
NT computer games
RT hand eye coordination

videodisks
DG Types and Forms of Materials
BT disks

videos
SG Communications
     Visual and Performing Arts
NT music videos
RT documentaries
     film
     pornography
     television

videotapes
DG Types and Forms of Materials
BT tapes

Vietnam War
DG Historical Periods

Vietnamese
DG National and Regional Descriptors
BT Asian

Vietnamese American
DG Ethnic, Racial, and Religious
     Descriptors

viewer ratings
SG Communications
BT ratings
RT opinion polls
     public opinion

village communes
SG International Women
     Social Sciences and Culture
BT communes

violence
SG Social Sciences and Culture
NT domestic violence
     lynching
     sexual violence
     violence against children
     violence against women
RT abuse
     accidents
     aggressive behavior
     anger
     assault
     battered women
     child abuse
     civil disobedience
     counseling
     crimes
     elder abuse
     masochism
     patriarchy
     physical abuse
     pornography
     prevention
     protest actions
     rape
     riots
     sexual abuse
     television

(cont.)

violence (*cont.*)
  RT   terrorism
        verbal abuse
        victims
        violence in the media
        war

violence against children
  SG   Social Sciences and Culture
  BT   violence
  RT   child abuse
        child pornography

violence against women
  SG   Social Sciences and Culture
  BT   violence
  RT   crimes of honor
        crimes of passion
        cultural sadism
        eve teasing
        foot binding
        misogyny
        objectification
        pornography
        prostitution
        rape
        sex crimes
        slave rape
        street harassment
        weapons
        witch burning

violence in the media
  SG   Communications
  RT   images of women
        pornography
        violence

viragos
  SN   *Defined both as loud, overbearing wo-*
        men or shrews and as women of
        great stature, strength, and courage
        possessing "masculine" qualities of
        body and mind.
  SG   Social Sciences and Culture
  BT   images of women
  RT   amazons

                                      (*cont.*)

viragos (*cont.*)
  RT   perceptual bias

virgin birth
  SG   Language, Literature, Religion, and
        Philosophy
  RT   immaculate conception
        impregnation
        madonna
        Virgin Mary

Virgin Mary
  SG   Language, Literature, Religion, and
        Philosophy
  BT   images of women
  RT   cult of the virgin
        goddesses
        immaculate conception
        madonna
        Mother/Father God
        virgin birth

virginity
  SG   Natural Sciences and Health
  RT   celibacy
        chastity
        defloration
        hymen
        hymenoplasty
        marriage
        purity
        sexual abstinence
        virginity tests
        vows of chastity
        wedding nights

virginity tests
  SN   *Gynecologic examination performed to*
        determine virginity.
  SG   Natural Sciences and Health
        International Women
        Law, Government, and Public Policy
  BT   tests
  RT   virginity

UF=Use for   BT=Broader term   NT=Narrower term   RT=Related term   493

virgins

SG Language, Literature, Religion, and
    Philosophy
Natural Sciences and Health
BT images of girls
images of women
RT canonization
ideal woman
purity
saints

vision

SG Natural Sciences and Health
Social Sciences and Culture
RT eyeglasses

visionaries

SG Language, Literature, Religion, and
    Philosophy
RT female spirituality
mediums
mysticism
prophets
psychics
seers
shamans

visions

SG Language, Literature, Religion, and
    Philosophy
RT dreams
mysticism
prophecy
seers

visitation rights

SG Law, Government, and Public Policy
Social Sciences and Culture
BT rights
RT custodial parents
custody
noncustodial parents

visiting homemakers

SG Economics and Employment
Social Sciences and Culture
BT homemakers

(cont.)

visiting homemakers *(cont.)*

BT service occupations

visiting nurses

SG Economics and Employment
Natural Sciences and Health
BT nurses

visiting scholars

SG Education
BT scholars

visual arts

SG Visual and Performing Arts
UF fine arts
BT arts
NT architecture
cartoons
collage
comic strips
craft arts
decorative arts
drawing
engraving
fiber art
graphics
metal art
miniatures
mural art
painting
photography
portraits
poster art
printmaking
sculpture
visual diaries
RT aesthetics
art
art conservation
commercial art
design
film
film festivals
iconography
media arts
museums
performance art

(cont.)

SN=Scope note   SG=Subject group   DG=Delimiters group   USE=Use

visual arts (*cont.*)
  RT performing arts

visual diaries
  SG Language, Literature, Religion, and
        Philosophy
      Visual and Performing Arts
  DG Types and Forms of Materials
  BT diaries
      visual arts
  RT artists' books

visual impairments
  SG Natural Sciences and Health
  BT disabilities
  NT blindness
  RT disabled

visual perception
  SG Social Sciences and Culture
  BT perception

vital statistics
  SG Economics and Employment
      Social Sciences and Culture
  BT demographic measurements
  NT birth rates
      divorce rates
      fertility rates
      marriage rates
      mortality rates
      sex ratio

vocal music
  SG Visual and Performing Arts
  BT music
  NT choral music
      madrigals
      opera
      songs

vocational aptitude
  SG Economics and Employment
      Education
  BT aptitude
  RT career satisfaction
      job satisfaction
                                    (*cont.*)

vocational aptitude (*cont.*)
  RT job skills

vocational choice
  USE **career choice**

vocational counseling
  USE **occupational counseling**

vocational education
  SG Education
  BT education

vocational nurses
  SG Economics and Employment
      Natural Sciences and Health
  BT nurses

vocational rehabilitation
  SG Economics and Employment
      Education
  BT rehabilitation

voice
  SN *Narrative point of view.*
  SG Language, Literature, Religion, and
        Philosophy
  RT narratives
      prose

volleyball
  SG Natural Sciences and Health
  BT sports

voluntarism
  USE **volunteer work**

voluntary organizations
  SG Economics and Employment
  BT nonprofit organizations
  NT private voluntary organizations
  RT auxiliaries
      careers
      charities
      community relations
      philanthropy
      public service
                                    (*cont.*)

UF=Use for   BT=Broader term   NT=Narrower term   RT=Related term

voluntary organizations *(cont.)*
- RT   social services
- tax exempt status
- volunteer work
- volunteers

volunteer occupations
- SG   Economics and Employment
- BT   occupations
- NT   chairpersons
- community organizers
- directors
- trustees
- volunteers
- RT   legal and political occupations

volunteer work
- SG   Economics and Employment
- UF   voluntarism
- volunteering
- BT   work
- RT   altruism
- careers
- charitable work
- hobbies
- in kind contributions
- parent teacher organizations
- philanthropy
- social change
- social class
- social structure
- unpaid employment
- voluntary organizations
- volunteers
- women in
- work experience
- work history

volunteering
- USE **volunteer work**

volunteers
- SG   Economics and Employment
- Social Sciences and Culture
- BT   female intensive occupations
- service occupations
- volunteer occupations

(cont.)

volunteers *(cont.)*
- NT   docents
- RT   change agents
- club women
- laity
- social class
- upper class
- voluntary organizations
- volunteer work
- workers

voluptuousness
- SG   Social Sciences and Culture
- RT   images of women

voodoo
- DG   Cultural and Political Movements

voter registration
- SG   History and Social Change
- Law, Government, and Public Policy
- RT   civil rights movements
- discrimination
- voting
- voting rights

voting
- SG   Law, Government, and Public Policy
- RT   eligibility
- political action
- political participation
- political representation
- poll tax
- voter registration

voting behavior
- SG   History and Social Change
- BT   behavior
- RT   gender gap
- political parties
- politics

voting records
- SG   Law, Government, and Public Policy
- BT   records
- RT   ethnic groups
- gender gap

(cont.)

SN=Scope note   SG=Subject group   DG=Delimiters group   USE=Use

voting records (*cont.*)
- RT people of color

voting rights
- SG History and Social Change
  Law, Government, and Public Policy
- BT rights
- RT enfranchisement
  poll tax
  suffrage
  voter registration

votive rites
- SG Language, Literature, Religion, and
  Philosophy
- BT rites

vows
- SG Language, Literature, Religion, and
  Philosophy
  Law, Government, and Public Policy
- NT marriage vows
  vows of obedience
  vows of silence

vows of chastity
- SG Language, Literature, Religion, and
  Philosophy
- RT abstinence
  asceticism
  celibacy
  chastity
  novitiates
  nuns
  purity
  religious orders
  virginity
  women religious

vows of obedience
- SG Language, Literature, Religion, and
  Philosophy
- BT vows
- RT religious orders

vows of poverty
- SG Language, Literature, Religion, and
  Philosophy
- RT poverty
  religious orders

vows of silence
- SG Language, Literature, Religion, and
  Philosophy
- BT vows
- RT religious orders

vulnerability
- SG Natural Sciences and Health
  Social Sciences and Culture
- BT emotions

vulva
- SG Natural Sciences and Health
- BT genitals

vulvectomy
- SG Natural Sciences and Health
- BT female circumcision
- RT genital mutilation

wage differential
- USE **wage gap**

wage discrimination
- SG Economics and Employment
- BT discrimination
- RT comparable worth
  equal pay for equal work
  pay equity
  wage gap

wage earners
- SG Economics and Employment
- UF working men
  working women
  workmen
- NT wage earning women

wage earning mothers
- SG Economics and Employment
  Social Sciences and Culture

(*cont.*)

UF=Use for   BT=Broader term   NT=Narrower term   RT=Related term

wage earning mothers (*cont.*)
- UF   working mothers
- BT   mothers
       wage earning women
- RT   mothers working outside the home

wage earning wives
- SG   Economics and Employment
       Social Sciences and Culture
- UF   working wives
- BT   wage earning women
       wives
- RT   wives working outside the home

wage earning women
- SG   Economics and Employment
       Social Sciences and Culture
- UF   career girls
       working women
- BT   wage earners
       women
- NT   wage earning mothers
       wage earning wives
- RT   employment
       pin money
       women working outside the home

wage gap
- SG   Economics and Employment
- UF   earnings gap
       wage differential
- RT   comparable worth
       discriminatory practices
       economic value of women's work
       equal pay
       equal pay for equal work
       low pay
       occupational sex segregation
       pay equity
       wage discrimination
       wages

wage increases
- SG   Economics and Employment
- RT   performance appraisal

wage labor
- SG   Economics and Employment
- RT   paid employment
       unpaid labor force
       women working outside the home

wages
- SG   Economics and Employment
- UF   pay
       salaries
- NT   back pay
       equal pay
       low pay
- RT   benefits
       compensation packages
       income
       money
       pay equity
       wage gap

wages for housework
- SG   Economics and Employment
       Social Sciences and Culture
- RT   economic value of women's work
       household labor

waifs
- SG   History and Social Change
- BT   images of girls
       images of women

wailing
- SG   Language, Literature, Religion, and
       Philosophy
- BT   mourning

waiters
- SG   Economics and Employment
- UF   waitresses
- BT   service occupations

waiters' assistants
- SG   Economics and Employment
- UF   busboys
- BT   service occupations

waitresses
USE **waiters**

want ads
DG   Types and Forms of Materials

war
SG   History and Social Change
Law, Government, and Public Policy
RT   aggressive behavior
machismo
militarism
peace
violence
war crimes
warfare

war crimes
SG   Law, Government, and Public Policy
BT   crimes
RT   war

wards
SG   Law, Government, and Public Policy
Social Sciences and Culture
RT   guardians

warfare
SG   Law, Government, and Public Policy
NT   biological warfare
guerrilla warfare
nuclear warfare
traditional warfare
RT   antiwar movement
disarmament
military
military defense
war
weapons

washerwomen
USE **launderers**

WASP
USE **White Anglo Saxon Protestant**

watchmakers
SG   Economics and Employment
Science and Technology
BT   craft occupations

watchmen
USE **guards**

water
SN   *A basic human need, especially affect-*
ing women's lives in developing
countries.
SG   International Women
Science and Technology
RT   basic human needs
developing nations
irrigation
third world
water pollution

water management
SG   International Women
Science and Technology
BT   management
RT   sanitation

water pollution
SG   International Women
Science and Technology
BT   pollution
RT   corporate responsibility
environmental health
water

water resources
SG   International Women
Science and Technology
BT   natural resources

water utilities
SG   Law, Government, and Public Policy
Science and Technology
BT   utilities

wealth
SG   Economics and Employment
NT   inherited wealth
RT   affluence   *(cont.)*

---

wealth (*cont.*)
RT capital
    class identity
    dual economy
    images of women
    income
    living standards
    money
    prestige
    privilege
    social class
    social status
    titles (nobility)
    wealth distribution
    women living in poverty

wealth distribution
SG Economics and Employment
    Law, Government, and Public Policy
RT capital
    class
    economic equity
    income distribution
    inequality
    poverty
    socioeconomic status
    wealth

weapons
SG Law, Government, and Public Policy
RT gun control laws
    military trade
    violence against women
    warfare

weather reporters
SG Economics and Employment
UF weathermen
BT reporters

weathermen
USE **meteorologists**
    weather reporters

weavers
SG Economics and Employment
    Visual and Performing Arts
                                    (*cont.*)

weavers (*cont.*)
BT craft artists

weaving
SG Visual and Performing Arts
BT craft arts

wedding ceremonies
SG Language, Literature, Religion, and
    Philosophy
BT ceremonies
RT brides
    bridesmaids
    grooms
    marriage
    marriage licenses
    rites
    wedding nights
    wedding rings

wedding nights
SG Social Sciences and Culture
RT honeymoons
    marriage customs
    sex
    virginity
    wedding ceremonies

wedding rings
SG Social Sciences and Culture
BT rings
RT wedding ceremonies

weight lifting
SG Natural Sciences and Health
BT sports

weight perception
SG Natural Sciences and Health
BT perception
RT body image
    diets
    eating disorders

welders
SG Economics and Employment
Science and Technology
Visual and Performing Arts
BT craft occupations

welfare
SG Law, Government, and Public Policy
Social Sciences and Culture
NT child welfare
maternal and infant welfare
public welfare
social welfare
RT economically disadvantaged
family finances
food stamps
public assistance
social services
supplementary benefits
welfare system

welfare agencies
SG Law, Government, and Public Policy
Social Sciences and Culture
BT social agencies

welfare economics
SG Economics and Employment
Social Sciences and Culture
BT economics

welfare fraud
SG Law, Government, and Public Policy
BT fraud

welfare mothers
SG Law, Government, and Public Policy
Social Sciences and Culture
BT mothers
RT attitudes
stereotyping

welfare programs
SG Law, Government, and Public Policy
Social Sciences and Culture
BT programs
RT agencies
(cont.)

welfare programs (cont.)
RT social policy

welfare reform
SG Law, Government, and Public Policy
BT reforms
RT child care
social policy
training

welfare rights
SG Law, Government, and Public Policy
BT rights

welfare state
SG Economics and Employment
Law, Government, and Public Policy
RT nationalization
social policy
Social Security

welfare system
SG Law, Government, and Public Policy
RT social policy
welfare

wellness
SG Natural Sciences and Health
RT disease prevention
health
health seeking behavior
holistic medicine
illness
mental health

Welsh
DG National and Regional Descriptors
BT European

West German
DG National and Regional Descriptors
BT European

West Indian
DG National and Regional Descriptors
BT Latin American
NT Barbadan
(cont.)

West Indian (*cont.*)
- NT Cuban
    - Dominican
    - Grenadan
    - Haitian
    - Jamaican
    - Trinidadian

Western
- DG National and Regional Descriptors
- BT United States

wet nurses
- SG Natural Sciences and Health
- BT child care workers
- RT breast feeding
    - mammies

White
- DG Ethnic, Racial, and Religious
    - Descriptors

White Anglo Saxon Protestant
- DG Ethnic, Racial, and Religious
    - Descriptors
- UF WASP

white collar crime
- SG Law, Government, and Public Policy
- BT crime
- RT corruption

white collar workers
- SG Economics and Employment
- BT workers
- RT pink collar workers

White man
- USE **Caucasian**

white slavery
- SG Social Sciences and Culture
- BT slavery

wholesale trade industry
- SG Economics and Employment
- BT industries

whores
- USE **prostitutes**

WIC
- USE **Women, Infants, and Children Nutrition Program**

wicca
- SN *Practice of witchcraft within framework of women's spiritual identity; term also used for wise women healers.*
- SG Language, Literature, Religion, and Philosophy
- DG Cultural and Political Movements
- RT goddess worship
    - mother goddess
    - religion
    - spiritual feminism
    - spirituality
    - thealogy
    - wisdom
    - witchcraft
    - witches

wicking
- SN *A source of infection from IUDs.*
- SG Natural Sciences and Health
- RT intrauterine devices

widowerhood
- USE **widowers**

widowers
- SG Social Sciences and Culture
- UF widowerhood
- BT men
- RT death

widowhood
- USE **widows**

widows
- SG Social Sciences and Culture
- UF widowhood
- BT images of women
    - women

(*cont.*)

widows (*cont.*)
- RT death
  - suttee
  - women in transition
  - women living in poverty

wife abuse
- SG Social Sciences and Culture
- BT spouse abuse
- RT battered women
  - marital violence

wife rape
- USE **domestic rape**

wigs
- SG Natural Sciences and Health
  - Social Sciences and Culture
- RT appearance
  - body image
  - chemotherapy
  - coiffures
  - hair
  - hair loss
  - images of women

wills
- SG Law, Government, and Public Policy
- DG Types and Forms of Materials
- BT legal documents
- RT executors

wisdom
- SG Language, Literature, Religion, and
  - Philosophy
- RT crones
  - healers
  - holy women
  - mentors
  - mothers
  - older women
  - shamans
  - wicca
  - witches

witch burning
- SG History and Social Change
  - Language, Literature, Religion, and
  - Philosophy
- RT gynocide
  - martyrs
  - patriarchal religion
  - religious repression
  - violence against women

witch hunts
- SG History and Social Change
- RT witch persecutions

witch persecutions
- SG History and Social Change
- BT persecution
- RT gynocide
  - religious repression
  - witch hunts

witchcraft
- SG Language, Literature, Religion, and
  - Philosophy
- UF the Craft
- RT devil
  - healing
  - magic
  - spiritual feminism
  - thealogy
  - wicca
  - witches

witches
- SG History and Social Change
  - Language, Literature, Religion, and
  - Philosophy
- BT images of women
  - women
- RT covens
  - crones
  - female spirituality
  - healers
  - heretics
  - holy women
  - martyrs
  - religious refugees

(*cont.*)

UF=Use for   BT=Broader term   NT=Narrower term   RT=Related term

witches (cont.)
RT saints
     wicca
     wisdom
     witchcraft

withdrawal
SG Natural Sciences and Health
     Social Sciences and Culture
RT addiction
     dependent behavior
     learned helplessness
     narcotic drugs
     substance abuse

wives
SG Social Sciences and Culture
UF married women
BT women
     spouses
NT cowives
     first wives
     former wives
     runaway wives
     wage earning wives
     wives working outside the home
RT birth name
     divorce
     economic value of women's work
     husbands
     polygyny

wives working outside the home
SG Economics and Employment
     Social Sciences and Culture
UF working wives
BT wives
     women working outside the home
RT child care
     homemakers
     household division of labor
     wage earning wives

wolfing
USE **street harassment**

woman power
SG History and Social Change
BT power
RT activism
     anlu
     consciousness raising
     feminism
     sisterhood
     women's organizations

the woman question
SN *Historical term referring to extensive public and scholarly discussions about the social and political status of women.*
SG History and Social Change
     Social Sciences and Culture
RT feminine mystique
     feminism
     private sphere
     suffrage
     woman's rights

woman the gatherer
SG Social Sciences and Culture
BT images of women
RT man the hunter
     sex role stereotyping
     women's roles

woman's rights
SN *Refers to pre-1920 period.*
SG History and Social Change
     Language, Literature, Religion, and Philosophy
BT rights
RT feminism
     first wave feminism
     protofeminism
     suffrage
     the woman question
     women's history
     women's rights

womanculture
USE **women's culture**

---

womanhood
  SG Social Sciences and Culture
  RT cult of true womanhood
      images of women

womanism
  SN *Name for a distinctly Black woman's*
      perspective, although used by both
      Black and non-Black women.
  SG History and Social Change
      Language, Literature, Religion, and
        Philosophy
      Social Sciences and Culture
  DG Cultural and Political Movements
  RT Black feminism
      Black women's studies
      female chauvinism
      feminist theory
      sexual politics
      sisterhood
      spiritual feminism
      womanist theology
      womanist writing
      women's culture

womanist theology
  SG Language, Literature, Religion, and
        Philosophy
  BT theology
  RT feminist theology
      thealogy
      womanism

womanist writing
  SG Language, Literature, Religion, and
        Philosophy
  BT writing
  RT Black women's studies
      cultural feminism
      female authored texts
      feminist writing
      texts
      womanism
      women's media

womanizers
  SG History and Social Change
      Social Sciences and Culture
  RT philanderers

womanspirit
  SG Language, Literature, Religion, and
        Philosophy
  RT goddesses
      spiritual feminism
      women's culture

womb
  USE **uterus**

womb envy
  SG Natural Sciences and Health
      Social Sciences and Culture
  RT male pregnancy
      penis envy

women
  SN *Use the term* **woman** *or* **women** *to refer*
      to socially or culturally based refer-
      ences to gender, **female** *or* **females** *to*
      refer to biologically based references
      to sex.
  SG History and Social Change
      Natural Sciences and Health
      Social Sciences and Culture
  UF ladies
  NT actresses (historical)
      amazons
      assemblywomen
      baronesses
      battered women
      beauty queens
      brides
      businesswomen
      club women
      concubines
      congresswomen
      countesses
      courtesans
      crones
      dames
      daughters

                                            (cont.)

UF=Use for   BT=Broader term   NT=Narrow term   RT=Related term   505

women (*cont.*)

NT   duchesses
       ethnic women
       fallen women
       First Ladies (historical)
       geishas
       governesses
       granddaughters
       grandmothers
       heroines (historical)
       holy women
       homeless women
       hostesses (historical)
       ladies (historical)
       ladies (nobility)
       laywomen
       lesbians
       medicine women
       midwives
       mistresses
       mothers
       nonorgasmic women
       nymphs
       older women
       ombudswomen
       peeresses
       princesses
       queens
       reentry women
       rural women
       seamstresses (historical)
       single women
       sisters
       spinsters
       wage earning women
       widows
       witches
       wives
       women identified women
       women in transition
       women living in poverty
       women of color
       women of valor
       women religious
       women working outside the home

RT   females
       girls

                   (cont.)

women (*cont.*)

RT   images of women

women and

SN   *Use in postcoordination to refer to gender-related issues affecting women in various content areas.*

SG   Economics and Employment
       History and Social Change

RT   women in

women college students

SG   Education
BT   college students
RT   date rape
       reentry students
       reentry women
       sororities
       women's colleges

women identified women

SN   *Women whose primary friendships and support structures are with other women.*

SG   Social Sciences and Culture
BT   women
RT   female female relationships
       female friendships
       lesbianism
       lesbians
       relationships
       sisterhood
       support systems

women in

SN   *Use in postcoordination to refer to existence, roles, and impact of women in occupations and disciplines.*

SG   Economics and Employment
       Education
       History and Social Change

RT   affirmative action
       canon
       critical mass
       discrimination
       female intensive occupations
       invisibility

                   (cont.)

    SN=Scope note   SG=Subject group   DG=Delimiters group   USE=Use

women in (*cont.*)

RT   male intensive occupations
quotas
tipping
volunteer work
women and

women in development

SG   International Women
Law, Government, and Public Policy

RT   development
development studies
economic value of women's work
impact on women
interdisciplinary studies
multinational corporations
third world

women in politics

SG   Law, Government, and Public Policy

RT   appointed officials
gender gap
legal and political occupations
legislatures
political candidates
political office
politics
social legislation

women in science

SG   Economics and Employment
Natural Sciences and Health
Science and Technology

RT   scientific and technical occupations

women in the military

SG   Law, Government, and Public Policy

RT   battlefields
military
military combat
military spouses

women in transition

SG   Economics and Employment
Education
Social Sciences and Culture

BT   women

(*cont.*)

women in transition (*cont.*)

RT   displaced homemakers
divorce
older women
reentry women
widows

Women, Infants, and Children Nutrition Program

SN   *Supplemental food program, part of the National School Lunch Amendments of 1982.*

DG   Laws and Regulations

UF   WIC

RT   children living in poverty
nutrition
women living in poverty

women intensive careers

USE **female intensive occupations**

women intensive occupations

USE **female intensive occupations**

women intensive professions

USE **female intensive occupations**

women living in poverty

SG   Economics and Employment
Social Sciences and Culture

UF   feminization of poverty

BT   women

RT   Aid to Families with Dependent Children
at risk populations
child support
children living in poverty
community property laws
divorce
divorce laws
economic equity
economically disadvantaged
homeless women
impoverishment of women
living conditions
living standards
lower class
older adults

(*cont.*)

UF=Use for   BT=Broader term   NT=Narrower term   RT=Related term

women living in poverty *(cont.)*
- RT older women
  pauperization of women
  poverty
  single parent families
  teenage mothers
  wealth
  widows
  Women, Infants, and Children Nutrition
  Program

women of color
- SN *See Delimiters Display: Ethnic, Racial,*
  and Religious Descriptors for more
  specific terms.
- SG History and Social Change
  Social Sciences and Culture
- UF minority women
- BT people of color
  women
- RT ethnic women
  immigrants
  race
  stereotyping

women of valor
- SG Language, Literature, Religion, and
  Philosophy
  Social Sciences and Culture
- BT heroes
  women
- RT courage
  heroines (historical)

women owned business
- SG Economics and Employment
- BT business
- RT business ownership
  businesswomen
  entrepreneurs
  family owned business
  home based business
  minority owned business
  small business

women religious
- SG Economics and Employment
  Language, Literature, Religion, and
  Philosophy
- BT female intensive occupations
  religious workers
  women
- NT clergywomen
  nuns
  priestesses
- RT clergy
  convents
  female spirituality
  holy women
  laywomen
  ministers
  monasticism
  novitiates
  patriarchal religion
  priests
  religious orders
  spiritual feminism
  vows of chastity
  women's ordination

women working outside the home
- SG Economics and Employment
  Social Sciences and Culture
- UF working women
- BT women
- NT mothers working outside the home
  wives working outside the home
- RT feminine mystique
  pin money
  wage earning women
  wage labor

women's art
- SG Visual and Performing Arts
- BT art
- RT alternative spaces
  art matronage
  arts
  one woman art shows

women's athletics

- SG Communications
      Education
      Natural Sciences and Health
- BT athletics
- RT collegiate athletics
      Title IX (education)

women's centers

- SG Education
      Social Sciences and Culture
- BT centers

women's colleges

- SG Education
- BT single sex colleges
- RT alumnae
      women college students

women's culture

- SG Language, Literature, Religion, and
      Philosophy
      Social Sciences and Culture
- UF womanculture
- BT culture
- NT lesbian culture
- RT ankh
      Beguinism
      biculturalism
      community
      invisibility
      male norms
      matriarchy
      mikiri
      mikveh
      tshiwila
      womanism
      womanspirit
      women's language
      yin

Women's Educational Equity Act

- DG Laws and Regulations
- RT educational equity

women's groups

- SG History and Social Change

(*cont.*)

women's groups (*cont.*)

- BT groups
- NT professional women's groups
- RT coalition politics
      consciousness raising groups
      feminist organizations
      social clubs
      support systems

women's health movement

- SG History and Social Change
      Natural Sciences and Health
- DG Cultural and Political Movements
- BT women's movement
- RT cancer
      healing
      health
      health advocates
      health care
      health seeking behavior

women's history

- SG History and Social Change
- UF history of women
- BT history
- RT foremothers
      heroines (historical)
      herstory
      literary canon
      protofeminism
      suffrage movements
      woman's rights

women's language

- SG Language, Literature, Religion, and
      Philosophy
- BT language
- RT bilingualism
      language skills
      male norms
      mother tongue
      social dialects
      women's culture

women's lib

USE **women's liberation**

---

women's liberation

SG History and Social Change
UF women's lib
BT liberation
RT feminism
      feminist movement
      men's liberation
      women's movement

women's liberation movement

USE **women's movement**

women's literature

SG History and Social Change
      Language, Literature, Religion, and
        Philosophy
BT literature
NT lesbian literature
RT female authored texts
      feminist writing
      literary canon

women's magazines

SG Communications
      Language, Literature, Religion, and
        Philosophy
BT magazines
      women's media
RT feminist publications

women's media

SG Communications
      History and Social Change
BT mass media
NT feminist publications
      women's magazines
RT book stores
      communications equity
      communications industry
      equal access
      feminist writing
      freedom of the press
      journalism
      media coverage
      media portrayal
      media stereotyping
      newspapers

(cont.)

women's media *(cont.)*

RT press coverage
      social change
      womanist writing
      women's movement

women's movement

SG History and Social Change
DG Cultural and Political Movements
UF women's liberation movement
BT social movements
NT international women's movement
      women's health movement
RT feminism
      feminist movement
      suffrage movements
      women's liberation
      women's media

women's music

SG Visual and Performing Arts
BT music
RT all women ensembles
      feminist music
      music festivals

women's networks

SG History and Social Change
      Social Sciences and Culture
BT networks
NT old girl networks
RT female female relationships
      queen bee syndrome
      women's organizations

women's ordination

SG Language, Literature, Religion, and
        Philosophy
BT ordination
RT clergy
      nuns
      patriarchal religion
      priests
      religion
      religious orders
      women religious

women's organizations

    SG History and Social Change
BT organizations
NT feminist organizations
      nongovernmental women's organizations
      sororities
RT coalition politics
      collaboration
      woman power
      women's networks

women's pages

    SG Communications
RT advice columns
      journalism
      newspapers

women's rights

    SG History and Social Change
      Law, Government, and Public Policy
UF rights of women
BT rights
RT abortion movement
      bioethics
      feminism
      freedom of choice
      protofeminism
      woman's rights

women's roles

    SG History and Social Change
      Social Sciences and Culture
BT roles
RT femininity
      gender development
      gender ideology
      sex role stereotyping
      socialization
      woman the gatherer

women's shelters

    SG Social Sciences and Culture
BT shelters
RT crisis centers
      crisis intervention
      domestic violence
      spouse abuse

women's studies

    SG Education
      History and Social Change
      Social Sciences and Culture
BT interdisciplinary studies
NT Black women's studies
      Jewish women's studies
      Latina studies
RT Chicana studies
      cross cultural studies
      ethnic studies
      feminist studies
      gender studies
      mainstreaming
      men's studies

Wonder Woman

    SG Communications
      History and Social Change
BT images of women
RT comic strips

woodworkers

    SG Economics and Employment
      Visual and Performing Arts
BT construction occupations
      workers
RT craft arts

word processing

    SG Communications
      Economics and Employment
      Science and Technology
RT automation
      data entry operators
      secretaries
      typewriters
      video display terminals

work

    SN *Use of a more specific term is recommended.*
    SG Economics and Employment
      Social Sciences and Culture
NT charitable work
      church work
      culture work

(cont.)

work (*cont.*)
- NT   extension work
      home based work
      office work
      piecework
      shift work
      social work
      volunteer work
- RT   alternative work arrangements
      employment
      labor
      occupations
      work ethic
      work experience

work alienation
- SG   Economics and Employment
- BT   alienation
- RT   job alienation
      work attitudes

work attitudes
- SG   Economics and Employment
- BT   attitudes
- RT   absenteeism
      motivation
      work alienation
      work incentives

work ethic
- SG   Economics and Employment
- RT   motivation
      work

work experience
- SG   Economics and Employment
- BT   experience
- RT   volunteer work
      work
      work history

work force
- USE   **labor force**

work hazards
- SG   Natural Sciences and Health
- UF   occupational hazards

(cont.)

work hazards (*cont.*)
- UF   office hazards
- BT   hazards
- NT   reproductive hazards at work
- RT   health hazards
      occupational health and safety
      offices (facilities)
      unfair labor practices
      video display terminals

work history
- SG   Economics and Employment
- RT   labor force participation
      volunteer work
      work experience

work hours
- SG   Economics and Employment
- UF   man hours
- NT   shift work
- RT   compressed workweek
      employment
      employment schedules
      flexible work schedules
      workaholics

work incentive programs
- SG   Economics and Employment
      Law, Government, and Public Policy
- BT   programs
- RT   federal assistance programs

work incentives
- SG   Economics and Employment
- BT   incentives
- RT   efficiency
      work attitudes

work reentry
- SG   Economics and Employment
- RT   employment
      job hunting

work release programs
- SG   Economics and Employment
      Law, Government, and Public Policy
- BT   programs

(cont.)

work release programs (*cont.*)
RT probation
    restitution

work sharing
USE **job sharing**

work space
SG Economics and Employment
    Social Sciences and Culture
RT architecture
    ergonomics
    quality of work life
    space

work styles
SG Economics and Employment
NT management styles
RT efficiency

workaholics
SG Economics and Employment
    Social Sciences and Culture
RT superwoman syndrome
    work hours

workbooks
DG Types and Forms of Materials

workers
SG Economics and Employment
UF unskilled workers
    working men
    working women
    workmen
NT blue collar workers
    child care workers
    clothing workers
    construction workers
    extension workers
    factory workers
    farm workers
    food service workers
    foreign workers
    government workers
    health care workers
    home based workers

(*cont.*)

workers (*cont.*)
NT hotel workers
    household workers
    laborers
    library workers
    longshore workers
    metalworkers
    migrant workers
    operators
    paralegal workers
    pieceworkers
    pink collar workers
    pregnant workers
    printing workers
    prison workers
    railroad workers
    religious workers
    road workers
    sanitation workers
    social workers
    steelworkers
    temporary workers
    undocumented workers
    white collar workers
    woodworkers
RT animatrices rurales
    braceros
    careers
    manual labor
    occupations
    social class
    unemployment
    volunteers
    working class

working class
SG Economics and Employment
    Social Sciences and Culture
BT class
RT blue collar workers
    classism
    craft occupations
    factory workers
    maternal and infant welfare
    proletariat
    workers

working conditions
>   SG   Economics and Employment
> BT   conditions

working men
> USE **wage earners**
>   **workers**

working mothers
> USE **mothers working outside the home**
>   **wage earning mothers**

working papers
>   DG   Types and Forms of Materials
> BT   legal documents

working parents
>   SG   Economics and Employment
>   Social Sciences and Culture
> BT   parents
> RT   after school programs
>   balancing work and family life
>   child care leave
>   dual career couples
>   latchkey children
>   support systems

working wives
> USE **wage earning wives**
>   **wives working outside the home**

working women
> USE **wage earners**
>   **wage earning women**
>   **women working outside the home**
>   **workers**

workmen
> USE **wage earners**
>   **workers**

workplace
>   SG   Economics and Employment
> RT   labor unions
>   organizing
>   unions

workplace nurseries
>   SG   Economics and Employment
>   Social Sciences and Culture
> BT   corporate day care centers
>   nurseries

works in progress
>   DG   Types and Forms of Materials

workshops
>   SG   History and Social Change
>   Social Sciences and Culture
> BT   activities
> RT   conferences
>   educational activities

world views
>   SG   Language, Literature, Religion, and
>   Philosophy
> RT   belief systems
>   cosmology

World War I
>   DG   Historical Periods

World War II
>   DG   Historical Periods

worship
>   SG   Language, Literature, Religion, and
>   Philosophy
> NT   goddess worship
> RT   ceremonies
>   deity
>   divinity
>   domestic rites
>   goddesses
>   gods
>   rites
>   totemism

wrestling
>   SG   Natural Sciences and Health
> BT   sports

wrinkles
>   SG   Natural Sciences and Health

(cont.)

wrinkles (*cont.*)
- RT   body image
  - face lifts
  - skin

writers
- SG   Communications
  - Economics and Employment
  - Language, Literature, Religion, and Philosophy
  - Visual and Performing Arts
- BT   arts, entertainment, and media occupations
  - professional occupations
- NT   translators
- RT   artists
  - authors
  - copywriters
  - critics
  - editors
  - journalists
  - novelists
  - playwrights
  - poets
  - reporters

writing
- SG   Communications
  - Language, Literature, Religion, and Philosophy
- NT   creative writing
  - descriptive writing
  - feminist writing
  - proposal writing
  - technical writing
  - womanist writing
- RT   authors
  - communication
  - correspondence
  - criticism
  - figurative language
  - humanities
  - journalism
  - language skills
  - literacy
  - literature
  - written language

written language
- SG   Language, Literature, Religion, and Philosophy
- BT   language
- NT   braille
- RT   language structure
  - writing

yearbooks
- DG   Types and Forms of Materials

yin
- SN   *Chinese feminine life force.*
- SG   International Women
  - Language, Literature, Religion, and Philosophy
- RT   women's culture

young adults
- SG   Education
  - Social Sciences and Culture
- DG   Age Levels
- BT   adults

young children
- SG   Education
  - Social Sciences and Culture
- DG   Age Levels
- BT   children
- NT   infants
  - preschool children

youth employment
- SG   Economics and Employment
  - Education
- BT   employment

youth movement
- SG   Education
  - History and Social Change
- DG   Cultural and Political Movements
- BT   social movements

youth services
- SG   Social Sciences and Culture
- BT   social services

youth unemployment
> SG Economics and Employment
>   Education
> BT unemployment

Yugoslav
> DG National and Regional Descriptors
> BT European

Zairean
> DG National and Regional Descriptors
> BT African

Zambian
> DG National and Regional Descriptors
> BT African

zero population growth
> SG Law, Government, and Public Policy
>   Natural Sciences and Health
> BT population growth
> RT population planning

Zimbabwean
> DG National and Regional Descriptors
> BT African

zionism
> DG Cultural and Political Movements

zoning
> SG Economics and Employment
>   Law, Government, and Public Policy
>   Social Sciences and Culture
> RT neighborhoods
>   rural planning
>   urban planning

zoology
> SG Natural Sciences and Health
> BT biological sciences
> NT primate studies
> RT anthropology
>   social sciences

ROTATED
DISPLAY

human rights violations
domestic violence
family violence USE **domestic violence**
Family Violence Prevention and Services Act
household violence USE **domestic violence**
marital violence
sexual violence
ROTATING TERM ⎯⎯⎯⎯⎯⎯⎯→ violence
violence against children
violence against women
violence in the media
viragos
cult of the virgin
virgin birth

```
                                a room of one's own
                  queen for     a day
                                ability
               academic         ability
                artistic        ability
                    math        ability
              nonverbal         ability
                  verbal        ability
             differently        abled
                                ableism
                                abnormal psychology
                                abolition
                                aboriginals  USE  indigenous
                                abortifacient agents
                                abortion
                                abortion clinics
                                abortion counseling
                                abortion laws
                                abortion mills  USE  abortion clinics
                                abortion movement
                                abortion rights
                criminal        abortion
                 induced        abortion
             spontaneous        abortion
             therapeutic        abortion
                   study        abroad
                                absentee fathers
                                absentee mothers
                                absenteeism
                                abstention
                                abstinence
                  sexual        abstinence
                                abstract expressionism
                                abstract reasoning
                                abstracts
                                abuse
                 alcohol        abuse
                   child        abuse
                    drug        abuse
                   elder        abuse
               emotional        abuse
                 husband        abuse
                physical        abuse
                  sexual        abuse
                  spouse        abuse
               substance        abuse
                  verbal        abuse
```

```
                          wife  abuse
                                academia
                                academic ability
                                academic achievement
                                academic aptitude
                                academic aspirations
                                academic awards
                                academic degrees  USE  degrees
                                academic disciplines
                                academic enrichment
                                academic failure
                                academic freedom
                                academic rank
                                academic standards
                                academies
                      military  academies
                                access  USE  equal access
                  barrier free  access
                         equal  access
                                accidental death
                                accidents
                          home  accidents
                       traffic  accidents
                        public  accommodations
                                accountants
                                accounting
                                accreditation
                                acculturation
                      academic  achievement
                                achievement
                                achievement motivation  USE  achievement need
                                achievement need
                                acne
                                acoustics
                                acquaintance rape
                                acquired immune deficiency syndrome
                                acronyms
             Age Discrimination  Act of 1975
                  Civil Rights  Act of 1964
      Civil Rights Restoration  Act of 1987
 Civil Service Spouse Retirement Equity  Act
Comprehensive Employment and Training  Act of 1973
               Economic Equity  Act of 1987
          Economic Recovery Tax  Act of 1981
       Equal Credit Opportunity  Act of 1974
                     Equal Pay  Act of 1963
                     Equal Pay  Act of 1970 (Great Britain)
```

519

Family and Medical Leave Act of 1987
Family Violence Prevention and Services Act
Federal Equitable Pay Practices Act of 1987
Job Training Partnership Act
National School Lunch Act Amendments of 1982
Pregnancy Discrimination Act of 1978
Public Health Service Act
Retirement Equity Act of 1984
Tax Reform Act of 1985
Uniformed Services Former Spouses' Protection Act
Women's Educational Equity Act
acting
affirmative action
affirmative action hiring
affirmative action officers
affirmative action suits
class action suits
community action
political action
political action committees
social action
mass actions
protest actions
activism
political activism
activists
political activists
activities
educational activities
extracurricular activities
leisure activities
social activities
actors
aspiring actors
actresses USE **actors**
actresses (historical)
acts
self actualization
actuarials
ad feminam
ad hominem
Adam
addiction
drug addiction
forms of address
insurance adjusters
adjustment

emotional adjustment
marital adjustment
psychological adjustment
social adjustment
administration
administrative assistants
administrative costs
administrative support occupations
administrators
college administrators
admissions
admissions criteria
open door admissions
adolescence
adolescent pregnancy USE **teenage pregnancy**
adolescents
adopted children
adoption
international adoption
interracial adoption
adoptive parents
adornment
want ads
adult basic education
adult child relationships
adult development
adult education
adult illiteracy
adult learning
adult literacy
adult students
adultery USE **extramarital affairs**
adults
middle aged adults
old old adults
older adults
young adults
advanced degrees USE **graduate degrees**
adventurers
advertisements
job advertisements
advertising
advertising industry
advice columns
advice shows
advocacy
advocacy groups

advocates
consumer advocates
health advocates
legal advocates
mental health advocates
peace advocates
aerobic exercise
aerobics USE **aerobic exercise**
aerospace engineering
aestheticism
aesthetics
AFDC USE **Aid to Families With Dependent Children**
community affairs USE **public affairs**
extramarital affairs
foreign affairs USE **international relations**
international affairs USE **international relations**
public affairs
affection
alienation of affection
forms of affection
affiliation
political party affiliations USE **political parties**
affirmative action
affirmative action hiring
affirmative action officers
affirmative action suits
affluence
Afghan
African
African studies
South African
Afro American
Afro American studies
Afro Caribbean
Afros
after school day care centers
after school programs
morning after pill USE **diethylstilbestrol**
crimes against children
crimes against the elderly
crimes against women
discrimination against the disabled
violence against children
violence against women
age

age discrimination
Age Discrimination Act of 1975
age of consent
age stereotypes
childbearing age
maternal age
middle age
old age USE **older adults**
retirement age
school age children
aged USE **older adults**
middle aged adults
ageism
agencies
employment agencies
federal agencies
government agencies
intelligence agencies
modeling agencies
private agencies
public agencies
social agencies
state agencies
welfare agencies
abortifacient agents
agents
airline reservation agents
change agents
insurance agents
menstruation inducing agents
real estate agents
travel agents
Middle Ages
aggression USE **aggressive behavior**
aggressive behavior
aging
agnosticism
agoraphobia
agreements
prenuptial agreements
separation agreements
agribusiness
agricultural economics
agricultural extension
agricultural industry
agricultural, fishing, and forestry occupations
agriculture

subsistence	agriculture
	aid
	Aid to Families with Dependent Children
federal	aid
financial	aid
foreign	aid
foreign	aid policy
ladies'	aid societies
legal	aid services
state	aid
student	aid USE **student financial aid**
student financial	aid
teacher	aides
	AIDS USE **acquired immune deficiency syndrome**
hearing	aids
sexual	aids
	air pollution
	air transportation
	airline reservation agents
	airline stewardesses USE **flight attendants**
	airlines USE **air transportation**
	Alaskan Indian
	Alaskan Native
Native	Alaskan
	Albanian
	albums
photograph	albums
record	albums
	alcohol abuse
fetal	alcohol syndrome
	alcoholism
	Aleut
	Algerian
	alienation
	alienation of affection
job	alienation
work	alienation
	aliens USE **immigrants**
illegal	aliens USE **illegal immigrants**
	alimony
	all volunteer military force
	all women ensembles
	allegory
	alliances
blame	allocation
	alma mater
	almanacs

                              living alone
                                     aloofness
                                     alternative employment
                                     alternative programs
                                     alternative schools
                                     alternative spaces
                                     alternative work arrangements
                                     altruism
                                     alumnae
                                     alumnae/i
                                     alumni
                                     alumni/ae
                                     amateur athletics
                                     amazons
                                     ambiguity
                                     ambition
                      Equal Rights Amendment
        Child Support Enforcement Amendments of 1984
                        Education Amendments of 1972
                        Education Amendments of 1985
        National School Lunch Act Amendments of 1982
                                     amenorrhea
                                     Amerasian
                            Afro American
                            Afro American studies
                                     American Indian
                                     American Indian studies
                                     American studies
                           Anglo American
                           Asian American
                           Asian American studies
                   Asian Pacific American
                           Black American studies USE **Afro American studies**
                       Cambodian American
                       Caribbean American
                         Central American
                         Chinese American
                           Cuban American
                            Euro American
                         Filipino American
                           Greek American
                         Haitian American
                        Hispanic American
                     Indochinese American
                          Italian American
                        Japanese American
                          Korean American

Latin American
Latin American studies
Mexican American
Native American USE **American Indian**
Native American studies USE **American Indian studies**
North American
Polish American
Portuguese American
Samoan American
South American USE **Latin American**
Spanish American
Thai American
Vietnamese American
amniocentesis
anal sex
cohort analysis
content analysis
contextual analysis
cost benefit analysis
data analysis
qualitative analysis
quantitative analysis
statistical analysis
systems analysts
analytical psychology
anarcha feminism
anarchism
anarchy
anatomy
ancestor spirits
ancestors
anchors
agricultural, fishing, and forestry occupations
arts and crafts movement
arts, entertainment, and media occupations
balancing work and family life
Comprehensive Employment and Training Act of 1973
D and C USE **dilatation and curettage**
death and dying
dilatation and curettage
Family and Medical Leave Act of 1987
Family Violence Prevention and Services Act
information and referral centers
legal and political occupations
marketing and sales occupations
marriage and family law
maternal and infant welfare

occupational health and safety
professional and related services industry
race, class, and gender studies
racial and ethnic differences
Retirement and Disability System Authorization
rock and roll
scientific and technical occupations
separation of church and state
tests and measurements USE **testing**
tool and die makers
track and field
women and
Women, Infants, and Children Nutrition Program
androcentrism
androgens
androgyny
anecdotes
anemia
iron deficiency anemia
sickle cell anemia
anesthesia
general anesthesia
local anesthesia
obstetrical anesthesia
anesthesiologists
angel in the house
angels
anger
Anglo American
Anglo Saxon
White Anglo Saxon Protestant
Angolan
angora
anima
animal behavior
animal caretakers
animals
laboratory animals
animation
animatrices rurales
animus
ankh
anlu
annals
Orphan Annie
anniversaries
annotations

announcements
announcers
annual reports
annulment
congenital anomalies USE **birth defects**
anonymous
anorexia nervosa
antebellum
antenuptial contracts USE **prenuptial agreements**
anthologies
anthropologists
anthropology
cultural anthropology
economic anthropology
medical anthropology
political anthropology
anthropometry
anthropomorphism
anti ERA movement
antiabortion movement
antiapartheid movement
antichoice USE **antiabortion movement**
antidepressant drugs
antidiscrimination laws USE **discrimination laws**
antifeminism
antiilliteracy movements
antilynching campaign
antinuclear movement
antiques
antiquity
antisemitism
antisepsis
antisocial behavior
antisuffrage movement
antithesis
antitrust legislation
antiwar movement
anxiety
computer anxiety USE **computer avoidance**
math anxiety USE **math avoidance**
science anxiety USE **science avoidance**
apartheid
apathy
aphrodisiacs
Appalachian
appearance
physical appearance

appendices
appetite depressants
appetite disorders USE **eating disorders**
applications
applied linguistics
applied mathematics
applied research
appointed officials
appointive positions USE **government appointments**
government appointments
judicial appointments
performance appraisal
apprenticeships
appropriate technology
appropriations
approval need
academic aptitude
aptitude
aptitude tests
language aptitude
vocational aptitude
Arab
Saudi Arabian
arbitration
archaeologists
archaeology
archery
architects
landscape architects
architecture
archives
area studies
rural areas
urban areas
Argentine
arguments
Armageddon
armament USE **militarism**
armed forces
armed services USE **armed forces**
Armenian
arms control
arousal
arranged marriage
alternative work arrangements
domestic arrangements

financial arrangements
living arrangements
flower arranging
arson
art
art conservation
art criticism
art exhibits USE **art shows**
art history
art matronage
art music
art preservation
art shows
art symbols
art theory
art therapy
body art
children's art
commercial art
computer art USE **electronic art**
cunt art
electronic art
erotic art
fiber art
folk art
metal art
multimedia art
mural art
naive art
one woman art shows
performance art
political art
poster art
primitive art
public art
religious art
tribal art
video art
women's art
articles
artifacts
artificial insemination
artificial intelligence
artisans
artistic ability
artists
artists' books

          craft artists
                arts
                arts and crafts movement
                arts organizations
                arts, entertainment, and media occupations
          craft arts
     decorative arts
       domestic arts
            fine arts USE **performing arts**
            fine arts USE **visual arts**
        literary arts USE **literature**
         martial arts
          media arts
     performing arts
        theater arts USE **theater**
         visual arts
                asbestos
                asceticism
                Asian
                Asian American
                Asian American studies
                Asian Pacific
                Asian Pacific American
                Asian studies
      academic aspirations
                aspirations
       parental aspirations
       political aspirations
                aspiring actors
                assault
         sexual assault
     freedom of assembly
         global assembly lines
                assemblymen
                assemblywomen
                assertive behavior
                assertiveness USE **assertive behavior**
                assertiveness training
                assessment
        quality assessment
                assessments
                assimilation patterns
                assistance programs
  dependent care assistance programs
        federal assistance programs
         public assistance
          state assistance programs

technical assistance
administrative assistants
laboratory assistants
physicians' assistants
research assistants
teaching assistants
waiters' assistants
assistantships
associate degrees
free association
associations
assumable mortgages
astrology
astronautics USE **space sciences**
astronauts
astronomers
astronomy
political asylum
at risk populations
reproductive hazards at work
atheism
athletes
professional athletes
amateur athletics
athletics
collegiate athletics
professional athletics
women's athletics
Middle Atlantic
North Atlantic
South Atlantic
atlases
attachment
educational attainment
school attendance
attendants
birth attendants USE **midwives**
flight attendants
attention
selective attention
attitude change
attitudes
family attitudes
judicial attitudes
occupational attitudes
parental attitudes
social attitudes

　　　　　　　　　　　　　　supervisor attitudes
　　　　　　　　　　　　　　　　　work attitudes
　　　　　　　　　　　　　　　　　　　attorneys USE **lawyers**
　　　　　　　　　　　　　　　　sexual attraction
　　　　　　　　　　　　　　　　　　　audiotapes
　　　　　　　　　　　　　　　　　　　auditory perception
　　　　　　　　　　　　　　　　　　　aunts
　　　　　　　　　　　　　　　　maiden aunts
　　　　　　　　　　　　　　　　　　　Australian
　　　　　　　　　　　　　　　　　　　Austrian
　　　　　　　　　　　　　　　　　　　auteur theory USE **auteurism**
　　　　　　　　　　　　　　　　　　　auteurism
　　　　　　　　　　　　　　　　female authored texts
　　　　　　　　　　　　　　　　　　　authoritarian child rearing practices
　　　　　　　　　　　　　　　　　　　authoritarian personality
　　　　　　　　　　　　　　　　　　　authoritarianism
　　　　　　　　　　　　　　　　　　　authority
Retirement and Disability System Authorization
　　　　　　　　　　　　　　　　　　　authors
　　　　　　　　　　　　　　　　　　　autism
　　　　　　　　　　　　　　　　　　　autobiographies
　　　　　　　　　　　　　　　　　　　autobiography
　　　　　　　　　　　　　　　　　　　autoeroticism USE **masturbation**
　　　　　　　　　　　　　　　　　　　automation
　　　　　　　　　　　　　　　　　　　automobile insurance
　　　　　　　　　　　　　　　　　　　automobile repair
　　　　　　　　　　　　　　　　　　　autonomy
　　　　　　　　　　　　　　　　　　　auxiliaries
　　　　　　　　　　　　　　　ladies' auxiliaries USE **auxiliaries**
　　　　　　　　　　　　　　　　　　　avant garde
　　　　　　　　　　　　　　　　　　　aversion therapy
　　　　　　　　　　　　　　　　　　　aviation
　　　　　　　　　　　　　　　　　　　aviatrices USE **pilots**
　　　　　　　　　　　　　　　　　　　avoidance behavior
　　　　　　　　　　　　　　　computer avoidance
　　　　　　　　　　　　　　　　　math avoidance
　　　　　　　　　　　　　　　science avoidance
　　　　　　　　　　　　　　　　Great Awakening
　　　　　　　　　　　　　　　academic awards
　　　　　　　　　　　　　　　　　　　awards
　　　　　　　　　　　　　　professional awards
　　　　　　　　　　　　　　　　sports awards
　　　　　　　　　　　　　　　　career awareness
　　　　　　　　　　　　　　　　　　　babies USE **infants**
　　　　　　　　　　　　　　　　　blue babies
　　　　　　　　　　　　　　test tube babies USE **in vitro fertilization**
　　　　　　　　　　　　　　　　　　　babysitters

babysitting
bachelors
bachelors' degrees
back pay
backlash
bag ladies USE **homeless women**
bakers
balance of payments
balancing work and family life
balding USE **hair loss**
crystal ball gazing
ballads
ballet
balls USE **testicles**
charity balls
society balls
Bangladeshi
bangs
bank tellers
bankers
banking industry
banks
multinational banks
sperm banks
transnational banks USE **multinational banks**
banners
baptism
Barbadan
barbers
collective bargaining
barmaids USE **cocktail servers**
baronesses
Baroque Period
barren USE **infertility**
barrier free access
barriers to employment USE **job discrimination**
barristers
bartenders
barter
bas mitzvah USE **bat mitzvah**
bas reliefs
basal body temperature
baseball
competency based tests
home based business
home based careers
home based work

home based workers
adult basic education
basic education
basic human needs
basic skills
basketball
basketry
bastards
bat mitzvah
bathing suits
battered women
battlefields
beadwork
beauticians
beauty
beauty contests
beauty parlors
beauty queens
beauty standards
bedrooms
queen bee syndrome
Beguinism
aggressive behavior
animal behavior
antisocial behavior
assertive behavior
avoidance behavior
behavior
behavior change
behavior modification
cognitive behavior modification
collective behavior USE **group behavior**
competitive behavior
compliant behavior
compulsive behavior
conforming behavior
consumer behavior
deferential behavior
delinquent behavior
dependent behavior
destructive behavior
deviant behavior
grooming behavior
group behavior
health behavior
health seeking behavior
help seeking behavior

helping behavior
learned behavior
manipulative behavior
nonconforming behavior
nonjudgmental behavior
nonverbal behavior
organizational behavior
parental behavior
passive behavior
psychosexual behavior
rebellious behavior
risk taking behavior
self destructive behavior
selfish behavior
sex role behavior
sexual behavior
social behavior
submissive behavior
voting behavior
behavioral objectives
behavioral research
behavioral sciences USE **social sciences**
behaviorism
Belgian
belief systems
religious beliefs
bellboys USE **bellhops**
bellhops
chastity belts
cost benefit analysis
benefits
dependent benefits
educational benefits
employee benefits
flexible benefits
fringe benefits
maternity benefits
paternity benefits
pension benefits
retirement benefits
supplementary benefits
veteran benefits
benign tumors
bereavement
bestiality
betrothal
betrothed

bias
gender bias
perceptual bias
race bias
research bias
social bias
test bias
textbook bias
biblical literature USE **religious literature**
bibliographies
bicultural education
biculturalism
bicycling
bigamy
bigotry
bikinis
bilineal kinship
bilingual education
bilingualism
bills
double bind
foot binding
binge purge syndrome USE **bulimia**
biobibliographies
biochemistry
bioethics
biofeedback
biographies
biography
biological clock
biological determinism
biological fathers USE **birth fathers**
biological influences
biological mothers USE **birth mothers**
biological parents USE **birth parents**
biological sciences
biological warfare
biologism
biologists
biology
biopsy
birth USE **childbirth**
birth attendants USE **midwives**
birth certificates
birth control
birth control methods USE **contraception**
birth control pills USE **oral contraceptives**

birth defects
birth fathers
birth mothers
birth name
birth order
birth parents
birth rates
child birth USE **childbirth**
home birth
virgin birth
birthing
birthing centers
birthing rooms
multiple births
bisexuality
bitches
bitterness
Black
Black American studies USE **Afro American studies**
Black colleges
Black feminism
black markets
Black movement
Black Muslim
Black power movement
Black studies USE **Afro American studies**
Black women's studies
historically Black colleges USE **Black colleges**
blame
blame allocation
self blame
blaming the victim
blended families
blind dates
blind review
blindness
block grants
blockbusting
blondes
blood
blood tests
high blood pressure USE **hypertension**
bloomers
blue babies
blue collar workers
blues

bluestockings
boarding schools
boards
boards of directors
boards of governors USE **governing boards**
boards of regents USE **governing boards**
boards of trustees USE **governing boards**
governing boards
Ouija boards
school boards USE **governing boards**
boat operators
bodies
basal body temperature
body art
body building
body hair
body image
body language
body odor
body politics
mind/ body split
upper body strength
Bolivian
bolshevism
bomfog
bondage
bonding
female bonding
male bonding
book clubs
book conservation
book lists
book reviews
book stores
bookbinders
bookkeepers
booklets
bookplates
artists' books
books
reference books
boredom
botany
Botswanan
bottle feeding
boudoirs
Outward Bound programs

boundary markers
bouquets
bourgeoisie
bowling
boy preference of parents
old boy networks
boycotts
economic boycotts
boys
delivery boys USE **deliverers**
braceros
braids
braille
brain
brainwashing
brassieres
Brazilian
breadwinners USE **householders**
career break
breakfasts
breast cancer
breast diseases
breast examination
breast feeding
breast implants
breast prostheses
breast pumps
breast self examination
breasts
bricklayers
bride burning
bride price
brides
child brides
mail order brides
bridesmaids
bridewealth USE **dowry**
legal briefs
Equal Pay Act of 1970 (Great Britain)
National Health Service (Great Britain)
broadcasters
broadcasts
broadsides
brochures
broken home USE **single parent families**
brothels
brother sister incest

brotherhood of man USE **humanity**
brothers
brothers in law
brunches
Brunhilde
Buddhism
Buddhist
budget cuts
budget deficits
budget process
federal budget
military budget
budgeting
budgets
body building
building industry USE **construction industry**
consensus building
built environment
Bulgarian
bulimia
bulletins
bullfighters
bumper stickers
bundling
bureaucracy
bureaus
burglaries
burial
burlesque
Burmese
bride burning
witch burning
burnout
Burundian
bus drivers
busboys USE **waiters' assistants**
business
business correspondence
business ethics
business ownership
business security
family owned business
home based business
minority owned business
small business
women owned business
businesses

businessmen
businesspeople
businesswomen
busing
butch
butchers
butt lifts USE **cosmetic surgery**
buttocks
buttons
credit by examination
marriage by proxy
bylaws
Byzantine Period
D and C USE **dilatation and curettage**
cabinetmakers
cable television
caesarian section
caffeine
Cajun
calcium deficiency
calendars
Calvinism
Cambodian
Cambodian American
camera operators
cameramen USE **camera operators**
cameramen USE **photographers**
Cameroonian
camp followers
antilynching campaign
campaigns
election campaigns
literacy campaigns
political campaigns USE **election campaigns**
concentration camps
peace camps
campus safety USE **campus security**
campus security
Canadian
Canadian Indian studies
Native Canadian
breast cancer
cancer
cervical cancer
candidates
job candidates

<pre>
        political candidates
                 canoeing
                 canon
                 canon law   USE **religious law**
        literary canon
                 canonization
                 capital
                 capital punishment   USE **death penalty**
          human capital
           seed capital
        venture capital
                 capitalism
                 capitalist economic development models
        venture capitalists
        cervical caps
                 car insurance   USE **automobile insurance**
                 car pools
                 car repair   USE **automobile repair**
                 carcinogens
                 cardiovascular diseases
   after school day care centers
                 care
           child care
           child care leave
           child care licensing
           child care policy
           child care workers
       child day care centers
       community care
   corporate day care centers
            day care
            day care centers
      dependent care
      dependent care assistance programs
      Dependent Care Tax Credit
    drop in day care centers
         elderly care
     elderly day care centers
employer supported day care
        ethic of care
        extended care facilities
          health care
          health care costs
          health care delivery
          health care facilities
          health care legislation
          health care occupations
</pre>

health care policy
health care providers
health care services
health care utilization
health care workers
home health care
infant care
medical care
multicultural health care services
prenatal care
respite care   USE   **elderly day care centers**
Title XX (Dependent Care)

career awareness
career break
career change
career choice
career counseling
career education
career family conflict
career feminism
career girls   USE   **wage earning women**
career guidance   USE   **career counseling**
career interest inventories
career ladders
career mapping
career mobility   USE   **occupational mobility**
career opportunities
career planning
career satisfaction
career strategies

dual career couples
dual career families
flexible career patterns
two career couples   USE   **dual career couples**
two career families   USE   **dual career families**

careers

dual careers
female dominated careers   USE   **female intensive occupations**
home based careers
male dominated careers   USE   **male dominated employment**
nontraditional careers   USE   **female intensive occupations**
nontraditional careers   USE   **male intensive occupations**
second careers
women intensive careers   USE   **female intensive occupations**

caregivers

primary caregivers
animal caretakers

caretakers USE **caregivers**
Afro Caribbean
Caribbean
Caribbean American
caricatures
carpenters
mail carriers
cartels
Cartesianism
cartoonists
cartoons
case studies
court cases
caseworkers USE **social workers**
cassettes
caste
casting
colorblind casting
cross cultural casting
castrating females
castration
castration complex
catalogs
cathartic therapy
cathedrals
cathode ray tubes USE **video display terminals**
Catholic
Roman Catholic
Catholicism
Roman Catholicism
Caucasian
caucuses
causal factors USE **influences**
glass ceiling
celebrations
celibacy
sickle cell anemia
cellulite
censorship
census
censuses
after school day care centers
birthing centers
centers
child day care centers
corporate day care centers
crisis centers

day care centers
drop in day care centers
elderly day care centers
information and referral centers
neighborhood health centers
rape crisis centers
training centers
women's centers
Central American
ceramics
ceremonies
graduation ceremonies
marriage ceremonies
master of ceremonies
mistress of ceremonies USE **master of ceremonies**
wedding ceremonies
birth certificates
death certificates
certification
cervical cancer
cervical caps
cervical mucus
cervix
CETA USE **Comprehensive Employment and Training Act of 1973**
Chadian
chador
chairpersons
chamber music
chambermaids USE **hotel workers**
attitude change
behavior change
career change
change
change agents
change of life USE **menopause**
midcareer change
sex change
social change
channeling
chanteuses
chants
chaperones
chapters
population characteristics
social characteristics
fictional characters

charisma
charitable work
charities
charity balls
charts
charwomen USE **janitors**
chastity
chastity belts
vows of chastity
chattels
chauvinism
female chauvinism
male chauvinism
male chauvinist pig USE **male chauvinism**
coat check girls USE **coat checkers**
hat check girls USE **hat checkers**
coat checkers
hat checkers
cheerleaders
cheesecake
chefs
chemical dependency USE **drug addiction**
chemical engineering
chemical industry
chemical warfare USE **biological warfare**
chemistry
chemists
chemotherapy
Chicana
Chicana studies
chief executives
adult child relationships
authoritarian child rearing practices
child abuse
child birth USE **childbirth**
child brides
child care
child care leave
child care licensing
child care policy
child care workers
child custody
child day care centers
child development
child labor
child marriage
child molesting USE **child abuse**

child neglect
child pornography
child psychology
child rearing practices
child support
Child Support Enforcement Amendments of 1984
child welfare
nonsexist child rearing practices
parent child relationships
permissive child rearing practices
unborn child USE **fetuses**
childbearing
childbearing age
early childbearing
late childbearing
childbed fever USE **puerperal fever**
childbirth
childbirth training
labor (childbirth)
natural childbirth
premature childbirth
childfree marriage
childhood
early childhood education
childless couples
childlessness
adopted children
Aid to Families with Dependent Children
children
children living in poverty
children's art
children's culture
children's groups
children's literature
children's music
children's relationships
children's rights
couples with children
crimes against children
dependent children
foster children
history of children
impact on children
latchkey children
legitimization of children
preschool children
school age children

sick children
valuing children
violence against children
Women, Infants, and Children Nutrition Program
young children
Chilean
china painting
Chinese
Chinese American
chiropodists
chiropractors
chivalry
career choice
freedom of choice
occupational choice   USE   **career choice**
vocational choice   USE   **career choice**
choirs
right to choose   USE   **prochoice**
choral music
chorus dancers
chorus girls   USE   **chorus dancers**
chorus lines
choruses
Christian
Christianity
chromosome disorders
chronicles
chronologies
church music   USE   **religious music**
church work
separation of church and state
churches
house churches
storefront churches
cigarettes   USE   **smoking**
Cinderella
cinema   USE   **film**
cinematography   USE   **film**
circles
circular reasoning
female circumcision
male circumcision
circus performers
large cities   USE   **urban areas**
citizen groups
senior citizens
citizenship

city government
city planning USE **urban planning**
inner city
civic education
civil disobedience
civil engineering
civil law
civil lawsuits
civil liberties
civil religion
civil rights
Civil Rights Act of 1964
civil rights commissions
civil rights legislation
civil rights movements
Civil Rights Restoration Act of 1987
civil service
Civil Service Spouse Retirement Equity Act
Civil War
Title IV (Civil Rights)
Title VI (Civil Rights)
Title VII (Civil Rights)
civility
clamydia
clans
class
class action suits
class consciousness
class differences
class discrimination
class division
class formation
class identity
class ideology
economic class
lower class
middle class
middle class families
race, class, and gender studies
social class
socioeconomic class
upper class
upper class families
working class
classes
classical conditioning
classical economics

classical music USE **art music**
Classical Period
classicism
industrial classification
classism
classless society
cleaners
cleaning
cleaning women USE **cleaners**
cleanliness
cleavage
clergy
clergymen
clergywomen
clerical occupations
clerks
cliches
lawyer client relationships
climacteric
clinical psychology
clinical trials
abortion clinics
clinics
clippings
cliques
clitoral orgasm
clitoridectomy
clitoris
biological clock
cloning
closeted lesbians
clothes USE **clothing**
clothing
clothing workers
protective clothing
club women
book clubs
clubs
garden clubs
night clubs
private clubs
social clubs
coaches
labor coaching
coal miners
coalition politics
coalitions

Pacific Coast
Ivory Coaster
coat check girls USE **coat checkers**
coat checkers
cocaine
cocktail parties
cocktail servers
domestic code
codependency
codes
dress codes
codices
coeds USE **college students**
coeducation
coffee klatches
cognition
cognitive behavior modification
cognitive development
cognitive dissonance
cognitive processes
cognitive science
cohabitation
cohort analysis
cohorts
coiffures
coins
coitus USE **sexual intercourse**
coitus interruptus
collaboration
collaborative theater
collage
blue collar workers
pink collar workers
white collar crime
white collar workers
data collection
collections
slide collections
collective bargaining
collective behavior USE **group behavior**
collective farms
collectives
college administrators
college credits
college presidents
college students
women college students

```
                     Black  colleges
                            colleges
                 community  colleges
                 four year  colleges
         historically Black colleges   USE   **Black colleges**
                    junior  colleges
                   private  colleges
                    public  colleges
                single sex  colleges
                  two year  colleges
                   women's  colleges
                            collegiate athletics
                            colloquia
                            Colombian
                            Colonial Period
                            colonialism
                            color perception
            people of  color
                 skin  color
            women of  color
                            colorblind casting
                            colorists
                            colostrum
                            columnists
               advice  columns
                            columns
             personal  columns
             military  combat
                            comedians
                            comediennes   USE   **comedians**
                            comedy
                            comic strips
                            coming out
                            commentaries
                            commentators
                            commercial art
                            commercial credit
                            commercial sex
                            commercial television
                            commercials
                radio  commercials
           television  commercials
Equal Employment Opportunity  Commission
         civil rights  commissions
                            commissions
                            commissions on the status of women
   equal opportunities  commissions
```

human relations commissions
commitment
committees
political action committees
search committees
common law marriage
communal families
communal groups
communes
village communes
communicable diseases
communication
communication satellites
communication styles
interpersonal communication
nonverbal communication
oral communication USE **verbal communication**
spiritual communication
verbal communication
communications
communications equity
communications industry
satellite communications
holy communion
communism
communist economic development models
Communist Party
communities
faith communities
lesbian communities
utopian communities
community
community action
community affairs USE **public affairs**
community care
community colleges
community development
community education
community health services
community organizers
community problems
community property laws
community relations
community responsibility
community schools
commuter marriage
commuting students

compact disks
companies
companionate marriage
comparable worth
comparative psychology
comparative religion
ethnic comparisons USE **racial and ethnic differences**
racial comparisons USE **racial and ethnic differences**
compendiums
compensation packages
unemployment compensation
compensatory education
competence
minimum competencies
competency based tests
competitive behavior
compilations
completion complex
castration complex
completion complex
Electra complex
female Oedipus complex
Oedipus complex
complexes
complexion
contract compliance
compliant behavior
compliments
composers
compositions
compositors
Comprehensive Employment and Training Act of
 1973
compressed workweek
compromise
compulsions USE **compulsive behavior**
compulsive behavior
compulsive sexuality USE **hypersexuality**
obsessive compulsive disorders
compulsory education
compulsory heterosexuality
compulsory sterilization USE **involuntary
 sterilization**
computer anxiety USE **computer avoidance**
computer art USE **electronic art**
computer avoidance
computer equipment operators

computer equity
computer games
computer literacy
computer music
computer programmers
computer programming
computer programs
computer science
computer searches USE **information retrieval
services**
computer security
computer terminals
computers
concentration camps
concept papers
self concept
conception
immaculate conception
conceptual errors
concert music USE **art music**
concerts
concordances
concubinage
concubines
concupiscence USE **lust**
classical conditioning
conditioning
operant conditioning
psychological conditioning USE **conditioning**
social conditioning
conditions
factory conditions
industrial conditions
living conditions
rural conditions
socioeconomic conditions
working conditions
condoms
conductors
train conductors
confederations
conferences
confession
lack of confidence
math confidence
self confidence
confidentiality

records confidentiality
confirmation
property confiscation
career family conflict
conflict
conflict of interest
conflict resolution
culture conflict
family conflict
interrole conflict
marital conflict
role conflict
social conflict
conforming behavior
conformity USE **conforming behavior**
confrontation
congenital anomalies USE **birth defects**
congregations
Congress
congresses
congressional hearings
congressmen
congresswomen
consanguinity
conscientious objection
class consciousness
consciousness
consciousness raising
consciousness raising groups
false consciousness
stream of consciousness
consensual union
consensus
consensus building
age of consent
consent USE **informed consent**
consent orders
informed consent
art conservation
book conservation
conservation
energy conservation
soil conservation
conservatism
conservative movement
conservatives
conservatories

consortia
constitution
constitutions
cultural constraints
construction industry
construction occupations
construction workers
social construction of gender
social construction of reality
consultants
consumer advocates
consumer behavior
consumer credit
consumer economy
consumer health organizations
consumer information
consumer installment loans
consumer power
consumer problems
consumer protection
consumerism
consumers
consumption
contact dykes
contact sports
contacts
content analysis
beauty contests
contextual analysis
Health Insurance Continuation
continuing education
continuing education units
contraception
injectable contraceptives
oral contraceptives
contract compliance
contract renewal
antenuptial contracts USE **prenuptial agreements**
contracts
labor contracts
marriage contracts
in kind contributions
arms control
birth control
birth control methods USE **contraception**
birth control pills USE **oral contraceptives**
control

gun control laws
locus of control
population control
self control
social control
conventional mortgages
conventions
political conventions
convents
conversation
cookbooks
cooking
cooks
cooperative education
cooperatives
health cooperatives
hand eye coordination
coordinators
coparenting
coping strategies
copulation USE **sexual intercourse**
copyright laws
copywriters
umbilical cord
core curriculum
corporate day care centers
corporate husbands USE **corporate spouses**
corporate law
corporate liability
corporate policy
corporate relocation policy
corporate responsibility
corporate spouses
corporate takeovers
corporate wives USE **corporate spouses**
multinational corporation policy
corporations
multinational corporations
transnational corporations USE **multinational corporations**
correctional facilities USE **prisons**
correctional officers
correctional rehabilitation
business correspondence
correspondence
correspondence courses
personal correspondence
correspondents

corruption
corsages
corsets
cosmetic surgery
cosmetics
cosmetologists
cosmetology
cosmology
cost benefit analysis
cost of living
Costa Rican
administrative costs
costs
educational costs
health care costs
housing costs
costume design
cotillions
cottage industry
electronic cottage
councils
abortion counseling
career counseling
counseling
economic counseling
family counseling
genetic counseling
group counseling
individual counseling
job counseling   USE **occupational counseling**
marriage counseling
occupational counseling
school counseling
sex counseling
sexual counseling   USE **sex counseling**
vocational counseling   USE **occupational counseling**
counselors
Counter Reformation
counterculture
countertransference
countesses
developed countries   USE **developed nations**
developing countries   USE **developing nations**
country music
county courts
county government
childless couples

couples
couples with children
dual career couples
gay couples
gay male couples
lesbian couples
married couples
two career couples USE **dual career couples**
coups
courage
course evaluation
course objectives
correspondence courses
court cases
court decisions
Supreme Court
courtesans
courtly love
courtroom transcripts
trials (courtroom)
county courts
courts
family courts
federal courts
juvenile courts
state courts
courtship customs
cousins
covens
media coverage
press coverage
television coverage
coverture
cowboys USE **ranch hands**
cowgirls USE **ranch hands**
cowives
coyness
craft artists
craft arts
craft occupations
the Craft USE **witchcraft**
arts and crafts movement
crafts USE **craft arts**
craftsmen USE **artisans**
craftsmen USE **craft artists**
craftsmen USE **craftspersons**
craftspersons

creation myths
creative thinking
creative writing
creativity
creches
credentials
commercial credit
consumer credit
credit
credit by examination
credit for experience
credit fraud
Dependent Care Tax Credit
equal credit
Equal Credit Opportunity Act of 1974
tuition tax credit
utility credit
college credits
credits
Creole
crew
crib death USE **sudden infant death syndrome**
cricket
crime
crime prevention
crime victims
organized crime
white collar crime
crimes
crimes against children
crimes against the elderly
crimes against women
crimes of honor
crimes of passion
property crimes
sex crimes
victimless crimes
war crimes
criminal abortion
criminal justice
criminal law
criminal lawsuits
criminals
criminology
crisis centers
crisis intervention
crisis shelters

identity crisis
midlife crisis
rape crisis centers
admissions criteria
criteria
evaluation criteria
critical mass
art criticism
criticism
dance criticism
feminist criticism
film criticism
literary criticism
music criticism
phallic criticism
psychoanalytic criticism
theater criticism
critics
crocheting
crones
cross cultural casting
cross cultural feminism
cross cultural research
cross cultural studies
cross dressing
cross sex identity
CRT USE **video display terminals**
legal cruelty
cruising
crying
crystal ball gazing
Cuban
Cuban American
cubism
cult of the virgin
cult of true womanhood
cults
cross cultural casting
cross cultural feminism
cross cultural research
cross cultural studies
cultural anthropology
cultural constraints
cultural feminism
cultural groups
cultural heritage
cultural identity

cultural imperialism
cultural influences
cultural sadism
cultural status
children's culture
culture
culture conflict
culture work
dominant culture
folk culture
gay culture
gay female culture USE **lesbian culture**
gay male culture
lesbian culture
majority culture
material culture
myths (folk culture) USE **mythology**
popular culture
women's culture
cunnilingus
cunning
cunt art
cunts
curators
dilatation and curettage
curfew
curiosity
curlers
curls
curricula
core curriculum
curriculum
curriculum guides
curriculum integration
curriculum transformation USE **curriculum integration**
hidden curriculum
nonsexist curriculum
custodial parents
child custody
custody
custody decrees
joint custody USE **shared custody**
shared custody
courtship customs
customs
dating customs

```
        inheritance customs
          marriage customs
             tribal customs
             budget cuts
             lumber cutters
          menstrual cycle
       reproductive cycle
               life cycles
                    Cypriot
                    cysts
                    Czechoslovakian
                    D and C  USE  dilatation and curettage
                    dadaism
                    dames
                    dance
                    dance criticism
       experimental dance
               folk dance
             modern dance
             sacred dance
             chorus dancers
                    dancers
                    dances
                    Danish
                    Darwinism
             social Darwinism
                    data
                    data analysis
                    data collection
                    data entry operators
                    data processing
                    data processors
                    data sets
                    date rape
               blind dates
                    dating
                    dating customs
                    dating services
                    daughter right
             father daughter incest
             father daughter relationships
             mother daughter incest
             mother daughter relationships
                    daughters
                    daughters in law
       after school day care centers
              child day care centers
```

corporate day care centers
day care
day care centers
drop in day care centers
elderly day care centers
employer supported day care
four day workweek
queen for a day
three day measles USE **rubella**
daydreams
nom de lait
deaconesses USE **deacons**
deacons
deafness
New Deal
deans
accidental death
crib death USE **sudden infant death syndrome**
death
death and dying
death certificates
death notices USE **obituaries**
death penalty
premature death
sudden infant death syndrome
dowry deaths
debt
debutantes
International Decade for Women
decision making
court decisions
declarations
population decline
declining neighborhoods
decolonization
deconstruction
decorative arts
custody decrees
divorce decrees
defamation
birth defects
genetic defects
defense mechanisms
military defense
self defense
deferential behavior
acquired immune deficiency syndrome

calcium	deficiency
iron	deficiency anemia
budget	deficits
	deficits
	defloration
external	degree programs
academic	degrees USE **degrees**
advanced	degrees USE **graduate degrees**
associate	degrees
bachelors'	degrees
	degrees
doctoral	degrees
graduate	degrees
honorary	degrees
masters'	degrees
professional	degrees
undergraduate	degrees
	deindustrialization
	deinstitutionalization
	deism
	deity
	delayed parenthood
	delegates
juvenile	delinquency
	delinquent behavior
	deliverers
	delivery USE **childbirth**
	delivery boys USE **deliverers**
	delivery rooms
health care	delivery
	deliverymen USE **deliverers**
	democracy
	Democratic Party
	democratic socialism
	demographic measurements
	demographic transition
	demographics USE **demographic measurements**
	demography
	demonstrations
	den mothers
	denial
self	denial
	dental hygienists
vagina	dentata
	dentistry
	dentists
	deodorants

departments
chemical dependency USE **drug addiction**
dependency USE **dependent behavior**
Aid to Families with Dependent Children
dependent behavior
dependent benefits
dependent care
dependent care assistance programs
Dependent Care Tax Credit
dependent children
Title XX (Dependent Care)
dependents
military dependents
depilation USE **hair removal**
depilatories
Depo Provera
depreciation
appetite depressants
depression
economic depression
Great Depression
involuntary depression
postnatal depression USE **postpartum depression**
postpartum depression
deprivation
depth perception
DES USE **diethylstilbestrol**
job descriptions
descriptive linguistics
descriptive writing
desegregation
desegregation methods
school desegregation
desertion
desex
costume design
design
experimental design
fashion design
graphic design
house design
interior design
research design
textile design
designers
desirable neighborhoods
desire

```
                          sexual  desire
                                  deskilling
                                  despair
                                  despotism
                     enlightened  despotism
                                  destructive behavior
                            self  destructive behavior
                                  detectives
                         genetic  determinants
                            self  determination
                             sex  determination
                      biological  determinism
                                  determinism
                                  devaluation
                                  developed countries  USE  **developed nations**
                                  developed nations
                           group  developed theater
                                  developing countries  USE  **developing nations**
                                  developing nations
                           adult  development
             capitalist economic  development models
                           child  development
                       cognitive  development
              communist economic  development models
                       community  development
                                  development
                                  development specialists
                                  development studies
                        economic  development
                        economic  development models
                        economic  development theory
                       emotional  development
                        employee  development
                          gender  development
                      individual  development
                          infant  development
                    intellectual  development
                             job  development
                        language  development
                Marxist economic  development models
                           moral  development
                           motor  development
                        muscular  development
                  organizational  development
                       perceptual  development
                        personal  development  USE  **individual development**
                     personality  development
```

569

physical development
professional development
rural development
sensory development
sex role development
skill development
social development
socialist economic development models
technology development
urban development
verbal development
women in development
developmental disabilities
developmental psychology
deviance USE **deviant behavior**
deviant behavior
intrauterine devices
labor saving devices
devil
diabetes
sugar diabetes USE **diabetes**
diagnoses
diagrams
dialects
social dialects
diaper services
diaphragms
diaries
visual diaries
false dichotomies
dichotomy
dictionaries
right to die
tool and die makers
diet pills
diet therapy
dietetics
diethylstilbestrol
dieticians
dieting
diets
class differences
differences
gender differences
learning differences
racial and ethnic differences
sex differences

social differences
wage differential USE **wage gap**
differently abled
diffusion
digests
dilatation and curettage
sexual dimorphism
dinners
diplomacy
diplomas
diplomats
directions
directories
boards of directors
directors
directors (film) USE **film directors**
film directors
developmental disabilities
disabilities
learning disabilities
disability discrimination USE **discrimination
against the disabled**
disability insurance
pregnancy disability
Retirement and Disability System Authorization
disabled
discrimination against the disabled
rights of the disabled
disadvantaged
disadvantaged groups
doubly disadvantaged
economically disadvantaged
educationally disadvantaged
socially disadvantaged
disarmament
nuclear disarmament
discipline
academic disciplines
disclosure laws
self disclosure
discographies
discourse
age discrimination
Age Discrimination Act of 1975
class discrimination
disability discrimination USE **discrimination against the
disabled**

discrimination
discrimination against the disabled
discrimination laws
double discrimination
housing discrimination
institutional discrimination
job discrimination
pregnancy discrimination
Pregnancy Discrimination Act of 1978
racial discrimination
religious discrimination
reverse discrimination
sex discrimination
sex discrimination in education
sex discrimination in employment
social discrimination USE **discrimination**
structural discrimination
wage discrimination
discriminatory language
discriminatory legislation
discriminatory practices
discussion groups
disease prevention
fibrocystic disease
heart disease
iatrogenic disease
breast diseases
cardiovascular diseases
communicable diseases
diseases
hereditary diseases
occupational diseases
sexually transmitted diseases
venereal diseases USE **sexually transmitted diseases**
ritual disfigurement
dishwashers
disinformation
disk jockeys
diskettes USE **disks**
compact disks
disks
laser disks
civil disobedience
appetite disorders USE **eating disorders**
chromosome disorders
disorders
eating disorders

gynecologic disorders
menstrual disorders
mental disorders
obsessive compulsive disorders
personality disorders
psychosomatic disorders
displaced homemakers
video display terminals
sewage disposal
labor disputes
information dissemination
dissent
dissertations
cognitive dissonance
long distance marriage USE **commuter marriage**
income distribution
population distribution
wealth distribution
distributive justice
diuretics
divers
diversity
ethnic diversity
gender diversity
racial diversity
divestiture
divine kingship
divining
divinity
class division
division of labor
household division of labor
international division of labor
sexual division of labor
divorce
divorce decrees
divorce laws
divorce rates
no fault divorce
docents
doctor patient relationships USE **patient doctor relationships**
patient doctor relationships
doctoral degrees
doctors USE **physicians**
documentaries
documentation

documents
government documents
legal documents
dogma
dogmatism
doll making
dolls
domestic arrangements
domestic arts
domestic code
domestic food production
domestic labor   USE   **household labor**
domestic rape
domestic relations
domestic rites
domestic roles
domestic services
domestic values
domestic violence
domesticity
domestics   USE   **household workers**
domicile rights
dominance
lateral dominance
dominant culture
female dominated careers   USE   **female intensive occupations**
female dominated occupations   USE   **female intensive occupations**
female dominated professions   USE   **female intensive occupations**
male dominated careers   USE   **male dominated employment**
male dominated employment
Dominican
prima donnas
donors
open door admissions
dormitories
double bind
double discrimination
double standard
doubly disadvantaged
dowry
dowry deaths
draft   USE   **military draft**
draft resistance

military draft
drafters
drafts
draftsmen USE **drafters**
drag USE **cross dressing**
drama
dramatists
drawing
drawings
dreams
dress USE **clothing**
dress codes
dress reform
cross dressing
dressing for success
dressmakers
dressmaking
drinking
drinking prohibition
sex drive
bus drivers
drivers
taxi drivers
truck drivers
drop in day care centers
dropouts
drug abuse
drug addiction
drug dumping
drug industry USE **pharmaceutical industry**
drug overdoses
drug rehabilitation
drug side effects
drug tests
drug therapy
drug use
antidepressant drugs
drugs
fertility drugs
narcotic drugs
nonprescription drugs
prescription drugs
psychotropic drugs
hair dryers
dual career couples
dual career families
dual careers

                     dual economy
                     dual roles
                     dual worker families   USE   **two income families**
                     dualism
                     duchesses
                     due process
         drug dumping
                     Dutch
                     dutch treat
         jury duty
                     dybbuks
    death and dying
      contact dykes
                     dykes   USE   **lesbians**
        group dynamics
      sexual dysfunction
                     dysmenorrhea
                     dysphoria
                     early childbearing
                     early childhood education
                     early experience
                     early retirement
                     earned income
        wage earners
        wage earning mothers
        wage earning wives
        wage earning women
                     earnings
                     earnings gap   USE   **wage gap**
                     earnings sharing
      pierced ears
                     earth mother
                     earth sciences
      mother earth
                     East German
                     Eastern
     Middle Eastern
       Near Eastern   USE   **Middle Eastern**
       Near Eastern studies
                     eating disorders
                     eclecticism
                     ecofeminism
                     ecological factors
                     ecology
                     econometrics
   capitalist economic development models
  communist economic development models

economic anthropology
economic boycotts
economic class
economic counseling
economic depression
economic development
economic development models
economic development theory
economic equity
Economic Equity Act of 1987
economic factors
economic geography
economic growth
economic history
economic indicators
economic policy
economic power
Economic Recovery Tax Act of 1981
economic refugees
economic sanctions
economic status
economic structure
economic theory
economic trends
economic value of women's work
Marxist economic development models
political economic systems
socialist economic development models
economically disadvantaged
agricultural economics
classical economics
economics
family economics
health economics
home economics
home economics extension work
household economics
neoclassical economics
welfare economics
economies of scale
economists
home economists
consumer economy
dual economy
economy
global economy
informal economy

                          mixed economy
                   underground economy
                             l' ecriture feminine
                                 ectogenesis USE **in vitro fertilization**
                                 ectopic pregnancy
                                 Ecuadoran
                                 ecumenism
                  Garden of Eden
                                 editions
                                 editorials
                                 editors
              adult basic education
                    adult education
                    basic education
                bicultural education
                 bilingual education
                   career education
                    civic education
               community education
            compensatory education
              compulsory education
               continuing education
               continuing education units
              cooperative education
        early childhood education
                                 education
                                 Education Amendments of 1972
                                 Education Amendments of 1985
                                 education occupations
               elementary education
    elementary secondary education
                   family education
                 graduate education
                   health education
                   higher education
                 informal education USE **nonformal education**
                 inservice education
                  medical education
               nondegree education
               nonformal education
            nontraditional education
                  nursing education
                 physical education ·
           postsecondary education
                preschool education
                  primary education
                  private education

professional education
progressive education
public education
religious education
remedial education
secondary education
sex discrimination in education
sex education
single sex education
special education
teacher education
technical education
Title IX (Education)
vocational education
educational activities
educational attainment
educational benefits
educational costs
educational equity
educational facilities
educational financing USE **educational costs**
educational legislation
educational methods
educational objectives
educational opportunities
educational policy
educational programs
educational psychology
educational reform
educational subsidies
educational television
equal educational opportunity
Women's Educational Equity Act
educationally disadvantaged
educators
EEOC USE **Equal Employment Opportunity Commission**
drug side effects
efficiency
egalitarian families
ego
Egyptian
ejaculation
elder abuse
elderhostel
crimes against the elderly
elderly USE **older adults**

elderly care
elderly day care centers
elderly households
elected officials
election campaigns
elections
Electra complex
electric utilities
electrical engineering
electricians
electroconvulsive therapy
electrolysis
electronic art
electronic cottage
electronic mail
electronic media
electronic music
electronics industry
elegies
elementary education
elementary schools
elementary secondary education
eligibility
elites
Elizabethan Period
emancipation
embroidery
embryo transfer
embryology
embryos
emergency medical services
emmenagogues USE **menstruation inducing agents**
emotional abuse
emotional adjustment
emotional development
emotional experience
emotional problems
emotionalism
emotions
empathy
employed mothers USE **mothers working outside the home**
self employed USE **self employment**
employee benefits
employee development
employee records
employees

employer supported day care

employers

alternative employment

barriers to employment USE **job discrimination**

Comprehensive Employment and Training Act of 1973

employment

employment agencies

employment opportunities

employment patterns

employment practices

employment schedules

employment training USE **job training**

equal employment opportunity

Equal Employment Opportunity Commission

federal employment

household employment

male dominated employment

minority employment

nontraditional employment

paid employment

part time employment

self employment

sex discrimination in employment

state employment

temporary employment

unpaid employment

youth employment

empowerment

empty nest

encounter groups

encyclopedias

end time thinking

endogamy

endometriosis

endowments

physical endurance

energy

energy conservation

nuclear energy

renewable energy sources

solar energy

Child Support Enforcement Amendments of 1984

enforcement

law enforcement

enfranchisement

engagement

aerospace engineering

chemical engineering
civil engineering
electrical engineering
engineering
genetic engineering
mechanical engineering
nuclear engineering
engineers
English
engravers
engraving
enlightened despotism
Enlightenment
enlisted personnel
military enlistment
academic enrichment
enrollment
all women ensembles
free enterprise
enterprises
entertainers
entertaining USE **social entertaining**
social entertaining
arts, entertainment, and media occupations
entertainment
entertainment industry
sports enthusiasts
entitlement programs
entrepreneurs
data entry operators
built environment
environment
family environment
permissive environment
social environment
urban environment
environmental hazards
environmental health
environmental medicine
environmental movement
environmental racism
environmental sciences
environmentalism
single sex environments
smokefree environments
penis envy
pronoun envy

womb envy
ephemera
epics
epidemiology
epigrams
episiotomy
epistemology
epithets
equal access
equal credit
Equal Credit Opportunity Act of 1974
equal educational opportunity
equal employment opportunity
Equal Employment Opportunity Commission
equal opportunities commissions
equal opportunity
equal pay
Equal Pay Act of 1963
Equal Pay Act of 1970 (Great Britain)
equal pay for equal work
equal pay for equal work
equal pay legislation
equal protection under the law
equal rights
Equal Rights Amendment
equal rights legislation
equality
racial equality
sex equality USE **sexual equality**
sexual equality
equilibrium
computer equipment operators
heavy equipment operators
Federal Equitable Pay Practices Act of 1987
Civil Service Spouse Retirement Equity Act
communications equity
computer equity
economic equity
Economic Equity Act of 1987
educational equity
equity
equity funding
pay equity
race equity
Retirement Equity Act of 1984
sex equity
sexual equity USE **sex equity**

Women's Educational Equity Act
high school equivalency programs
anti ERA movement
ERA USE **Equal Rights Amendment**
ergonomics
erogenous zones USE **arousal**
erotic art
erotic literature
erotica
eroticism
conceptual errors
escorts
Eskimo
ESP USE **extrasensory perception**
essayists
essays
essentialism
real estate
real estate agents
self esteem
estradiol
estrogen replacement therapy
estrogens
estrus
ethclass
ethic of care
work ethic
business ethics
ethics
feminist ethics
medical ethics
political ethics
religious ethics
Ethiopian
ethnic comparisons USE **racial and ethnic differences**
ethnic diversity
ethnic groups
ethnic intimidation
ethnic neighborhoods
ethnic relations
ethnic studies
ethnic women
racial and ethnic differences
ethnicity
ethnography
ethnology

ethnomethodology
ethnomusicology
ethologists
ethology
etiquette
eucharist USE **holy communion**
eugenic sterilization
eugenics
eulogies
eunuchs
Euro American
European
euthanasia
course evaluation
evaluation
evaluation criteria
job evaluation
medical evaluation
mental evaluation
personnel evaluation
evaluations
evangelism
evangelists
Eve
eve teasing
fund raising events
evil
evil spirits
evolution
human evolution
breast examination
breast self examination
credit by examination
pelvic examination
physical examination
self examination
examinations
insurance examiners
excerpts
exchange rate
exchange students
exchange theory
stock exchanges
sexual excitement
excommunication
Executive Order 11246
executive recruitment

executive search firms
executive spouses USE **corporate spouses**
chief executives
executives
executors
executrixes USE **executors**
tax exempt status
aerobic exercise
exercise
isometric exercise
exhibitionism
exhibitions
art exhibits USE **art shows**
exhusbands USE **former husbands**
exile
existentialism
exogamy
life expectancy
expectations
role expectations
credit for experience
early experience
emotional experience
experience
gay experience
gay female experience USE **lesbian experience**
gay male experience
lesbian experience
minority experience
religious experience
work experience
experiential learning
experimental dance
experimental design
experimental psychology
experimental theater
experts
expiation
exploitation
sexual exploitation
explorers
expositions
expressing milk
abstract expressionism
expressionism
extended care facilities
extended families

extended kinship network USE **extended families**
agricultural extension
extension work
extension workers
home economics extension work
external degree programs
menstrual extraction
extractive industry
extracurricular activities
extramarital affairs
extrasensory perception
extroversion
exwives USE **former wives**
hand eye coordination
eyeglasses
Fabianism
fables
face lifts
faces
correctional facilities USE **prisons**
educational facilities
extended care facilities
facilities
health care facilities
offices (facilities)
religious facilities
facism
factions
Rh factor
rhesus factor USE **Rh factor**
factories
causal factors USE **influences**
ecological factors
economic factors
performance factors
psychological factors
racial factors
factory conditions
factory workers
faculty
faculty retrenchment
fads
faghag
academic failure
failure
fear of failure
fainting

	fair play
laissez	faire
	fairness
	fairy tales
	faith
	faith communities
	faith healers
	Falkland Islander
	fallen women
	fallopian tubes
	false consciousness
	false dichotomies
	false generics
	false pregnancy USE **pseudopregnancy**
	falsies USE **padding**
Aid to	Families with Dependent Children
blended	families
communal	families
dual career	families
dual worker	families USE **two income families**
egalitarian	families
extended	families
	families
fatherless	families
foster	families
heads of	families
interethnic	families
interracial	families
interreligious	families
low income	families
middle class	families
motherless	families
nuclear	families
one parent	families USE **single parent families**
single parent	families
surrogate	families
two career	families USE **dual career families**
two income	families
upper class	families
balancing work and	family life
career	family conflict
	Family and Medical Leave Act of 1987
	family attitudes
	family conflict
	family counseling
	family courts
	family economics

family education
family environment
family farms
family finances
family history
family income
family influence
family life
family medicine
family mobility
family owned business
family planning
family policy
family practice USE **family medicine**
family practitioners
family problems
family recipes
family relationships
family responsibility
family rights
family roles
family size
family structure
family therapy
family violence USE **domestic violence**
Family Violence Prevention and Services Act
ideal family size USE **family size**
marriage and family law
natural family planning USE **rhythm method**
the family USE **families**
famine
fantasies
rape fantasies
sexual fantasies
farce
farm workers
farmers
farming
tenant farming
collective farms
family farms
farms
fascism
fashion
fashion design
fashion illustration
fashion photography

fashion shows
fasting
fat liberation
fat oppression
femmes fatales
father daughter incest
father daughter relationships
father son incest
father son relationships
God the father
Mother/ Father God
fatherhood USE **fathers**
fatherhood USE **parenthood**
fathering
fatherless families
absentee fathers
biological fathers USE **birth fathers**
birth fathers
fathers
fathers (religious) USE **priests**
fathers in law
gay fathers
runaway fathers
single fathers
surrogate fathers
teenage fathers
unmarried fathers USE **single fathers**
fatigue
no fault divorce
no fault insurance
faulty generalization
fear
fear of failure
fear of success
federal agencies
federal aid
federal assistance programs
federal budget
federal courts
federal employment
Federal Equitable Pay Practices Act of 1987
federal government
federal legislation
federal regulations
federal taxes
federalism
federally sponsored research

federations
feedback
bottle feeding
breast feeding
feelings USE **emotions**
fellatio
fellowships
postdoctoral fellowships
female authored texts
female bonding
female chauvinism
female circumcision
female dominated careers USE **female intensive occupations**
female dominated occupations USE **female intensive occupations**
female dominated professions USE **female intensive occupations**
female female relationships
female female relationships
female friendships
female headed households
female homosexuality USE **lesbianism**
female homosexuals USE **lesbians**
female hypersexuality
female impersonators
female intensive occupations
female male friendships
female male relationships
female Oedipus complex
female sexual slavery
female sexuality
female societies
female spirituality
gay female culture USE **lesbian culture**
gay female experience USE **lesbian experience**
male female friendships USE **female male friendships**
male female relationships USE **female male relationships**
castrating females
females
ad feminam
feminine mystique
feminine principle
l'ecriture feminine
femininity
anarcha feminism

Black feminism
career feminism
cross cultural feminism
cultural feminism
feminism
first wave feminism
global feminism
international feminism USE **global feminism**
lesbian feminism
liberal feminism
mainstream feminism
Marxist feminism
nonaligned feminism
psychoanalytic feminism
radical feminism
socialist feminism
spiritual feminism
feminist criticism
feminist ethics
feminist methods
feminist movement
feminist music
feminist organizations
feminist perspective
feminist publications
feminist scholarship
feminist studies
feminist theology
feminist theory
feminist therapy
feminist writing
feminists
male feminists
feminization of occupations USE **tipping**
feminization of poverty USE **pauperization of women**
feminization of poverty USE **women living in poverty**
feminization of professions USE **tipping**
femmage
femme
femmes fatales
fencing
fertility
fertility drugs
fertility rates
fertility rites

fertilization
in vitro fertilization
festivals
film festivals
music festivals
fetal alcohol syndrome
fetal monitoring
fetuses
feudalism
feuds
childbed fever USE **puerperal fever**
puerperal fever
fiber art
fibrocystic disease
fiction
pulp fiction
science fiction
fictional characters
field hockey
track and field
fieldwork
fifth world
fire fighters
figurative language
figures of speech USE **figurative language**
files
Filipino
Filipino American
directors (film) USE **film directors**
film
film criticism
film directors
film festivals
film producers
filmographies
films
filmstrips
finance
family finances
finances
personal finances
financial aid
financial arrangements
financial management
financial occupations
financial planners
financial planning

financial resources
financial statements
student financial aid
financiers
educational financing USE **educational costs**
fine arts USE **performing arts**
fine arts USE **visual arts**
finishing schools
Finnish
fire fighters
fire prevention
firemen USE **fire fighters**
firing
executive search firms
first husbands
First Ladies USE **governors' spouses**
First Ladies USE **presidential spouses**
First Ladies (historical)
first wave feminism
first wives
fiscal policy
fish sellers
fishermen USE **fishers**
fishers
agricultural, fishing, and forestry occupations
fishwives USE **fish sellers**
physical fitness
hot flashes
flexible benefits
flexible career patterns
flexible hours USE **flexible work schedules**
flexible work schedules
flexitime USE **flexible work schedules**
flight attendants
flirtation
flirts
flowcharts
flower arranging
flower painting
flowers
flyers
folk art
folk culture
folk dance
folk healers
folk literature
folk medicine

folk music
myths (folk culture) USE **mythology**
folklore USE **folk culture**
folklorists
camp followers
domestic food production
food
food for work
food industry
food marketing
food preparation
food preparation occupations
food processing
food service workers
food stamps
food technology
foot binding
football
credit for experience
dressing for success
equal pay for equal work
food for work
International Decade for Women
queen for a day
wages for housework
all volunteer military force
labor force
labor force participation
labor force rates
labor force statistics
multinational labor force
reduction in force
unpaid labor force
work force USE **labor force**
forced retirement
armed forces
task forces
forecasting
foreign affairs USE **international relations**
foreign aid
foreign aid policy
foreign investment policy
foreign service
foreign students
foreign workers
foremen USE **supervisors**
foremothers

foreplay
agricultural, fishing, and forestry occupations
forgiveness
formalism
class formation
race formation
state formation
former husbands
former spouses
former wives
Uniformed Services Former Spouses' Protection Act
forms of address
forms of affection
infant formula
fortune tellers
fortune telling
forums
fossil hominids
foster children
foster families
foster grandparents
foster homes
foster parents
foundations
four day workweek
four year colleges
fourth world
franchise
fraternal twins
fraternities
credit fraud
fraud
insurance fraud
welfare fraud
barrier free access
free association
free enterprise
free love USE **sexual liberation**
free schools
free speech
free trade zones
nuclear free zones
academic freedom
freedom
freedom from oppression
freedom of assembly
freedom of choice

freedom of information
freedom of speech
freedom of the press
freedom of worship
religious freedom   USE   **freedom of worship**
reproductive freedom
sexual freedom
freedoms
French
French Revolution
Freudianism
girl Fridays   USE   **administrative assistants**
friends
female friendships
female male friendships
friendships
male female friendships   USE   **female male friendships**
male friendships
frigidity   USE   **nonorgasmic women**
fringe benefits
freedom from oppression
frontier life
frustration
fund raising
fund raising events
fundamentalism
equity funding
funding
pension funds
funeral rites
furniture
future
future studies
futurism
G spot
gallantry
galleries
Gambian
gambling
game shows
game theory
computer games
games
Olympic Games
video games
gang rape
gangs

earnings gap USE **wage gap**
gender gap
generation gap
wage gap
avant garde
garden clubs
Garden of Eden
gardeners
gardens
garment industry
gas utilities
gatekeeping
woman the gatherer
gay couples
gay culture
gay experience
gay fathers
gay female culture USE **lesbian culture**
gay female experience USE **lesbian experience**
gay literature
gay male couples
gay male culture
gay male experience
gay male literature
gay male marriage
gay male relationships
gay males USE **gay men**
gay marriage
gay men
gay pride
gay relationships
gay rights
gay stepfathers
gay stepmothers USE **lesbian stepmothers**
gay studies
gay women USE **lesbians**
gay/straight split
gays
gazetteers
crystal ball gazing
geishas
gender
gender bias
gender development
gender differences
gender diversity
gender gap

gender identity
gender ideology
gender marking
gender roles
gender studies
race, class, and gender studies
sex/ gender systems
social construction of gender
general anesthesia
faulty generalization
generation gap
income generation
generative grammar
generic pronouns
false generics
genetic counseling
genetic defects
genetic determinants
genetic engineering
genetic screening
geneticists
genetics
population genetics
genital herpes
genital mutilation
genitalia USE **genitals**
genitals
genocide
literary genres USE **literature**
geographic mobility
economic geography
geography
social geography
geologists
geology
geriatrics
East German
German
German measles USE **rubella**
West German
gerontology
gestalt therapy
gestation USE **pregnancy**
gestation period
gestures
Ghanaian
ghettos

job ghettos
gigolos
girdles
girl Fridays USE **administrative assistants**
girl preference of parents
girl watching USE **street harassment**
new girl networks USE **old girl networks**
old girl networks
career girls USE **wage earning women**
chorus girls USE **chorus dancers**
coat check girls USE **coat checkers**
girls
hat check girls USE **hat checkers**
images of girls
mill girls USE **factory workers**
glamour
pituitary gland
thyroid gland
glands
lymph glands
mammary glands
glass ceiling
glassmakers
glaziers
global assembly lines
global economy
global feminism
global security
global village
glossaries
glossolalia
gnosticism
goals USE **objectives**
God the father
Mother/Father God
goddess worship
mother goddess
goddesses
gods
golf
gonorrhea
gospel music
gossip
Gothic style
governance
governesses
governing boards

city	government
county	government
federal	government
	government
	government agencies
	government appointments
	government documents
	government workers
local	government
municipal	government USE **city government**
state	government
student	government
boards of	governors USE **governing boards**
	governors
	governors' spouses
	graciousness
intermediate	grades
	graduate degrees
	graduate education
	graduation ceremonies
	graffiti
generative	grammar
	grammar
transformational	grammar
	gramsevika
	grandchildren
	granddaughters
	grandfathers
	grandmothers
foster	grandparents
	grandparents
	grandsons
	granny midwives USE **lay midwives**
	grant proposals
	grant writing USE **proposal writing**
block	grants
	grants
research	grants
tuition	grants
	grapevine
	graphic design
	graphics
	graphs
	grass roots
	gray power
Equal Pay Act of 1970	(Great Britain)
	Great Awakening

Great Depression

National Health Service (Great Britain)

greed

Greek

Greek American

Grenadan

grief

grievance procedures

grooming behavior

grooms

gross income

group behavior

group counseling

group developed theater

group dynamics

group marriage

group process

group sex

group therapy

advocacy groups

children's groups

citizen groups

communal groups

consciousness raising groups

cultural groups

disadvantaged groups

discussion groups

encounter groups

ethnic groups

groups

heterogeneous groups

homogeneous groups

minority groups

mixed sex groups

pressure groups

professional women's groups

religious groups

special interest groups

study groups

support groups

women's groups

economic growth

growth   USE   **physical development**

population growth

zero population growth

guaranteed income

guardians

legal guardians
guards
security guards
Guatemalan
guerrilla warfare
career guidance USE **career counseling**
guidelines
curriculum guides
guides
how to guides
spirit guides
tour guides
guilt
Guinean
Papua New Guinean
gun control laws
Guyanese
gymnastics
gynarchy
gynecologic disorders
gynecology
gynocide
gynocologists
gynocriticism
Gypsy
hagiography
haiku
body hair
hair
hair dryers
hair loss
hair removal
hair straightening
hair styles
pubic hair
hairdressers
Haitian
Haitian American
halfway houses
residence halls
hand eye coordination
handbooks
handicapped USE **disabled**
mentally handicapped
handicrafts USE **craft arts**
handmade
laying on of hands

                              ranch hands
                                    happiness
                             sexual harassment
                             street harassment
                                    harems
                                    harlots
                                    hat check girls USE **hat checkers**
                                    hat checkers
                                    hate
                                    Hawaiian
                                    hazardous waste
                     environmental hazards
                                    hazards
                            health hazards
                         household hazards
                          industrial hazards
                       occupational hazards USE **work hazards**
                             office hazards USE **work hazards**
                       reproductive hazards at work
                               work hazards
                                    he/man language
                                    Head Start programs
                                    headaches
                           migraine headaches
                            tension headaches
                            female headed households
                                    headhunters USE **executive recruitment**
                            subject headings
                                    headmasters USE **principals**
                                    headmistresses USE **principals**
                                    heads of families
                                    heads of households USE **householders**
                                    heads of state
                              faith healers
                               folk healers
                                    healers
                             native healers
                                    healing
                         community health services
                          consumer health organizations
                     environmental health
                                    health
                                    health advocates
                                    health behavior
                                    health care
                                    health care costs
                                    health care delivery

health care facilities
health care legislation
health care occupations
health care policy
health care providers
health care services
health care utilization
health care workers
health cooperatives
health economics
health education
health hazards
health insurance
Health Insurance Continuation
health maintenance organizations
health seeking behavior
health services USE **health care services**
holistic health
home health care
maternal health service
mental health
mental health advocates
mental health issues
mental health treatment
multicultural health care services
national health insurance
National Health Service (Great Britain)
neighborhood health centers
occupational health and safety
physical health
public health
Public Health Service Act
reproductive health
school health services
Title VII (Public Health)
Title VIII (Public Health)
Title X (Public Health)
women's health movement
hearing
hearing aids
hearing impairments
congressional hearings
hearings
heart disease
heavy equipment operators
high heeled shoes
Hegelianism

Hellenic Period
help seeking behavior
self help
helping behavior
helplessness USE **learned helplessness**
learned helplessness
hemlines
herbal remedies
herbs
hereditary diseases
heredity
heresies
heretics
cultural heritage
hermaphrodites
hermaphroditism
hermeneutics
heroes
heroic women USE **heroes**
heroin
heroines USE **heroes**
heroines (historical)
genital herpes
herpes simplex virus type II USE **genital herpes**
herstory
heterogeneous groups
heterosexism
heterosexual privilege
heterosexual relationships
compulsory heterosexuality
heterosexuality
heterosexuals USE **heterosexuality**
hidden curriculum
hidjab
hierarchy
high blood pressure USE **hypertension**
high heeled shoes
high priestesses
high school equivalency programs
high schools
junior high schools
higher education
Hindu
Hinduism
hips
affirmative action hiring
hiring policy

hirsutism
Hispanic
Hispanic American
Hispanic studies USE **Latina studies**
historians
actresses (historical)
First Ladies (historical)
heroines (historical)
historical linguistics
hostesses (historical)
ladies (historical)
seamstresses (historical)
historically Black colleges USE **Black colleges**
histories
life histories
oral histories
historiography
art history
economic history
family history
history
history of children
history of religion
history of science
history of women USE **women's history**
intellectual history
labor history
literary history
music history
oral history
social history
women's history
work history
HMOs USE **health maintenance organizations**
hobbies
field hockey
ice hockey
holistic health
holistic medicine
holistic music
holocaust
holy communion
holy matrimony
holy men
holy women
broken home USE **single parent families**
home accidents

home based business
home based careers
home based work
home based workers
home birth
home economics
home economics extension work
home economists
home health care
home improvement loans
home labor USE **household labor**
home life
home remedies
home schooling
home study
mothers working outside the home
wives working outside the home
women working outside the home
homeless
homeless men
homeless women
homemaker rights
homemaker service
displaced homemakers
homemakers
visiting homemakers
homemaking
homeowners
foster homes
homes USE **housing**
maternity homes
nursing homes
homesteading
homicide USE **murder**
homilies
ad hominem
fossil hominids
homoeroticism
homogeneous groups
homophile movement
homophobia
homosexual marriage USE **gay marriage**
homosexual relationships USE **gay relationships**
female homosexuality USE **lesbianism**
homosexuality
male homosexuality
female homosexuals USE **lesbians**

homosexuals USE **gays**

male homosexuals USE **gay men**

Honduran

honesty

honeymoons

crimes of honor

honorary degrees

honorary societies

hookers USE **prostitutes**

rug hooking

hormone therapy

hormones

pituitary hormones

sex hormones

horticulture

hosiery

hospices

hospitals

mental hospitals

hostels

hostesses USE **hosts**

hostesses (historical)

hostility

hosts

hosts (media) USE **television personalities**

hot flashes

hot lines

hotel workers

flexible hours USE **flexible work schedules**

man hours USE **work hours**

work hours

angel in the house

house churches

house design

house husbands USE **homemakers**

House of Representatives

house wives USE **homemakers**

housecleaners

housecleaning

household division of labor

household economics

household employment

household hazards

household labor

household violence USE **domestic violence**

household workers

unpaid household labor

householders
elderly households
female headed households
heads of households USE **householders**
households
low income households
househusbands USE **homemakers**
housekeepers
housekeeping services
housemothers
housepainters
halfway houses
houses
housewares
housewives USE **homemakers**
housework
wages for housework
housing
housing costs
housing discrimination
housing subsidies
public housing
segregated housing
student housing
subsidized housing USE **public housing**
temporary housing
how to guides
hugging
basic human needs
human capital
human evolution
human interest
human needs
human relations
human relations commissions
human resources
human rights
human rights violations
human services
humanism
humanists
humanitarianism
humanities
humanity
humor
sense of humor
Hungarian

```
                    hunger
         man the    hunter
             job    hunting
           witch    hunts
                    husband abuse
       corporate    husbands   USE   corporate spouses
           first    husbands
          former    husbands
           house    husbands   USE   homemakers
                    husbands
       political    husbands   USE   political spouses
         runaway    husbands
                    hygiene
      industrial    hygiene
        personal    hygiene
          dental    hygienists
                    hymen
                    hymenoplasty
                    hymns
          female    hypersexuality
                    hypersexuality
            male    hypersexuality
                    hypertension
                    hyphenated names
                    hypnotism
                    hypochondria
                    hysterectomy
                    hysteria
                    iatrogenic disease
                    ice hockey
                    ice skating
                    Icelandic
                    iconoclasts
                    iconography
                    icons
                    ideal family size   USE   family size
                    ideal woman
                    idealism
                    identical twins
        sex role    identification   USE   sexual identity
           women    identified women
           class    identity
       cross sex    identity
        cultural    identity
          gender    identity
                    identity
                    identity crisis
```

sex identity   USE   **sexual identity**
sexual identity
social identity
class ideology
gender ideology
ideology
political ideology
sacred ideology
illegal aliens   USE   **illegal immigrants**
illegal immigrants
illegitimacy
adult illiteracy
illiteracy
illness
mental illness   USE   **mental disorders**
terminal illness
fashion illustration
illustration
illustrators
body image
image
self image   USE   **self concept**
imagery
images of girls
images of women
imagination
immaculate conception
illegal immigrants
immigrants
immigration
immigration policy
immigration quotas
immorality
acquired immune deficiency syndrome
impact on children
impact on women
hearing impairments
visual impairments
cultural imperialism
imperialism   USE   **colonialism**
female impersonators
impersonators
male impersonators
breast implants
impotence
impoverishment of women
impregnation

                                        impressionism
                        home improvement loans
                                        improvisation
                                        impurity
                        angel in the house
                     brothers in law
             children living in poverty
                  daughters in law
                          drop in day care centers
                    fathers in law
                                        in kind contributions
                                        in laws
                                        in vitro fertilization
                    mothers in law
                 reduction in force
                      rooming in
      sex discrimination in education
      sex discrimination in employment
                    sisters in law
                       sons in law
                 speaking in tongues USE **glossolalia**
                    traffic in women USE **sex tourism**
                  violence in the media
                    women in
                    women in development
                    women in politics
                    women in science
                    women in the military
                    women in transition
            women living in poverty
                     works in progress
                                        inbreeding
                                        incarceration
                                        incarnation
                      work incentive programs
                                        incentives
               monetary incentives
                       tax incentives
                      work incentives
          brother sister incest
       father daughter incest
              father son incest
                                        incest
                                        incest victims
       mother daughter incest
            mother son incest
                                        incidental music

earned income
family income
gross income
guaranteed income
income
income distribution
income generation
income tax
low income families
low income households
minimum income
net income
transfer income
two income families
Rh incompatibility
wage increases
incubi
independence
independent scholars
independent study
indexes
Alaskan Indian
American Indian
American Indian studies
Canadian Indian studies
Indian
West Indian
economic indicators
social indicators
socioeconomic indicators
urban indicators
indigenous
indigenous populations
individual counseling
individual development
individualism
individuality
Indochinese
Indochinese American
indoctrination
Indonesian
induced abortion
induced labor
menstruation inducing agents
industrial classification
industrial conditions
industrial hazards

industrial hygiene
industrial policy USE **corporate policy**
industrial psychology
industrial relations
Industrial Revolution
industrialization
industries
advertising industry
agricultural industry
banking industry
building industry USE **construction industry**
chemical industry
communications industry
construction industry
cottage industry
drug industry USE **pharmaceutical industry**
electronics industry
entertainment industry
extractive industry
food industry
garment industry
insurance industry
manufacturing industry
mining industry
motion picture industry
music industry
oil industry
personal service industry
pharmaceutical industry
professional and related services industry
publishing industry
retail trade industry
sex industry
textile industry
tobacco industry
transportation industry
wholesale trade industry
inequality
infant care
infant development
infant formula
infant mortality
maternal and infant welfare
sudden infant death syndrome
infanticide
infants
premature infants

Women, Infants, and Children Nutrition Program
vaginal infections
infertility
infibulation
infidelity
inflation
family influence
influence
parent influence
peer influence
political influence
sibling influence
biological influences
cultural influences
influences
prenatal influences
religious influences
social influences
informal economy
informal education   USE   **nonformal education**
informal language
informal sector
consumer information
freedom of information
information
information and referral centers
information dissemination
information processing
information retrieval
information retrieval services
information sciences
information scientists
information services
information storage
information theory
public information
informed consent
ingratiation
inheritance customs
inheritance rights
inherited wealth
initiation rites
initiative
injectable contraceptives
inner city
innocence
innovation

sit	ins
teach	ins
	insanity
artificial	insemination
	insemination
self	insemination
	inservice education
	inspectors
consumer	installment loans
	instigators
	instincts
	institutes
	institutional discrimination
	institutional racism
	institutional sexism
	institutions
	instructions
	instrument makers
	instrumental music
automobile	insurance
car	insurance USE **automobile insurance**
disability	insurance
health	insurance
Health	Insurance Continuation
	insurance
	insurance adjusters
	insurance agents
	insurance examiners
	insurance fraud
	insurance industry
liability	insurance
life	insurance
medical	insurance USE **health insurance**
national health	insurance
no fault	insurance
unemployment	insurance
	insured loans
curriculum	integration
	integration
school	integration
	integrity
	intellectual development
	intellectual history
	intellectuals
artificial	intelligence
	intelligence
	intelligence agencies

intelligence tests
female intensive occupations
male intensive occupations
women intensive careers USE **female intensive**
occupations
women intensive occupations USE **female intensive**
occupations
women intensive professions USE **female intensive**
occupations
intercaste marriage
sexual intercourse
interdisciplinary studies
career interest inventories
conflict of interest
human interest
interest rates
prime interest rate
public interest
special interest groups
interethnic families
interfaith marriage
interior design
intermediate grades
intern programs
international adoption
international affairs USE **international relations**
International Decade for Women
international division of labor
international feminism USE **global feminism**
international marriage
international perspective
international policy
international relations
international trade policy
international women's movement
internment
internships
interpersonal communication
interpersonal relationships USE **personal**
relationships
interpreters
interracial adoption
interracial families
interracial marriage
interracial relations
interreligious families
interrole conflict

interruptions
coitus interruptus
crisis intervention
interviewers
interviewing
interviews
intimacy
ethnic intimidation
intimidation
sexual intimidation
lactose intolerance
intramurals
intrauterine devices
introversion
intuition
Inuit
inventions
career interest inventories
inventors
investigations
investigative journalism
foreign investment policy
investments
investors
invisibility
involuntary depression
involuntary sterilization
Iranian
Iraqi
Irish
Northern Irish
iron deficiency anemia
ironers
ironing
irony
irrationalism
irrigation
Islam
Falkland Islander
Pacific Islander
isolation
isolationism
isometric exercise
Israeli
mental health issues
social issues
Italian

Italian American
IUDs USE **intrauterine devices**
Ivory Coaster
jails USE **prisons**
Jamaican
janitors
Japanese
Japanese American
jargon
jazz
jazz musicians
jealousy
jewelry
jewelry makers
Jewish
Jewish women's studies
job advertisements
job alienation
job candidates
job counseling USE **occupational counseling**
job descriptions
job development
job discrimination
job evaluation
job ghettos
job hunting
job layoffs
job market
job mobility USE **occupational mobility**
job performance
job placement
job recruitment
job responsibility
job retraining
job rewards
job satisfaction
job search USE **job hunting**
job search methods
job security
job segregation USE **occupational segregation**
job sharing
job skills
job standards
job stress USE **occupational stress**
job training
Job Training Partnership Act
on the job training

jobs USE **occupations**
nose jobs USE **cosmetic surgery**
disk jockeys
jockeys
jogging USE **running**
johns
joint custody USE **shared custody**
jokes
investigative journalism
journalism
sports journalism
journalists
journals
journals (periodicals)
joy
Judaism
judges
judicial appointments
judicial attitudes
judicial process
judiciary
judiciary system
judo
Jungianism
junior colleges
junior high schools
juries
jurors
jury duty
criminal justice
distributive justice
justice
juvenile justice system
juvenile courts
juvenile delinquency
juvenile justice system
juvenile offenders
juvenile prostitution
Kantianism
karate
keening
Kenyan
keypunch operators USE **data entry operators**
kibbutzim
kidnapping
in kind contributions
kindergarten

kinesics
kinesthetic perception
divine kingship
bilineal kinship
extended kinship network　USE　**extended families**
kinship
matrilineal kinship
patrilineal kinship
unilineal kinship
kissing
kitchens
coffee klatches
knitting
knitting machine operators
right to know legislation
knowledge
sociology of knowledge
subjective knowledge
Korean
Korean American
Korean War
l'ecriture feminine
labels
labia
child labor
division of labor
domestic labor　USE　**household labor**
home labor　USE　**household labor**
household division of labor
household labor
induced labor
international division of labor
labor
labor (childbirth)
labor coaching
labor contracts
labor disputes
labor force
labor force participation
labor force rates
labor force statistics
labor history
labor law reform
labor laws　USE　**labor legislation**
labor legislation
labor market
labor movement

labor policy
labor relations
labor saving devices
labor supply
labor theory of value
labor turnover
labor unions
manual labor
multinational labor force
nonwage labor USE **unpaid employment**
piecework labor policy
regional labor workers USE **migrant workers**
sexual division of labor
unfair labor practices
unpaid household labor
unpaid labor force
wage labor
laboratories
laboratory animals
laboratory assistants
laborers
unskilled laborers USE **laborers**
lace making
lack of confidence
lacrosse
lactation
lactose intolerance
career ladders
bag ladies USE **homeless women**
First Ladies USE **governors' spouses**
First Ladies USE **presidential spouses**
First Ladies (historical)
ladies USE **women**
ladies (historical)
ladies (nobility)
ladies' aid societies
ladies' auxiliaries USE **auxiliaries**
laissez faire
nom de lait
laity
land reform
land rights
land settlement
land tenure
land use
land use technology
landlords

```
                      slum  landlords
                            landscape architects
                      body  language
             discriminatory  language
                  figurative  language
                   he/man  language
                   informal  language
                            language
                            language aptitude
                            language development
                            language skills
                            language structure
                 nonsexist  language
                 nonverbal  language
                patriarchal  language
                  religious  language
                     sexist  language
                      sign  language
                 women's  language
                   written  language
             programming  languages
                       Sri  Lankan
                            Laotian
                            larceny
                            large cities   USE   **urban areas**
                            laser disks
                            last rites
                            latchkey children
                            late childbearing
                            lateral dominance
                            Latin American
                            Latin American studies
                            Latina
                            Latina studies
                            laughter
                            launderers
                            laundresses   USE   **launderers**
                            laundry
              brothers in  law
                   canon  law   USE   **religious law**
                     civil  law
                 common  law marriage
                corporate  law
                  criminal  law
             daughters in  law
   equal protection under the  law
                 fathers in  law
```

labor law reform
law
law enforcement
marriage and family law
mothers in law
religious law
sisters in law
sons in law
abortion laws
antidiscrimination laws USE **discrimination laws**
community property laws
copyright laws
disclosure laws
discrimination laws
divorce laws
gun control laws
in laws
labor laws USE **labor legislation**
laws
property laws
tax laws
civil lawsuits
criminal lawsuits
lawsuits
lawyer client relationships
lawyers
lay midwives
laying on of hands
laymen
job layoffs
laypeople USE **laity**
laywomen
political leaders
leadership
leadership roles
leadership skills
leadership training
student leadership
tea leaf reading
leagues
learned behavior
learned helplessness
adult learning
experiential learning
learning
learning differences
learning disabilities

learning motivation
lifelong learning
prior learning USE **credit for experience**
social learning USE **socialization**
child care leave
Family and Medical Leave Act of 1987
maternity leave
parental leave
paternity leave
pregnancy leave
sick leave
Lebanese
lectures
ledgers
left wing organizations
new left
legal advocates
legal aid services
legal and political occupations
legal briefs
legal cruelty
legal documents
legal guardians
legal responsibility
legal services
legal settlements
legal status
legal system
legends
antitrust legislation
civil rights legislation
discriminatory legislation
educational legislation
equal pay legislation
equal rights legislation
federal legislation
health care legislation
labor legislation
legislation
local legislation
minimum wage legislation
protective legislation
right to know legislation
social legislation
state legislation
legislators
legislatures

                    legitimacy
                    legitimization of children
                    legs
                    leisure
                    leisure activities
                    Leninism
             Sierra Leonean
                    lesbian communities
                    lesbian couples
                    lesbian culture
                    lesbian experience
                    lesbian feminism
                    lesbian literature
                    lesbian marriage
                    lesbian mothers
                    lesbian movement
                    lesbian relationships
                    lesbian separatism
                    lesbian stepmothers
                    lesbian studies
                    lesbianism
          closeted lesbians
                    lesbians
                    lesbophobia
                    lesson plans
                    letter writers
                    letters
                    letters of recommendation
                    levirate
         corporate liability
                    liability
                    liability insurance
           limited liability
          women's lib USE **women's liberation**
                    libel
                    liberal feminism
                    liberalism
                    liberals
               fat liberation
                    liberation
                    liberation struggles
                    liberation theology
             men's liberation
            sexual liberation
           women's liberation
           women's liberation movement USE **women's movement**
                    Liberian

Libertarian Party
libertarianism
civil liberties
Statue of Liberty
libido USE **sex drive**
librarians
libraries
library science
library workers
librettos
Libyan
licenses
marriage licenses
child care licensing
licensing
lieder
lies
balancing work and family life
change of life USE **menopause**
family life
frontier life
home life
life cycles
life expectancy
life histories
life insurance
life sciences USE **biological sciences**
life skills
life span
life styles
quality of life
quality of work life
right to life USE **antiabortion movement**
lifelong learning
weight lifting
butt lifts USE **cosmetic surgery**
face lifts
tubal ligation
tubal ligation reversal
Lilith
limericks
limited liability
lineage
chorus lines
global assembly lines
hot lines
lingerie

linguistic sexism
applied linguistics
descriptive linguistics
historical linguistics
linguistics
structural linguistics
suction lipectomy USE **liposuction surgery**
liposuction surgery
listening
book lists
lists
adult literacy
computer literacy
literacy
literacy campaigns
literary arts USE **literature**
literary canon
literary criticism
literary genres USE **literature**
literary history
literary symbols
literary theory
biblical literature USE **religious literature**
children's literature
erotic literature
folk literature
gay literature
gay male literature
lesbian literature
literature
nonsexist literature
oral literature
religious literature
travel literature
utopian literature
women's literature
litigation USE **lawsuits**
liturgies
children living in poverty
cost of living
living alone
living arrangements
living conditions
living standards
living together USE **cohabitation**
rural living
standards of living USE **living standards**

women living in poverty
consumer installment loans
home improvement loans
insured loans
loans
student loans
lobbying
local anesthesia
local government
local legislation
local politics
locker rooms
locus of control
lodges
logic
logical thinking
logs
Lolita
loneliness
long distance marriage   USE   **commuter marriage**
long term memory
longshore workers
longshoremen   USE   **longshore workers**
lookism
hair loss
loss
loss of self
courtly love
free love   USE   **sexual liberation**
love
love potions
maternal love
romantic love
unrequited love
lovemaking
lovers
low income families
low income households
low pay
lower class
loyalty
loyalty oaths
lubricants
lullabies
lumber cutters
lumbermen   USE   **lumber cutters**
National School Lunch Act Amendments of 1982

lunches
lust
Luxembourgian
lying
lymph glands
lynching
lyric poetry
lyricists
lyrics
knitting machine operators
machine operators
sewing machine operators
machinery
machinists
machismo
macroeconomics
madonna
madrigals
magazines
women's magazines
magic
magistrates
magnetic tapes
maiden aunts
maiden name USE **birth name**
maidenhead USE **hymen**
maids USE **household workers**
old maids
electronic mail
mail carriers
mail order brides
mainstream feminism
mainstreaming
health maintenance organizations
majority culture
majority rule
moral majority
instrument makers
jewelry makers
tool and die makers
makeup
decision making
doll making
lace making
policy making
textile making
Malaysian

female male friendships
female male relationships
gay male couples
gay male culture
gay male experience
gay male literature
gay male marriage
gay male relationships
male bonding
male chauvinism
male chauvinist pig USE **male chauvinism**
male circumcision
male dominated careers USE **male dominated
employment**
male dominated employment
male female friendships USE **female male
friendships**
male female relationships USE **female male
relationships**
male feminists
male friendships
male homosexuality
male homosexuals USE **gay men**
male hypersexuality
male impersonators
male intensive occupations
male male relationships
male male relationships
male norms
male nurses USE **nurses**
male pregnancy
male sexuality
male standards
gay males USE **gay men**
males
Malian
malignant tumors
malnutrition
Maltese
Malthusianism
mammary glands
mammies
mammography
brotherhood of man USE **humanity**
he/ man language
man
man hours USE **work hours**

marital

man the hunter
White man USE **Caucasian**
financial management
management
management practices
management styles
management techniques
management theory
management training
money management
personal management
personnel management
time management
water management
managerial occupations
managers
middle managers
manicurists
manipulative behavior
manipulators
mankind USE **humanity**
manmade USE **handmade**
manmade USE **manufactured**
mannequins
manners
manpower USE **human resources**
manpower USE **labor force**
manpower USE **personnel**
manual labor
manuals
sex manuals
manufactured
manufacturers
manufacturing industry
manufacturing occupations
manumission
manuscripts
career mapping
maps
maquiladora
marathons
marches
marginality
marianismo
marijuana
marital adjustment
marital conflict

marital property reform
marital rape USE **domestic rape**
marital roles
marital satisfaction
marital stability
marital status
marital violence
boundary markers
job market
labor market
market research
food marketing
marketing and sales occupations
black markets
markets
stock markets
gender marking
tribal markings
arranged marriage
child marriage
childfree marriage
common law marriage
commuter marriage
companionate marriage
gay male marriage
gay marriage
group marriage
homosexual marriage USE **gay marriage**
intercaste marriage
interfaith marriage
international marriage
interracial marriage
lesbian marriage
long distance marriage USE **commuter marriage**
marriage
marriage and family law
marriage by proxy
marriage ceremonies
marriage contracts
marriage counseling
marriage customs
marriage licenses
marriage proposals
marriage rates
marriage tax
marriage vows
posthumous marriage

teenage marriage
trial marriage
married couples
married men USE **husbands**
married students
married women USE **wives**
martial arts
martyrdom
martyrs
Marxism
Marxist economic development models
Marxist feminism
Virgin Mary
masculine pronouns
masculinity
masochism
critical mass
mass actions
mass media
massage
massage parlors
massage therapy USE **massage**
masseuses
mastectomy
master of ceremonies
masters' degrees
masturbation
matchmakers
alma mater
material culture
materialism
maternal age
maternal and infant welfare
maternal health service
maternal love
maternal mortality
maternity
maternity benefits
maternity homes
maternity leave
maternity rights
maternity wards
math USE **mathematics**
math ability
math anxiety USE **math avoidance**
math avoidance
math confidence

                 mathematical models
                 mathematicians
       applied mathematics
                 mathematics
                 matriarchs
                 matriarchy
                 matricentric societies
                 matricide
                 matrilineal kinship
                 matrilineal societies
                 matrilocal residences
         holy matrimony
                 matrimony USE **marriage**
          art matronage
                 matronymy
                 mature students USE **adult students**
                 maturity
                 Mauritanian
                 mayors
                 MCP USE **male chauvinism**
    German measles USE **rubella**
                 measles
  three day measles USE **rubella**
                 measurement
  demographic measurements
                 measurements
     tests and measurements USE **testing**
                 mechanical engineering
                 mechanics
     defense mechanisms
arts, entertainment, and media occupations
     electronic media
        hosts (media) USE **television personalities**
          mass media
                 media USE **mass media**
                 media arts
                 media coverage
                 media portrayal
                 media reform
                 media stereotyping
        mixed media
    networks (media)
         print media
  violence in the media
     women's media
                 mediation
                 mediators

Medicaid
emergency medical services
Family and Medical Leave Act of 1987
medical anthropology
medical care
medical education
medical ethics
medical evaluation
medical insurance USE **health insurance**
medical oppression
medical procedures
medical records
medical sciences
medical sociology
Medicare
environmental medicine
family medicine
folk medicine
holistic medicine
medicine USE **medical sciences**
medicine women
preventive medicine
socialized medicine
Medieval Period
meditation
meditation music
mediums
physical mediums
spiritual mediums
meetings
planning meetings
prayer meetings
union membership
memoirs
memoranda
long term memory
memory
short term memory
memos
gay men
holy men
homeless men
married men USE **husbands**
men
men's liberation
men's movement
men's roles

men's studies
older men
single men
unmarried men USE **single men**
working men USE **wage earners**
working men USE **workers**
menarche
menopause
menses USE **menstruation**
menstrual cycle
menstrual disorders
menstrual extraction
menstrual taboos
menstruation
menstruation inducing agents
mental disorders
mental evaluation
mental health
mental health advocates
mental health issues
mental health treatment
mental hospitals
mental illness USE **mental disorders**
mental retardation
mentally handicapped
mentors
mercantilism
merchandisers
merchants
mergers
mermaids
metal art
metalworkers
metaphors
metaphysics
meteorologists
rhythm method
scientific method
methodologies
methodology USE **methods**
birth control methods USE **contraception**
desegregation methods
educational methods
feminist methods
job search methods
methods
research methods

Mexican
Mexican American
microeconomics
microfiche
microfilm
microinequities
midcareer change
middle age
middle aged adults
Middle Ages
Middle Atlantic
middle class
middle class families
Middle Eastern
middle managers
middle schools
midlife
midlife crisis
Midwestern
midwifery
granny midwives USE **lay midwives**
lay midwives
midwives
migraine headaches
migrant workers
migration
migration patterns
rural migration
seasonal migration
urban migration
mikiri
mikveh
militance
militarism
all volunteer military force
military
military academies
military budget
military combat
military defense
military dependents
military draft
military enlistment
military personnel
military rank
military recruitment
military services USE **armed forces**

military spouses
military trade
women in the military
expressing milk
milk
milk substitutes
mother's milk
mill girls USE **factory workers**
millenarian movements
millenialism
milliners
millinery trade
abortion mills USE **abortion clinics**
mime
mind
mind/body split
mineral resources
coal miners
miniatures
minimum competencies
minimum income
minimum wage legislation
mining industry
miniskirts
ministers
prime ministers
minor parties
minorities USE **ethnic groups**
minorities USE **people of color**
minority employment
minority experience
minority groups
minority owned business
minority studies USE **ethnic studies**
minority women USE **ethnic women**
minority women USE **women of color**
miracles
misandry
miscarriage
miscegenation
misogyny
missionaries
missionary societies
mistress of ceremonies USE **master of ceremonies**
mistresses
bas mitzvah USE **bat mitzvah**
bat mitzvah

mixed economy
mixed media
mixed sex groups
mixers
career mobility USE **occupational mobility**
family mobility
geographic mobility
job mobility USE **occupational mobility**
mobility
occupational mobility
social mobility
upward mobility
model programs
modeling agencies
capitalist economic development models
communist economic development models
economic development models
Marxist economic development models
mathematical models
models
models (paradigms)
role models
socialist economic development models
modern dance
modernism
modernization
modesty
behavior modification
cognitive behavior modification
child molesting USE **child abuse**
momism
monasteries
monasticism
monetary incentives
monetary policy
money
money management
pin money
Mongolian
fetal monitoring
monogamy
monographs
monopolies
monotheism
moonlighting
moral development
moral majority

moral reasoning
moral reform
morality
morals USE **morality**
morbidity
mores
Mormon
Mormonism
morning after pill USE **diethylstilbestrol**
Moroccan
morphology
infant mortality
maternal mortality
mortality
mortality rates
occupational mortality
assumable mortgages
conventional mortgages
mortgages
mortuary science
Moslem USE **Muslim**
mosques
earth mother
mother daughter incest
mother daughter relationships
mother earth
mother goddess
mother nature
mother right
mother son incest
mother son relationships
mother superiors
mother syndrome
mother tongue
Mother/Father God
mother's milk
motherhood USE **mothers**
motherhood USE **parenthood**
mothering
motherless families
absentee mothers
biological mothers USE **birth mothers**
birth mothers
den mothers
employed mothers USE **mothers working outside the home**
lesbian mothers
mothers

mothers in law
mothers working outside the home
runaway mothers
single mothers
surrogate mothers
teenage mothers
unmarried mothers USE **single mothers**
unwed mothers USE **single mothers**
wage earning mothers
welfare mothers
working mothers USE **mothers working outside the home**
working mothers USE **wage earning mothers**
motion picture industry
motion pictures USE **films**
achievement motivation USE **achievement need**
learning motivation
motivation
student motivation
teacher motivation
motor development
motor skills
mountaineering
mourning
abortion movement
anti ERA movement
antiabortion movement
antiapartheid movement
antinuclear movement
antisuffrage movement
antiwar movement
arts and crafts movement
Black movement
Black power movement
conservative movement
environmental movement
feminist movement
homophile movement
international women's movement
labor movement
lesbian movement
men's movement
prochoice movement USE **abortion movement**
temperance movement
women's health movement
women's liberation movement USE **women's movement**
women's movement
youth movement

antiilliteracy movements
civil rights movements
millenarian movements
movements USE **social movements**
nationalist movements
nativistic movements
peace movements
religious movements
revolutionary movements
social movements
suffrage movements
movers
movies USE **films**
Ms
cervical mucus
mullahs
multicultural health care services
multimedia art
multinational banks
multinational corporation policy
multinational corporations
multinational labor force
multiple births
multiple roles
municipal government USE **city government**
municipalities
mural art
murder
murderers
muscular development
museums
art music
chamber music
children's music
choral music
church music USE **religious music**
classical music USE **art music**
computer music
concert music USE **art music**
country music
electronic music
feminist music
folk music
gospel music
holistic music
incidental music
instrumental music

```
     meditation music
               music
               music criticism
               music festivals
               music history
               music industry
               music theory
               music therapy
               music videos
   orchestral music
    political music
     popular music
      protest music
    religious music
      sacred music  USE  religious music
       salon music
       sheet music
       tribal music
        vocal music
      women's music
               musical theater
               musicals
          jazz musicians
               musicians
               musicology
         Black Muslim
               Muslim
       genital mutilation
               mysteries
               mysticism
      feminine mystique
               mythology
      creation myths
               myths
               myths (folk culture)  USE  mythology
               nags
               naive art
         birth name
        maiden name  USE  birth name
               name rights
           pen name
         slave name
    hyphenated names
               names
               Namibian
               naming
               nannies
```

sanitary napkins
narcissism
narcotic drugs
narcotics USE **narcotic drugs**
narratives
personal narratives
national health insurance
National Health Service (Great Britain)
National School Lunch Act Amendments of 1982
national security
nationalism
nationalist movements
nationalist revolutions
nationality
nationalization
developed nations
developing nations
underdeveloped nations USE **developing nations**
Alaskan Native
Native Alaskan
Native American USE **American Indian**
Native American studies USE **American Indian studies**
Native Canadian
native healers
nativistic movements
natural childbirth
natural family planning USE **rhythm method**
natural resources
natural sciences
natural selection
naturalism
naturalists
naturalization
mother nature
nature
Nazism
Near Eastern USE **Middle Eastern**
Near Eastern studies
achievement need
approval need
needlepoint
needlework
needleworkers USE **clothing workers**
basic human needs
human needs
psychological needs

negative reinforcement
child neglect
negotiation
negotiators
Negro USE **Black**
neighborhood health centers
neighborhood preservation
declining neighborhoods
desirable neighborhoods
ethnic neighborhoods
neighborhoods
neoclassical economics
neoclassicism
neocolonialism
neoconservatism
neoorthodoxy
neophytes USE **novices**
neoplatonism
neopositivism
Nepalese
nephews
nepotism
anorexia nervosa
nervous system
nervousness
empty nest
net income
extended kinship network USE **extended families**
network ratings
network theory
networking
networks
networks (media)
new girl networks USE **old girl networks**
old boy networks
old girl networks
social networks USE **networks**
women's networks
neuroses
New Deal
new girl networks USE **old girl networks**
new left
New Zealander
Papua New Guinean
news services
newsletters
newspapers

Nicaraguan
nieces
Nigerian
Nigerois
night clubs
wedding night
wedding nights
nihilism
no fault divorce
no fault insurance
ladies (nobility)
titles (nobility)
noise pollution
nom de lait
nominations
nonaligned feminism
nonconforming behavior
noncustodial parents
nondegree education
nondegree programs
nonfiction
nonformal education
nongovernmental organizations
nongovernmental women's organizations
nonjudgmental behavior
nonorgasmic women
nonprescription drugs
nonprofit organizations
nonsexist child rearing practices
nonsexist curriculum
nonsexist language
nonsexist literature
nonsexist textbooks
nontraditional careers USE **female intensive
occupations**
nontraditional careers USE **male intensive
occupations**
nontraditional education
nontraditional employment
nontraditional occupations USE **female intensive
occupations**
nontraditional occupations USE **male intensive
occupations**
nontraditional work patterns
nonverbal ability
nonverbal behavior
nonverbal communication

nonverbal language
nonviolence
nonwage labor USE **unpaid employment**
normal schools
male norms
norms
North American
North Atlantic
Northeastern
Northern
Northern Irish
Northwestern
Norwegian
nose jobs USE **cosmetic surgery**
notes
death notices USE **obituaries**
notices
novelists
novellas
novels
novices
novitiates
nuclear disarmament
nuclear energy
nuclear engineering
nuclear families
nuclear free zones
nuclear power USE **nuclear energy**
nuclear warfare
the nude
nudity
nuns
nurse practitioners
nurseries
workplace nurseries
nursery schools
nursery songs
male nurses USE **nurses**
nurses
practical nurses
registered nurses
visiting nurses
vocational nurses
wet nurses
nursing
nursing education
nursing homes

nurturance
nurturers
nurturing
nutrition
Women, Infants, and Children Nutrition Program
nutritionists
nymphomania USE **female hypersexuality**
nymphs
loyalty oaths
obedience
vows of obedience
obesity
obituaries
objectification
conscientious objection
behavioral objectives
course objectives
educational objectives
objectives
organizational objectives
training objectives
objectivity
sex objects
obscenity
observance
participant observation
obsessive compulsive disorders
obstetrical anesthesia
obstetricians
obstetrics
occupational attitudes
occupational choice USE **career choice**
occupational counseling
occupational diseases
occupational hazards USE **work hazards**
occupational health and safety
occupational mobility
occupational mortality
occupational options
occupational patterns
occupational perceptions USE **occupational attitudes**
occupational roles
occupational segregation
occupational sex segregation
occupational status
occupational stress

occupational therapists
occupational training   USE   **job training**
occupational trends
administrative support occupations
agricultural, fishing, and forestry occupations
arts, entertainment, and media occupations
clerical occupations
construction occupations
craft occupations
education occupations
female dominated occupations   USE   **female intensive occupations**
female intensive occupations
feminization of occupations   USE   **tipping**
financial occupations
food preparation occupations
health care occupations
legal and political occupations
male intensive occupations
managerial occupations
manufacturing occupations
marketing and sales occupations
nontraditional occupations   USE   **female intensive occupations**
nontraditional occupations   USE   **male intensive occupations**
occupations
paraprofessional occupations
professional occupations
protective service occupations
scientific and technical occupations
service occupations
transportation occupations
volunteer occupations
women intensive occupations   USE   **female intensive occupations**
oceanography
odalisques
odes
body odor
female Oedipus complex
Oedipus complex
a room of one's own
Age Discrimination Act of 1975
age of consent
alienation of affection
balance of payments
boards of directors
boards of governors   USE   **governing boards**
boards of regents   USE   **governing boards**
boards of trustees   USE   **governing boards**

boy preference of parents
brotherhood of man USE **humanity**
change of life USE **menopause**
Child Support Enforcement Amendments of 1984
Civil Rights Act of 1964
Civil Rights Restoration Act of 1987
commissions on the status of women
Comprehensive Employment and Training Act of 1973
conflict of interest
cost of living
crimes of honor
crimes of passion
cult of the virgin
cult of true womanhood
division of labor
Economic Equity Act of 1987
Economic Recovery Tax Act of 1981
economic value of women's work
economies of scale
Education Amendments of 1972
Education Amendments of 1985
Equal Credit Opportunity Act of 1974
Equal Pay Act of 1963
Equal Pay Act of 1970 (Great Britain)
ethic of care
Family and Medical Leave Act of 1987
fear of failure
fear of success
Federal Equitable Pay Practices Act of 1987
feminization of occupations USE **tipping**
feminization of poverty USE **pauperization of women**
feminization of poverty USE **women living in poverty**
feminization of professions USE **tipping**
figures of speech USE **figurative language**
forms of address
forms of affection
freedom of assembly
freedom of choice
freedom of information
freedom of speech
freedom of the press
freedom of worship
Garden of Eden
girl preference of parents
heads of families
heads of households USE **householders**
heads of state

history of children
history of religion
history of science
history of women USE **women's history**
House of Representatives
household division of labor
images of girls
images of women
impoverishment of women
international division of labor
labor theory of value
lack of confidence
laying on of hands
legitimization of children
letters of recommendation
locus of control
loss of self
master of ceremonies
mistress of ceremonies USE **master of ceremonies**
National School Lunch Act Amendments of 1982
pauperization of women
people of color
Pregnancy Discrimination Act of 1978
prisoners of war
quality of life
quality of work life
Retirement Equity Act of 1984
rights of the disabled
rights of women USE **women's rights**
rites of passage
sense of humor
separation of church and state
sexual division of labor
social construction of gender
social construction of reality
sociology of knowledge
standards of living USE **living standards**
Statue of Liberty
status of women
stream of consciousness
subordination of women
Tax Reform Act of 1985
veiling of women
vows of chastity
vows of obedience
vows of poverty
vows of silence

women of color
women of valor
juvenile offenders
offenders USE **criminals**
sex offenses USE **sex crimes**
office hazards USE **work hazards**
office parties
office work
political office
presidential office
vice presidential office
affirmative action officers
correctional officers
parole officers
police officers
probation officers
offices (facilities)
appointed officials
elected officials
officials
public officials
sports officials
offshore production plants
oil industry
old age USE **older adults**
old boy networks
old girl networks
old maids
old old adults
old old adults
old wives' tales
older adults
older men
older students USE **adult students**
older women
Olympic Games
ombudsmen
ombudswomen
commissions on the status of women
impact on children
impact on women
laying on of hands
on the job training
a room of one's own
one parent families USE **single parent families**
one woman art shows
oophorectomy

open door admissions
opera
opera singers
operant conditioning
soap operas
operations   USE   **surgical procedures**
operations researchers
boat operators
camera operators
computer equipment operators
data entry operators
heavy equipment operators
keypunch operators   USE   **data entry operators**
knitting machine operators
machine operators
operators
press operators
sewing machine operators
telephone operators
opinion polls
public opinion
public opinion polls   USE   **opinion polls**
career opportunities
educational opportunities
employment opportunities
equal opportunities commissions
opportunities
Equal Credit Opportunity Act of 1974
equal educational opportunity
equal employment opportunity
Equal Employment Opportunity Commission
equal opportunity
fat oppression
freedom from oppression
medical oppression
oppression
political oppression
sexual oppression
optimism
occupational options
stock options
optometrists
optometry
oral communication   USE   **verbal communication**
oral contraceptives
oral histories
oral history

oral literature
oral sex
oral tradition
orators
oratory
orchestral music
birth order
Executive Order 11246
mail order brides
consent orders
religious orders
restraining orders
ordination
women's ordination
social organization
organizational behavior
organizational development
organizational objectives
organizational psychology
organizational theory
arts organizations
consumer health organizations
feminist organizations
health maintenance organizations
left wing organizations
nongovernmental organizations
nongovernmental women's organizations
nonprofit organizations
organizations
parent teacher organizations
private voluntary organizations
right wing organizations
social organizations
voluntary organizations
women's organizations
organized crime
community organizers
organizing
clitoral orgasm
orgasm
vaginal orgasm
Oriental studies USE **Asian studies**
original sin
Orphan Annie
orthodoxy
osteoporosis
significant others

<pre>
                                Ouija boards
                        coming out
                                outlaws
                                outlines
                                outplacement
                                outreach programs
        mothers working outside the home
          wives working outside the home
          women working outside the home
                                Outward Bound programs
                                outwork
                                ovariectomy USE **oophorectomy**
                                ovaries
                                overachievement
                          drug overdoses
                                oviducts
                                ovulation
                                ovum
        a room of one's own
                 family owned business
               minority owned business
                  women owned business
              business ownership
              property ownership
                  Asian Pacific
                  Asian Pacific American
                                Pacific
                                Pacific Coast
                                Pacific Islander
                  South Pacific
                                pacifism
          compensation packages
                                PACs USE **political action committees**
                                padding
               women's pages
                                paid employment
                                pain
                                painters
                   sign painters
                  china painting
                 flower painting
                                painting
                                paintings
                                Pakistani
                                Palestinian
                                palimony
                                palm reading
</pre>

                palmistry USE **palm reading**

       pen pals

                pamphlets

                Panamanian

                panels

                pantheism

                pantheon

                pants

                pantyhose USE **hosiery**

                Pap smear

                Papanicolaou smear USE **Pap smear**

                paperhangers

  concept papers

                papers

  position papers

  working papers

                Papua New Guinean

                parables

                parades

   models (paradigms)

                paradigms

                paradise

                Paraguayan

                paralegal workers

                paralegals

                paramedics

                paranoia

                paraprofessional occupations

                paraprofessionals

                parapsychology

      one parent families USE **single parent families**

                parent child relationships

                parent influence

                parent teacher organizations

                parent teacher relationships

   single parent families

                parental aspirations

                parental attitudes

                parental behavior

                parental leave

                parental rights

  delayed parenthood

                parenthood

  planned parenthood

                parenting

                parenting rewards

   shared parenting

adoptive parents
biological parents USE **birth parents**
birth parents
boy preference of parents
custodial parents
foster parents
girl preference of parents
noncustodial parents
parents
single parents
working parents
pariahs
parliaments
beauty parlors
massage parlors
parody
parole officers
part time employment
part time students
part time work USE **part time employment**
parthenogenesis
participant observation
labor force participation
political participation
cocktail parties
minor parties
office parties
parties
political parties
third parties USE **minor parties**
partners
Job Training Partnership Act
private parts USE **genitals**
Communist Party
Democratic Party
Libertarian Party
political party affiliations USE **political parties**
Republican Party
Socialist Party
rites of passage
passages
passing
crimes of passion
passion
passive behavior
patents
paternity

paternity benefits
paternity leave
paternity rights
paternity suits
patience
doctor patient relationships   USE   **patient doctor relationships**
patient doctor relationships
physician patient relationships   USE   **patient doctor relationships**
patriarchal language
patriarchal religion
patriarchs
patriarchy
patricide
patrilineal kinship
patriotism
patronymy
assimilation patterns
employment patterns
flexible career patterns
migration patterns
nontraditional work patterns
occupational patterns
pauperization of women
back pay
equal pay
Equal Pay Act of 1963
Equal Pay Act of 1970 (Great Britain)
equal pay for equal work
equal pay legislation
Federal Equitable Pay Practices Act of 1987
low pay
pay   USE   **wages**
pay equity
balance of payments
peace
peace advocates
peace camps
peace movements
peasants
pedagogy
pedestals
pediatricians
pediatrics
pedicurists
peer influence

peer relationships
peeresses
peers
pelvic examination
pen name
pen pals
death penalty
penance
penis
penis envy
pension benefits
pension funds
pensions USE **pension benefits**
people of color
street people USE **homeless**
auditory perception
color perception
depth perception
extrasensory perception
kinesthetic perception
perception
perception skills
self perception
social perception
spatial perception
tactual perception
visual perception
weight perception
occupational perceptions USE **occupational attitudes**
perceptual bias
perceptual development
perfection
job performance
performance
performance appraisal
performance art
performance factors
performance spaces
performances
circus performers
performers
performing arts
perfume
Baroque Period
Byzantine Period
Classical Period
Colonial Period

Elizabethan Period
gestation period
Hellenic Period
Medieval Period
period USE **menstruation**
postnatal period
Progressive Period
Romantic Period
Victorian Period
journals (periodicals)
periodicals
permanents
permissive child rearing practices
permissive environment
sexual permissiveness
perquisites
persecution
witch persecutions
personal columns
personal correspondence
personal development USE **individual development**
personal finances
personal hygiene
personal management
personal narratives
personal relationships
personal service industry
personal space
personal values
television personalities
authoritarian personality
personality
personality development
personality disorders
personality problems
personality tests
personality traits
enlisted personnel
military personnel
personnel
personnel evaluation
personnel management
personnel recruitment USE **job recruitment**
sales personnel
school personnel
feminist perspective
international perspective

perspiration
Peruvian
pessimism
pets
phallic criticism
phallocentrism
phallogocentrism
phallus
pharmaceutical industry
pharmacists
pharmacology
phenomenalism
phenomenology
pheromones
philanderers
philanthropists
philanthropy
philosophers
philosophy
political philosophy
phobias
phonograph records
phonology
photograph albums
photographers
photographs
fashion photography
photography
photojournalism
phrenology
physical abuse
physical appearance
physical development
physical education
physical endurance
physical examination
physical fitness
physical health
physical mediums
physical sciences
physical strength
physical therapists
physical therapy
stress (physical)
physician patient relationships USE **patient doctor relationships**
physicians

physicians' assistants
physicists
physics
physiological psychology
physiologists
physiology
pica
pickets
motion picture industry
motion pictures   USE   **films**
pictures
piecework
piecework labor policy
pieceworkers
pierced ears
male chauvinist pig   USE   **male chauvinism**
morning after pill   USE   **diethylstilbestrol**
the pill   USE   **oral contraceptives**
birth control pills   USE   **oral contraceptives**
diet pills
pilots
pimps
pin money
pink collar workers
pinups
pioneers
pirates
pituitary gland
pituitary hormones
placebos
job placement
placenta
planned parenthood
financial planners
urban planners
career planning
city planning   USE   **urban planning**
family planning
financial planning
natural family planning   USE   **rhythm method**
planning
planning meetings
population planning
rural planning
urban planning
lesson plans
plans

	plantations
offshore production	plants
	plasterers
	plastic surgery
	plates
	Platonism
fair	play
	play
	playbooks
	playgrounds
	playgroups
team	playing
	plays
	playwrights
	pleasure
	plenary sessions
	plumbers
	pluralism
religious	pluralism
	PMS USE **premenstrual syndrome**
	podiatrists
lyric	poetry
	poetry
	poets
	polemics
	police officers
	policemen USE **police officers**
child care	policy
corporate	policy
corporate relocation	policy
economic	policy
educational	policy
family	policy
fiscal	policy
foreign aid	policy
foreign investment	policy
health care	policy
hiring	policy
immigration	policy
industrial	policy USE **corporate policy**
international	policy
international trade	policy
labor	policy
monetary	policy
multinational corporation	policy
piecework labor	policy
	policy

                                    policy making
                   population policy
                        public policy
                        public policy programs
                        social policy
                                    Polish
                                    Polish American
                                    politeness
                legal and political occupations
                                    political action
                                    political action committees
                                    political activism
                                    political activists
                                    political anthropology
                                    political art
                                    political aspirations
                                    political asylum
                                    political campaigns USE **election campaigns**
                                    political candidates
                                    political conventions
                                    political economic systems
                                    political ethics
                                    political husbands USE **political spouses**
                                    political ideology
                                    political influence
                                    political leaders
                                    political music
                                    political office
                                    political oppression
                                    political participation
                                    political parties
                                    political party affiliations USE **political parties**
                                    political philosophy
                                    political power
                                    political prisoners
                                    political refugees
                                    political representation
                                    political repression
                                    political rights
                                    political sanctions
                                    political science
                                    political spouses
                                    political status
                                    political systems
                                    political theory
                                    political wives USE **political spouses**
                                    politicians USE **elected officials**

body politics
coalition politics
local politics
politics
sexual politics
women in politics
poll tax
polling USE **opinion polls**
opinion polls
polls USE **opinion polls**
public opinion polls USE **opinion polls**
air pollution
noise pollution
pollution
water pollution
polyandry
polygamy
polygyny
polytheism
ponytails
car pools
poor USE **poverty**
popular culture
popular music
population characteristics
population control
population decline
population distribution
population genetics
population growth
population planning
population policy
population trends
zero population growth
at risk populations
indigenous populations
populism
child pornography
pornography
portraits
media portrayal
Portuguese
Portuguese American
position papers
appointive positions USE **government appointments**
positive reinforcement
positivism

spirit possession
possessiveness
posslq
postdoctoral fellowships
poster art
posters
posthumous marriage
postindustrial society
postmodernism
postnatal depression USE **postpartum depression**
postnatal period
postpartum depression
postsecondary education
poststructuralism
love potions
potluck suppers
potters
pottery
tea pouring
children living in poverty
feminization of poverty USE **pauperization of women**
feminization of poverty USE **women living in poverty**
poverty
rural poverty
vows of poverty
women living in poverty
Black power movement
consumer power
economic power
gray power
nuclear power USE **nuclear energy**
political power
power
power structure
woman power
powerlessness
practical nurses
family practice USE **family medicine**
authoritarian child rearing practices
child rearing practices
discriminatory practices
employment practices
Federal Equitable Pay Practices Act of 1987
management practices
nonsexist child rearing practices
permissive child rearing practices
religious practices

sexual practices USE **sexual behavior**
unfair labor practices
family practitioners
nurse practitioners
pragmatism
prayer
prayer meetings
preaching
predestination
boy preference of parents
girl preference of parents
sexual preference
veteran preference
prefixes
adolescent pregnancy USE **teenage pregnancy**
ectopic pregnancy
false pregnancy USE **pseudopregnancy**
male pregnancy
pregnancy
pregnancy disability
pregnancy discrimination
Pregnancy Discrimination Act of 1978
pregnancy leave
pregnancy prevention
pregnancy trimesters
sympathetic pregnancy
teenage pregnancy
tubal pregnancy
unwanted pregnancy
pregnant students
pregnant workers
prehistory
prejudice
premarital relations
premature childbirth
premature death
premature infants
premenstrual syndrome
premenstrual tension
prenatal care
prenatal influences
prenuptial agreements
food preparation
food preparation occupations
preparatory schools
preRaphaelites
preschool children

preschool education
preschools
prescription drugs
sex preselection
art preservation
neighborhood preservation
preservation
presidency
presidential office
presidential spouses
vice presidential office
college presidents
presidents
vice presidents
freedom of the press
press coverage
press operators
press services USE **news services**
the press USE **print media**
pressmen USE **press operators**
high blood pressure USE **hypertension**
pressure groups
prestige
crime prevention
disease prevention
Family Violence Prevention and Services Act
fire prevention
pregnancy prevention
prevention
rape prevention
preventive medicine
bride price
gay pride
pride
high priestesses
priestesses
priests
prima donnas
primary caregivers
primary education
primary schools
primate studies
prime interest rate
prime ministers
primitive art
primitivism
primness

princesses
principals
feminine principle
print media
printers
printing workers
printmakers
printmaking
prints
prior learning USE **credit for experience**
priorities
prison workers
political prisoners
prisoners
prisoners of war
prisons
privacy
privacy rights
private agencies
private clubs
private colleges
private education
private parts USE **genitals**
private schools
private sector
private sphere
private voluntary organizations
privatization
heterosexual privilege
privilege
prizes
probation
probation officers
problem solving
community problems
consumer problems
emotional problems
family problems
personality problems
problems
research problems
sexual problems
social problems
grievance procedures
medical procedures
procedures USE **methods**
selection procedures

surgical procedures
proceedings
budget process
due process
group process
judicial process
process
cognitive processes
processes
data processing
food processing
information processing
word processing
data processors
prochoice
prochoice movement USE **abortion movement**
procreation
film producers
domestic food production
offshore production plants
productivity
profanity
professional and related services industry
professional athletes
professional athletics
professional awards
professional degrees
professional development
professional education
professional occupations
professional recognition
professional sports
professional status
professional women's groups
professionalism
female dominated professions USE **female intensive occupations**
feminization of professions USE **tipping**
professions USE **occupations**
women intensive professions USE **female intensive occupations**
professors
profits
progesterone
progestins
program ratings
Women, Infants, and Children Nutrition Program
computer programmers
computer programming

programming languages
after school programs
alternative programs
assistance programs
computer programs
dependent care assistance programs
educational programs
entitlement programs
external degree programs
federal assistance programs
Head Start programs
high school equivalency programs
intern programs
model programs
nondegree programs
outreach programs
Outward Bound programs
programs
public policy programs
residency programs
state assistance programs
welfare programs
work incentive programs
work release programs
progress
works in progress
progressive education
Progressive Period
progressivism
drinking prohibition
Prohibition
smoking prohibition
social prohibitions
projection
proletariat
prolife USE **antiabortion movement**
promiscuity
promotions
proms
pronoun envy
generic pronouns
masculine pronouns
pronouns
proofs
propaganda
community property laws
marital property reform

property confiscation
property crimes
property laws
property ownership
property rights
property settlements
property taxes
prophecy
prophets
proposal writing
grant proposals
marriage proposals
proposals
proprietary schools
prose
breast prostheses
prostheses
prostitutes
juvenile prostitution
prostitution
consumer protection
equal protection under the law
protection
Uniformed Services Former Spouses' Protection Act
protective clothing
protective legislation
protective service occupations
protest
protest actions
protest music
Protestant
White Anglo Saxon Protestant
Protestantism
protests USE **protest actions**
protofeminism
Depo Provera
proverbs
health care providers
provosts
marriage by proxy
pseudonyms
pseudopregnancy
psychiatrists
psychiatry
psychic readings
psychics
psychoanalysis

psychoanalytic criticism
psychoanalytic feminism
psychodrama
psycholinguistics
psychological adjustment
psychological conditioning USE **conditioning**
psychological factors
psychological needs
psychological repression
psychological stress
psychological testing
psychological tests USE **psychological testing**
psychologists
abnormal psychology
analytical psychology
child psychology
clinical psychology
comparative psychology
developmental psychology
educational psychology
experimental psychology
industrial psychology
organizational psychology
physiological psychology
psychology
social psychology
psychometry
psychopharmacology
psychosexual behavior
psychosomatic disorders
psychosurgery
psychotherapists
psychotherapy
psychotropic drugs
puberty
pubic hair
public accommodations
public affairs
public agencies
public art
public assistance
public colleges
public education
public health
Public Health Service Act
public housing
public information

public interest
public officials
public opinion
public opinion polls USE **opinion polls**
public policy
public policy programs
public radio
public relations
public relations specialists
public schools
public sector
public service
public speaking
public sphere
public television
public transportation
public utilities
public welfare
Title VII (Public Health)
Title VIII (Public Health)
Title X (Public Health)
feminist publications
publications
publicity
publishers
publishing industry
puerperal fever
Puerto Rican
pulp fiction
breast pumps
capital punishment USE **death penalty**
punishment
puns
puppetry
purdah
binge purge syndrome USE **bulimia**
purification rites
purists
puritanism
purity
purses
puzzles
quadruplets USE **multiple births**
qualitative analysis
quality assessment
quality of life
quality of work life

quantitative analysis
queen bee syndrome
queen for a day
beauty queens
queens
the woman question
questionnaires
quilting
quilts USE **quilting**
quintuplets USE **multiple births**
immigration quotas
quotas
student quotas
quotations
rabbis
race
race bias
race equity
race formation
race relations
race, class, and gender studies
racial and ethnic differences
racial comparisons USE **racial and ethnic differences**
racial discrimination
racial diversity
racial equality
racial factors
racial stereotypes
racial stratification
environmental racism
institutional racism
racism
racist rape
raconteurs
racquetball
radiation therapy
radical feminism
radicalism
radicals
public radio
radio
radio commercials
rage
rail transportation
railroad workers
underground railroad

consciousness raising
consciousness raising groups
fund raising
fund raising events
rallies
ranch hands
random sampling
academic rank
military rank
rank
acquaintance rape
date rape
domestic rape
gang rape
marital rape USE **domestic rape**
racist rape
rape
rape crisis centers
rape fantasies
rape prevention
rape victims
slave rape
spouse rape USE **domestic rape**
wife rape USE **domestic rape**
rapists
raps
exchange rate
prime interest rate
birth rates
divorce rates
fertility rates
interest rates
labor force rates
marriage rates
mortality rates
turnover rates
unemployment rates
ratification
treaty ratification
network ratings
program ratings
ratings
viewer ratings
sex ratio
rationalism
rationality
cathode ray tubes USE **video display terminals**

reaction times
palm reading
reading
tarot reading
tea leaf reading
psychic readings
readings
real estate
real estate agents
realism
social realism
social construction of reality
authoritarian child rearing practices
child rearing practices
nonsexist child rearing practices
permissive child rearing practices
reason
abstract reasoning
circular reasoning
moral reasoning
rebellions
rebellious behavior
rebirth
recall
receptionists
receptions
recession
recidivism
family recipes
recipes
professional recognition
recognition
letters of recommendation
reconciliation
Reconstruction
reconstructive surgery
record albums
employee records
medical records
phonograph records
records
records confidentiality
school records
voting records
Economic Recovery Tax Act of 1981
recreation
executive recruitment

job recruitment
military recruitment
personnel recruitment USE **job recruitment**
student recruitment
redlining
reduction in force
reel to reel tapes
reel to reel tapes
reentry students
reentry women
work reentry
referees
reference books
references
referenda
information and referral centers
dress reform
educational reform
labor law reform
land reform
marital property reform
media reform
moral reform
social reform
tax reform
Tax Reform Act of 1985
welfare reform
Counter Reformation
Reformation
reformatories
reformers
reforms
religious reforms
economic refugees
political refugees
refugees
religious refugees
boards of regents USE **governing boards**
regional labor workers USE **migrant workers**
regional studies
registered nurses
voter registration
slide registries
federal regulations
regulations
state regulations
correctional rehabilitation

drug rehabilitation
rehabilitation
vocational rehabilitation
reincarnation
negative reinforcement
positive reinforcement
reinforcement
rejection
professional and related services industry
community relations
domestic relations
ethnic relations
human relations
human relations commissions
industrial relations
international relations
interracial relations
labor relations
premarital relations
public relations
public relations specialists
race relations
social relations
adult child relationships
children's relationships
doctor patient relationships   USE   **patient doctor relationships**
family relationships
father daughter relationships
father son relationships
female female relationships
female male relationships
gay male relationships
gay relationships
heterosexual relationships
homosexual relationships   USE   **gay relationships**
interpersonal relationships   USE   **personal relationships**
lawyer client relationships
lesbian relationships
male female relationships   USE   **female male relationships**
male male relationships
mother daughter relationships
mother son relationships
parent child relationships
parent teacher relationships
patient doctor relationships
peer relationships
personal relationships

physician patient	relationships	USE **patient doctor relationships**
	relationships	
same sex	relationships	USE **female female relationships**
same sex	relationships	USE **male male relationships**
sexual	relationships	
sibling	relationships	
teacher student	relationships	
	relativism	
	relaxation	
work	release programs	
bas	reliefs	
civil	religion	
comparative	religion	
history of	religion	
patriarchal	religion	
	religion	
state	religion	
	religions	
fathers	(religious)	USE **priests**
	religious art	
	religious beliefs	
	religious discrimination	
	religious education	
	religious ethics	
	religious experience	
	religious facilities	
	religious freedom	USE **freedom of worship**
	religious groups	
	religious influences	
	religious language	
	religious law	
	religious literature	
	religious movements	
	religious music	
	religious orders	
	religious pluralism	
	religious practices	
	religious reforms	
	religious refugees	
	religious repression	
	religious sanctions	
	religious schools	
	religious symbols	
	religious traditions	
	religious values	
	religious workers	
the	religious right	

women religious
corporate relocation policy
relocation
remarriage
remedial education
herbal remedies
home remedies
remedies
hair removal
Renaissance
renewable energy sources
contract renewal
urban renewal
rent
automobile repair
car repair USE **automobile repair**
repairers
repairmen USE **repairers**
estrogen replacement therapy
reporters
weather reporters
science reporting
annual reports
reports
status reports
political representation
representation
House of Representatives
representatives
political repression
psychological repression
religious repression
repression
sexual repression
reprints
reproduction
reproductive cycle
reproductive freedom
reproductive hazards at work
reproductive health
reproductive rights
reproductive technologies
Republican Party
reputations
applied research
behavioral research
cross cultural research

federally sponsored research
market research
research
research assistants
research bias
research design
research grants
research methods
research problems
scientific research
social science research
sponsored research
state sponsored research
operations researchers
researchers
airline reservation agents
resettlement USE **land settlement**
rural resettlement
residence halls
matrilocal residences
residency programs
residential security
draft resistance
resistance
conflict resolution
financial resources
human resources
mineral resources
natural resources
resources
water resources
self respect
respite care USE **elderly day care centers**
community responsibility
corporate responsibility
family responsibility
job responsibility
legal responsibility
responsibility
restitution
Civil Rights Restoration Act of 1987
restraining orders
resumes
retail trade
retail trade industry
mental retardation
Civil Service Spouse Retirement Equity Act

```
            early retirement
           forced retirement
                  retirement
                  retirement age
                  Retirement and Disability System Authorization
                  retirement benefits
                  Retirement Equity Act of 1984
             job retraining
                  retreats
         faculty retrenchment
     information retrieval
     information retrieval services
                  returning women  USE  reentry women
            role reversal
             sex reversal
   sterilization reversal
  tubal ligation reversal
       vasectomy reversal
                  reverse discrimination
           blind review
                  reviewers
            book reviews
                  reviews
                  revisionism
                  revivals
          French Revolution
      Industrial Revolution
                  revolution
          sexual revolution
                  revolutionary movements
                  Revolutionary War
      nationalist revolutions
        socialist revolutions
             job rewards
       parenting rewards
                  Rh factor
                  Rh incompatibility
                  rhesus factor  USE  Rh factor
                  rhetoric
                  rhythm method
           Costa Rican
          Puerto Rican
                  RIF  USE  reduction in force
        daughter right
          mother right
                  right to choose  USE  prochoice
                  right to die
```

right to know legislation
right to life USE **antiabortion movement**
right to work
right wing organizations
the religious right
abortion rights
children's rights
civil rights
Civil Rights Act of 1964
civil rights commissions
civil rights legislation
civil rights movements
Civil Rights Restoration Act of 1987
domicile rights
equal rights
Equal Rights Amendment
equal rights legislation
family rights
gay rights
homemaker rights
human rights
human rights violations
inheritance rights
land rights
maternity rights
name rights
parental rights
paternity rights
political rights
privacy rights
property rights
reproductive rights
rights
rights of the disabled
rights of women USE **women's rights**
Title IV (Civil Rights)
Title VI (Civil Rights)
Title VII (Civil Rights)
uxorial rights
visitation rights
voting rights
welfare rights
woman's rights
women's rights
rings
wedding rings
riots

```
                          at risk populations
                             risk taking
                             risk taking behavior
                             risks
                 domestic rites
                 fertility rites
                  funeral rites
                initiation rites
                     last rites
              purification rites
                             rites
                             rites of passage
                   votive rites
                             ritual disfigurement
                             rituals  USE  rites
                             road workers
                             roasts
                             rock and roll
                             rococo style
                             role conflict
                             role expectations
                             role models
                             role reversal
                       sex role behavior
                       sex role development
                       sex role identification  USE  sexual identity
                       sex role stereotyping
                 domestic roles
                     dual roles
                   family roles
                   gender roles
               leadership roles
                   marital roles
                    men's roles
                 multiple roles
             occupational roles
                             roles
                       sex roles
                  women's roles
                 rock and roll
                             roller skating
                             Roman Catholic
                             Roman Catholicism
                             romance
                             romances
                             Romanesque
                             romantic love
```

```
                              Romantic Period
                              romanticism
                              roofers
                        a     room of one's own
                              rooming in
              birthing       rooms
              delivery       rooms
                locker       rooms
                              rooms
                   tea       rooms
                 grass       roots
                              royalty
                              rubella
                              rug hooking
              majority       rule
                              Rumanian
                              runaway fathers
                              runaway husbands
                              runaway mothers
                              runaway shops
                              runaway wives
                              runaways
                              running
                              rural areas
                              rural conditions
                              rural development
                              rural living
                              rural migration
                              rural planning
                              rural poverty
                              rural resettlement
                              rural women
            animatrices      rurales
                              Russian
      a room of one'         s own
     Black women'            s studies
         children'           s art
         children'           s culture
         children'           s groups
         children'           s literature
         children'           s music
         children'           s relationships
         children'           s rights
economic value of women'     s work
international women'          s movement
     Jewish women'           s studies
             men'            s liberation
```

men' s movement
men' s roles
men' s studies
mother' s milk
nongovernmental women' s organizations
professional women' s groups
woman' s rights
women' s art
women' s athletics
women' s centers
women' s colleges
women' s culture
Women' s Educational Equity Act
women' s groups
women' s health movement
women' s history
women' s language
women' s lib   USE   **women's liberation**
women' s liberation
women' s liberation movement   USE   **women's movement**
women' s literature
women' s magazines
women' s media
women' s movement
women' s music
women' s networks
women' s ordination
women' s organizations
women' s pages
women' s rights
women' s roles
women' s shelters
women' s studies
sacraments
sacred dance
sacred ideology
sacred music   USE   **religious music**
sacred space
sacred texts
sacrifice
self sacrifice
cultural sadism
sadism
sadness
sadomasochism
safe sex
campus safety   USE   **campus security**

occupational health and safety
safety
sailing
saints
salaries   USE   **wages**
marketing and sales occupations
sales personnel
sales taxes
salesgirls   USE   **saleswomen**
salesmen
saleswomen
salon music
salons
Salvadoran
salvation
same sex relationships   USE   **female female relationships**
same sex relationships   USE   **male male relationships**
Samoan American
samplers
samples
random sampling
sampling
economic sanctions
political sanctions
religious sanctions
sanctions
sanctuaries
sanitary napkins
sanitation
sanitation workers
sanity
satellite communications
communication satellites
satellites
satire
career satisfaction
job satisfaction
marital satisfaction
satisfaction
sexual satisfaction
Saudi Arabian
labor saving devices
Anglo Saxon
White Anglo Saxon Protestant
economies of scale

scales
Scandinavian
employment schedules
flexible work schedules
schedules
school schedules
schizophrenia
independent scholars
scholars
unaffiliated scholars USE **independent scholars**
visiting scholars
feminist scholarship
scholarship
scholarships
after school day care centers
after school programs
high school equivalency programs
National School Lunch Act Amendments of 1982
school age children
school attendance
school boards USE **governing boards**
school counseling
school desegregation
school health services
school integration
school personnel
school records
school schedules
school segregation
home schooling
alternative schools
boarding schools
community schools
elementary schools
finishing schools
free schools
high schools
junior high schools
middle schools
normal schools
nursery schools
preparatory schools
primary schools
private schools
proprietary schools
public schools
religious schools

schools
secondary schools
single sex schools
cognitive science
computer science
history of science
library science
mortuary science
political science
science
science anxiety USE **science avoidance**
science avoidance
science fiction
science reporting
social science research
women in science
behavioral sciences USE **social sciences**
biological sciences
earth sciences
environmental sciences
information sciences
life sciences USE **biological sciences**
medical sciences
natural sciences
physical sciences
social sciences
space sciences
veterinary sciences
scientific and technical occupations
scientific method
scientific research
information scientists
scientists
social scientists
scientology
scolds
scores
Scotch
genetic screening
screenplays
scripts
scrotum
sculptors
sculpture
soft sculpture
seafarers
seamstresses USE **tailors**

seamstresses (historical)
seances
executive search firms
job search USE **job hunting**
job search methods
search committees
computer searches USE **information retrieval services**
seasonal migration
seclusion
second careers
elementary secondary education
secondary education
secondary schools
secret societies
secretaries
caesarian section
informal sector
private sector
public sector
sects
secularism
secularization
business security
campus security
computer security
global security
job security
national security
residential security
security
security guards
Social Security
seduction
seductresses
seed capital
health seeking behavior
help seeking behavior
seers
segregated housing
job segregation USE **occupational segregation**
occupational segregation
occupational sex segregation
school segregation
segregation
sex segregation
natural selection
selection procedures

```
                          sex  selection
                               selective attention
                       breast  self examination
                      loss of  self
                               self actualization
                               self blame
                               self concept
                               self confidence
                               self control
                               self defense
                               self denial
                               self destructive behavior
                               self determination
                               self disclosure
                               self employed  USE  self employment
                               self employment
                               self esteem
                               self examination
                               self help
                               self image  USE  self concept
                               self insemination
                               self perception
                               self respect
                               self sacrifice
                               self sufficiency
                               self understanding
                               selfish behavior
                         fish  sellers
                               semantics
                               seminaries
                               seminars
                               semiotics
                               Senate
                               senators
                               Senegalese
                               senior citizens
                               seniority
                               sensation
                               sense of humor
                               sensitivity
                               sensitivity training
                               sensory development
                               sensuality
                               sentencing
                               separate spheres
                               separation
                               separation agreements
```

separation of church and state
lesbian separatism
separatism
seraglios
serials
series
sermons
servants USE **household workers**
cocktail servers
civil service
Civil Service Spouse Retirement Equity Act
food service workers
foreign service
homemaker service
maternal health service
National Health Service (Great Britain)
personal service industry
protective service occupations
Public Health Service Act
public service
service occupations
armed services USE **armed forces**
community health services
dating services
diaper services
domestic services
emergency medical services
Family Violence Prevention and Services Act
health care services
health services USE **health care services**
housekeeping services
human services
information retrieval services
information services
legal aid services
legal services
military services USE **armed forces**
multicultural health care services
news services
press services USE **news services**
professional and related services industry
school health services
services
social services
Uniformed Services Former Spouses' Protection Act
victim services
youth services

plenary sessions
sessions
data sets
land settlement
legal settlements
property settlements
sewage disposal
sewers
sewing
sewing machine operators
anal sex
commercial sex
cross sex identity
group sex
mixed sex groups
occupational sex segregation
oral sex
safe sex
same sex relationships USE **female female relationships**
same sex relationships USE **male male relationships**
sex
sex change
sex counseling
sex crimes
sex determination
sex differences
sex discrimination
sex discrimination in education
sex discrimination in employment
sex drive
sex education
sex equality USE **sexual equality**
sex equity
sex hormones
sex identity USE **sexual identity**
sex industry
sex manuals
sex objects
sex offenses USE **sex crimes**
sex preselection
sex ratio
sex reversal
sex role behavior
sex role development
sex role identification USE **sexual identity**
sex role stereotyping
sex roles

sex segregation
sex selection
sex stereotypes
sex therapy USE **sex counseling**
sex tourism
sex/gender systems
single sex colleges
single sex education
single sex environments
single sex schools
institutional sexism
linguistic sexism
sexism
sexist language
sextuplets USE **multiple births**
female sexual slavery
sexual abstinence
sexual abuse
sexual aids
sexual assault
sexual attraction
sexual behavior
sexual counseling USE **sex counseling**
sexual desire
sexual dimorphism
sexual division of labor
sexual dysfunction
sexual equality
sexual equity USE **sex equity**
sexual excitement
sexual exploitation
sexual fantasies
sexual freedom
sexual harassment
sexual identity
sexual intercourse
sexual intimidation
sexual liberation
sexual oppression
sexual permissiveness
sexual politics
sexual practices USE **sexual behavior**
sexual preference
sexual problems
sexual relationships
sexual repression
sexual revolution

	sexual satisfaction
	sexual slavery
	sexual stratification
	sexual violence
compulsive	sexuality USE **hypersexuality**
female	sexuality
male	sexuality
	sexuality
	sexually transmitted diseases
	shamans
	shared custody
	shared parenting
earnings	sharing
job	sharing
work	sharing USE **job sharing**
	sheet music
crisis	shelters
	shelters
women's	shelters
	sheriffs
	shift work
tee	shirts
	shock therapy USE **electroconvulsive therapy**
toxic	shock syndrome
high heeled	shoes
	shoplifting
runaway	shops
	short stories
	short term memory
	showers
advice	shows
art	shows
fashion	shows
game	shows
one woman art	shows
	shows
talk	shows
	shunning
	sibling influence
	sibling relationships
	siblings
	sick children
	sick leave
	sickle cell anemia
drug	side effects
	Sierra Leonean
	sign language

sign painters
significant others
silence
vows of silence
herpes simplex virus type II   USE   **genital herpes**
original sin
sin
opera singers
singers
torch singers
single fathers
single men
single mothers
single parent families
single parents
single sex colleges
single sex education
single sex environments
single sex schools
single women
singles
sirens
sissies
brother sister incest
sisterhood
sisters
sisters in law
sit ins
family size
ideal family size   USE   **family size**
ice skating
roller skating
skepticism
sketches
skiing
skill development
skill training
skilled trades
basic skills
job skills
language skills
leadership skills
life skills
motor skills
perception skills
skills
social skills

                    spatial skills
                            skin
                            skin color
                            skirts
                            skits
                            slang
                            slapstick
                            slave name
                            slave rape
                            slave songs
      female sexual slavery
             sexual slavery
                            slavery
              white slavery
                            slaves
                            Slavic
                            Slavic studies
                            sleep
                            slide collections
                            slide registries
                            slide tapes
                            slides
                            slimming USE **dieting**
                            slogans
                            slum landlords
                            slums
                            small business
                      Pap smear
        Papanicolaou smear USE **Pap smear**
                            smiling
                            smokefree environments
                            smoking
                            smoking prohibition
                            snakes
                            Snow White
                            soap operas
                            soccer
                            social action
                            social activities
                            social adjustment
                            social agencies
                            social attitudes
                            social behavior
                            social bias
                            social change
                            social characteristics
                            social class

social clubs
social conditioning
social conflict
social construction of gender
social construction of reality
social control
social Darwinism
social development
social dialects
social differences
social discrimination USE **discrimination**
social entertaining
social environment
social geography
social history
social identity
social indicators
social influences
social issues
social learning USE **socialization**
social legislation
social mobility
social movements
social networks USE **networks**
social organization
social organizations
social perception
social policy
social problems
social prohibitions
social psychology
social realism
social reform
social relations
social science research
social sciences
social scientists
Social Security
social services
social skills
social status
social stratification
social structure
social studies
social support systems USE **support systems**
social system USE **social structure**
social trends

social values
social welfare
social work
social workers
democratic socialism
socialism
utopian socialism
socialist economic development models
socialist feminism
Socialist Party
socialist revolutions
socialization
socialized medicine
socially disadvantaged
female societies
honorary societies
ladies' aid societies
matricentric societies
matrilineal societies
missionary societies
secret societies
societies
stateless societies
classless society
postindustrial society
society
society balls
sociobiologists
sociobiology
socioeconomic class
socioeconomic conditions
socioeconomic indicators
socioeconomic status
sociolinguistics
sociologists
medical sociology
sociology
sociology of knowledge
sociopathology
sodomy
soft sculpture
softball
software
soil conservation
solar energy
solitude
soloists

solstice
problem solving
Somalian
somnambulism
father son incest
father son relationships
mother son incest
mother son relationships
nursery songs
slave songs
songs
sonnets
sons
sons in law
sororal twins
sororate
sororities
renewable energy sources
South African
South American USE **Latin American**
South Atlantic
South Pacific
Southern
Southwestern
personal space
sacred space
space
space sciences
work space
alternative spaces
performance spaces
life span
Spanish
Spanish American
spatial perception
spatial skills
public speaking
speaking in tongues USE **glossolalia**
special education
special interest groups
development specialists
public relations specialists
speculums
figures of speech USE **figurative language**
free speech
freedom of speech
speech

speech therapists
speeches
spending
sperm
sperm banks
spermicides
private sphere
public sphere
separate spheres
sphinx
spies
spinning
spinsters
spirit guides
spirit possession
ancestor spirits
evil spirits
spirits
spiritual communication
spiritual feminism
spiritual mediums
spiritualism
spiritualists
female spirituality
spirituality
spirituals
gay/straight split
mind/body split
spokesmen USE **spokespersons**
spokespersons
federally sponsored research
sponsored research
state sponsored research
sponsors
spontaneous abortion
contact sports
professional sports
sports
sports awards
sports enthusiasts
sports journalism
sports officials
sportscasters
sportsmanship USE **fair play**
sportsmen USE **sports enthusiasts**
G spot
Civil Service Spouse Retirement Equity Act

	spouse abuse
	spouse rape USE **domestic rape**
	spouse support
corporate	spouses
executive	spouses USE **corporate spouses**
former	spouses
governors'	spouses
military	spouses
political	spouses
presidential	spouses
	spouses
Uniformed Services Former	Spouses' Protection Act
	spreadsheets
	squash
	squatters
	Sri Lankan
marital	stability
	staff
support	staff
	stamina USE **physical endurance**
food	stamps
	stamps
double	standard
	standardized tests
academic	standards
beauty	standards
job	standards
living	standards
male	standards
	standards
	standards of living USE **living standards**
	starlets USE **aspiring actors**
Head	Start programs
	starvation
heads of	state
separation of church and	state
	state agencies
	state aid
	state assistance programs
	state courts
	state employment
	state formation
	state government
	state legislation
	state regulations
	state religion
	state sponsored research

```
                        state taxes
              the state
          welfare state
                        stateless societies
        financial statements
                        statements
                        states
            United States
                        statesmanship  USE  **diplomacy**
                        statesmen  USE  **diplomats**
                        statesmen  USE  **political leaders**
                        statistical analysis
                        statisticians
       labor force statistics
                        statistics
             vital statistics
                        Statue of Liberty
                        statues
commissions on the status of women
          cultural status
          economic status
             legal status
           marital status
       occupational status
          political status
       professional status
            social status
     socioeconomic status
                        status
                        status of women
                        status reports
        tax exempt status
                        statutes
                        steelworkers
                        steering
                        stenographers
                        stepchildren
              gay stepfathers
                        stepfathers
              gay stepmothers  USE  **lesbian stepmothers**
          lesbian stepmothers
                        stepmothers
                        stepparents
              age stereotypes
           racial stereotypes
              sex stereotypes
                        stereotypes
```

media stereotyping
sex role stereotyping
stereotyping
sterility
compulsory sterilization USE **involuntary sterilization**
eugenic sterilization
involuntary sterilization
sterilization
sterilization reversal
stevedores USE **longshore workers**
airline stewardesses USE **flight attendants**
stewardesses USE **flight attendants**
bumper stickers
stigmas
stillbirth
stimulants
stock exchanges
stock markets
stock options
stockbrokers
information storage
storefront churches
book stores
short stories
stories
storytelling
gay/ straight split
hair straightening
straights
career strategies
coping strategies
strategies
survival strategies
racial stratification
sexual stratification
social stratification
stratification
stream of consciousness
street harassment
street people USE **homeless**
street theater
street vendors
physical strength
upper body strength
job stress USE **occupational stress**
occupational stress
psychological stress

stress
stress (physical)
strikes
strippers
comic strips
structural discrimination
structural linguistics
structural unemployment
structuralism
economic structure
family structure
language structure
power structure
social structure
liberation struggles
struggles
strumpets
stubbornness
student aid   USE   **student financial aid**
student financial aid
student government
student housing
student leadership
student loans
student motivation
student quotas
student recruitment
teacher student relationships
adult students
college students
commuting students
exchange students
foreign students
married students
mature students   USE   **adult students**
older students   USE   **adult students**
part time students
pregnant students
reentry students
students
transfer students
women college students
African studies
Afro American studies
American Indian studies
American studies
area studies

Asian American studies
Asian studies
Black American studies   USE   **Afro American studies**
Black studies   USE   **Afro American studies**
Black women's studies
Canadian Indian studies
case studies
Chicana studies
cross cultural studies
development studies
ethnic studies
feminist studies
future studies
gay studies
gender studies
Hispanic studies   USE   **Latina studies**
interdisciplinary studies
Jewish women's studies
Latin American studies
Latina studies
lesbian studies
men's studies
minority studies   USE   **ethnic studies**
Native American studies   USE   **American Indian studies**
Near Eastern studies
Oriental studies   USE   **Asian studies**
primate studies
race, class, and gender studies
regional studies
Slavic studies
social studies
studies
time use studies
women's studies
home study
independent study
study abroad
study groups
Gothic style
rococo style
communication styles
hair styles
life styles
management styles
work styles
subconscious
subculture

subject headings
subjective knowledge
subjectivism
subjugation
submissive behavior
subordination
subordination of women
educational subsidies
housing subsidies
subsidies
transportation subsidies
subsidized housing USE **public housing**
subsistence agriculture
substance abuse
substitute teaching
milk substitutes
suburbs
subway workers
dressing for success
fear of success
success
succubi
suction lipectomy USE **liposuction surgery**
Sudanese
sudden infant death syndrome
self sufficiency
suffrage
suffrage movements
suffragettes USE **suffragists**
suffragists
sugar diabetes USE **diabetes**
suicide
affirmative action suits
bathing suits
class action suits
paternity suits
suits USE **lawsuits**
summaries
superego
superintendents
mother superiors
supermom
superstitions
supervisor attitudes
supervisors
superwoman
superwoman syndrome

potluck suppers
suppers
supplementary benefits
labor supply
administrative support occupations
child support
Child Support Enforcement Amendments of 1984
social support systems USE **support systems**
spouse support
support groups
support staff
support systems
employer supported day care
Supreme Court
surgeons
cosmetic surgery
liposuction surgery
plastic surgery
reconstructive surgery
surgery
surgical procedures
Surinamese
surnames
surrealism
surrogate families
surrogate fathers
surrogate mothers
surrogates
surveys
survival strategies
survivors
suttee
sweatshops
Swedish
swimming
Swiss
swooning
syllabi
symbolism
art symbols
literary symbols
religious symbols
symbols
sympathetic pregnancy
sympathy
symposia
synagogues

synchrony
acquired immune deficiency syndrome
binge purge syndrome USE **bulimia**
fetal alcohol syndrome
mother syndrome
premenstrual syndrome
queen bee syndrome
sudden infant death syndrome
superwoman syndrome
toxic shock syndrome
synergy
synopses
syntax
syphilis
Syrian
judiciary system
juvenile justice system
legal system
nervous system
Retirement and Disability System Authorization
social system USE **social structure**
welfare system
belief systems
political economic systems
political systems
sex/gender systems
social support systems USE **support systems**
support systems
systems analysts
systems theory
transit systems
value systems
tables
menstrual taboos
taboos
tactual perception
Tahitian
tailors
Taiwanese
corporate takeovers
risk taking
risk taking behavior
talent
fairy tales
old wives' tales
talk
talk shows

tampons
tank tops
Tanzanian
magnetic tapes
reel to reel tapes
slide tapes
tapes
tapestry
tarot
tarot reading
task forces
tattoos
Dependent Care Tax Credit
Economic Recovery Tax Act of 1981
income tax
marriage tax
poll tax
tax exempt status
tax incentives
tax laws
tax reform
Tax Reform Act of 1985
tuition tax credit
taxation
federal taxes
property taxes
sales taxes
state taxes
taxes
taxi drivers
tea leaf reading
tea pouring
tea rooms
teach ins
parent teacher organizations
parent teacher relationships
teacher aides
teacher education
teacher motivation
teacher student relationships
teacher training USE **teacher education**
teachers
substitute teaching
teaching
teaching assistants
team playing
teas

teases
eve teasing
scientific and technical occupations
technical assistance
technical education
technical writing
technicians
management techniques
reproductive technologies
appropriate technology
food technology
land use technology
technology
technology development
technology transfer
tee shirts
teenage fathers
teenage marriage
teenage mothers
teenage pregnancy
teenagers
telecommunications
telecommuting
teleconferences
teleconferencing
telephone operators
telephones
cable television
commercial television
educational television
public television
television
television commercials
television coverage
television personalities
bank tellers
fortune tellers
fortune telling
temperance movement
basal body temperature
temples
temporary employment
temporary housing
temporary workers
temps USE **temporary workers**
temptation
temptresses

tenant farming
tennis
premenstrual tension
tension headaches
land tenure
tenure
tenure track
long term memory
short term memory
terminal illness
computer terminals
video display terminals
territoriality
terrorism
terrorists
test bias
test tube babies   USE   **in vitro fertilization**
testicles
testimonials
testimony
psychological testing
testing
testosterone
aptitude tests
blood tests
competency based tests
drug tests
intelligence tests
personality tests
psychological tests   USE   **psychological testing**
standardized tests
tests
tests and measurements   USE   **testing**
virginity tests
textbook bias
nonsexist textbooks
textbooks
textile design
textile industry
textile making
female authored texts
sacred texts
texts
Thai
Thai American
angel in the house
blaming the victim

```
                 commissions on the status of women
                  crimes against the elderly
                      cult of the virgin
          discrimination against the disabled
           equal protection under the law
                    freedom of the press
                           God the father
                           man the hunter
       mothers working outside the home
                            on the job training
                     rights of the disabled
                               the Craft  USE  witchcraft
                               the family  USE  families
                               the nude
                               the pill  USE  oral contraceptives
                               the press  USE  print media
                               the religious right
                               the state
                               the woman question
                    violence in the media
         wives working outside the home
                        woman the gatherer
                     women in the military
        women working outside the home
                               thealogy
                 collaborative theater
                 experimental theater
              group developed theater
                       musical theater
                        street theater
                               theater
                               theater arts  USE  theater
                               theater criticism
                               theaters
                               theatre  USE  theater
                               theism
                      feminist theology
                    liberation theology
                               theology
                     womanist theology
                           art theory
                        auteur theory  USE  auteurism
         economic development theory
                      economic theory
                      exchange theory
                      feminist theory
                          game theory
```

```
              information  theory
                   labor  theory of value
                 literary  theory
              management  theory
                   music  theory
                 network  theory
            organizational  theory
                political  theory
                 systems  theory
                          theory
                          therapeutic abortion
            occupational  therapists
                physical  therapists
                 speech  therapists
                          therapists
                     art  therapy
                aversion  therapy
                cathartic  therapy
                    diet  therapy
                    drug  therapy
        electroconvulsive  therapy
    estrogen replacement  therapy
                  family  therapy
                 feminist  therapy
                 gestalt  therapy
                  group  therapy
                hormone  therapy
                massage  therapy    USE   **massage**
                   music  therapy
                physical  therapy
                radiation  therapy
                     sex  therapy    USE   **sex counseling**
                  shock  therapy    USE   **electroconvulsive therapy**
                          therapy
                          thermography
                          thesauri
                          theses
                 creative  thinking
                end time  thinking
                 logical  thinking
                          thinness
                          third parties   USE   **minor parties**
                          third world
                          three day measles   USE   **rubella**
                          thyroid gland
                          Tibetan
                end time  thinking
```

part time employment
part time students
part time work USE **part time employment**
time
time management
time use studies
reaction times
tipping
Title IV (Civil Rights)
Title IX (Education)
Title VI (Civil Rights)
Title VII (Civil Rights)
Title VII (Public Health)
Title VIII (Public Health)
Title X (Public Health)
Title XX (Dependent Care)
titles
titles (nobility)
Aid to Families with Dependent Children
barriers to employment USE **job discrimination**
how to guides
reel to reel tapes
right to choose USE **prochoice**
right to die
right to know legislation
right to life USE **antiabortion movement**
right to work
tobacco
tobacco industry
Togan
living together USE **cohabitation**
tokenism
tolerance
tomboys
tombstones
mother tongue
speaking in tongues USE **glossolalia**
tool and die makers
tank tops
torch singers
totalitarianism
totemism
touching
tour guides
sex tourism
toxemia
toxic shock syndrome

toxic waste   USE   **hazardous waste**

toys

tenure track

track and field

free trade zones

international trade policy

military trade

millinery trade

retail trade

retail trade industry

trade unions

wholesale trade industry

skilled trades

trades

oral tradition

traditional warfare

traditionalism

religious traditions

traditions

traffic accidents

traffic in women   USE   **sex tourism**

tragedy

train conductors

trainers

assertiveness training

childbirth training

Comprehensive Employment and Training Act of 1973

employment training   USE   **job training**

job training

Job Training Partnership Act

leadership training

management training

occupational training   USE   **job training**

on the job training

sensitivity training

skill training

teacher training   USE   **teacher education**

training

training centers

training objectives

personality traits

traits

trances

tranquilizers

transcendentalism

courtroom transcripts

transcripts

embryo transfer
technology transfer
transfer income
transfer students
transference
curriculum transformation USE **curriculum integration**
transformational grammar
transit systems
demographic transition
women in transition
transitions
translations
translators
sexually transmitted diseases
transnational banks USE **multinational banks**
transnational corporations USE **multinational corporations**
air transportation
public transportation
rail transportation
transportation
transportation industry
transportation occupations
transportation subsidies
transsexualism USE **transsexuality**
transsexuality
transsexuals USE **transsexuality**
transvestites
trashing
travel agents
travel literature
travelogues
dutch treat
treaties
treatises
mental health treatment
treatment
treatments
treaty ratification
economic trends
occupational trends
population trends
social trends
trends
trial marriage
clinical trials
trials (courtroom)

tribadism

tribal art

tribal customs

tribal markings

tribal music

tricks

pregnancy trimesters

trimness

Trinidadian

triplets USE **multiple births**

Trotskyism

troubadours

trousers USE **pants**

truck drivers

cult of true womanhood

trust

boards of trustees USE **governing boards**

trustees

tshiwila

tubal ligation

tubal ligation reversal

tubal pregnancy

test tube babies USE **in vitro fertilization**

tube tying USE **tubal ligation**

cathode ray tubes USE **video display terminals**

fallopian tubes

tummy tucks USE **cosmetic surgery**

tuition grants

tuition tax credit

tummy tucks USE **cosmetic surgery**

benign tumors

malignant tumors

tumors

Tunisian

Turkish

labor turnover

turnover rates

tutoring

fraternal twins

identical twins

sororal twins

twins

two career couples USE **dual career couples**

two career families USE **dual career families**

two income families

two year colleges

tube tying USE **tubal ligation**

                              herpes simplex virus type II USE **genital herpes**
                                                      typesetters
                                                      typewriters
                                                      typists
                                                      typography
                                                      tyranny
                                                      Ugandan
                                                      ulcers
                                                      ultrasound
                                                      umbilical cord
                                                      unaffiliated scholars USE **independent scholars**
                                                      unborn child USE **fetuses**
                                                      uncleanliness
                                                      uncles
                                                      unconscious
                                 equal protection under the law
                                                      underachievement
                                                      underdeveloped nations USE **developing nations**
                                                      underdevelopment
                                                      underemployment
                                                      undergraduate degrees
                                                      underground economy
                                                      underground railroad
                                             self understanding
                                                      underwear
                                                      underwriters
                                                      undocumented workers
                                                      unemployed USE **unemployment**
                                       structural unemployment
                                                      unemployment
                                                      unemployment compensation
                                                      unemployment insurance
                                                      unemployment rates
                                             youth unemployment
                                                      unfair labor practices
                                                      Uniformed Services Former Spouses' Protection Act
                                                      unilineal kinship
                                     consensual union
                                                      union
                                                      union membership
                                             labor unions
                                             trade unions
                                                      unions
                                                      unisex
                                                      United States
                         continuing education units
                                                      universities

unmarried fathers USE **single fathers**
unmarried men USE **single men**
unmarried mothers USE **single mothers**
unmarried women USE **single women**
unpaid employment
unpaid household labor
unpaid labor force
unrequited love
unskilled laborers USE **laborers**
unskilled workers USE **workers**
untouchables
unwanted pregnancy
unwed mothers USE **single mothers**
upper body strength
upper class
upper class families
Upper Voltan
upward mobility
urban areas
urban development
urban environment
urban indicators
urban migration
urban planners
urban planning
urban renewal
urbanization
Uruguayan

drug use
land use
land use technology
time use studies

usherettes USE **ushers**
ushers
uterus
utilitarianism

electric utilities
gas utilities
public utilities
utilities
water utilities

utility credit

health care utilization
utopian communities
utopian literature
utopian socialism
utopianism

utopias
uxorial rights
uxoriousness
uzr
vacations
vagina
vagina dentata
vaginal infections
vaginal orgasm
vaginismus
vaginitis
women of valor
economic value of women's work
labor theory of value
value
value systems
domestic values
personal values
religious values
social values
values
valuing children
vampires
vamps
vandalism
vasectomy
vasectomy reversal
vaudeville
VD USE **sexually transmitted diseases**
VDT USE **video display terminals**
vegetarianism
veiling of women
veils
street vendors
vendors
venereal diseases USE **sexually transmitted diseases**
Venezuelan
venture capital
venture capitalists
verbal ability
verbal abuse
verbal communication
verbal development
veteran benefits
veteran preference
veterans

veterinarians
veterinary sciences
viability
vibrators
vice presidential office
vice presidents
blaming the victim
victim services
victimization
victimless crimes
crime victims
incest victims
rape victims
victims
Victorian Period
video art
video display terminals
video games
videodisks
music videos
videos
videotapes
Vietnam War
Vietnamese
Vietnamese American
viewer ratings
world views
global village
village communes
human rights violations
domestic violence
family violence USE **domestic violence**
Family Violence Prevention and Services Act
household violence USE **domestic violence**
marital violence
sexual violence
violence
violence against children
violence against women
violence in the media
viragos
cult of the virgin
virgin birth
Virgin Mary
virginity
virginity tests
virgins

herpes simplex virus type II　USE　**genital herpes**
　　　　　　　　　　　vision
　　　　　　　　　　　visionaries
　　　　　　　　　　　visions
　　　　　　　　　　　visitation rights
　　　　　　　　　　　visiting homemakers
　　　　　　　　　　　visiting nurses
　　　　　　　　　　　visiting scholars
　　　　　　　　　　　visual arts
　　　　　　　　　　　visual diaries
　　　　　　　　　　　visual impairments
　　　　　　　　　　　visual perception
　　　　　　　　　　　vital statistics
　　　　　　　　　in vitro fertilization
　　　　　　　　　　　vocal music
　　　　　　　　　　　vocational aptitude
　　　　　　　　　　　vocational choice　USE　**career choice**
　　　　　　　　　　　vocational counseling　USE　**occupational counseling**
　　　　　　　　　　　vocational education
　　　　　　　　　　　vocational nurses
　　　　　　　　　　　vocational rehabilitation
　　　　　　　　　　　voice
　　　　　　　　　　　volleyball
　　　　　　　Upper Voltan
　　　　　　　　　　　voluntarism　USE　**volunteer work**
　　　　　　　private voluntary organizations
　　　　　　　　　　　voluntary organizations
　　　　　　　　　all volunteer military force
　　　　　　　　　　　volunteer occupations
　　　　　　　　　　　volunteer work
　　　　　　　　　　　volunteering　USE　**volunteer work**
　　　　　　　　　　　volunteers
　　　　　　　　　　　voluptuousness
　　　　　　　　　　　voodoo
　　　　　　　　　　　voter registration
　　　　　　　　　　　voting
　　　　　　　　　　　voting behavior
　　　　　　　　　　　voting records
　　　　　　　　　　　voting rights
　　　　　　　　　　　votive rites
　　　　　　　marriage vows
　　　　　　　　　　　vows
　　　　　　　　　　　vows of chastity
　　　　　　　　　　　vows of obedience
　　　　　　　　　　　vows of poverty
　　　　　　　　　　　vows of silence
　　　　　　　　　　　vulnerability

vulva

vulvectomy

minimum wage legislation

wage differential USE **wage gap**

wage discrimination

wage earners

wage earning mothers

wage earning wives

wage earning women

wage gap

wage increases

wage labor

wages

wages for housework

waifs

wailing

waiters

waiters' assistants

waitresses USE **waiters**

want ads

Civil War

Korean War

prisoners of war

Revolutionary War

Vietnam War

war

war crimes

World War I

World War II

maternity wards

wards

biological warfare

chemical warfare USE **biological warfare**

guerrilla warfare

nuclear warfare

traditional warfare

warfare

washerwomen USE **launderers**

WASP USE **White Anglo Saxon Protestant**

hazardous waste

toxic waste USE **hazardous waste**

girl watching USE **street harassment**

watchmakers

watchmen USE **guards**

water

water management

water pollution

water resources
water utilities
first wave feminism
inherited wealth
wealth
wealth distribution
weapons
weather reporters
weathermen USE **meteorologists**
weathermen USE **weather reporters**
weavers
weaving
wedding ceremonies
wedding nights
wedding rings
weight lifting
weight perception
welders
child welfare
maternal and infant welfare
public welfare
social welfare
welfare
welfare agencies
welfare economics
welfare fraud
welfare mothers
welfare programs
welfare reform
welfare rights
welfare state
welfare system
wellness
Welsh
West German
West Indian
Western
wet nurses
Snow White
White
White Anglo Saxon Protestant
white collar crime
white collar workers
White man USE **Caucasian**
white slavery
wholesale trade industry

whores USE **prostitutes**

WIC USE **Women, Infants, and Children Nutrition Program**

wicca

wicking

widowerhood USE **widowers**

widowers

widowhood USE **widows**

widows

wife abuse

wife rape USE **domestic rape**

wigs

wills

left wing organizations

right wing organizations

wisdom

witch burning

witch hunts

witch persecutions

witchcraft

witches

Aid to Families with Dependent Children

couples with children

withdrawal

corporate wives USE **corporate spouses**

first wives

former wives

house wives USE **homemakers**

old wives' tales

political wives USE **political spouses**

runaway wives

wage earning wives

wives

wives working outside the home

working wives USE **wage earning wives**

working wives USE **wives working outside the home**

wolfing USE **street harassment**

ideal woman

one woman art shows

the woman question

woman power

woman the gatherer

woman's rights

Wonder Woman

womanculture USE **women's culture**

cult of true womanhood

womanhood

womanism
womanist theology
womanist writing
womanizers
womanspirit
womb USE **uterus**
womb envy
all women ensembles
battered women
Black women's studies
cleaning women USE **cleaners**
club women
commissions on the status of women
crimes against women
economic value of women's work
ethnic women
fallen women
gay women USE **lesbians**
heroic women USE **heroes**
history of women USE **women's history**
holy women
homeless women
images of women
impact on women
impoverishment of women
International Decade for Women
international women's movement
Jewish women's studies
married women USE **wives**
medicine women
minority women USE **ethnic women**
minority women USE **women of color**
nongovernmental women's organizations
nonorgasmic women
older women
pauperization of women
professional women's groups
reentry women
returning women USE **reentry women**
rights of women USE **women's rights**
rural women
single women
status of women
subordination of women
traffic in women USE **sex tourism**
unmarried women USE **single women**
veiling of women

violence against women
wage earning women
women
women and
women college students
women identified women
women identified women
women in
women in development
women in politics
women in science
women in the military
women in transition
women intensive careers USE **female intensive occupations**
women intensive occupations USE **female intensive occupations**
women intensive professions USE **female intensive occupations**
women living in poverty
women of color
women of valor
women owned business
women religious
women working outside the home
Women, Infants, and Children Nutrition Program
women's art
women's athletics
women's centers
women's colleges
women's culture
Women's Educational Equity Act
women's groups
women's health movement
women's history
women's language
women's lib USE **women's liberation**
women's liberation
women's liberation movement USE **women's movement**
women's literature
women's magazines
women's media
women's movement
women's music
women's networks
women's ordination

women's organizations
women's pages
women's rights
women's roles
women's shelters
women's studies
working women USE **wage earners**
working women USE **wage earning women**
working women USE **women working outside the home**
working women USE **workers**
Wonder Woman
woodworkers
word processing
alternative work arrangements
balancing work and family life
charitable work
church work
culture work
economic value of women's work
equal pay for equal work
extension work
flexible work schedules
food for work
home based work
home economics extension work
nontraditional work patterns
office work
part time work USE **part time employment**
quality of work life
reproductive hazards at work
right to work
shift work
social work
volunteer work
work
work alienation
work attitudes
work ethic
work experience
work force USE **labor force**
work hazards
work history
work hours
work incentive programs
work incentives
work reentry
work release programs

work sharing   USE   **job sharing**
work space
work styles
workaholics
workbooks
dual worker families   USE   **two income families**
blue collar workers
child care workers
clothing workers
construction workers
extension workers
factory workers
farm workers
food service workers
foreign workers
government workers
health care workers
home based workers
hotel workers
household workers
library workers
longshore workers
migrant workers
paralegal workers
pink collar workers
pregnant workers
printing workers
prison workers
railroad workers
regional labor workers   USE   **migrant workers**
religious workers
road workers
sanitation workers
social workers
subway workers
temporary workers
undocumented workers
unskilled workers   USE   **workers**
white collar workers
workers
mothers working outside the home
wives working outside the home
women working outside the home
working class
working conditions
working men   USE   **wage earners**
working men   USE   **workers**

working mothers USE **mothers working outside the home**

working mothers USE **wage earning mothers**

working papers

working parents

working wives USE **wage earning wives**

working wives USE **wives working outside the home**

working women USE **wage earners**

working women USE **wage earning women**

working women USE **women working outside the home**

working women USE **workers**

workmen USE **wage earners**

workmen USE **workers**

workplace

workplace nurseries

works in progress

workshops

compressed workweek

four day workweek

fifth world

fourth world

third world

world views

World War I

World War II

freedom of worship

goddess worship

worship

comparable worth

wrestling

wrinkles

letter writers

writers

creative writing

descriptive writing

feminist writing

grant writing USE **proposal writing**

proposal writing

technical writing

womanist writing

writing

written language

four year colleges

two year colleges

yearbooks

yin
young adults
young children
youth employment
youth movement
youth services
youth unemployment
Yugoslav
Zairean
Zambian
New Zealander
zero population growth
Zimbabwean
zionism
erogenous zones USE **arousal**
free trade zones
nuclear free zones
zoning
zoology

HIERARCHICAL
DISPLAY

READ UP FOR BROADER TERMS

: women
:: workers
::: occupations
:: professional occupations
: religious workers
:: occupations
: female intensive occupations
MAIN TERM → **women religious**
. clergywomen
. nuns
.. mother superiors
. priestesses
.. high priestesses

READ DOWN FOR NARROWER TERMS

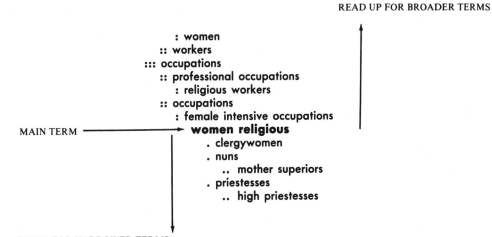

ability
- academic ability
- artistic ability
- math ability
- nonverbal ability
- verbal ability

ableism

:: social sciences
: psychology
abnormal psychology

abolition

abortifacient agents

abortion
- criminal abortion
- induced abortion
- spontaneous abortion
- therapeutic abortion

:: facilities
: clinics
abortion clinics

: counseling
abortion counseling

: laws
abortion laws

: social movements
abortion movement

: rights
abortion rights

:: men
: fathers
absentee fathers

:: women
: mothers
absentee mothers

absenteeism

abstention

abstinence
- sexual abstinence

: cognitive processes
abstract reasoning

abuse
- child abuse
- elder abuse
- emotional abuse
- physical abuse
- sexual abuse
- spouse abuse
  - .. husband abuse
  - .. wife abuse
- substance abuse
  - .. alcohol abuse
  - .. drug abuse
- verbal abuse

academia

: ability
academic ability

: achievement
academic achievement

: aptitude
academic aptitude

: aspirations
academic aspirations

: awards
academic awards

academic disciplines

academic enrichment

: failure
academic failure

: freedoms
academic freedom

: rank
academic rank

: standards
academic standards

:: facilities
: educational facilities
academies
. military academies

: death
accidental death

accidents
. home accidents
. traffic accidents

:: occupations
: professional occupations
:: occupations
: financial occupations
accountants

accounting

accreditation

acculturation

achievement
. academic achievement
. overachievement
. underachievement

:: human needs
: psychological needs
achievement need

acne

acoustics

::: violence
:: sexual violence
: rape
acquaintance rape
. date rape

::: diseases
:: communicable diseases
: sexually transmitted diseases
:: diseases
: communicable diseases
acquired immune deficiency syndrome

acting

activism
. political activism

activists
. political activists

activities
. campaigns
.. election campaigns
. celebrations
. conferences
.. teleconferences
. conventions
.. political conventions
. educational activities
.. classes
.. colloquia
.. discussion groups
.. lectures
.. seminars
.. study groups
.. teach ins
. exhibitions
. expositions
. extracurricular activities
. festivals
.. film festivals
.. music festivals
. forums
. fund raising events
.. charity balls
. hearings
.. congressional hearings
. leisure activities
. mass actions
.. rallies
. meetings
.. planning meetings
.. prayer meetings
. panels
. parades
. performances

(cont.)

. .. . Narrower term

activities (*cont.*)
. protest actions
.. boycotts
... economic boycotts
.. civil disobedience
.. demonstrations
.. marches
.. pickets
.. rebellions
.. riots
.. sit ins
.. strikes
. readings
. retreats
. revivals
. roasts
. shows
.. advice shows
.. art shows
... one woman art
shows
.. fashion shows
.. game shows
.. talk shows
. social activities
.. breakfasts
.. brunches
.. coffee klatches
.. dances
... charity balls
... cotillions
... mixers
... proms
... society balls
.. dating
... blind dates
.. dinners
.. lunches
.. parties
... cocktail parties
... office parties
.. receptions
.. suppers
... potluck suppers
.. teas
. symposia
. testimonials
. workshops

:: occupations
: arts, entertainment, and media
occupations
actors
. aspiring actors

: women
actresses (historical)

actuarials

ad feminam

ad hominem

Adam

addiction
. drug addiction

adjustment
. emotional adjustment
. marital adjustment
. psychological adjustment
. social adjustment

administration

:: occupations
: female intensive occupations
:: occupations
: administrative support occupations
administrative assistants

: costs
administrative costs

: occupations
**administrative support
occupations**
. administrative assistants
. clerical occupations
.. bank tellers
.. bookkeepers
.. clerks
.. computer equipment
operators
.. data entry operators
.. mail carriers
.. receptionists
.. secretaries
.. stenographers
.. telephone operators

(*cont.*)

administrative support occupations (*cont.*)
.. typists
. data processors
. operations researchers
. supervisors

:: occupations
: managerial occupations
administrators
. college administrators

admissions
. open door admissions

: criteria
admissions criteria

adolescence

: teenagers
adolescents

: children
adopted children

adoption
. international adoption
. interracial adoption

: parents
adoptive parents

adornment

::: education
:: elementary secondary education
: elementary education
:: education
: basic education
adult basic education

: relationships
adult child relationships
. parent child relationships
.. father daughter relationships
.. father son relationships
.. mother daughter relationships

(*cont.*)

adult child relationships (*cont.*)
.. mother son relationships

:: development
: individual development
adult development

: education
adult education

: illiteracy
adult illiteracy

: learning
adult learning

: literacy
adult literacy

: students
adult students

adults
. middle aged adults
. old old adults
. older adults
.. older men
.. older women
.. senior citizens
. young adults

adventurers

advertisements

advertising

: industries
advertising industry

: columns
advice columns

:: activities
: shows
advice shows

advocacy

. .. . Narrower term

: groups
advocacy groups

advocates
. consumer advocates
. health advocates
.. mental health advocates
. legal advocates
. peace advocates

: exercise
aerobic exercise

: engineering
aerospace engineering

aesthetics

:: human needs
: psychological needs
affection

affiliation

affirmative action

:: employment practices
::: policy
:: corporate policy
: hiring policy
affirmative action hiring

:: occupations
: female intensive occupations
:: occupations
: education occupations
affirmative action officers

: lawsuits
affirmative action suits

affluence

:: interdisciplinary studies
: area studies
African studies

:: interdisciplinary studies
: ethnic studies
Afro American studies
. Black women's studies

: hair styles
Afros

::: facilities
:: centers
: day care centers
after school day care centers

: programs
after school programs

age
. childbearing age
. maternal age
. middle age
. retirement age

: discrimination
age discrimination

age of consent

: stereotypes
age stereotypes

ageism

: organizations
agencies
. employment agencies
. federal agencies
. government agencies
. intelligence agencies
. modeling agencies
. private agencies
. public agencies
.. state agencies
. social agencies
.. welfare agencies

:: occupations
: service occupations
:: occupations
: female intensive occupations
agents
. airline reservation agents
. insurance agents
. real estate agents
. travel agents

: behavior
aggressive behavior

aging

::: disorders
:: mental disorders
: phobias
agoraphobia

: business
agribusiness

:: social sciences
: economics
agricultural economics

agricultural extension

: occupations
agricultural, fishing, and forestry occupations
. braceros
. development specialists
. divers
. extension workers
.. animatrices rurales
.. gramsevika
. farm workers
. farmers
. fishers
. gardeners
. lumber cutters
. migrant workers
. ranch hands

: industries
agricultural industry

agriculture
. subsistence agriculture

aid
. federal aid
. financial aid
.. student financial aid
... assistantships
... fellowships
.... postdoctoral fellowships
... scholarships
. foreign aid
. state aid

: pollution
air pollution

: transportation
air transportation

::: occupations
:: service occupations
::: occupations
:: female intensive occupations
: agents
airline reservation agents

:: abuse
: substance abuse
alcohol abuse

: diseases
alcoholism

: emotions
alienation
. job alienation
. work alienation

alienation of affection

alimony

::: organizations
:: military
: armed forces
all volunteer military force

all women ensembles

:: language
: figurative language
allegory

: organizations
alliances

: images of women
alma mater

: attitudes
aloofness

: employment
alternative employment

: programs
alternative programs

::: facilities
:: educational facilities
: schools
alternative schools

: space
alternative spaces

**alternative work
arrangements**

altruism

alumnae

alumnae/i

alumni

alumni/ae

: athletics
amateur athletics

: women
: images of women
amazons

:: language
: figurative language
ambiguity

ambition

::: disorders
:: gynecologic disorders
: menstrual disorders
amenorrhea

:: interdisciplinary studies
: ethnic studies
American Indian studies

:: interdisciplinary studies
: area studies
American studies

: medical procedures
amniocentesis

:: behavior
: sexual behavior
anal sex

:: social sciences
: psychology
analytical psychology

: feminism
anarcha feminism

:: natural sciences
: biological sciences
anatomy

: spirits
ancestor spirits

ancestors

:: occupations
: arts, entertainment, and media
occupations
anchors

androcentrism

::: bodies
:: hormones
: sex hormones
androgens
. testosterone

androgyny

: diseases
anemia
. iron deficiency anemia

anesthesia
. general anesthesia
. local anesthesia
. obstetrical anesthesia

:: occupations
: health care occupations
anesthesiologists

: images of women
angel in the house

: images of women
: images of girls
angels

: emotions
anger
. rage

angora

anima

: behavior
animal behavior
. grooming behavior

::: occupations
:: education occupations
: laboratory assistants
:: occupations
: health care occupations
animal caretakers

animals
. laboratory animals

:: arts
: media arts
animation

:: workers
::: occupations
:: female intensive occupations
::: occupations
:: agricultural, fishing, and forestry
occupations
: extension workers
animatrices rurales

animus

ankh

anlu

anniversaries

:: occupations
: arts, entertainment, and media
occupations
announcers

annulment

anonymous

:: disorders
: eating disorders
anorexia nervosa

::: occupations
:: professional occupations
::: occupations
:: education occupations
: social scientists
anthropologists

: social sciences
anthropology
. archaeology
. cultural anthropology
. economic anthropology
. ethnography
. ethnology
. medical anthropology
. political anthropology

anthropometry

anthropomorphism

: social movements
anti ERA movement

: social movements
antiabortion movement

: social movements
antiapartheid movement

:: drugs
: psychotropic drugs
antidepressant drugs

antifeminism

: social movements
antiilliteracy movements

: social movements
antilynching campaign

: social movements
antinuclear movement

antiques

antisemitism

antisepsis

: behavior
antisocial behavior

: social movements
antisuffrage movement

:: language
: figurative language
antithesis

: legislation
antitrust legislation

:: social movements
: peace movements
antiwar movement

: emotions
anxiety

apartheid

: emotions
apathy

: sexual aids
aphrodisiacs

appearance
. physical appearance

appetite depressants
. diet pills

applications

:: humanities
: linguistics
applied linguistics

: mathematics
applied mathematics

: research
applied research

: officials
:: occupations
: legal and political occupations
appointed officials

::: training
:: job training
: on the job training
apprenticeships

: technology
appropriate technology

appropriations

:: human needs
: psychological needs
approval need

aptitude
. academic aptitude
. language aptitude
. vocational aptitude

: testing
aptitude tests

arbitration

::: occupations
:: professional occupations
::: occupations
:: education occupations
: social scientists
archaeologists

:: social sciences
: anthropology
archaeology

: sports
archery

:: occupations
: professional occupations
architects
. landscape architects

:: arts
: visual arts
architecture

: interdisciplinary studies
area studies
. African studies
. American studies
. Asian studies
. Latin American studies
. Near Eastern studies
. regional studies
. Slavic studies

arguments

Armageddon

:: organizations
: military
armed forces
. all volunteer military force

arms control

arousal

: marriage
arranged marriage

:: crimes
: property crimes
arson

art
. body art
. children's art
. commercial art
.. graphics
.. illustration
... fashion illustration
.. typography
. cunt art
. electronic art
. erotic art
. folk art
. multimedia art
. naive art
. performance art
. political art
. primitive art
. public art
. religious art
. tribal art
. women's art

: conservation
art conservation

: criticism
art criticism

:: social sciences
:: humanities
: history
art history

art matronage

::: arts
:: performing arts
: music
art music

: preservation
art preservation

:: activities
: shows
art shows
. one woman art shows

: symbols
art symbols

: theory
art theory

: therapy
art therapy

:: technology
: reproductive technologies
: insemination
artificial insemination

: intelligence
artificial intelligence

:: occupations
: arts, entertainment, and media
occupations
artisans

: ability
artistic ability

:: occupations
: professional occupations
:: occupations
: arts, entertainment, and media
occupations
artists

: books
artists' books

arts
. media arts
.. animation
.. electronic art
.. film
... documentaries
.. video art
. performing arts
.. dance
... ballet
... experimental dance
... folk dance
... modern dance
... sacred dance
.. mime
.. music
... art music
... blues
... chamber music
... children's music
... computer music
... electronic music
... feminist music
... holistic music
... incidental music
... instrumental music
... jazz
... meditation music
... orchestral music
... political music
.... protest music
... popular music
.... country music
.... folk music
.... rock and roll
... religious music
.... chants
.... gospel music
.... hymns
.... spirituals
... salon music
... tribal music
... vocal music
.... choral music
.... madrigals
.... opera
.... songs
..... ballads
..... lieder
..... lullabies
..... nursery songs

(cont.)

arts (*cont.*)
- ..... slave songs
- ... women's music
- .. theater
- ... collaborative theater
- ... drama
- .... comedy
- ..... farce
- ..... skits
- .... tragedy
- ... experimental theater
- ... group developed
  theater
- ... improvisation
- ... musical theater
- ... street theater
- ... vaudeville
- . visual arts
- .. architecture
- .. cartoons
- .. collage
- ... femmage
- .. comic strips
- .. craft arts
- ... basketry
- ... beadwork
- ... ceramics
- ... china painting
- ... doll making
- ... flower painting
- ... lace making
- ... needlework
- .... crocheting
- .... embroidery
- .... knitting
- .... needlepoint
- ... pottery
- ... puppetry
- ... quilting
- ... rug hooking
- ... spinning
- ... tapestry
- ... textile making
- ... weaving
- .. decorative arts
- .. drawing
- .. engraving
- .. fiber art
- .. graphics
- .. metal art
- .. miniatures
- .. mural art

(*cont.*)

arts (*cont.*)
- .. painting
- .. photography
- ... fashion photography
- .. portraits
- .. poster art
- .. printmaking
- .. sculpture
- ... bas reliefs
- ... soft sculpture
- .. visual diaries

: occupations
**arts, entertainment, and
media occupations**
- . actors
- .. aspiring actors
- . anchors
- . announcers
- . artisans
- . artists
- . authors
- . broadcasters
- . bullfighters
- . camera operators
- . cartoonists
- . circus performers
- . coaches
- . columnists
- . comedians
- . commentators
- . composers
- . conductors
- . copywriters
- . craftspersons
- . critics
- . dancers
- .. chorus dancers
- . designers
- . disk jockeys
- . drafters
- . dramatists
- . editors
- . entertainers
- . essayists
- . film directors
- . film producers
- . geishas
- . glassmakers
- . hostesses (historical)
- . hosts
- . illustrators

(*cont.*)

. .. . Narrower term

**arts, entertainment, and
media occupations** (*cont.*)
. impersonators
.. female impersonators
.. male impersonators
. instrument makers
. jewelry makers
. jockeys
. journalists
.. correspondents
. lyricists
. models
. musicians
.. jazz musicians
.. troubadours
. novelists
. orators
. painters
. performers
.. prima donnas
.. soloists
. photographers
. playwrights
. poets
. printers
. printmakers
. professional athletes
. public relations specialists
. publishers
. reporters
.. weather reporters
. reviewers
. sculptors
. singers
.. chanteuses
.. opera singers
.. torch singers
. sports officials
. sportscasters
. strippers
. television personalities
. writers
.. translators

: organizations
arts organizations

asbestos

asceticism

:: interdisciplinary studies
: ethnic studies
Asian American studies

:: interdisciplinary studies
: area studies
Asian studies

aspirations
. academic aspirations
. parental aspirations
. political aspirations

::: occupations
:: arts, entertainment, and media
occupations
: actors
aspiring actors

assault
. sexual assault

: men
:: officials
::: occupations
:: legal and political occupations
: elected officials
assemblymen

: women
:: officials
::: occupations
:: legal and political occupations
: elected officials
assemblywomen

: behavior
assertive behavior

: training
assertiveness training

assessment
. quality assessment

assimilation patterns

: programs
assistance programs
. dependent care assistance
programs
. federal assistance programs
. state assistance programs

::: aid
:: financial aid
: student financial aid
assistantships

: degrees
associate degrees

: organizations
associations

: mortgages
assumable mortgages

astrology

:: occupations
: scientific and technical occupations
astronauts

::: occupations
:: scientific and technical occupations
::: occupations
:: professional occupations
::: occupations
:: education occupations
: scientists
astronomers

:: natural sciences
: physical sciences
astronomy

at risk populations

athletes
. professional athletes

athletics
. amateur athletics
. collegiate athletics
. professional athletics
. women's athletics

attachment

:: occupations
: service occupations
:: occupations
: female intensive occupations
attendants

attention
. selective attention

: change
attitude change

attitudes
. aloofness
. bigotry
. family attitudes
. judicial attitudes
. occupational attitudes
. optimism
. parental attitudes
. pessimism
. politeness
. primness
. social attitudes
. stubbornness
. supervisor attitudes
. trust
. work attitudes

:: cognitive processes
: perception
auditory perception

aunts
. maiden aunts

auteurism

: child rearing practices
**authoritarian child rearing
practices**

: personality
authoritarian personality

authoritarianism

authority

. .. . Narrower term

:: occupations
: arts, entertainment, and media
occupations
authors

:: disorders
: mental disorders
autism

::::: humanities
:::: literature
:: prose
: nonfiction
autobiography

automation

: insurance
automobile insurance

automobile repair

autonomy

: organizations
auxiliaries

: therapy
aversion therapy

aviation

: behavior
avoidance behavior
. computer avoidance
. math avoidance
. science avoidance

awards
. academic awards
. professional awards
. sports awards

:: workers
::: occupations
:: service occupations
::: occupations
:: female intensive occupations
: child care workers
babysitters

::: care
:: dependent care
: child care
babysitting

: men
bachelors

:: degrees
: undergraduate degrees
bachelors' degrees

: wages
back pay

backlash

::: occupations
:: service occupations
: food preparation occupations
bakers

balance of payments

**balancing work and family
life**

::::: arts
:::: performing arts
::: music
:: vocal music
: songs
::: humanities
:: literature
: poetry
ballads

::: arts
:: performing arts
: dance
ballet

: hair styles
bangs

:: occupations
: female intensive occupations
::: occupations
:: administrative support occupations
: clerical occupations
bank tellers

:: occupations
: financial occupations
bankers

: industries
banking industry

: organizations
banks
. multinational banks

::: spiritual communication
:: rites
: sacraments
baptism

:: occupations
: service occupations
barbers

: women
: titles (nobility)
: images of women
baronesses

barrier free access

::: occupations
:: professional occupations
::: occupations
:: legal and political occupations
: lawyers
barristers

:: occupations
: service occupations
bartenders

barter

::: arts
:: visual arts
: sculpture
bas reliefs

basal body temperature

: sports
baseball

: education
basic education
. adult basic education

: human needs
basic human needs

: skills
basic skills

: sports
basketball

::: arts
:: visual arts
: craft arts
basketry

bastards

:: spiritual communication
: rites
bat mitzvah

: clothing
bathing suits
. bikinis

: women
battered women

battlefields

::: arts
:: visual arts
: craft arts
beadwork

. .. . Narrower term

:: occupations
  : service occupations
:: occupations
  : female intensive occupations
    beauticians

    beauty

    beauty contests

    beauty parlors

: women
: images of women
    beauty queens

: standards
    beauty standards

: rooms
    bedrooms

    Beguinism

    behavior
    . aggressive behavior
    . animal behavior
      .. grooming behavior
    . antisocial behavior
    . assertive behavior
    . avoidance behavior
      .. computer avoidance
      .. math avoidance
      .. science avoidance
    . competitive behavior
    . compliant behavior
    . compulsive behavior
      .. hypersexuality
        ... female
              hypersexuality
        ... male hypersexuality
    . conforming behavior
    . consumer behavior
    . deferential behavior
    . delinquent behavior
    . dependent behavior
    . destructive behavior
      .. self destructive behavior
    . deviant behavior
    . group behavior

(cont.)

behavior *(cont.)*
. health behavior
  .. health seeking behavior
. help seeking behavior
  .. self help
. helping behavior
. learned behavior
. manipulative behavior
. nonconforming behavior
. nonjudgmental behavior
. nonverbal behavior
. organizational behavior
. parental behavior
. passive behavior
. psychosexual behavior
. risk taking behavior
. selfish behavior
. sex role behavior
  .. flirtation
. sexual behavior
  .. anal sex
  .. foreplay
  .. group sex
  .. masturbation
  .. oral sex
    ... cunnilingus
    ... fellatio
  .. sexual intercourse
  .. tribadism
. social behavior
  .. manners
    ... gallantry
    ... graciousness
. submissive behavior
. voting behavior

: change
  behavior change

  behavior modification
  . cognitive behavior
    modification

: objectives
  behavioral objectives

:: research
: social science research
  behavioral research

  belief systems

:: occupations
: service occupations
  bellhops

  benefits
  . dependent benefits
  . educational benefits
  . employee benefits
  . flexible benefits
  . fringe benefits
  . maternity benefits
  . paternity benefits
  . retirement benefits
    .. pension benefits
  . supplementary benefits
  . veteran benefits

: tumors
  benign tumors

  bereavement

  bestiality

  betrothal

  betrothed

  bias
  . gender bias
  . perceptual bias
  . race bias
  . research bias
  . social bias
  . test bias
  . textbook bias

: education
  bicultural education

  biculturalism

: sports
  bicycling

  bigamy

: attitudes
  bigotry

:: clothing
: bathing suits
  bikinis

: kinship
  bilineal kinship

: education
  bilingual education

  bilingualism

:: natural sciences
: biological sciences
  biochemistry

::: humanities
:: philosophy
: ethics
  bioethics

: feedback
  biofeedback

:::: humanities
::: literature
:: prose
: nonfiction
  biography

  biological clock

  biological determinism

: influences
  biological influences

: natural sciences
  biological sciences
  . anatomy
  . biochemistry
  . biology
  . botany
  . ecology
  . embryology
  . ethology
  . genetics
    .. population genetics
  . physiology
  . sociobiology

(cont.)

biological sciences (*cont.*)
. zoology
.. primate studies

: warfare
biological warfare

biologism

::: occupations
:: scientific and technical occupations
::: occupations
:: professional occupations
::: occupations
:: education occupations
: scientists
biologists

:: natural sciences
: biological sciences
biology

: medical procedures
biopsy

:: documents
: legal documents
birth certificates

birth control
. sterilization
.. eugenic sterilization
.. involuntary sterilization

birth defects

:: men
: fathers
birth fathers

:: women
: mothers
birth mothers

:: names
: surnames
birth name

birth order

: parents
birth parents

::: measurements
:: demographic measurements
: vital statistics
birth rates

birthing

:: facilities
: centers
birthing centers

: rooms
birthing rooms

: sexuality
bisexuality

: images of women
bitches

: emotions
bitterness

::: facilities
:: educational facilities
: colleges
Black colleges

: feminism
Black feminism

: markets
black markets

: social movements
Black movement
. Black power movement

:: social movements
: Black movement
Black power movement

:: interdisciplinary studies
: women's studies
::: interdisciplinary studies
:: ethnic studies
: Afro American studies
Black women's studies

blame
. self blame

blame allocation

blaming the victim

: families
blended families

::: activities
:: social activities
: dating
blind dates

blind review

:: disabilities
: visual impairments
blindness

:: funding
: grants
block grants

: discriminatory practices
blockbusting

: images of women
: images of girls
blondes

: bodies
blood

: tests
blood tests

: clothing
bloomers

::: children
:: young children
: infants
blue babies

: workers
blue collar workers

::: arts
:: performing arts
: music
blues

: images of women
bluestockings

::: facilities
:: educational facilities
: schools
boarding schools

: organizations
boards
. boards of directors
. governing boards

:: organizations
: boards
boards of directors

:: occupations
: transportation occupations
:: workers
: operators
boat operators

bodies
. blood
. brain
. breasts
. buttocks
. cervical mucus
. cervix
. faces
. genitals
.. clitoris
.. labia
.. penis
.. scrotum
.. testicles

(cont.)

. .. . Narrower term

bodies (*cont.*)
.. vulva
. glands
.. lymph glands
.. mammary glands
.. pituitary gland
.. thyroid gland
. hair
.. body hair
.. pubic hair
. hips
. hormones
.. pituitary hormones
.. sex hormones
... androgens
.... testosterone
... estrogens
... progestins
.... progesterone
. legs
. nervous system
. ovaries
. oviducts
. ovum
. perspiration
. skin
. sperm
. vagina
.. hymen

: art
body art

body building

:: bodies
: hair
body hair

: image
body image

:: language
: nonverbal language
body language

body odor

:: politics
: sexual politics
body politics

bomfog

bondage

bonding
. female bonding
. male bonding

:: organizations
: clubs
book clubs

: conservation
book conservation

book stores

:: workers
::: occupations
:: manufacturing occupations
: printing workers
bookbinders

:: occupations
: female intensive occupations
::: occupations
:: administrative support occupations
: clerical occupations
bookkeepers

: emotions
boredom

:: natural sciences
: biological sciences
botany

bottle feeding

: rooms
boudoirs

boundary markers

: flowers
bouquets

bourgeoisie

: sports
bowling

boy preference of parents

:: activities
: protest actions
boycotts
. economic boycotts

: children
boys

:: occupations
: agricultural, fishing, and forestry
  occupations
braceros

: hair styles
braids

:: language
: written language
braille

: bodies
brain

brainwashing

: clothing
brassieres

:: activities
: social activities
breakfasts

:: diseases
: cancer
breast cancer

: diseases
breast diseases

::: evaluation
:: medical evaluation
: physical examination
breast examination
. breast self examination

breast feeding

breast implants

: prostheses
breast prostheses

breast pumps

:::: evaluation
::: medical evaluation
:: physical examination
: breast examination
breast self examination

: bodies
breasts

::: occupations
:: craft occupations
: construction occupations
bricklayers

: murder
bride burning

bride price

: women
: images of women
brides
. child brides
. mail order brides

bridesmaids

:: occupations
: arts, entertainment, and media
  occupations
broadcasters

broadcasts

: facilities
brothels

: incest
brother sister incest

: men
brothers

: in laws
  brothers in law

:: activities
: social activities
  brunches

: images of women
  Brunhilde

  budget cuts

: deficits
  budget deficits

: process
  budget process

  budgeting

  budgets

: environment
  built environment

:: disorders
: eating disorders
  bulimia

:: occupations
: arts, entertainment, and media
    occupations
  bullfighters

:: customs
: courtship customs
  bundling

  bureaucracy

: organizations
  bureaus

:: crimes
: property crimes
  burglaries

  burial

  burlesque

  burnout

::: occupations
:: transportation occupations
: drivers
  bus drivers

  business
    . agribusiness
    . family owned business
    . home based business
    . minority owned business
    . small business
    . women owned business

: correspondence
  business correspondence

::: humanities
:: philosophy
: ethics
  business ethics

  business ownership

: security
  business security

: organizations
  businesses

: men
: businesspeople
  businessmen

  businesspeople
    . businessmen
    . businesswomen

: women
: businesspeople
  businesswomen

:: methods
: desegregation methods
  busing

  butch

::: occupations
  :: service occupations
    : food preparation occupations
     butchers

    : bodies
     buttocks

::: occupations
  :: craft occupations
    : construction occupations
     cabinetmakers

::: mass media
  :: electronic media
    : television
     cable television

  :: medical procedures
    : surgical procedures
     caesarian section

    : stimulants
     caffeine

     calcium deficiency

  :: workers
    : operators
  :: occupations
    : arts, entertainment, and media
     occupations
     camera operators

     camp followers

    : activities
     campaigns
      . election campaigns

    : security
     campus security

  :: interdisciplinary studies
    : ethnic studies
     Canadian Indian studies

: diseases
  cancer
    . breast cancer
    . cervical cancer

  candidates
    . job candidates
    . political candidates

: sports
  canoeing

  canon
    . literary canon

  canonization

  capital
    . human capital
    . seed capital
    . venture capital

: economic development models
  capitalist economic
    development models

  car pools

  carcinogens

: diseases
  cardiovascular diseases
    . heart disease

  care
    . community care
    . day care
     .. employer supported day
      care
    . dependent care
     .. child care
      ... babysitting
      ... infant care
     .. elderly care
    . health care
     .. home health care
     .. medical care
     .. prenatal care

  career awareness

  career break

: change
career change
. midcareer change

career choice

: counseling
career counseling

: education
career education

: conflict
career family conflict

: feminism
career feminism

: testing
career interest inventories

:: mobility
: occupational mobility
career ladders

career mapping

: opportunities
career opportunities

: planning
career planning

: satisfaction
career satisfaction

: strategies
career strategies

careers
. dual careers
. home based careers
. second careers

:: occupations
: female intensive occupations
caregivers
. primary caregivers

caricatures

::: occupations
:: craft occupations
: construction occupations
carpenters

: organizations
cartels

:: occupations
: arts, entertainment, and media
occupations
cartoonists

:: arts
: visual arts
cartoons

:: methods
: research methods
case studies

caste

casting
. colorblind casting
. cross cultural casting

: images of women
castrating females

castration

: complexes
castration complex

: therapy
cathartic therapy
. psychodrama

:: facilities
: religious facilities
cathedrals

: organizations
caucuses

: activities
celebrations

　　　　　　　　　　　　　　　: :: ::: :::: :::::: Broader term

celibacy

cellulite

censorship

census

: facilities
centers
. birthing centers
. crisis centers
.. rape crisis centers
. day care centers
.. after school day care
centers
.. child day care centers
.. corporate day care
centers
... workplace nurseries
.. drop in day care centers
.. elderly day care centers
. information and referral
centers
. neighborhood health centers
. training centers
. women's centers

::: arts
:: visual arts
: craft arts
ceramics

ceremonies
. graduation ceremonies
. marriage ceremonies
. wedding ceremonies

certification

:: diseases
: cancer
cervical cancer

: contraception
cervical caps

: bodies
cervical mucus

: bodies
cervix

: clothing
chador

:: occupations
: volunteer occupations
:: occupations
: education occupations
chairpersons

::: arts
:: performing arts
: music
chamber music

change
. attitude change
. behavior change
. career change
.. midcareer change
. sex change
. social change

change agents

: spiritual communication
channeling

::: occupations
:: arts, entertainment, and media
occupations
: singers
chanteuses

:: spiritual communication
:::: arts
::: performing arts
:: music
: religious music
chants

chaperones

charisma

: work
charitable work

:: organizations
: nonprofit organizations
charities

:: activities
: fund raising events
::: activities
:: social activities
: dances
charity balls

chastity

chastity belts

: images of women
chattels

chauvinism
. female chauvinism
. male chauvinism

: images of women
: images of girls
cheerleaders

cheesecake

::: occupations
:: service occupations
: food preparation occupations
chefs

: engineering
chemical engineering

: industries
chemical industry

:: natural sciences
: physical sciences
chemistry

::: occupations
:: scientific and technical occupations
::: occupations
:: professional occupations
::: occupations
:: education occupations
: scientists
chemists

: therapy
: medical procedures
chemotherapy

::: interdisciplinary studies
:: women's studies
::: interdisciplinary studies
:: ethnic studies
: Latina studies
Chicana studies

::: occupations
:: managerial occupations
: executives
chief executives

: abuse
child abuse

:: women
:: images of women
: brides
child brides

:: care
: dependent care
child care
. babysitting
. infant care

child care leave

: licensing
child care licensing

: policy
child care policy

: workers
:: occupations
: service occupations
:: occupations
: female intensive occupations
child care workers
. babysitters
. governesses
. nannies
. wet nurses

: custody
child custody
. shared custody

::: facilities
:: centers
: day care centers
child day care centers

:: development
: individual development
child development
. infant development

: labor
child labor

: marriage
child marriage

child neglect

: pornography
child pornography

:: social sciences
: psychology
child psychology

child rearing practices
. authoritarian child rearing
practices
. nonsexist child rearing
practices
. permissive child rearing
practices

child support

: welfare
child welfare

childbearing
. early childbearing
. late childbearing

: age
childbearing age

childbirth
. labor (childbirth)
.. induced labor
. natural childbirth
. premature childbirth

: training
childbirth training

: marriage
childfree marriage

childhood

: couples
childless couples

childlessness

children
. adopted children
. boys
. children living in poverty
. dependent children
. foster children
. girls
. grandchildren
.. granddaughters
.. grandsons
. latchkey children
. school age children
. sick children
. stepchildren
. young children
.. infants
... blue babies
... premature infants
.. preschool children

: children
children living in poverty

: art
  children's art

: culture
  children's culture

: groups
  children's groups

:: humanities
: literature
  children's literature

::: arts
:: performing arts
: music
  children's music

: relationships
  children's relationships

: rights
  children's rights

::: arts
:: visual arts
: craft arts
  china painting

:: occupations
: professional occupations
:: occupations
: health care occupations
  chiropodists

:: occupations
: professional occupations
:: occupations
: health care occupations
  chiropractors

chivalry

choirs

:::: arts
::: performing arts
:: music
: vocal music
  choral music

::: occupations
:: arts, entertainment, and media
  occupations
: dancers
  chorus dancers

chorus lines

choruses

: disorders
  chromosome disorders

:::: humanities
::: literature
:: prose
: nonfiction
  chronicles

: work
  church work

:: facilities
: religious facilities
  churches
    . house churches
    . storefront churches

: images of women
: images of girls
  Cinderella

: organizations
  circles

: conceptual errors
  circular reasoning

:: occupations
: arts, entertainment, and media
  occupations
  circus performers

: groups
citizen groups

citizenship

: government
city government

: education
civic education

:: activities
: protest actions
civil disobedience

: engineering
civil engineering

: law
civil law

: lawsuits
civil lawsuits

civil liberties
. civil rights
. due process
. freedom of assembly
. freedom of speech
. freedom of worship

: religion
civil religion

: rights
: civil liberties
civil rights

:: organizations
: commissions
civil rights commissions

: legislation
civil rights legislation

: social movements
civil rights movements

civil service

civility

::: diseases
:: communicable diseases
: sexually transmitted diseases
clamydia

: organizations
clans

class
. class division
. economic class
. ethclass
. lower class
. middle class
. social class
. socioeconomic class
. upper class
. working class

: lawsuits
class action suits

class consciousness

: differences
class differences

: discrimination
class discrimination

: class
class division

class formation

: identity
class identity

: ideology
class ideology

:: activities
: educational activities
classes

: conditioning
classical conditioning

:: social sciences
: economics
classical economics

classism

: society
classless society

:: occupations
: service occupations
cleaners
. housecleaners
. janitors

cleaning

cleanliness

cleavage

:: workers
::: occupations
:: professional occupations
: religious workers
clergy
. clergymen
. clergywomen
. ministers
. mullahs
. priests
. rabbis

: men
::: workers
:::: occupations
::: professional occupations
:: religious workers
: clergy
clergymen

:: women
::: workers
:::: occupations
::: professional occupations
:: religious workers
::: occupations
:: female intensive occupations
: women religious
::: workers
:::: occupations
::: professional occupations
:: religious workers
: clergy
clergywomen

:: occupations
: administrative support occupations
clerical occupations
. bank tellers
. bookkeepers
. clerks
. computer equipment
operators
. data entry operators
. mail carriers
. receptionists
. secretaries
. stenographers
. telephone operators
. typists

:: occupations
: female intensive occupations
::: occupations
:: administrative support occupations
: clerical occupations
clerks

cliches

climacteric

:: social sciences
: psychology
clinical psychology

clinical trials

: facilities
clinics
. abortion clinics

cliques

: orgasm
clitoral orgasm

: female circumcision
clitoridectomy

:: bodies
: genitals
clitoris

:: technology
: reproductive technologies
cloning

:: women
:: gays
: lesbians
closeted lesbians

clothing
. bathing suits
.. bikinis
. bloomers
. brassieres
. chador
. high heeled shoes
. hosiery
. lingerie
.. corsets
.. girdles
. pants
. protective clothing
. purses
. skirts
.. miniskirts
. tank tops
. tee shirts
. underwear
. veils

: workers
:: occupations
: manufacturing occupations
:: occupations
: female intensive occupations
clothing workers
. dressmakers
. knitting machine operators
. milliners

(cont.)

clothing workers *(cont.)*
. seamstresses (historical)
. sewers
. sewing machine operators
. tailors

: women
club women

: organizations
clubs
. book clubs
. garden clubs
. night clubs
. private clubs
. social clubs

:: occupations
: education occupations
:: occupations
: arts, entertainment, and media
occupations
coaches

:: occupations
: craft occupations
coal miners

: politics
coalition politics

: organizations
coalitions

:: occupations
: service occupations
:: occupations
: female intensive occupations
coat checkers

:: drugs
: narcotic drugs
cocaine

::: activities
:: social activities
: parties
cocktail parties

:: occupations
: service occupations
cocktail servers

codependency

: education
coeducation

:: activities
: social activities
coffee klatches

cognition

: behavior modification
cognitive behavior modification

:: development
: individual development
cognitive development
. intellectual development
. perceptual development

cognitive dissonance

cognitive processes
. abstract reasoning
. creative thinking
. decision making
. logical thinking
. memory
.. long term memory
.. recall
.. recognition
.. short term memory
. perception
.. auditory perception
.. color perception
.. depth perception
.. extrasensory perception
.. kinesthetic perception
.. self perception
.. social perception
.. spatial perception
.. tactual perception
.. visual perception
.. weight perception
. problem solving

: science
cognitive science

cohabitation

:: methods
: research methods
cohort analysis

: groups
cohorts

coiffures

coins

: contraception
coitus interruptus

collaboration

::: arts
:: performing arts
: theater
collaborative theater

:: arts
: visual arts
collage
. femmage

collective bargaining

: farms
:: organizations
: collectives
collective farms

: organizations
collectives
. collective farms

::: occupations
:: managerial occupations
: administrators
college administrators

: credits
college credits

:: occupations
: education occupations
college presidents

: students
college students
. women college students

:: facilities
: educational facilities
colleges
. Black colleges
. community colleges
. junior colleges
. private colleges
. public colleges
. single sex colleges
.. women's colleges
. two year colleges

: athletics
collegiate athletics

:: activities
: educational activities
colloquia

colonialism
. neocolonialism

:: cognitive processes
: perception
color perception

: casting
colorblind casting

::: occupations
:: service occupations
::: occupations
:: female intensive occupations
: cosmetologists
colorists

colostrum

:: occupations
: arts, entertainment, and media
occupations
columnists

columns
. advice columns
. personal columns

:: occupations
: arts, entertainment, and media
occupations
comedians

:::: arts
::: performing arts
:: theater
::: humanities
:: literature
: drama
comedy
. farce
. skits

:: arts
: visual arts
comic strips

coming out

:: occupations
: arts, entertainment, and media
occupations
commentators

: art
commercial art
. graphics
. illustration
.. fashion illustration
. typography

: credit
commercial credit

: sex
commercial sex

::: mass media
:: electronic media
: television
commercial television

---

commercials
. radio commercials
. television commercials

: organizations
commissions
. civil rights commissions
. commissions on the status of
women
. equal opportunities
commissions
.. Equal Employment
Opportunity
Commission
. human relations commissions

:: organizations
: commissions
**commissions on the status of
women**

commitment

: organizations
committees
. political action committees
. search committees

: marriage
common law marriage

: families
:: groups
: communal groups
communal families

: groups
communal groups
. communal families

: organizations
communes
. kibbutzim
. village communes

: diseases
communicable diseases
. acquired immune deficiency
syndrome
. sexually transmitted diseases
.. acquired immune
deficiency syndrome
.. clamydia
.. genital herpes
.. gonorrhea
.. syphilis

communication
. interpersonal communication
. nonverbal communication
.. gestures
. verbal communication
.. conversation
.. gossip
.. talk

: satellites
communication satellites

communication styles

communications
. telecommunications

: equity
communications equity

: industries
communications industry

: political systems
communism

: economic development models
**communist economic
development models**

:: organizations
: political parties
Communist Party

communities
. faith communities
. lesbian communities
. utopian communities

community

community action

: care
community care

::: facilities
:: educational facilities
: colleges
community colleges

: development
community development

: education
community education

:: services
: health care services
community health services

:: occupations
: volunteer occupations
:: occupations
: service occupations
community organizers

: problems
community problems

: laws
community property laws

: relationships
community relations

: responsibility
community responsibility

::: facilities
:: educational facilities
: schools
community schools

: marriage
commuter marriage

: students
commuting students

: organizations
companies

: marriage
companionate marriage

:: equity
: pay equity
comparable worth

:: social sciences
: psychology
comparative psychology

:: interdisciplinary studies
: cross cultural studies
comparative religion

compensation packages

: education
compensatory education

competence
. minimum competencies

: testing
competency based tests

: behavior
competitive behavior

: complexes
completion complex

complexes
. castration complex
. completion complex
. Electra complex
. Oedipus complex
.. female Oedipus complex

complexion

: behavior
compliant behavior

compliments

:: occupations
: arts, entertainment, and media occupations
composers

:: workers
::: occupations
:: manufacturing occupations
: printing workers
compositors

compressed workweek

compromise

: behavior
compulsive behavior
. hypersexuality
.. female hypersexuality
.. male hypersexuality

: education
compulsory education

:: sexuality
: heterosexuality
compulsory heterosexuality

:: behavior
: avoidance behavior
computer avoidance

:: workers
: operators
::: occupations
:: administrative support occupations
: clerical occupations
computer equipment operators

: equity
computer equity

:: games
: video games
computer games

: literacy
computer literacy

::: arts
:: performing arts
: music
computer music

:: occupations
: scientific and technical occupations
computer programmers

computer programming

: information sciences
computer science

: security
computer security

: computers
computer terminals

computers
. computer terminals

concentration camps

conception

conceptual errors
. circular reasoning
. faulty generalization

concerts

concubinage

: women
: images of women
concubines

conditioning
. classical conditioning
. operant conditioning
. social conditioning

conditions
. factory conditions
. industrial conditions
. living conditions
. rural conditions

(cont.)

conditions (*cont.*)
. working conditions

: contraception
condoms

:: occupations
: arts, entertainment, and media
occupations
conductors

: organizations
confederations

: activities
conferences
. teleconferences

::: spiritual communication
:: rites
: sacraments
confession

confidentiality
. records confidentiality

::: spiritual communication
:: rites
: sacraments
confirmation

conflict
. career family conflict
. conflict of interest
. culture conflict
. family conflict
. marital conflict
. role conflict
.. interrole conflict
. social conflict

: conflict
conflict of interest

conflict resolution

: behavior
conforming behavior

confrontation

:: groups
: religious groups
congregations

Congress
. House of Representatives
. Senate

: organizations
congresses

:: activities
: hearings
congressional hearings

::: officials
:::: occupations
::: legal and political occupations
:: elected officials
: representatives
: men
congressmen

: women
::: officials
:::: occupations
::: legal and political occupations
:: elected officials
: representatives
congresswomen

consanguinity

conscientious objection

consciousness
. false consciousness

consciousness raising

: groups
consciousness raising groups

: union
consensual union

consensus
. consensus building

: consensus
consensus building

consent orders

conservation
. art conservation
. book conservation
. energy conservation
. soil conservation

: social movements
conservative movement

conservatives

:: facilities
: educational facilities
conservatories

: organizations
consortia

constitution

: industries
construction industry

:: occupations
: craft occupations
construction occupations
. bricklayers
. cabinetmakers
. carpenters
. construction workers
. electricians
. glaziers
. heavy equipment operators
. housepainters
. inspectors
. paperhangers
. plasterers
. plumbers
. roofers
. woodworkers

: workers
::: occupations
:: craft occupations
: construction occupations
construction workers

:: occupations
: professional occupations
consultants

: advocates
consumer advocates

: behavior
consumer behavior

: credit
consumer credit

: economy
consumer economy

: organizations
**consumer health
organizations**

: information
consumer information

: loans
consumer installment loans

: power
consumer power

: problems
consumer problems

consumer protection

consumerism

consumers

consumption

:: women
:: gays
: lesbians
contact dykes

: sports
contact sports

contacts

:: methods
: research methods
content analysis

:: methods
: research methods
contextual analysis

: education
continuing education

: credits
continuing education units

contraception
. cervical caps
. coitus interruptus
. condoms
. diaphragms
. injectable contraceptives
.. Depo Provera
. intrauterine devices
. oral contraceptives
. rhythm method
. spermicides

contract compliance

contract renewal

:: documents
: legal documents
contracts
. labor contracts
. marriage contracts
.. prenuptial agreements

control
. self control
. social control

: mortgages
conventional mortgages

: activities
conventions
. political conventions

:: facilities
: religious facilities
convents

:: communication
: verbal communication
conversation

cooking

::: occupations
:: service occupations
: food preparation occupations
:: occupations
: female intensive occupations
cooks

: education
cooperative education

: organizations
cooperatives
. health cooperatives

:: occupations
: managerial occupations
:: occupations
: education occupations
coordinators

: parenting
coparenting

: strategies
coping strategies

: laws
copyright laws

:: occupations
: arts, entertainment, and media
occupations
copywriters

: curriculum
core curriculum

::: facilities
:: centers
: day care centers
corporate day care centers
. workplace nurseries

: law
corporate law

: liability
corporate liability

: policy
corporate policy
. corporate relocation policy
. foreign investment policy
. hiring policy
.. affirmative action hiring
.. job advertisements
.. veteran preference
. multinational corporation
policy
.. drug dumping
.. global assembly lines
.. offshore production
plants
.. piecework labor policy

:: policy
: corporate policy
corporate relocation policy

: responsibility
corporate responsibility

: spouses
corporate spouses

corporate takeovers

: organizations
corporations
. monopolies
. multinational corporations
. networks (media)

::: occupations
:: service occupations
: protective service occupations
correctional officers
. parole officers
. probation officers

: rehabilitation
correctional rehabilitation

correspondence
. business correspondence
. personal correspondence

correspondence courses

::: occupations
:: arts, entertainment, and media
occupations
: journalists
correspondents

corruption

: flowers
corsages

:: clothing
: lingerie
corsets

:: medical sciences
: surgery
cosmetic surgery

cosmetics

:: occupations
: service occupations
:: occupations
: female intensive occupations
cosmetologists
. colorists
. manicurists
. pedicurists

cosmetology

cosmology

:: methods
: research methods
cost benefit analysis

cost of living

costs
. administrative costs
. educational costs
. health care costs
. housing costs

: design
costume design

::: activities
:: social activities
: dances
cotillions

: industries
cottage industry

: organizations
councils

counseling
. abortion counseling
. career counseling
. economic counseling
. family counseling
. genetic counseling
. group counseling
. individual counseling
. marriage counseling
. occupational counseling
. school counseling
. sex counseling

:: occupations
: professional occupations
:: occupations
: female intensive occupations
:: occupations
: education occupations
counselors

: culture
counterculture

: transference
countertransference

: women
: titles (nobility)
: images of women
countesses

:::: arts
::: performing arts
:: music
: popular music
country music

: courts
county courts

: government
county government

couples
. childless couples
. couples with children
. dual career couples
. gay couples
.. gay male couples
.. lesbian couples
. married couples

: couples
couples with children

coups

courage

: evaluation
course evaluation

: objectives
course objectives

court cases

court decisions

: women
: images of women
courtesans

:: emotions
: love
courtly love

courts
. county courts
. family courts
. federal courts
. juvenile courts
. state courts
. Supreme Court

: customs
courtship customs
. bundling
. marriage proposals

cousins

:: groups
: religious groups
covens

coverture

:: women
:: spouses
: wives
cowives

coyness

craft artists
. potters
. weavers

:: arts
: visual arts
craft arts
. basketry
. beadwork
. ceramics
. china painting
. doll making
. flower painting
. lace making
. needlework
.. crocheting
.. embroidery
.. knitting
.. needlepoint
. pottery

(cont.)

craft arts *(cont.)*
. puppetry
. quilting
. rug hooking
. spinning
. tapestry
. textile making
. weaving

: occupations
craft occupations
. coal miners
. construction occupations
.. bricklayers
.. cabinetmakers
.. carpenters
.. construction workers
.. electricians
.. glaziers
.. heavy equipment
operators
.. housepainters
.. inspectors
.. paperhangers
.. plasterers
.. plumbers
.. roofers
.. woodworkers
. engravers
. machinists
. mechanics
. repairers
. sign painters
. technicians
. tool and die makers
. watchmakers
. welders

:: occupations
: arts, entertainment, and media
occupations
craftspersons

::::: humanities
:::: literature
::: folk literature
:: mythology
creation myths

: cognitive processes
creative thinking

: writing
creative writing

:: human needs
: psychological needs
creativity

: nurseries
creches

credentials

credit
. commercial credit
. consumer credit
. equal credit
. tuition tax credit
. utility credit

: credits
credit by examination

: credits
credit for experience

: fraud
credit fraud

credits
. college credits
. continuing education units
. credit by examination
. credit for experience

: sports
crew

: sports
cricket

crime
. organized crime
. white collar crime

: prevention
crime prevention

: victims
crime victims

crimes
. crimes against children
. crimes against the elderly
. crimes against women
. crimes of honor
. crimes of passion
. property crimes
.. arson
.. burglaries
.. larceny
.. shoplifting
.. vandalism
. sex crimes
. victimless crimes
. war crimes

: crimes
crimes against children

: crimes
crimes against the elderly

: crimes
crimes against women

: crimes
crimes of honor

: crimes
crimes of passion

: abortion
criminal abortion

: justice
criminal justice

: law
criminal law

: lawsuits
criminal lawsuits

criminals
. rapists

. .. . Narrower term

: social sciences
criminology

:: facilities
: centers
crisis centers
. rape crisis centers

crisis intervention

:: housing
: temporary housing
:: facilities
: shelters
crisis shelters

criteria
. admissions criteria
. evaluation criteria

critical mass

criticism
. art criticism
. dance criticism
. feminist criticism
. film criticism
. gynocriticism
. literary criticism
. music criticism
. phallic criticism
. psychoanalytic criticism
. theater criticism

:: occupations
: arts, entertainment, and media
occupations
critics

:::: arts
::: visual arts
:: craft arts
: needlework
crocheting

: women
: images of women
crones

: casting
cross cultural casting

: feminism
cross cultural feminism

: research
cross cultural research

: interdisciplinary studies
cross cultural studies
. comparative religion

cross dressing

:: identity
: sexual identity
cross sex identity

cruising

crying

: fortune telling
crystal ball gazing

cult of the virgin

cult of true womanhood

cults

:: social sciences
: anthropology
cultural anthropology

cultural constraints

: feminism
cultural feminism

: groups
cultural groups

cultural heritage

: identity
cultural identity

cultural imperialism

: influences
cultural influences

: sadism
cultural sadism

: status
cultural status

culture
. children's culture
. counterculture
. dominant culture
. folk culture
 .. old wives' tales
. gay culture
 .. gay male culture
 .. lesbian culture
. majority culture
. material culture
. popular culture
. subculture
. women's culture
 .. lesbian culture

: conflict
culture conflict

: work
culture work

::: behavior
:: sexual behavior
: oral sex
cunnilingus

cunning

: art
cunt art

: images of women
cunts

curators

curfew

: emotions
curiosity

curlers

: hair styles
curls

curriculum
. core curriculum
. hidden curriculum
. nonsexist curriculum

: integration
curriculum integration

: parents
custodial parents

custody
. child custody
 .. shared custody

:: documents
: legal documents
custody decrees

customs
. courtship customs
 .. bundling
 .. marriage proposals
. dating customs
. inheritance customs
. marriage customs
 .. endogamy
 .. exogamy
 .. levirate
 .. polygamy
  ... polyandry
  ... polygyny
 .. sororate
. taboos
. tribal customs

cysts

: women
: titles (nobility)
: images of women
dames

. .. . Narrower term

:: arts
: performing arts
dance
. ballet
. experimental dance
. folk dance
. modern dance
. sacred dance

: criticism
dance criticism

:: occupations
: arts, entertainment, and media occupations
dancers
. chorus dancers

:: activities
: social activities
dances
. charity balls
. cotillions
. mixers
. proms
. society balls

data analysis
. statistical analysis

data collection
. sampling
.. random sampling

:: workers
: operators
:: occupations
: female intensive occupations
::: occupations
:: administrative support occupations
: clerical occupations
data entry operators

data processing

:: occupations
: female intensive occupations
:: occupations
: administrative support occupations
data processors

:::: violence
::: sexual violence
:: rape
: acquaintance rape
date rape

:: activities
: social activities
dating
. blind dates

: customs
dating customs

: services
dating services

daughter right

: women
daughters

: in laws
daughters in law

: care
day care
. employer supported day care

:: facilities
: centers
day care centers
. after school day care centers
. child day care centers
. corporate day care centers
.. workplace nurseries
. drop in day care centers
. elderly day care centers

: dreams
daydreams

: laity
deacons

:: disabilities
: hearing impairments
deafness

:: occupations
: education occupations
  deans

  death
  . accidental death
  . dowry deaths
  . premature death

  death and dying

:: documents
: legal documents
  death certificates

  death penalty

  debt

: images of women
: images of girls
  debutantes

: cognitive processes
  decision making

: neighborhoods
  declining neighborhoods
    . slums

  decolonization

  deconstruction

:: arts
: visual arts
  decorative arts

  defamation

: psychological factors
  defense mechanisms
    . denial
    . projection

: behavior
  deferential behavior

  deficits
    . budget deficits

  defloration

degrees
  . associate degrees
  . graduate degrees
    .. doctoral degrees
    .. masters' degrees
  . honorary degrees
  . professional degrees
  . undergraduate degrees
    .. bachelors' degrees

deindustrialization

deinstitutionalization

deity

: parenthood
  delayed parenthood

  delegates

: behavior
  delinquent behavior

:: occupations
: service occupations
  deliverers

: rooms
  delivery rooms

: political systems
  democracy

:: organizations
: political parties
  Democratic Party

: measurements
  demographic measurements
  . population characteristics
  . population decline
  . population distribution
  . population growth
    .. zero population growth
  . vital statistics
    .. birth rates
    .. divorce rates
    .. fertility rates
    .. marriage rates
    .. mortality rates

(cont.)

. .. . Narrower term

demographic measurements (*cont.*)
.. sex ratio

demographic transition

: social sciences
demography

:: activities
: protest actions
demonstrations

:: women
: mothers
: images of women
den mothers

:: psychological factors
: defense mechanisms
denial

:: occupations
: health care occupations
:: occupations
: female intensive occupations
dental hygienists

: medical sciences
dentistry

:: occupations
: professional occupations
:: occupations
: health care occupations
dentists

deodorants

: organizations
departments

: behavior
dependent behavior

: benefits
dependent benefits

: care
dependent care
. child care
.. babysitting
.. infant care
. elderly care

:: programs
: assistance programs
**dependent care assistance
programs**

: children
dependent children

dependents

depilatories

:: contraception
: injectable contraceptives
Depo Provera

depreciation

:: disorders
: mental disorders
depression
. involuntary depression
. postpartum depression

deprivation

:: cognitive processes
: perception
depth perception

:: humanities
: linguistics
descriptive linguistics

: writing
descriptive writing

desegregation
. school desegregation

: methods
desegregation methods
. busing

desertion

desex

design
. costume design
. experimental design
. fashion design
. graphic design
. house design
. interior design
. textile design

:: occupations
: arts, entertainment, and media
occupations
designers

: neighborhoods
desirable neighborhoods

: emotions
desire
. sexual desire

deskilling

: emotions
despair

: behavior
destructive behavior
. self destructive behavior

::: occupations
:: service occupations
: protective service occupations
detectives

devaluation

developed nations

developing nations

development
. community development
. economic development
. employee development
. individual development
.. adult development

(cont.)

development *(cont.)*
.. child development
... infant development
.. cognitive development
... intellectual
development
... perceptual
development
.. emotional development
.. gender development
.. language development
... verbal development
.. moral development
... ethic of care
... moral reasoning
.. personality development
.. physical development
... motor development
... muscular
development
... sensory development
.. sex role development
.. skill development
.. social development
. job development
. organizational development
. professional development
. rural development
. technology development
. urban development

:: occupations
: financial occupations
:: occupations
: agricultural, fishing, and forestry
occupations
development specialists

: interdisciplinary studies
development studies

: disabilities
developmental disabilities

:: social sciences
: psychology
developmental psychology

: behavior
deviant behavior

. .. . Narrower term

devil

: diseases
diabetes

diagnoses

dialects
. social dialects

:: services
: domestic services
diaper services

: contraception
diaphragms

::::: humanities
:::: literature
:: prose
: nonfiction
diaries
. visual diaries

dichotomy
. false dichotomies
.. mind/body split

: appetite depressants
diet pills

: therapy
diet therapy

dietetics

diethylstilbestrol

:: occupations
: professional occupations
:: occupations
: health care occupations
:: occupations
: female intensive occupations
dieticians

dieting

diets

differences
. class differences
. gender differences
. learning differences
. racial and ethnic differences
. sex differences
. social differences

differently abled

diffusion

:: medical procedures
: surgical procedures
dilatation and curettage

:: activities
: social activities
dinners

diplomacy

diplomas

:: occupations
: legal and political occupations
diplomats

:: occupations
: volunteer occupations
directors

disabilities
. developmental disabilities
. hearing impairments
.. deafness
. learning disabilities
. mental retardation
. pregnancy disability
. visual impairments
.. blindness

: insurance
disability insurance

disabled

disadvantaged
. doubly disadvantaged
. economically disadvantaged
. educationally disadvantaged

(cont.)

disadvantaged (*cont.*)
. socially disadvantaged

: groups
disadvantaged groups

disarmament
. nuclear disarmament

discipline

: laws
disclosure laws

discourse

discrimination
. age discrimination
. class discrimination
. discrimination against the disabled
. double discrimination
. housing discrimination
. institutional discrimination
.. institutional racism
.. institutional sexism
. job discrimination
. microinequities
. pregnancy discrimination
. racial discrimination
. religious discrimination
. reverse discrimination
. sex discrimination
.. sex discrimination in education
.. sex discrimination in employment
. structural discrimination
. wage discrimination

: discrimination
discrimination against the disabled

: laws
discrimination laws

: language
discriminatory language
. sexist language
.. he/man language
.. patriarchal language

: legislation
discriminatory legislation

discriminatory practices
. blockbusting
. glass ceiling
. redlining
. segregation
.. occupational segregation
... occupational sex segregation
.. school segregation
.. sex segregation
. steering

: groups
:: activities
: educational activities
discussion groups

: prevention
disease prevention

diseases
. alcoholism
. anemia
.. iron deficiency anemia
. breast diseases
. cancer
.. breast cancer
.. cervical cancer
. cardiovascular diseases
.. heart disease
. communicable diseases
.. acquired immune deficiency syndrome
.. sexually transmitted diseases
... acquired immune deficiency syndrome
... clamydia
... genital herpes
... gonorrhea
... syphilis
. diabetes

(*cont.*)

. .. . Narrower term

diseases (*cont.*)
. drug addiction
. fetal alcohol syndrome
. fibrocystic disease
. hereditary diseases
. hypertension
. iatrogenic disease
. measles
. occupational diseases
. osteoporosis
. puerperal fever
. rubella
. sickle cell anemia
. sudden infant death
   syndrome
. toxic shock syndrome

:: occupations
 : service occupations
  dishwashers

disinformation

:: occupations
 : arts, entertainment, and media
  occupations
  disk jockeys

disorders
. chromosome disorders
. eating disorders
  .. anorexia nervosa
  .. bulimia
. gynecologic disorders
  .. menstrual disorders
    ... amenorrhea
    ... dysmenorrhea
    ... endometriosis
  .. vaginismus
  .. vaginitis
. mental disorders
  .. autism
  .. depression
    ... involuntary
      depression
    ... postpartum
      depression
  .. hysteria
  .. neuroses
  .. phobias
    ... agoraphobia

         (*cont.*)

disorders (*cont.*)
    ... homophobia
     .... lesbophobia
  .. schizophrenia
. obsessive compulsive
  disorders
. personality disorders
. premenstrual tension
. psychosomatic disorders

::: occupations
 :: female intensive occupations
  : homemakers
  displaced homemakers

dissent

: justice
distributive justice

: drugs
diuretics

:: occupations
 : agricultural, fishing, and forestry
  occupations
  divers

diversity
. ethnic diversity
. gender diversity
. racial diversity

divestiture

divine kingship

: spiritual communication
divining

divinity

division of labor
. household division of labor
. international division of
  labor
. sexual division of labor

divorce
. no fault divorce

:: documents
: legal documents
divorce decrees

: laws
divorce laws

::: measurements
:: demographic measurements
: vital statistics
divorce rates

::: occupations
:: volunteer occupations
::: occupations
:: service occupations
::: occupations
:: female intensive occupations
: volunteers
docents

:: degrees
: graduate degrees
doctoral degrees

::: arts
:: media arts
: film
documentaries

documents
. government documents
. legal documents
.. birth certificates
.. contracts
... labor contracts
... marriage contracts
.... prenuptial
agreements
.. custody decrees
.. death certificates
.. divorce decrees
.. legal briefs
.. licenses
... marriage licenses
.. property settlements
.. restraining orders
.. separation agreements
.. wills
.. working papers

dogma

dogmatism

::: arts
:: visual arts
: craft arts
doll making

dolls

domestic arrangements

domestic arts

domestic code

domestic food production

::: violence
:: sexual violence
: rape
domestic rape

: relationships
domestic relations

:: spiritual communication
: rites
domestic rites

: roles
domestic roles

: services
domestic services
. diaper services
. homemaker service

: values
domestic values

: violence
domestic violence
. marital violence

domesticity

: rights
domicile rights

. .. . Narrower term

dominance

: culture
dominant culture

donors

:: housing
: student housing
dormitories

double bind

: discrimination
double discrimination

double standard

: disadvantaged
doubly disadvantaged

dowry

: death
dowry deaths

: resistance
draft resistance

:: occupations
: arts, entertainment, and media
  occupations
drafters

::: arts
:: performing arts
: theater
:: humanities
: literature
drama
  . comedy
   .. farce
   .. skits
  . tragedy

:: occupations
: arts, entertainment, and media
  occupations
dramatists

:: arts
: visual arts
drawing

dreams
  . daydreams

dress codes

: reforms
dress reform

dressing for success

:: workers
::: occupations
:: manufacturing occupations
::: occupations
:: female intensive occupations
: clothing workers
dressmakers

dressmaking

drinking

: social prohibitions
drinking prohibition

:: occupations
: transportation occupations
drivers
  . bus drivers
  . taxi drivers
  . truck drivers

::: facilities
:: centers
: day care centers
drop in day care centers

dropouts

:: abuse
: substance abuse
drug abuse

: diseases
: addiction
drug addiction

::: policy
:: corporate policy
: multinational corporation policy
drug dumping

drug overdoses

: rehabilitation
drug rehabilitation

drug side effects

: tests
drug tests

: therapy
drug therapy

drug use

drugs
. diuretics
. fertility drugs
. narcotic drugs
.. cocaine
.. heroin
.. marijuana
. nonprescription drugs
. oral contraceptives
. prescription drugs
. psychotropic drugs
.. antidepressant drugs
.. tranquilizers

: couples
dual career couples

: families
dual career families

: careers
dual careers

dual economy

:: roles
: multiple roles
dual roles

dualism

: women
: titles (nobility)
: images of women
duchesses

: civil liberties
due process

dutch treat

:: spirits
: evil spirits
dybbuks

::: disorders
:: gynecologic disorders
: menstrual disorders
dysmenorrhea

dysphoria

: childbearing
early childbearing

: education
early childhood education
. preschool education
. primary education

: experience
early experience

: retirement
early retirement

: income
earned income

earnings

earnings sharing

:: women
: mothers
: images of women
earth mother

:: natural sciences
: physical sciences
earth sciences
. geology
. oceanography

: disorders
eating disorders
. anorexia nervosa
. bulimia

: feminism
ecofeminism

: influences
ecological factors

:: natural sciences
: biological sciences
ecology

econometrics

:: social sciences
: anthropology
economic anthropology

::: activities
:: protest actions
: boycotts
economic boycotts

: class
economic class

: counseling
economic counseling

economic depression

: development
economic development

**economic development
models**
. capitalist economic
development models
. communist economic
development models
. Marxist economic
development models

(cont.)

**economic development
models** *(cont.)*
. socialist economic
development models

:: theory
: economic theory
**economic development
theory**

: equity
economic equity

: influences
economic factors

:: social sciences
: geography
economic geography

economic growth

:: social sciences
:: humanities
: history
economic history

: socioeconomic indicators
economic indicators

: policy
economic policy

: power
economic power

: refugees
economic refugees

: sanctions
economic sanctions

: status
economic status

economic structure

: :: ::: :::: ::::: Broader term

: theory
economic theory
  . economic development
    theory

: trends
economic trends

economic value of women's work

: disadvantaged
economically disadvantaged

: social sciences
economics
  . agricultural economics
  . classical economics
  . health economics
  . macroeconomics
  . microeconomics
  . neoclassical economics
  . welfare economics

economies of scale

::: occupations
:: professional occupations
::: occupations
:: education occupations
: social scientists
:: occupations
: financial occupations
economists

economy
  . consumer economy
  . global economy
  . mixed economy
  . underground economy

l'ecriture feminine

: pregnancy
ectopic pregnancy

ecumenism

editorials

:: occupations
: arts, entertainment, and media
  occupations
editors

education
  . adult education
  . basic education
    .. adult basic education
  . bicultural education
  . bilingual education
  . career education
  . civic education
  . coeducation
  . community education
  . compensatory education
  . compulsory education
  . continuing education
  . cooperative education
  . early childhood education
    .. preschool education
    .. primary education
  . elementary secondary
    education
    .. elementary education
      ... adult basic education
      ... intermediate grades
      ... primary education
    .. secondary education
      ... high school
          equivalency
          programs
      ... high schools
        .... junior high
             schools
  . family education
  . health education
  . inservice education
  . medical education
  . nondegree education
  . nonformal education
  . nontraditional education
  . nursing education
  . physical education
  . postsecondary education
    .. higher education
      ... four year colleges
      ... graduate education
      ... two year colleges
  . private education
  . professional education
  . progressive education

(cont.)

. .. . Narrower term

education (*cont.*)
. public education
. religious education
. remedial education
. sex education
. single sex education
. special education
. teacher education
. technical education
. vocational education

: occupations
education occupations
. affirmative action officers
. chairpersons
. coaches
. college presidents
. coordinators
. counselors
. deans
. educators
. faculty
. home economists
. housemothers
. humanists
.. historians
.. philosophers
. laboratory assistants
.. animal caretakers
. librarians
. library workers
. principals
. professors
. provosts
. research assistants
. researchers
. scholars
.. independent scholars
.. visiting scholars
. school personnel
. scientists
.. astronomers
.. biologists
.. chemists
.. ethologists
.. geneticists
.. geologists
.. meteorologists
.. physicists
.. sociobiologists
. social scientists
.. anthropologists

(cont.)

education occupations (*cont.*)
.. archaeologists
.. economists
.. historians
.. psychologists
.. sociologists
.. urban planners
. superintendents
. teacher aides
. teachers
. teaching assistants
. vice presidents

: activities
educational activities
. classes
. colloquia
. discussion groups
. lectures
. seminars
. study groups
. teach ins

educational attainment

: benefits
educational benefits

: costs
educational costs

: equity
educational equity

: facilities
educational facilities
. academies
.. military academies
. colleges
.. Black colleges
.. community colleges
.. junior colleges
.. private colleges
.. public colleges
.. single sex colleges
... women's colleges
.. two year colleges
. conservatories
. elderhostel
. kindergarten
. libraries

(cont.)

educational facilities (*cont.*)
. schools
  .. alternative schools
  .. boarding schools
  .. community schools
  .. elementary schools
  .. free schools
  .. high schools
    ... junior high schools
  .. middle schools
  .. normal schools
  .. nursery schools
  .. preschools
  .. primary schools
  .. private schools
    ... finishing schools
    ... preparatory schools
  .. proprietary schools
  .. public schools
  .. religious schools
  .. secondary schools
  .. single sex schools
. seminaries
. universities

: legislation
educational legislation

: methods
educational methods

: objectives
educational objectives

: opportunities
educational opportunities
. equal educational
  opportunity

: policy
educational policy

: programs
educational programs
. external degree programs
. Head Start programs
. high school equivalency
  programs
. nondegree programs

:: social sciences
: psychology
educational psychology

: reforms
educational reform

: subsidies
educational subsidies

::: mass media
:: electronic media
: television
educational television

: disadvantaged
educationally disadvantaged

:: occupations
: female intensive occupations
:: occupations
: education occupations
educators

efficiency

: families
egalitarian families

ego

ejaculation

: abuse
elder abuse

:: facilities
: educational facilities
elderhostel

:: care
: dependent care
elderly care

::: facilities
:: centers
: day care centers
elderly day care centers

: households
elderly households

: officials
:: occupations
: legal and political occupations
elected officials
. assemblymen
. assemblywomen
. governors
. mayors
. representatives
.. congressmen
.. congresswomen
. senators

:: activities
: campaigns
election campaigns

elections

: complexes
Electra complex

:: organizations
: utilities
electric utilities

: engineering
electrical engineering

::: occupations
:: craft occupations
: construction occupations
electricians

: therapy
electroconvulsive therapy

electrolysis

:: arts
: media arts
: art
electronic art

electronic cottage

electronic mail

: mass media
electronic media
. radio
.. public radio
. television
.. cable television
.. commercial television
.. educational television
.. public television

::: arts
:: performing arts
: music
electronic music

: industries
electronics industry

::: humanities
:: literature
: poetry
elegies

:: education
: elementary secondary education
elementary education
. adult basic education
. intermediate grades
. primary education

::: facilities
:: educational facilities
: schools
elementary schools

: education
**elementary secondary
education**
. elementary education
.. adult basic education
.. intermediate grades
.. primary education
. secondary education
.. high school equivalency
programs
.. high schools
... junior high schools

eligibility

elites

emancipation

:::: arts
  ::: visual arts
    :: craft arts
     : needlework
      embroidery

    :: technology
     : reproductive technologies
      embryo transfer

    :: natural sciences
     : biological sciences
      embryology

      embryos

    :: services
     : health care services
      emergency medical services

     : abuse
      emotional abuse

     : adjustment
      emotional adjustment

    :: development
     : individual development
      emotional development

     : experience
      emotional experience

     : problems
      emotional problems

      emotionalism

      emotions
       . alienation
        .. job alienation
        .. work alienation
       . anger
        .. rage
       . anxiety
       . apathy
       . bitterness

                (*cont.*)

emotions (*cont.*)
 . boredom
 . curiosity
 . desire
  .. sexual desire
 . despair
 . empathy
 . fear
  .. fear of failure
  .. fear of success
 . frustration
 . greed
 . grief
 . guilt
 . happiness
 . hate
 . hostility
 . jealousy
 . joy
 . loneliness
 . love
  .. courtly love
  .. maternal love
  .. romantic love
  .. unrequited love
 . lust
 . passion
 . pleasure
 . rage
 . sadness
 . sympathy
 . trust
 . vulnerability

: emotions
 empathy

: benefits
 employee benefits

: development
 employee development

: records
 employee records

 employees

. .. . Narrower term

:: care
: day care
employer supported day care

employers

employment
. alternative employment
. federal employment
. household employment
. male dominated employment
. minority employment
. nontraditional employment
. paid employment
. part time employment
.. job sharing
. self employment
. state employment
. temporary employment
. underemployment
. unpaid employment
.. unpaid household labor
. youth employment

:: organizations
: agencies
employment agencies

: opportunities
employment opportunities
. equal employment
opportunity

employment patterns

employment practices
. hiring policy
.. affirmative action hiring
.. job advertisements
.. veteran preference
. job descriptions
. job recruitment
.. executive recruitment
. promotions

: schedules
employment schedules
. flexible work schedules

empowerment

empty nest

: groups
encounter groups

end time thinking

:: customs
: marriage customs
endogamy

::: disorders
:: gynecologic disorders
: menstrual disorders
endometriosis

endowments

energy
. nuclear energy
. solar energy

: conservation
energy conservation

enforcement

enfranchisement

engagement

engineering
. aerospace engineering
. chemical engineering
. civil engineering
. electrical engineering
. mechanical engineering
. nuclear engineering

:: occupations
: scientific and technical occupations
:: occupations
: professional occupations
engineers

:: occupations
: craft occupations
engravers

:: arts
: visual arts
engraving

: personnel
enlisted personnel

enrollment

: organizations
enterprises

:: occupations
: arts, entertainment, and media
occupations
entertainers

entertainment

: industries
entertainment industry
. motion picture industry
. music industry

: programs
entitlement programs

entrepreneurs

environment
. built environment
. family environment
. permissive environment
. single sex environments
. smokefree environments
. social environment
. urban environment

: hazards
environmental hazards

: health
environmental health

: medical sciences
environmental medicine

: social movements
environmental movement

: racism
environmental racism

: natural sciences
environmental sciences

::: humanities
:: literature
: poetry
epics

epidemiology

::: humanities
:: literature
: poetry
epigrams

:: medical procedures
: surgical procedures
episiotomy

:: humanities
: philosophy
epistemology

:: language
: figurative language
epithets

equal access

: credit
equal credit

: equal opportunity
:: opportunities
: educational opportunities
**equal educational
opportunity**

: equal opportunity
:: opportunities
: employment opportunities
**equal employment
opportunity**

::: organizations
:: commissions
: equal opportunities commissions
**Equal Employment
Opportunity Commission**

:: organizations
: commissions
**equal opportunities
commissions**
. Equal Employment
Opportunity Commission

equal opportunity
. equal educational
opportunity
. equal employment
opportunity

: wages
equal pay

:: equity
: pay equity
equal pay for equal work

: legislation
equal pay legislation

: protection
**equal protection under the
law**

: rights
equal rights

: legislation
equal rights legislation

equality
. racial equality
. sexual equality

equilibrium

equity
. communications equity
. computer equity
. economic equity
. educational equity

(cont.)

equity *(cont.)*
. pay equity
.. comparable worth
.. equal pay for equal
work
. race equity
. sex equity

equity funding

ergonomics

: erotica
: art
erotic art

:: humanities
: literature
: erotica
erotic literature

erotica
. erotic art
. erotic literature

eroticism

:: occupations
: service occupations
escorts

:: occupations
: arts, entertainment, and media
occupations
essayists

:::: humanities
::: literature
:: prose
: nonfiction
essays

essentialism

estradiol

:: therapy
: hormone therapy
**estrogen replacement
therapy**

::: bodies
:: hormones
: sex hormones
estrogens

estrus

: class
ethclass

::: development
:: individual development
: moral development
ethic of care

:: humanities
: philosophy
ethics
. bioethics
. business ethics
. feminist ethics
. medical ethics
. political ethics
. religious ethics

: diversity
ethnic diversity

: groups
ethnic groups

: intimidation
ethnic intimidation

: neighborhoods
ethnic neighborhoods
. ghettos

: relationships
ethnic relations

: interdisciplinary studies
ethnic studies
. Afro American studies
.. Black women's studies
. American Indian studies
. Asian American studies
. Canadian Indian studies
. Jewish women's studies

(cont.)

ethnic studies *(cont.)*
. Latina studies
.. Chicana studies

: women
ethnic women

ethnicity

:: social sciences
: anthropology
ethnography

:: social sciences
: anthropology
ethnology

ethnomethodology

ethnomusicology

::: occupations
:: scientific and technical occupations
::: occupations
:: professional occupations
::: occupations
:: education occupations
: scientists
ethologists

: social sciences
:: natural sciences
: biological sciences
ethology

etiquette

:: birth control
: sterilization
eugenic sterilization

eugenics

eulogies

eunuchs

euthanasia

evaluation
. course evaluation
. job evaluation
. medical evaluation
.. physical examination
... breast examination
.... breast self
examination
... pelvic examination
. mental evaluation
. personnel evaluation
.. performance appraisal

: criteria
evaluation criteria

:: workers
::: occupations
:: professional occupations
: religious workers
evangelists

: images of women
Eve

eve teasing

evil

: spirits
evil spirits
. dybbuks
. incubi
. succubi

evolution
. human evolution
.. fossil hominids

exchange rate

: students
exchange students

: theory
exchange theory

excommunication

:: employment practices
: job recruitment
executive recruitment

: organizations
executive search firms

:: occupations
: managerial occupations
executives
. chief executives

executors

exercise
. aerobic exercise
. isometric exercise

exhibitionism

: activities
exhibitions

exile

:: customs
: marriage customs
exogamy

expectations

experience
. early experience
. emotional experience
. gay experience
.. gay male experience
.. lesbian experience
. religious experience
. work experience

: learning
experiential learning

::: arts
:: performing arts
: dance
experimental dance

: design
experimental design

:: social sciences
: psychology
experimental psychology

::: arts
:: performing arts
: theater
experimental theater

experts

expiation

exploitation
. sexual exploitation

:: occupations
: professional occupations
explorers

: activities
expositions

expressing milk

:: facilities
: health care facilities
extended care facilities

: families
extended families

: work
extension work
. home economics extension
work

: workers
:: occupations
: female intensive occupations
:: occupations
: agricultural, fishing, and forestry
occupations
extension workers
. animatrices rurales
. gramsevika

:: programs
: educational programs
external degree programs

: industries
extractive industry
. mining industry
. oil industry

: activities
extracurricular activities

extramarital affairs

:: cognitive processes
: perception
extrasensory perception

extroversion

eyeglasses

::: humanities
:: literature
: folk literature
fables

face lifts

: bodies
faces

facilities
. brothels
. centers
.. birthing centers
.. crisis centers
... rape crisis centers
.. day care centers
... after school day care
centers
... child day care
centers
... corporate day care
centers
.... workplace
nurseries
... drop in day care
centers
... elderly day care
centers
.. information and referral
centers
.. neighborhood health
centers
.. training centers
(*cont.*)

facilities (*cont.*)
.. women's centers
. clinics
.. abortion clinics
. educational facilities
.. academies
... military academies
.. colleges
... Black colleges
... community colleges
... junior colleges
... private colleges
... public colleges
... single sex colleges
.... women's colleges
... two year colleges
.. conservatories
.. elderhostel
.. kindergarten
.. libraries
.. schools
... alternative schools
... boarding schools
... community schools
... elementary schools
... free schools
... high schools
.... junior high
schools
... middle schools
... normal schools
... nursery schools
... preschools
... primary schools
... private schools
.... finishing schools
.... preparatory
schools
... proprietary schools
... public schools
... religious schools
... secondary schools
... single sex schools
.. seminaries
.. universities
. foster homes
. health care facilities
.. extended care facilities
.. hospices
.. hospitals
... maternity wards

(*cont.*)

facilities (*cont.*)
... mental hospitals
.. neighborhood health
centers
.. nursing homes
. hostels
. houses
.. halfway houses
. laboratories
. lodges
. maternity homes
. museums
. offices (facilities)
. prisons
. reformatories
. religious facilities
.. cathedrals
.. churches
... house churches
... storefront churches
.. convents
.. monasteries
.. mosques
.. synagogues
.. temples
. seraglios
. shelters
.. crisis shelters
.. women's shelters
. theaters

facism

: groups
factions

factories

: conditions
factory conditions

: workers
:: occupations
: manufacturing occupations
factory workers

:: occupations
: professional occupations
:: occupations
: education occupations
faculty

faculty retrenchment

fads

faghag

failure
. academic failure

fainting

fair play

fairness

::: humanities
:: literature
: folk literature
fairy tales

faith

:: groups
: religious groups
: communities
faith communities

::: occupations
:: health care occupations
::: occupations
:: female intensive occupations
: healers
faith healers

: women
: images of women
fallen women

fallopian tubes

: consciousness
false consciousness

: dichotomy
false dichotomies
. mind/body split

false generics

families
. blended families
. communal families
. dual career families

(cont.)

families (*cont.*)
. egalitarian families
. extended families
. fatherless families
. foster families
. interethnic families
. interracial families
. interreligious families
. low income families
. middle class families
. motherless families
. nuclear families
. single parent families
. surrogate families
. two income families
. upper class families

: attitudes
family attitudes

: conflict
family conflict

: counseling
family counseling

: courts
family courts

family economics

: education
family education

: environment
family environment

: farms
family farms

: finances
family finances

::: social sciences
::: humanities
:: history
: social history
family history

: income
family income

: influence
family influence
. parent influence
. sibling influence

family life

: medical sciences
family medicine

: mobility
family mobility

: business
family owned business

: planning
family planning

:: policy
: social policy
family policy

:: occupations
: health care occupations
family practitioners

: problems
family problems

: recipes
family recipes

: relationships
family relationships
. sibling relationships

: responsibility
family responsibility

: rights
family rights

: roles
family roles

family size

family structure

: therapy
family therapy

famine

fantasies
. rape fantasies
. sexual fantasies

::::: arts
:::: performing arts
::: theater
:::: humanities
::: literature
:: drama
: comedy
farce

: workers
:: occupations
: agricultural, fishing, and forestry
occupations
farm workers

:: occupations
: agricultural, fishing, and forestry
occupations
farmers

farming
. tenant farming

farms
. collective farms
. family farms

fashion

: design
fashion design

::: art
:: commercial art
: illustration
fashion illustration

::: arts
:: visual arts
: photography
fashion photography

:: activities
: shows
fashion shows

: spiritual communication
fasting

: liberation
fat liberation

: oppression
fat oppression

: incest
father daughter incest

::: relationships
:: adult child relationships
: parent child relationships
::: relationships
:: personal relationships
: female male relationships
father daughter relationships

: incest
father son incest

::: relationships
:: adult child relationships
: parent child relationships
::: relationships
:: personal relationships
: male male relationships
father son relationships

: parenting
fathering

: families
fatherless families

: men
fathers
. absentee fathers
. birth fathers
. gay fathers
. runaway fathers
. single fathers
. stepfathers
.. gay stepfathers
. surrogate fathers
. teenage fathers

: men
: in laws
fathers in law

fatigue

: conceptual errors
faulty generalization

: emotions
fear
. fear of failure
. fear of success

:: emotions
: fear
fear of failure

:: emotions
: fear
fear of success

:: organizations
: agencies
federal agencies

: aid
federal aid

:: programs
: assistance programs
federal assistance programs

federal budget
. military budget

: courts
  federal courts

: employment
  federal employment

: government
  federal government

: legislation
  federal legislation

: regulations
  federal regulations

: taxes
  federal taxes

:: research
: sponsored research
  federally sponsored research

: organizations
  federations

  feedback
    . biofeedback

::: behavior
:: sexual behavior
: oral sex
  fellatio

::: aid
:: financial aid
: student financial aid
  fellowships
    . postdoctoral fellowships

: texts
  female authored texts

: bonding
  female bonding

: chauvinism
  female chauvinism

female circumcision
  . clitoridectomy
  . vulvectomy

:: relationships
: personal relationships
  female female relationships
    . female friendships
    . lesbian relationships
    . mother daughter
      relationships

::: relationships
:: personal relationships
: friendships
::: relationships
:: personal relationships
: female female relationships
  female friendships

: households
  female headed households

:: sexuality
::: behavior
:: compulsive behavior
: hypersexuality
  female hypersexuality

::: occupations
:: arts, entertainment, and media
    occupations
: impersonators
  female impersonators

: occupations
  female intensive occupations
    . administrative assistants
    . affirmative action officers
    . agents
      .. airline reservation agents
      .. insurance agents
      .. real estate agents
      .. travel agents
    . attendants
    . bank tellers
    . beauticians
    . bookkeepers

(cont.)

female intensive occupations (*cont.*)

. caregivers
.. primary caregivers
. child care workers
.. babysitters
.. governesses
.. nannies
.. wet nurses
. clerks
. clothing workers
.. dressmakers
.. knitting machine
operators
.. milliners
.. seamstresses (historical)
.. sewers
.. sewing machine
operators
.. tailors
. coat checkers
. cooks
. cosmetologists
.. colorists
.. manicurists
.. pedicurists
. counselors
. data entry operators
. data processors
. dental hygienists
. dieticians
. educators
. extension workers
.. animatrices rurales
.. gramsevika
. flight attendants
. food service workers
. fortune tellers
. geishas
. hairdressers
. hat checkers
. healers
.. faith healers
.. folk healers
.. native healers
. health care workers
. home economists
. homemakers
.. displaced homemakers
.. visiting homemakers
. hostesses (historical)

(*cont.*)

female intensive occupations

(*cont.*)
. household workers
.. housecleaners
. housekeepers
. housemothers
. ironers
. launderers
. librarians
. library workers
. masseuses
. medicine women
. midwives
.. lay midwives
. milliners
. models
. nurse practitioners
. nurses
.. practical nurses
.. registered nurses
.. visiting nurses
.. vocational nurses
. nutritionists
. paralegals
. physical therapists
. physicians' assistants
. pink collar workers
. prostitutes
. psychics
. receptionists
. saleswomen
. secretaries
. seers
. social workers
. stenographers
. strippers
. teacher aides
. teachers
. telephone operators
. tour guides
. typists
. volunteers
.. docents
. women religious
.. clergywomen
.. nuns
... mother superiors
.. priestesses
... high priestesses

. .. . Narrower term

::: relationships
:: personal relationships
: friendships
::: relationships
:: personal relationships
: female male relationships
female male friendships

:: relationships
: personal relationships
female male relationships
. father daughter relationships
. female male friendships
. mother son relationships

:: complexes
: Oedipus complex
female Oedipus complex

:: slavery
: sexual slavery
female sexual slavery

: sexuality
female sexuality

:: organizations
: societies
female societies

: spirituality
female spirituality

females

feminine mystique

feminine principle

femininity

feminism
. anarcha feminism
. Black feminism
. career feminism
. cross cultural feminism
. cultural feminism
. ecofeminism
. first wave feminism
. global feminism
. lesbian feminism
. liberal feminism

(cont.)

feminism (*cont.*)
. mainstream feminism
. Marxist feminism
. nonaligned feminism
. protofeminism
. psychoanalytic feminism
. radical feminism
. socialist feminism
. spiritual feminism

: criticism
feminist criticism

::: humanities
:: philosophy
: ethics
feminist ethics

: methods
feminist methods

: social movements
feminist movement

::: arts
:: performing arts
: music
feminist music

:: organizations
: women's organizations
feminist organizations

feminist perspective

:: mass media
: women's media
::: mass media
:: print media
: publications
feminist publications

: scholarship
feminist scholarship

: interdisciplinary studies
feminist studies

:: humanities
: theology
feminist theology
. thealogy

: theory
feminist theory

: therapy
feminist therapy

: writing
feminist writing

feminists
. male feminists

::: arts
:: visual arts
: collage
femmage

femme

: images of women
femmes fatales

: sports
fencing

fertility

:: technology
: reproductive technologies
: drugs
fertility drugs

::: measurements
:: demographic measurements
: vital statistics
fertility rates

:: spiritual communication
: rites
fertility rites

fertilization
. in vitro fertilization

: activities
festivals
. film festivals
. music festivals

: diseases
fetal alcohol syndrome

: medical procedures
fetal monitoring

fetuses

feuds

:: arts
: visual arts
fiber art

: diseases
fibrocystic disease

::: humanities
:: literature
: prose
fiction
. mysteries
. novels
.. novellas
. pulp fiction
. romances
. science fiction
. short stories

fictional characters

: sports
field hockey

fieldwork

fifth world

: language
figurative language
. allegory
. ambiguity
. antithesis
. epithets
. imagery
. irony
. metaphors

(cont.)

figurative language (*cont.*)
. puns

:: arts
: media arts
film
. documentaries

: criticism
film criticism

:: occupations
: arts, entertainment, and media
occupations
film directors

:: activities
: festivals
film festivals

:: occupations
: arts, entertainment, and media
occupations
film producers

films

finance

finances
. family finances
. personal finances

: aid
financial aid
. student financial aid
.. assistantships
.. fellowships
... postdoctoral
fellowships
.. scholarships

financial arrangements

: management
financial management

: occupations
financial occupations
. accountants
. bankers
. development specialists
. economists
. financial planners
. financiers
. insurance adjusters
. insurance examiners
. philanthropists
. stockbrokers
. venture capitalists

:: occupations
: financial occupations
financial planners

: planning
financial planning

: resources
financial resources

:: occupations
: financial occupations
financiers

:::: facilities
::: educational facilities
:: schools
: private schools
finishing schools

::: occupations
:: service occupations
: protective service occupations
fire fighters

: prevention
fire prevention

firing

:: spouses
:: men
: husbands
first husbands

: women
:: spouses
: political spouses
First Ladies (historical)

: feminism
first wave feminism

:: women
:: spouses
: wives
first wives

: policy
fiscal policy

fish sellers

:: occupations
: agricultural, fishing, and forestry
occupations
fishers

: benefits
flexible benefits

flexible career patterns

:: schedules
: employment schedules
flexible work schedules

:: occupations
: transportation occupations
:: occupations
: female intensive occupations
flight attendants

:: behavior
: sex role behavior
flirtation

: images of women
flirts

flower arranging

::: arts
:: visual arts
: craft arts
flower painting

flowers
. bouquets
. corsages

: art
folk art

: culture
folk culture
. old wives' tales

::: arts
:: performing arts
: dance
folk dance

::: occupations
:: health care occupations
::: occupations
:: female intensive occupations
: healers
folk healers

:: humanities
: literature
folk literature
. fables
. fairy tales
. legends
. mythology
.. creation myths
. parables
. proverbs

: medical sciences
folk medicine

:::: arts
::: performing arts
:: music
: popular music
folk music

folklorists

food
. food for work

: food
food for work

: industries
food industry

food marketing

food preparation

:: occupations
: service occupations
food preparation occupations
. bakers
. butchers
. chefs
. cooks

food processing

: workers
:: occupations
: service occupations
:: occupations
: female intensive occupations
food service workers

: stamps
food stamps

: technology
food technology

foot binding

: sports
football

: retirement
forced retirement

forecasting

: aid
foreign aid

:: policy
: international policy
foreign aid policy

:: policy
: corporate policy
foreign investment policy

foreign service

: students
foreign students

: workers
foreign workers

:: women
: mothers
foremothers

:: behavior
: sexual behavior
foreplay

forgiveness

:: spouses
:: men
: husbands
:: spouses
: former spouses
former husbands

: spouses
former spouses
. former husbands
. former wives

:: women
:: spouses
: wives
:: spouses
: former spouses
former wives

forms of address
. Ms

forms of affection
. hugging
. kissing
. listening
. lovemaking
. touching

:: occupations
: service occupations
:: occupations
: female intensive occupations
fortune tellers

fortune telling
. crystal ball gazing
. Ouija boards
. palm reading
. tarot reading
. tea leaf reading

: activities
forums

:: evolution
: human evolution
fossil hominids

: children
foster children

: families
foster families

: grandparents
foster grandparents

: facilities
foster homes

: parents
foster parents

:: organizations
: nonprofit organizations
foundations

four day workweek

::: education
:: postsecondary education
: higher education
four year colleges

fourth world

franchise

: twins
fraternal twins

fraternities

fraud
. credit fraud
. insurance fraud
. welfare fraud

free association

free enterprise

::: facilities
:: educational facilities
: schools
free schools

: speech
free speech

free trade zones

freedom

freedom from oppression

: civil liberties
freedom of assembly

freedom of choice

freedom of information

: civil liberties
freedom of speech

freedom of the press

: civil liberties
freedom of worship

freedoms
. academic freedom
. reproductive freedom
. sexual freedom

friends

:: relationships
: personal relationships
friendships
. female friendships
. female male friendships
. male friendships

: benefits
fringe benefits

frontier life

: emotions
frustration

fund raising

: activities
fund raising events
. charity balls

fundamentalism

funding
. grants
.. block grants
.. research grants
.. tuition grants
. in kind contributions

:: spiritual communication
: rites
funeral rites

furniture

: interdisciplinary studies
future studies

futurism

G spot

::: behavior
:: social behavior
: manners
gallantry

galleries

gambling

:: activities
: shows
game shows

: theory
game theory

games
. video games
.. computer games

:::: violence
:: sexual violence
: rape
gang rape

gangs

:: organizations
: clubs
garden clubs

Garden of Eden

:: occupations
: agricultural, fishing, and forestry
occupations
gardeners

gardens

: industries
garment industry
. millinery trade

:: organizations
: utilities
gas utilities

gatekeeping

: couples
  gay couples
   . gay male couples
   . lesbian couples

: culture
  gay culture
   . gay male culture
   . lesbian culture

: experience
  gay experience
   . gay male experience
   . lesbian experience

:: men
 : fathers
  gay fathers

:: humanities
 : literature
  gay literature
   . gay male literature
   . lesbian literature

:: couples
 : gay couples
  gay male couples

:: culture
 : gay culture
  gay male culture

:: experience
 : gay experience
  gay male experience

::: humanities
 :: literature
  : gay literature
   gay male literature

:: marriage
 : gay marriage
  gay male marriage

::: relationships
 :: personal relationships
  : male male relationships
::: relationships
 :: personal relationships
  : gay relationships
   gay male relationships

: marriage
  gay marriage
   . gay male marriage
   . lesbian marriage

: men
: gays
  gay men

: pride
  gay pride

:: relationships
 : personal relationships
  gay relationships
   . gay male relationships
   . lesbian relationships

: rights
  gay rights

::: men
 :: fathers
  : stepfathers
   gay stepfathers

  : interdisciplinary studies
   gay studies
    . lesbian studies

gay/straight split

gays
 . gay men
 . lesbians
  .. closeted lesbians
  .. contact dykes

: women
: images of women
:: occupations
: female intensive occupations
:: occupations
: arts, entertainment, and media
   occupations
geishas

gender

: bias
gender bias

:: development
: individual development
gender development

: differences
gender differences

: diversity
gender diversity

gender gap

: identity
gender identity

: ideology
gender ideology

gender marking

: roles
gender roles

: interdisciplinary studies
gender studies

: anesthesia
general anesthesia

generation gap

: grammar
generative grammar

: pronouns
generic pronouns

: counseling
genetic counseling

genetic defects

genetic determinants

genetic engineering

: medical procedures
genetic screening

::: occupations
:: scientific and technical occupations
::: occupations
:: professional occupations
::: occupations
:: education occupations
: scientists
geneticists

:: natural sciences
: biological sciences
genetics
. population genetics

::: diseases
:: communicable diseases
: sexually transmitted diseases
genital herpes

genital mutilation

: bodies
genitals
. clitoris
. labia
. penis
. scrotum
. testicles
. vulva

genocide

: mobility
geographic mobility

: social sciences
geography
  . economic geography
  . social geography

::: occupations
  :: scientific and technical occupations
::: occupations
  :: professional occupations
::: occupations
  :: education occupations
   : scientists
    geologists

::: natural sciences
  :: physical sciences
   : earth sciences
    geology

   : medical sciences
    geriatrics

   : social sciences
   : interdisciplinary studies
    gerontology

   : therapy
    gestalt therapy

    gestation period

:: communication
  : nonverbal communication
   gestures

:: neighborhoods
  : ethnic neighborhoods
   ghettos

:: occupations
  : service occupations
   gigolos

:: clothing
  : lingerie
   girdles

   girl preference of parents

: children
girls

glamour

: bodies
glands
  . lymph glands
  . mammary glands
  . pituitary gland
  . thyroid gland

: discriminatory practices
glass ceiling

:: occupations
  : arts, entertainment, and media
   occupations
   glassmakers

::: occupations
  :: craft occupations
   : construction occupations
    glaziers

::: policy
  :: corporate policy
   : multinational corporation policy
    global assembly lines

   : economy
    global economy

   : feminism
    global feminism

   : security
    global security

    global village

   : spiritual communication
    glossolalia

   : gods
    God the father

   : worship
    goddess worship

: images of women
  goddesses
    . mother goddess
    . Mother/Father God

  gods
    . God the father
    . Mother/Father God

  : sports
    golf

::: diseases
  :: communicable diseases
    : sexually transmitted diseases
      gonorrhea

  :: spiritual communication
::::: arts
  ::: performing arts
    :: music
      : religious music
        gospel music

  :: communication
    : verbal communication
      gossip

      governance

    : women
  :: workers
::: occupations
  :: service occupations
::: occupations
  :: female intensive occupations
    : child care workers
      governesses

  :: organizations
    : boards
      governing boards

      government
        . city government
        . county government
        . federal government
        . local government
        . state government
        . student government

:: organizations
  : agencies
    government agencies

    government appointments

  : workers
:: occupations
  : service occupations
:: occupations
  : legal and political occupations
    government workers

:: officials
::: occupations
  :: legal and political occupations
    : elected officials
      governors

:: spouses
  : political spouses
    governors' spouses

::: behavior
  :: social behavior
    : manners
      graciousness

    : degrees
      graduate degrees
        . doctoral degrees
        . masters' degrees

::: education
  :: postsecondary education
    : higher education
      graduate education

    : ceremonies
      graduation ceremonies

      grammar
        . generative grammar
        . transformational grammar

:: workers
::: occupations
:: female intensive occupations
::: occupations
:: agricultural, fishing, and forestry
    occupations
: extension workers
gramsevika

: children
grandchildren
  . granddaughters
  . grandsons

: women
:: children
: grandchildren
granddaughters

: men
: grandparents
grandfathers

: women
: grandparents
grandmothers

grandparents
  . foster grandparents
  . grandfathers
  . grandmothers

: men
:: children
: grandchildren
grandsons

: proposals
grant proposals

: funding
grants
  . block grants
  . research grants
  . tuition grants

grapevine

: design
graphic design

:: arts
: visual arts
:: art
: commercial art
graphics

grass roots

: power
gray power

: emotions
greed

: emotions
grief

grievance procedures

:: behavior
: animal behavior
grooming behavior

: men
grooms

: income
gross income

: behavior
group behavior

: counseling
group counseling

::: arts
:: performing arts
: theater
group developed theater

group dynamics

: marriage
group marriage

: process
group process

:: behavior
: sexual behavior
group sex

: therapy
group therapy

groups
. advocacy groups
. children's groups
. citizen groups
. cohorts
. communal groups
.. communal families
. consciousness raising groups
. cultural groups
. disadvantaged groups
. discussion groups
. encounter groups
. ethnic groups
. factions
. heterogeneous groups
. homogeneous groups
. minority groups
. mixed sex groups
. pressure groups
. religious groups
.. congregations
.. covens
.. faith communities
.. sects
. special interest groups
. study groups
. support groups
. women's groups
.. professional women's
groups

: income
guaranteed income

guardians
. legal guardians

::: occupations
:: service occupations
: protective service occupations
guards
. security guards

: warfare
guerrilla warfare

: emotions
guilt

: laws
gun control laws

: sports
gymnastics

gynarchy

: disorders
gynecologic disorders
. menstrual disorders
.. amenorrhea
.. dysmenorrhea
.. endometriosis
. vaginismus
. vaginitis

: medical sciences
gynecology

: murder
gynocide

:: occupations
: health care occupations
gynocologists

: criticism
gynocriticism

hagiography

::: humanities
:: literature
: poetry
haiku

: bodies
hair
. body hair
. pubic hair

hair dryers

hair loss

hair removal

hair straightening

hair styles
. Afros
. bangs
. braids
. curls
. ponytails

:: occupations
: service occupations
:: occupations
: female intensive occupations
hairdressers

:: housing
: temporary housing
:: facilities
: houses
halfway houses

:: skills
: motor skills
hand eye coordination

handmade

: emotions
happiness

harems

: images of women
harlots

:: occupations
: service occupations
:: occupations
: female intensive occupations
hat checkers

: emotions
hate

hazardous waste

hazards
. environmental hazards
. health hazards
. household hazards
. industrial hazards
. work hazards
.. reproductive hazards at
work

::: language
:: discriminatory language
: sexist language
he/man language

:: programs
: educational programs
Head Start programs

headaches
. migraine headaches
. tension headaches

heads of families

:: occupations
: legal and political occupations
heads of state

:: occupations
: health care occupations
:: occupations
: female intensive occupations
healers
. faith healers
. folk healers
. native healers

healing

health
. environmental health
. holistic health
. mental health
. occupational health and
safety
. physical health
.. physical fitness
... physical endurance

(cont.)

health (*cont.*)
      ... physical strength
        .... upper body
                 strength
  . reproductive health

: advocates
health advocates
  . mental health advocates

: behavior
health behavior
  . health seeking behavior

: care
health care
  . home health care
  . medical care
  . prenatal care

: costs
health care costs

health care delivery

: facilities
health care facilities
  . extended care facilities
  . hospices
  . hospitals
    .. maternity wards
    .. mental hospitals
  . neighborhood health centers
  . nursing homes

: legislation
health care legislation

: occupations
health care occupations
  . anesthesiologists
  . animal caretakers
  . chiropodists
  . chiropractors
  . dental hygienists
  . dentists
  . dieticians
  . family practitioners
  . gynocologists
  . healers
    .. faith healers

(*cont.*)

health care occupations (*cont.*)
    .. folk healers
    .. native healers
  . health care workers
  . medicine women
  . midwives
    .. lay midwives
  . nurse practitioners
  . nurses
    .. practical nurses
    .. registered nurses
    .. visiting nurses
    .. vocational nurses
  . nutritionists
  . obstetricians
  . optometrists
  . paramedics
  . pediatricians
  . pharmacists
  . physicians
  . physicians' assistants
  . podiatrists
  . psychiatrists
  . psychologists
  . surgeons
  . therapists
    .. occupational therapists
    .. physical therapists
    .. psychotherapists
    .. speech therapists
  . veterinarians

: policy
health care policy

health care providers

: services
health care services
  . community health services
  . emergency medical services
  . maternal health service
  . multicultural health care
    services
  . school health services

health care utilization

: :: ::: :::: ::::: Broader term

: workers
:: occupations
: health care occupations
:: occupations
: female intensive occupations
health care workers

:: organizations
: cooperatives
health cooperatives

:: social sciences
: economics
health economics

: education
health education

: hazards
health hazards

: insurance
health insurance
. Medicaid
. Medicare
. national health insurance

: organizations
**health maintenance
organizations**

:: behavior
: health behavior
health seeking behavior

hearing

hearing aids

: disabilities
hearing impairments
. deafness

: activities
hearings
. congressional hearings

:: diseases
: cardiovascular diseases
heart disease

:: occupations
: transportation occupations
:: workers
: operators
::: occupations
:: craft occupations
: construction occupations
heavy equipment operators

: behavior
help seeking behavior
. self help

: behavior
helping behavior

hemlines

: remedies
herbal remedies

herbs

: diseases
hereditary diseases

heredity

heresies

heretics

hermaphrodites

hermaphroditism

hermeneutics

heroes
. women of valor

:: drugs
: narcotic drugs
heroin

: women
heroines (historical)

herstory

: groups
  heterogeneous groups

  heterosexism

: privilege
  heterosexual privilege

: relationships
  heterosexual relationships

: sexuality
  heterosexuality
    . compulsory heterosexuality

: curriculum
  hidden curriculum

  hidjab

  hierarchy

: clothing
  high heeled shoes

::: women
:::: workers
::::: occupations
::::: professional occupations
::: religious workers
:::: occupations
::: female intensive occupations
:: women religious
: priestesses
  high priestesses

::: education
:: elementary secondary education
: secondary education
:: programs
: educational programs
  **high school equivalency
  programs**

::: education
:: elementary secondary education
: secondary education
::: facilities
:: educational facilities
: schools
  high schools
    . junior high schools

:: education
: postsecondary education
  higher education
    . four year colleges
    . graduate education
    . two year colleges

: bodies
  hips

: employment practices
:: policy
: corporate policy
  hiring policy
    . affirmative action hiring
    . job advertisements
    . veteran preference

  hirsutism

::: occupations
:: professional occupations
::: occupations
:: education occupations
: social scientists
::: occupations
:: education occupations
: humanists
  historians

:: humanities
: linguistics
  historical linguistics

:::: humanities
::: literature
:: prose
: nonfiction
  histories
    . life histories
    . oral histories

:: social sciences
:: humanities
: history
historiography

: social sciences
: humanities
history
. art history
. economic history
. historiography
. history of children
. history of religion
. history of science
. intellectual history
. labor history
. literary history
. music history
. oral history
. social history
.. family history
. women's history

:: social sciences
:: humanities
: history
history of children

:: social sciences
:: humanities
: history
history of religion

:: social sciences
:: humanities
: history
history of science

hobbies

: health
holistic health

: medical sciences
holistic medicine

::: arts
:: performing arts
: music
holistic music

holocaust

::: spiritual communication
:: rites
: sacraments
holy communion

::: spiritual communication
:: rites
: sacraments
holy matrimony

: men
holy men

: women
holy women

: accidents
home accidents

: business
home based business

: careers
home based careers

: work
home based work

: workers
home based workers

home birth

home economics

:: work
: extension work
home economics extension work

:: occupations
: scientific and technical occupations
:: occupations
: female intensive occupations
:: occupations
: education occupations
home economists

:: care
: health care
home health care

: loans
home improvement loans

home life

: remedies
home remedies

home schooling

home study

homeless
. homeless men
. homeless women

: men
: homeless
homeless men

: women
: homeless
homeless women

: rights
homemaker rights

:: services
: domestic services
homemaker service

:: occupations
: female intensive occupations
homemakers
. displaced homemakers
. visiting homemakers

homemaking

homeowners

homesteading

homilies

homoeroticism

: groups
homogeneous groups

: social movements
homophile movement

::: disorders
:: mental disorders
: phobias
homophobia
. lesbophobia

: sexuality
homosexuality
. lesbianism
. male homosexuality

honesty

honeymoons

: degrees
honorary degrees

:: organizations
: societies
honorary societies

: therapy
hormone therapy
. estrogen replacement
therapy

: bodies
hormones
. pituitary hormones
. sex hormones
.. androgens
... testosterone
.. estrogens
.. progestins
... progesterone

horticulture

: clothing
hosiery

:: facilities
: health care facilities
hospices

:: facilities
: health care facilities
hospitals
. maternity wards
. mental hospitals

:: housing
: temporary housing
: facilities
hostels

: women
:: occupations
: female intensive occupations
:: occupations
: arts, entertainment, and media
occupations
hostesses (historical)

: emotions
hostility

:: occupations
: arts, entertainment, and media
occupations
hosts

hot flashes

hot lines

: workers
:: occupations
: service occupations
hotel workers

::: facilities
:: religious facilities
: churches
house churches

: design
house design

: Congress
House of Representatives

:: workers
::: occupations
:: service occupations
::: occupations
:: female intensive occupations
: household workers
::: occupations
:: service occupations
: cleaners
housecleaners

:: labor
: household labor
housecleaning

: division of labor
household division of labor

household economics

: employment
household employment

: hazards
household hazards

: labor
household labor
. housecleaning
. unpaid household labor

: workers
:: occupations
: service occupations
:: occupations
: female intensive occupations
household workers
. housecleaners

householders

households
. elderly households
. female headed households
. low income households

:: occupations
  : service occupations
:: occupations
  : female intensive occupations
    housekeepers

  : services
    housekeeping services

:: women
  : mothers
:: occupations
  : female intensive occupations
:: occupations
  : education occupations
    housemothers

::: occupations
  :: craft occupations
    : construction occupations
      housepainters

  : facilities
    houses
     . halfway houses

housewares

housework

housing
  . public housing
  . segregated housing
  . student housing
    .. dormitories
    .. residence halls
  . temporary housing
    .. crisis shelters
    .. halfway houses
    .. hostels

  : costs
    housing costs

  : discrimination
    housing discrimination

  : subsidies
    housing subsidies

: forms of affection
  hugging

: capital
  human capital

: evolution
  human evolution
    . fossil hominids

human interest

human needs
  . basic human needs
  . psychological needs
    .. achievement need
    .. affection
    .. approval need
    .. creativity
    .. intimacy
    .. personal space
    .. self actualization
    .. self concept
    .. self esteem
    .. self respect
    .. self sufficiency

: relationships
  human relations

:: organizations
  : commissions
    human relations commissions

: resources
  human resources
    . labor force
      .. multinational labor force
      .. unpaid labor force
        ... unpaid household labor
    . labor supply

: rights
  human rights

human rights violations

: services
human services
. social services
.. victim services
.. youth services

:: occupations
: education occupations
humanists
. historians
. philosophers

humanitarianism

humanities
. history
.. art history
.. economic history
.. historiography
.. history of children
.. history of religion
.. history of science
.. intellectual history
.. labor history
.. literary history
.. music history
.. oral history
.. social history
... family history
.. women's history
. linguistics
.. applied linguistics
.. descriptive linguistics
.. historical linguistics
.. morphology
.. phonology
.. psycholinguistics
.. semantics
.. sociolinguistics
.. structural linguistics
.. syntax
. literature
.. children's literature
.. drama
... comedy
.... farce
.... skits
... tragedy
.. erotic literature
.. folk literature
... fables
... fairy tales

(cont.)

humanities *(cont.)*
... legends
... mythology
.... creation myths
... parables
... proverbs
.. gay literature
... gay male literature
... lesbian literature
.. nonsexist literature
.. oral literature
.. poetry
... ballads
... elegies
... epics
... epigrams
... haiku
... limericks
... lyric poetry
... odes
... sonnets
.. prose
... fiction
.... mysteries
.... novels
..... novellas
.... pulp fiction
.... romances
.... science fiction
.... short stories
... nonfiction
.... autobiography
.... biography
.... chronicles
.... diaries
..... visual diaries
.... essays
.... histories
..... life histories
..... oral histories
.... journals
.... letters
.... memoirs
.... parody
.... satire
.. religious literature
.. travel literature
.. utopian literature
.. women's literature
... lesbian literature
. musicology

(cont.)

. .. . Narrower term

humanities (*cont.*)
. philosophy
.. epistemology
.. ethics
... bioethics
... business ethics
... feminist ethics
... medical ethics
... political ethics
... religious ethics
.. logic
.. metaphysics
.. phenomenology
.. political philosophy
.. semiotics
. theology
.. feminist theology
... thealogy
.. liberation theology
.. womanist theology

humanity

humor

hunger

:: abuse
: spouse abuse
husband abuse

: spouses
: men
husbands
. first husbands
. former husbands
. runaway husbands

hygiene
. industrial hygiene
. personal hygiene

:: bodies
: vagina
hymen

hymenoplasty

:: spiritual communication
:::: arts
::: performing arts
:: music
: religious music
hymns

: sexuality
:: behavior
: compulsive behavior
hypersexuality
. female hypersexuality
. male hypersexuality

: diseases
hypertension

: names
hyphenated names

hypnotism

hypochondria

:: medical procedures
: surgical procedures
hysterectomy

:: disorders
: mental disorders
hysteria

: diseases
iatrogenic disease

: sports
ice hockey

: sports
ice skating

iconoclasts

iconography

icons

: images of women
ideal woman

: twins
identical twins

identity
. class identity
. cultural identity
. gender identity
. sexual identity
.. cross sex identity
. social identity

identity crisis

ideology
. class ideology
. gender ideology
. political ideology
. sacred ideology

: immigrants
illegal immigrants

illegitimacy

illiteracy
. adult illiteracy

illness
. terminal illness

:: art
: commercial art
illustration
. fashion illustration

:: occupations
: arts, entertainment, and media
occupations
illustrators

image
. body image

:: language
: figurative language
imagery

images of girls
. angels
. blondes
. cheerleaders
. Cinderella
. debutantes

(cont.)

images of girls (*cont.*)
. Orphan Annie
. sissies
. sisters
. tomboys
. virgins
. waifs

images of women
. alma mater
. amazons
. angel in the house
. angels
. baronesses
. beauty queens
. bitches
. blondes
. bluestockings
. brides
.. child brides
.. mail order brides
. Brunhilde
. castrating females
. chattels
. cheerleaders
. Cinderella
. concubines
. countesses
. courtesans
. crones
. cunts
. dames
. debutantes
. den mothers
. duchesses
. earth mother
. Eve
. fallen women
. femmes fatales
. flirts
. geishas
. goddesses
.. mother goddess
.. Mother/Father God
. harlots
. ideal woman
. instigators
. ladies (historical)
. ladies (nobility)
. Lilith
. Lolita
. madonna

(cont.)

. .. . Narrower term

images of women (*cont.*)
. mammies
. manipulators
. mannequins
. mermaids
. mother earth
. mother nature
. mothers in law
. nags
. nuns
.. mother superiors
. nurturers
. odalisques
. old maids
. princesses
. prostitutes
. queen for a day
. queens
. scolds
. seductresses
. sirens
. sisters
. Snow White
. sphinx
. spinsters
. Statue of Liberty
. stepmothers
.. lesbian stepmothers
. strumpets
. succubi
. superwoman
. teases
. temptresses
. vagina dentata
. vampires
. vamps
. viragos
. Virgin Mary
. virgins
. waifs
. widows
. witches
. woman the gatherer
. Wonder Woman

imagination

: religious beliefs
immaculate conception

immigrants
. illegal immigrants

immigration

:: policy
: international policy
immigration policy

: quotas
immigration quotas

immorality

impact on children

impact on women

:: occupations
: arts, entertainment, and media occupations
impersonators
. female impersonators
. male impersonators

: sexual dysfunction
impotence

impoverishment of women

impregnation

::: arts
:: performing arts
: theater
improvisation

impurity

: funding
in kind contributions

in laws
. brothers in law
. daughters in law
. fathers in law
. mothers in law
. sisters in law
. sons in law

:: technology
: reproductive technologies
: fertilization
   in vitro fertilization

inbreeding

incarceration

: religious beliefs
   incarnation

incentives
. monetary incentives
. tax incentives
. work incentives

incest
. brother sister incest
. father daughter incest
. father son incest
. mother daughter incest
. mother son incest

: victims
   incest victims

::: arts
:: performing arts
: music
   incidental music

income
. earned income
. family income
. gross income
. guaranteed income
. minimum income
. net income
. transfer income

income distribution

income generation

: taxes
   income tax

:: spirits
: evil spirits
   incubi

independence

::: occupations
:: education occupations
: scholars
   independent scholars

independent study

indigenous populations

: counseling
   individual counseling

: development
   individual development
. adult development
. child development
.. infant development
. cognitive development
.. intellectual development
.. perceptual development
. emotional development
. gender development
. language development
.. verbal development
. moral development
.. ethic of care
.. moral reasoning
. personality development
. physical development
.. motor development
.. muscular development
.. sensory development
. sex role development
. skill development
. social development

individualism

individuality

indoctrination

: abortion
   induced abortion

:: childbirth
: labor (childbirth)
   induced labor

industrial classification

: conditions
industrial conditions

: hazards
industrial hazards

: hygiene
industrial hygiene

:: social sciences
: psychology
industrial psychology

: relationships
industrial relations

industrialization

industries
. advertising industry
. agricultural industry
. banking industry
. chemical industry
. communications industry
. construction industry
. cottage industry
. electronics industry
. entertainment industry
.. motion picture industry
.. music industry
. extractive industry
.. mining industry
.. oil industry
. food industry
. garment industry
.. millinery trade
. insurance industry
. manufacturing industry
. mining industry
. personal service industry
. pharmaceutical industry
. professional and related
    services industry
. publishing industry
. retail trade industry
. sex industry
. textile industry
. tobacco industry
. transportation industry

(cont.)

industries *(cont.)*
. wholesale trade industry

inequality

::: care
:: dependent care
: child care
infant care

:::: development
:: individual development
: child development
infant development

infant formula

: mortality
infant mortality
. stillbirth

: murder
infanticide

:: children
: young children
infants
. blue babies
. premature infants

infertility

infibulation

infidelity

inflation

influence
. family influence
.. parent influence
.. sibling influence
. peer influence
. political influence

influences
. biological influences
. cultural influences
. ecological factors
. economic factors
. performance factors
. prenatal influences
. racial factors

(cont.)

: :: ::: :::: ::::: Broader term

influences (*cont.*)
. religious influences
. social influences

: informal sector
informal economy

: language
informal language
. slang

informal sector
. informal economy

information
. consumer information
. public information

:: facilities
: centers
**information and referral
centers**

information dissemination

:: services
: information services
information processing

:: services
: information services
information retrieval

:: services
: information services
information retrieval services

information sciences
. computer science
. library science

:: occupations
: scientific and technical occupations
:: occupations
: professional occupations
information scientists

: services
information services
. information processing
. information retrieval
. information retrieval services
. information storage
. news services

:: services
: information services
information storage

: theory
information theory

informed consent

ingratiation

: customs
inheritance customs

: rights
inheritance rights

: wealth
inherited wealth

:: spiritual communication
: rites
initiation rites

initiative

: contraception
injectable contraceptives
. Depo Provera

: urban areas
inner city

innocence

innovation

insanity

insemination
. artificial insemination
. self insemination

: education
inservice education

::: occupations
:: craft occupations
: construction occupations
inspectors

: images of women
instigators

instincts

: organizations
institutes

: discrimination
institutional discrimination
. institutional racism
. institutional sexism

: racism
:: discrimination
: institutional discrimination
institutional racism

: sexism
:: discrimination
: institutional discrimination
institutional sexism

: organizations
institutions

:: occupations
: arts, entertainment, and media
occupations
instrument makers

::: arts
:: performing arts
: music
instrumental music

insurance
. automobile insurance
. disability insurance
. health insurance
.. Medicaid
.. Medicare

(cont.)

insurance *(cont.)*
.. national health insurance
. liability insurance
. life insurance
. no fault insurance
. unemployment insurance

:: occupations
: financial occupations
insurance adjusters

:: occupations
: marketing and sales occupations
::: occupations
:: service occupations
::: occupations
:: female intensive occupations
: agents
insurance agents

:: occupations
: financial occupations
insurance examiners

: fraud
insurance fraud

: industries
insurance industry

: loans
insured loans

integration
. curriculum integration
. school integration

integrity

::: development
:: individual development
: cognitive development
intellectual development

:: social sciences
:: humanities
: history
intellectual history

intellectuals

intelligence
. artificial intelligence

:: organizations
: agencies
intelligence agencies

: testing
intelligence tests

: marriage
intercaste marriage

interdisciplinary studies
. area studies
.. African studies
.. American studies
.. Asian studies
.. Latin American studies
.. Near Eastern studies
.. regional studies
.. Slavic studies
. cross cultural studies
.. comparative religion
. development studies
. ethnic studies
.. Afro American studies
... Black women's
studies
.. American Indian studies
.. Asian American studies
.. Canadian Indian studies
.. Jewish women's studies
.. Latina studies
... Chicana studies
. feminist studies
. future studies
. gay studies
.. lesbian studies
. gender studies
. gerontology
. men's studies
. race, class, and gender
studies
. women's studies
.. Black women's studies
.. Jewish women's studies
.. Latina studies
... Chicana studies

: socioeconomic indicators
interest rates
. prime interest rate

: families
interethnic families

: marriage
interfaith marriage

: design
interior design

::: education
:: elementary secondary education
: elementary education
intermediate grades

: programs
intern programs

: adoption
international adoption

**International Decade for
Women**

: division of labor
**international division of
labor**

: marriage
international marriage

international perspective

: policy
international policy
. foreign aid policy
. immigration policy
. international trade policy

: relationships
international relations

:: policy
: international policy
international trade policy

:: social movements
  : women's movement
    international women's
    movement

    internment

    internships

  : communication
    interpersonal communication

:: occupations
  : legal and political occupations
    interpreters

  : adoption
    interracial adoption

  : families
    interracial families

  : marriage
    interracial marriage

  : relationships
    interracial relations

  : families
    interreligious families

:: conflict
  : role conflict
    interrole conflict

    interruptions

    interviewers

:: methods
  : research methods
    interviewing

    interviews

:: human needs
  : psychological needs
    intimacy

intimidation
  . ethnic intimidation
  . sexual intimidation

intramurals

: contraception
  intrauterine devices

introversion

: knowledge
  intuition

inventions

:: occupations
  : scientific and technical occupations
    inventors

    investigations

: journalism
  investigative journalism

  investments

  investors

  invisibility

::: disorders
:: mental disorders
  : depression
    involuntary depression

:: birth control
  : sterilization
    involuntary sterilization

:: diseases
  : anemia
    iron deficiency anemia

:: occupations
  : service occupations
:: occupations
  : female intensive occupations
    ironers

    ironing

:: language
: figurative language
irony

irrigation

isolation

: exercise
isometric exercise

::: occupations
:: service occupations
: cleaners
janitors

jargon

::: arts
:: performing arts
: music
jazz

::: occupations
:: arts, entertainment, and media
occupations
: musicians
jazz musicians

: emotions
jealousy

jewelry
. rings
.. wedding rings

:: occupations
: arts, entertainment, and media
occupations
jewelry makers

:: interdisciplinary studies
: women's studies
:: interdisciplinary studies
: ethnic studies
Jewish women's studies

:: employment practices
::: policy
:: corporate policy
: hiring policy
job advertisements

:: emotions
: alienation
job alienation

: candidates
job candidates

: employment practices
job descriptions

: development
job development

: discrimination
job discrimination

: evaluation
job evaluation

job ghettos

job hunting

job layoffs

job market

: performance
job performance

job placement

: employment practices
job recruitment
. executive recruitment

job responsibility

job retraining

job rewards

: satisfaction
job satisfaction

: methods
job search methods

: security
job security

:: employment
: part time employment
job sharing

: skills
job skills

: standards
job standards

: training
job training
. on the job training
.. apprenticeships

:: occupations
: arts, entertainment, and media
occupations
jockeys

johns

jokes

journalism
. investigative journalism
. photojournalism
. sports journalism

:: occupations
: arts, entertainment, and media
occupations
journalists
. correspondents

::::: humanities
:::: literature
::: prose
:: nonfiction
journals

: emotions
joy

:: occupations
: professional occupations
:: occupations
: legal and political occupations
judges

judicial appointments

: attitudes
judicial attitudes

: process
judicial process

: legal system
judiciary

judiciary system

: sports
: martial arts
judo

::: facilities
:: educational facilities
: colleges
junior colleges

::::: education
:::: elementary secondary education
::: secondary education
::::: facilities
:::: educational facilities
::: schools
: high schools
junior high schools

juries

jurors

jury duty

justice
. criminal justice
. distributive justice

:: legal system
: juvenile justice system
: courts
juvenile courts

juvenile delinquency

: legal system
juvenile justice system
. juvenile courts

juvenile offenders

: prostitution
juvenile prostitution

: sports
: martial arts
karate

: mourning
keening

:: organizations
: communes
kibbutzim

kidnapping

:: facilities
: educational facilities
kindergarten

kinesics

:: cognitive processes
: perception
kinesthetic perception

kinship
. bilineal kinship
. matrilineal kinship
. patrilineal kinship
. unilineal kinship

: forms of affection
kissing

: rooms
kitchens

:::: arts
::: visual arts
:: craft arts
: needlework
knitting

::: workers
:: operators
: machine operators
:: workers
::: occupations
:: manufacturing occupations
::: occupations
:: female intensive occupations
: clothing workers
knitting machine operators

knowledge
. intuition
. subjective knowledge

labels

:: bodies
: genitals
labia

labor
. child labor
. household labor
.. housecleaning
.. unpaid household labor
. manual labor

: childbirth
labor (childbirth)
. induced labor

labor coaching

::: documents
:: legal documents
: contracts
labor contracts

labor disputes

:: resources
  : human resources
    labor force
      . multinational labor force
      . unpaid labor force
        .. unpaid household labor

    labor force participation

  : labor force statistics
    labor force rates

    labor force statistics
      . labor force rates

:: social sciences
:: humanities
  : history
    labor history

  : reforms
    labor law reform

  : legislation
    labor legislation

    labor market

  : social movements
    labor movement

  : policy
    labor policy
      . piecework labor policy

  : relationships
    labor relations

    labor saving devices

:: resources
  : human resources
    labor supply

  : theory
    labor theory of value

    labor turnover

:: organizations
  : unions
    labor unions

  : facilities
    laboratories

  : animals
    laboratory animals

:: occupations
  : education occupations
    laboratory assistants
      . animal caretakers

  : workers
    laborers

::: arts
:: visual arts
  : craft arts
    lace making

    lack of confidence

  : sports
    lacrosse

    lactation

    lactose intolerance

  : women
  : images of women
    ladies (historical)

  : women
  : titles (nobility)
  : images of women
    ladies (nobility)

:: organizations
  : societies
    ladies' aid societies

    laissez faire

laity
. deacons
. laymen
. laywomen

: reforms
land reform

: rights
land rights

land settlement
. rural resettlement

land tenure

land use

: technology
land use technology

landlords
. slum landlords

::: occupations
:: professional occupations
: architects
landscape architects

language
. discriminatory language
.. sexist language
... he/man language
... patriarchal language
. figurative language
.. allegory
.. ambiguity
.. antithesis
.. epithets
.. imagery
.. irony
.. metaphors
.. puns
. informal language
.. slang
. nonsexist language
. nonverbal language
.. body language
. programming languages
. religious language
. sign language
. women's language

(cont.)

language *(cont.)*
. written language
.. braille

: aptitude
language aptitude

:: development
: individual development
language development
. verbal development

: skills
language skills

language structure

:: crimes
: property crimes
larceny

::: spiritual communication
:: rites
: sacraments
last rites

: children
latchkey children

: childbearing
late childbearing

lateral dominance

:: interdisciplinary studies
: area studies
Latin American studies

:: interdisciplinary studies
: women's studies
:: interdisciplinary studies
: ethnic studies
Latina studies
. Chicana studies

laughter

:: occupations
  : service occupations
:: occupations
  : female intensive occupations
    launderers

    laundry

    law
      . civil law
      . corporate law
      . criminal law
      . marriage and family law
      . religious law

    law enforcement

    laws
      . abortion laws
      . community property laws
      . copyright laws
      . disclosure laws
      . discrimination laws
      . divorce laws
      . gun control laws
      . property laws
      . tax laws

    lawsuits
      . affirmative action suits
      . civil lawsuits
      . class action suits
      . criminal lawsuits
      . paternity suits

  : relationships
    lawyer client relationships

:: occupations
  : professional occupations
:: occupations
  : legal and political occupations
    lawyers
      . barristers

:: women
::: occupations
  :: health care occupations
::: occupations
  :: female intensive occupations
    : midwives
      lay midwives

    laying on of hands

: men
: laity
    laymen

: women
: laity
    laywomen

    leadership
      . student leadership

: roles
    leadership roles

: skills
    leadership skills

: training
    leadership training

: organizations
    leagues

: behavior
    learned behavior

    learned helplessness

    learning
      . adult learning
      . experiential learning
      . lifelong learning

: differences
    learning differences

: disabilities
    learning disabilities

: motivation
    learning motivation

:: activities
  : educational activities
    lectures

: organizations
left wing organizations

: advocates
legal advocates

:: services
: legal services
legal aid services

: occupations
**legal and political
occupations**
. appointed officials
. diplomats
. elected officials
.. assemblymen
.. assemblywomen
.. governors
.. mayors
.. representatives
... congressmen
... congresswomen
.. senators
. government workers
. heads of state
. interpreters
. judges
. lawyers
.. barristers
. legislators
. magistrates
. mediators
. military personnel
. negotiators
. presidents
. prime ministers
. public officials
. vice presidents

legal cruelty

: documents
legal documents
. birth certificates
. contracts
.. labor contracts
.. marriage contracts
... prenuptial
agreements
. custody decrees

(cont.)

legal documents *(cont.)*
. death certificates
. divorce decrees
. legal briefs
. licenses
.. marriage licenses
. property settlements
. restraining orders
. separation agreements
. wills
. working papers

: surrogates
: guardians
legal guardians

: responsibility
legal responsibility

: services
legal services
. legal aid services

legal settlements

: status
legal status

legal system
. judiciary
. juvenile justice system
.. juvenile courts

::: humanities
:: literature
: folk literature
legends

legislation
. antitrust legislation
. civil rights legislation
. discriminatory legislation
. educational legislation
. equal pay legislation
. equal rights legislation
. federal legislation
. health care legislation
. labor legislation
. local legislation
. minimum wage legislation
. protective legislation
. right to know legislation

(cont.)

. .. . Narrower term

legislation (*cont.*)
  . social legislation
  . state legislation

:: occupations
  : legal and political occupations
    legislators

  : organizations
    legislatures

    legitimacy

    legitimization of children

: bodies
  legs

  leisure

: activities
  leisure activities

: communities
  lesbian communities

:: couples
  : gay couples
    lesbian couples

:: culture
  : women's culture
:: culture
  : gay culture
    lesbian culture

:: experience
  : gay experience
    lesbian experience

  : feminism
    lesbian feminism

::: humanities
  :: literature
    : women's literature
::: humanities
  :: literature
    : gay literature
      lesbian literature

:: marriage
  : gay marriage
    lesbian marriage

:: women
  : mothers
    lesbian mothers

  : social movements
    lesbian movement

::: relationships
  :: personal relationships
    : gay relationships
::: relationships
  :: personal relationships
    : female female relationships
      lesbian relationships

  : separatism
    lesbian separatism

::: women
  :: mothers
  :: images of women
    : stepmothers
      lesbian stepmothers

:: interdisciplinary studies
  : gay studies
    lesbian studies

:: sexuality
  : homosexuality
    lesbianism

: women
: gays
  lesbians
    . closeted lesbians
    . contact dykes

::::: disorders
:::: mental disorders
::   phobias
:   homophobia
  lesbophobia

  letter writers

::::: humanities
:::: literature
::   prose
:   nonfiction
  letters

  letters of recommendation

::   customs
:   marriage customs
  levirate

  liability
    . corporate liability
    . limited liability

:   insurance
  liability insurance

  libel

:   feminism
  liberal feminism

  liberals

  liberation
    . fat liberation
    . men's liberation
    . sexual liberation
    . women's liberation

:   struggles
  liberation struggles

::   humanities
:   theology
  liberation theology

::   organizations
:   political parties
  Libertarian Party

::   occupations
:   professional occupations
::   occupations
:   female intensive occupations
::   occupations
:   education occupations
  librarians

::   facilities
:   educational facilities
  libraries

:   information sciences
  library science

:   workers
::   occupations
:   female intensive occupations
::   occupations
:   education occupations
  library workers

  librettos

::   documents
:   legal documents
  licenses
    . marriage licenses

  licensing
    . child care licensing

:::::: arts
::::: performing arts
:::: music
::   vocal music
:   songs
  lieder

  lies

  life cycles

  life expectancy

:::::: humanities
::::: literature
:::: prose
::   nonfiction
:   histories
  life histories

: insurance
life insurance

: skills
life skills

life span

life styles

: learning
lifelong learning

: images of women
Lilith

::: humanities
:: literature
: poetry
limericks

: liability
limited liability

lineage

: clothing
lingerie
. corsets
. girdles

: sexism
linguistic sexism

: humanities
linguistics
. applied linguistics
. descriptive linguistics
. historical linguistics
. morphology
. phonology
. psycholinguistics
. semantics
. sociolinguistics
. structural linguistics
. syntax

::: medical sciences
:: surgery
: plastic surgery
liposuction surgery

: forms of affection
listening

literacy
. adult literacy
. computer literacy

literacy campaigns

: canon
literary canon

: criticism
literary criticism

:: social sciences
:: humanities
: history
literary history

: symbols
literary symbols

: theory
literary theory

: humanities
literature
. children's literature
. drama
.. comedy
... farce
... skits
.. tragedy
. erotic literature
. folk literature
.. fables
.. fairy tales
.. legends
.. mythology
... creation myths
.. parables
.. proverbs
. gay literature
.. gay male literature

(cont.)

literature (*cont.*)
.. lesbian literature
. nonsexist literature
. oral literature
. poetry
.. ballads
.. elegies
.. epics
.. epigrams
.. haiku
.. limericks
.. lyric poetry
.. odes
.. sonnets
. prose
.. fiction
... mysteries
... novels
.... novellas
... pulp fiction
... romances
... science fiction
... short stories
.. nonfiction
... autobiography
... biography
... chronicles
... diaries
.... visual diaries
... essays
... histories
.... life histories
.... oral histories
... journals
... letters
... memoirs
... parody
... satire
. religious literature
. travel literature
. utopian literature
. women's literature
.. lesbian literature

liturgies

living alone

living arrangements

: conditions
living conditions

: standards
living standards

loans
. consumer installment loans
. home improvement loans
. insured loans
. student loans

lobbying

: anesthesia
local anesthesia

: government
local government

: legislation
local legislation

: politics
local politics

: rooms
locker rooms

: psychological factors
locus of control

: facilities
lodges

:: humanities
: philosophy
logic

: cognitive processes
logical thinking

: images of women
Lolita

: emotions
loneliness

:: cognitive processes
: memory
long term memory

: workers
longshore workers

lookism

loss

loss of self

: emotions
love
. courtly love
. maternal love
. romantic love
. unrequited love

love potions

: forms of affection
lovemaking

lovers

: families
low income families

: households
low income households

: wages
low pay

: class
lower class

loyalty

loyalty oaths

lubricants

:::::: arts
::::: performing arts
:::: music
::: vocal music
: songs
lullabies

:: occupations
: agricultural, fishing, and forestry occupations
lumber cutters

:: activities
: social activities
lunches

: emotions
lust

lying

:: bodies
: glands
lymph glands

: violence
lynching

::: humanities
:: literature
: poetry
lyric poetry

:: occupations
: arts, entertainment, and media occupations
lyricists

lyrics

:: workers
: operators
machine operators
. knitting machine operators
. sewing machine operators

machinery

:: occupations
: craft occupations
machinists

machismo

:: social sciences
: economics
macroeconomics

: images of women
madonna

:::: arts
::: performing arts
:: music
: vocal music
madrigals

::: mass media
:: print media
: periodicals
magazines
. women's magazines

magic

:: occupations
: legal and political occupations
magistrates

: aunts
maiden aunts

::: occupations
:: administrative support occupations
: clerical occupations
mail carriers

:: women
:: images of women
: brides
mail order brides

: feminism
mainstream feminism

mainstreaming

: culture
majority culture

majority rule

makeup

: bonding
male bonding

: chauvinism
male chauvinism

:: medical procedures
: surgical procedures
male circumcision

: employment
male dominated employment

: feminists
male feminists

::: relationships
:: personal relationships
: male male relationships
::: relationships
:: personal relationships
: friendships
male friendships

:: sexuality
: homosexuality
male homosexuality

:: sexuality
::: behavior
:: compulsive behavior
: hypersexuality
male hypersexuality

::: occupations
:: arts, entertainment, and media occupations
: impersonators
male impersonators

: occupations
male intensive occupations

:: relationships
: personal relationships
male male relationships
. father son relationships
. gay male relationships
. male friendships

: norms
male norms

: pregnancy
male pregnancy

: sexuality
male sexuality

: standards
male standards

males

: tumors
malignant tumors

malnutrition

:: bodies
: glands
mammary glands

: images of women
mammies

: medical procedures
mammography

man

man the hunter

management
. financial management
. money management
. personal management
. personnel management
. time management
. water management

management practices

: work styles
management styles

management techniques

: theory
management theory

: training
management training

: occupations
managerial occupations
. administrators
.. college administrators
. coordinators
. executives
.. chief executives
. managers
.. middle managers
. presidents
. underwriters
. vice presidents

:: occupations
: managerial occupations
managers
. middle managers

::: occupations
:: service occupations
::: occupations
:: female intensive occupations
: cosmetologists
manicurists

: behavior
manipulative behavior

: images of women
manipulators

: images of women
mannequins

:: behavior
: social behavior
manners
. gallantry
. graciousness

: labor
manual labor

manufactured

:: occupations
: manufacturing occupations
manufacturers

: industries
manufacturing industry

: occupations
manufacturing occupations
. clothing workers
.. dressmakers
.. knitting machine
operators
.. milliners
.. seamstresses (historical)
.. sewers
.. sewing machine
operators
.. tailors
. factory workers
. manufacturers
. metalworkers
. printing workers
.. bookbinders
.. compositors
.. press operators
.. printers
.. typesetters
. steelworkers

manumission

maquiladora

marathons

:: activities
: protest actions
marches

marginality

marianismo

:: drugs
: narcotic drugs
marijuana

: adjustment
marital adjustment

: conflict
marital conflict

: reforms
marital property reform

: roles
marital roles

: satisfaction
marital satisfaction

marital stability

: status
marital status

:: violence
: domestic violence
marital violence

:: research
: social science research
market research

: occupations
**marketing and sales
occupations**
. insurance agents
. merchandisers
. real estate agents
. sales personnel
.. salesmen
.. saleswomen
. stockbrokers
. vendors
.. street vendors

markets
. black markets

marriage
. arranged marriage
. child marriage
. childfree marriage
. common law marriage
. commuter marriage
. companionate marriage
. gay marriage
.. gay male marriage
.. lesbian marriage
. group marriage
. intercaste marriage
. interfaith marriage

(cont.)

marriage (*cont.*)
. international marriage
. interracial marriage
. marriage by proxy
. posthumous marriage
. remarriage
. teenage marriage
. trial marriage

: law
marriage and family law

: marriage
marriage by proxy

: ceremonies
marriage ceremonies

::: documents
:: legal documents
: contracts
marriage contracts
. prenuptial agreements

: counseling
marriage counseling

: customs
marriage customs
. endogamy
. exogamy
. levirate
. polygamy
.. polyandry
.. polygyny
. sororate

::: documents
:: legal documents
: licenses
marriage licenses

:: customs
: courtship customs
marriage proposals

::: measurements
:: demographic measurements
: vital statistics
marriage rates

marriage tax

: vows
marriage vows

: couples
married couples

: students
married students

martial arts
. judo
. karate

martyrdom

martyrs

: economic development models
Marxist economic development models

: feminism
Marxist feminism

: pronouns
masculine pronouns

masculinity

masochism

: activities
mass actions
. rallies

mass media
. electronic media
.. radio
... public radio
.. television
... cable television
... commercial television
... educational television

(*cont.*)

: :: ::: :::: ::::: Broader term

mass media (*cont.*)
... public television
. print media
.. periodicals
... journals (periodicals)
... magazines
.... women's
magazines
... newsletters
... newspapers
.. publications
... feminist publications
. women's media
.. feminist publications
.. women's magazines

massage

massage parlors

:: occupations
: female intensive occupations
masseuses

:: medical procedures
: surgical procedures
mastectomy

master of ceremonies

:: degrees
: graduate degrees
masters' degrees

:: behavior
: sexual behavior
masturbation

matchmakers

: culture
material culture

: age
maternal age

: welfare
maternal and infant welfare

:: services
: health care services
maternal health service

:: emotions
: love
maternal love

: mortality
maternal mortality

maternity

: benefits
maternity benefits

: facilities
maternity homes

: parental leave
maternity leave

: rights
maternity rights

::: facilities
:: health care facilities
: hospitals
maternity wards

: ability
math ability

:: behavior
: avoidance behavior
math avoidance

math confidence

mathematical models

:: occupations
: scientific and technical occupations
:: occupations
: professional occupations
mathematicians

mathematics
. applied mathematics
. statistics

matriarchs

matriarchy

: society
matricentric societies

: murder
matricide

: kinship
matrilineal kinship

: society
matrilineal societies

matrilocal residences

: naming
matronymy

maturity

:: officials
::: occupations
:: legal and political occupations
: elected officials
mayors

: diseases
measles

measurement

: engineering
mechanical engineering

:: occupations
: craft occupations
mechanics

: arts
media arts
. animation
. electronic art
. film
.. documentaries
. video art

media coverage
. press coverage
. television coverage

media portrayal

: reforms
media reform

: stereotyping
media stereotyping

mediation

:: occupations
: legal and political occupations
mediators

:: insurance
: health insurance
Medicaid

:: social sciences
: anthropology
medical anthropology

:: care
: health care
medical care

: education
medical education

::: humanities
:: philosophy
: ethics
medical ethics

: evaluation
medical evaluation
. physical examination
.. breast examination
... breast self
examination
.. pelvic examination

: oppression
medical oppression

medical procedures
. amniocentesis
. biopsy
. chemotherapy
. fetal monitoring
. genetic screening
. mammography
. Pap smear
. radiation therapy
. surgical procedures
  .. caesarian section
  .. dilatation and curettage
  .. episiotomy
  .. hysterectomy
  .. male circumcision
  .. mastectomy
  .. oophorectomy
  .. tubal ligation
  .. vasectomy
. thermography
. ultrasound

: records
medical records

medical sciences
. dentistry
. environmental medicine
. family medicine
. folk medicine
. geriatrics
. gynecology
. holistic medicine
. nursing
. obstetrics
. pediatrics
. pharmacology
. preventive medicine
. psychiatry
. surgery
  .. cosmetic surgery
  .. plastic surgery
    ... liposuction surgery
  .. psychosurgery
  .. reconstructive surgery

:: social sciences
: sociology
medical sociology

:: insurance
: health insurance
Medicare

: women
:: occupations
: health care occupations
:: occupations
: female intensive occupations
medicine women

: spiritual communication
meditation

::: arts
:: performing arts
: music
meditation music

:: workers
::: occupations
:: professional occupations
: religious workers
mediums
. physical mediums
. spiritual mediums

: activities
meetings
. planning meetings
. prayer meetings

:::: humanities
::: literature
:: prose
: nonfiction
memoirs

: cognitive processes
memory
. long term memory
. recall
. recognition
. short term memory

men
. assemblymen
. bachelors
. brothers
. businessmen
. clergymen

(cont.)

men (*cont.*)
. congressmen
. fathers
.. absentee fathers
.. birth fathers
.. gay fathers
.. runaway fathers
.. single fathers
.. stepfathers
... gay stepfathers
.. surrogate fathers
.. teenage fathers
. fathers in law
. gay men
. grandfathers
. grandsons
. grooms
. holy men
. homeless men
. husbands
.. first husbands
.. former husbands
.. runaway husbands
. laymen
. older men
. ombudsmen
. single men
. sons
. widowers

: liberation
men's liberation

: social movements
men's movement

: roles
men's roles

: interdisciplinary studies
men's studies

menarche

menopause

menstrual cycle

:: disorders
: gynecologic disorders
menstrual disorders
. amenorrhea
. dysmenorrhea
. endometriosis

menstrual extraction

menstrual taboos

menstruation

menstruation inducing agents

: disorders
mental disorders
. autism
. depression
.. involuntary depression
.. postpartum depression
. hysteria
. neuroses
. phobias
.. agoraphobia
.. homophobia
... lesbophobia
. schizophrenia

: evaluation
mental evaluation

: health
mental health

:: advocates
: health advocates
mental health advocates

mental health issues

: treatment
mental health treatment

::: facilities
:: health care facilities
: hospitals
mental hospitals

: disabilities
mental retardation

mentally handicapped

mentors

:: occupations
  : marketing and sales occupations
   merchandisers

merchants

mergers

: images of women
  mermaids

:: arts
  : visual arts
   metal art

  : workers
:: occupations
  : manufacturing occupations
   metalworkers

:: language
  : figurative language
   metaphors

:: humanities
  : philosophy
   metaphysics

::: occupations
:: scientific and technical occupations
::: occupations
:: professional occupations
::: occupations
:: education occupations
  : scientists
   meteorologists

methods
  . desegregation methods
   .. busing
  . educational methods
  . feminist methods
  . job search methods
  . research methods
   .. case studies
   .. cohort analysis
   .. content analysis

(*cont.*)

methods (*cont.*)
  .. contextual analysis
  .. cost benefit analysis
  .. interviewing
  .. participant observation
  .. qualitative analysis
  .. quantitative analysis

:: social sciences
  : economics
   microeconomics

: discrimination
  microinequities

:: change
  : career change
   midcareer change

: age
  middle age

: adults
  middle aged adults

: class
  middle class

: families
  middle class families

::: occupations
:: managerial occupations
  : managers
   middle managers

::: facilities
:: educational facilities
  : schools
   middle schools

midlife

midlife crisis

midwifery

: women
:: occupations
: health care occupations
:: occupations
: female intensive occupations
midwives
. lay midwives

: headaches
migraine headaches

: workers
:: occupations
: agricultural, fishing, and forestry
occupations
migrant workers

migration
. rural migration
. seasonal migration
. urban migration

migration patterns

mikiri

mikveh

militance

militarism

: organizations
military
. armed forces
.. all volunteer military
force

::: facilities
:: educational facilities
: academies
military academies

: federal budget
military budget

military combat

military defense

military dependents
. military spouses

military draft

military enlistment

: personnel
:: occupations
: legal and political occupations
military personnel

: rank
military rank

military recruitment

: spouses
: military dependents
military spouses

military trade

milk
. milk substitutes

: milk
milk substitutes

:: occupations
: female intensive occupations
:: workers
::: occupations
:: manufacturing occupations
::: occupations
:: female intensive occupations
: clothing workers
milliners

:: industries
: garment industry
millinery trade

:: arts
: performing arts
mime

mind

:: dichotomy
: false dichotomies
mind/body split

:: resources
: natural resources
mineral resources

:: arts
: visual arts
miniatures

: competence
minimum competencies

: income
minimum income

: legislation
minimum wage legislation

: industries
:: industries
: extractive industry
mining industry

:: clothing
: skirts
miniskirts

::: workers
:::: occupations
::: professional occupations
:: religious workers
: clergy
ministers

:: organizations
: political parties
minor parties

: employment
minority employment

minority experience

: groups
minority groups

: business
minority owned business

miracles

misandry

miscarriage

miscegenation

misogyny

:: workers
::: occupations
:: professional occupations
: religious workers
missionaries

:: organizations
: societies
missionary societies

: women
mistresses

: economy
mixed economy

mixed media

: groups
mixed sex groups

::: activities
:: social activities
: dances
mixers

mobility
. family mobility
. geographic mobility
. occupational mobility
.. career ladders
. social mobility
. upward mobility

: programs
model programs

:: organizations
: agencies
modeling agencies

:: occupations
: female intensive occupations
:: occupations
: arts, entertainment, and media
occupations
models

models (paradigms)

::: arts
:: performing arts
: dance
modern dance

modernization

modesty

momism

:: facilities
: religious facilities
monasteries

monasticism

: incentives
monetary incentives

: policy
monetary policy

money
. pin money

: management
money management

monogamy

:: organizations
: corporations
monopolies

monotheism

moonlighting

:: development
: individual development
moral development
. ethic of care
. moral reasoning

moral majority

::: development
:: individual development
: moral development
moral reasoning

: reforms
moral reform

morality

morbidity

mores

:: humanities
: linguistics
morphology

mortality
. infant mortality
.. stillbirth
. maternal mortality
. occupational mortality

::: measurements
:: demographic measurements
: vital statistics
mortality rates

mortgages
. assumable mortgages
. conventional mortgages

mortuary science

:: facilities
: religious facilities
mosques

: incest
mother daughter incest

::: relationships
:: adult child relationships
: parent child relationships
::: relationships
:: personal relationships
: female female relationships
**mother daughter
relationships**

: images of women
mother earth

:: images of women
: goddesses
mother goddess

: images of women
mother nature

mother right

: incest
mother son incest

::: relationships
:: adult child relationships
: parent child relationships
::: relationships
:: personal relationships
: female male relationships
mother son relationships

::: women
:::: workers
::::: occupations
::::: professional occupations
::: religious workers
:::: occupations
::: female intensive occupations
:: women religious
:: images of women
: nuns
mother superiors

mother syndrome

mother tongue

: gods
:: images of women
: goddesses
Mother/Father God

mother's milk

: parenting
mothering

: families
motherless families

: women
mothers
. absentee mothers
. birth mothers
. den mothers
. earth mother
. foremothers
. housemothers
. lesbian mothers
. mothers in law
. mothers working outside the
home
. runaway mothers
. single mothers
. stepmothers
.. lesbian stepmothers
. supermom
. surrogate mothers
. teenage mothers
. wage earning mothers
. welfare mothers

:: women
: mothers
: in laws
: images of women
mothers in law

:: women
: women working outside the home
:: women
: mothers
**mothers working outside the
home**

:: industries
: entertainment industry
motion picture industry

motivation
. learning motivation
. student motivation
. teacher motivation

::: development
:: individual development
: physical development
motor development

: skills
motor skills
. hand eye coordination

: sports
mountaineering

mourning
. keening
. wailing

:: occupations
: transportation occupations
movers

: forms of address
Ms

::: workers
:::: occupations
::: professional occupations
:: religious workers
: clergy
mullahs

:: services
: health care services
**multicultural health care
services**

: art
multimedia art

:: organizations
: banks
multinational banks

:: policy
: corporate policy
**multinational corporation
policy**
. drug dumping
. global assembly lines
. offshore production plants
. piecework labor policy

:: organizations
: corporations
multinational corporations

::: resources
:: human resources
: labor force
multinational labor force

multiple births

: roles
multiple roles
. dual roles

: urban areas
municipalities

:: arts
: visual arts
mural art

murder
. bride burning
. gynocide
. infanticide
. matricide
. patricide

murderers

::: development
:: individual development
: physical development
muscular development

: facilities
  museums

:: arts
: performing arts
  music
    . art music
    . blues
    . chamber music
    . children's music
    . computer music
    . electronic music
    . feminist music
    . holistic music
    . incidental music
    . instrumental music
    . jazz
    . meditation music
    . orchestral music
    . political music
      .. protest music
    . popular music
      .. country music
      .. folk music
      .. rock and roll
    . religious music
      .. chants
      .. gospel music
      .. hymns
      .. spirituals
    . salon music
    . tribal music
    . vocal music
      .. choral music
      .. madrigals
      .. opera
      .. songs
        ... ballads
        ... lieder
        ... lullabies
        ... nursery songs
        ... slave songs
    . women's music

: criticism
  music criticism

:: activities
: festivals
  music festivals

:: social sciences
:: humanities
: history
  music history

:: industries
: entertainment industry
  music industry

: theory
  music theory

: therapy
  music therapy

: videos
  music videos

::: arts
:: performing arts
: theater
  musical theater

  musicals

:: occupations
: arts, entertainment, and media
  occupations
  musicians
    . jazz musicians
    . troubadours

: humanities
  musicology

:::: humanities
::: literature
:: prose
: fiction
  mysteries

  mysticism

::: humanities
:: literature
: folk literature
  mythology
    . creation myths

  myths

: images of women
nags

: art
naive art

: rights
name rights

names
. hyphenated names
. nom de lait
. pen name
. surnames
.. birth name
.. slave name

naming
. matronymy
. patronymy

:: workers
::: occupations
:: service occupations
::: occupations
:: female intensive occupations
: child care workers
nannies

narcissism

: drugs
narcotic drugs
. cocaine
. heroin
. marijuana

narratives
. personal narratives

:: insurance
: health insurance
national health insurance

**National Health Service
(Great Britain)**

: security
national security

nationalism

: social movements
nationalist movements

: revolution
nationalist revolutions

nationality

nationalization

::: occupations
:: health care occupations
::: occupations
:: female intensive occupations
: healers
native healers

: childbirth
natural childbirth

: resources
natural resources
. mineral resources
. water resources

natural sciences
. biological sciences
.. anatomy
.. biochemistry
.. biology
.. botany
.. ecology
.. embryology
.. ethology
.. genetics
... population genetics
.. physiology
.. sociobiology
.. zoology
... primate studies
. environmental sciences
. physical sciences
.. astronomy
.. chemistry
.. earth sciences
... geology
... oceanography
.. physics
.. space sciences

natural selection

:: occupations
: scientific and technical occupations
naturalists

naturalization

nature

:: interdisciplinary studies
: area studies
Near Eastern studies

:::: arts
::: visual arts
:: craft arts
: needlework
needlepoint

::: arts
:: visual arts
: craft arts
needlework
. crocheting
. embroidery
. knitting
. needlepoint

: reinforcement
negative reinforcement

negotiation

:: occupations
: legal and political occupations
negotiators

:: facilities
: health care facilities
:: facilities
: centers
neighborhood health centers

: preservation
neighborhood preservation

neighborhoods
. declining neighborhoods
.. slums
. desirable neighborhoods
(cont.)

neighborhoods *(cont.)*
. ethnic neighborhoods
.. ghettos

:: social sciences
: economics
neoclassical economics

nephews

nepotism

: bodies
nervous system

nervousness

: income
net income

: ratings
network ratings

: theory
network theory

networking

networks
. old boy networks
. women's networks
.. old girl networks

:: organizations
: corporations
networks (media)

:: disorders
: mental disorders
neuroses

new left

:: services
: information services
news services

::: mass media
  :: print media
    : periodicals
      newsletters

::: mass media
  :: print media
    : periodicals
      newspapers

      nieces

  :: organizations
    : clubs
      night clubs

    : divorce
      no fault divorce

    : insurance
      no fault insurance

    : pollution
      noise pollution

    : names
      nom de lait

      nominations

    : feminism
      nonaligned feminism

    : behavior
      nonconforming behavior

    : parents
      noncustodial parents

    : education
      nondegree education

  :: programs
    : educational programs
      nondegree programs

:::: humanities
  :: literature
    : prose
      nonfiction
        . autobiography
        . biography
        . chronicles
        . diaries
          .. visual diaries
        . essays
        . histories
          .. life histories
          .. oral histories
        . journals
        . letters
        . memoirs
        . parody
        . satire

    : education
      nonformal education

  :: organizations
    : nonprofit organizations
      nongovernmental organizations
        . nongovernmental women's organizations

  :: organizations
    : women's organizations
::: organizations
  :: nonprofit organizations
    : nongovernmental organizations
      nongovernmental women's organizations

    : behavior
      nonjudgmental behavior

    : women
      nonorgasmic women

    : drugs
      nonprescription drugs

: organizations
nonprofit organizations
. charities
. foundations
. nongovernmental
organizations
.. nongovernmental
women's organizations
. voluntary organizations
.. private voluntary
organizations

: child rearing practices
**nonsexist child rearing
practices**

: curriculum
nonsexist curriculum

: language
nonsexist language

:: humanities
: literature
nonsexist literature

: textbooks
nonsexist textbooks

: education
nontraditional education

: employment
nontraditional employment

nontraditional work patterns

: ability
nonverbal ability

: behavior
nonverbal behavior

: communication
nonverbal communication
. gestures

: language
nonverbal language
. body language

nonviolence

::: facilities
:: educational facilities
: schools
normal schools

norms
. male norms

:: occupations
: arts, entertainment, and media
occupations
novelists

::::: humanities
:::: literature
::: prose
:: fiction
: novels
novellas

:::: humanities
::: literature
:: prose
: fiction
novels
. novellas

novices

novitiates

: disarmament
nuclear disarmament

: energy
nuclear energy

: engineering
nuclear engineering

: families
nuclear families

nuclear free zones

: warfare
nuclear warfare

the nude

nudity

:: women
::: workers
:::: occupations
::: professional occupations
:: religious workers
::: occupations
:: female intensive occupations
: women religious
: images of women
nuns
. mother superiors

:: occupations
: health care occupations
:: occupations
: female intensive occupations
nurse practitioners

nurseries
. creches
. workplace nurseries

::: facilities
:: educational facilities
: schools
nursery schools

::::: arts
:::: performing arts
::: music
:: vocal music
: songs
nursery songs

:: occupations
: health care occupations
:: occupations
: female intensive occupations
nurses
. practical nurses
. registered nurses
. visiting nurses
. vocational nurses

: medical sciences
nursing

: education
nursing education

:: facilities
: health care facilities
nursing homes

nurturance

: images of women
nurturers

nurturing

nutrition

:: occupations
: health care occupations
:: occupations
: female intensive occupations
nutritionists

: women
nymphs

obedience

obesity

obituaries

objectification

objectives
. behavioral objectives
. course objectives
. educational objectives
. organizational objectives
. training objectives

objectivity

obscenity

observance

: disorders
**obsessive compulsive
disorders**

: anesthesia
obstetrical anesthesia

:: occupations
: health care occupations
obstetricians

: medical sciences
obstetrics

: attitudes
occupational attitudes

: counseling
occupational counseling

: diseases
occupational diseases

: safety
: health
occupational health and safety

: mobility
occupational mobility
. career ladders

: mortality
occupational mortality

occupational options

occupational patterns

: roles
occupational roles

:: discriminatory practices
: segregation
occupational segregation
. occupational sex segregation

::: discriminatory practices
:: segregation
: occupational segregation
occupational sex segregation

: status
occupational status

: stress
occupational stress

::: occupations
:: professional occupations
::: occupations
:: health care occupations
: therapists
occupational therapists

: trends
occupational trends

occupations
. administrative support occupations
.. administrative assistants
.. clerical occupations
... bank tellers
... bookkeepers
... clerks
... computer equipment operators
... data entry operators
... mail carriers
... receptionists
... secretaries
... stenographers
... telephone operators
... typists
.. data processors
.. operations researchers
.. supervisors
. agricultural, fishing, and forestry occupations
.. braceros
.. development specialists
.. divers
.. extension workers
... animatrices rurales
... gramsevika
.. farm workers
.. farmers
.. fishers
.. gardeners
.. lumber cutters
.. migrant workers

(cont.)

. .. . Narrower term

occupations (*cont.*)
.. ranch hands
. arts, entertainment, and
   media occupations
.. actors
... aspiring actors
.. anchors
.. announcers
.. artisans
.. artists
.. authors
.. broadcasters
.. bullfighters
.. camera operators
.. cartoonists
.. circus performers
.. coaches
.. columnists
.. comedians
.. commentators
.. composers
.. conductors
.. copywriters
.. craftspersons
.. critics
.. dancers
... chorus dancers
.. designers
.. disk jockeys
.. drafters
.. dramatists
.. editors
.. entertainers
.. essayists
.. film directors
.. film producers
.. geishas
.. glassmakers
.. hostesses (historical)
.. hosts
.. illustrators
.. impersonators
... female impersonators
... male impersonators
.. instrument makers
.. jewelry makers
.. jockeys
.. journalists
... correspondents
.. lyricists
.. models

             (*cont.*)

occupations (*cont.*)
.. musicians
... jazz musicians
... troubadours
.. novelists
.. orators
.. painters
.. performers
... prima donnas
... soloists
.. photographers
.. playwrights
.. poets
.. printers
.. printmakers
.. professional athletes
.. public relations
   specialists
.. publishers
.. reporters
... weather reporters
.. reviewers
.. sculptors
.. singers
... chanteuses
... opera singers
... torch singers
.. sports officials
.. sportscasters
.. strippers
.. television personalities
.. writers
... translators
. craft occupations
.. coal miners
.. construction occupations
... bricklayers
... cabinetmakers
... carpenters
... construction workers
... electricians
... glaziers
... heavy equipment
   operators
... housepainters
... inspectors
... paperhangers
... plasterers
... plumbers
... roofers
... woodworkers
.. engravers

             (*cont.*)

: :: ::: :::: ::::: Broader term

occupations (*cont.*)

.. machinists
.. mechanics
.. repairers
.. sign painters
.. technicians
.. tool and die makers
.. watchmakers
.. welders
. education occupations
.. affirmative action
officers
.. chairpersons
.. coaches
.. college presidents
.. coordinators
.. counselors
.. deans
.. educators
.. faculty
.. home economists
.. housemothers
.. humanists
... historians
... philosophers
.. laboratory assistants
... animal caretakers
.. librarians
.. library workers
.. principals
.. professors
.. provosts
.. research assistants
.. researchers
.. scholars
... independent scholars
... visiting scholars
.. school personnel
.. scientists
... astronomers
... biologists
... chemists
... ethologists
... geneticists
... geologists
... meteorologists
... physicists
... sociobiologists
.. social scientists
... anthropologists
... archaeologists
... economists

(*cont.*)

occupations (*cont.*)

... historians
... psychologists
... sociologists
... urban planners
.. superintendents
.. teacher aides
.. teachers
.. teaching assistants
.. vice presidents
. female intensive occupations
.. administrative assistants
.. affirmative action
officers
.. agents
... airline reservation
agents
... insurance agents
... real estate agents
... travel agents
.. attendants
.. bank tellers
.. beauticians
.. bookkeepers
.. caregivers
... primary caregivers
.. child care workers
... babysitters
... governesses
... nannies
... wet nurses
.. clerks
.. clothing workers
... dressmakers
... knitting machine
operators
... milliners
... seamstresses
(historical)
... sewers
... sewing machine
operators
... tailors
.. coat checkers
.. cooks
.. cosmetologists
... colorists
... manicurists
... pedicurists
.. counselors
.. data entry operators
.. data processors

(*cont.*)

. .. . Narrower term

occupations (*cont.*)
- .. dental hygienists
- .. dieticians
- .. educators
- .. extension workers
  - ... animatrices rurales
  - ... gramsevika
- .. flight attendants
- .. food service workers
- .. fortune tellers
- .. geishas
- .. hairdressers
- .. hat checkers
- .. healers
  - ... faith healers
  - ... folk healers
  - ... native healers
- .. health care workers
- .. home economists
- .. homemakers
  - ... displaced
    homemakers
  - ... visiting homemakers
- .. hostesses (historical)
- .. household workers
  - ... housecleaners
- .. housekeepers
- .. housemothers
- .. ironers
- .. launderers
- .. librarians
- .. library workers
- .. masseuses
- .. medicine women
- .. midwives
  - ... lay midwives
- .. milliners
- .. models
- .. nurse practitioners
- .. nurses
  - ... practical nurses
  - ... registered nurses
  - ... visiting nurses
  - ... vocational nurses
- .. nutritionists
- .. paralegals
- .. physical therapists
- .. physicians' assistants
- .. pink collar workers
- .. prostitutes
- .. psychics
- .. receptionists

(*cont.*)

occupations (*cont.*)
- .. saleswomen
- .. secretaries
- .. seers
- .. social workers
- .. stenographers
- .. strippers
- .. teacher aides
- .. teachers
- .. telephone operators
- .. tour guides
- .. typists
- .. volunteers
  - ... docents
- .. women religious
  - ... clergywomen
  - ... nuns
    - .... mother superiors
  - ... priestesses
    - .... high priestesses
- . financial occupations
  - .. accountants
  - .. bankers
  - .. development specialists
  - .. economists
  - .. financial planners
  - .. financiers
  - .. insurance adjusters
  - .. insurance examiners
  - .. philanthropists
  - .. stockbrokers
  - .. venture capitalists
- . health care occupations
  - .. anesthesiologists
  - .. animal caretakers
  - .. chiropodists
  - .. chiropractors
  - .. dental hygienists
  - .. dentists
  - .. dieticians
  - .. family practitioners
  - .. gynocologists
  - .. healers
    - ... faith healers
    - ... folk healers
    - ... native healers
  - .. health care workers
  - .. medicine women
  - .. midwives
    - ... lay midwives
  - .. nurse practitioners

(*cont.*)

: :: ::: :::: ::::: Broader term

occupations (*cont.*)

.. nurses
... practical nurses
... registered nurses
... visiting nurses
... vocational nurses
.. nutritionists
.. obstetricians
.. optometrists
.. paramedics
.. pediatricians
.. pharmacists
.. physicians
.. physicians' assistants
.. podiatrists
.. psychiatrists
.. psychologists
.. surgeons
.. therapists
... occupational therapists
... physical therapists
... psychotherapists
... speech therapists
.. veterinarians
. legal and political occupations
.. appointed officials
.. diplomats
.. elected officials
... assemblymen
... assemblywomen
... governors
... mayors
... representatives
.... congressmen
.... congresswomen
... senators
.. government workers
.. heads of state
.. interpreters
.. judges
.. lawyers
... barristers
.. legislators
.. magistrates
.. mediators
.. military personnel
.. negotiators
.. presidents
.. prime ministers
.. public officials

(*cont.*)

occupations (*cont.*)

.. vice presidents
. male intensive occupations
. managerial occupations
.. administrators
... college administrators
.. coordinators
.. executives
... chief executives
.. managers
... middle managers
.. presidents
.. underwriters
.. vice presidents
. manufacturing occupations
.. clothing workers
... dressmakers
... knitting machine operators
... milliners
... seamstresses (historical)
... sewers
... sewing machine operators
... tailors
.. factory workers
.. manufacturers
.. metalworkers
.. printing workers
... bookbinders
... compositors
... press operators
... printers
... typesetters
.. steelworkers
. marketing and sales occupations
.. insurance agents
.. merchandisers
.. real estate agents
.. sales personnel
... salesmen
... saleswomen
.. stockbrokers
.. vendors
... street vendors
. paraprofessional occupations
.. paralegals
.. paramedics
.. physicians' assistants

(*cont.*)

. .. . Narrower term

occupations (*cont.*)
- .. teacher aides
- .. technicians
- . professional occupations
  - .. accountants
  - .. architects
    - ... landscape architects
  - .. artists
  - .. chiropodists
  - .. chiropractors
  - .. consultants
  - .. counselors
  - .. dentists
  - .. dieticians
  - .. engineers
  - .. explorers
  - .. faculty
  - .. information scientists
  - .. judges
  - .. lawyers
    - ... barristers
  - .. librarians
  - .. mathematicians
  - .. optometrists
  - .. pharmacists
  - .. physicians
  - .. podiatrists
  - .. psychologists
  - .. registered nurses
  - .. religious workers
    - ... clergy
      - .... clergymen
      - .... clergywomen
      - .... ministers
      - .... mullahs
      - .... priests
      - .... rabbis
    - ... evangelists
    - ... mediums
      - .... physical mediums
      - .... spiritual mediums
    - ... missionaries
    - ... prophets
    - ... seers
    - ... spirit guides
    - ... spiritualists
    - ... women religious
      - .... clergywomen

(cont.)

occupations (*cont.*)
- .... nuns
  - ..... mother superiors
- .... priestesses
  - ..... high priestesses
- .. researchers
- .. scientists
  - ... astronomers
  - ... biologists
  - ... chemists
  - ... ethologists
  - ... geneticists
  - ... geologists
  - ... meteorologists
  - ... physicists
  - ... sociobiologists
- .. social scientists
  - ... anthropologists
  - ... archaeologists
  - ... economists
  - ... historians
  - ... psychologists
  - ... sociologists
  - ... urban planners
- .. social workers
- .. statisticians
- .. systems analysts
- .. teachers
- .. therapists
  - ... occupational therapists
  - ... physical therapists
  - ... psychotherapists
  - ... speech therapists
- .. veterinarians
- .. writers
  - ... translators
- . scientific and technical occupations
  - .. astronauts
  - .. computer programmers
  - .. engineers
  - .. home economists
  - .. information scientists
  - .. inventors
  - .. mathematicians
  - .. naturalists
  - .. physiologists
  - .. scientists
    - ... astronomers

(cont.)

occupations (*cont.*)

... biologists
... chemists
... ethologists
... geneticists
... geologists
... meteorologists
... physicists
... sociobiologists
.. statisticians
.. systems analysts
. service occupations
.. agents
... airline reservation
    agents
... insurance agents
... real estate agents
... travel agents
.. attendants
.. barbers
.. bartenders
.. beauticians
.. bellhops
.. child care workers
... babysitters
... governesses
... nannies
... wet nurses
.. cleaners
... housecleaners
... janitors
.. coat checkers
.. cocktail servers
.. community organizers
.. cosmetologists
... colorists
... manicurists
... pedicurists
.. deliverers
.. dishwashers
.. escorts
.. food preparation
    occupations
... bakers
... butchers
... chefs
... cooks
.. food service workers
.. fortune tellers
.. gigolos
.. government workers
.. hairdressers

(*cont.*)

occupations (*cont.*)

.. hat checkers
.. hotel workers
.. household workers
... housecleaners
.. housekeepers
.. ironers
.. launderers
.. prostitutes
.. protective service
    occupations
... correctional officers
.... parole officers
.... probation
        officers
... detectives
... fire fighters
... guards
.... security guards
... police officers
... prison workers
... sheriffs
.. sanitation workers
.. tour guides
.. ushers
.. visiting homemakers
.. volunteers
... docents
.. waiters
.. waiters' assistants
. transportation occupations
.. boat operators
.. drivers
... bus drivers
... taxi drivers
... truck drivers
.. flight attendants
.. heavy equipment
    operators
.. movers
.. pilots
.. railroad workers
... train conductors
.. road workers
.. seafarers
.. subway workers
... train conductors
. volunteer occupations
.. chairpersons
.. community organizers
.. directors
.. trustees

(*cont.*)

. .. . Narrower term

occupations (*cont.*)
    .. volunteers
      ... docents

::: natural sciences
  :: physical sciences
    : earth sciences
    oceanography

    : images of women
    odalisques

::: humanities
  :: literature
    : poetry
    odes

    : complexes
    Oedipus complex
     . female Oedipus complex

::: activities
  :: social activities
    : parties
    office parties

    : work
    office work

    : facilities
    offices (facilities)

    officials
     . appointed officials
     . elected officials
      .. assemblymen
      .. assemblywomen
      .. governors
      .. mayors
      .. representatives
       ... congressmen
       ... congresswomen
      .. senators
     . public officials
     . sports officials

::: policy
  :: corporate policy
    : multinational corporation policy
    offshore production plants

  :: industries
    : extractive industry
    oil industry

    : networks
    old boy networks

  :: networks
    : women's networks
    old girl networks

    : images of women
    old maids

    : adults
    old old adults

  :: culture
    : folk culture
    old wives' tales

    : adults
    older adults
     . older men
     . older women
     . senior citizens

  :: adults
    : older adults
    : men
    older men

    : women
  :: adults
    : older adults
    older women

    Olympic Games

    : men
    ombudsmen

    : women
    ombudswomen

:: training
: job training
on the job training
. apprenticeships

::: activities
:: shows
: art shows
one woman art shows

:: medical procedures
: surgical procedures
oophorectomy

: admissions
open door admissions

:::: arts
::: performing arts
:: music
: vocal music
opera

::: occupations
:: arts, entertainment, and media occupations
: singers
opera singers

: conditioning
operant conditioning

:: occupations
: administrative support occupations
operations researchers

: workers
operators
. boat operators
. camera operators
. computer equipment operators
. data entry operators
. heavy equipment operators
. machine operators
.. knitting machine operators
.. sewing machine operators
. press operators

(cont.)

operators (cont.)
. telephone operators

opinion polls

opportunities
. career opportunities
. educational opportunities
.. equal educational opportunity
. employment opportunities
.. equal employment opportunity

oppression
. fat oppression
. medical oppression
. political oppression
. sexual oppression

: attitudes
optimism

:: occupations
: professional occupations
:: occupations
: health care occupations
optometrists

optometry

: drugs
: contraception
oral contraceptives

:: social sciences
:: humanities
: history
oral history

:: humanities
: literature
oral literature

:: behavior
: sexual behavior
oral sex
. cunnilingus
. fellatio

: traditions
oral tradition

:: occupations
: arts, entertainment, and media
  occupations
orators

oratory

::: arts
:: performing arts
: music
orchestral music

::: spiritual communication
:: rites
: sacraments
ordination
. women's ordination

: behavior
organizational behavior

: development
organizational development

: objectives
organizational objectives

:: social sciences
: psychology
organizational psychology

: theory
organizational theory

organizations
. agencies
.. employment agencies
.. federal agencies
.. government agencies
.. intelligence agencies
.. modeling agencies
.. private agencies
.. public agencies
... state agencies
.. social agencies
... welfare agencies
. alliances
. arts organizations

(cont.)

organizations *(cont.)*
. associations
. auxiliaries
. banks
.. multinational banks
. boards
.. boards of directors
.. governing boards
. bureaus
. businesses
. cartels
. caucuses
. circles
. clans
. clubs
.. book clubs
.. garden clubs
.. night clubs
.. private clubs
.. social clubs
. coalitions
. collectives
.. collective farms
. commissions
.. civil rights commissions
.. commissions on the
  status of women
.. equal opportunities
  commissions
... Equal Employment
    Opportunity
    Commission
.. human relations
  commissions
. committees
.. political action
  committees
.. search committees
. communes
.. kibbutzim
.. village communes
. companies
. confederations
. congresses
. consortia
. consumer health
  organizations
. cooperatives
.. health cooperatives
. corporations
.. monopolies

(cont.)

organizations (*cont.*)
- .. multinational corporations
- .. networks (media)
- . councils
- . departments
- . enterprises
- . executive search firms
- . federations
- . health maintenance organizations
- . institutes
- . institutions
- . leagues
- . left wing organizations
- . legislatures
- . military
  - .. armed forces
    - ... all volunteer military force
- . nonprofit organizations
  - .. charities
  - .. foundations
  - .. nongovernmental organizations
    - ... nongovernmental women's organizations
  - .. voluntary organizations
    - ... private voluntary organizations
- . parent teacher organizations
- . parliaments
- . pension funds
- . political parties
  - .. Communist Party
  - .. Democratic Party
  - .. Libertarian Party
  - .. minor parties
  - .. Republican Party
  - .. Socialist Party
- . religious orders
- . right wing organizations
- . social organizations
- . societies
  - .. female societies
  - .. honorary societies
  - .. ladies' aid societies
  - .. missionary societies
  - .. secret societies
- . stock exchanges
- . task forces

(*cont.*)

organizations (*cont.*)
- . unions
  - .. labor unions
  - .. trade unions
- . utilities
  - .. electric utilities
  - .. gas utilities
  - .. public utilities
  - .. water utilities
- . women's organizations
  - .. feminist organizations
  - .. nongovernmental women's organizations
  - .. sororities

: crime
organized crime

organizing

orgasm
- . clitoral orgasm
- . vaginal orgasm

:: religious beliefs
: sin
original sin

: images of girls
Orphan Annie

: diseases
osteoporosis

: fortune telling
Ouija boards

outlaws

outplacement

: programs
outreach programs

: programs
Outward Bound programs

outwork

. .. . Narrower term

: bodies
ovaries

: achievement
overachievement

: bodies
oviducts

ovulation

: bodies
ovum

pacifism

padding

: employment
paid employment

pain

:: occupations
: arts, entertainment, and media
  occupations
painters

:: arts
: visual arts
painting

palimony

: fortune telling
palm reading

: activities
panels

pantheon

: clothing
pants

: medical procedures
Pap smear

::: occupations
:: craft occupations
: construction occupations
paperhangers

::: humanities
:: literature
: folk literature
parables

: activities
parades

paradigms

paradise

: workers
paralegal workers

:: occupations
: paraprofessional occupations
:: occupations
: female intensive occupations
paralegals

:: occupations
: paraprofessional occupations
:: occupations
: health care occupations
paramedics

paranoia

: occupations
paraprofessional occupations
  . paralegals
  . paramedics
  . physicians' assistants
  . teacher aides
  . technicians

paraprofessionals

parapsychology

:: relationships
  : adult child relationships
    parent child relationships
     . father daughter relationships
     . father son relationships
     . mother daughter
       relationships
     . mother son relationships

:: influence
  : family influence
    parent influence

  : organizations
    parent teacher organizations

  : relationships
    parent teacher relationships

  : aspirations
    parental aspirations

  : attitudes
    parental attitudes

  : behavior
    parental behavior

    parental leave
     . maternity leave
     . paternity leave

  : rights
    parental rights

    parenthood
     . delayed parenthood
     . planned parenthood

    parenting
     . coparenting
     . fathering
     . mothering
     . shared parenting

    parenting rewards

    parents
     . adoptive parents
     . birth parents
     . custodial parents
     . foster parents

(cont.)

parents (*cont.*)
  . noncustodial parents
  . single parents
   .. single fathers
   .. single mothers
  . stepparents
  . working parents

pariahs

  : organizations
parliaments

:::: humanities
 ::: literature
  :: prose
   : nonfiction
    parody

:::: occupations
 ::: service occupations
  :: protective service occupations
   : correctional officers
    parole officers

   : employment
    part time employment
     . job sharing

   : students
    part time students

   : reproduction
    parthenogenesis

  :: methods
   : research methods
    participant observation

  :: activities
   : social activities
    parties
     . cocktail parties
     . office parties

    partners

    passages

    passing

: emotions
passion

: behavior
passive behavior

patents

paternity

: benefits
paternity benefits

: parental leave
paternity leave

: rights
paternity rights

: lawsuits
paternity suits

patience

: relationships
patient doctor relationships

::: language
:: discriminatory language
: sexist language
patriarchal language

: religion
patriarchal religion

patriarchs

patriarchy

: murder
patricide

: kinship
patrilineal kinship

patriotism

: naming
patronymy

pauperization of women

: equity
pay equity
. comparable worth
. equal pay for equal work

peace

: advocates
peace advocates

peace camps

: social movements
peace movements
. antiwar movement

peasants

pedagogy

pedestals

:: occupations
: health care occupations
pediatricians

: medical sciences
pediatrics

::: occupations
:: service occupations
::: occupations
:: female intensive occupations
: cosmetologists
pedicurists

: influence
peer influence

: relationships
peer relationships

: women
: titles (nobility)
peeresses

peers

::: evaluation
:: medical evaluation
: physical examination
pelvic examination

: names
pen name

pen pals

penance

:: bodies
: genitals
penis

penis envy

:: benefits
: retirement benefits
pension benefits

: organizations
pension funds

people of color
. women of color

: cognitive processes
perception
. auditory perception
. color perception
. depth perception
. extrasensory perception
. kinesthetic perception
. self perception
. social perception
. spatial perception
. tactual perception
. visual perception
. weight perception

: skills
perception skills

: bias
perceptual bias

::: development
:: individual development
: cognitive development
perceptual development

perfection

performance
. job performance

:: evaluation
: personnel evaluation
performance appraisal

: art
performance art

: influences
performance factors

: space
performance spaces

: activities
performances

:: occupations
: arts, entertainment, and media
occupations
performers
. prima donnas
. soloists

: arts
performing arts
. dance
.. ballet
.. experimental dance
.. folk dance
.. modern dance
.. sacred dance
. mime
. music
.. art music
.. blues
.. chamber music
.. children's music
.. computer music
.. electronic music
.. feminist music
.. holistic music

(cont.)

. .. . Narrower term

performing arts (*cont.*)
.. incidental music
.. instrumental music
.. jazz
.. meditation music
.. orchestral music
.. political music
... protest music
.. popular music
... country music
... folk music
... rock and roll
.. religious music
... chants
... gospel music
... hymns
... spirituals
.. salon music
.. tribal music
.. vocal music
... choral music
... madrigals
... opera
... songs
.... ballads
.... lieder
.... lullabies
.... nursery songs
.... slave songs
.. women's music
. theater
.. collaborative theater
.. drama
... comedy
.... farce
.... skits
... tragedy
.. experimental theater
.. group developed theater
.. improvisation
.. musical theater
.. street theater
.. vaudeville

perfume

:: mass media
: print media
periodicals
. journals (periodicals)
. magazines
.. women's magazines
. newsletters
. newspapers

permanents

: child rearing practices
permissive child rearing practices

: environment
permissive environment

perquisites

persecution
. witch persecutions

: columns
personal columns

: correspondence
personal correspondence

: finances
personal finances

: hygiene
personal hygiene

: management
personal management

: narratives
personal narratives

: relationships
personal relationships
. female female relationships
.. female friendships
.. lesbian relationships
.. mother daughter relationships
. female male relationships
.. father daughter relationships

(*cont.*)

personal relationships (*cont.*)
   .. female male friendships
   .. mother son relationships
  . friendships
   .. female friendships
   .. female male friendships
   .. male friendships
  . gay relationships
   .. gay male relationships
   .. lesbian relationships
  . male male relationships
   .. father son relationships
   .. gay male relationships
   .. male friendships

: industries
personal service industry

: space
:: human needs
: psychological needs
personal space

: values
personal values

personality
  . authoritarian personality

:: development
: individual development
personality development

: disorders
personality disorders

: problems
personality problems

: testing
personality tests

: traits
personality traits

personnel
  . enlisted personnel
  . military personnel
  . sales personnel
   .. salesmen

(*cont.*)

personnel (*cont.*)
  .. saleswomen
 . school personnel

: evaluation
personnel evaluation
  . performance appraisal

: management
personnel management

: bodies
perspiration

: attitudes
pessimism

pets

: criticism
phallic criticism

phallocentrism
  . phallogocentrism

: phallocentrism
phallogocentrism

phallus

: industries
pharmaceutical industry

:: occupations
: professional occupations
:: occupations
: health care occupations
pharmacists

: medical sciences
pharmacology

:: humanities
: philosophy
phenomenology

pheromones

philanderers

. .. . Narrower term

:: occupations
: financial occupations
philanthropists

philanthropy

::: occupations
:: education occupations
: humanists
philosophers

: humanities
philosophy
. epistemology
. ethics
.. bioethics
.. business ethics
.. feminist ethics
.. medical ethics
.. political ethics
.. religious ethics
. logic
. metaphysics
. phenomenology
. political philosophy
. semiotics

:: disorders
: mental disorders
phobias
. agoraphobia
. homophobia
.. lesbophobia

:: humanities
: linguistics
phonology

:: occupations
: arts, entertainment, and media
occupations
photographers

:: arts
: visual arts
photography
. fashion photography

: journalism
photojournalism

: spiritual communication
phrenology

: abuse
physical abuse

: appearance
physical appearance

:: development
: individual development
physical development
. motor development
. muscular development
. sensory development

: education
physical education

::: health
:: physical health
: physical fitness
physical endurance

:: evaluation
: medical evaluation
physical examination
. breast examination
.. breast self examination
. pelvic examination

:: health
: physical health
physical fitness
. physical endurance
. physical strength
.. upper body strength

: health
physical health
. physical fitness
.. physical endurance
.. physical strength
... upper body strength

::: workers
:::: occupations
::: professional occupations
:: religious workers
: mediums
physical mediums

: natural sciences
physical sciences
. astronomy
. chemistry
. earth sciences
.. geology
.. oceanography
. physics
. space sciences

::: health
:: physical health
: physical fitness
physical strength
. upper body strength

::: occupations
:: professional occupations
::: occupations
:: health care occupations
: therapists
:: occupations
: female intensive occupations
physical therapists

: therapy
physical therapy

:: occupations
: professional occupations
:: occupations
: health care occupations
physicians

:: occupations
: paraprofessional occupations
:: occupations
: health care occupations
:: occupations
: female intensive occupations
physicians' assistants

::: occupations
:: scientific and technical occupations
::: occupations
:: professional occupations
::: occupations
:: education occupations
: scientists
physicists

:: natural sciences
: physical sciences
physics

:: social sciences
: psychology
physiological psychology

:: occupations
: scientific and technical occupations
physiologists

:: natural sciences
: biological sciences
physiology

pica

:: activities
: protest actions
pickets

: work
piecework

::: policy
:: corporate policy
: multinational corporation policy
:: policy
: labor policy
piecework labor policy

: workers
pieceworkers

pierced ears

:: occupations
: transportation occupations
pilots

pimps

: money
pin money

: workers
:: occupations
: female intensive occupations
pink collar workers

pinups

pioneers

pirates

:: bodies
: glands
pituitary gland

:: bodies
: hormones
pituitary hormones

placebos

placenta

: parenthood
planned parenthood

planning
. career planning
. family planning
. financial planning
. population planning
. rural planning
. urban planning

:: activities
: meetings
planning meetings

plantations

::: occupations
:: craft occupations
: construction occupations
plasterers

:: medical sciences
: surgery
plastic surgery
. liposuction surgery

play

playgrounds

playgroups

plays

:: occupations
: arts, entertainment, and media occupations
playwrights

: emotions
pleasure

: sessions
plenary sessions

::: occupations
:: craft occupations
: construction occupations
plumbers

pluralism
. religious pluralism

:: occupations
: professional occupations
:: occupations
: health care occupations
podiatrists

:: humanities
: literature
poetry
. ballads
. elegies
. epics
. epigrams
. haiku
. limericks
. lyric poetry
. odes
. sonnets

:: occupations
: arts, entertainment, and media
occupations
poets

polemics

::: occupations
:: service occupations
: protective service occupations
police officers

policy
. child care policy
. corporate policy
.. corporate relocation
policy
.. foreign investment policy
.. hiring policy
... affirmative action
hiring
... job advertisements
... veteran preference
.. multinational corporation
policy
... drug dumping
... global assembly lines
... offshore production
plants
... piecework labor
policy
. economic policy
. educational policy
. fiscal policy
. health care policy
. international policy
.. foreign aid policy
.. immigration policy
.. international trade policy
. labor policy
.. piecework labor policy
. monetary policy
. population policy
. public policy
. social policy
.. family policy

policy making

: attitudes
politeness

political action

:: organizations
: committees
political action committees

: activism
political activism

: activists
political activists

:: social sciences
: anthropology
political anthropology

: art
political art

: aspirations
political aspirations

political asylum

: candidates
political candidates

:: activities
: conventions
political conventions

political economic systems

::: humanities
:: philosophy
: ethics
political ethics

: ideology
political ideology

: influence
political influence

political leaders

::: arts
  :: performing arts
    : music
      political music
        . protest music

      political office

  : oppression
    political oppression

    political participation

  : organizations
    political parties
      . Communist Party
      . Democratic Party
      . Libertarian Party
      . minor parties
      . Republican Party
      . Socialist Party

  :: humanities
    : philosophy
      political philosophy

  : power
    political power

  : prisoners
    political prisoners

  : refugees
    political refugees

  : representation
    political representation

  : repression
    political repression

  : rights
    political rights

  : sanctions
    political sanctions

  : social sciences
    political science

: spouses
  political spouses
    . First Ladies (historical)
    . governors' spouses
    . presidential spouses

: status
  political status

  political systems
    . communism
    . democracy
    . democratic socialism
    . socialism
      .. democratic socialism
      .. utopian socialism

: theory
  political theory

  politics
    . coalition politics
    . local politics
    . sexual politics
      .. body politics

  poll tax

  pollution
    . air pollution
    . noise pollution
    . water pollution

::: customs
  :: marriage customs
    : polygamy
      polyandry

:: customs
  : marriage customs
    polygamy
      . polyandry
      . polygyny

::: customs
  :: marriage customs
    : polygamy
      polygyny

: hair styles
ponytails

: culture
popular culture

::: arts
:: performing arts
: music
popular music
. country music
. folk music
. rock and roll

:: measurements
: demographic measurements
population characteristics

population control

:: measurements
: demographic measurements
population decline

:: measurements
: demographic measurements
population distribution

::: natural sciences
:: biological sciences
: genetics
population genetics

:: measurements
: demographic measurements
population growth
. zero population growth

: planning
population planning

: policy
population policy

: trends
population trends

populism

pornography
. child pornography

:: arts
: visual arts
portraits

: reinforcement
positive reinforcement

possessiveness

posslq

:::: aid
::: financial aid
:: student financial aid
: fellowships
postdoctoral fellowships

:: arts
: visual arts
poster art

: marriage
posthumous marriage

: society
postindustrial society

postnatal period

::: disorders
:: mental disorders
: depression
postpartum depression

: education
postsecondary education
. higher education
.. four year colleges
.. graduate education
.. two year colleges

poststructuralism

::: activities
:: social activities
: suppers
potluck suppers

: craft artists
potters

::: arts
:: visual arts
: craft arts
pottery

poverty
. rural poverty

power
. consumer power
. economic power
. gray power
. political power
. woman power

power structure

powerlessness

::: occupations
:: health care occupations
::: occupations
:: female intensive occupations
: nurses
practical nurses

: spiritual communication
prayer

:: activities
: meetings
prayer meetings

preaching

: religious beliefs
predestination

prefixes

pregnancy
. ectopic pregnancy
. male pregnancy
. pseudopregnancy
. sympathetic pregnancy
. teenage pregnancy
. tubal pregnancy
. unwanted pregnancy

: disabilities
pregnancy disability

: discrimination
pregnancy discrimination

pregnancy leave

: prevention
pregnancy prevention

pregnancy trimesters

: students
pregnant students

: workers
pregnant workers

prejudice

:: relationships
: sexual relationships
premarital relations

: childbirth
premature childbirth

: death
premature death

::: children
:: young children
: infants
premature infants

premenstrual syndrome

: disorders
premenstrual tension

:: care
: health care
prenatal care

: influences
prenatal influences

:::: documents
::: legal documents
:: contracts
: marriage contracts
prenuptial agreements

:::: facilities
::: educational facilities
:: schools
: private schools
preparatory schools

:: children
: young children
preschool children

:: education
: early childhood education
preschool education

::: facilities
:: educational facilities
: schools
preschools

: drugs
prescription drugs

preservation
. art preservation
. neighborhood preservation

presidency

presidential office

:: spouses
: political spouses
presidential spouses

:: occupations
: managerial occupations
:: occupations
: legal and political occupations
presidents

: media coverage
press coverage

:: workers
::: occupations
:: manufacturing occupations
: printing workers
:: workers
: operators
press operators

: groups
pressure groups

prestige

prevention
. crime prevention
. disease prevention
. fire prevention
. pregnancy prevention
. rape prevention

: medical sciences
preventive medicine

pride
. gay pride

:: women
::: workers
:::: occupations
::: professional occupations
:: religious workers
::: occupations
:: female intensive occupations
: women religious
priestesses
. high priestesses

::: workers
:::: occupations
::: professional occupations
:: religious workers
: clergy
priests

::: occupations
:: arts, entertainment, and media
occupations
: performers
prima donnas

::: occupations
:: female intensive occupations
: caregivers
primary caregivers

::: education
:: elementary secondary education
: elementary education
:: education
: early childhood education
primary education

::: facilities
:: educational facilities
: schools
primary schools

::: natural sciences
:: biological sciences
: zoology
primate studies

:: socioeconomic indicators
: interest rates
prime interest rate

:: occupations
: legal and political occupations
prime ministers

: art
primitive art

: attitudes
primness

: women
: titles (nobility)
: images of women
princesses

:: occupations
: education occupations
principals

: mass media
print media
. periodicals
.. journals (periodicals)
.. magazines
... women's magazines
.. newsletters
.. newspapers
. publications
.. feminist publications

:: workers
::: occupations
:: manufacturing occupations
: printing workers
:: occupations
: arts, entertainment, and media occupations
printers

: workers
:: occupations
: manufacturing occupations
printing workers
. bookbinders
. compositors
. press operators
. printers
. typesetters

:: occupations
: arts, entertainment, and media occupations
printmakers

:: arts
: visual arts
printmaking

priorities

: workers
::: occupations
:: service occupations
: protective service occupations
prison workers

prisoners
. political prisoners
. prisoners of war

: prisoners
prisoners of war

: facilities
prisons

privacy

: rights
privacy rights

:: organizations
: agencies
private agencies

:: organizations
: clubs
private clubs

::: facilities
:: educational facilities
: colleges
private colleges

: education
private education

::: facilities
:: educational facilities
: schools
private schools
. finishing schools
. preparatory schools

private sector

: separate spheres
private sphere

::: organizations
:: nonprofit organizations
: voluntary organizations
**private voluntary
organizations**

privatization

privilege
. heterosexual privilege

prizes

probation

:::: occupations
::: service occupations
:: protective service occupations
: correctional officers
probation officers

: cognitive processes
problem solving

problems
. community problems
. consumer problems
. emotional problems
. family problems
. personality problems
. research problems
. sexual problems
. social problems

process
. budget process
. group process
. judicial process

prochoice

procreation

productivity

profanity

: industries
**professional and related
services industry**

: athletes
:: occupations
: arts, entertainment, and media
occupations
professional athletes

: athletics
professional athletics

: professional recognition
: awards
   professional awards

: degrees
   professional degrees

: development
   professional development

: education
   professional education

: occupations
   professional occupations
    . accountants
    . architects
      .. landscape architects
    . artists
    . chiropodists
    . chiropractors
    . consultants
    . counselors
    . dentists
    . dieticians
    . engineers
    . explorers
    . faculty
    . information scientists
    . judges
    . lawyers
      .. barristers
    . librarians
    . mathematicians
    . optometrists
    . pharmacists
    . physicians
    . podiatrists
    . psychologists
    . registered nurses
    . religious workers
      .. clergy
        ... clergymen
        ... clergywomen
        ... ministers
        ... mullahs
        ... priests
        ... rabbis
      .. evangelists
      .. mediums
        ... physical mediums

            (cont.)

professional occupations *(cont.)*
        ... spiritual mediums
    .. missionaries
    .. prophets
    .. seers
    .. spirit guides
    .. spiritualists
    .. women religious
      ... clergywomen
      ... nuns
        .... mother superiors
      ... priestesses
        .... high priestesses
  . researchers
  . scientists
    .. astronomers
    .. biologists
    .. chemists
    .. ethologists
    .. geneticists
    .. geologists
    .. meteorologists
    .. physicists
    .. sociobiologists
  . social scientists
    .. anthropologists
    .. archaeologists
    .. economists
    .. historians
    .. psychologists
    .. sociologists
    .. urban planners
  . social workers
  . statisticians
  . systems analysts
  . teachers
  . therapists
    .. occupational therapists
    .. physical therapists
    .. psychotherapists
    .. speech therapists
  . veterinarians
  . writers
    .. translators

professional recognition
  . professional awards

: sports
   professional sports

   : status
   professional status

  :: groups
   : women's groups
   professional women's groups

   professionalism

 :: occupations
  : education occupations
  professors

  profits

:::: bodies
 ::: hormones
  :: sex hormones
   : progestins
   progesterone

::: bodies
 :: hormones
  : sex hormones
  progestins
   . progesterone

 : ratings
 program ratings

 : language
 programming languages

 programs
  . after school programs
  . alternative programs
  . assistance programs
   .. dependent care
    assistance programs
   .. federal assistance
    programs
   .. state assistance
    programs
  . educational programs
   .. external degree
    programs
   .. Head Start programs
   .. high school equivalency
    programs
   .. nondegree programs
  . entitlement programs

(cont.)

programs (*cont.*)
 . intern programs
 . model programs
 . outreach programs
 . Outward Bound programs
 . public policy programs
 . residency programs
 . welfare programs
 . work incentive programs
 . work release programs

progress

: education
progressive education

:: psychological factors
: defense mechanisms
projection

proletariat

promiscuity

: employment practices
promotions

::: activities
:: social activities
: dances
proms

pronoun envy

pronouns
 . generic pronouns
 . masculine pronouns

propaganda

property confiscation

: crimes
property crimes
 . arson
 . burglaries
 . larceny
 . shoplifting
 . vandalism

. .. . Narrower term

: laws
property laws

property ownership

: rights
property rights

:: documents
: legal documents
property settlements

: taxes
:: taxes
: state taxes
property taxes

prophecy

:: workers
::: occupations
:: professional occupations
: religious workers
prophets

: writing
proposal writing

::: facilities
:: educational facilities
: schools
proprietary schools

:: humanities
: literature
prose
. fiction
.. mysteries
.. novels
... novellas
.. pulp fiction
.. romances
.. science fiction
.. short stories
. nonfiction
.. autobiography
.. biography
.. chronicles
.. diaries
... visual diaries
.. essays

(cont.)

prose (cont.)
.. histories
... life histories
... oral histories
.. journals
.. letters
.. memoirs
.. parody
.. satire

prostheses
. breast prostheses

:: occupations
: service occupations
: images of women
:: occupations
: female intensive occupations
prostitutes

prostitution
. juvenile prostitution

protection
. equal protection under the
law

: clothing
protective clothing

: legislation
protective legislation

:: occupations
: service occupations
**protective service
occupations**
. correctional officers
.. parole officers
.. probation officers
. detectives
. fire fighters
. guards
.. security guards
. police officers
. prison workers
. sheriffs

protest

: activities
protest actions
  . boycotts
    .. economic boycotts
  . civil disobedience
  . demonstrations
  . marches
  . pickets
  . rebellions
  . riots
  . sit ins
  . strikes

::::: arts
:::: performing arts
::: music
: political music
protest music

: feminism
protofeminism

::: humanities
:: literature
: folk literature
proverbs

:: occupations
: education occupations
provosts

pseudonyms

: pregnancy
pseudopregnancy

:: occupations
: health care occupations
psychiatrists

: medical sciences
psychiatry

: spiritual communication
psychic readings

:: occupations
: female intensive occupations
psychics

psychoanalysis

: criticism
psychoanalytic criticism

: feminism
psychoanalytic feminism

:: therapy
: cathartic therapy
psychodrama

:: humanities
: linguistics
psycholinguistics

: adjustment
psychological adjustment

psychological factors
  . defense mechanisms
    .. denial
    .. projection
  . locus of control

: human needs
psychological needs
  . achievement need
  . affection
  . approval need
  . creativity
  . intimacy
  . personal space
  . self actualization
  . self concept
  . self esteem
  . self respect
  . self sufficiency

: repression
psychological repression

: stress
psychological stress

: testing
psychological testing

. .. . Narrower term

::: occupations
:: professional occupations
::: occupations
:: education occupations
: social scientists
:: occupations
: professional occupations
:: occupations
: health care occupations
psychologists

: social sciences
psychology
. abnormal psychology
. analytical psychology
. child psychology
. clinical psychology
. comparative psychology
. developmental psychology
. educational psychology
. experimental psychology
. industrial psychology
. organizational psychology
. physiological psychology
. social psychology

: spiritual communication
psychometry

psychopharmacology

: behavior
psychosexual behavior

: disorders
psychosomatic disorders

:: medical sciences
: surgery
psychosurgery

::: occupations
:: professional occupations
::: occupations
:: health care occupations
: therapists
psychotherapists

: therapy
psychotherapy

: drugs
psychotropic drugs
. antidepressant drugs
. tranquilizers

puberty

:: bodies
: hair
pubic hair

public accommodations

public affairs

:: organizations
: agencies
public agencies
. state agencies

: art
public art

public assistance

::: facilities
:: educational facilities
: colleges
public colleges

: education
public education

public health

: housing
public housing

: information
public information

public interest

: officials
:: occupations
: legal and political occupations
public officials

public opinion

: :: ::: :::: :::::: Broader term

: policy
public policy

: programs
public policy programs

::: mass media
:: electronic media
: radio
public radio

: relationships
public relations

:: occupations
: arts, entertainment, and media
occupations
public relations specialists

::: facilities
:: educational facilities
: schools
public schools

public sector

public service

public speaking

: separate spheres
public sphere

::: mass media
:: electronic media
: television
public television

: transportation
public transportation

:: organizations
: utilities
public utilities

: welfare
public welfare

:: mass media
: print media
publications
. feminist publications

publicity

:: occupations
: arts, entertainment, and media
occupations
publishers

: industries
publishing industry

: diseases
puerperal fever

:::: humanities
::: literature
:: prose
: fiction
pulp fiction

punishment

:: language
: figurative language
puns

::: arts
:: visual arts
: craft arts
puppetry

purdah

:: spiritual communication
: rites
purification rites

purists

purity

: clothing
purses

. .. . Narrower term   907

:: methods
: research methods
  qualitative analysis

: assessment
  quality assessment

  quality of life
    . quality of work life

: quality of life
  quality of work life

:: methods
: research methods
  quantitative analysis

  queen bee syndrome

: images of women
  queen for a day

: women
: titles (nobility)
: images of women
  queens

::: arts
:: visual arts
: craft arts
  quilting

  quotas
    . immigration quotas
    . student quotas

::: workers
:::: occupations
::: professional occupations
:: religious workers
: clergy
  rabbis

  race

: bias
  race bias

: interdisciplinary studies
  race, class, and gender studies

: equity
  race equity

  race formation

: relationships
  race relations

: differences
  racial and ethnic differences

: discrimination
  racial discrimination

: diversity
  racial diversity

: equality
  racial equality

: influences
  racial factors

: stereotypes
  racial stereotypes

:: stratification
: social stratification
  racial stratification

  racism
    . environmental racism
    . institutional racism

::: violence
:: sexual violence
: rape
  racist rape

  raconteurs

: sports
  racquetball

: therapy
: medical procedures
radiation therapy

: feminism
radical feminism

radicals

:: mass media
: electronic media
radio
. public radio

: commercials
radio commercials

: emotions
:: emotions
: anger
rage

: transportation
rail transportation

: workers
:: occupations
: transportation occupations
railroad workers
. train conductors

:: activities
: mass actions
rallies

:: occupations
: agricultural, fishing, and forestry
occupations
ranch hands

:: data collection
: sampling
random sampling

rank
. academic rank
. military rank

:: violence
: sexual violence
rape
. acquaintance rape
.. date rape
. domestic rape
. gang rape
. racist rape
. slave rape

::: facilities
:: centers
: crisis centers
rape crisis centers

: fantasies
rape fantasies

: prevention
rape prevention

: victims
rape victims

: criminals
rapists

raps

ratification
. treaty ratification

ratings
. network ratings
. program ratings
. viewer ratings

rationality

reaction times

reading

: activities
readings

real estate

:: occupations
: marketing and sales occupations
::: occupations
:: service occupations
::: occupations
:: female intensive occupations
: agents
real estate agents

reason

:: activities
: protest actions
rebellions

rebellious behavior

: religious beliefs
rebirth

:: cognitive processes
: memory
recall

:: occupations
: female intensive occupations
::: occupations
:: administrative support occupations
: clerical occupations
receptionists

:: activities
: social activities
receptions

recession

recidivism

recipes
. family recipes

:: cognitive processes
: memory
recognition

reconciliation

:: medical sciences
: surgery
reconstructive surgery

records
. employee records
. medical records
. school records
. voting records

: confidentiality
records confidentiality

recreation

: discriminatory practices
redlining

reduction in force

: students
reentry students

: women
reentry women

referees

references

: facilities
reformatories

reformers

reforms
. dress reform
. educational reform
. labor law reform
. land reform
. marital property reform
. media reform
. moral reform
. religious reforms
. social reform
. welfare reform

refugees
. economic refugees
. political refugees
. religious refugees

:: interdisciplinary studies
: area studies
regional studies

:: occupations
: professional occupations
::: occupations
:: health care occupations
::: occupations
:: female intensive occupations
: nurses
registered nurses

regulations
. federal regulations
. state regulations

rehabilitation
. correctional rehabilitation
. drug rehabilitation
. vocational rehabilitation

: religious beliefs
reincarnation

reinforcement
. negative reinforcement
. positive reinforcement

rejection

relationships
. adult child relationships
.. parent child relationships
... father daughter
relationships
... father son
relationships
... mother daughter
relationships
... mother son
relationships
. children's relationships
. community relations
. domestic relations
. ethnic relations
. family relationships
.. sibling relationships
. heterosexual relationships
. human relations
. industrial relations
. international relations
. interracial relations
. labor relations
. lawyer client relationships
. parent teacher relationships
. patient doctor relationships
(cont.)

relationships *(cont.)*
. peer relationships
. personal relationships
.. female female
relationships
... female friendships
... lesbian relationships
... mother daughter
relationships
.. female male
relationships
... father daughter
relationships
... female male
friendships
... mother son
relationships
.. friendships
... female friendships
... female male
friendships
... male friendships
.. gay relationships
... gay male
relationships
... lesbian relationships
.. male male relationships
... father son
relationships
... gay male
relationships
... male friendships
. public relations
. race relations
. sexual relationships
.. premarital relations
. social relations
. teacher student relationships

relaxation

religion
. civil religion
. patriarchal religion
. state religion

religions

: art
religious art

. .. . Narrower term

religious beliefs
- . immaculate conception
- . incarnation
- . predestination
- . rebirth
- . reincarnation
- . salvation
- . sin
  - .. original sin

: discrimination
religious discrimination

: education
religious education

::: humanities
:: philosophy
: ethics
religious ethics

: experience
religious experience

: facilities
religious facilities
- . cathedrals
- . churches
  - .. house churches
  - .. storefront churches
- . convents
- . monasteries
- . mosques
- . synagogues
- . temples

: groups
religious groups
- . congregations
- . covens
- . faith communities
- . sects

: influences
religious influences

: language
religious language

: law
religious law

:: humanities
: literature
religious literature

: social movements
religious movements

: spiritual communication
::: arts
:: performing arts
: music
religious music
- . chants
- . gospel music
- . hymns
- . spirituals

: organizations
religious orders

: pluralism
religious pluralism

religious practices

: reforms
religious reforms

: refugees
religious refugees

: repression
religious repression

the religious right

: sanctions
religious sanctions

::: facilities
:: educational facilities
: schools
religious schools

: symbols
religious symbols

: :: ::: :::: ::::: Broader term

: traditions
religious traditions

: values
religious values

: workers
:: occupations
: professional occupations
religious workers
. clergy
.. clergymen
.. clergywomen
.. ministers
.. mullahs
.. priests
.. rabbis
. evangelists
. mediums
.. physical mediums
.. spiritual mediums
. missionaries
. prophets
. seers
. spirit guides
. spiritualists
. women religious
.. clergywomen
.. nuns
... mother superiors
.. priestesses
... high priestesses

relocation

: marriage
remarriage

: education
remedial education

remedies
. herbal remedies
. home remedies

renewable energy sources
. solar energy

rent

:: occupations
: craft occupations
repairers

:: occupations
: arts, entertainment, and media
occupations
reporters
. weather reporters

representation
. political representation

:: officials
::: occupations
:: legal and political occupations
: elected officials
representatives
. congressmen
. congresswomen

repression
. political repression
. psychological repression
. religious repression
. sexual repression

reproduction
. parthenogenesis

reproductive cycle

: freedoms
reproductive freedom

:: hazards
: work hazards
**reproductive hazards at
work**

: health
reproductive health

: rights
reproductive rights

: technology
reproductive technologies
. artificial insemination
. cloning
. embryo transfer

(cont.)

reproductive technologies (*cont.*)
- fertility drugs
- in vitro fertilization
- sperm banks

:: organizations
: political parties
  Republican Party

reputations

research
- applied research
- cross cultural research
- scientific research
- social science research
 - .. behavioral research
 - .. market research
- sponsored research
 - .. federally sponsored research
 - .. state sponsored research

:: occupations
: education occupations
  research assistants

: bias
  research bias

research design

:: funding
: grants
  research grants

: methods
  research methods
- case studies
- cohort analysis
- content analysis
- contextual analysis
- cost benefit analysis
- interviewing
- participant observation
- qualitative analysis
- quantitative analysis

: problems
  research problems

:: occupations
: professional occupations
:: occupations
: education occupations
  researchers

:: housing
: student housing
  residence halls

: programs
  residency programs

: security
  residential security

resistance
- draft resistance

resources
- financial resources
- human resources
 - .. labor force
   - ... multinational labor force
   - ... unpaid labor force
     - .... unpaid household labor
 - .. labor supply
- natural resources
 - .. mineral resources
 - .. water resources

responsibility
- community responsibility
- corporate responsibility
- family responsibility
- legal responsibility

restitution

:: documents
: legal documents
  restraining orders

resumes

: trades
  retail trade

: industries
retail trade industry

retirement
. early retirement
. forced retirement

: age
retirement age

: benefits
retirement benefits
. pension benefits

: activities
retreats

: discrimination
reverse discrimination

:: occupations
: arts, entertainment, and media
    occupations
reviewers

: activities
revivals

revolution
. nationalist revolutions
. sexual revolution
. socialist revolutions

: social movements
revolutionary movements

Rh factor

Rh incompatibility

rhetoric

: contraception
rhythm method

: rights
right to die

: legislation
right to know legislation

: rights
right to work

: organizations
right wing organizations

rights
. abortion rights
. children's rights
. civil rights
. domicile rights
. equal rights
. family rights
. gay rights
. homemaker rights
. human rights
. inheritance rights
. land rights
. maternity rights
. name rights
. parental rights
. paternity rights
. political rights
. privacy rights
. property rights
. reproductive rights
. right to die
. right to work
. rights of the disabled
. uxorial rights
. visitation rights
. voting rights
. welfare rights
. woman's rights
. women's rights

: rights
rights of the disabled

: jewelry
rings
. wedding rings

:: activities
: protest actions
riots

risk taking

: behavior
risk taking behavior

---

risks

: spiritual communication
  rites
    . bat mitzvah
    . domestic rites
    . fertility rites
    . funeral rites
    . initiation rites
    . purification rites
    . rites of passage
    . sacraments
      .. baptism
      .. confession
      .. confirmation
      .. holy communion
      .. holy matrimony
      .. last rites
      .. ordination
        ... women's ordination
    . votive rites

:: spiritual communication
  : rites
    rites of passage

    ritual disfigurement

  : workers
:: occupations
  : transportation occupations
    road workers

  : activities
    roasts

:::: arts
  ::: performing arts
    :: music
      : popular music
        rock and roll

      : conflict
        role conflict
          . interrole conflict

        role expectations

        role models

        role reversal

roles
  . domestic roles
  . family roles
  . gender roles
  . leadership roles
  . marital roles
  . men's roles
  . multiple roles
    .. dual roles
  . occupational roles
  . sex roles
  . women's roles

: sports
  roller skating

  romance

:::: humanities
  ::: literature
    :: prose
      : fiction
        romances

  :: emotions
    : love
      romantic love

::: occupations
  :: craft occupations
    : construction occupations
      roofers

  : rooms
    a room of one's own

    rooming in

    rooms
      . a room of one's own
      . bedrooms
      . birthing rooms
      . boudoirs
      . delivery rooms
      . kitchens
      . locker rooms

    royalty

: diseases
  rubella

::: arts
:: visual arts
 : craft arts
   rug hooking

:: men
 : fathers
   runaway fathers

:: spouses
:: men
 : husbands
   runaway husbands

:: women
 : mothers
   runaway mothers

   runaway shops

:: women
:: spouses
 : wives
   runaway wives

   runaways

 : sports
   running

   rural areas

 : conditions
   rural conditions

 : development
   rural development

   rural living

 : migration
   rural migration

 : planning
   rural planning

: poverty
  rural poverty

: land settlement
  rural resettlement

: women
  rural women

:: spiritual communication
 : rites
   sacraments
    . baptism
    . confession
    . confirmation
    . holy communion
    . holy matrimony
    . last rites
    . ordination
     .. women's ordination

 : spiritual communication
::: arts
:: performing arts
 : dance
   sacred dance

 : ideology
   sacred ideology

 : space
   sacred space

 : texts
   sacred texts

 : spiritual communication
   sacrifice

   sadism
    . cultural sadism

 : emotions
   sadness

   sadomasochism

 : sex
   safe sex

safety
. occupational health and
  safety

: sports
sailing

saints

: personnel
:: occupations
: marketing and sales occupations
sales personnel
. salesmen
. saleswomen

:: taxes
: state taxes
sales taxes

:: personnel
::: occupations
:: marketing and sales occupations
: sales personnel
salesmen

:: personnel
::: occupations
:: marketing and sales occupations
: sales personnel
:: occupations
: female intensive occupations
saleswomen

::: arts
:: performing arts
: music
salon music

salons

: religious beliefs
salvation

samplers

: data collection
sampling
. random sampling

sanctions
. economic sanctions
. political sanctions
. religious sanctions

sanctuaries

sanitary napkins

sanitation

: workers
:: occupations
: service occupations
sanitation workers

sanity

satellite communications

satellites
. communication satellites

:::: humanities
::: literature
:: prose
: nonfiction
satire

satisfaction
. career satisfaction
. job satisfaction
. marital satisfaction
. sexual satisfaction

schedules
. employment schedules
.. flexible work schedules
. school schedules

:: disorders
: mental disorders
schizophrenia

:: occupations
: education occupations
scholars
. independent scholars
. visiting scholars

scholarship
. feminist scholarship

::: aid
:: financial aid
: student financial aid
scholarships

: children
school age children

school attendance

: counseling
school counseling

: desegregation
school desegregation

:: services
: health care services
school health services

: integration
school integration

: personnel
:: occupations
: education occupations
school personnel

: records
school records

: schedules
school schedules

:: discriminatory practices
: segregation
school segregation

:: facilities
: educational facilities
schools
. alternative schools
. boarding schools
. community schools
. elementary schools
. free schools
. high schools
.. junior high schools
. middle schools
. normal schools

(cont.)

schools *(cont.)*
. nursery schools
. preschools
. primary schools
. private schools
.. finishing schools
.. preparatory schools
. proprietary schools
. public schools
. religious schools
. secondary schools
. single sex schools

science
. cognitive science

:: behavior
: avoidance behavior
science avoidance

:::: humanities
::: literature
:: prose
: fiction
science fiction

science reporting

: occupations
scientific and technical occupations
. astronauts
. computer programmers
. engineers
. home economists
. information scientists
. inventors
. mathematicians
. naturalists
. physiologists
. scientists
.. astronomers
.. biologists
.. chemists
.. ethologists
.. geneticists
.. geologists
.. meteorologists
.. physicists
.. sociobiologists
. statisticians

(cont.)

. .. . Narrower term   919

scientific and technical occupations (*cont.*)
. systems analysts

scientific method

: research
scientific research

:: occupations
: scientific and technical occupations
:: occupations
: professional occupations
:: occupations
: education occupations
scientists
. astronomers
. biologists
. chemists
. ethologists
. geneticists
. geologists
. meteorologists
. physicists
. sociobiologists

: images of women
scolds

scores

screenplays

scripts

:: bodies
: genitals
scrotum

:: occupations
: arts, entertainment, and media occupations
sculptors

:: arts
: visual arts
sculpture
. bas reliefs
. soft sculpture

:: occupations
: transportation occupations
seafarers

: women
:: workers
::: occupations
:: manufacturing occupations
::: occupations
:: female intensive occupations
: clothing workers
seamstresses (historical)

seances

:: organizations
: committees
search committees

: migration
seasonal migration

seclusion

: careers
second careers

:: education
: elementary secondary education
secondary education
. high school equivalency programs
. high schools
.. junior high schools

::: facilities
:: educational facilities
: schools
secondary schools

:: organizations
: societies
secret societies

:: occupations
: female intensive occupations
::: occupations
:: administrative support occupations
: clerical occupations
secretaries

:: groups
: religious groups
sects

secularization

security
. business security
. campus security
. computer security
. global security
. job security
. national security
. residential security

:::: occupations
::: service occupations
:: protective service occupations
: guards
security guards

seduction

: images of women
seductresses

: capital
seed capital

:: workers
::: occupations
:: professional occupations
: religious workers
:: occupations
: female intensive occupations
seers

: housing
segregated housing

: discriminatory practices
segregation
. occupational segregation
.. occupational sex
segregation
. school segregation
. sex segregation

selection procedures

: attention
selective attention

:: human needs
: psychological needs
self actualization

: blame
self blame

:: human needs
: psychological needs
self concept

self confidence

: control
self control

self defense

self denial

:: behavior
: destructive behavior
self destructive behavior

self determination

self disclosure

: employment
self employment

:: human needs
: psychological needs
self esteem

self examination

:: behavior
: help seeking behavior
self help

: insemination
self insemination

:: cognitive processes
: perception
self perception

:: human needs
: psychological needs
self respect

self sacrifice

:: human needs
: psychological needs
self sufficiency

self understanding

: behavior
selfish behavior

:: humanities
: linguistics
semantics

:: facilities
: educational facilities
seminaries

:: activities
: educational activities
seminars

:: humanities
: philosophy
semiotics

: Congress
Senate

:: officials
::: occupations
:: legal and political occupations
: elected officials
senators

:: adults
: older adults
senior citizens

seniority

sensation

sense of humor

sensitivity

: training
sensitivity training

::: development
:: individual development
: physical development
sensory development

sensuality

sentencing

separate spheres
. private sphere
. public sphere

separation

:: documents
: legal documents
separation agreements

separation of church and state

separatism
. lesbian separatism

: facilities
seraglios

serials

sermons

: occupations
service occupations
. agents
.. airline reservation agents
.. insurance agents
.. real estate agents
.. travel agents
. attendants
. barbers
. bartenders
. beauticians
. bellhops
. child care workers
.. babysitters
.. governesses
.. nannies

(cont.)

service occupations (*cont.*)
.. wet nurses
. cleaners
.. housecleaners
.. janitors
. coat checkers
. cocktail servers
. community organizers
. cosmetologists
.. colorists
.. manicurists
.. pedicurists
. deliverers
. dishwashers
. escorts
. food preparation occupations
.. bakers
.. butchers
.. chefs
.. cooks
. food service workers
. fortune tellers
. gigolos
. government workers
. hairdressers
. hat checkers
. hotel workers
. household workers
.. housecleaners
. housekeepers
. ironers
. launderers
. prostitutes
. protective service
    occupations
.. correctional officers
... parole officers
... probation officers
.. detectives
.. fire fighters
.. guards
... security guards
.. police officers
.. prison workers
.. sheriffs
. sanitation workers
. tour guides
. ushers
. visiting homemakers
. volunteers
.. docents
. waiters

(*cont.*)

service occupations (*cont.*)
. waiters' assistants

services
. dating services
. domestic services
.. diaper services
.. homemaker service
. health care services
.. community health
    services
.. emergency medical
    services
.. maternal health service
.. multicultural health care
    services
.. school health services
. housekeeping services
. human services
.. social services
... victim services
... youth services
. information services
.. information processing
.. information retrieval
.. information retrieval
    services
.. information storage
.. news services
. legal services
.. legal aid services

sessions
. plenary sessions

sewage disposal

:: workers
::: occupations
:: manufacturing occupations
::: occupations
:: female intensive occupations
: clothing workers
sewers

sewing

. .. . Narrower term

::: workers
  :: operators
    : machine operators
  :: workers
::: occupations
  :: manufacturing occupations
::: occupations
  :: female intensive occupations
    : clothing workers
      sewing machine operators

      sex
        . commercial sex
        . safe sex

    : change
      sex change

    : counseling
      sex counseling

    : crimes
      sex crimes

      sex determination

    : differences
      sex differences

    : discrimination
      sex discrimination
        . sex discrimination in
          education
        . sex discrimination in
          employment

  :: discrimination
    : sex discrimination
      **sex discrimination in
        education**

  :: discrimination
    : sex discrimination
      **sex discrimination in
        employment**

      sex drive

    : education
      sex education

    : equity
      sex equity

  :: bodies
    : hormones
      sex hormones
        . androgens
          .. testosterone
        . estrogens
        . progestins
          .. progesterone

    : industries
      sex industry

    : manuals
      sex manuals

      sex objects

    : sex selection
      sex preselection

::: measurements
  :: demographic measurements
    : vital statistics
      sex ratio

      sex reversal

    : behavior
      sex role behavior
        . flirtation

  :: development
    : individual development
      sex role development

    : stereotyping
      sex role stereotyping

    : roles
      sex roles

  :: discriminatory practices
    : segregation
      sex segregation

sex selection
. sex preselection

: stereotypes
sex stereotypes

sex tourism

sex/gender systems

sexism
. institutional sexism
. linguistic sexism

:: language
: discriminatory language
sexist language
. he/man language
. patriarchal language

: abstinence
sexual abstinence

: abuse
sexual abuse

sexual aids
. aphrodisiacs
. vibrators

:: violence
: sexual violence
: assault
sexual assault

sexual attraction

: behavior
sexual behavior
. anal sex
. foreplay
. group sex
. masturbation
. oral sex
.. cunnilingus
.. fellatio
. sexual intercourse
. tribadism

:: emotions
: desire
sexual desire

sexual dimorphism

: division of labor
sexual division of labor

sexual dysfunction
. impotence

: equality
sexual equality

sexual excitement

: exploitation
sexual exploitation

: fantasies
sexual fantasies

: freedoms
sexual freedom

sexual harassment
. street harassment

: identity
sexual identity
. cross sex identity

:: behavior
: sexual behavior
sexual intercourse

: intimidation
sexual intimidation

: liberation
sexual liberation

: oppression
sexual oppression

sexual permissiveness

. .. . Narrower term

: politics
sexual politics
. body politics

sexual preference

: problems
sexual problems

: relationships
sexual relationships
. premarital relations

: repression
sexual repression

: revolution
sexual revolution

: satisfaction
sexual satisfaction

: slavery
sexual slavery
. female sexual slavery

:: stratification
: social stratification
sexual stratification

: violence
sexual violence
. rape
.. acquaintance rape
... date rape
.. domestic rape
.. gang rape
.. racist rape
.. slave rape
. sexual assault

sexuality
. bisexuality
. female sexuality
. heterosexuality
.. compulsory
heterosexuality
. homosexuality
.. lesbianism

(cont.)

sexuality *(cont.)*
.. male homosexuality
. hypersexuality
.. female hypersexuality
.. male hypersexuality
. male sexuality
. transsexuality

:: diseases
: communicable diseases
sexually transmitted diseases
. acquired immune deficiency
syndrome
. clamydia
. genital herpes
. gonorrhea
. syphilis

shamans

:: custody
: child custody
shared custody

: parenting
shared parenting

sheet music

: facilities
shelters
. crisis shelters
. women's shelters

::: occupations
:: service occupations
: protective service occupations
sheriffs

: work
shift work

:: crimes
: property crimes
shoplifting

:::: humanities
::: literature
:: prose
: fiction
short stories

:: cognitive processes
: memory
short term memory

showers

: activities
shows
. advice shows
. art shows
.. one woman art shows
. fashion shows
. game shows
. talk shows

shunning

:: influence
: family influence
sibling influence

:: relationships
: family relationships
sibling relationships

siblings

: children
sick children

sick leave

: diseases
sickle cell anemia

: language
sign language

:: occupations
: craft occupations
sign painters

significant others

silence

: religious beliefs
sin
. original sin

:: occupations
: arts, entertainment, and media occupations
singers
. chanteuses
. opera singers
. torch singers

:: parents
: single parents
:: men
: fathers
single fathers

: men
single men

:: parents
: single parents
:: women
: mothers
single mothers

: families
single parent families

: parents
single parents
. single fathers
. single mothers

::: facilities
:: educational facilities
: colleges
single sex colleges
. women's colleges

: education
single sex education

: environment
single sex environments

. .. . Narrower term

::: facilities
:: educational facilities
: schools
single sex schools

: women
single women

singles

: images of women
sirens

: images of girls
sissies

sisterhood

: women
: images of women
: images of girls
sisters

: in laws
sisters in law

:: activities
: protest actions
sit ins

: sports
skiing

:: development
: individual development
skill development

: training
skill training

: trades
skilled trades

skills
. basic skills
. job skills
. language skills
. leadership skills
. life skills

(cont.)

skills *(cont.)*
. motor skills
.. hand eye coordination
. perception skills
. social skills
. spatial skills

: bodies
skin

skin color

: clothing
skirts
. miniskirts

::::: arts
:::: performing arts
::: theater
:::: humanities
::: literature
:: drama
: comedy
skits

:: language
: informal language
slang

slapstick

:: names
: surnames
slave name

::: violence
:: sexual violence
: rape
slave rape

::::: arts
:::: performing arts
::: music
:: vocal music
: songs
slave songs

: :: ::: :::: ::::: Broader term

slavery
. sexual slavery
.. female sexual slavery
. white slavery

slaves

:: interdisciplinary studies
: area studies
Slavic studies

sleep

: landlords
slum landlords

:: neighborhoods
: declining neighborhoods
slums

: business
small business

smiling

: environment
smokefree environments

smoking

: social prohibitions
smoking prohibition

snakes

: images of women
Snow White

soap operas

: sports
soccer

social action

: activities
social activities
. breakfasts
. brunches
. coffee klatches
. dances
.. charity balls

(cont.)

social activities *(cont.)*
.. cotillions
.. mixers
.. proms
.. society balls
. dating
.. blind dates
. dinners
. lunches
. parties
.. cocktail parties
.. office parties
. receptions
. suppers
.. potluck suppers
. teas

: adjustment
social adjustment

:: organizations
: agencies
social agencies
. welfare agencies

: attitudes
social attitudes

: behavior
social behavior
. manners
.. gallantry
.. graciousness

: bias
social bias

: change
social change

social characteristics

: class
social class

:: organizations
: clubs
social clubs

: conditioning
social conditioning

: conflict
social conflict

: social construction of reality
social construction of gender

social construction of reality
. social construction of gender

: control
social control

:: development
: individual development
social development

: dialects
social dialects

: differences
social differences

social entertaining

: environment
social environment

:: social sciences
: geography
social geography

:: social sciences
:: humanities
: history
social history
. family history

: identity
social identity

: socioeconomic indicators
social indicators

: influences
social influences

social issues

: legislation
social legislation

: mobility
social mobility

social movements
. abortion movement
. anti ERA movement
. antiabortion movement
. antiapartheid movement
. antiilliteracy movements
. antilynching campaign
. antinuclear movement
. antisuffrage movement
. Black movement
.. Black power movement
. civil rights movements
. conservative movement
. environmental movement
. feminist movement
. homophile movement
. labor movement
. lesbian movement
. men's movement
. nationalist movements
. peace movements
.. antiwar movement
. religious movements
. revolutionary movements
. suffrage movements
. temperance movement
. women's movement
.. international women's
movement
.. women's health
movement
. youth movement

social organization

: organizations
social organizations

:: cognitive processes
: perception
social perception

: policy
  social policy
  . family policy

: problems
  social problems

  social prohibitions
  . drinking prohibition
  . smoking prohibition

:: social sciences
: psychology
  social psychology

: reforms
  social reform

: relationships
  social relations

: research
  social science research
  . behavioral research
  . market research

social sciences
  . anthropology
  .. archaeology
  .. cultural anthropology
  .. economic anthropology
  .. ethnography
  .. ethnology
  .. medical anthropology
  .. political anthropology
  . criminology
  . demography
  . economics
  .. agricultural economics
  .. classical economics
  .. health economics
  .. macroeconomics
  .. microeconomics
  .. neoclassical economics
  .. welfare economics
  . ethology
  . geography
  .. economic geography
  .. social geography
  . gerontology

(*cont.*)

social sciences (*cont.*)
  . history
  .. art history
  .. economic history
  .. historiography
  .. history of children
  .. history of religion
  .. history of science
  .. intellectual history
  .. labor history
  .. literary history
  .. music history
  .. oral history
  .. social history
  ... family history
  .. women's history
  . political science
  . psychology
  .. abnormal psychology
  .. analytical psychology
  .. child psychology
  .. clinical psychology
  .. comparative psychology
  .. developmental
     psychology
  .. educational psychology
  .. experimental psychology
  .. industrial psychology
  .. organizational
     psychology
  .. physiological psychology
  .. social psychology
  . social studies
  . sociobiology
  . sociology
  .. medical sociology
  .. sociology of knowledge

:: occupations
: professional occupations
:: occupations
: education occupations
  social scientists
  . anthropologists
  . archaeologists
  . economists
  . historians
  . psychologists
  . sociologists
  . urban planners

Social Security

:: services
: human services
social services
. victim services
. youth services

: skills
social skills

: status
social status

: stratification
social stratification
. racial stratification
. sexual stratification

social structure

: social sciences
social studies

: trends
social trends

: values
social values

: welfare
social welfare

: work
social work

: workers
:: occupations
: professional occupations
:: occupations
: female intensive occupations
social workers

: political systems
socialism
. democratic socialism
. utopian socialism

: economic development models
**socialist economic
development models**

: feminism
socialist feminism

:: organizations
: political parties
Socialist Party

: revolution
socialist revolutions

socialization

socialized medicine

: disadvantaged
socially disadvantaged

: organizations
societies
. female societies
. honorary societies
. ladies' aid societies
. missionary societies
. secret societies

society
. classless society
. matricentric societies
. matrilineal societies
. postindustrial society
. stateless societies

::: activities
:: social activities
: dances
society balls

::: occupations
:: scientific and technical occupations
::: occupations
:: professional occupations
::: occupations
:: education occupations
: scientists
sociobiologists

: social sciences
:: natural sciences
: biological sciences
sociobiology

: class
socioeconomic class

socioeconomic conditions

socioeconomic indicators
. economic indicators
. interest rates
.. prime interest rate
. social indicators
. unemployment rates
. urban indicators

: status
socioeconomic status

:: humanities
: linguistics
sociolinguistics

::: occupations
:: professional occupations
::: occupations
:: education occupations
: social scientists
sociologists

: social sciences
sociology
. medical sociology
. sociology of knowledge

:: social sciences
: sociology
sociology of knowledge

sociopathology

sodomy

::: arts
:: visual arts
: sculpture
soft sculpture

: sports
softball

: conservation
soil conservation

: renewable energy sources
: energy
solar energy

solitude

::: occupations
:: arts, entertainment, and media occupations
: performers
soloists

solstice

somnambulism

:::: arts
::: performing arts
:: music
: vocal music
songs
. ballads
. lieder
. lullabies
. nursery songs
. slave songs

::: humanities
:: literature
: poetry
sonnets

: men
sons

: in laws
sons in law

: twins
sororal twins

:: customs
: marriage customs
sororate

:: organizations
: women's organizations
sororities

space
. alternative spaces
. performance spaces
. personal space
. sacred space

:: natural sciences
: physical sciences
space sciences

:: cognitive processes
: perception
spatial perception

: skills
spatial skills

: education
special education

: groups
special interest groups

speculums

speech
. free speech

::: occupations
:: professional occupations
::: occupations
:: health care occupations
: therapists
speech therapists

speeches

spending

: bodies
sperm

:: technology
: reproductive technologies
sperm banks

: contraception
spermicides

: images of women
sphinx

spies

::: arts
:: visual arts
: craft arts
spinning

: women
: images of women
spinsters

:: workers
::: occupations
:: professional occupations
: religious workers
spirit guides

spirit possession

spirits
. ancestor spirits
. evil spirits
.. dybbuks
.. incubi
.. succubi

spiritual communication
. channeling
. divining
. fasting
. glossolalia
. meditation
. phrenology
. prayer
. psychic readings
. psychometry
. religious music
.. chants
.. gospel music
.. hymns
.. spirituals
. rites
.. bat mitzvah
.. domestic rites
.. fertility rites
.. funeral rites

(cont.)

spiritual communication (*cont.*)
.. initiation rites
.. purification rites
.. rites of passage
.. sacraments
... baptism
... confession
... confirmation
... holy communion
... holy matrimony
... last rites
... ordination
.... women's
ordination
.. votive rites
. sacred dance
. sacrifice
. trances

: feminism
spiritual feminism

::: workers
:::: occupations
::: professional occupations
:: religious workers
: mediums
spiritual mediums

spiritualism

:: workers
:::: occupations
:: professional occupations
: religious workers
spiritualists

spirituality
. female spirituality

:: spiritual communication
:::: arts
::: performing arts
:: music
: religious music
spirituals

spokespersons

: research
sponsored research
. federally sponsored research
. state sponsored research

sponsors

: abortion
spontaneous abortion

sports
. archery
. baseball
. basketball
. bicycling
. bowling
. canoeing
. contact sports
. crew
. cricket
. fencing
. field hockey
. football
. golf
. gymnastics
. ice hockey
. ice skating
. judo
. karate
. lacrosse
. mountaineering
. professional sports
. racquetball
. roller skating
. running
. sailing
. skiing
. soccer
. softball
. squash
. swimming
. tennis
. track and field
. volleyball
. weight lifting
. wrestling

: awards
sports awards

sports enthusiasts

: journalism
sports journalism

: officials
:: occupations
: arts, entertainment, and media
occupations
sports officials

:: occupations
: arts, entertainment, and media
occupations
sportscasters

: abuse
spouse abuse
. husband abuse
. wife abuse

spouse support

spouses
. corporate spouses
. former spouses
.. former husbands
.. former wives
. husbands
.. first husbands
.. former husbands
.. runaway husbands
. military spouses
. political spouses
.. First Ladies (historical)
.. governors' spouses
.. presidential spouses
. wives
.. cowives
.. first wives
.. former wives
.. runaway wives
.. wage earning wives
.. wives working outside
the home

: sports
squash

squatters

staff
. support staff

stamps
. food stamps

: testing
standardized tests

standards
. academic standards
. beauty standards
. job standards
. living standards
. male standards

starvation

the state

::: organizations
:: agencies
: public agencies
state agencies

: aid
state aid

:: programs
: assistance programs
state assistance programs

: courts
state courts

: employment
state employment

state formation

: government
state government

: legislation
state legislation

: regulations
state regulations

: religion
state religion

:: research
 : sponsored research
   state sponsored research

 : taxes
   state taxes
     . property taxes
     . sales taxes

 : society
   stateless societies

   states

 : data analysis
   statistical analysis

:: occupations
 : scientific and technical occupations
:: occupations
 : professional occupations
   statisticians

 : mathematics
   statistics

 : images of women
   Statue of Liberty

   statues

   status
     . cultural status
     . economic status
     . legal status
     . marital status
     . occupational status
     . political status
     . professional status
     . social status
     . socioeconomic status
     . status of women
     . tax exempt status

 : status
   status of women

 : workers
:: occupations
 : manufacturing occupations
   steelworkers

 : discriminatory practices
   steering

:: occupations
 : female intensive occupations
::: occupations
:: administrative support occupations
 : clerical occupations
   stenographers

 : children
   stepchildren

:: men
 : fathers
   stepfathers
     . gay stepfathers

:: women
 : mothers
 : images of women
   stepmothers
     . lesbian stepmothers

 : parents
   stepparents

   stereotypes
     . age stereotypes
     . racial stereotypes
     . sex stereotypes

   stereotyping
     . media stereotyping
     . sex role stereotyping

   sterility

 : birth control
   sterilization
     . eugenic sterilization
     . involuntary sterilization

   sterilization reversal
     . tubal ligation reversal
     . vasectomy reversal

. .. . Narrower term

stigmas

:: mortality
  : infant mortality
    stillbirth

    stimulants
      . caffeine

  : organizations
    stock exchanges

    stock markets

    stock options

:: occupations
  : marketing and sales occupations
:: occupations
  : financial occupations
    stockbrokers

::: facilities
  :: religious facilities
    : churches
      storefront churches

      stories

      storytelling

      straights

      strategies
        . career strategies
        . coping strategies
        . survival strategies

      stratification
        . social stratification
          .. racial stratification
          .. sexual stratification

      stream of consciousness

  : sexual harassment
    street harassment

::: arts
  :: performing arts
    : theater
      street theater

::: occupations
  :: marketing and sales occupations
    : vendors
      street vendors

      stress
        . occupational stress
        . psychological stress

      stress (physical)

:: activities
  : protest actions
    strikes

:: occupations
  : female intensive occupations
:: occupations
  : arts, entertainment, and media
      occupations
    strippers

  : discrimination
    structural discrimination

:: humanities
  : linguistics
    structural linguistics

  : unemployment
    structural unemployment

    structuralism

    struggles
      . liberation struggles

  : images of women
    strumpets

  : attitudes
    stubbornness

: :: ::: :::: ::::: Broader term

:: aid
: financial aid
   student financial aid
      . assistantships
      . fellowships
         .. postdoctoral fellowships
      . scholarships

: government
   student government

: housing
   student housing
      . dormitories
      . residence halls

: leadership
   student leadership

: loans
   student loans

: motivation
   student motivation

: quotas
   student quotas

   student recruitment

   students
      . adult students
      . college students
         .. women college students
      . commuting students
      . exchange students
      . foreign students
      . married students
      . part time students
      . pregnant students
      . reentry students
      . transfer students

   study abroad

: groups
:: activities
: educational activities
   study groups

subconscious

: culture
   subculture

: knowledge
   subjective knowledge

subjugation

: behavior
   submissive behavior

subordination
   . subordination of women

: subordination
   subordination of women

subsidies
   . educational subsidies
   . housing subsidies
   . transportation subsidies

: agriculture
   subsistence agriculture

: abuse
   substance abuse
      . alcohol abuse
      . drug abuse

: teaching
   substitute teaching

suburbs

:: occupations
: transportation occupations
   subway workers
      . train conductors

success

: images of women
:: spirits
: evil spirits
   succubi

: diseases
**sudden infant death
syndrome**

suffrage

: social movements
suffrage movements

suffragists

suicide
. suttee

superego

:: occupations
: education occupations
superintendents

:: women
: mothers
supermom

superstitions

: attitudes
supervisor attitudes

:: occupations
: administrative support occupations
supervisors

: images of women
superwoman

superwoman syndrome

:: activities
: social activities
suppers
. potluck suppers

: benefits
supplementary benefits

: groups
support groups

: staff
support staff

support systems

: courts
Supreme Court

:: occupations
: health care occupations
surgeons

: medical sciences
surgery
. cosmetic surgery
. plastic surgery
.. liposuction surgery
. psychosurgery
. reconstructive surgery

: medical procedures
surgical procedures
. caesarian section
. dilatation and curettage
. episiotomy
. hysterectomy
. male circumcision
. mastectomy
. oophorectomy
. tubal ligation
. vasectomy

: names
surnames
. birth name
. slave name

: surrogates
: families
surrogate families

: surrogates
:: men
: fathers
surrogate fathers

: surrogates
:: women
: mothers
surrogate mothers

surrogates
. legal guardians
. surrogate families
. surrogate fathers
. surrogate mothers

: strategies
survival strategies

survivors

: suicide
suttee

sweatshops

: sports
swimming

swooning

symbolism

symbols
. art symbols
. literary symbols
. religious symbols

: pregnancy
sympathetic pregnancy

: emotions
sympathy

: activities
symposia

:: facilities
: religious facilities
synagogues

synchrony

synergy

:: humanities
: linguistics
syntax

::: diseases
:: communicable diseases
: sexually transmitted diseases
syphilis

:: occupations
: scientific and technical occupations
:: occupations
: professional occupations
systems analysts

: theory
systems theory

: customs
taboos

:: cognitive processes
: perception
tactual perception

:: workers
::: occupations
:: manufacturing occupations
::: occupations
:: female intensive occupations
: clothing workers
tailors

talent

:: communication
: verbal communication
talk

:: activities
: shows
talk shows

tampons

: clothing
tank tops

::: arts
:: visual arts
: craft arts
tapestry

tarot

: fortune telling
tarot reading

: organizations
task forces

tattoos

: status
tax exempt status

: incentives
tax incentives

: laws
tax laws

tax reform

taxation

taxes
. federal taxes
. income tax
. property taxes
. state taxes
.. property taxes
.. sales taxes

::: occupations
:: transportation occupations
: drivers
taxi drivers

: fortune telling
tea leaf reading

tea pouring

tea rooms

:: activities
: educational activities
teach ins

:: occupations
: paraprofessional occupations
:: occupations
: female intensive occupations
:: occupations
: education occupations
teacher aides

: education
teacher education

: motivation
teacher motivation

: relationships
teacher student relationships

:: occupations
: professional occupations
:: occupations
: female intensive occupations
:: occupations
: education occupations
teachers

teaching
. substitute teaching

:: occupations
: education occupations
teaching assistants

team playing

:: activities
: social activities
teas

: images of women
teases

technical assistance

: education
technical education

: writing
technical writing

:: occupations
  : paraprofessional occupations
:: occupations
  : craft occupations
    technicians

    technology
      . appropriate technology
      . food technology
      . land use technology
      . reproductive technologies
        .. artificial insemination
        .. cloning
        .. embryo transfer
        .. fertility drugs
        .. in vitro fertilization
        .. sperm banks

  : development
    technology development

    technology transfer

  : clothing
    tee shirts

:: men
  : fathers
    teenage fathers

  : marriage
    teenage marriage

:: women
  : mothers
    teenage mothers

  : pregnancy
    teenage pregnancy

    teenagers
      . adolescents

  : communications
    telecommunications

    telecommuting

:: activities
  : conferences
    teleconferences

    teleconferencing

:: workers
  : operators
:: occupations
  : female intensive occupations
::: occupations
  :: administrative support occupations
    : clerical occupations
      telephone operators

      telephones

:: mass media
  : electronic media
    television
      . cable television
      . commercial television
      . educational television
      . public television

  : commercials
    television commercials

  : media coverage
    television coverage

:: occupations
  : arts, entertainment, and media
    occupations
      television personalities

  : social movements
    temperance movement

:: facilities
  : religious facilities
    temples

  : employment
    temporary employment

: housing
  temporary housing
  . crisis shelters
  . halfway houses
  . hostels

: workers
  temporary workers

  temptation

: images of women
  temptresses

: farming
  tenant farming

: sports
  tennis

: headaches
  tension headaches

  tenure

  tenure track

: illness
  terminal illness

  territoriality

  terrorism

  terrorists

: bias
  test bias

:: bodies
: genitals
  testicles

  testimony

  testing
  . aptitude tests
  . career interest inventories
  . competency based tests
  . examinations
  . intelligence tests
  . personality tests

(cont.)

testing *(cont.)*
  . psychological testing
  . standardized tests

:::: bodies
::: hormones
:: sex hormones
: androgens
  testosterone

  tests
  . blood tests
  . drug tests
  . virginity tests

: bias
  textbook bias

  textbooks
  . nonsexist textbooks

: design
  textile design

: industries
  textile industry

::: arts
:: visual arts
: craft arts
  textile making

  texts
  . female authored texts
  . sacred texts

::: humanities
:: theology
: feminist theology
  thealogy

:: arts
: performing arts
  theater
  . collaborative theater
  . drama
  .. comedy
  ... farce
  ... skits
  .. tragedy
  . experimental theater

(cont.)

theater (*cont.*)
. group developed theater
. improvisation
. musical theater
. street theater
. vaudeville

: criticism
theater criticism

: facilities
theaters

: humanities
theology
. feminist theology
.. thealogy
. liberation theology
. womanist theology

theory
. art theory
. economic theory
.. economic development
    theory
. exchange theory
. feminist theory
. game theory
. information theory
. labor theory of value
. literary theory
. management theory
. music theory
. network theory
. organizational theory
. political theory
. systems theory

: abortion
therapeutic abortion

:: occupations
: professional occupations
:: occupations
: health care occupations
therapists
. occupational therapists
. physical therapists
. psychotherapists
. speech therapists

therapy
. art therapy
. aversion therapy
. cathartic therapy
.. psychodrama
. chemotherapy
. diet therapy
. drug therapy
. electroconvulsive therapy
. family therapy
. feminist therapy
. gestalt therapy
. group therapy
. hormone therapy
.. estrogen replacement
    therapy
. music therapy
. physical therapy
. psychotherapy
. radiation therapy

: medical procedures
thermography

thinness

third world

:: bodies
: glands
thyroid gland

time

: management
time management

time use studies

tipping

titles

titles (nobility)
. baronesses
. countesses
. dames
. duchesses
. ladies (nobility)
. peeresses
. princesses
. queens

---

tobacco

: industries
tobacco industry

tokenism

tolerance

: images of girls
tomboys

:: occupations
: craft occupations
tool and die makers

::: occupations
:: arts, entertainment, and media
occupations
: singers
torch singers

totemism

: forms of affection
touching

:: occupations
: service occupations
:: occupations
: female intensive occupations
tour guides

toxemia

: diseases
toxic shock syndrome

toys

: sports
track and field

:: organizations
: unions
trade unions

trades
. retail trade
. skilled trades

: warfare
traditional warfare

traditions
. oral tradition
. religious traditions

: accidents
traffic accidents

:::: arts
::: performing arts
:: theater
::: humanities
:: literature
: drama
tragedy

::: occupations
:: transportation occupations
: subway workers
:: workers
::: occupations
:: transportation occupations
: railroad workers
train conductors

trainers

training
. assertiveness training
. childbirth training
. job training
.. on the job training
... apprenticeships
. leadership training
. management training
. sensitivity training
. skill training

:: facilities
: centers
training centers

: objectives
training objectives

traits
. personality traits

: spiritual communication
trances

:: drugs
: psychotropic drugs
tranquilizers

: income
transfer income

: students
transfer students

transference
. countertransference

: grammar
transformational grammar

transit systems

transitions

::: occupations
:: professional occupations
::: occupations
:: arts, entertainment, and media
occupations
: writers
translators

transportation
. air transportation
. public transportation
. rail transportation

: industries
transportation industry

: occupations
transportation occupations
. boat operators
. drivers
.. bus drivers
.. taxi drivers
.. truck drivers
. flight attendants
. heavy equipment operators
. movers
. pilots

(*cont.*)

transportation occupations
(*cont.*)
. railroad workers
.. train conductors
. road workers
. seafarers
. subway workers
.. train conductors

: subsidies
transportation subsidies

: sexuality
transsexuality

transvestites

trashing

::: occupations
:: service occupations
::: occupations
:: female intensive occupations
: agents
travel agents

:: humanities
: literature
travel literature

treatment
. mental health treatment

: ratification
treaty ratification

trends
. economic trends
. occupational trends
. population trends
. social trends

: marriage
trial marriage

trials (courtroom)

:: behavior
: sexual behavior
tribadism

: art
  tribal art

: customs
  tribal customs

  tribal markings

::: arts
:: performing arts
: music
  tribal music

  tricks

  trimness

::: occupations
:: arts, entertainment, and media
  occupations
: musicians
  troubadours

::: occupations
:: transportation occupations
: drivers
  truck drivers

: emotions
: attitudes
  trust

:: occupations
: volunteer occupations
  trustees

  tshiwila

:: medical procedures
: surgical procedures
  tubal ligation

: sterilization reversal
  tubal ligation reversal

: pregnancy
  tubal pregnancy

:: funding
: grants
  tuition grants

: credit
  tuition tax credit

  tumors
   . benign tumors
   . malignant tumors

  turnover rates

  tutoring

  twins
   . fraternal twins
   . identical twins
   . sororal twins

: families
  two income families

::: education
:: postsecondary education
: higher education
::: facilities
:: educational facilities
: colleges
  two year colleges

:: workers
::: occupations
:: manufacturing occupations
: printing workers
  typesetters

  typewriters

:: occupations
: female intensive occupations
::: occupations
:: administrative support occupations
: clerical occupations
  typists

:: art
: commercial art
  typography

  tyranny

ulcers

: medical procedures
ultrasound

umbilical cord

uncleanliness

uncles

unconscious

: achievement
underachievement

underdevelopment

: employment
underemployment

: degrees
undergraduate degrees
  . bachelors' degrees

: economy
underground economy

underground railroad

: clothing
underwear

:: occupations
 : managerial occupations
underwriters

: workers
undocumented workers

unemployment
  . structural unemployment
  . youth unemployment

unemployment compensation

: insurance
unemployment insurance

: socioeconomic indicators
unemployment rates

unfair labor practices

: kinship
unilineal kinship

union
  . consensual union

union membership

: organizations
unions
  . labor unions
  . trade unions

unisex

:: facilities
 : educational facilities
universities

: employment
unpaid employment
  . unpaid household labor

:::: resources
 ::: human resources
  :: labor force
   : unpaid labor force
  :: employment
   : unpaid employment
  :: labor
   : household labor
unpaid household labor

::: resources
 :: human resources
  : labor force
unpaid labor force
  . unpaid household labor

:: emotions
 : love
unrequited love

untouchables

: pregnancy
unwanted pregnancy

:::: health
  ::: physical health
    :: physical fitness
      : physical strength
        upper body strength

      : class
        upper class

      : families
        upper class families

      : mobility
        upward mobility

        urban areas
          . inner city
          . municipalities

      : development
        urban development

      : environment
        urban environment

      : socioeconomic indicators
        urban indicators

      : migration
        urban migration

  ::: occupations
    :: professional occupations
  ::: occupations
    :: education occupations
      : social scientists
        urban planners

      : planning
        urban planning

        urban renewal

        urbanization

    :: occupations
      : service occupations
        ushers

        uterus

: organizations
  utilities
    . electric utilities
    . gas utilities
    . public utilities
    . water utilities

: credit
  utility credit

: communities
  utopian communities

:: humanities
  : literature
    utopian literature

    utopias

  : rights
    uxorial rights

    uxoriousness

    uzr

    vacations

  : bodies
    vagina
      . hymen

  : images of women
    vagina dentata

    vaginal infections

  : orgasm
    vaginal orgasm

:: disorders
  : gynecologic disorders
    vaginismus

:: disorders
  : gynecologic disorders
    vaginitis

    value

    value systems

values
  . domestic values
  . personal values
  . religious values
  . social values

valuing children

: images of women
vampires

: images of women
vamps

:: crimes
  : property crimes
vandalism

:: medical procedures
  : surgical procedures
vasectomy

: sterilization reversal
vasectomy reversal

::: arts
  :: performing arts
    : theater
vaudeville

vegetarianism

veiling of women

: clothing
veils

:: occupations
  : marketing and sales occupations
vendors
    . street vendors

: capital
venture capital

:: occupations
  : financial occupations
venture capitalists

: ability
verbal ability

: abuse
verbal abuse

: communication
verbal communication
  . conversation
  . gossip
  . talk

::: development
  :: individual development
    : language development
verbal development

: benefits
veteran benefits

:: employment practices
::: policy
  :: corporate policy
    : hiring policy
veteran preference

veterans

:: occupations
  : professional occupations
:: occupations
  : health care occupations
veterinarians

veterinary sciences

viability

: sexual aids
vibrators

vice presidential office

:: occupations
  : managerial occupations
:: occupations
  : legal and political occupations
:: occupations
  : education occupations
vice presidents

::: services
:: human services
: social services
victim services

victimization

: crimes
victimless crimes

victims
. crime victims
. incest victims
. rape victims

:: arts
: media arts
video art

video display terminals

: games
video games
. computer games

videos
. music videos

: ratings
viewer ratings

:: organizations
: communes
village communes

violence
. domestic violence
.. marital violence
. lynching
. sexual violence
.. rape
... acquaintance rape
.... date rape
... domestic rape
... gang rape
... racist rape
... slave rape
.. sexual assault
. violence against children
. violence against women

: violence
violence against children

: violence
violence against women

violence in the media

: images of women
viragos

virgin birth

: images of women
Virgin Mary

virginity

: tests
virginity tests

: images of women
: images of girls
virgins

vision

visionaries

visions

: rights
visitation rights

:: occupations
: service occupations
::: occupations
:: female intensive occupations
: homemakers
visiting homemakers

::: occupations
:: health care occupations
::: occupations
:: female intensive occupations
: nurses
visiting nurses

::: occupations
:: education occupations
: scholars
visiting scholars

: arts
visual arts
. architecture
. cartoons
. collage
  .. femmage
. comic strips
. craft arts
  .. basketry
  .. beadwork
  .. ceramics
  .. china painting
  .. doll making
  .. flower painting
  .. lace making
  .. needlework
    ... crocheting
    ... embroidery
    ... knitting
    ... needlepoint
  .. pottery
  .. puppetry
  .. quilting
  .. rug hooking
  .. spinning
  .. tapestry
  .. textile making
  .. weaving
. decorative arts
. drawing
. engraving
. fiber art
. graphics
. metal art
. miniatures
. mural art
. painting
. photography
  .. fashion photography
. portraits
. poster art
. printmaking
. sculpture
  .. bas reliefs
  .. soft sculpture
. visual diaries

:: arts
: visual arts
::::: humanities
:::: literature
::: prose
:: nonfiction
: diaries
visual diaries

: disabilities
visual impairments
. blindness

:: cognitive processes
: perception
visual perception

:: measurements
: demographic measurements
vital statistics
. birth rates
. divorce rates
. fertility rates
. marriage rates
. mortality rates
. sex ratio

::: arts
:: performing arts
: music
vocal music
. choral music
. madrigals
. opera
. songs
  .. ballads
  .. lieder
  .. lullabies
  .. nursery songs
  .. slave songs

: aptitude
vocational aptitude

: education
vocational education

. .. . Narrower term

::: occupations
  :: health care occupations
::: occupations
  :: female intensive occupations
    : nurses
      vocational nurses

    : rehabilitation
      vocational rehabilitation

      voice

    : sports
      volleyball

:: organizations
  : nonprofit organizations
    voluntary organizations
      . private voluntary
        organizations

  : occupations
    volunteer occupations
      . chairpersons
      . community organizers
      . directors
      . trustees
      . volunteers
        .. docents

  : work
    volunteer work

:: occupations
  : volunteer occupations
:: occupations
  : service occupations
:: occupations
  : female intensive occupations
    volunteers
      . docents

    voluptuousness

    voter registration

    voting

  : behavior
    voting behavior

: records
  voting records

: rights
  voting rights

:: spiritual communication
  : rites
    votive rites

    vows
      . marriage vows
      . vows of obedience
      . vows of silence

    vows of chastity

: vows
  vows of obedience

  vows of poverty

: vows
  vows of silence

: emotions
  vulnerability

:: bodies
  : genitals
    vulva

  : female circumcision
    vulvectomy

  : discrimination
    wage discrimination

    wage earners
      . wage earning women
        .. wage earning mothers
        .. wage earning wives

:: women
:: wage earners
  : wage earning women
:: women
  : mothers
    wage earning mothers

:: women
:: spouses
: wives
:: women
:: wage earners
: wage earning women
wage earning wives

: women
: wage earners
wage earning women
. wage earning mothers
. wage earning wives

wage gap

wage increases

wage labor

wages
. back pay
. equal pay
. low pay

wages for housework

: images of women
: images of girls
waifs

: mourning
wailing

:: occupations
: service occupations
waiters

:: occupations
: service occupations
waiters' assistants

war

: crimes
war crimes

wards

warfare
. biological warfare
. guerrilla warfare
. nuclear warfare
. traditional warfare

:: occupations
: craft occupations
watchmakers

water

: management
water management

: pollution
water pollution

:: resources
: natural resources
water resources

:: organizations
: utilities
water utilities

wealth
. inherited wealth

wealth distribution

weapons

::: occupations
:: arts, entertainment, and media
occupations
: reporters
weather reporters

: craft artists
weavers

::: arts
:: visual arts
: craft arts
weaving

: ceremonies
wedding ceremonies

wedding nights

:: jewelry
: rings
wedding rings

: sports
weight lifting

:: cognitive processes
: perception
weight perception

:: occupations
: craft occupations
welders

welfare
. child welfare
. maternal and infant welfare
. public welfare
. social welfare

::: organizations
:: agencies
: social agencies
welfare agencies

:: social sciences
: economics
welfare economics

: fraud
welfare fraud

:: women
: mothers
welfare mothers

: programs
welfare programs

: reforms
welfare reform

: rights
welfare rights

welfare state

welfare system

wellness

:: workers
::: occupations
:: service occupations
::: occupations
:: female intensive occupations
: child care workers
wet nurses

: crime
white collar crime

: workers
white collar workers

: slavery
white slavery

: industries
wholesale trade industry

wicca

wicking

: men
widowers

: women
: images of women
widows

:: abuse
: spouse abuse
wife abuse

wigs

:: documents
: legal documents
wills

wisdom

witch burning

witch hunts

: persecution
witch persecutions

witchcraft

: women
: images of women
witches

withdrawal

: women
: spouses
wives
. cowives
. first wives
. former wives
. runaway wives
. wage earning wives
. wives working outside the
   home

:: women
: women working outside the home
:: women
:: spouses
: wives
**wives working outside the
home**

: power
woman power

the woman question

: images of women
woman the gatherer

: rights
woman's rights

womanhood

womanism

:: humanities
: theology
womanist theology

: writing
womanist writing

womanizers

womanspirit

womb envy

women
. actresses (historical)
. amazons
. assemblywomen
. baronesses
. battered women
. beauty queens
. brides
.. child brides
.. mail order brides
. businesswomen
. club women
. concubines
. congresswomen
. countesses
. courtesans
. crones
. dames
. daughters
. duchesses
. ethnic women
. fallen women
. First Ladies (historical)
. geishas
. governesses
. granddaughters
. grandmothers
. heroines (historical)
. holy women
. homeless women
. hostesses (historical)
. ladies (historical)
. ladies (nobility)
. laywomen
. lesbians
.. closeted lesbians
.. contact dykes
. medicine women
. midwives
.. lay midwives
. mistresses
. mothers
.. absentee mothers
.. birth mothers
.. den mothers
.. earth mother
.. foremothers

(cont.)

. .. . Narrower term   957

women (*cont.*)
   .. housemothers
   .. lesbian mothers
   .. mothers in law
   .. mothers working outside
       the home
   .. runaway mothers
   .. single mothers
   .. stepmothers
    ... lesbian stepmothers
   .. supermom
   .. surrogate mothers
   .. teenage mothers
   .. wage earning mothers
   .. welfare mothers
. nonorgasmic women
. nymphs
. older women
. ombudswomen
. peeresses
. princesses
. queens
. reentry women
. rural women
. seamstresses (historical)
. single women
. sisters
. spinsters
. wage earning women
   .. wage earning mothers
   .. wage earning wives
. widows
. witches
. wives
   .. cowives
   .. first wives
   .. former wives
   .. runaway wives
   .. wage earning wives
   .. wives working outside
       the home
. women identified women
. women in transition
. women living in poverty
. women of color
. women of valor
. women religious
   .. clergywomen

(*cont.*)

women (*cont.*)
   .. nuns
    ... mother superiors
   .. priestesses
    ... high priestesses
. women working outside the
   home
   .. mothers working outside
       the home
   .. wives working outside
       the home

women and

:: students
: college students
women college students

: women
women identified women

women in

women in development

women in politics

women in science

women in the military

: women
women in transition

: women
women living in poverty

: women
: people of color
women of color

: women
: heroes
women of valor

: business
women owned business

: women
:: workers
::: occupations
:: professional occupations
: religious workers
:: occupations
: female intensive occupations
women religious
. clergywomen
. nuns
.. mother superiors
. priestesses
.. high priestesses

: women
women working outside the home
. mothers working outside the home
. wives working outside the home

: art
women's art

: athletics
women's athletics

:: facilities
: centers
women's centers

:::: facilities
::: educational facilities
:: colleges
: single sex colleges
women's colleges

: culture
women's culture
. lesbian culture

: groups
women's groups
. professional women's groups

:: social movements
: women's movement
women's health movement

:: social sciences
:: humanities
: history
women's history

: language
women's language

: liberation
women's liberation

:: humanities
: literature
women's literature
. lesbian literature

:: mass media
: women's media
:::: mass media
::: print media
:: periodicals
: magazines
women's magazines

: mass media
women's media
. feminist publications
. women's magazines

: social movements
women's movement
. international women's movement
. women's health movement

::: arts
:: performing arts
: music
women's music

: networks
women's networks
. old girl networks

:::: spiritual communication
::: rites
:: sacraments
: ordination
women's ordination

. .. . Narrower term

: organizations
  women's organizations
    . feminist organizations
    . nongovernmental women's
       organizations
    . sororities

  women's pages

: rights
  women's rights

: roles
  women's roles

:: facilities
  : shelters
    women's shelters

: interdisciplinary studies
  women's studies
    . Black women's studies
    . Jewish women's studies
    . Latina studies
      .. Chicana studies

: images of women
  Wonder Woman

: workers
::: occupations
  :: craft occupations
    : construction occupations
      woodworkers

  word processing

  work
    . charitable work
    . church work
    . culture work
    . extension work
      .. home economics
          extension work
    . home based work
    . office work
    . piecework
    . shift work
    . social work
    . volunteer work

:: emotions
: alienation
  work alienation

: attitudes
  work attitudes

  work ethic

: experience
  work experience

: hazards
  work hazards
    . reproductive hazards at work

  work history

  work hours

: programs
  work incentive programs

: incentives
  work incentives

  work reentry

: programs
  work release programs

  work space

  work styles
    . management styles

  workaholics

  workers
    . blue collar workers
    . child care workers
      .. babysitters
      .. governesses
      .. nannies
      .. wet nurses
    . clothing workers
      .. dressmakers
      .. knitting machine
          operators
      .. milliners
      .. seamstresses (historical)
      .. sewers

                                        (*cont.*)

workers (*cont.*)

.. sewing machine
   operators
.. tailors
. construction workers
. extension workers
.. animatrices rurales
.. gramsevika
. factory workers
. farm workers
. food service workers
. foreign workers
. government workers
. health care workers
. home based workers
. hotel workers
. household workers
.. housecleaners
. laborers
. library workers
. longshore workers
. metalworkers
. migrant workers
. operators
.. boat operators
.. camera operators
.. computer equipment
   operators
.. data entry operators
.. heavy equipment
   operators
.. machine operators
... knitting machine
    operators
... sewing machine
    operators
.. press operators
.. telephone operators
. paralegal workers
. pieceworkers
. pink collar workers
. pregnant workers
. printing workers
.. bookbinders
.. compositors
.. press operators
.. printers
.. typesetters
. prison workers

(*cont.*)

workers (*cont.*)

. railroad workers
.. train conductors
. religious workers
.. clergy
... clergymen
... clergywomen
... ministers
... mullahs
... priests
... rabbis
.. evangelists
.. mediums
... physical mediums
... spiritual mediums
.. missionaries
.. prophets
.. seers
.. spirit guides
.. spiritualists
.. women religious
... clergywomen
... nuns
.... mother superiors
... priestesses
.... high priestesses
. road workers
. sanitation workers
. social workers
. steelworkers
. temporary workers
. undocumented workers
. white collar workers
. woodworkers

: class
   working class

: conditions
   working conditions

: parents
   working parents

   workplace

: nurseries
::::: facilities
:::: centers
::: day care centers
:: corporate day care centers
workplace nurseries

: activities
workshops

world views

worship
. goddess worship

: sports
wrestling

wrinkles

:: occupations
: professional occupations
:: occupations
: arts, entertainment, and media
   occupations
writers
. translators

writing
. creative writing
. descriptive writing
. feminist writing
. proposal writing
. technical writing
. womanist writing

: language
written language
. braille

yin

: adults
young adults

: children
young children
. infants
.. blue babies
.. premature infants
. preschool children

: employment
youth employment

: social movements
youth movement

::: services
:: human services
: social services
youth services

: unemployment
youth unemployment

::::: measurements
:: demographic measurements
: population growth
zero population growth

zoning

:: natural sciences
: biological sciences
zoology
. primate studies

SUBJECT GROUP
DISPLAY

Communications
Economics and Employment
Education
History and Social Change
International Women
Language, Literature, Religion, and Philosophy
Law, Government, and Public Policy
Natural Sciences and Health
Science and Technology
Social Sciences and Culture
Visual and Performing Arts

Communications

acting
actors
actresses (historical)
ad feminam
ad hominem
advertisements
advertising
advertising industry
advice columns
advice shows
amateur athletics
anchors
announcers
art shows
artists
arts, entertainment, and media
  occupations
athletes
athletics
authors
bomfog
book clubs
book conservation
book stores
braille
brainwashing
broadcasters
broadcasts
business correspondence
cable television
caricatures
cartoonists
cartoons
censorship
children's literature
circus performers
collegiate athletics
columnists
columns
comedians
comic strips
commentators
commercial television
commercials
communication

communication satellites
communications
communications equity
communications industry
community relations
compositors
computer games
computer terminals
computers
confidentiality
copyright laws
copywriters
correspondence
correspondents
critics
cultural sadism
curators
desex
designers
disinformation
disk jockeys
documentaries
editorials
editors
electronic cottage
electronic mail
electronic media
entertainers
entertainment industry
essayists
feminist publications
feminist writing
film directors
film producers
free speech
freedom of information
freedom of speech
freedom of the press
game shows
grapevine
graphics
hosts
hot lines
illustration
illustrators

image
imagery
images of girls
images of women
indoctrination
information
information and referral centers
information dissemination
information processing
information retrieval
information retrieval services
information services
information storage
information theory
intelligence agencies
interviewers
interviews
investigative journalism
jokes
journalism
journalists
libel
librarians
libraries
library science
library workers
licensing
magazines
mass media
media coverage
media portrayal
media reform
media stereotyping
models
motion picture industry
music industry
music videos
network ratings
networks (media)
news services
newsletters
newspapers
nonsexist language
opinion polls
oral history

oral literature
oral tradition
orators
oratory
performances
performers
periodicals
personal columns
political rights
popular culture
pornography
preservation
press coverage
print media
printers
printing workers
privacy
professional athletes
professional athletics
professional sports
program ratings
propaganda
proposal writing
protest actions
public art
public information
public interest
public opinion
public radio
public relations

public relations specialists
public speaking
public television
publications
publicity
publishers
publishing industry
queen for a day
radio
radio commercials
ratings
receptionists
records confidentiality
regulations
reporters
reviewers
roasts
satellite communications
satellites
satire
science reporting
serials
shows
sign language
sign painters
singers
soap operas
social entertaining
speeches
spokespersons

sports
sports enthusiasts
sports journalism
sportscasters
storytelling
talk shows
telecommunications
teleconferencing
telephone operators
telephones
television
television commercials
television coverage
television personalities
typesetters
typewriters
video display terminals
video games
videos
viewer ratings
violence in the media
women's athletics
women's magazines
women's media
women's pages
Wonder Woman
word processing
writers
writing

Economics and Employment

absenteeism
accountants
accounting
actors
actuarials
administration
administrative assistants
administrative costs
administrative support
  occupations
administrators
adventurers
advertising industry
aerospace engineering
affirmative action

affirmative action hiring
affirmative action officers
affirmative action suits
affluence
age discrimination
agencies
agents
agribusiness
agricultural economics
agricultural, fishing, and forestry
  occupations
agricultural industry
agriculture
aid
airline reservation agents

alimony
alternative employment
alternative work arrangements
ambition
anchors
anesthesiologists
animal caretakers
announcers
anthropologists
antiapartheid movement
antitrust legislation
applications
appointed officials
apprenticeships
arbitration

archaeologists
architects
armed forces
artisans
artists
arts, entertainment, and media
  occupations
aspirations
assessment
assistance programs
assumable mortgages
astronauts
astronomers
athletes
attendants
authors
automobile insurance
automobile repair
awards
babysitters
babysitting
back pay
bakers
balance of payments
bank tellers
bankers
banking industry
banks
barbers
barristers
bartenders
barter
basic human needs
beauticians
beauty parlors
bellhops
benefits
biologists
birth rates
black markets
blaming the victim
blue collar workers
boards
boards of directors
boat operators
bookbinders
bookkeepers
bourgeoisie
boycotts

bricklayers
bride price
broadcasters
budget cuts
budget deficits
budget process
budgeting
budgets
bullfighters
burnout
bus drivers
business
business correspondence
business ethics
business ownership
business security
businesses
businessmen
businesspeople
businesswomen
butchers
butlers
cabinetmakers
camera operators
candidates
capital
career break
career change
career choice
career counseling
career feminism
career ladders
career mapping
career opportunities
career planning
career satisfaction
career strategies
careers
carpenters
cartels
cartoonists
caste
chairpersons
charitable work
charities
charity balls
cheerleaders
chefs
chemical engineering

chemical industry
chemists
chief executives
child care leave
child care workers
child pornography
children living in poverty
church work
circus performers
civil engineering
civil service
class
class discrimination
class division
class identity
class ideology
classical economics
classless society
cleaners
cleaning
clergy
clergymen
clergywomen
clerical occupations
clerks
clothing workers
coaches
coal miners
coat checkers
cocktail servers
collective bargaining
college administrators
college presidents
colorists
columnists
comedians
commentators
commercial credit
commercial sex
community development
community organizers
community property laws
community relations
comparable worth
compensation packages
composers
compositors
compressed workweek
computer equipment operators

computer programmers
conductors
conflict of interest
conflict resolution
congressmen
congresswomen
consensus
construction industry
construction occupations
construction workers
consultants
consumer advocates
consumer behavior
consumer credit
consumer economy
consumer health organizations
consumer information
consumer installment loans
consumer power
consumer problems
consumer protection
consumerism
consumers
consumption
contacts
contract compliance
contract renewal
contracts
conventional mortgages
cooking
cooks
coordinators
copywriters
corporate day care centers
corporate law
corporate liability
corporate policy
corporate relocation policy
corporate responsibility
corporate spouses
corporate takeovers
corporations
correctional officers
correspondents
cosmetologists
cosmetology
cost benefit analysis
cost of living
costs

cottage industry
counselors
craft occupations
craftspersons
credentials
credit
credit fraud
critics
curators
dancers
data entry operators
data processing
data processors
deacons
deans
debt
decision making
deficits
deindustrialization
deliverers
demographic measurements
dental hygienists
dentistry
dentists
dependent benefits
dependent care
dependent care assistance
    programs
depreciation
desertion
designers
deskilling
detectives
devaluation
development
development specialists
dieticians
diplomats
directors
disability insurance
disadvantaged
disadvantaged groups
dishwashers
disk jockeys
divers
divestiture
division of labor
divorce rates
docents

domestic food production
drafters
dramatists
dress codes
dressing for success
dressmakers
dressmaking
drivers
dual career couples
dual career families
dual careers
dual economy
dutch treat
early retirement
earned income
earnings
earnings sharing
econometrics
economic anthropology
economic boycotts
economic class
economic counseling
economic depression
economic development
economic development models
economic development theory
economic equity
economic factors
economic geography
economic growth
economic history
economic indicators
economic policy
economic power
economic refugees
economic status
economic structure
economic theory
economic trends
economic value of women's
    work
economically disadvantaged
economics
economies of scale
economists
economy
editors
education occupations
educational benefits

educators
efficiency
elderly households
elected officials
electricians
electronic cottage
electronics industry
eligibility
employee benefits
employee development
employee records
employees
employer supported day care
employers
employment
employment agencies
employment opportunities
employment patterns
employment practices
employment schedules
endowments
engineers
engravers
entertainers
entertainment industry
entrepreneurs
equal credit
equal educational opportunity
equal employment opportunity
Equal Employment Opportunity
    Commission
equal pay
equal pay for equal work
equal pay legislation
equilibrium
equity funding
escorts
essayists
ethclass
ethologists
exchange rate
executive recruitment
executive search firms
executives
executors
experts
explorers
extension work
extension workers

extractive industry
factories
factory conditions
factory workers
faculty
failure
fair play
family economics
family farms
family finances
family income
family owned business
famine
farm workers
farmers
farming
farms
federal aid
federal assistance programs
federal budget
federal employment
feedback
female headed households
female intensive occupations
fertility rates
fifth world
film directors
film producers
finance
finances
financial arrangements
financial management
financial occupations
financial planners
financial planning
financial resources
financiers
fire fighters
firing
First Ladies (historical)
fiscal policy
fish sellers
fishers
flexible benefits
flexible career patterns
flexible work schedules
flight attendants
folk healers
folklorists

food
food for work
food industry
food marketing
food preparation occupations
food processing
food service workers
forced retirement
forecasting
foreign aid
foreign aid policy
foreign investment policy
foreign workers
fortune tellers
foster parents
foundations
four day workweek
fourth world
franchise
free enterprise
free trade zones
fringe benefits
fund raising
fund raising events
funding
gambling
game theory
gardeners
garment industry
gatekeeping
geishas
geneticists
geographic mobility
geologists
glass ceiling
glassmakers
glaziers
global assembly lines
global economy
governance
governesses
government workers
governors
gramsevika
grant proposals
grievance procedures
gross income
guaranteed income
guards

hairdressers
handmade
hat checkers
hazards
heads of families
heads of state
healers
health care workers
health economics
health maintenance
   organizations
heavy equipment operators
hierarchy
hiring policy
historians
home based business
home based careers
home based work
home based workers
home economics
home economics extension work
home economists
home improvement loans
homemaker service
homemaking
homeowners
homesteading
hostesses (historical)
hosts
hotel workers
housecleaners
housecleaning
household division of labor
household economics
household employment
household labor
household workers
householders
households
housekeepers
housekeeping services
housemothers
housepainters
housework
housing
housing costs
housing subsidies
human capital
human resources

humanists
illustrators
impact on children
impact on women
impoverishment of women
in kind contributions
incentives
income
income distribution
income generation
income tax
industrial classification
industrial conditions
industrial hygiene
industrial psychology
industrial relations
industrialization
industries
infant care
inflation
informal economy
informal sector
information scientists
inherited wealth
inspectors
institutional discrimination
instrument makers
insurance
insurance adjusters
insurance agents
insurance examiners
insurance industry
insured loans
interest rates
intern programs
international division of labor
international policy
internships
interpreters
inventors
investigations
investments
investors
ironers
ironing
janitors
jazz musicians
jewelry makers
job advertisements

job alienation
job candidates
job descriptions
job development
job discrimination
job evaluation
job ghettos
job hunting
job layoffs
job market
job performance
job placement
job recruitment
job responsibility
job retraining
job rewards
job satisfaction
job search methods
job security
job sharing
job skills
job standards
job training
jockeys
journalists
judges
jurors
knitting machine operators
labor
labor contracts
labor disputes
labor force
labor force participation
labor force rates
labor force statistics
labor market
labor policy
labor relations
labor saving devices
labor supply
labor theory of value
labor turnover
labor unions
laborers
lace making
laissez faire
land tenure
land use
landlords

landscape architects
launderers
laundry
lawyers
lay midwives
leadership roles
leadership skills
leadership training
legal and political occupations
legislators
letters of recommendation
liability
liability insurance
librarians
library workers
licensing
life insurance
limited liability
living standards
loans
longshore workers
low income families
low income households
low pay
lower class
lumber cutters
lyricists
machine operators
machinists
macroeconomics
magistrates
mail carriers
male dominated employment
male intensive occupations
mammies
management
management practices
management styles
management techniques
management theory
management training
managerial occupations
managers
manicurists
mannequins
manual labor
manufactured
manufacturers
manufacturing industry

manufacturing occupations
marital property reform
market research
marketing and sales occupations
markets
marriage rates
marriage tax
maternity benefits
maternity leave
maternity rights
mathematicians
mayors
mechanics
mediators
mentors
merchandisers
merchants
mergers
metalworkers
meteorologists
microeconomics
microinequities
midcareer change
middle class
middle managers
midwives
migrant workers
military budget
military personnel
military trade
milliners
millinery trade
minimum income
mining industry
ministers
minority employment
minority owned business
missionaries
mixed economy
modeling agencies
models
modernization
monetary incentives
monetary policy
money
money management
monopolies
moonlighting
mortality rates

mortgages
mothers working outside the
  home
movers
multinational banks
multinational corporations
multinational labor force
music industry
musicians
nannies
nationalization
naturalists
negotiation
negotiators
neoclassical economics
nepotism
net income
network theory
no fault insurance
nominations
nongovernmental women's
  organizations
nonprofit organizations
nontraditional employment
nontraditional work patterns
novelists
novices
nuclear engineering
nuns
nurse practitioners
nurses
nursing
nutritionists
obstetricians
occupational attitudes
occupational counseling
occupational diseases
occupational health and safety
occupational mobility
occupational mortality
occupational options
occupational patterns
occupational roles
occupational segregation
occupational sex segregation
occupational status
occupational stress
occupational therapists
occupational trends

occupations
office parties
office work
offices (facilities)
offshore production plants
old boy networks
old girl networks
ombudsmen
ombudswomen
on the job training
opera singers
operations researchers
operators
optometrists
orators
organizational behavior
organizational development
organizational objectives
organizational psychology
organizational theory
organizations
outplacement
outwork
paid employment
painters
palm reading
paperhangers
paralegal workers
paralegals
paramedics
paraprofessional occupations
paraprofessionals
parental leave
parole officers
part time employment
partners
paternity benefits
paternity leave
pauperization of women
pay equity
pension benefits
pension funds
performance appraisal
performers
perquisites
personal finances
personal management
personal service industry
personnel

personnel evaluation
personnel management
pharmaceutical industry
pharmacists
philanthropists
philosophers
photographers
physical therapists
physicians
physicians' assistants
physicists
physiologists
piecework
piecework labor policy
pieceworkers
pilots
pin money
pink collar workers
plasterers
playwrights
plumbers
podiatrists
poets
police officers
political action committees
political leaders
poll tax
population characteristics
population decline
population distribution
population growth
population trends
postindustrial society
potters
poverty
practical nurses
pregnancy disability
pregnancy discrimination
pregnancy leave
pregnant workers
preparatory schools
presidency
presidents
press operators
prestige
priests
prime interest rate
prime ministers
principals

printers
printing workers
printmakers
priorities
prison workers
private sector
private voluntary organizations
privatization
privilege
probation officers
productivity
professional and related services
   industry
professional athletes
professional athletics
professional awards
professional development
professional occupations
professional recognition
professional sports
professional women's groups
professionalism
professors
profits
proletariat
promotions
property taxes
prostitutes
protective clothing
protective service occupations
provosts
psychiatrists
psychics
psychologists
psychotherapists
public affairs
public officials
public relations
public relations specialists
public sector
public service
publishers
publishing industry
quality of work life
queen bee syndrome
quotas
rabbis
race equity
railroad workers

ranch hands
real estate
real estate agents
receptionists
recession
records
reduction in force
reentry students
reentry women
references
registered nurses
religious workers
relocation
rent
repairers
reporters
representatives
reproductive hazards at work
research assistants
research grants
researchers
restitution
resumes
retail trade
retail trade industry
retirement
retirement age
retirement benefits
reviewers
right to work
road workers
role models
roofers
runaway shops
rural development
rural planning
rural poverty
rural women
sales personnel
sales taxes
salesmen
saleswomen
sanitation workers
schedules
scholars
school personnel
school schedules
scientific and technical
    occupations

scientists
sculptors
seafarers
seamstresses (historical)
search committees
seasonal migration
second careers
secretaries
security guards
seed capital
seers
selection procedures
self employment
senators
seniority
service occupations
sewers
sewing
sewing machine operators
sex discrimination in
    employment
sex equity
sex industry
sexual division of labor
sexual harassment
sheriffs
shift work
sick leave
sign painters
singers
skill development
skill training
skilled trades
small business
social class
social indicators
social scientists
social work
social workers
socialized medicine
socially disadvantaged
society balls
socioeconomic class
socioeconomic conditions
socioeconomic indicators
socioeconomic status
sociologists
speech therapists
spending

spies
spokespersons
sports officials
sportscasters
spouse support
staff
standards
state aid
state assistance programs
state employment
statisticians
steelworkers
stenographers
stock exchanges
stock markets
stock options
stockbrokers
street vendors
strippers
structural unemployment
subsistence agriculture
subway workers
superintendents
supermom
supervisor attitudes
supervisors
superwoman
superwoman syndrome
supplementary benefits
support staff
surgeons
sweatshops
systems analysts
tailors
tax incentives
tax laws
tax reform
taxation
taxi drivers
tea pouring
teacher aides
teachers
team playing
technical assistance
technicians
telecommuting
telephone operators
television personalities
temporary employment

temporary workers
tenant farming
tenure
textile industry
therapists
third world
time management
time use studies
tipping
tobacco
tobacco industry
tokenism
tool and die makers
tour guides
trade unions
trades
traffic accidents
train conductors
trainers
training
transfer income
translators
transportation industry
transportation occupations
travel agents
trends
truck drivers
trustees
turnover rates
two income families
typesetters
typewriters
typists
underdevelopment
underemployment
underground economy
underwriters
undocumented workers
unemployment
unemployment compensation
unemployment insurance
unemployment rates
unfair labor practices
union membership

unions
unpaid employment
unpaid household labor
unpaid labor force
upper class
urban indicators
urban planners
ushers
vacations
value
vendors
venture capital
venture capitalists
veteran benefits
veteran preference
veterans
veterinarians
vice presidents
video display terminals
visiting homemakers
visiting nurses
vital statistics
vocational aptitude
vocational nurses
vocational rehabilitation
voluntary organizations
volunteer occupations
volunteer work
volunteers
wage discrimination
wage earners
wage earning mothers
wage earning wives
wage earning women
wage gap
wage increases
wage labor
wages
wages for housework
waiters
waiters' assistants
watchmakers
wealth
wealth distribution

weather reporters
weavers
welders
welfare economics
welfare state
white collar workers
wholesale trade industry
wives working outside the home
women and
women in
women in science
women in transition
women living in poverty
women owned business
women religious
women working outside the
  home
woodworkers
word processing
work
work alienation
work attitudes
work ethic
work experience
work history
work hours
work incentive programs
work incentives
work reentry
work release programs
work space
work styles
workaholics
workers
working class
working conditions
working parents
workplace
workplace nurseries
writers
youth employment
youth unemployment
zoning

Education

ability
abortion counseling
academia
academic ability
academic achievement
academic aptitude
academic aspirations
academic awards
academic disciplines
academic enrichment
academic failure
academic freedom
academic rank
academic standards
academies
accreditation
achievement
achievement need
administrative costs
administrators
admissions
admissions criteria
adolescents
adult basic education
adult education
adult illiteracy
adult learning
adult literacy
adult students
advice shows
advocacy
advocacy groups
advocates
affirmative action officers
affirmative action suits
African studies
Afro American studies
after school day care centers
after school programs
age
agricultural extension
alma mater
alternative employment
alternative programs
alternative schools

alumnae
alumnae/i
alumni
alumni/ae
amateur athletics
American Indian studies
American studies
antiilliteracy movements
applications
apprenticeships
aptitude tests
area studies
artistic ability
Asian American studies
Asian studies
assessment
assistance programs
assistantships
associate degrees
at risk populations
athletes
athletics
awards
bachelors' degrees
basic education
basic skills
bicultural education
bilingual education
bilingualism
Black colleges
Black women's studies
blaming the victim
blind review
boarding schools
boards
boycotts
busing
campus security
Canadian Indian studies
career awareness
career counseling
career education
career interest inventories
career ladders
career mapping

career opportunities
career planning
career strategies
case studies
certification
chairpersons
cheerleaders
Chicana studies
child care
child day care centers
children
children's groups
civic education
coaches
coeducation
cohorts
college administrators
college credits
college presidents
college students
colleges
collegiate athletics
community colleges
community education
community schools
commuting students
compensatory education
competence
competency based tests
compulsory education
computer games
consultants
contact sports
content analysis
contextual analysis
continuing education
continuing education units
contract compliance
contract renewal
cooperative education
coordinators
core curriculum
correspondence courses
counselors
course evaluation

course objectives
creches
credentials
credit by examination
credit for experience
credits
criminology
criteria
critical mass
cross cultural studies
curiosity
curriculum
curriculum integration
data analysis
data collection
day care
day care centers
deans
degrees
departments
desegregation
desegregation methods
desex
development studies
differences
diplomas
discrimination against the disabled
doctoral degrees
dormitories
double bind
dress codes
dropouts
drug rehabilitation
early childhood education
education
education occupations
educational activities
educational attainment
educational benefits
educational costs
educational equity
educational facilities
educational legislation
educational methods
educational objectives
educational opportunities
educational policy
educational programs

educational psychology
educational reform
educational subsidies
educational television
educationally disadvantaged
educators
elderhostel
elementary education
elementary schools
elementary secondary education
employer supported day care
enrollment
entitlement programs
equal educational opportunity
equal employment opportunity
equity funding
ethnic studies
evaluation criteria
exchange students
experiential learning
experimental design
experts
extension work
external degree programs
extracurricular activities
facilities
faculty
faculty retrenchment
family education
federal aid
federally sponsored research
fellowships
feminist scholarship
feminist studies
financial aid
finishing schools
foreign students
four year colleges
fraternities
free schools
future studies
futurism
gangs
gatekeeping
gay studies
gender studies
governing boards
graduate degrees
graduate education

graduation ceremonies
grants
grapevine
hand eye coordination
Head Start programs
health education
heterogeneous groups
hidden curriculum
high school equivalency programs
high schools
higher education
home economists
home schooling
home study
homogeneous groups
honorary degrees
honorary societies
housemothers
humanists
humanities
illiteracy
independent scholars
independent study
information processing
inservice education
institutional racism
institutional sexism
institutions
intellectuals
intelligence
intelligence tests
interdisciplinary studies
intermediate grades
intern programs
internships
interviews
intramurals
Jewish women's studies
job development
job retraining
job training
junior colleges
junior high schools
kindergarten
knowledge
laboratories
laboratory assistants
language aptitude

language development
language skills
latchkey children
Latin American studies
Latina studies
learning
learning differences
learning motivation
lesbian studies
letters of recommendation
libraries
library workers
life skills
lifelong learning
literacy
literacy campaigns
loans
locker rooms
married students
martial arts
masters' degrees
math ability
math avoidance
math confidence
measurement
medical education
men's studies
mentally handicapped
mentors
mergers
microinequities
midcareer change
middle aged adults
middle schools
military academies
minimum competencies
model programs
Near Eastern studies
networks
nondegree education
nondegree programs
nonformal education
nonsexist curriculum
nonsexist textbooks
nontraditional education
nonverbal ability
normal schools
norms
nurseries

nursery schools
nursing education
old boy networks
old girl networks
Olympic Games
open door admissions
outreach programs
Outward Bound programs
paraprofessionals
parent teacher organizations
parent teacher relationships
part time students
pedagogy
physical education
playgrounds
playgroups
postdoctoral fellowships
postsecondary education
pregnancy prevention
pregnant students
preparatory schools
preschool children
preschool education
preschools
primary education
primary schools
primate studies
principals
private colleges
private education
private schools
prizes
probation
probation officers
problem solving
professional degrees
professional education
professional recognition
professors
programs
progressive education
proposal writing
proprietary schools
protest actions
provosts
public colleges
public education
public schools
qualitative analysis

quantitative analysis
race, class, and gender studies
race equity
rank
reading
records
reentry students
reentry women
referees
references
regional studies
religious education
religious schools
remedial education
research
research assistants
research bias
research design
research grants
research methods
research problems
researchers
residence halls
residency programs
rhetoric
rights of the disabled
sampling
scholars
scholarship
scholarships
school age children
school attendance
school counseling
school desegregation
school health services
school integration
school personnel
school records
school schedules
school segregation
schools
science avoidance
scientific research
search committees
secondary education
secondary schools
selection procedures
seminaries
sex discrimination in education

sex equity
sex segregation
sexual harassment
single sex colleges
single sex education
single sex environments
single sex schools
skill development
skill training
Slavic studies
social development
social scientists
social studies
sororities
special education
sponsored research
sponsors
sports
standardized tests
standards
state aid
state sponsored research
statistical analysis
student financial aid
student government
student housing
student leadership
student loans
student motivation

student quotas
student recruitment
students
study abroad
subjective knowledge
substitute teaching
superintendents
talent
teach ins
teacher aides
teacher education
teacher motivation
teacher student relationships
teachers
teaching
teaching assistants
team playing
technical education
tenure
tenure track
test bias
testing
textbook bias
textbooks
time use studies
training
training centers
training objectives
transfer students

trustees
tuition grants
tuition tax credit
tutoring
two year colleges
underachievement
undergraduate degrees
universities
verbal ability
vice presidents
video games
visiting scholars
vocational aptitude
vocational education
vocational rehabilitation
women college students
women in
women in transition
women's athletics
women's centers
women's colleges
women's studies
young adults
young children
youth employment
youth movement
youth unemployment

History and Social Change

ableism
abolition
abortion
abortion movement
acquired immune deficiency
  syndrome
activism
activities
adventurers
advocacy
advocacy groups
advocates
affirmative action hiring
affirmative action officers
affirmative action suits
Afro American studies

ageism
alliances
amazons
anarcha feminism
androcentrism
androgyny
anima
animus
anti ERA movement
antiabortion movement
antiapartheid movement
antifeminism
antilynching campaign
antinuclear movement
antisemitism
antisuffrage movement

antiwar movement
archaeologists
arms control
art history
Asian American studies
associations
backlash
beauty
beauty contests
beauty standards
Beguinism
biculturalism
biologism
Black feminism
Black movement
Black power movement

Black women's studies
bloomers
bluestockings
body politics
bonding
book stores
boycotts
brassieres
breakfasts
brunches
bureaus
butch
campaigns
career feminism
castrating females
caucuses
census
centers
change
change agents
charitable work
charities
chattels
chauvinism
Chicana studies
children's culture
chivalry
circles
civil disobedience
civil rights
civil rights commissions
civil rights movements
class consciousness
class differences
class discrimination
classes
classism
clinics
clitoridectomy
closeted lesbians
clubs
coalition politics
coalitions
cocktail parties
collaboration
collectives
colloquia
colonialism
coming out

commissions
commissions on the status of
  women
committees
communes
communications equity
communities
community action
community organizers
companies
concentration camps
confederations
conferences
congresses
conscientious objection
consciousness raising
consciousness raising groups
consensus
consensus building
consent orders
conservative movement
consortia
constitution
contact dykes
conventions
cooperatives
coordinators
corporate responsibility
corsets
councils
coups
crisis centers
cross cultural feminism
cross cultural studies
cruising
cult of true womanhood
cultural constraints
cultural feminism
cultural imperialism
daughter right
deconstruction
demonstrations
desex
dinners
disadvantaged groups
discrimination against the
  disabled
discussion groups
dissent

diversity
divestiture
documents
domestic code
double discrimination
doubly disadvantaged
dowry
draft resistance
dress reform
ecofeminism
economic history
educational activities
enforcement
enfranchisement
enterprises
environmental movement
Equal Employment Opportunity
  Commission
equal opportunities commissions
equal rights legislation
equality
ethnic diversity
ethnic intimidation
ethnic neighborhoods
eugenic sterilization
eugenics
eunuchs
exhibitions
expositions
facism
faghag
false consciousness
family history
fat liberation
federations
female bonding
female chauvinism
female friendships
female sexual slavery
female societies
females
feminine mystique
feminine principle
feminism
feminist criticism
feminist ethics
feminist methods
feminist movement
feminist music

feminist organizations
feminist perspective
feminist scholarship
feminist studies
feminist theory
feminists
femme
fifth world
first wave feminism
foremothers
forums
fourth world
freedom
freedoms
friendships
frontier life
fund raising events
gay couples
gay culture
gay experience
gay fathers
gay literature
gay male couples
gay male culture
gay male experience
gay male literature
gay male marriage
gay marriage
gay men
gay pride
gay rights
gay stepfathers
gay studies
gay/straight split
gays
gender
gender bias
gender development
gender differences
gender diversity
gender gap
gender ideology
gender roles
gender studies
genocide
geographic mobility
girdles
global feminism
global security

goddesses
grass roots
gray power
gynarchy
gynocriticism
halfway houses
harems
harlots
heroes
heroines (historical)
herstory
heterosexism
heterosexual privilege
high heeled shoes
historians
histories
historiography
history
history of children
history of religion
holocaust
home life
homoeroticism
homophile movement
homophobia
homosexuality
human needs
human relations commissions
human rights
humanity
ideal woman
image
images of girls
images of women
industrialization
infanticide
inherited wealth
institutes
institutional discrimination
institutional racism
institutional sexism
institutions
integration
intellectual history
interdisciplinary studies
International Decade for
    Women
international perspective
international women's movement

internment
interracial relations
investigations
invisibility
job discrimination
kitchens
labels
labor history
labor movement
laboratories
ladies (historical)
ladies' aid societies
Latina studies
leadership
leagues
learned helplessness
lectures
left wing organizations
lesbian communities
lesbian couples
lesbian culture
lesbian experience
lesbian feminism
lesbian literature
lesbian marriage
lesbian mothers
lesbian movement
lesbian separatism
lesbian studies
lesbianism
lesbians
lesbophobia
liberal feminism
liberation
life histories
lingerie
literary canon
literary history
lobbying
lodges
lookism
lunches
lynching
machismo
mainstream feminism
mainstreaming
male bonding
male chauvinism
male feminists

male friendships
male homosexuality
male norms
males
mammies
man
manumission
marches
martyrs
Marxist feminism
mass actions
material culture
matricentric societies
meetings
men
men's liberation
men's movement
men's roles
men's studies
militance
minority experience
misandry
miscegenation
misogyny
missionary societies
mixers
mobility
moral reform
mother right
Ms
murderers
music history
mythology
myths
names
nationalist movements
nationalist revolutions
naturalization
new left
newsletters
nonaligned feminism
nonviolence
objectification
occupational sex segregation
odalisques
old girl networks
oppression
organizing
outlaws

panels
parades
parties
passing
patriarchy
peace
peace advocates
peace camps
peace movements
peasants
persecution
phallic criticism
philanderers
philanthropists
philanthropy
pickets
pioneers
pirates
planning meetings
plenary sessions
political activism
political activists
political economic systems
political philosophy
political theory
poll tax
polyandry
polygamy
polygyny
postindustrial society
potluck suppers
power
powerlessness
prayer meetings
prejudice
press coverage
private clubs
private sphere
professional women's groups
progress
protest
protest actions
protest music
protofeminism
psychoanalytic criticism
psychoanalytic feminism
public sphere
publicity
race bias

race, class, and gender studies
race equity
racial discrimination
racial equality
racial stratification
racism
radical feminism
radicals
rallies
raps
readings
rebellions
receptions
reformers
reproductive freedom
reproductive rights
resistance
retreats
revivals
revolution
revolutionary movements
right wing organizations
rights
riots
roles
a room of one's own
sacred space
sanctuaries
seclusion
seductresses
seminars
sensitivity training
separate spheres
separatism
seraglios
sessions
sex discrimination
sex discrimination in education
sex equity
sex segregation
sex/gender systems
sexism
sexual equality
sexual freedom
sexual liberation
sexual oppression
sexual politics
sexual revolution
shelters

sirens
sisterhood
sit ins
slave name
slave rape
slave songs
slavery
slaves
social action
social activities
social change
social clubs
social construction of gender
social construction of reality
social history
social issues
social mobility
social movements
social policy
social prohibitions
social reform
social trends
social welfare
socialist feminism
socialist revolutions
society
solstice
sororities
spiritual feminism
the state
Statue of Liberty
status of women

straights
strikes
structural discrimination
struggles
strumpets
study groups
subordination
subordination of women
suffrage
suffrage movements
suffragists
superwoman
superwoman syndrome
suppers
support groups
symposia
task forces
teach ins
teas
teleconferences
temperance movement
temptresses
theaters
tokenism
trashing
troubadours
tyranny
underground railroad
union membership
utopias
vamps
voter registration

voting behavior
voting rights
waifs
war
witch burning
witch hunts
witch persecutions
witches
woman power
the woman question
woman's rights
womanism
womanizers
women
women and
women in
women of color
women's groups
women's health movement
women's history
women's liberation
women's literature
women's media
women's movement
women's networks
women's organizations
women's rights
women's roles
women's studies
Wonder Woman
workshops
youth movement

International Women

adventurers
African studies
agribusiness
agricultural extension
aid
anarcha feminism
animatrices rurales
antiilliteracy movements
antinuclear movement
apartheid
appropriate technology
area studies
Asian studies

balance of payments
baronesses
basic human needs
Black feminism
black markets
braceros
Canadian Indian studies
capitalist economic development
   models
caste
chador
Chicana studies
civil disobedience

civil rights
class consciousness
collective farms
colonialism
communist economic
   development models
concubines
corporate policy
countesses
coups
cross cultural feminism
cross cultural research
cross cultural studies

cultural feminism
cultural groups
cultural heritage
cultural identity
cultural imperialism
cultural influences
culture
culture conflict
dames
decolonization
deindustrialization
demographic transition
developed nations
developing nations
development
development specialists
development studies
diplomacy
diplomats
domestic food production
dowry
dowry deaths
drug dumping
dual economy
duchesses
economic development
economic development models
economic development theory
economic sanctions
empowerment
ethnic studies
eugenic sterilization
eve teasing
exchange rate
exile
explorers
extension work
extension workers
famine
farms
female sexual slavery
feminism
fifth world
food for work
foot binding
foreign aid
foreign aid policy
foreign investment policy
foreign service

foreign students
foreign workers
fourth world
free trade zones
freedom from oppression
geishas
genocide
global assembly lines
global economy
global feminism
global security
global village
government agencies
gramsevika
grass roots
heads of state
housing
human rights violations
hunger
illegal immigrants
illiteracy
immigrants
immigration policy
impact on children
impact on women
impoverishment of women
income generation
indigenous populations
infant formula
informal economy
informal sector
intercaste marriage
international adoption
International Decade for
    Women
international division of labor
international marriage
international perspective
international policy
international relations
international trade policy
international women's movement
interpreters
ladies (nobility)
laissez faire
land reform
land settlement
land tenure
land use

Latin American studies
Latina studies
lesbian feminism
liberal feminism
liberation struggles
literacy
literacy campaigns
majority culture
malnutrition
manumission
maquiladora
Marxist economic development
    models
Marxist feminism
midwifery
midwives
migrant workers
migration
migration patterns
modernization
multinational banks
multinational corporation policy
multinational labor force
municipalities
nationalist movements
nationalist revolutions
nationality
Near Eastern studies
negotiators
nongovernmental organizations
nongovernmental women's
    organizations
nutrition
offshore production plants
oil industry
oppression
pariahs
parliaments
peace advocates
peace movements
peasants
peeresses
piecework
piecework labor policy
plantations
political asylum
political prisoners
political refugees
political rights

political sanctions
political systems
population control
population planning
population policy
presidents
prime ministers
princesses
private voluntary organizations
property confiscation
prostitutes
psychoanalytic feminism
purdah
queens
radical feminism
refugees
regional studies
religious refugees
religious sanctions
relocation
revolutionary movements
right to work
runaway shops
rural areas
rural conditions
rural development

rural living
rural migration
rural planning
rural poverty
rural resettlement
rural women
sanctions
sanitation
seasonal migration
seclusion
sex industry
sex tourism
Slavic studies
slums
small business
socialist economic development
   models
socialist feminism
socialist revolutions
spies
starvation
state formation
state sponsored research
street vendors
subsistence agriculture
suttee

technical assistance
technology transfer
terrorism
terrorists
third world
titles (nobility)
tribal markings
underdevelopment
undocumented workers
unpaid household labor
untouchables
urban areas
urban development
urban migration
urban renewal
veiling of women
vendors
vice presidents
village communes
virginity tests
water
water management
water pollution
water resources
women in development
yin

Language, Literature, Religion, and Philosophy

abstinence
abstract reasoning
Adam
advice columns
aesthetics
allegory
altruism
ambiguity
American studies
ancestor spirits
ancestors
angel in the house
angels
ankh
anonymous
anthropomorphism
antisemitism
antithesis
applied linguistics

Armageddon
artists
artists' books
arts
arts, entertainment, and media
   occupations
asceticism
astrology
authors
autobiography
ballads
baptism
bat mitzvah
belief systems
betrothal
bilingualism
bioethics
biography
biological determinism

birth name
book clubs
braille
burial
burlesque
business ethics
canon
canonization
cathedrals
celebrations
celibacy
ceremonies
channeling
chants
chastity
children's literature
chivalry
choirs
chronicles

church work
churches
Cinderella
circular reasoning
civil religion
cleanliness
clergy
clergymen
clergywomen
cliches
comedy
communication
communication styles
comparative religion
conceptual errors
confession
confirmation
conflict of interest
congregations
contextual analysis
convents
conversation
correspondence
cosmology
courage
courtly love
covens
creation myths
creative thinking
creative writing
criticism
critics
crones
crystal ball gazing
cult of the virgin
cults
culture work
deacons
death penalty
debutantes
deconstruction
deity
descriptive linguistics
descriptive writing
devil
dialects
diaries
dichotomy
discipline

discourse
discriminatory language
divine kingship
divining
divinity
documents
dogma
dogmatism
domestic code
domestic rites
domestic values
drama
dramatists
dreams
dualism
dybbuks
earth mother
l'ecriture feminine
ecumenism
editors
elegies
end time thinking
epics
epigrams
epistemology
epithets
equality
erotic literature
erotica
essayists
essays
essentialism
ethics
etiquette
eulogies
evangelists
Eve
evil
evil spirits
excommunication
expiation
fables
fairy tales
faith
faith communities
faith healers
fallen women
false dichotomies
false generics

fantasies
farce
faulty generalization
female authored texts
female spirituality
feminine principle
feminist criticism
feminist ethics
feminist publications
feminist scholarship
feminist theology
feminist writing
feminists
femmes fatales
fiction
fictional characters
figurative language
folk healers
folk literature
folklorists
forgiveness
forms of address
fortune telling
freedom of assembly
freedom of worship
fundamentalism
futurism
Garden of Eden
gay literature
gay male literature
gender marking
generative grammar
generic pronouns
gestures
glossolalia
God the father
goddess worship
goddesses
gods
gossip
grammar
greed
gynocriticism
hagiography
haiku
he/man language
healers
healing
heresies

heretics
hermeneutics
heroes
heroines (historical)
high priestesses
historical linguistics
histories
history of religion
holy communion
holy matrimony
holy men
holy women
homilies
honesty
house churches
humanists
humanitarianism
humanities
humor
hyphenated names
iconography
icons
ideology
illiteracy
illustration
imagery
images of girls
images of women
imagination
immaculate conception
immorality
impregnation
impurity
incarnation
incubi
informal language
initiation rites
integrity
interruptions
invisibility
irony
irrigation
isolation
jargon
Jewish women's studies
jokes
journals
keening
kinesics

knowledge
laity
language
language aptitude
language development
language skills
language structure
last rites
laying on of hands
laymen
laywomen
legends
lesbian literature
letter writers
letters
liberation theology
librettos
lies
Lilith
limericks
linguistic sexism
linguistics
listening
literacy
literary canon
literary criticism
literary history
literary symbols
literary theory
literature
liturgies
logic
logical thinking
Lolita
love
loyalty
lying
lyric poetry
madonna
man
marianismo
marriage ceremonies
marriage vows
martyrdom
martyrs
masculine pronouns
matronymy
meditation
mediums

memoirs
menstrual taboos
mermaids
metaphors
metaphysics
mikveh
mind
mind/body split
ministers
miracles
misogyny
missionaries
monasteries
monasticism
monotheism
moral development
moral majority
moral reasoning
moral reform
morality
morphology
mosques
mother earth
mother goddess
mother superiors
mother tongue
Mother/Father God
mullahs
mysteries
mysticism
mythology
names
naming
narratives
native healers
nature
nonfiction
nonsexist language
nonsexist literature
nonverbal language
novelists
novellas
novels
novices
novitiates
nuns
nymphs
observance
odes

oral history
oral literature
oral tradition
orators
oratory
ordination
Ouija boards
pacifism
palm reading
pantheon
parables
paradise
parody
passages
patience
patriarchal language
patriarchal religion
patriotism
patronymy
pen name
pen pals
penance
performances
personal correspondence
personal narratives
phallic criticism
phallocentrism
phallogocentrism
phallus
phenomenology
philosophers
philosophy
phonology
phrenology
physical mediums
plays
playwrights
pluralism
poetry
poets
polemics
political philosophy
popular culture
poststructuralism
prayer
preaching
predestination
prefixes
priestesses

priests
printers
procreation
profanity
programming languages
pronoun envy
pronouns
prophecy
prophets
proposal writing
prose
proverbs
pseudonyms
psychic readings
psychics
psychoanalytic criticism
psycholinguistics
psychometry
publishers
pulp fiction
puns
purification rites
purists
purity
rabbis
racial equality
raconteurs
rationality
reason
rebirth
reincarnation
religion
religions
religious beliefs
religious education
religious ethics
religious experience
religious facilities
religious groups
religious influences
religious language
religious law
religious literature
religious movements
religious music
religious orders
religious pluralism
religious practices
religious reforms

religious refugees
religious repression
the religious right
religious sanctions
religious symbols
religious traditions
religious values
religious workers
retreats
reviewers
rhetoric
rites
rites of passage
romances
sacraments
sacred dance
sacred ideology
sacred space
sacred texts
sacrifice
saints
salons
salvation
satire
science fiction
scripts
seances
sects
secularization
seduction
seductresses
seers
self denial
semantics
seminaries
semiotics
separation of church and state
sermons
sexist language
sexual equality
shamans
short stories
shunning
sign language
silence
sin
sirens
skits
slang

slapstick
slave name
snakes
Snow White
social dialects
social reform
sociolinguistics
solstice
sonnets
sphinx
spirit guides
spirit possession
spirits
spiritual communication
spiritual feminism
spiritual mediums
spiritualism
spiritualists
spirituality
state religion
storefront churches
stories
storytelling
stream of consciousness
structural linguistics
structuralism
subjective knowledge
succubi
superstitions
suttee
symbolism
symbols
synagogues
syntax
talk
tarot

tarot reading
tea leaf reading
technical writing
temperance movement
temples
temptation
temptresses
texts
thealogy
theology
titles
tolerance
totemism
traditions
tragedy
trances
transformational grammar
transitions
translators
travel literature
troubadours
trust
uncleanliness
union
unrequited love
utopian communities
utopian literature
value systems
values
vampires
verbal abuse
verbal communication
verbal development
victims
virgin birth
Virgin Mary

virgins
visionaries
visions
visual diaries
voice
votive rites
vows
vows of chastity
vows of obedience
vows of poverty
vows of silence
wailing
wedding ceremonies
wicca
wisdom
witch burning
witchcraft
witches
woman's rights
womanism
womanist theology
womanist writing
womanspirit
women of valor
women religious
women's culture
women's language
women's literature
women's magazines
women's ordination
world views
worship
writers
writing
written language
yin

Law, Government, and Public Policy

abortion
abortion clinics
abortion laws
abortion rights
adoptive parents
advocacy
advocacy groups
advocates
affirmative action

affirmative action suits
age discrimination
age of consent
agencies
aid
alienation of affection
alimony
all volunteer military force
alternative programs

anlu
annulment
anti ERA movement
antifeminism
antilynching campaign
antitrust legislation
apartheid
appointed officials
appropriations

arbitration
arms control
arson
assault
assemblymen
assemblywomen
assistance programs
at risk populations
authoritarianism
back pay
balance of payments
baronesses
barrier free access
barristers
bastards
battered women
battlefields
bigamy
birth fathers
birth mothers
birth parents
black markets
blaming the victim
block grants
blockbusting
boards of directors
boycotts
brothels
budget cuts
budget deficits
budget process
budgeting
budgets
bureaucracy
burglaries
busing
candidates
census
child care leave
child care licensing
child care policy
child custody
child labor
child neglect
child support
children's rights
citizen groups
citizenship
city government

civic education
civil disobedience
civil law
civil lawsuits
civil liberties
civil religion
civil rights
civil rights commissions
civil rights legislation
civil service
class action suits
class ideology
clerks
colonialism
commissions on the status of
  women
communism
Communist Party
community action
community property laws
community responsibility
comparable worth
compromise
concentration camps
conflict of interest
conflict resolution
Congress
congressional hearings
congressmen
congresswomen
consensual union
consensus building
consent orders
conservatives
constitution
consumer protection
contract compliance
contracts
copyright laws
corporate law
correctional officers
correctional rehabilitation
corruption
countesses
county courts
county government
coups
court cases
court decisions

courts
coverture
credit fraud
crime
crime prevention
crime victims
crimes
crimes against children
crimes against the elderly
crimes against women
crimes of honor
crimes of passion
criminal abortion
criminal justice
criminal law
criminal lawsuits
criminals
criminology
cultural imperialism
curfew
custodial parents
custody decrees
dames
day care
day care centers
death certificates
death penalty
debt
declining neighborhoods
decolonization
defamation
deficits
deinstitutionalization
delegates
democracy
Democratic Party
dependent care
desegregation
desegregation methods
desirable neighborhoods
detectives
diplomacy
diplomats
disarmament
disclosure laws
discrimination against the
  disabled
discrimination laws
discriminatory legislation

discriminatory practices
disinformation
distributive justice
divine kingship
divorce decrees
divorce laws
domicile rights
drinking prohibition
duchesses
due process
earnings sharing
economic equity
economic sanctions
economic status
economic theory
economics
educational equity
educational legislation
educational policy
educational subsidies
elected officials
election campaigns
elections
electric utilities
enforcement
enfranchisement
enlisted personnel
entitlement programs
equal access
Equal Employment Opportunity
   Commission
equal opportunities commissions
equal opportunity
equal pay legislation
equal protection under the law
equal rights
equal rights legislation
equity
ethnic intimidation
ethnic neighborhoods
executors
family courts
family policy
family rights
famine
father daughter incest
father son incest
federal agencies
federal aid

federal assistance programs
federal budget
federal courts
federal employment
federal government
federal legislation
federal regulations
federal taxes
federally sponsored research
financial aid
financial arrangements
fire prevention
food stamps
foreign aid
foreign aid policy
foreign service
fraud
free speech
freedom
freedom from oppression
freedom of assembly
freedom of choice
freedom of information
freedom of the press
freedom of worship
freedoms
gangs
gas utilities
gay rights
gender gap
ghettos
global security
government
government agencies
government appointments
government workers
governors
governors' spouses
gray power
guerrilla warfare
gun control laws
heads of state
health care legislation
health insurance
hearings
homeless
homemaker rights
hostels
House of Representatives

housing
housing costs
housing discrimination
housing subsidies
human relations commissions
human rights
human rights violations
ideology
illegal immigrants
immigration
immigration policy
immigration quotas
immorality
impact on children
impact on women
in vitro fertilization
incarceration
incest
incest victims
income tax
independence
inequality
infant care
influence
inheritance rights
inner city
inspectors
institutional racism
institutional sexism
institutions
insurance
insurance fraud
integration
intelligence agencies
International Decade for
   Women
international policy
international relations
international trade policy
internment
interpreters
interracial adoption
investigations
judges
judicial appointments
judicial attitudes
judicial process
judiciary
judiciary system

juries
jurors
jury duty
justice
juvenile courts
juvenile delinquency
juvenile justice system
juvenile offenders
juvenile prostitution
kidnapping
labor disputes
labor law reform
labor legislation
labor policy
ladies (nobility)
laissez faire
land rights
landlords
larceny
law
law enforcement
laws
lawsuits
lawyer client relationships
lawyers
leadership roles
legal advocates
legal aid services
legal and political occupations
legal cruelty
legal documents
legal guardians
legal responsibility
legal services
legal settlements
legal status
legal system
legislation
legislators
legislatures
legitimacy
legitimization of children
liability
libel
liberals
Libertarian Party
licenses
licensing
lobbying

local government
local legislation
local politics
loyalty oaths
magistrates
majority rule
marital property reform
marriage and family law
marriage licenses
maternity leave
maternity rights
matricide
mayors
mediation
mediators
Medicaid
Medicare
mikiri
militarism
military
military academies
military budget
military combat
military defense
military dependents
military draft
military enlistment
military personnel
military rank
military recruitment
military spouses
military trade
minimum wage legislation
minor parties
monetary policy
moral majority
mother daughter incest
mother son incest
multinational corporation policy
municipalities
murder
murderers
name rights
national health insurance
National Health Service (Great
    Britain)
national security
nationalism
nationalist movements

nationalist revolutions
nationality
nationalization
naturalization
negotiation
negotiators
neighborhoods
new left
nominations
noncustodial parents
nongovernmental organizations
nuclear disarmament
nuclear free zones
nuclear warfare
officials
ombudsmen
ombudswomen
opinion polls
organized crime
pacifism
paralegal workers
paralegals
parental leave
parental rights
parliaments
parole officers
patents
paternity leave
paternity rights
paternity suits
patriotism
pay equity
peace advocates
peace camps
peace movements
peeresses
piecework labor policy
planning
pluralism
polemics
police officers
policy
policy making
political action
political action committees
political activism
political activists
political anthropology
political aspirations

political asylum
political candidates
political conventions
political economic systems
political ethics
political ideology
political influence
political music
political office
political oppression
political participation
political parties
political philosophy
political power
political prisoners
political refugees
political representation
political repression
political rights
political sanctions
political spouses
political status
political systems
political theory
politics
poll tax
population planning
population policy
populism
pornography
power structure
pregnancy discrimination
pregnancy leave
presidency
presidential office
presidential spouses
presidents
press coverage
pressure groups
prevention
princesses
prison workers
prisoners
prisoners of war
prisons
privacy
privacy rights
private agencies
private sphere

privatization
probation
probation officers
process
prochoice
propaganda
property confiscation
property crimes
property laws
property rights
property settlements
property taxes
protective legislation
protective service occupations
psychological repression
public accommodations
public affairs
public agencies
public assistance
public health
public housing
public interest
public officials
public opinion
public policy
public policy programs
public sector
public service
public sphere
public utilities
public welfare
publicity
punishment
queens
quotas
race equity
ratification
recidivism
records
records confidentiality
redlining
reformatories
reforms
refugees
regulations
religious pluralism
religious repression
the religious right
religious sanctions

representation
representatives
reproductive freedom
reproductive rights
Republican Party
resistance
restitution
restraining orders
revolutionary movements
rhetoric
right to die
right to know legislation
right wing organizations
rights
rights of the disabled
riots
runaway fathers
runaway husbands
runaway mothers
runaway wives
runaways
rural planning
rural resettlement
safe sex
sales taxes
sanctions
security
security guards
segregated housing
Senate
senators
sentencing
separate spheres
separation agreements
separation of church and state
sex crimes
sex equity
sexual harassment
sexual violence
sheriffs
shoplifting
slum landlords
smoking prohibition
social agencies
social issues
social legislation
social policy
Social Security
socialism

Socialist Party
socialist revolutions
socialized medicine
special interest groups
spies
spokespersons
sponsored research
spouse support
the state
state agencies
state aid
state assistance programs
state courts
state employment
state formation
state government
state legislation
state regulations
state religion
state sponsored research
state taxes
stateless societies
states
steering
strikes
student housing
subsidies
suffrage
Supreme Court
survivors
tax exempt status
tax incentives
tax laws

tax reform
taxation
taxes
temporary housing
terrorism
terrorists
testimony
third world
titles (nobility)
traditional warfare
transfer income
transit systems
transportation subsidies
treaty ratification
trials (courtroom)
tyranny
urban development
urban planners
urban planning
urban renewal
utilities
utility credit
uxorial rights
valuing children
vandalism
veteran preference
veterans
vice presidential office
vice presidents
victim services
victimization
victimless crimes
virginity tests

visitation rights
voter registration
voting
voting records
voting rights
vows
war
war crimes
wards
warfare
water utilities
wealth distribution
weapons
welfare
welfare agencies
welfare fraud
welfare mothers
welfare programs
welfare reform
welfare rights
welfare state
welfare system
white collar crime
wills
women in development
women in politics
women in the military
women's rights
work incentive programs
work release programs
zero population growth
zoning

Natural Sciences and Health

ableism
abortifacient agents
abortion
abortion clinics
abortion counseling
abstinence
accidental death
accidents
acne
acquired immune deficiency
  syndrome
addiction

advice shows
aerobic exercise
aging
agoraphobia
alcohol abuse
alcoholism
amateur athletics
amenorrhea
amniocentesis
anal sex
anatomy
androgens

anemia
anesthesia
anesthesiologists
animal behavior
animal caretakers
animals
anorexia nervosa
anthropometry
antidepressant drugs
antisepsis
aphrodisiacs
appetite depressants

archery
arousal
art therapy
artificial insemination
asbestos
athletes
athletics
auditory perception
autism
aversion therapy
basal body temperature
baseball
basketball
benign tumors
bestiality
bicycling
biochemistry
bioethics
biofeedback
biological clock
biological determinism
biological influences
biological sciences
biological warfare
biologism
biologists
biology
biopsy
birth certificates
birth control
birth defects
birth fathers
birth mothers
birth parents
birthing
birthing centers
birthing rooms
blindness
blood
blood tests
blue babies
bodies
body building
body hair
body image
body odor
bondage
bonding
botany

bottle feeding
bowling
boy preference of parents
boys
brain
brassieres
breast cancer
breast diseases
breast examination
breast feeding
breast implants
breast prostheses
breast pumps
breast self examination
breasts
bulimia
buttocks
caesarian section
caffeine
calcium deficiency
cancer
canoeing
carcinogens
cardiovascular diseases
care
caregivers
castration
castration complex
cellulite
cervical cancer
cervical caps
cervical mucus
cervix
chefs
chemistry
chemotherapy
childbearing
childbearing age
childbirth
childbirth training
childless couples
chiropodists
chiropractors
chromosome disorders
clamydia
cleanliness
cleavage
climacteric
clinical trials

clinics
clitoral orgasm
clitoris
cloning
clothing
cocaine
codependency
coitus interruptus
collegiate athletics
color perception
colostrum
communicable diseases
community care
community health services
complexes
complexion
compulsory heterosexuality
conception
conditioning
condoms
consumer health organizations
contact sports
contraception
cooking
cooks
corsets
cosmetic surgery
cosmetics
crew
cricket
crying
cunnilingus
cysts
dancers
data analysis
data collection
daughter right
deafness
death and dying
death certificates
defloration
deinstitutionalization
delayed parenthood
delivery rooms
dental hygienists
dentistry
dentists
deodorants
dependent care

depilatories
Depo Provera
depression
depth perception
desire
development
developmental disabilities
diabetes
diagnoses
diaphragms
diet pills
diet therapy
dietetics
diethylstilbestrol
dieticians
dieting
diets
differently abled
dilatation and curettage
disabilities
disability insurance
disabled
discrimination against the
    disabled
disease prevention
diseases
disorders
diuretics
donors
dreams
drinking
drug abuse
drug addiction
drug dumping
drug overdoses
drug rehabilitation
drug side effects
drug tests
drug therapy
drug use
drugs
dysmenorrhea
dysphoria
early childbearing
eating disorders
ectopic pregnancy
ego
ejaculation
electroconvulsive therapy

electrolysis
embryo transfer
embryology
embryos
emergency medical services
emotional abuse
emotions
endometriosis
environmental health
environmental medicine
epidemiology
episiotomy
eroticism
essentialism
estradiol
estrogen replacement therapy
estrogens
estrus
ethology
eugenic sterilization
eugenics
eunuchs
evolution
exercise
exhibitionism
experimental design
expressing milk
extended care facilities
eyeglasses
face lifts
faces
fainting
faith healers
fallopian tubes
family medicine
family planning
family practitioners
family recipes
family therapy
famine
fasting
fat liberation
fat oppression
father daughter incest
father son incest
fathering
fatigue
fellatio
female bonding

female circumcision
female hypersexuality
female Oedipus complex
female sexuality
females
feminist therapy
fencing
fertility
fertility drugs
fertilization
fetal alcohol syndrome
fetal monitoring
fetuses
fibrocystic disease
field hockey
flowers
folk healers
folk medicine
food
food preparation
food preparation occupations
foot binding
football
foreplay
forms of affection
fraternal twins
G spot
gardeners
gardens
gay male experience
gay male relationships
gay relationships
gender development
gender identity
gender roles
general anesthesia
genetic counseling
genetic defects
genetic determinants
genetic engineering
genetic screening
geneticists
genetics
genital herpes
genital mutilation
genitals
geriatrics
gestation period
girdles

girl preference of parents
girls
glands
golf
gonorrhea
group behavior
group sex
gymnastics
gynecologic disorders
gynecology
gynocologists
hair
hair loss
hair removal
hand eye coordination
hazards
headaches
healers
healing
health
health advocates
health behavior
health care
health care costs
health care delivery
health care facilities
health care legislation
health care occupations
health care policy
health care providers
health care services
health care utilization
health care workers
health cooperatives
health economics
health education
health hazards
health insurance
health maintenance
    organizations
health seeking behavior
hearing
hearing aids
hearing impairments
heart disease
herbal remedies
herbs
hereditary diseases
heredity

hermaphrodites
hermaphroditism
heroin
heterosexual relationships
high heeled shoes
hips
hirsutism
holistic health
holistic medicine
home birth
home health care
home remedies
homoeroticism
homophobia
homosexuality
hormone therapy
hormones
horticulture
hospices
hospitals
hot flashes
household hazards
hugging
hunger
hygiene
hymen
hymenoplasty
hypersexuality
hypertension
hypnotism
hypochondria
hysterectomy
hysteria
iatrogenic disease
ice hockey
ice skating
identical twins
identity
identity crisis
illness
impotence
impregnation
in vitro fertilization
inbreeding
incest
incest victims
induced abortion
induced labor
industrial hygiene

infant formula
infant mortality
infants
infertility
infibulation
influences
informed consent
injectable contraceptives
insanity
insemination
instincts
intrauterine devices
involuntary depression
involuntary sterilization
iron deficiency anemia
isometric exercise
jockeys
judo
karate
labia
labor (childbirth)
labor coaching
laboratory animals
laboratory assistants
lacrosse
lactation
lactose intolerance
late childbearing
lateral dominance
lay midwives
laying on of hands
learning disabilities
legs
lesbian relationships
lesbophobia
life cycles
life skills
life span
liposuction surgery
local anesthesia
loss of self
love potions
lubricants
lymph glands
male bonding
male circumcision
male homosexuality
male hypersexuality
male pregnancy

male sexuality
males
malignant tumors
malnutrition
mammary glands
mammography
manicurists
marathons
marijuana
martial arts
masochism
massage
masseuses
mastectomy
masturbation
maternal age
maternal and infant welfare
maternal health service
maternal love
maternal mortality
maternity
maternity homes
maternity rights
maternity wards
measles
Medicaid
medical anthropology
medical care
medical education
medical ethics
medical evaluation
medical oppression
medical procedures
medical records
medical sciences
medical sociology
Medicare
medicine women
men
menarche
menopause
menstrual cycle
menstrual disorders
menstrual extraction
menstrual taboos
menstruation
menstruation inducing agents
mental disorders
mental evaluation

mental health
mental health advocates
mental health issues
mental health treatment
mental hospitals
mental retardation
mentally handicapped
midwifery
midwives
migraine headaches
milk
milk substitutes
mind
mind/body split
miscarriage
morbidity
mortality
mortuary science
mother daughter incest
mother right
mother son incest
mother's milk
mothering
motivation
motor development
motor skills
mountaineering
multicultural health care services
multiple births
muscular development
music therapy
narcotic drugs
national health insurance
National Health Service (Great
   Britain)
native healers
natural childbirth
natural sciences
natural selection
naturalists
neighborhood health centers
nervous system
nervousness
neuroses
nom de lait
nonorgasmic women
nonprescription drugs
nurse practitioners
nurses

nursing
nursing education
nursing homes
nurturance
nurturers
nurturing
nutrition
nutritionists
obesity
obsessive compulsive disorders
obstetrical anesthesia
obstetricians
obstetrics
occupational diseases
occupational health and safety
occupational patterns
occupational stress
occupational therapists
old old adults
old wives' tales
Olympic Games
oophorectomy
optometrists
optometry
oral contraceptives
oral sex
orgasm
osteoporosis
ovaries
oviducts
ovulation
ovum
pain
Pap smear
paramedics
paranoia
paraprofessionals
parapsychology
parental rights
parenthood
parenting
parenting rewards
parthenogenesis
paternity
paternity rights
patient doctor relationships
pediatricians
pediatrics
pelvic examination

penis
perception skills
personal hygiene
personality disorders
perspiration
phallus
pharmaceutical industry
pharmacists
pharmacology
pheromones
phobias
physical appearance
physical development
physical education
physical endurance
physical examination
physical fitness
physical health
physical strength
physical therapists
physical therapy
physicians
physicians' assistants
physiological psychology
physiologists
physiology
pica
pierced ears
pituitary gland
pituitary hormones
placebos
placenta
planned parenthood
plastic surgery
podiatrists
population control
population genetics
population planning
postnatal period
postpartum depression
practical nurses
pregnancy
pregnancy disability
pregnancy discrimination
pregnancy prevention
pregnancy trimesters
pregnant workers
premature childbirth
premature infants

premenstrual syndrome
premenstrual tension
prenatal care
prenatal influences
prescription drugs
prevention
preventive medicine
primary caregivers
primate studies
privacy
procreation
professional athletics
progesterone
progestins
prostheses
protective clothing
pseudopregnancy
psychiatrists
psychiatry
psychics
psychoanalysis
psychopharmacology
psychosomatic disorders
psychosurgery
psychotherapists
psychotropic drugs
puberty
pubic hair
puerperal fever
quality of life
racquetball
radiation therapy
reaction times
reconstructive surgery
records
registered nurses
rehabilitation
remedies
reproduction
reproductive cycle
reproductive freedom
reproductive hazards at work
reproductive health
reproductive technologies
research
research assistants
research bias
research design
research methods

research problems
researchers
residency programs
Rh factor
Rh incompatibility
rhythm method
right to die
rights
rights of the disabled
roller skating
rooming in
rubella
running
sadism
sadomasochism
safety
sailing
sampling
sanitary napkins
sanitation
schizophrenia
school health services
science
scientific and technical
   occupations
scientific method
scientists
scrotum
self examination
self insemination
self perception
sense of humor
sensory development
sewage disposal
sex
sex change
sex counseling
sex determination
sex differences
sex drive
sex education
sex hormones
sex manuals
sex preselection
sex reversal
sex selection
sexual abstinence
sexual aids
sexual attraction

sexual behavior
sexual desire
sexual dimorphism
sexual dysfunction
sexual excitement
sexual identity
sexual intercourse
sexual preference
sexual problems
sexual relationships
sexual repression
sexual satisfaction
sexual violence
sexuality
sexually transmitted diseases
shared parenting
sick children
sick leave
sickle cell anemia
skiing
skin
smokefree environments
smoking
soccer
socialized medicine
sociobiologists
sociobiology
sodomy
softball
somnambulism
sororal twins
spatial perception
spatial skills
speculums
speech
speech therapists
sperm
sperm banks
spermicides
spontaneous abortion
sports
sports awards
sports officials
squash
starvation
statistical analysis
stepchildren
sterility

sterilization
sterilization reversal
stillbirth
stimulants
stream of consciousness
stress
stress (physical)
subconscious
substance abuse
sudden infant death syndrome
surgeons
surgery
surgical procedures
swimming
swooning
sympathetic pregnancy
sympathy
synchrony
syphilis
tampons
technicians
teenage pregnancy
tennis
tension headaches
terminal illness
testicles
testosterone
tests
therapeutic abortion
therapists
therapy
thermography
thinness
thyroid gland
toxemia
toxic shock syndrome
track and field
tranquilizers
transsexuality
transvestites
treatment
tribadism
trimness
trust
tubal ligation
tubal ligation reversal
tubal pregnancy
tumors

twins
ulcers
ultrasound
umbilical cord
uncleanliness
unwanted pregnancy
upper body strength
uterus
vagina
vaginal infections
vaginal orgasm
vaginismus
vaginitis
vasectomy
vasectomy reversal
vegetarianism
veterinarians
veterinary sciences
viability
vibrators
virginity
virginity tests
virgins
vision
visiting nurses
visual impairments
vocational nurses
volleyball
vulnerability
vulva
vulvectomy
weight lifting
weight perception
wellness
wet nurses
wicking
wigs
withdrawal
womb envy
women
women in science
women's athletics
women's health movement
work hazards
wrestling
wrinkles
zero population growth
zoology

Science and Technology

acoustics
aerospace engineering
air pollution
air transportation
antinuclear movement
applied mathematics
appropriate technology
artificial intelligence
astronauts
astronomers
astronomy
automation
aviation
boat operators
built environment
bus drivers
cancer
chemical engineering
chemists
civil engineering
coal miners
cohort analysis
communication satellites
computer avoidance
computer equity
computer games
computer literacy
computer programmers
computer programming
computer science
computer security
computer terminals
conservation
construction industry
craft occupations
data analysis
data collection
data processors
deindustrialization
divers
divining
drivers
earth sciences
ecological factors
ecology

electric utilities
electrical engineering
electricians
electronics industry
energy
energy conservation
enforcement
engineering
engineers
engravers
environmental hazards
environmental movement
environmental racism
environmental sciences
ergonomics
experimental design
extractive industry
factory workers
federally sponsored research
fire fighters
flight attendants
food technology
gas utilities
geography
geologists
geology
glaziers
hazardous waste
heavy equipment operators
history of science
home economists
industrial conditions
industrial hazards
industrialization
industries
influences
information sciences
information scientists
information theory
innovation
inventions
inventors
irrigation
laborers
land use technology

machinery
machinists
manufacturing occupations
math ability
mathematical models
mathematicians
mathematics
mechanical engineering
mechanics
mineral resources
mining industry
models (paradigms)
mother earth
movers
natural resources
naturalists
nature
noise pollution
nuclear disarmament
nuclear energy
nuclear engineering
objectivity
oceanography
oil industry
operations researchers
paradigms
paraprofessionals
physical sciences
physicists
physics
pilots
plumbers
pollution
problem solving
programming languages
public information
public transportation
public utilities
rail transportation
railroad workers
random sampling
renewable energy sources
repairers
reproductive technologies
research

research assistants
research bias
research design
research methods
research problems
researchers
resources
sampling
satellite communications
science
science reporting
scientific and technical
  occupations
scientific method
scientific research
scientists
seafarers

social construction of reality
soil conservation
solar energy
space sciences
state sponsored research
statistical analysis
statisticians
statistics
systems analysts
technical assistance
technicians
technology
technology development
telecommunications
telecommuting
telephones
tests

tool and die makers
train conductors
transportation
typewriters
urban environment
utilities
utility credit
video display terminals
watchmakers
water
water management
water pollution
water resources
water utilities
welders
women in science
word processing

Social Sciences and Culture

ableism
abnormal psychology
abortion counseling
absentee fathers
absentee mothers
abstention
abstinence
abstract reasoning
abuse
acculturation
achievement
achievement need
acquaintance rape
acquired immune deficiency
  syndrome
activism
activists
activities
ad feminam
adjustment
adolescence
adolescents
adopted children
adoption
adoptive parents
adornment
adult child relationships
adult development

adults
affection
affiliation
African studies
Afro American studies
Afros
age
age of consent
age stereotypes
ageism
aggressive behavior
alienation
alienation of affection
alliances
aloofness
ambition
American Indian studies
American studies
analytical psychology
ancestors
angel in the house
anger
angora
anima
animus
ankh
anlu
anniversaries

annulment
anonymous
anthropologists
anthropology
anthropometry
anthropomorphism
antifeminism
antisemitism
antisocial behavior
anxiety
apathy
appearance
applied research
approval need
aptitude
aptitude tests
archaeologists
archaeology
area studies
arguments
arranged marriage
arts
Asian American studies
Asian studies
aspirations
assault
assertive behavior
assertiveness training

assimilation patterns
associations
astrology
athletics
attachment
attention
attitude change
attitudes
aunts
authoritarian child rearing
   practices
authoritarian personality
authoritarianism
authority
autonomy
auxiliaries
avoidance behavior
babysitters
babysitting
bachelors
balancing work and family life
bangs
bastards
bathing suits
battered women
beauty
beauty parlors
beauty queens
beauty standards
bedrooms
behavior
behavior change
behavior modification
behavioral objectives
behavioral research
bereavement
betrothal
betrothed
bias
biculturalism
bigamy
bigotry
bikinis
bilineal kinship
biological warfare
biologism
birth fathers
birth mothers
birth name

birth order
birth parents
birth rates
bisexuality
bitches
bitterness
Black women's studies
blame
blame allocation
blaming the victim
blended families
blind dates
blind review
blondes
blood
boards
body image
body language
body politics
bondage
bonding
boredom
boudoirs
boundary markers
bouquets
bourgeoisie
boy preference of parents
boys
braids
breakfasts
bride burning
bride price
brides
bridesmaids
brothels
brother sister incest
brothers
brothers in law
brunches
Brunhilde
built environment
bundling
bureaus
burnout
butlers
camp followers
campaigns
Canadian Indian studies
car pools

care
career break
career family conflict
caregivers
case studies
caste
cathartic therapy
caucuses
celebrations
celibacy
centers
change
chaperones
charisma
charity balls
chastity
chastity belts
chattels
cheesecake
Chicana studies
child abuse
child brides
child care
child care leave
child care workers
child custody
child day care centers
child development
child labor
child marriage
child neglect
child pornography
child psychology
child rearing practices
child support
child welfare
childfree marriage
childhood
childlessness
children
children living in poverty
children's culture
children's groups
children's relationships
circles
citizen groups
civility
clans
class

class consciousness
class differences
class discrimination
class division
class formation
class identity
class ideology
classes
classical conditioning
classism
classless society
cleaning
clinical psychology
clinics
cliques
closeted lesbians
clothing
club women
coalitions
cocktail parties
codependency
coffee klatches
cognition
cognitive behavior modification
cognitive development
cognitive dissonance
cognitive processes
cognitive science
cohabitation
cohort analysis
cohorts
coiffures
colloquia
commercial sex
commitment
committees
common law marriage
communal families
communal groups
communes
communication
communication styles
communities
community
community action
community care
community development
community organizers
community problems

community responsibility
commuter marriage
companies
companionate marriage
comparative psychology
competitive behavior
completion complex
complexes
compliant behavior
compliments
compromise
compulsive behavior
compulsory heterosexuality
concubinage
concubines
conditioning
conditions
confederations
conferences
conflict
conflict resolution
conforming behavior
confrontation
congresses
consanguinity
consciousness
consensual union
consortia
consumer behavior
consumerism
consumption
content analysis
contextual analysis
control
conventions
coparenting
coping strategies
corporate day care centers
corporate spouses
corsages
cosmetology
cotillions
councils
counseling
counselors
counterculture
countertransference
couples
couples with children

courtesans
courtship customs
cousins
coverture
cowives
coyness
creative thinking
creativity
creches
crisis centers
crisis intervention
crisis shelters
critical mass
cross cultural research
cross cultural studies
cross dressing
cross sex identity
crying
crystal ball gazing
cult of true womanhood
cultural anthropology
cultural constraints
cultural groups
cultural heritage
cultural identity
cultural influences
cultural sadism
cultural status
culture
culture conflict
cunning
cunts
curlers
curls
custodial parents
custody
customs
dances
data analysis
data collection
date rape
dating
dating customs
dating services
daughter right
daughters
daughters in law
day care
day care centers

daydreams
death
death and dying
debutantes
decision making
declining neighborhoods
defense mechanisms
deferential behavior
delayed parenthood
delinquent behavior
demographic measurements
demographic transition
demography
den mothers
denial
departments
dependent behavior
dependent care
dependent care assistance
  programs
dependent children
dependents
deprivation
desertion
desirable neighborhoods
despair
destructive behavior
development studies
developmental psychology
deviant behavior
diagnoses
diaper services
differences
diffusion
dinners
disadvantaged groups
discipline
discrimination
discussion groups
displaced homemakers
diversity
divining
divorce
divorce rates
dogmatism
dolls
domestic arrangements
domestic arts
domestic code

domestic rape
domestic relations
domestic roles
domestic services
domestic values
domestic violence
domesticity
dominance
dominant culture
donors
double bind
double discrimination
double standard
doubly disadvantaged
dowry deaths
dreams
dressing for success
drinking prohibition
drop in day care centers
dual career couples
dual career families
dual careers
dual roles
dutch treat
early experience
economic anthropology
economic class
economic geography
economic status
economic structure
economics
educational activities
educational psychology
efficiency
egalitarian families
ego
elder abuse
elderly care
elderly day care centers
elderly households
Electra complex
electroconvulsive therapy
electronic cottage
elites
emancipation
emotional abuse
emotional adjustment
emotional development
emotional experience

emotional problems
emotionalism
emotions
empathy
employer supported day care
empowerment
empty nest
encounter groups
end time thinking
endogamy
engagement
enterprises
environment
epidemiology
escorts
essentialism
ethclass
ethic of care
ethnic diversity
ethnic groups
ethnic intimidation
ethnic neighborhoods
ethnic relations
ethnic studies
ethnic women
ethnicity
ethnography
ethnology
ethnomethodology
ethnomusicology
ethologists
ethology
etiquette
euthanasia
evaluation
eve teasing
evolution
exchange theory
exhibitions
exile
exogamy
expectations
experience
experimental design
experimental psychology
experts
exploitation
expositions
extended families

extramarital affairs
extrasensory perception
extroversion
eyeglasses
faces
facilities
facism
factions
fads
faghag
fair play
fairness
false consciousness
families
family attitudes
family conflict
family counseling
family economics
family education
family environment
family finances
family income
family influence
family life
family mobility
family owned business
family policy
family problems
family recipes
family relationships
family responsibility
family rights
family roles
family size
family structure
family therapy
fashion
father daughter incest
father daughter relationships
father son incest
father son relationships
fathering
fatherless families
fathers
fathers in law
fear
fear of failure
fear of success
federations

female bonding
female female relationships
female friendships
female headed households
female impersonators
female male friendships
female male relationships
female societies
females
feminine mystique
femininity
feminist studies
femmes fatales
fertility rates
fertility rites
feuds
fieldwork
first husbands
first wives
flirtation
flirts
flowers
folk culture
folklorists
food marketing
food preparation
food stamps
former husbands
former spouses
former wives
forms of affection
fortune tellers
fortune telling
forums
fossil hominids
foster children
foster families
foster grandparents
foster homes
foster parents
fraternal twins
free association
friends
friendships
frustration
fund raising events
funeral rites
future studies
gallantry

gambling
game theory
games
gang rape
gangs
garden clubs
gay couples
gay culture
gay experience
gay fathers
gay male couples
gay male culture
gay male experience
gay male marriage
gay male relationships
gay marriage
gay men
gay pride
gay relationships
gay stepfathers
gay studies
gay/straight split
gays
gender
gender bias
gender differences
gender diversity
gender ideology
gender roles
gender studies
generation gap
gerontology
gestalt therapy
ghettos
gigolos
girl preference of parents
girls
glamour
global village
governesses
graciousness
grandchildren
granddaughters
grandfathers
grandmothers
grandparents
grandsons
gray power
grief

grooming behavior
grooms
group behavior
group counseling
group dynamics
group marriage
group process
group therapy
groups
guardians
guilt
gynarchy
gynocide
hair dryers
hair straightening
hair styles
halfway houses
happiness
harlots
hate
heads of families
help seeking behavior
helping behavior
hemlines
heterogeneous groups
heterosexism
heterosexual privilege
heterosexual relationships
heterosexuality
hidjab
hierarchy
history of children
hobbies
home accidents
home based work
home economics
home economists
home life
homeless
homeless men
homeless women
homemakers
homemaking
homesteading
homoeroticism
homogeneous groups
homophobia
homosexuality
honeymoons

hosiery
hostesses (historical)
hostility
hosts
house design
housecleaners
housecleaning
household division of labor
household hazards
household workers
householders
households
housekeepers
houses
housewares
housework
housing costs
housing discrimination
housing subsidies
hugging
human evolution
human interest
human needs
human relations
human resources
human services
humanity
husband abuse
husbands
iconoclasts
identical twins
identity
identity crisis
illegitimacy
images of girls
images of women
immorality
impact on children
impact on women
impersonators
impoverishment of women
in laws
incest
incest victims
indigenous populations
individual counseling
individual development
individualism
individuality

industrial psychology
infant care
infant development
infants
infidelity
influence
influences
ingratiation
inheritance customs
initiation rites
initiative
inner city
innocence
innovation
insanity
instigators
institutes
institutional racism
institutional sexism
institutions
intellectual development
intellectuals
intercaste marriage
interdisciplinary studies
interethnic families
interfaith marriage
international adoption
international marriage
interpersonal communication
interracial adoption
interracial families
interracial marriage
interracial relations
interreligious families
interrole conflict
interruptions
interviewers
interviewing
interviews
intimacy
intimidation
introversion
intuition
invisibility
ironing
jealousy
johns
joy
juvenile delinquency

1005

juvenile offenders
juvenile prostitution
kibbutzim
kinesics
kinesthetic perception
kinship
kissing
kitchens
labor saving devices
laboratories
lace making
lack of confidence
ladies (historical)
ladies' aid societies
landlords
latchkey children
Latin American studies
Latina studies
laughter
laundry
lawyer client relationships
leadership roles
leagues
learned behavior
learned helplessness
lectures
left wing organizations
legitimacy
legitimization of children
leisure
leisure activities
lesbian communities
lesbian couples
lesbian culture
lesbian experience
lesbian marriage
lesbian mothers
lesbian relationships
lesbian stepmothers
lesbian studies
lesbians
lesbophobia
levirate
life cycles
life expectancy
life histories
life span
life styles
lineage

lingerie
linguistic sexism
listening
living alone
living arrangements
living conditions
locker rooms
locus of control
lodges
logical thinking
loneliness
long term memory
loss
loss of self
love
love potions
lovemaking
lovers
low income families
low income households
lower class
lunches
lust
lying
lynching
machismo
maiden aunts
mail order brides
mainstreaming
majority culture
male bonding
male circumcision
male friendships
male impersonators
male male relationships
male norms
male standards
males
man
man the hunter
manipulative behavior
manipulators
mannequins
manners
manumission
marginality
marianismo
marital adjustment
marital conflict

marital property reform
marital roles
marital satisfaction
marital stability
marital status
marital violence
marriage
marriage by proxy
marriage contracts
marriage counseling
marriage customs
marriage proposals
marriage rates
marriage tax
married couples
martial arts
masculinity
mass actions
massage parlors
matchmakers
maternal and infant welfare
maternal love
maternity homes
maternity leave
mathematical models
matriarchs
matriarchy
matricentric societies
matrilineal kinship
matrilineal societies
matrilocal residences
matronymy
maturity
measurement
mediation
medical anthropology
medical sociology
meetings
memory
men
men's roles
men's studies
mergers
methods
middle age
middle aged adults
middle class
middle class families
midlife

midlife crisis
mikiri
military dependents
mind
miniskirts
minority experience
minority groups
misandry
miscegenation
mistresses
mixed sex groups
mixers
mobility
models (paradigms)
modernization
modesty
momism
monogamy
moral development
moral reasoning
morbidity
mores
mortality rates
mother daughter incest
mother daughter relationships
mother nature
mother right
mother son incest
mother son relationships
mother syndrome
mothering
motherless families
mothers
mothers in law
mothers working outside the
    home
motivation
mourning
multiple roles
mythology
myths
nags
nannies
narcissism
Near Eastern studies
negative reinforcement
neighborhood preservation
neighborhoods
nephews

nervous system
nervousness
networking
neuroses
nieces
no fault divorce
nonconforming behavior
noncustodial parents
nonjudgmental behavior
nonsexist child rearing practices
nonverbal behavior
nonverbal communication
nonviolence
novices
nuclear families
nudity
nurseries
nurturance
nurturers
nurturing
obedience
obituaries
objectification
objectives
objectivity
obscenity
obsessive compulsive disorders
occupational sex segregation
odalisques
Oedipus complex
office parties
offices (facilities)
old boy networks
old girl networks
old maids
old old adults
old wives' tales
older adults
older men
older women
operant conditioning
opportunities
optimism
organizational psychology
organizations
original sin
Orphan Annie
Ouija boards
outreach programs

overachievement
padding
palimony
panels
pants
parades
paradigms
paranoia
parent child relationships
parent influence
parental aspirations
parental attitudes
parental behavior
parental leave
parental rights
parenthood
parenting
parenting rewards
parents
pariahs
participant observation
parties
partners
passages
passion
passive behavior
paternity leave
paternity rights
patience
patriarchs
patriarchy
patricide
patrilineal kinship
pauperization of women
peasants
pedestals
pedicurists
peer influence
peer relationships
peers
pen pals
penis envy
people of color
perception
perception skills
perceptual bias
perceptual development
perfection
performance

performance factors
perfume
permanents
permissive child rearing
    practices
permissive environment
persecution
personal columns
personal management
personal relationships
personal space
personal values
personality
personality development
personality problems
personality tests
personality traits
perspiration
pessimism
pets
phallocentrism
philanderers
phrenology
physical abuse
physical appearance
physiological psychology
pierced ears
pimps
pin money
pinups
planning meetings
play
playgrounds
playgroups
pleasure
plenary sessions
politeness
political anthropology
political science
political spouses
political status
polyandry
polygamy
polygyny
ponytails
popular culture
population characteristics
population decline
population distribution

population genetics
population growth
population policy
population trends
pornography
positive reinforcement
possessiveness
posslq
posthumous marriage
postindustrial society
poverty
prayer meetings
pregnancy discrimination
pregnancy leave
premarital relations
premature death
prenuptial agreements
preschool children
prestige
pride
prima donnas
primary caregivers
primate studies
primness
priorities
privacy
private sphere
privilege
problems
process
professional status
projection
proletariat
promiscuity
proms
property ownership
prostitutes
prostitution
protection
protest
psychodrama
psychological adjustment
psychological factors
psychological needs
psychological repression
psychological stress
psychological testing
psychologists
psychology

psychometry
psychopharmacology
psychosexual behavior
psychotherapy
public assistance
public interest
public service
public sphere
public welfare
punishment
purdah
purists
purity
purses
qualitative analysis
quality assessment
quality of life
quantitative analysis
queen for a day
race
race bias
race, class, and gender studies
race formation
race relations
racial and ethnic differences
racial discrimination
racial diversity
racial factors
racial stereotypes
racial stratification
racism
racist rape
raconteurs
rage
rallies
random sampling
rape
rape crisis centers
rape fantasies
rape prevention
rape victims
rapists
raps
readings
rebellious behavior
recall
receptions
recipes
recognition

reconciliation
recreation
reentry women
regional studies
reinforcement
rejection
relationships
relaxation
religious discrimination
remarriage
repression
reputations
research
research assistants
research bias
research design
research methods
research problems
researchers
residential security
responsibility
retirement age
retreats
reverse discrimination
revivals
right to die
rings
risk taking
risk taking behavior
risks
rites of passage
ritual disfigurement
role conflict
role expectations
role models
role reversal
roles
romance
romantic love
a room of one's own
rooms
royalty
runaway fathers
runaway husbands
runaway mothers
runaway wives
runaways
rural areas
rural conditions

rural living
rural migration
rural planning
rural poverty
rural resettlement
rural women
sacred dance
sacred space
sacrifice
sadness
safe sex
sampling
sanctuaries
sanity
satisfaction
school age children
scolds
seasonal migration
seclusion
secret societies
secularization
seduction
seductresses
segregated housing
segregation
selective attention
self actualization
self blame
self concept
self confidence
self control
self defense
self denial
self destructive behavior
self determination
self disclosure
self esteem
self help
self perception
self respect
self sacrifice
self sufficiency
self understanding
selfish behavior
seminars
senior citizens
sensation
sensitivity
sensuality

separate spheres
separation
seraglios
services
sessions
sewing
sex
sex counseling
sex discrimination
sex discrimination in
    employment
sex industry
sex objects
sex ratio
sex role behavior
sex role development
sex role stereotyping
sex roles
sex segregation
sex selection
sex stereotypes
sex/gender systems
sexism
sexual abstinence
sexual abuse
sexual assault
sexual attraction
sexual exploitation
sexual fantasies
sexual freedom
sexual identity
sexual intimidation
sexual liberation
sexual oppression
sexual permissiveness
sexual politics
sexual relationships
sexual slavery
sexual stratification
sexual violence
shamans
shared custody
shared parenting
shelters
short term memory
showers
shunning
sibling influence
sibling relationships

siblings
significant others
silence
single fathers
single men
single mothers
single parent families
single parents
single sex environments
single women
singles
sissies
sisters
sisters in law
skills
skin color
skirts
slave rape
Slavic studies
sleep
smiling
smoking prohibition
social activities
social adjustment
social agencies
social attitudes
social behavior
social bias
social characteristics
social class
social conditioning
social conflict
social construction of gender
social construction of reality
social control
social development
social differences
social entertaining
social environment
social geography
social identity
social indicators
social influences
social mobility
social organization
social organizations
social perception
social policy
social problems

social prohibitions
social psychology
social relations
social science research
social sciences
social scientists
Social Security
social services
social skills
social status
social stratification
social structure
social studies
social trends
social values
social welfare
social work
socialization
socially disadvantaged
societies
society
society balls
sociobiologists
sociobiology
socioeconomic class
socioeconomic conditions
socioeconomic indicators
socioeconomic status
sociologists
sociology
sociology of knowledge
sociopathology
solitude
somnambulism
sons
sons in law
sororal twins
sororate
space
spinsters
sports awards
sports enthusiasts
spouse abuse
spouse support
spouses
squatters
standards
state formation
stateless societies

statistical analysis
status
status of women
stepchildren
stepfathers
stepmothers
stepparents
stereotypes
stereotyping
stigmas
stimulants
straights
strategies
stratification
stream of consciousness
street harassment
structural discrimination
structural unemployment
strumpets
stubbornness
study groups
subconscious
subculture
subjective knowledge
subjugation
submissive behavior
subordination
subordination of women
suburbs
success
suicide
superego
supermom
superwoman syndrome
suppers
support systems
surnames
surrogate families
surrogate fathers
surrogate mothers
surrogates
survival strategies
symbolism
symbols
sympathy
symposia
synergy
systems theory
taboos

tactual perception
tank tops
tarot
tarot reading
task forces
tattoos
tea leaf reading
tea pouring
tea rooms
teas
teases
tee shirts
teenage fathers
teenage marriage
teenage mothers
teenagers
teleconferences
temporary housing
temptresses
terminal illness
territoriality
testing
tests
theaters
theory
therapists
therapy
thinness
time
tomboys
totemism
touching
toys
traditions
training objectives
traits
transference
transitions
trashing
trends
trial marriage
tribal customs
tribal markings
tricks
trust
tshiwila
twins
two income families

uncles
unconscious
underachievement
underwear
unilineal kinship
unisex
unrequited love
untouchables
upper class
upper class families
upward mobility
urban areas
urban environment
urban indicators
urban migration
urbanization
utopian communities
uxoriousness
uzr
vacations
vagina dentata
values
valuing children
veiling of women
veils
verbal development
victim services
victimization
victims
video games
village communes
violence
violence against children
violence against women
viragos
vision
visitation rights
visiting homemakers
visual perception
vital statistics
volunteers
voluptuousness
vulnerability
wage earning mothers
wage earning wives
wage earning women
wages for housework
wards

wedding night
wedding nights
wedding rings
welfare
welfare agencies
welfare economics
welfare mothers
welfare programs
white slavery
widowers
widows
wife abuse
wigs
withdrawal
wives
wives working outside the home
the woman question
woman the gatherer
womanhood
womanism
womanizers
womb envy
women
women identified women
women in transition
women living in poverty
women of color
women of valor
women working outside the
  home
women's centers
women's culture
women's networks
women's roles
women's shelters
women's studies
work
work space
workaholics
working class
working parents
workplace nurseries
workshops
young adults
young children
youth services
zoning

Visual and Performing Arts

acoustics
acting
actors
actresses (historical)
aesthetics
all women ensembles
alternative spaces
animation
anonymous
antiques
apprenticeships
architects
architecture
art
art conservation
art criticism
art history
art matronage
art music
art preservation
art shows
art symbols
art theory
art therapy
artisans
artistic ability
artists
artists' books
arts
arts, entertainment, and media
   occupations
arts organizations
aspiring actors
auteurism
authors
ballads
ballet
bas reliefs
basketry
beadwork
blues
body art
book conservation
Brunhilde
camera operators

canon
cartoonists
cartoons
casting
cathedrals
ceramics
chamber music
chanteuses
chants
children's art
children's music
china painting
choirs
choral music
chorus dancers
chorus lines
choruses
circus performers
clothing
coins
collaborative theater
collage
colorblind casting
comedians
comic strips
commercial art
composers
computer music
concerts
conductors
conservation
conservatories
costume design
country music
craft artists
craft arts
craftspersons
creativity
criticism
critics
crocheting
cross cultural casting
cult of the virgin
culture work
cunt art

curators
dance
dance criticism
dancers
dances
deconstruction
decorative arts
design
designers
disk jockeys
docents
documentaries
doll making
domestic arts
drafters
drama
dramatists
drawing
dreams
dressmakers
electronic art
electronic music
embroidery
engravers
engraving
entertainers
entertainment
erotic art
erotica
ethnomusicology
experimental dance
experimental theater
fashion design
fashion illustration
fashion photography
fashion shows
feminist music
femmage
festivals
fiber art
film
film criticism
film directors
film festivals
film producers

films
flower arranging
flower painting
folk art
folk dance
folk music
furniture
galleries
geishas
glassmakers
gospel music
graphic design
graphics
group developed theater
handmade
heroes
holistic music
hosts
humor
hymns
iconography
illustrators
imagery
images of girls
images of women
improvisation
incidental music
instrument makers
instrumental music
interior design
invisibility
jazz
jazz musicians
jewelry
jewelry makers
knitting
landscape architects
librettos
lieder
lullabies
lyricists
lyrics
madonna
madrigals
magic
makeup
master of ceremonies
media arts
meditation music

metal art
metalworkers
milliners
mime
miniatures
mixed media
models
modern dance
motion picture industry
multimedia art
mural art
museums
music
music criticism
music festivals
music history
music industry
music theory
music therapy
music videos
musical theater
musicals
musicians
musicology
naive art
needlepoint
needlework
night clubs
the nude
nursery songs
one woman art shows
opera
opera singers
orators
orchestral music
painters
painting
performance art
performance spaces
performances
performers
performing arts
photographers
photography
photojournalism
plays
playwrights
poets
political art

political music
popular music
portraits
poster art
potters
pottery
primitive art
printers
printmakers
printmaking
protest music
public art
puppetry
quilting
religious art
religious music
reviewers
rock and roll
rug hooking
salon music
salons
samplers
satire
scores
screenplays
scripts
sculptors
sculpture
sewing machine operators
sheet music
sign painters
singers
skits
slave songs
soft sculpture
soloists
songs
sphinx
spinning
spirituals
stamps
statues
street theater
strippers
symbolism
symbols
tailors
talent
tapestry

textile design
textile making
theater
theater criticism
torch singers
tribal art
tribal music
troubadours

typography
vamps
vaudeville
video art
videos
visual arts
visual diaries
vocal music

weavers
weaving
welders
women's art
women's music
woodworkers
writers

USE/DO NOT USE
DISPLAY

USE	DO NOT USE
acquired immune deficiency syndrome	AIDS ◄————————————— ACRONYM
GENER-NEUTRAL ——► actors	actresses
PEFERRED USAGE birth mothers	biological mothers
cosmetic surgery	butt lifts ◄————————————— SLANG
prisons	correctional facilities ◄———— EUPHEMISM
single women	unmarried women ◄———— EMBEDDED NORM
PEFERRED SPELLING——► theater	theater arts
work hours	man hours ◄————————— FALSE GENERIC

USE	DO NOT USE
abortion clinics	abortion mills
abortion movement	prochoice movement
achievement need	achievement motivation
acquired immune deficiency syndrome	AIDS
actors	actresses
administrative assistants	girl Fridays
adult students	mature students
adult students	older students
aerobic exercise	aerobics
Afro American studies	Black American studies
Afro American studies	Black studies
aggressive behavior	aggression
Aid to Families With Dependent Children	AFDC
air transportation	airlines
American Indian	Native American
American Indian studies	Native American studies
antiabortion movement	antichoice
antiabortion movement	prolife
antiabortion movement	right to life
armed forces	armed services
armed forces	military services
arousal	erogenous zones
art music	classical music
art music	concert music
art shows	art exhibits
artisans	craftsmen
Asian studies	Oriental studies
aspiring actors	starlets
assertive behavior	assertiveness
auteurism	auteur theory
automobile insurance	car insurance
automobile repair	car repair
auxiliaries	ladies' auxiliaries
bat mitzvah	bas mitzvah
bellhops	bellboys
biological sciences	life sciences
biological warfare	chemical warfare
birth defects	congenital anomalies
birth fathers	biological fathers
birth mothers	biological mothers
birth name	maiden name
birth parents	biological parents
Black	Negro

USE	DO NOT USE
Black colleges	historically Black colleges
bulimia	binge purge syndrome
camera operators	cameramen
campus security	campus safety
career choice	occupational choice
career choice	vocational choice
career counseling	career guidance
caregivers	caretakers
Caucasian	White man
child abuse	child molesting
childbirth	birth
childbirth	child birth
childbirth	delivery
chorus dancers	chorus girls
city government	municipal government
cleaners	cleaning women
clothing	clothes
clothing	dress
clothing workers	needleworkers
coat checkers	coat check girls
cocktail servers	barmaids
cohabitation	living together
college students	coeds
colonialism	imperialism
comedians	comediennes
commuter marriage	long distance marriage
Comprehensive Employment and Training Act of 1973	CETA
compulsive behavior	compulsions
computer avoidance	computer anxiety
conditioning	psychological conditioning
conforming behavior	conformity
construction industry	building industry
contraception	birth control methods
corporate policy	industrial policy
corporate spouses	corporate husbands
corporate spouses	corporate wives
corporate spouses	executive spouses
cosmetic surgery	butt lifts
cosmetic surgery	nose jobs
cosmetic surgery	tummy tucks
craft artists	craftsmen
craft arts	crafts
craft arts	handicrafts

USE	DO NOT USE
craftspersons	craftsmen
credit for experience	prior learning
criminals	offenders
cross dressing	drag
curriculum integration	curriculum transformation
data entry operators	keypunch operators
deacons	deaconesses
death penalty	capital punishment
degrees	academic degrees
deliverers	delivery boys
deliverers	deliverymen
demographic measurements	demographics
dependent behavior	dependency
developed nations	developed countries
developing nations	developing countries
developing nations	underdeveloped nations
deviant behavior	deviance
diabetes	sugar diabetes
diethylstilbestrol	DES
diethylstilbestrol	morning after pill
dieting	slimming
dilatation and curettage	D and C
diplomacy	statesmanship
diplomats	statesmen
disabled	handicapped
discrimination	social discrimination
discrimination against the disabled	disability discrimination
discrimination laws	antidiscrimination laws
disks	diskettes
domestic rape	marital rape
domestic rape	spouse rape
domestic rape	wife rape
domestic violence	family violence
domestic violence	household violence
dowry	bridewealth
drafters	draftsmen
drug addiction	chemical dependency
dual career couples	two career couples
dual career families	two career families
eating disorders	appetite disorders
educational costs	educational financing
elderly day care centers	respite care
elected officials	politicians

USE	DO NOT USE
election campaigns	political campaigns
electroconvulsive therapy	shock therapy
electronic art	computer art
emotions	feelings
equal access	access
Equal Employment Opportunity Commission	EEOC
Equal Rights Amendment	ERA
ethnic groups	minorities
ethnic studies	minority studies
ethnic women	minority women
executive recruitment	headhunters
executors	executrixes
extended families	extended kinship network
extramarital affairs	adultery
extrasensory perception	ESP
factory workers	mill girls
fair play	sportsmanship
families	the family
family medicine	family practice
family size	ideal family size
fathers	fatherhood
female female relationships	same sex relationships
female hypersexuality	nymphomania
female intensive occupations	female dominated careers
female intensive occupations	female dominated occupations
female intensive occupations	female dominated professions
female intensive occupations	nontraditional careers
female intensive occupations	nontraditional occupations
female intensive occupations	women intensive careers
female intensive occupations	women intensive occupations
female intensive occupations	women intensive professions
female male friendships	male female friendships
female male relationships	male female relationships
fetuses	unborn child
figurative language	figures of speech

USE	DO NOT USE
film	cinema
film	cinematography
film directors	directors (film)
films	motion pictures
films	movies
fire fighters	firemen
fish sellers	fishwives
fishers	fishermen
flexible work schedules	flexible hours
flexible work schedules	flexitime
flight attendants	airline stewardesses
flight attendants	stewardesses
folk culture	folklore
former husbands	exhusbands
former wives	exwives
freedom of worship	religious freedom
gay marriage	homosexual marriage
gay men	gay males
gay men	male homosexuals
gay relationships	homosexual relationships
gays	homosexuals
genital herpes	herpes simplex virus type II
genitals	genitalia
genitals	private parts
global feminism	international feminism
glossolalia	speaking in tongues
governing boards	boards of governors
governing boards	boards of regents
governing boards	boards of trustees
governing boards	school boards
government appointments	appointive positions
governors' spouses	First Ladies
graduate degrees	advanced degrees
group behavior	collective behavior
guards	watchmen
hair loss	balding
hair removal	depilation
handmade	manmade
hat checkers	hat check girls
hazardous waste	toxic waste
health care services	health services
health insurance	medical insurance
health maintenance organizations	HMOs
heroes	heroic women

USE	DO NOT USE
heroes	heroines
heterosexuality	heterosexuals
holy communion	eucharist
homeless	street people
homeless women	bag ladies
homemakers	house husbands
homemakers	house wives
homemakers	househusbands
homemakers	housewives
hosiery	pantyhose
hosts	hostesses
hotel workers	chambermaids
household labor	domestic labor
household labor	home labor
household workers	domestics
household workers	maids
household workers	servants
householders	breadwinners
householders	heads of households
housing	homes
human resources	manpower
humanity	brotherhood of man
humanity	mankind
husbands	married men
hymen	maidenhead
hypersexuality	compulsive sexuality
hypertension	high blood pressure
illegal immigrants	illegal aliens
immigrants	aliens
in vitro fertilization	ectogenesis
in vitro fertilization	test tube babies
independent scholars	unaffiliated scholars
indigenous	aboriginals
individual development	personal development
infants	babies
infertility	barren
influences	causal factors
information retrieval services	computer searches
informed consent	consent
international relations	foreign affairs
international relations	international affairs
intrauterine devices	IUDs
involuntary sterilization	compulsory sterilization
janitors	charwomen

USE	DO NOT USE
job discrimination	barriers to employment
job hunting	job search
job recruitment	personnel recruitment
job sharing	work sharing
job training	employment training
job training	occupational training
labor force	manpower
labor force	work force
labor legislation	labor laws
laborers	unskilled laborers
laity	laypeople
land settlement	resettlement
Latin American	South American
Latina studies	Hispanic studies
launderers	laundresses
launderers	washerwomen
lawsuits	litigation
lawsuits	suits
lawyers	attorneys
lay midwives	granny midwives
learned helplessness	helplessness
lesbian culture	gay female culture
lesbian experience	gay female experience
lesbian stepmothers	gay stepmothers
lesbianism	female homosexuality
lesbians	dykes
lesbians	female homosexuals
lesbians	gay women
liposuction surgery	suction lipectomy
literature	literary arts
literature	literary genres
living standards	standards of living
longshore workers	longshoremen
longshore workers	stevedores
lumber cutters	lumbermen
lust	concupiscence
male chauvinism	male chauvinist pig
male chauvinism	MCP
male dominated employment	male dominated careers
male intensive occupations	nontraditional careers
male intensive occupations	nontraditional occupations
male male relationships	same sex relationships
manufactured	manmade
marriage	matrimony

USE	DO NOT USE
mass media	media
massage	massage therapy
master of ceremonies	mistress of ceremonies
masturbation	autoeroticism
math avoidance	math anxiety
mathematics	math
medical sciences	medicine
menopause	change of life
menstruation	menses
menstruation	period
menstruation inducing agents	emmenagogues
mental disorders	mental illness
meteorologists	weathermen
methods	methodology
methods	procedures
Middle Eastern	Near Eastern
midwives	birth attendants
migrant workers	regional labor workers
militarism	armament
military draft	draft
minor parties	third parties
morality	morals
mothers	motherhood
mothers working outside the home	employed mothers
mothers working outside the home	working mothers
multinational banks	transnational banks
multinational corporations	transnational corporations
multiple births	quadruplets
multiple births	quintuplets
multiple births	sextuplets
multiple births	triplets
murder	homicide
Muslim	Moslem
mythology	myths (folk culture)
narcotic drugs	narcotics
networks	social networks
news services	press services
nonformal education	informal education
nonorgasmic women	frigidity
novices	neophytes
nuclear energy	nuclear power
nurses	male nurses

USE	DO NOT USE
obituaries	death notices
objectives	goals
occupational attitudes	occupational perceptions
occupational counseling	job counseling
occupational counseling	vocational counseling
occupational mobility	career mobility
occupational mobility	job mobility
occupational segregation	job segregation
occupational stress	job stress
occupations	jobs
occupations	professions
old girl networks	new girl networks
older adults	aged
older adults	elderly
older adults	old age
oophorectomy	ovariectomy
opinion polls	polling
opinion polls	polls
opinion polls	public opinion polls
oral contraceptives	birth control pills
oral contraceptives	the pill
padding	falsies
palm reading	palmistry
pants	trousers
Pap smear	Papanicolaou smear
parenthood	fatherhood
parenthood	motherhood
part time employment	part time work
patient doctor relationships	doctor patient relationships
patient doctor relationships	physician patient relationships
pauperization of women	feminization of poverty
pension benefits	pensions
people of color	minorities
performing arts	fine arts
personal relationships	interpersonal relationships
personnel	manpower
pharmaceutical industry	drug industry
photographers	cameramen
physical development	growth
physical endurance	stamina
physicians	doctors
pilots	aviatrices
police officers	policemen

USE	DO NOT USE
political action committees	PACs
political leaders	statesmen
political parties	political party affiliations
political spouses	political husbands
political spouses	political wives
postpartum depression	postnatal depression
poverty	poor
pregnancy	gestation
premenstrual syndrome	PMS
prenuptial agreements	antenuptial contracts
presidential spouses	First Ladies
press operators	pressmen
priests	fathers (religious)
principals	headmasters
principals	headmistresses
print media	the press
prisons	correctional facilities
prisons	jails
prochoice	right to choose
proposal writing	grant writing
prostitutes	hookers
prostitutes	whores
protest actions	protests
pseudopregnancy	false pregnancy
psychological testing	psychological tests
public affairs	community affairs
public housing	subsidized housing
puerperal fever	childbed fever
quilting	quilts
racial and ethnic differences	ethnic comparisons
racial and ethnic differences	racial comparisons
ranch hands	cowboys
ranch hands	cowgirls
reduction in force	RIF
reentry women	returning women
religious law	canon law
religious literature	biblical literature
religious music	church music
religious music	sacred music
repairers	repairmen
Rh factor	rhesus factor
rhythm method	natural family planning
rites	rituals

USE	DO NOT USE
rubella	German measles
rubella	three day measles
running	jogging
saleswomen	salesgirls
science avoidance	science anxiety
self concept	self image
self employment	self employed
sex counseling	sex therapy
sex counseling	sexual counseling
sex crimes	sex offenses
sex drive	libido
sex equity	sexual equity
sex tourism	traffic in women
sexual behavior	sexual practices
sexual equality	sex equality
sexual identity	sex identity
sexual identity	sex role identification
sexual intercourse	coitus
sexual intercourse	copulation
sexual liberation	free love
sexually transmitted diseases	VD
sexually transmitted diseases	venereal diseases
shared custody	joint custody
single fathers	unmarried fathers
single men	unmarried men
single mothers	unmarried mothers
single mothers	unwed mothers
single parent families	broken home
single parent families	one parent families
single women	unmarried women
smoking	cigarettes
social entertaining	entertaining
social movements	movements
social sciences	behavioral sciences
social structure	social system
social workers	caseworkers
socialization	social learning
space sciences	astronautics
spokespersons	spokesmen
sports enthusiasts	sportsmen
street harassment	girl watching
street harassment	wolfing
student financial aid	student aid

USE	DO NOT USE
sudden infant death syndrome	crib death
suffragists	suffragettes
supervisors	foremen
support systems	social support systems
surgical procedures	operations
tailors	seamstresses
teacher education	teacher training
teenage pregnancy	adolescent pregnancy
television personalities	hosts (media)
temporary workers	temps
testicles	balls
testing	tests and measurements
theater	theater arts
theater	theatre
tipping	feminization of occupations
tipping	feminization of professions
transsexuality	transsexualism
transsexuality	transsexuals
tubal ligation	tube tying
two income families	dual worker families
unemployment	unemployed
unpaid employment	nonwage labor
urban areas	large cities
urban planning	city planning
ushers	usherettes
uterus	womb
verbal communication	oral communication
video display terminals	cathode ray tubes
video display terminals	CRT
video display terminals	VDT
visual arts	fine arts
volunteer work	voluntarism
volunteer work	volunteering
wage earners	working men
wage earners	working women
wage earners	workmen
wage earning mothers	working mothers
wage earning wives	working wives
wage earning women	career girls
wage earning women	working women
wage gap	earnings gap
wage gap	wage differential
wages	pay
wages	salaries

USE	DO NOT USE
waiters	waitresses
waiters' assistants	busboys
weather reporters	weathermen
White Anglo Saxon Protestant	WASP
widowers	widowerhood
widows	widowhood
witchcraft	the Craft
wives	married women
wives working outside the home	working wives
women	ladies
women living in poverty	feminization of poverty
women of color	minority women
women working outside the home	working women
Women, Infants, and Children Nutrition Program	WIC
women's culture	womanculture
women's history	history of women
women's liberation	women's lib
women's movement	women's liberation movement
women's rights	rights of women
work hazards	occupational hazards
work hazards	office hazards
work hours	man hours
workers	unskilled workers
workers	working men
workers	working women
workers	workmen

DO NOT USE	USE
aboriginals	indigenous
abortion mills	abortion clinics
academic degrees	degrees
access	equal access
achievement motivation	achievement need
actresses	actors
adolescent pregnancy	teenage pregnancy
adultery	extramarital affairs
advanced degrees	graduate degrees
aerobics	aerobic exercise
AFDC	Aid to Families With Dependent Children
aged	older adults
aggression	aggressive behavior
AIDS	acquired immune deficiency syndrome
airline stewardesses	flight attendants
airlines	air transportation
aliens	immigrants
antenuptial contracts	prenuptial agreements
antichoice	antiabortion movement
antidiscrimination laws	discrimination laws
appetite disorders	eating disorders
appointive positions	government appointments
armament	militarism
armed services	armed forces
art exhibits	art shows
assertiveness	assertive behavior
astronautics	space sciences
attorneys	lawyers
auteur theory	auteurism
autoeroticism	masturbation
aviatrices	pilots
babies	infants
bag ladies	homeless women
balding	hair loss
balls	testicles
barmaids	cocktail servers
barren	infertility
barriers to employment	job discrimination
bas mitzvah	bat mitzvah
behavioral sciences	social sciences
bellboys	bellhops
biblical literature	religious literature
binge purge syndrome	bulimia
biological fathers	birth fathers
biological mothers	birth mothers

DO NOT USE	USE
biological parents	birth parents
birth	childbirth
birth attendants	midwives
birth control methods	contraception
birth control pills	oral contraceptives
Black American studies	Afro American studies
Black studies	Afro American studies
boards of governors	governing boards
boards of regents	governing boards
boards of trustees	governing boards
breadwinners	householders
bridewealth	dowry
broken home	single parent families
brotherhood of man	humanity
building industry	construction industry
busboys	waiters' assistants
butt lifts	cosmetic surgery
cameramen	camera operators
cameramen	photographers
campus safety	campus security
canon law	religious law
capital punishment	death penalty
car insurance	automobile insurance
car repair	automobile repair
career girls	wage earning women
career guidance	career counseling
career mobility	occupational mobility
caretakers	caregivers
caseworkers	social workers
cathode ray tubes	video display terminals
causal factors	influences
CETA	Comprehensive Employment and Training Act of 1973
chambermaids	hotel workers
change of life	menopause
charwomen	janitors
chemical dependency	drug addiction
chemical warfare	biological warfare
child birth	childbirth
child molesting	child abuse
childbed fever	puerperal fever
chorus girls	chorus dancers
church music	religious music
cigarettes	smoking
cinema	film
cinematography	film

DO NOT USE	USE
city planning	urban planning
classical music	art music
cleaning women	cleaners
clothes	clothing
coat check girls	coat checkers
coeds	college students
coitus	sexual intercourse
collective behavior	group behavior
comediennes	comedians
community affairs	public affairs
compulsions	compulsive behavior
compulsive sexuality	hypersexuality
compulsory sterilization	involuntary sterilization
computer anxiety	computer avoidance
computer art	electronic art
computer searches	information retrieval services
concert music	art music
concupiscence	lust
conformity	conforming behavior
congenital anomalies	birth defects
consent	informed consent
copulation	sexual intercourse
corporate husbands	corporate spouses
corporate wives	corporate spouses
correctional facilities	prisons
cowboys	ranch hands
cowgirls	ranch hands
crafts	craft arts
craftsmen	artisans
craftsmen	craft artists
craftsmen	craftspersons
crib death	sudden infant death syndrome
CRT	video display terminals
curriculum transformation	curriculum integration
D and C	dilatation and curettage
deaconesses	deacons
death notices	obituaries
delivery	childbirth
delivery boys	deliverers
deliverymen	deliverers
demographics	demographic measurements
dependency	dependent behavior
depilation	hair removal
DES	diethylstilbestrol
developed countries	developed nations

DO NOT USE	USE
developing countries	developing nations
deviance	deviant behavior
directors (film)	film directors
disability discrimination	discrimination against the disabled
diskettes	disks
doctor patient relationships	patient doctor relationships
doctors	physicians
domestic labor	household labor
domestics	household workers
draft	military draft
draftsmen	drafters
drag	cross dressing
dress	clothing
drug industry	pharmaceutical industry
dual worker families	two income families
dykes	lesbians
earnings gap	wage gap
ectogenesis	in vitro fertilization
educational financing	educational costs
EEOC	Equal Employment Opportunity Commission
elderly	older adults
emmenagogues	menstruation inducing agents
employed mothers	mothers working outside the home
employment training	job training
entertaining	social entertaining
ERA	Equal Rights Amendment
erogenous zones	arousal
ESP	extrasensory perception
ethnic comparisons	racial and ethnic differences
eucharist	holy communion
executive spouses	corporate spouses
executrixes	executors
exhusbands	former husbands
extended kinship network	extended families
exwives	former wives
false pregnancy	pseudopregnancy
falsies	padding
family practice	family medicine
family violence	domestic violence
fatherhood	fathers
fatherhood	parenthood
fathers (religious)	priests
feelings	emotions
female dominated careers	female intensive occupations

DO NOT USE	USE
female dominated occupations	female intensive occupations
female dominated professions	female intensive occupations
female homosexuality	lesbianism
female homosexuals	lesbians
feminization of occupations	tipping
feminization of poverty	pauperization of women
feminization of poverty	women living in poverty
feminization of professions	tipping
figures of speech	figurative language
fine arts	performing arts
fine arts	visual arts
firemen	fire fighters
First Ladies	governors' spouses
First Ladies	presidential spouses
fishermen	fishers
fishwives	fish sellers
flexible hours	flexible work schedules
flexitime	flexible work schedules
folklore	folk culture
foreign affairs	international relations
foremen	supervisors
free love	sexual liberation
frigidity	nonorgasmic women
gay female culture	lesbian culture
gay female experience	lesbian experience
gay males	gay men
gay stepmothers	lesbian stepmothers
gay women	lesbians
genitalia	genitals
German measles	rubella
gestation	pregnancy
girl Fridays	administrative assistants
girl watching	street harassment
goals	objectives
granny midwives	lay midwives
grant writing	proposal writing
growth	physical development
handicapped	disabled
handicrafts	craft arts
hat check girls	hat checkers
headhunters	executive recruitment
headmasters	principals
headmistresses	principals

DO NOT USE	USE
heads of households	householders
health services	health care services
helplessness	learned helplessness
heroic women	heroes
heroines	heroes
herpes simplex virus type II	genital herpes
heterosexuals	heterosexuality
high blood pressure	hypertension
Hispanic studies	Latina studies
historically Black colleges	Black colleges
history of women	women's history
HMOs	health maintenance organizations
home labor	household labor
homes	housing
homicide	murder
homosexual marriage	gay marriage
homosexual relationships	gay relationships
homosexuals	gays
hookers	prostitutes
hostesses	hosts
hosts (media)	television personalities
house husbands	homemakers
house wives	homemakers
household violence	domestic violence
househusbands	homemakers
housewives	homemakers
ideal family size	family size
illegal aliens	illegal immigrants
imperialism	colonialism
industrial policy	corporate policy
informal education	nonformal education
international affairs	international relations
international feminism	global feminism
interpersonal relationships	personal relationships
IUDs	intrauterine devices
jails	prisons
job counseling	occupational counseling
job mobility	occupational mobility
job search	job hunting
job segregation	occupational segregation
job stress	occupational stress
jobs	occupations
jogging	running
joint custody	shared custody

DO NOT USE	USE
keypunch operators	data entry operators
labor laws	labor legislation
ladies	women
ladies' auxiliaries	auxiliaries
large cities	urban areas
laundresses	launderers
laypeople	laity
libido	sex drive
life sciences	biological sciences
literary arts	literature
literary genres	literature
litigation	lawsuits
living together	cohabitation
long distance marriage	commuter marriage
longshoremen	longshore workers
lumbermen	lumber cutters
maiden name	birth name
maidenhead	hymen
maids	household workers
male chauvinist pig	male chauvinism
male dominated careers	male dominated employment
male female friendships	female male friendships
male female relationships	female male relationships
male homosexuals	gay men
male nurses	nurses
man hours	work hours
mankind	humanity
manmade	handmade
manmade	manufactured
manpower	human resources
manpower	labor force
manpower	personnel
marital rape	domestic rape
married men	husbands
married women	wives
massage therapy	massage
math	mathematics
math anxiety	math avoidance
matrimony	marriage
mature students	adult students
MCP	male chauvinism
media	mass media
medical insurance	health insurance
medicine	medical sciences
menses	menstruation

DO NOT USE	USE
mental illness	mental disorders
methodology	methods
military services	armed forces
mill girls	factory workers
minorities	ethnic groups
minorities	people of color
minority studies	ethnic studies
minority women	ethnic women
minority women	women of color
mistress of ceremonies	master of ceremonies
morals	morality
morning after pill	diethylstilbestrol
Moslem	Muslim
motherhood	mothers
motherhood	parenthood
motion pictures	films
movements	social movements
movies	films
municipal government	city government
myths (folk culture)	mythology
narcotics	narcotic drugs
Native American	American Indian
Native American studies	American Indian studies
natural family planning	rhythm method
Near Eastern	Middle Eastern
needleworkers	clothing workers
Negro	Black
neophytes	novices
new girl networks	old girl networks
nontraditional careers	female intensive occupations
nontraditional careers	male intensive occupations
nontraditional occupations	female intensive occupations
nontraditional occupations	male intensive occupations
nonwage labor	unpaid employment
nose jobs	cosmetic surgery
nuclear power	nuclear energy
nymphomania	female hypersexuality
occupational choice	career choice
occupational hazards	work hazards
occupational perceptions	occupational attitudes
occupational training	job training
offenders	criminals
office hazards	work hazards
old age	older adults
older students	adult students

DO NOT USE	USE
one parent families	single parent families
operations	surgical procedures
oral communication	verbal communication
Oriental studies	Asian studies
ovariectomy	oophorectomy
PACs	political action committees
palmistry	palm reading
pantyhose	hosiery
Papanicolaou smear	Pap smear
part time work	part time employment
pay	wages
pensions	pension benefits
period	menstruation
personal development	individual development
personnel recruitment	job recruitment
physician patient relationships	patient doctor relationships
PMS	premenstrual syndrome
policemen	police officers
political campaigns	election campaigns
political husbands	political spouses
political party affiliations	political parties
political wives	political spouses
politicians	elected officials
polling	opinion polls
polls	opinion polls
poor	poverty
postnatal depression	postpartum depression
press services	news services
pressmen	press operators
prior learning	credit for experience
private parts	genitals
procedures	methods
prochoice movement	abortion movement
professions	occupations
prolife	antiabortion movement
protests	protest actions
psychological conditioning	conditioning
psychological tests	psychological testing
public opinion polls	opinion polls
quadruplets	multiple births
quilts	quilting
quintuplets	multiple births
racial comparisons	racial and ethnic differences
regional labor workers	migrant workers

DO NOT USE	USE
religious freedom	freedom of worship
repairmen	repairers
resettlement	land settlement
respite care	elderly day care centers
returning women	reentry women
rhesus factor	Rh factor
RIF	reduction in force
right to choose	prochoice
right to life	antiabortion movement
rights of women	women's rights
rituals	rites
sacred music	religious music
salaries	wages
salesgirls	saleswomen
same sex relationships	female female relationships
same sex relationships	male male relationships
school boards	governing boards
science anxiety	science avoidance
seamstresses	tailors
self employed	self employment
self image	self concept
servants	household workers
sex equality	sexual equality
sex identity	sexual identity
sex offenses	sex crimes
sex role identification	sexual identity
sex therapy	sex counseling
sextuplets	multiple births
sexual counseling	sex counseling
sexual equity	sex equity
sexual practices	sexual behavior
shock therapy	electroconvulsive therapy
slimming	dieting
social discrimination	discrimination
social learning	socialization
social networks	networks
social support systems	support systems
social system	social structure
South American	Latin American
speaking in tongues	glossolalia
spokesmen	spokespersons
sportsmanship	fair play
sportsmen	sports enthusiasts
spouse rape	domestic rape
stamina	physical endurance

DO NOT USE	USE
standards of living	living standards
starlets	aspiring actors
statesmanship	diplomacy
statesmen	diplomats
statesmen	political leaders
stevedores	longshore workers
stewardesses	flight attendants
street people	homeless
student aid	student financial aid
subsidized housing	public housing
suction lipectomy	liposuction surgery
suffragettes	suffragists
sugar diabetes	diabetes
suits	lawsuits
teacher training	teacher education
temps	temporary workers
test tube babies	in vitro fertilization
tests and measurements	testing
the Craft	witchcraft
the family	families
the pill	oral contraceptives
the press	print media
theater arts	theater
theatre	theater
third parties	minor parties
three day measles	rubella
toxic waste	hazardous waste
traffic in women	sex tourism
transnational banks	multinational banks
transnational corporations	multinational corporations
transsexualism	transsexuality
transsexuals	transsexuality
triplets	multiple births
trousers	pants
tube tying	tubal ligation
tummy tucks	cosmetic surgery
two career couples	dual career couples
two career families	dual career families
unaffiliated scholars	independent scholars
unborn child	fetuses
underdeveloped nations	developing nations
unemployed	unemployment
unmarried fathers	single fathers
unmarried men	single men
unmarried mothers	single mothers

DO NOT USE	USE
unmarried women	single women
unskilled laborers	laborers
unskilled workers	workers
unwed mothers	single mothers
usherettes	ushers
VD	sexually transmitted diseases
VDT	video display terminals
venereal diseases	sexually transmitted diseases
vocational choice	career choice
vocational counseling	occupational counseling
voluntarism	volunteer work
volunteering	volunteer work
wage differential	wage gap
waitresses	waiters
washerwomen	launderers
WASP	White Anglo Saxon Protestant
watchmen	guards
weathermen	meteorologists
weathermen	weather reporters
White man	Caucasian
whores	prostitutes
WIC	Women, Infants, and Children Nutrition Program
widowerhood	widowers
widowhood	widows
wife rape	domestic rape
wolfing	street harassment
womanculture	women's culture
womb	uterus
women intensive careers	female intensive occupations
women intensive occupations	female intensive occupations
women intensive professions	female intensive occupations
women's lib	women's liberation
women's liberation movement	women's movement
work force	labor force
work sharing	job sharing
working men	wage earners
working men	workers
working mothers	mothers working outside the home
working mothers	wage earning mothers
working wives	wage earning wives
working wives	wives working outside the home
working women	wage earners

DO NOT USE	USE
working women	wage earning women
working women	women working outside the home
working women	workers
workmen	wage earners
workmen	workers

DELIMITERS DISPLAY

Age Levels
Cultural and Political Movements
Education Levels
Ethnic, Racial, and Religious Descriptors
Historical Periods
Laws and Regulations
National and Regional Descriptors
Types and Forms of Materials

Age Levels

children
. young children
.. infants
.. preschool children
. school age children

teenagers
. adolescents

adults
. young adults
. middle aged adults
. older adults
.. old old adults

Cultural and Political Movements

abortion movement
abstract expressionism
aestheticism
agnosticism
altruism
anarcha feminism
anarchism
anarchy
androcentrism
anthropomorphism
anti ERA movement
antiabortion movement
antiapartheid movement
antifeminism
antiilliteracy movements
antinuclear movement
antisemitism
antisuffrage movement
antiwar movement
apartheid
arts and crafts movement
asceticism
atheism
auteurism
authoritarianism
avant garde
Beguinism
behaviorism
biological determinism
Black feminism
Black movement
Black power movement
bolshevism
Buddhism
Calvinism
capitalism
Cartesianism

Catholicism
Christianity
civil rights movements
classicism
colonialism
communism
conservatism
conservative movement
consumerism
cross cultural feminism
cubism
cultural feminism
cultural imperialism
dadaism
Darwinism
deconstruction
deism
democracy
democratic socialism
despotism
determinism
dualism
eclecticism
ecumenism
enlightened despotism
environmental movement
environmentalism
essentialism
evangelism
existentialism
expressionism
Fabianism
fascism
federalism
feminism
feminist criticism
feminist movement

feudalism
first wave feminism
formalism
Freudianism
fundamentalism
futurism
global feminism
gnosticism
Gothic style
gynocriticism
Hegelianism
Hinduism
homophile movement
humanism
humanitarianism
idealism
impressionism
international women's movement
irrationalism
Islam
isolationism
Judaism
Jungianism
Kantianism
labor movement
Leninism
lesbian feminism
lesbian movement
lesbian separatism
lesbianism
liberal feminism
liberalism
libertarianism
mainstream feminism
Malthusianism
Marxism
Marxist feminism

materialism
men's movement
mercantilism
millenarian movements
millenialism
modernism
monasticism
monotheism
Mormonism
mysticism
nationalism
nativistic movements
naturalism
Nazism
neoclassicism
neocolonialism
neoconservatism
neoorthodoxy
neoplatonism
neopositivism
nihilism
nonaligned feminism
orthodoxy
pacifism
pantheism
patriotism
phallic criticism
phallocentrism
phallogocentrism
phenomenalism

Platonism
pluralism
polytheism
populism
positivism
postmodernism
poststructuralism
pragmatism
PreRaphaelites
primitivism
progressivism
Protestantism
protofeminism
psychoanalytic criticism
psychoanalytic feminism
puritanism
radical feminism
radicalism
rationalism
realism
relativism
religious pluralism
revisionism
rococo style
Roman Catholicism
Romanesque
romanticism
scientology
secularism
separatism

skepticism
social Darwinism
social realism
socialism
socialist feminism
spiritual feminism
spiritualism
structuralism
subjectivism
suffrage movements
surrealism
symbolism
temperance movement
theism
totalitarianism
traditionalism
transcendentalism
Trotskyism
utilitarianism
utopian socialism
utopianism
voodoo
wicca
womanism
women's health movement
women's movement
youth movement
zionism

Education Levels

early childhood education
. preschool education
. primary education

      elementary secondary education
      . elementary education
      .. adult basic education
      .. intermediate grades
      .. primary education
      . secondary education
      .. high school equivalency
        programs
      .. high schools
      ... junior high schools

postsecondary education
. higher education
.. two year colleges
.. four year colleges
.. graduate education

Ethnic, Racial, and Religious Descriptors

Afro American
Afro Caribbean
Alaskan Indian
Alaskan Native
Aleut
Amerasian
American Indian
Anglo American
Anglo Saxon
Arab
Armenian
Asian American
Asian Pacific
Asian Pacific American
Black
Black Muslim
Buddhist
Cajun
Cambodian American
Caribbean American
Catholic

Caucasian
Chicana
Chinese American
Christian
Creole
Cuban American
Eskimo
Euro American
Filipino American
Greek American
Gypsy
Haitian American
Hindu
Hispanic
Hispanic American
indigenous
Indochinese American
Inuit
Italian American
Japanese American
Jewish

Korean American
Latina
Mexican American
Mormon
Muslim
Native Alaskan
Native Canadian
Polish American
Portuguese American
Protestant
Puerto Rican
Roman Catholic
Samoan American
Slavic
Spanish American
Thai American
Vietnamese American
White
White Anglo Saxon Protestant

Historical Periods

1st–5th Centuries AD
6th–10th Centuries AD
11th Century
12th Century
13th Century
14th Century
15th Century
16th Century
17th Century
18th Century
1800–1809
1810–1819
1820–1829
1830–1839
1840–1849
1850–1859
1860–1869
1870–1879
1880–1889
1890–1899
19th Century
1900–1909

1910–1919
1920–1929
1930–1939
1940–1949
1950–1959
1960–1969
1970–1979
1980–
20th Century
21st Century
antebellum
antiquity
Baroque Period
Byzantine Period
Civil War
Classical Period
Colonial Period
Counter Reformation
Elizabethan Period
Enlightenment
French Revolution
future

Great Awakening
Great Depression
Hellenic Period
Industrial Revolution
Korean War
Medieval Period
Middle Ages
New Deal
prehistory
Progressive Period
Prohibition
Reconstruction
Reformation
Renaissance
Revolutionary War
Romantic Period
Victorian Period
Vietnam War
World War I
World War II

Laws and Regulations

Age Discrimination Act of 1975
Aid to Families with Dependent Children
Child Support Enforcement Amendments of 1984
Civil Rights Act of 1964
Civil Rights Restoration Act of 1987
Civil Service Spouse Retirement Equity Act
Comprehensive Employment and Training Act of 1973
Dependent Care Tax Credit
Economic Equity Act of 1987
Economic Recovery Tax Act of 1981
Education Amendments of 1972
Education Amendments of 1985
Equal Credit Opportunity Act of 1974
Equal Pay Act of 1963
Equal Pay Act of 1970 (Great Britain)
Equal Rights Amendment
Executive Order 11246
Family and Medical Leave Act of 1987
Family Violence Prevention and Services Act
Federal Equitable Pay Practices Act of 1987
Health Insurance Continuation
Job Training Partnership Act

Medicaid
Medicare
National Health Service (Great Britain)
National School Lunch Act Amendments of 1982
Pregnancy Discrimination Act of 1978
Public Health Service Act
Retirement and Disability System Authorization
Retirement Equity Act of 1984
Social Security
Tax Reform Act of 1985
Title IV (Civil Rights)
Title VI (Civil Rights)
Title VII (Civil Rights)
Title VII (Public Health)
Title VIII (Public Health)
Title IX (Education)
Title X (Public Health)
Title XX (Dependent Care)
Uniformed Services Former Spouses' Protection Act
Women, Infants, and Children Nutrition Program
Women's Educational Equity Act

National and Regional Descriptors

African
. Algerian
. Angolan
. Botswanan
. Burundian
. Cameroonian
. Chadian
. Egyptian
. Ethiopian
. Gambian
. Ghanaian
. Guinean
. Ivory Coaster
. Kenyan
. Liberian
. Libyan
. Malian
. Mauritanian
. Moroccan
. Namibian

. Nigerian
. Nigerois
. Senegalese
. Sierra Leonean
. Somalian
. South African
. Sudanese
. Tanzanian
. Togan
. Tunisian
. Ugandan
. Upper Voltan
. Zairean
. Zambian
. Zimbabwean

Asian
. Afghan
. Bangladeshi
. Burmese
. Cambodian

. Chinese
. Filipino
. Indian
. Indochinese
. Indonesian
. Japanese
. Korean
. Laotian
. Malaysian
. Mongolian
. Nepalese
. Pakistani
. Sri Lankan
. Taiwanese
. Thai
. Tibetan
. Vietnamese

European
. Albanian
. Austrian
. Belgian
. Bulgarian
. Czechoslovakian
. Dutch
. East German
. English
. French
. German
. Greek
. Hungarian
. Irish
. Italian
. Luxembourgian
. Maltese
. Northern Irish
. Polish
. Portuguese
. Rumanian
. Russian
. Scandinavian
.. Danish
.. Finnish
.. Icelandic
.. Norwegian
.. Swedish
. Scotch
. Spanish
. Swiss
. Turkish

. Welsh
. West German
. Yugoslav

Latin American
. Argentine
. Bolivian
. Brazilian
. Caribbean
. Central American
.. Costa Rican
.. Guatemalan
.. Honduran
.. Nicaraguan
.. Panamanian
.. Salvadoran
. Chilean
. Colombian
. Ecuadoran
. Falkland Islander
. Guyanese
. Mexican
. Paraguayan
. Peruvian
. Surinamese
. Uruguayan
. Venezuelan
. West Indian
.. Barbadan
.. Cuban
.. Dominican
.. Grenadan
.. Haitian
.. Jamaican
.. Trinidadian

Middle Eastern
. Cypriot
. Iranian
. Iraqi
. Israeli
. Lebanese
. Palestinian
. Saudi Arabian
. Syrian

North American
. Canadian
. United States
.. Appalachian

.. Eastern
.. Middle Atlantic
.. Midwestern
.. North Atlantic
.. Northeastern
.. Northern
.. Northwestern
.. Pacific Coast
.. South Atlantic
.. Southern

.. Southwestern
.. Western

Pacific
. Australian
. Hawaiian
. New Zealander
. Pacific Islander
. Papua New Guinean
. South Pacific
. Tahitian

Types and Forms of Materials

abstracts
acronyms
acts
advertisements
agreements
albums
almanacs
anecdotes
annals
annotations
announcements
: reports
annual reports
anthologies
appendices
archives
articles
artifacts
: books
artists' books
assessments
:: books
: reference books
atlases
: tapes
audiotapes
autobiographies
banners
bibliographies
bills
biobibliographies
biographies
book lists
: reviews
book reviews
booklets

bookplates
books
. artists' books
. cookbooks
. handbooks
. reference books
.. atlases
.. dictionaries
.. encyclopedias
.. thesauri
broadsides
brochures
budgets
bulletins
bumper stickers
buttons
bylaws
calendars
cartoons
case studies
: tapes
cassettes
catalogs
censuses
chapters
charts
. flowcharts
chronologies
clippings
codes
codices
collections
columns
comic strips
commentaries

: disks
  compact disks
  compendiums
  compilations
  compositions
  computer programs
: papers
  concept papers
  concordances
  constitutions
:: documents
  : legal documents
    contracts
  : books
    cookbooks
    courtroom transcripts
    curricula
  : guides
    curriculum guides
    data
    data sets
    declarations
    diagrams
    diaries
      . visual diaries
:: books
  : reference books
    dictionaries
    digests
    directions
    directories
    discographies
    disks
      . compact disks
      . laser disks
      . videodisks
    dissertations
    documentation
    documents
      . government documents
      . legal documents
    drafts
    drawings
    editions
    editorials
    electronic mail
:: books
  : reference books
    encyclopedias

ephemera
essays
eulogies
evaluations
examinations
excerpts
files
filmographies
films
filmstrips
: statements
  financial statements
: charts
  flowcharts
  flyers
  gazetteers
  glossaries
: documents
  government documents
  graffiti
  graphs
  guidelines
  guides
    . curriculum guides
    . how to guides
: books
  handbooks
  histories
    . life histories
    . oral histories
: guides
  how to guides
  indexes
  instructions
  interviews
  journals
: periodicals
  journals (periodicals)
: disks
  laser disks
  ledgers
:: documents
  : legal documents
    legal briefs
  : documents
    legal documents
      . contracts
      . legal briefs
      . licenses

. wills
. working papers
: plans
  lesson plans
  letters
  librettos
:: documents
  : legal documents
    licenses
  : histories
    life histories
    lists
    logs
  : periodicals
    magazines
  : tapes
    magnetic tapes
    manuals
      . sex manuals
    manuscripts
    maps
    measurements
    memoirs
    memoranda
    memos
    methodologies
    microfiche
    microfilm
    models (paradigms)
    monographs
    narratives
      . personal narratives
  : periodicals
    newsletters
  : periodicals
    newspapers
    notes
    notices
    novels
    obituaries
  : histories
    oral histories
    outlines
    pamphlets
    papers
      . concept papers
      . position papers
    periodicals
      . journals (periodicals)

. magazines
. newsletters
. newspapers
. serials
: narratives
  personal narratives
  phonograph records
  photograph albums
  photographs
  pictures
  plans
    . lesson plans
  plates
  playbooks
  plays
  poems
: papers
  position papers
  posters
  prints
  proceedings
  processes
  proofs
  proposals
    . grant proposals
  puzzles
  questionnaires
  quotations
  record albums
  records
: tapes
  reel to reel tapes
: books
  reference books
    . atlases
    . dictionaries
    . encyclopedias
    . thesauri
  referenda
  reports
    . annual reports
    . status reports
  reprints
  reviews
    . book reviews
  samples
  scales
  scores
  scripts

: periodicals
  serials
  series
: manuals
  sex manuals
  sheet music
  sketches
  slide collections
  slide registries
  slide tapes
  slides
  slogans
  software
  speeches
  spreadsheets
  statements
   . financial statements
  statues
: reports
  status reports
  statutes
  stories
  studies
  subject headings
  summaries
  surveys
  syllabi
  synopses
  tables
  tapes
   . audiotapes
   . cassettes

   . magnetic tapes
   . reel to reel tapes
   . videotapes
  testimonials
  tests
:: books
: reference books
  thesauri
  theses
  tombstones
  transcripts
  translations
  travelogues
  treaties
  treatises
  treatments
: disks
  videodisks
: tapes
  videotapes
: diaries
  visual diaries
  want ads
:: documents
: legal documents
  wills
  workbooks
:: documents
: legal documents
  working papers
  works in progress
  yearbooks